A NATION UNDER OUR FEET

A NATION UNDER OUR FEET

*Black Political Struggles in the
Rural South from Slavery
to the Great Migration*

STEVEN HAHN

THE BELKNAP PRESS OF
HARVARD UNIVERSITY PRESS
Cambridge, Massachusetts
London, England

Library of Congress Cataloging-in-Publication Data

Hahn, Steven, 1951–
A nation under our feet : Black political struggles in the rural South from slavery to
the great migration / Steven Hahn.
p. cm.
Includes bibliographical references and index.
ISBN 0-674-01169-4 (alk. paper)
1. African Americans—Southern States—Politics and government—19th century.
2. African Americans—Southern States—Politics and government—20th century.
3. African Americans—Social conditions—To 1964. 4. Southern States—Politics and
government—1865–1950. 5. Southern States—Race relations. 6. Southern States—
Rural conditions. I. Title.

E185.2H15 2003
975'.0049607301734—dc21   2003045326

For Stephanie

CONTENTS

Illustrations follow page 294.

A NATION UNDER OUR FEET

PROLOGUE

LOOKING OUT FROM SLAVERY

This is a book about extraordinary people who did extraordinary things under the most difficult of circumstances and, in the process, transformed themselves and the world in which they lived. It is about how African Americans in the rural South conducted politics and engaged in political struggle as slaves and as freedpeople, about how they constituted themselves as political actors in a society that tried to refuse them that part, and thus about how they gave powerful direction to America's revolutionary experience of disunion, emancipation, and nation-building. It is a book about how political relations and aspirations were forged at the grassroots, about how they took collective and institutional form, and about how they pressed on different arenas of social and political life. It is about the making and remaking of a distinctive African-American politics during the second half of the nineteenth century, and about the origins of popular black nationalism and the civil rights movement in the twentieth. And it is a book about the inspiring and dispiriting history of American democracy.

My interest in this very large subject began with a small episode that I encountered during my research and a problem that the episode posed. In late January 1868, less than a year after Radical Reconstruction had commenced, freedmen and women in the vicinity of Woodville, Mississippi, were, I learned, driving their employers to distraction. They were not, according to a federal agent on the scene, laboring "as faithfully as they should," and instead insisted "on having Saturday for themselves." But most irritating of all was their disposition to "leave work to attend public meetings and speakings of various kinds, and at difficult places" up to twenty-five miles distant, and to hold "private club meetings" closer to home.[1] The agent clearly identified features of an African-American political activism and culture in the very early period after emancipation, and I came to discover that it was only one example of rapid and widespread mobilizations of freedpeople across the former Confederate South. This alone commanded attention. Yet I was especially interested in the remarkable solidarities that these mobilizations displayed: solidarities that confounded Radical Republicans, who had worried that the legacy of slavery and the persistence of economic dependence would leave newly enfranchised freedmen at the political mercy of their former masters. Given the coercions and dangers of slavery and incipient freedom, how can we account for the development of these solidarities, for their dynamics and boundaries, for their responsibilities and compulsions? And what would such an accounting mean for our understanding of African Americans, the South, and the nation?

This book started as an effort to address these questions; it has turned into much more because of the directions, chronologically and conceptually, in which the questions led me. On the one hand, I began to look back at slavery and ahead toward the late nineteenth and early twentieth centuries because I could not imagine understanding what had happened near Woodville, Mississippi, without uncovering the foundations on which it built, and because the vitality of the moment there and elsewhere hinted at a longer and more complex story of political engagement than had generally been allowed. On the other hand, I had to think much more deeply about the nature of politics and political practice, about how unfranchised and disfranchised people might conduct politics, and about the relationship between different arenas of political activity.[2] Thus, rather than follow even the best of the scholarly literature in regarding slaves, who had no standing in the official arenas of civil and political society, as nonpolitical, prepolitical, or protopolitical—involved, at most, in acts of resistance and accommodation (a perspective not very different from that of their owners)—I have tried to identify constituent elements of slave politics and suggest how they alter our comprehension of what happened after slavery, not to mention our sense of the dynamics and dimensions of southern politics as a whole.

Indeed, I have sought a broad understanding of politics and the political that is relational and historical, and that encompasses collective struggles for what might be termed socially meaningful power. Which is to say that the appropriate conceptual universe of study must be determined by a specific social and historical context. What could sensibly be regarded as political activity at one time and place might not be regarded as political activity at another, while different forms of activity in any one time and place assume political character in relation to other forms of activity. A slave who defies the authority of his or her owner does something very different than a free worker who defies the authority of his or her employer, for slavery is a relation of direct personal domination in which there are few institutionalized avenues of negotiation. By its nature, the slave's defiance challenges the fictions of domination and submission around which slavery was constructed, and is thereby imbued with a political resonance that would not necessarily be true for the worker's defiance, which is mediated chiefly by the market. Yet in both cases, the acts of defiance may achieve political meaning and salience in relation to other acts and developments. A slave rebellion or a labor strike depends on solidarities nurtured by many small-scale acts of resistance and defiance, sometimes over extended periods of time, that sketch the axes of conflict, engender trust and support, and draw scattered ideas and aspirations into a collective project.[3]

My book focuses on the period in which African-American men in the South won and then lost the right to vote, and this might appear to simplify the problems of conceptual scope. But it has not. The advent of the elective franchise was itself the result of sensibilities, struggles, and mobilizations advanced by slaves and freedpeople before, during, and immediately after the Civil War. And once the franchise was obtained, its conduct and purposes could not be separated from the institutions, customs, and relations of black life, and from the participation and influence of women, who never held the franchise during these years, as well as men. Thus, I speak of the construction and reconstruction of what might be called social divisions of politics, and have bounded the study chronologically not by enfranchisement and disfranchisement, but rather by the latter years of slavery on the one side and the Great Migration of blacks from the South to the North on the other.

These are not the usual demarcations of African-American political—or, for that matter, social and cultural—history. Scholars are more likely to look at the era of slavery, or of the Civil War and Reconstruction, or of the Jim Crow South, in large part because these comport with the frames defined by conventional national political narratives. But such an approach does not allow us to see how the relations and developments of one era created both limits and possibilities in the next, and it tends to suggest that black politics was constructed and destroyed chiefly during Reconstruction. I have therefore chosen to encompass all of these eras because together they make up a coherent period in which black political struggles, inside and outside of the electoral arena, decisively shaped the South and the nation. These struggles speak directly to the revolutionary nature of the Civil War and emancipation, to the character and complexities of nineteenth-century southern and American politics, to the process of nation-building and sectional reconciliation, and eventually to the massive remapping of the country's political landscape in the twentieth century. Indeed, a powerful social and political consciousness that linked the first generation of black migrants in the urban North with those who remained behind in the rural and small-town South must be comprehended in relation to the lived experience of slavery and its immediate aftermath.

I have focused on the rural South (and mostly on the Confederate and former Confederate South), in part because that was where the overwhelming majority of African Americans lived during this time, but also because these rural areas were characterized by particular deployments of power and cultural forms whose political ramifications have been greatly underestimated. Within this broad setting, I have been sensitive to important variations in geography, racial demography, crop cultures, and local political traditions, and I regularly move from cotton, sugar, rice, and tobacco-growing areas to mixed-farming areas, or from areas with very large plantations to those with smaller plantations and farms, drawing suitable comparisons and contrasts. Readers will discover that African Americans in the southern countryside fashioned a range of political cultures as well as engaged in an array of political activities. At the same time, I try to identify significant commonalities across space that then had consequence over time: in the ways in which slaves widely sought to contest the power of their owners, circulate intelligence, interpret events, and cultivate relations suitable to a world of freedom as well as in the aspirations of freedpeople for family and community reconstitution, local justice, meaningful authority over their own spheres of life, and increasingly, social separatism from whites. The quest for what may be termed self-governance animated African-American politics across much of the rural South during the entire period, even if it assumed many different forms.

I am, of course, mindful of the risks in overemphasizing solidarities and cohesion among African Americans. This book is about the emergence of political communities and the threads that held them together in the face of tremendous countervailing pressures. But it is also—and necessarily—about the tensions and conflicts that erupted within those communities owing to specific relations of power, to rivalries nurtured by intense localism and competing kinship groups, to the coming of the franchise and party politics, to the requirements of political discipline, and to divisions between what may be called plantation-based and franchise-based styles of politics and political leadership. How and when the tensions and conflicts were held in check, and how and when they were not, are important parts of the story.

The subject of this book occupies a rather anomalous place in the current historical literature. On the one hand, there is a great deal of scholarship—often very impressive and sophisticated—on various aspects of African-American life during the second half of the nineteenth century; on the other hand, there remains relatively little on African-American politics during this period, especially for the rural areas, and thus there is not a well-developed historiography or major set of interpretations to engage. Because the book covers a very large territory—geographically, chronologically, and topically—it does intersect with a good many scholarly debates in southern and African-American history, and, where appropriate, I have my say. But in a

broader sense, there are related perspectives on African-American politics that my book challenges, and it would be helpful for readers to
understand what these challenges are.

Most of the relevant scholarship has been governed by something
of a liberal integrationist framework. It is a framework of analysis that
does not really incorporate slaves as political beings, that measures
politicization chiefly by what came to freedpeople from the outside,
and that privileges and lends legitimacy to certain sets of aspirations
(inclusion and assimilation, the pursuit of individual rights) while presenting other sets of aspirations (separatism and community development, the pursuit of collective rights, protonationalism) as the response
to failures and defeats. Slavery forms the "background." "Politics"
comes with freedom and the franchise, and arrives through the vehicles
of the Union army, the Freedmen's Bureau, the Republican party, and
black leaders who had for the most part been free before the Civil War.
And the goals of struggle are to be understood in close connection to
the liberal ideals of civil and political equality, economic opportunity,
and interracial democracy. Emigrationism, separatism, self-help, and
racial solidarity are seen to have been embraced largely after the struggles were defeated and the goals rejected.[4]

I had doubts about this perspective from the outset. But once the
implications of imagining slaves as political actors took hold, the
doubts became even deeper. For it seemed increasingly apparent that
slavery was not mere background or prologue; it was formative and
foundational. In countless ways, freedpeople built and drew on relations, institutions, infrastructures, and aspirations that they and their
ancestors had struggled for and constructed as slaves. Without this
legacy, activism and mobilization could not have taken place so rapidly
after slavery had been abolished; and without consideration of this
legacy, we cannot begin to understand how activism and mobilization
did take place, and around what sorts of issues. It seemed, in short,
that a serious study of African-American politics during this era needed
to look out from slavery onto the postemancipation world, and that
once it did so, that world would appear very different.

To look out from slavery is not to discount the powerful currents
of liberal and republican ideals that African Americans embraced and
advanced during the Civil War and Reconstruction, ideals that had

already been cultivated in the North by developing traditions of black public protest and in the South by the less visible circulation of people exposed to the political culture of the revolutionary Atlantic. Nor is it to emphasize continuity rather than change in political experience. It is instead to suggest that African Americans continually made and remade their politics and political history in complex relation to shifting events; they did not have their politics and political history made for them. In so doing, they often assimilated ideas and institutions from the outside to their own goals and practices, giving a distinctive shape to their political struggles and, by extension, to the interpretive significance of those struggles. Thus, in the pages that follow, I present kinship, labor, and circuits of communication and education (especially rumor) as fundamental components of slave and freed politics, and try to show how they enabled organization and solidarity, and then were reconfigured by the course and outcome of political contests.

This book is framed chronologically and thematically, and is divided into three parts. Part One is concerned with the elements and conduct of slave and freed politics before the coming of the franchise, and with the political roles of slaves and freedpeople in turning the Civil War into a massive social and political revolution. It explores kinship relations, labor practices, religious communalism, and forms of community regulation under slavery, as well as the circulation of political intelligence that educated and effectively organized slaves in many different parts of the South. Indeed, it suggests that slaves were far more conversant with local and national politics than has generally been recognized, and that they fashioned their own interpretations of the sectional conflict. These interpretations lent special meaning to the Union invasion of the Confederate South and encouraged them to launch what became the largest slave rebellion in modern history: a rebellion that began as flight from plantations and farms but soon involved new forms of politicization; and a rebellion that culminated in tens of thousands of former slaves taking up arms to help the Union army crush the Confederacy and complete the destruction of slavery. In the process, they began to imagine and enact new social and political possibilities, as well as new alliances to bring them into being. By the summer and fall of 1865, their expectations and political activity found expression both in formal demands for civil and political rights and in the explosion of rumors about federally sponsored land redistribution, which deepened the crisis of Presidential Reconstruction and prepared the way for its radical alternative.

Part Two focuses on Radical Reconstruction at the grassroots, on the making of a new political order in the former Confederate South, and on the advent of the elective franchise, which simultaneously availed itself of and transformed older forms of African-American political practice. It examines popular mobilizations in the countryside and their relation to labor reorganization and community reconstitution. It studies the emergence of new political leaders and new political institutions. And it explores the struggles for local power that the enfranchisement of black men and the projects of the Republican party made possible. The Union League figures very significantly in this history both because of its crucial role in organizing freedmen to participate in the electoral arena and because it exemplified the connections among the electoral and other, more inclusive, arenas of political activity. So, too, do the formidable challenges that African Americans faced in their efforts to participate in contests for public power: challenges that required communitywide involvement, harsh internal discipline and reprisals, secrecy, and armed self-defense. Indeed, I suggest that Reconstruction brought to light the paramilitary character of southern politics, which ex-slaves clearly grasped but which nonetheless compromised the interracial coalition on which the Republican party was based and made it very difficult for them to obtain and wield power. Radical Reconstruction did see remarkable political inversions on the local and state levels, and remarkable opportunities for newly freed slaves to build their own institutions and use the levers of the state to protect themselves and advance their goals. But it also proved to be a very painful lesson in the nature and boundaries of American democracy.

The toppling of Reconstruction governments in the former Confederate states ended a phase of African-American—and American—political history, but it by no means put an end to African-American political activities and struggles. Part Three explores a variety of forms that these took, emphasizing both the deeper impulses toward self-governance and separatism, and the emergence of new claims and projects inside and outside the electoral arena. Considerable attention is devoted to what I call grassroots emigrationism (looking to Liberia or to other parts of the United States), which took hold almost immediately after emancipation and then erupted into a mass movement in the cotton belt of the Deep South during the late 1870s. But I examine, as well, the coincidental and at times overlapping phenomenon of political biracialism, which involved electoral alliances with white insurgents (Readjusters, Independents, Populists) or white Democrats, and gave renewed pulse to the political life of the South before collapsing in the face of conflicting expectations and violence. I suggest that the 1880s may be regarded as a period of African-American political assertiveness on a number of fronts, including those advanced by the Knights of Labor and the Colored Farmers' Alliance, and that this very assertiveness helps account for the sweeping and ferocious nature of the white counterattack, marked as it was by lynching, disfranchisement, and the more general advent of Jim Crow. Together, these developments set the stage for the Great Migration and nourished the materials of African-American popular politics thereafter, beginning with Garveyism, which showed impressive, albeit little noticed, strength in the rural and small-town South and which simultaneously absorbed and elaborated various traditions of thought and practice.

This book, therefore, argues that African Americans in the rural South contributed to the making of a new political nation while they made themselves into a new people—a veritable nation as many of them came to understand it. Their politics and political struggles, that is, went into the making of two nations, deeply interconnected and stunningly distinct, imagined with a palpability and groundedness: nations alike embedded in persons, places, and land, in the relations and aspirations of rural family and community life, under their feet, as it were.

But this book also suggests that, in imagining a nation under their feet, African Americans exposed, in searing ways, the complex and contradictory relation between labor and political democracy in the United States. For we must remember that throughout the years covered by this book—when they were slaves, freedpeople, and a subject race—African Americans were also overwhelmingly workers. That they were predominantly rural workers may explain why such a recognition has not been readily made by many scholars, since even the best histories of working people have focused on urban and industrial sites, and have shown little interest in rural workers of any sort.[5] But

African Americans were more consistently a part of the nation's working class, over a more extended period of time, than any other social, ethnic, or racial group. Their many struggles thereby serve as crucial examples of how workers have energized the meaning of democracy at many points in our past. At the same time, their exclusions from arenas of civil and political life, the many obstacles they were made to surmount in the simplest exercise of their rights—let alone the wielding of power—and the political violence that routinely afflicted their communities and leaders must remind us, as well, of our democracy's deep historical problems with the full participation of its working people generally, and of its working people from ethnic and racial minorities in particular. African Americans demonstrated with great pain and at great cost that the problems resided at the heart of politics in the nineteenth and early twentieth centuries. They still do.

A Note on Language and Quotation

Some of the original source material on which I have drawn consists of interviews with slaves, ex-slaves, and freedpeople. When the interviewers were white, transcriptions often included their version of the subject's dialect and pronunciation, often in ways that appear demeaning. Where this has obviously occurred (as in many of the ex-slave narratives collected by the federal Works Progress Administration in the 1930s), I have taken the liberty in the text to change the spellings, and thus the pronunciations and inflections, but never the word or words—or the meanings—being conveyed by the interviewees. Specialists and interested readers may check the citation in my endnotes if they wish to see the original interviews and spellings.

PART I

❖

"The Jacobins of the Country"

OF CHAINS AND THREADS

> I build my house upon de rock,
> O yes, Lord!
> No wind, no storm can blow dem down,
> O yes, Lord!
> March on member, Bound to go;
> March on member, Bound to go;
> March on member, Bound to go;
> Bid 'em fare you well.
>
> "Bound to Go"

The whispering began even before the November election, and it spread rapidly in the weeks and months that followed. The "Black Republican" Abraham Lincoln had been elected President, and in the quarters, in the woods, on the roads, and at the county seats the slaves passed the word and considered what it meant. Some were absolutely convinced that freedom was at hand; indeed, on a plantation just outside Petersburg, Virginia, seventeen slaves marked Lincoln's inauguration by proclaiming that they were free and marching off of their master's property. For others, hopeful anticipation of great changes to come grew as news of the Civil War swept "like [a] whirlwin'" among them. Enough activity was soon to be detected, enough unrest was soon to be found, that anxious whites throughout the slave states began to circulate rumors and stories of insurrectionary plots and disturbances. Kate Stone, who lived with her widowed mother and siblings on their large cotton plantation in Louisiana, thus blamed the "trouble" among the house servants in June of 1861 on the "excitement in the air," and confided that "the Negroes are suspected of an intention to spring on the fourth of [July]."[1]

Independence Day 1861 proved more memorable for Abraham Lincoln's address assuring white southerners that he wished only to preserve the Union and omitting any mention of the institution of slavery. But northern armies had already set foot on Confederate soil, and when intelligence of the Yankees' whereabouts reached them, slaves often chose to follow their own interpretation of Lincoln's intentions and seek protection and freedom within Union lines. At first, young men figured disproportionately in their numbers, reflecting both the opportunities and hazards that flight from their owners entailed. Increasingly, however, entire families arrived, some "belonging to the same owner" and some hastily united from forced separations. After the Union army invaded the coast of South Carolina and then the lower Mississippi Valley, the flow of slaves taking flight swelled, encompassing many plantations and farms as well as multiple generations who frequently departed their places suddenly with their few articles of property, "their blankets, feather beds, chickens, pigs, and such like," representing "the net result of all their labors." Nearly 150,000 of the men eventually donned blue Yankee uniforms and fought to secure the defeat of the Confederacy and the liberation of their people.[2]

Many of the slaves who remained on their holdings for much, if not all, of the Civil War sought to advance the tide of change nonetheless. If their owners had fled in the face of Union forays, they took charge of the "abandoned" estate, farmed it on their own account, and kept order by their own rules and customs. If their owners, or owner's family, stayed, they looked to rearrange the balances of power and authority. They slowed the pace of work, devoted more time to their provision crops, ignored the master's commands, moved about as they wished or could, and generally tried to tend to their own affairs. John Houston Bills, owner of three plantations in Tennessee, was accordingly driven to distraction by 1864, as his diary amply registered: "My Negroes all at home, but working only as they see fit, doing little"; "some disposition amongst the servants to serve the federals rather than work on the farm"; "My people preparing cotton land for *themselves* at Cornucopia"; "Early this morning my man Jerry and Harriet his wife, their children, Simon and Mary with Vira 3 children Jerry[,] Hattie and . . . also Victoria and child and Angelina and child all off by RR there appears to be a general stampede"; "Negroes all going off with returning troops. some come back to urge others to go and they are easily persuaded"; "the females have quit entirely or nearly so [at Hickory Valley], four of the men come and go where and when they please"; and "many of my servants have run away and most of those left had as well be gone, they being totally demoralized and ungovernable." Little wonder that some wartime slaveholders ultimately offered their slaves small wages or shares of the crop to keep them at work and the operations afloat.[3]

The rapid circulation of news and rumor, the complex ties of family and kinship, the contests over the deployment of labor, the accumulation of petty property, the customs and institutions of internal authority and discipline—these were the means by which African-American slaves tried to give shape to the great struggle over the Union and slavery. They were, of course, the materials of day-to-day "resistance," lent wider field and consequence by civil war. But they were something more as well. They were the stuff of the slaves' "politics."

To speak of the slaves' politics may seem a contradiction in terms, for the slaves had no standing in the official arenas of either civil or political society. As chattel property and legal dependents, they were subject to the sovereign authority of their masters and thereby lacked, at least theoretically, the very essence of political beings: the ability to express and act according to their individual and collective wills. Southern slaveholders and their representatives, in fact, extolled the institution of slavery as the best guarantor of social and political stability precisely because it rendered the laboring class politically inert. They could scarcely acknowledge, let alone dignify, the disruptive or communal behaviors of their slaves as worthy of the name political, for by doing so they would undermine their own claims of absolute power. And yet the slaves did express and act according to their individual wills, fashion collective norms and aspirations, contest the authority of their owners on many fronts, build institutions to mobilize their resources and sensibilities, produce leaders who wielded significant influence, and, in ways we have still to appreciate fully, press on the official arenas of politics at the local, state, and national levels. To be sure, the slaves' politics composed a web of fragile threads, delicately devised and easily broken, that cannot be readily marked or measured. Masters and slaves necessarily conducted their political battles in a manner befitting the relationship that linked them: with stealth and indirection, with postures and fictions, with choreographed rituals and competitive scrambles. And with explosive force. Nonetheless, by the late 1850s these battles helped to bring the South and the nation into crisis, and when the Civil War broke out, the slaves' political experience not only came to notable effect; it would also be dramatically transformed.

❖

Slavery in the antebellum South was marked by great variations. In 1860, roughly four slaves in ten lived in the upper and border South, where farms rather than plantations generally predominated and mixed agriculture assumed considerable importance. Among them, nearly four in ten could be found in areas in which free people of color, slave hiring, and urban life were alike consequential. Farther south, most slaves worked on cotton plantations, but thousands of others worked on sugar or rice estates or on units given over to diversified farming; perhaps one in five throughout the Deep South resided on what could be regarded as a yeoman farm. A small group of slaves in rural districts and a larger one in towns and cities plied the skills of tradesmen, and an elite of sorts supervised the activities of field hands on some of the bigger agricultural holdings.[4] Yet wherever they may have labored, all slaves in the antebellum South had one thing in common: they were chained to their owners as individuals.

Slavery, quite simply, was a system of extreme personal domination in which a slave had no relationship that achieved legal sanction or recognition other than with the master, or with someone specifically designated by the master. Nothing was more central to the character of the institution or more debilitating to the slaves as human beings and political actors. Although jurists and legislators in most southern states sought, certainly by the late antebellum period, to provide minimal statutory protections to some relations among slaves—especially between mother and child—their efforts came to little effect. The slaves, therefore, were left peculiarly vulnerable and were encouraged to depend on and identify with their owners as a strategy of survival. As a result, slavery undermined the solidarities of the enslaved in a manner fundamentally different not only from the experience of free

laborers but also from that of most other servile laborers.[5] Consequently, the slaves' struggle to form relations among themselves and
to give those relations customary standing in the eyes of masters and
slaves alike was both the most basic and the most profound of political
acts in which they engaged.

As in the West African societies from which they originally came,
and as in most rural societies in the preindustrial world, kinship relations composed the social and political foundation of the slaves' world,
and the slaves pressed from the first to construct them as means of
achieving stability and resisting slavery. It was not an easy undertaking, for a combination of law, masterly prerogative, and demography
often conspired against them. Neither legal codes nor other official
institutions ever offered protection to slave marriages or other consanguineous relations; only the relation of mother and child had legal
bearing, because it defined the heritability of enslavement. Slaveowners
might accept, perhaps even encourage, slave marriages and might show
reluctance to break up families through sale or inheritance, but this
reflected an ethics of sovereignty rather than a prescriptive right, and
it was an ethics frequently observed in the breach, especially when the
burdens of debt or generational property transmission came to be felt.
In the formative period of southern slave society, moreover, as staple
agriculture developed and intensified, purchasers of African slaves
widely preferred males to females and thus created a marked sexual
imbalance in the slave population. This, together with the high rates
of slave mortality and morbidity that routinely stalked the rise of plantation systems, undermined the early establishment and elaboration of
family ties.[6]

The southern slave population began to reproduce itself naturally
sometime around the middle of the eighteenth century, and a structure
of kinship relations, expectations, and practices gradually took shape,
bolstered subsequently by the closing of the African slave trade and
the prevalence of crop cultures (principally cotton, tobacco, and grains)
that weighed somewhat less heavily on the material conditions of slave
laborers than sugar culture did elsewhere in the Western Hemisphere.
By the antebellum era, it appears that slaves commonly lived in simple
families, often nuclear in character, and had built complex and geographically extensive kinship networks, thanks in part to exogamous
marriage patterns. On large plantations with deep generational roots,

kinship could eventually have linked an individual slave to more than three-quarters of those resident.[7] Fictive kinship arrangements, deployed chiefly to serve as buffers against the many perils of slave life, helped tie other slaves to consanguineous kin groups, while kinship titles came to denote social hierarchies among slaves of a given community whether they were blood relations or not. The former Maryland slave Frederick Douglass thus recalled that the mechanics on Colonel Edward Lloyd's eastern shore plantation "were called 'uncles' by all the younger slaves, not because they really sustained that relationship to any, but as a mark of plantation etiquette, as a mark of respect, due from the younger to the older slaves." When the northern teacher Elizabeth Hyde Botume arrived on the coast of South Carolina soon after Union occupation to minister to the very large black population, it took her "months before [she] learned their family relations." "The terms 'bubber' for brother, and 'titty' for sister, with 'nanna' for mother, and 'mother' for grandmother, and 'father' for all leaders in church and society were so generally used," she marveled, "I was forced to believe that all belonged to one immense family."[8]

Impressive as it was for the slaves to have won room for family formation and the construction of kinship networks, it is easy to exaggerate the stability and resiliency of these relations. On farms and small plantations, fewer than half of the slaves at any one time lived in "standard nuclear families" (both parents and children), and even on larger plantations, the developmental cycle of birth, aging, and death made for periods of social and familial imbalance, at times casting slaves into a succession of different family settings. Slave sales were for the most part local, and likely stretched rather than broke family ties, but the antebellum cotton boom promoted an interregional migration that sent more than three-quarters of a million slaves from the upper and seaboard South to the lower South and Southwest between 1820 and 1860, perhaps 60 percent of whom went by means of the slave trade. According to the most careful estimate, one in three first marriages in the upper South may have been broken by such forced separations, and slave children who lived in the upper South at the beginning of this period stood about a 30 percent chance of being sold to the lower South before the end of it. Family relations and kinship networks were perpetually being severed and reconstituted, whether owing to sale, estate division, or the long-distance movement of entire plantations.

In the end, what may have mattered most was not so much the duration of these relations and networks as the obligations and responsibilities imposed so long as they did endure.[9]

These obligations and responsibilities created the sort of ties among slaves—generational and spatial—that could counterbalance the individuating dependencies that slavery was meant to enforce. They gave slaves support in daily contests of will with owners and managers, and in negotiating the personal travails that could have left them isolated and exposed. They augmented slaves' sources of sustenance, and aided them in fending off the many fears and destructive behaviors that the system encouraged. And they helped to bring sanctions against those who violated developing norms. Which is to say that the obligations and responsibilities of kinship were crucial to the achievement of the slaves' short-term political objectives: to protect themselves and each other from the worst of the regime's violence and exploitation; to carve out spheres of activity in which they could provide for themselves and establish relations and values suitable to a world without enslavement; and to turn a system based on the absolute power and personal domination of the master into one based on reciprocities, even if between parties with resources acknowledged to be vastly unequal.[10]

The struggle to achieve these objectives revolved around the activity so central to the lives of slaves that it has often been taken for granted: work.[11] Rural slaves spent most of their waking hours in the fields plowing, planting, hoeing, weeding, harvesting, and processing crops; tending to livestock; digging ditches; making and repairing fences; and cutting logs. The length of their workday, the pace and organization of their labor, and the range of their duties varied as to the staple crop and the size of the plantation or farm, but was everywhere subject to the discretionary authority of masters who, if they bothered to explain it (and few did), saw the involuntary labor of their slaves as a just return for the subsistence, protection, and direction they provided. So sweeping did some masters regard this authority that in the records of their agricultural operations the laborers—"hands"—became literal extensions of themselves. "Plowed ten acres," "planted the old willow field," "hoed fifty rows cotton," they might write. The slaves, not surprisingly, viewed matters differently. By their lights, the labor they performed represented an accommodation to the coercive power of their owners, and they sought not only to limit the reaches and damages of that power but also to draw some distinction between the time and services they "owed" the master and the time and rewards they could claim for themselves. Whereas the masters might regard concessions made in the ensuing contests as adjustments to the "inferior" abilities and sensibilities of their slaves, the slaves would regard such concessions as "rights" that could then become a basis for further rounds of "negotiation."[12] Over time, the labor system became increasingly complex and contradictory.

The slaves, to be sure, had limited manuevering room and incurred substantial risks. On the largest cotton, tobacco, and sugar plantations (those with fifty or more slaves), they were organized into gangs based on strength, skill, sex, and age, and placed under the direct supervision of a black driver or white overseer. The "main gang," "first gang," or "plow gang" generally consisted of adult males and of women between child-bearing and old age; the "second" or "hoe gang" was composed disproportionately of women of child-bearing age and older teenagers; and the "trash" gang included a mix of pregnant and nursing women, older men and women, and children doing their first rounds of field work. Where special skills were required of slaves, as in the processing of sugar, more of the field labor was performed by women, since skilled labor was almost exclusively the province of men. At all events, the field slaves worked from dawn to dusk.[13] Rice plantations, however, were organized by the task—a specific amount of work to be completed on a certain plot of land during a day—although the task assignments, too, marked the distinctions of strength, age, and sex: workers were known as "full-task," "three-quarter-task," "half-task," and "quarter-task" hands. The tasks were designed to require an entire day for the typical hand in each category to finish.[14]

Most slaves worked on smaller plantations and farms (with fewer than fifty slaves), where the division of labor was far less pronounced. Their duties were probably more diverse in character and the gangs, when organized, more haphazard in composition. But they were at least as subject to the direction and supervision of their owners, who were advised endlessly in the South's agricultural journals and newspapers to set clear expectations and leave as little initiative as possible to the slaves. Thus, whatever the circumstances of their labor, the slaves looked to influence the boundaries of those expectations so as to lighten their loads and minimize occasions for the infliction of punishments, and then to patrol those boundaries in their own manner.[15]

It had to be a collective undertaking, for individual acts of resistance to the master's directions were most easily detected and most likely to bring quick discipline. Even those acts that might appear to be individual in character—breaking tools, injuring draft animals, feigning illness—needed the cooperation of other slaves to be effective. As a result, the slaves struggled to infuse the organization of work with their kin relations. Where possible, kinship mediated early socialization to the skills, regimens, and rhythms of agricultural labor, as parents, grandparents, and fictive kin offered children instruction and example. And where possible, kinship mediated the labor process itself. Frank Bell, who grew up on a large Virginia wheat plantation where the master "put everybody in the field," explained both the logic and potential conflicts:

> Used to work in family groups, we did. Now we and my four brothers, never had no sisters, used to follow my mom and dad. In that way one could help the other when they got behind. All of us would pitch in and help Momma who wasn't very strong. 'Course in that way the man what was doing the cradling would always go no faster than the woman, who was most times his wife, could keep up. Old overseer on some plantations wouldn't let families work together, 'cause they ain't gonna work as fast as when they all mixed up, but Marse John Fallons had a black foreman, what was my mother's brother, my uncle. Moses Bell was his name and he always looked out for his kinfolk, especially my mother. Uncle Moses was a caution. Everybody scared of him, even old Marser.

Bell's experience may not have been all that unusual, since foremen and drivers were often deeply embedded in the community of field hands. But the practice of working in "family groups," when established, had probably been a good many confrontation-ridden years in the making.[16]

Slaves able to work in kin groups, or in gangs composed chiefly of kinfolk, did not escape punishment and abuse. Nothing could be more galling for a slave than to bear helpless witness to the beating of a parent, child, or other relation, and masters who permitted the practice perhaps imagined that it would thereby serve as a form of social control. Yet those slaves who did succeed in placing the imprint of kinship on the organization of labor not only were better able to give day-to-day assistance and protection to one another; they were also better able to secure the gains they did make. When Frederick Law Olmsted traveled to the rice districts of South Carolina in 1853, he was struck by how the slaves maintained the system of task labor. "It is looked upon in this region as a proscriptive right of the negroes to have this incitement to diligence offered them," he wrote, "and the man who denied it, or attempted to lessen it, would . . . experience much annoyance from the obstinate 'rascality' of the negroes." Such a man might even provoke "a general stampede" to the swamp. Olmsted apparently did not notice that the slaves who completed their tasks early helped older and slower kinfolk to finish before quitting the rice fields themselves.[17]

The success of slaves in some parts of the South by the mid-nineteenth century in delineating expectations as to time and work owed to the master and in enscribing reciprocities into the master-slave relation was reflected in the incidence of "paid" labor. In principle, slaveholders were entitled to all of the slaves' time and work, and certainly to whatever earnings were derived from hiring them out. But slaves managed to win time for themselves, set loose standards for various agricultural tasks, and avail themselves of opportunities opened by the rhythms governing various crop cultures. In sections of the upper South that had made the transition from tobacco to grains, in nonplantation districts near mines or transportation projects, and in rural areas that came within the orbit of larger towns and scattered manufacturing centers, the hiring of slaves on both short- and long-term bases became increasingly common, and slaveholders frequently allowed the slaves to retain at least a very small share of their wages as an incentive and reward. In cities like Baltimore, Richmond, New Orleans, and, to a lesser extent, Charleston—or in agricultural processing towns like Danville, Lynchburg, and Farmville, Virginia—slaves usually fed and lodged themselves, bargained with prospective employers, and might receive payments for "overwork." During his time in Baltimore, Frederick Douglass became so expert in the caulking trade that he could "command the highest wages paid to journeymen" and thereby "sought my own employment, made my own contracts, and collected my own earnings."[18]

In the wheat-growing tidewater of Virginia and eastern shore of Maryland, in the general farming areas of middle Kentucky and Tennessee, and in the hill and mountain counties of North Carolina, Georgia, and Alabama, larger slaveholders needed a full labor force only during harvest and, perhaps, planting season, and hired out slaves—especially those with skills—to neighboring farmers and craftsmen or to railroad, canal, and mining companies at other times of the year. Even in the plantation belt of the Deep South, where labor demands were more evenly distributed through the agricultural calendar, slaves occasionally performed such stints, of varying duration. Stephen Brooke, who "was a slave and belonged to Col. M. Jones of Madison County, Mississippi," scrambled to make the best of his. "[F]or several years before the war," he declared, "I was hired by [Jones] to the Mississippi Central Railroad Company as a brakeman on a passenger train" but also found "opportunities of making extra wages which I was permitted to keep for my own use." By the fall of 1858, Brooke had "accumulated about $300," which he used to buy a "wagon and one yoke of oxen" and "then hired my time from my . . . master and went to hauling with my team." Jones was probably not amused by the outcome: In 1863, Brooke loaded his wife and children in the wagon and had the oxen pull them to Vicksburg, where he enlisted in the Union army.[19]

Paid labor had wider meaning for the slaves at harvest time. Then, under pressures from commodity markets and approaching frosts, even masters who normally relied on gang labor designed tasks and commonly offered monetary incentives to those slaves who exceeded them. Charles Ball, sold south from Maryland to cotton plantations in South Carolina and Georgia, suggested how the parties wrangled to set the terms. The overseer, he recalled, would commence the cotton harvest by prescribing the standard for a day's picking, but by "Monday morning of the second week . . . he told us that he fixed the day's work at 50 pounds; and that all those who picked more than that would be paid a cent a pound for the overplus." Other slaveholders selected a date for the harvest's completion and rewarded their slaves if they met it; still others eventually took to tasking noncrop as well as harvest labor.[20]

Of greater symbolic importance were the payments that came to be associated with the slaves' "free time." By the antebellum period, slaves throughout the South had gained Sundays and, in some cases, half or all of Saturday for themselves. Most used the chance to rest, tend to the needs of their households, visit kinfolk on other plantations and farms, or worship. But more than a few did odd jobs for their owners or for neighboring planters and farmers, and they expected to be paid. "It is the custom in Louisiana," the kidnapped slave Solomon Northup later wrote, "to allow the slave to retain whatever compensation he may obtain for services performed on Sundays." Ex-slave John Cameron, who grew up on a plantation near Richmond, Virginia, was told that his master gave the slaves "every other Saturday for themselves" during which "they cut cordwood for Boss, women and all." "Most of the men cut two cords a day an the women one," Cameron claimed, and "Boss paid them a dollar a cord." Slaves in Beaufort Parish, South Carolina, occasionally left their rice plantations on Saturday nights and worked through Sunday for nonslaveholders who cultivated small farms on knolls and hammocks in the swamps.[21]

Paid labor seems to have developed in close connection with a larger system of production, provisioning, and exchange—what some historians have called an "internal economy"—that, by the 1850s, formed an integral part of the southern slave economy and the social relations of slavery.[22] It had become a common practice, especially on plantations, for masters to permit or tolerate a range of economic activities among the slaves that might include cultivating subsistence and market-garden plots; raising fowl and some livestock; making craft and other articles; as well as hunting, fishing, and gathering wild fruits and nuts. The rules governing these activities varied from place to place, and they reflected not only pressure from the slaves but also the circumstances of social life: the nature of the staple crop, the fluctuations of national and international markets, whether the slaveowner was resident or absentee, and the availability of local foodstuffs. In some instances, the slaves became principally responsible for feeding themselves and, as a consequence, were allocated more time for provisioning work and allowed to engage in exchanges both on and off the plantation. In other instances, the slaves continued to receive full rations and used their gardens and chicken coops merely to supplement their diets, with exchanges prohibited. In between, a considerable mix of possibilities emerged, with slaves producing different portions of their subsistence, perhaps raising small crops of the staple, trading in one or more markets, and accumulating limited quantities of money and personal property. The most elaborate examples were to be found in the rice and long-staple-cotton growing areas of the South Carolina and Georgia coast and in the sugar growing parishes of lower Louisiana, where planter absenteeism was more prevalent and plantations had especially large numbers of slaves. But evidence is mounting to suggest that this system of production, provisioning, and exchange was a general achievement of slaves from the Chesapeake to Texas, and that distinctions among the many examples were of degree rather than kind.

Wherever one looked, the system was organized around kin-based slave households and the allocation of arable plots, usually next to or near the slave cabins and from one-quarter acre to one acre in size. Rice and sugar slaves appear to have won use-rights to grounds on other parts of their plantations, and slaves in a variety of settings spoke about the allotment of "patches." Throughout, however, the plots and grounds were worked chiefly by family members, and only during those segments of time regarded as the slaves' own: in the evening after the completion of daily field labor, and on Saturday afternoons and Sundays. Those slaves who labored for their masters by the task could finish earlier and spend more time on their grounds, and this seems to have enabled the system to develop more fully in the rice districts. Even so, a robust adult slave would normally work in the rice fields for about nine hours before completing a task. The system would, therefore, always demand a good deal of extra labor and, by extension, the slaves' exploitation of themselves, their kin, and others in the household.[23]

At the same time, the slaves often gained leverage in determining what would be raised in the plots and grounds, how they would be worked, and how the results of their efforts would be disbursed. Most masters prohibited the cultivation of staple crops, fearing that it would encourage theft from the plantation supply headed for market, and in the case of rice and sugar, technological and capital requirements placed petty cultivation pretty much out of reach. But this merely established the outer boundaries of practices, and more than a few slaveholders did allow the slaves to grow small quantities of cotton and tobacco. On plantations in the South Carolina piedmont, the slaves' portion of the total cotton crop could range from as little as 2 percent to as much as 15 percent.[24] In general, though, the slaves concentrated on food crops and livestock and, where possible, raised an assortment of vegetables, melons, potatoes, and pumpkins. We still know relatively little about how the slaves organized production. A broad, though ill-defined, division of labor based on the sex and age of household members can be discerned. Male slaves did most of the hunting and fishing (especially if undertaken at night), most of the work involving craft skills, probably more of the work on those grounds located on the periphery of the plantations or devoted to cash crops, and probably most of the related activities taking slaves off of the plantations and farms. Female slaves may have been disproportionately responsible for tending the chickens and small livestock, and for working the garden plots if other grounds were cultivated; and they were almost entirely responsible for turning raw produce and materials into consumable food and clothing, and for cooking, spinning and weaving, quilting, sewing, and mending. Will Sheets, who lived on a modest-sized Georgia farm with seven other slaves, could recall that "they all knocked off from Work Saturday at 12 o'clock. The women washed, patched, and cleaned up, and the men worked in their own cotton patches what Marse Jeff [Southerland] give them." But these divisions were loose and traversable—even more by women than by men—and when females headed households, owing to off-plantation marriages or the permanent absence of a mate, they carried the primary burden of making the production and provisioning system viable.[25]

If slave households served as the units of petty production, they also served as the units of distribution and consumption, and participation in productive activities seems to have entitled members of the household to a roughly proportionate share of the produce. Direct contributions to the provisioning system may well have been more important than coresidency in establishing who was to be regarded as a "household member." Consider the story told by Charles Ball. Sold by a slave trader to the owner of a large South Carolina cotton plantation, Ball, who had been separated from his kin and had no kin relations on the estate, was assigned to live with one of the slave families there. He was received kindly, and, having already developed craft and foraging skills, soon proposed, significantly, "that I would bring all my earnings into the family stock, provided I might be treated as one of its members, and be allowed a portion of the proceeds of their patch or garden." "This offer," Ball reported, "was readily accepted and from this time we constituted one community, as long as I remained among the field hands on the plantation."[26]

The petty production and provisioning system generally embraced patterns of exchange that not only gave many slaves some experience in the marketplace and enabled them to accumulate a little money and a few possessions, but also came to symbolize reciprocal relations of several types. Most attention has focused on the question of whether the slaves could sell their produce to buyers off of the plantation or farm, in large part because this has been a vital point of contrast between slave culture in the antebellum South and that in the Caribbean during much of the late eighteenth and nineteenth centuries. For whereas slaves in the Caribbean typically brought the products of their provision grounds and handicrafts to "Sunday markets" and, in some cases, came to control most of the circulating currency on their island, their counterparts in the South seem to have had little to do with local and regional petty commodity markets, save for those markets in coastal South Carolina and Georgia and southern Louisiana.[27] Southern slaveholders struggled to restrict the potential trading opportunities and activities of their slaves, and in this they were aided by the tendency of planters and farmers alike to raise substantial food crops and to continue providing their slaves with at least basic rations. But we may well have underestimated the extent to which slaves in a great many locales—with or without their owners' approval—bought, sold, and bargained with merchants, shopkeepers, peddlers, and neighboring whites. A Mississippi planter acknowledged as much when announcing that he did not permit the slaves on his large estate "to have 'truck patches,' or to raise anything whatever for the market," yet felt obliged to "give to each head of a family and to every negro on Christmas day, five dollars and send them to the country town under the charge of an overseer or driver . . . in lieu thereof."[28]

Slaves who resided on or near major thoroughfares or close to market towns were perhaps best able to engage in such trading, and most likely to have reached some arrangement with their masters to do so. A slaveholder whose estate fronted one of Virginia's rivers told of a ship's captain asking permission "to purchase some eggs of his people" and then finding "nearly two bushels" brought out, "all the property of the slaves, and which they were willing to sell at four cents a dozen." Further inland, slaves gathered at the county seats on "court Sunday" or Whitsunday to conduct their trade, much to one observer's surprise, who remarked on "how much more cheerful they are than the court day collection of whites." On J. M. Gibson's large plantation in Warren County, Mississippi, each slave "family had its own chickens and melon patch," and they could send their produce into Vicksburg on wagons that made the trip twice a week. "In this way," Gibson remembered, "some pocket change was had by the slaves." Having spent a few years on a plantation just outside nearby Natchez, Samuel B. Smith found that some slaves had become highly conversant with the ways of the market. "The negroes living near the [Mississippi] river had better opportunities to trade and were better able to take care of themselves than those in the interior," he subsequently testified. "They all knew the value of money. They knew very well what things were worth, and . . . they could cipher and keep complicated accounts."[29]

For those slaves held in the interior districts, crossroads villages and hamlets often became prime trading sites. To the small shops and huts located there, housing storekeepers, mechanics, and farm laborers, the slaves might resort, "sometimes with and sometimes without the consent of the overseer"—often at night "after the overseer has retired to his bed." There a welcome reception could probably be found; the slaves were frequently deemed "better customers than many white people; because [they] always pay cash" and because the shopkeeper believed he could "demand whatever price he pleases for the goods." Yet the slaves learned to drive hard bargains of their own, and in some places "a considerable traffic is carried on . . . by barter." How considerable we cannot know, though if the complaints of slaveholders are any indication, such dealings were widespread and very irritating to them. Frederick Law Olmsted discovered that "the nuisance of petty traders dealing with the negroes" was "everywhere a great annoyance to the planters," who assumed it encouraged the slaves "to pilfer" and to mingle with lowly whites. In response, every slave state made trading with slaves illegal unless specifically permitted by the master or overseer, and localities occasionally roused their slave patrols to enforce the statutes. Nowhere was the traffic fully suppressed, however.[30]

Slaveholders, especially the wealthy and politically powerful, might attempt to solve the problem by forcing merchandisers and poor white folk out of the neighborhood, but they usually found it easier to create a market on their own property and buy up the slaves' produce themselves. Easier perhaps, though in the end not much less corrosive of the personal dependencies they tried to protect. A South Carolina rice planter, anxious to "allow his servants no excuse for dealing with [retailers]," had "a rule to purchase everything they desire to sell and give them a high price for it himself." Eggs quickly became "a circulating medium on the plantation" with a "par value . . . considered to be twelve for a dime, at which they [could] always be exchanged for cash, or left on deposit, without interest, at his kitchen." Instead of "tak[ing] money for the articles he has of them," the slaves put the "value" to a "regular account" they kept and used it, in part, to facilitate purchases from the store the planter opened and "supplied with articles they most want . . . at wholesale quantities," which gave "them a great advantage in dealing with him rather than the grog shops." As a result, a traveler noted, obviously mindful of the social inversion, "his slaves are sometimes his creditors to large amounts." John Burnside, master of the Houmas plantation in Ascension Parish, Louisiana, learned too how the social balances could shift under these circumstances when "an old negro brought up some ducks" and "offered the lot of six for three dollars." "Very well, Louis," Burnside responded with paternalist prerogative, "if you come tomorrow, I'll pay you." "No master," Louis replied, deferentially but firmly, "me want the money now." "But won't you give me credit, Louis?" Burnside asked. "Don't you think I'll pay the three dollars?" "Oh, pay some day, master, sure enough. Master good to pay the three dollar," Louis answered, "but this nigger want the money now to buy food and things for his little family." And, with what must have seemed an unsettling sophistication, Louis added: "They will trust master at Donaldsonville, but they won't trust this nigger."[31]

However Burnside and the rice planter chose to interpret these exchanges, the slaves could hardly have missed the main point: that these were *exchanges* involving reciprocal understandings, expectations, and obligations; that owing to their skills and labor, slaves could exert power and leverage in relations with their owners, giving the lie to claims about absolute authority on the one side and abject submission on the other. Indeed, the system of petty production, provisioning, and exchange permitted the slaves to enact various rituals of reciprocity that implicitly rejected the condition of enslavement and envisioned, if not insisted on, alternative possibilities. Some slaves took produce from their gardens, grounds, coops, or crafts and made small gifts to their masters in return for what they regarded as "considerations." When Charles Ball began to cast his fish nets into the river "with very good effect," he "gave a large fish to the overseer, and took three more to the great house." "These were the first fish that had been in the family this season," he wrote, lending special meaning to the gesture, for which he received "much praise" from "my master and young mistresses" and eventually "some respite from the labors of the cotton field."[32]

Such ritual gifting became more elaborate during the Christmas season. The slaveholders, following long-established custom, took the occasion of Christmas to demonstrate their wealth and benevolence by distributing gifts and sponsoring barbecues for their black, as well as white, "families." But the slaves did not simply play grateful servants to their masters' Lord Bountiful. Visiting plantations in Louisiana in December 1857, Thomas B. Thorpe, a correspondent from *Frank Leslie's Illustrated Newspaper,* wrote that Christmas was not just the "season when the planter makes presents of calico of flaming colors to the women and children, and a coat of extra fineness to patriarchal 'boys' of sixty-five and seventy." It was also "the time when negroes square their accounts with each other, and get 'master' and 'mistress' to pay up for innumerable eggs and chickens which they have from time to time, since the last settling day, furnished the 'big house.'" Thorpe found reason to call the event "a kind of jubilee." Nelson Ferebee, whose family owned a plantation in Camden County, North Carolina, described, though failed fully to grasp, an even more complex rite: "Christmas morning the slaves came to the master's with presents for the mistress, brooms, mats, buckets, etc., things which they had made themselves. In return, the mistress gave them handkerchiefs, worn clothing, ribbons, snuff, pipes, etc. The whole family would be assembled . . . Christmas greetings were exchanged and then a tub of eggnog or toddy was brought out. The master and a few of the older slaves drank to each other a 'Merry Christmas.' The tub was then taken to the 'Quarters.'" Ferebee's family doubtless saw their patriarch and head of household presiding over an event that confirmed the organic and hierarchical nature of the plantation community; the slaves could well have witnessed their own leaders, standing if only momentarily on a level plane with the master, trading respects and good wishes.[33]

That the slaves might look to Christmas as a time to "square accounts with each other" suggests a further dimension to their exchanges, and one that is usually ignored: exchanges between slaves and slave households. Petty production and provisioning helped to define the meaning and boundaries of slave households, and to give family and kinship a material basis, but it could also make for social differentiation among the slaves of a particular plantation or neighborhood. Although Charles Ball surely exaggerated when he insisted that there was a greater "diversity in the modes of life" among "the several households of our quarter" on a South Carolina estate than among "the several families of any white village in New York or Pennsylvania," he made a deeper point. The system favored those slaves with greater energy and initiative, those with craft skills and literacy, and those with larger families and more extensive kinship networks; and it could promote rivalries, jealousies, and destructive infighting. Especially when staple crops could be grown and sold or when slaves had to supply a substantial portion of their daily subsistence, the disparities in their harvests, earnings, and other resources might be significant and salient.[34]

Exchanges among slaves could, therefore, serve to redistribute goods and labor to those in need, reinforce ties of kinship and friendship, and reconfigure the boundaries of social life. Slaves might barter corn for beans, potatoes for melons, chickens for baskets, and food for help in the gardens. They might share their produce or perform services as obligations to kin or as gifts cementing relationships. A few might extend money loans to slaves on other plantations and farms, creating new ties between different groups of slaves or strengthening older ones. And they would use their vegetables, fruits, cakes, fowl, and game to nourish more general conviviality in the quarters.[35]

Indeed, these exchanges could also be generational, thereby sanctifying relations of kinship over time as well as space. There is as yet much to be learned about inheritance practices among slaves. But owing to the records of the Southern Claims Commission, constituted by the federal government to reimburse Union sympathizers in the South whose property was destroyed or confiscated by the Union army, we know that the practices developed and that they may have been both widespread and consequential. For when officials began to make inquiries in the early 1870s, freedpeople in districts stretching from Virginia to South Carolina and Georgia to Mississippi came forward and told how their pigs, chickens, horses, wagons, and other petty property lost during the war had been left them by parents, grandparents, and even more distant kin. And as some of the testimony revealed, the inherited property helped younger slaves form and partially sustain their own families and households. "My old parents used to raise poultry & pigs &c & they gave me some," one claimant, then sixty years of age, poignantly informed the commissioners. "[T]hat is how I got a start."[36]

It is easy, and sometimes tempting, to overstate the gains that slaves managed to make and to understate the limits and costs of those gains. The accumulation of property, when it occurred, was often the result of many years' worth of effort and it never secured more than a fragile basis of recognition. Those slaves who could claim proprietorship of a horse, a carriage, more than a few head of livestock, or a few dollars in cash were rarities—and probably not field hands—and even they ran the risk of losing everything in a moment of masterly whim. Most came to possess little more than some creature comforts of daily life, which barely satisfied the needs of the current generation, let alone the aspirations of the next one. Petty production, provisioning, and exchange did not, moreover, compose a sphere of "autonomy" under slavery or a distinct set of social and economic relations buried within the slave regime; they developed through the antagonistic struggle between master and slave and became embedded as a central component of the regime itself. To that extent, the purposes of masters may have been served as well if not better than those of slaves, for the masters' operational and supervisory costs were duly reduced, and the slaves were perhaps more firmly tied to the quarters. The chains of enslavement always proved stronger than the threads of kinship and custom.

But threads can be pliable and resilient in their own way, and if they remained ever vulnerable to slavery's chains—even if they helped, in some respects, to fortify those chains—they would also redefine the master-slave relation. By contesting the wills of their owners, forging complex ties to each other, etching out time and terrain that they could claim for themselves, turning privileges won into rights to be defended, and blending rituals of reciprocity into ostensible acts of deference and submission, the slaves transformed as well as resisted the southern system of slavery. They conducted, that is, a politics of slaves while simultaneously sketching the framework for a politics of freedpeople.

❖

For rural peoples the world over, in the centuries before the modernization of agriculture led to great migrations from country to town and city, the notion of "community" had immediacy and tangibility. It meant particular people to be encountered in face-to-face relations, as well as a particular place to be lived in and worked on. Community did not ordinarily involve or evoke harmonious or egalitarian relations; more often than not it was marked by multiple hierarchies, harsh regimens, and nasty legitimating sanctions. But it was grounded and bounded, with institutional articulations that could promote, at once, deep senses of social identification among members—including those of different rank or class—and deep suspicions of outsiders.[37]

If they had the means and wherewithal, southern slaveholders tried to build communities organized around the Big House, nearly self-sufficient in essential supplies, insulated from much of the social surroundings, and with strong ties of loyalty binding individual slaves to the plantation and the plantation owner. During the eighteenth century some of the great planter families of the Chesapeake and Carolina sought to do just this, and in the nineteenth century, the various plantation rituals of distribution together with the allocation of garden plots and provision grounds were clearly meant to define both the substance and boundaries of such communities. The effort was surely aided by the generally low population density of the southern countryside. Frederick Douglass described the "home plantation" of Colonel Edward Lloyd as "a secluded, dark, and out-of-the-way place, . . . far away from all the great thoroughfares, and . . . proximate to no town and village," noting that "every leaf and grain of the produce of this plantation, and those of the neighboring farms belonging to Col. Lloyd, are transported to Baltimore in Col. Lloyd's own vessels," and that "everything brought to the plantation comes through the same channel." The slaves might express their attachments to these plantation communities by touting the wealth and refinement of their owners as against the rougher, more common, and meaner figures cut by neighboring slaveholders. Douglass himself scornfully acknowledged the tendency of some slaves to "think their own masters are better than the masters of other slaves." "They seemed to think," he scoffed, "that the greatness of their masters was transferable to themselves."[38]

And yet, Douglass's own experience, first moving onto and then off the Lloyd estate, suggests that the cultural boundaries of large and relatively isolated plantations could be quite permeable, and that the slaves' notion of community may not have coincided with them. In Talbot County, Maryland, home of the Lloyd estate, more than one-third of all the slaves in 1860 lived on farms with fewer than ten slaves, and one in six lived on farms with fewer than five. For them, the prospects of forming families, all of whose members could reside on the same unit, was limited if not remote, and so their social worlds often linked them directly to slaves owned by other farmers and planters. In varying degrees this proved to be the case through much of the antebellum South. In districts having white population majorities and only a small number of plantations, most of the slaves lived on farms with fewer than ten slaves, and a substantial portion (ranging from one-seventh to more than one-third) lived on farms with fewer than five. If Carroll County, Georgia, where the slaves composed only 10 percent of the population, offers a useful illustration, well over half of them were on holdings in which they could not have been living in nuclear family settings. In black majority districts dominated by plantations, the distribution was quite different; nevertheless, between one-sixth and one-third of the slaves might be found on farms with fewer than ten slaves, and between one-third and one-half might be found on farms and small plantations with fewer than twenty. Even on large plantations that boasted dense internal networks of kinship, off-plantation or "abroad" marriages could be commonplace. At the time of his death in 1863, John C. Cohoon owned forty-seven slaves on his Cedar Vale plantation in Nansemond County, Virginia. Of those slaves, nine adults headed families, but only two, Rachel and David, were married; two of the others had been widowed and five had husbands on other farms or plantations.[39]

Based as it was on ties and obligations of kinship, the slaves' idea of community thus broke through the bounds of individual holdings as defined by the slave- and landowner and had a spatially fluid character. Although some masters used their resources to unite immediate families so as to bind them more firmly to one estate, and although masters were occasionally warned against allowing the slaves to "run about," both the incidence of abroad marriages and the slaves' practice of frowning on marriages to cousins ultimately subverted these efforts. Slaveholders simply could not have it all ways: they could not purchase and dispense with their slave property as the requirements of their households dictated while at the same time constructing tightly-knit communities of masters and dependents. Either reluctantly or willingly, they had to yield to demographic realities and pressure from their slaves, and to permit regular social interaction across farms and plantations. Most often, slaves won the ability to go off and join mates and other family members on Saturday nights and Sundays, so long as they were ready for field work on Monday morning; where the distance to be traveled was short, they might also have the opportunity to visit a night or two during the week. For their part, the slaves preferred in some instances to take mates who lived elsewhere, especially when their own master was unusually imperious or abusive.[40]

Community for the slaves, therefore, was a matter of people and of purpose, and its dimensions could vary widely. Everywhere it rested on the sustenance and protection of slave households, and its sites, on all save the smallest holdings, included the quarters, the garden plots, and the provision grounds. But the geographical and social net could become fairly large and diverse. In areas of the upper South, the prevalence of farms and smaller plantations, the frequency of slave hiring and "borrowing," and the legacy of Revolutionary-era manumissions meant that slaves routinely traversed wide stretches of the countryside and formed relations linking town and country, agriculture and industry, slave and freed. Archie Booker, who grew up a slave in Virginia, later recalled that "there was a free nigger town near by the plantation" and "my old boss used to hire some of them to work at harvest time." That he also knew that "some of the niggers in it was set free, some turned free, and some was free born," and that "they had little places of their own to work on," along with "stores, shops, and everything," suggests that movement was in both directions.[41]

In the lower South, and particularly in the plantation districts, however, the geographical reach of the slaves' community was more limited while the social fabric was more dense. There the slaves had better prospects for living in nuclear families and amid extended kin, and for lending these relations a firmer material basis. But they also had fewer opportunities for being hired out, experiencing urban life, or mingling with free people of color. Still, the threads of community normally extended over a number of adjacent plantations and farms, and both the occasions and sites of community could be multiple and varied: routine visitations of friends and kin on Saturday nights and Sundays, festivities marking harvests and holidays, and more clandestine meetings, beyond the masters' gaze, sometimes on the liminal unenclosed and public terrain between neighboring properties. Only on the very largest estates might the slaves' community be chiefly coterminus with the plantation's borders, and then, ironically, the cultural distance between master and slave was probably the most substantial. Charles Ball believed, "On the great cotton plantations . . . the field hands who live in the quarter are removed so far from the domestic circle of their master's family . . . that they know but little more of the transactions within the walls of the great house than if they were ten miles off." He might have been even more struck by the divide on the great rice estates some miles away, where planters often spent at least part of the year in Charleston, and by the ramifications for the slaves' culture. It was on plantations such as these that West African traditions and sensibilities survived most tenaciously. When, moreover, the plantations were several generations old, the slaves undoubtedly came to feel deep and lasting attachments to what they may have called the "home place." But the attachments rarely involved their white owners; they were to their forebears and to each other, and to the ground that they collectively nourished with their work and sweat and consecrated with the bones of their ancestors.[42]

Slave communities reflected and shaped the relations of power, authority, and prestige within them. Indeed, if community was to mean anything—if it was to involve cohesion and not just contact—it had to entail the organization and reproduction of social life, the construction and enforcement of cultural norms, and the development of leaders who could help direct collective aspirations and interpret the significance of wider events. Precisely because slaves were subject to the personal domination of their owners and had no rights that free people officially acknowledged, the project was immensely difficult and the institutional manifestations always shaky. And precisely because the conventional foundations of power and authority—the ownership of property—had only a very limited and customary basis among slaves, the social relations and expectations that slaves devised were necessarily a mix of inherited sensibilities, practical accommodations, and roles imposed on them. It may, in this connection, be useful to speak of "social divisions" of politics that various communities displayed.

Kinship, age, gender, and service-rendering skills stood as the main markers of these divisions. Especially where large plantations predominated, kinship formed the foundation not only of the slaves' world but also of social distinctions among them. Those slaves who formed sizable households and became part of extended families often were able both to accumulate resources and comforts more successfully and to hold other slaves in their debt, provoking an assortment of tensions and jealousies. More than a few observers thus remarked upon the "clannishness" they saw on some estates, with slaves "belonging to one family or one master 'ganged' together . . . always ready to fight for each other." Charles Colcock Jones, the Presbyterian minister and planter from densely black Liberty County, Georgia, found several internecine struggles erupting: "Families grow jealous and envious of their neighbors; some essay to be *leading* families; they overhear conversations and domestic disagreements; become privy to improper conduct . . . [and] depredate upon each other." The disputes, he added, could spill over to "adjoining plantations" and become "open breaches . . . with their neighbors," and the women seemed to be the lightning rods of family conflict, quarreling and fighting "more often than the men."[43]

The management and resolution of such disputes likely fell to slave elders, whose experience, wisdom, and kinship base thrust them into positions of leadership and respect. On particularly large estates, the heads of different families may have established informal "plantation councils" to maintain order and impose discipline. We know almost nothing of the workings of these councils or other such deliberative bodies, but we may suspect that they contributed to collective solidarities that usually held personal and familial altercations in check. Appropriately, Charles Colcock Jones had to concede that "the Negroes are scrupulous on one point; they make common cause, as servants, in

concealing their faults from their owners." "Inquiry elicits no information," he reported, and "the matter assumes the sacredness of a 'professional secret' for they remember that they may hereafter require the
same concealment . . . [and fear] having their names cast out as evil
among their brethren and being subjected to scorn, and perhaps personal violence or pecuniary injury."[44]

Plantation elders who exercised power and authority seemed to be
disproportionately, though not exclusively, male. A correspondent to
the *Southern Cultivator* said as much when noting that "on almost every
plantation of Negroes there is one among them who holds a kind of
magical sway over the minds and opinions of the rest; [and] to him
they look as their oracle." But exceptions suggest that the slaves did
not embrace the gender conventions that regulated the social and political worlds of their owners or the white population in general. When
on picket duty near Beaufort, South Carolina, in September 1862, John
E. Bryant, later a leading Georgia Republican, told therefore of visiting
Christiana, the "Queen of Little island." "Now about 45 years old"
and having been married to the plantation driver who "died some two
years ago," she "has for years exerted a wonderful influence over the
slaves and now her word is law." "All go to her for advice and do as
she advises," he discovered, and although she "has no education," she
did have "remarkable good sense," and it became "the fashion for the
officers on picket at [her plantation] to take dinner with the queen."
Bryant saw fit to mention that Christiana was "nearly white" and
"when . . . young she was pretty and a favorite of the master" while
her husband was "said to have been a smart man but black." Perhaps he
felt that this accounted for her "wonderful influence." In all likelihood,
Christiana's marriage to the driver put her in a position from which
real influence could be exerted and for which the slaves' norms provided room.[45]

The ability of some slave women—and especially of older slave
women—to achieve a place of honor and political power rested on
their decisive contributions to the material and cultural life of the quarters. Without question, they did much of the work of sustaining family
and kinship networks and of anchoring slave communities. They
shouldered the dual burdens of field labor for their owners and domestic responsibilities for their households on a daily basis; and although
on the larger plantations they were found disproportionately on the

hoe and trash gangs, this may have been because of their resistance strategies rather than due to gendered considerations concerning ability and strength. Ex-slave males widely remembered slave women being assigned the same tasks as the men. Solomon Northup was sufficiently impressed by the "four black girls" sent down from a neighboring plantation to cut trees with him that he felt obliged to add that "in the region of Bayou Boeuf they perform their share of all the labor required on the plantation. They plough, drag, drive team, clear wild lands, work on the highway, and so forth." The relegation of slave women to lighter field work, where it occurred, may instead have been the result of the frequent interruptions they inflicted on the plantation regimen owing to illness and child-bearing—interruptions that signaled their day-to-day struggles against the prerogatives of the master and in support of the needs of their families. Indeed, slave women, who also had well-deserved reputations for truculence, may have driven efforts to reorganize field work around kin groups, especially on holdings too small for a fully elaborated gang system.[46]

Slave women assumed prominent roles in related areas of social and cultural reproduction. They usually taught older children of both sexes the many skills involved in tending the fields, gardens, and livestock and in using farm implements. As cooks and seamstresses, they helped feed and clothe their kin and work mates. As midwives and nurses, they saw younger slave women through the trials of childbirth and nurtured slave children through the many challenges of their early years. As healers and folk doctors they attended to the medical concerns of slaves of all ages, while often winning the attention and solicitation of white owners. And as house slaves, whose numbers were predominantly female, they could spirit provisions from the larders and storerooms of their masters back into the quarters, supplementing the diets of their households and kin. Over the course of the life cycle, the status of women in the slave community increased owing to their work as nurses, midwives, caretakers, and educators, while the status of many men may have diminished as they lost the stamina and strength to perform tasks that customarily earned them respect. Older slave women were thereby positioned to command admiration and exercise authority.[47]

The openings available to slave women to wield power and authority, however, depended on their freedom from direct subordination to black men and their centrality to the stability and cultural integrity of slave communities. We still understand very little about how slaves sought to organize their domestic lives or construct their gender norms, and one surely must hesitate before describing relations between husbands and wives—or slave men and women generally—as "egalitarian." Undoubtedly, slaves came to be familiar with the antebellum gender conventions that prevailed among white slaveowners and perhaps in some cases they followed them. But neither law nor custom provided slave men with real leverage over slave women or gave slave women good reason to submit to slave men. Women could not expect men to serve as chief providers or as protectors against economic exploitation, corporal punishment, or sexual abuse. Although masters might designate slave men as "household heads" when they were present, slave households, as social and cultural units, revolved much more fully around women. When slaves found spouses on different plantations or farms, wives and mothers always had immediate responsibility for care of the children; with rare exception, husbands and fathers did the visiting. And when slave families were separated by sale, it was far more likely that mothers and children (and especially mothers and daughters) would manage to remain together. Thus, in a world of tremendous uncertainly and instability, slave women occupied the least volatile niche available, and so they became the chief keepers and transmitters of the community's culture. The slaves' society of the antebellum South may well have been "unusually female-centered."[48]

Like slave women, slave men who most effectively used the resources fashioned by African Americans to serve their communities might acquire special authority among them: those who demonstrated exceptional skills in provisioning families and kin; who had musical or verbal abilities that could entertain, move, and protect other slaves; who had knowledge and experience that healed, educated, and awed; who passed on the stories and traditions of the quarters; or who could question the master's power and prowess without inviting retribution. Some, such as those selected by the slaves to be "captains" or "generals" during annual corn shuckings, displayed multiple talents. They could sing, rhyme, improvise, and ridicule the master's pretensions while encouraging fellow slaves to work hard for the group.[49] But the social division of the slaves' politics also created important roles for those who could appropriate the skills and language of the slaveholders' world toward the similar end of building and fortifying community life. And, for a variety of reasons, this gave an important edge to slave men.

Community building took place between as well as on plantations and farms, as slaves not only formed and renewed relations with one another but also exchanged information, gossip, and rumor. Here the threads were those of communication that outside observers could scarcely glimpse, let alone trace. John Adams, having been warned by Georgia slaveholders in the Continental Congress that a British promise of freedom would mobilize twenty thousand slaves in short order, learned that "the negroes have a wonderful art of communicating intelligence among themselves; it will run several hundred miles in a week or fortnight." A northern teacher later wrote of "secret signs," of what she called "an underground telephone" much "like the underground railroad" which provided slaves with "their own way of gathering news from the whole country." It was, as former slaves would reveal, a communal undertaking, with lines and carriers running in many directions. On individual holdings, women and children were particularly well placed to overhear discussions in the parlors, dining rooms, and immediate environs of their owner's residence. Anna Baker, who spent her childhood as a slave in Monroe County, Mississippi, explained her delight at turning the tables on the nosy master: "Master would tell me, 'Loosanna, if you keep you ears open and tell me what de darkies talk about, there'll be something good in it for you. . . . But all the time I must a-had a right smart mind because I'd play around the white folks and hear what they'd say and then go tell the niggers." Other female or young slaves eavesdropped on conversations among whites while serving meals, tending the horses, or hiding in trees that shaded the Big House; some even would "crawl under the house and lie on the ground to hear master read the newspaper to missis."[50]

The channels of slave communication that linked plantations and farms to each other and to additional sites where information could be garnered included those events—Fourth of July barbecues, corn shuckings, marriages, and funerals—when black men, women, and children from the entire neighborhood had the opportunity to come together. But the channels were created and traveled principally by slaves who had more regular mobility, and these tended to be men.

Some had craft skills in local demand and were hired or "borrowed" out. Some drove coaches or wagons for their owners and journeyed to trading centers and the county courthouse, or piloted boats along the many waterways. Some were members of work gangs sent round to clear fields, chop wood, dig ditches and levees, and repair fences. And some sold the products of their gardens and provision grounds in nearby towns and hamlets (in the South, unlike in the Caribbean, such marketing was done chiefly by men). In the upper South, where the generally smaller slaveholding units meant that community and communication could be one and the same thing, these slaves—along with rural free blacks—played especially significant social and political roles. Booker T. Washington, who grew up on a remote farm in the foothills of Virginia's Blue Ridge Mountains, remembered learning something of the wider world from his stepfather, who was hired for lengthy stints to tobacco factories, railroad companies, and salt mines in the western part of the state but returned each year around Christmas and shared his experiences.[51]

If mobility and craft skills allowed some slaves, most of whom were men, to become crucial political actors, the acquisition of literacy elevated them to positions of great influence. The ability to read newspapers, broadsides, account books, and other documents, to write letters and passes, and to educate their children and fellow slaves was immensely empowering in a world increasingly dominated by commodities and electoral politics. It was also a source of community prestige in a world that officially, albeit haphazardly, regarded literacy instruction for slaves as a crime. Some slaves learned to read, and perhaps to write, from evangelical masters—often mistresses—who ignored legal prohibitions so that their bondpeople might become better acquainted with the Bible. Some learned from the children of their owners with whom they had close relations. Some, especially in cities, learned from literate free blacks. Far more, with stunning determination, taught themselves slowly and ingeniously through sound and pronunciation, frequently by manipulating whites into helping and by getting hold of Webster's blue-back speller.[52]

The Scots traveler David Macrae was told of slaves who gained literacy by observing a governess instruct white children, by studying the letters engraved on the master's plates and silver, and by "noticing the signboards above the shop doors and printing the letters on the dust on the stable floor." "It was only by trickery that I learned to read and write," George Washington Albright, a Mississippi slave who later served in the state senate, recalled. "[T]he white children on my plantation did their lessons in the kitchen in my mother's presence, and she picked up what information she could, and taught me. I got a primer and learned to read it." Frederick Douglass availed himself, first, of an amiable mistress and, then, of hungry white playmates who offered lessons in return for biscuits; he subsequently labored mightily, at one point with the assistance of a free black man, to instruct other rural slaves, who numbered as many as forty. By means of such "stolen" education and clandestine schooling—by a combination, that is, of individual creativity and collective struggle—the basic literacy rate among slaves, according to the leading authority, eventually reached, and may well have surpassed, 10 percent. And as was true in many traditional societies, the greater proportion was male. But together, those who had achieved literacy, male and female alike, quickly found themselves at the center of political life in slave, and later in freed, communities.[53]

If slave communities found quasi-institutional expression, it was most commonly in the religious congregations that they fashioned. In them, the varied threads of household, kinship, labor, gender, and leadership came to be joined with those of sensibility, ethics, aspiration, spirituality, and faith to create a social fabric both rich and varied, with many blends. One cannot fail to be struck both by the pervasiveness of spiritual concerns among the slaves and by the diverse ways in which those concerns became manifest over space and time. From the Chesapeake to Texas, there were biracial churches, independent black churches, praise houses, and brush arbors. And there emerged complex mixes of West African rituals and cosmology, folk customs, and Christian beliefs and practices, some of which had denominational affiliations. Yet however diverse, these congregations had, by the late antebellum period, become the principal means through which individual slaves and their families were formally initiated into a chosen community, collective norms were defined and imposed, leaders were mobilized and sustained, and events were discussed and interpreted. By the late

antebellum period, too, these congregations evinced a quiet millennialism that fed a proto-peasant consciousness. They were, in a very real
sense, the slaves' houses of politics as well as their houses of worship.

The formation of the slaves' religious congregations has a complex
history that can be traced, at least, to the mid-eighteenth century, when
the Great Awakening first attracted a substantial number to Christianity. Until then, few white Christians—most of whom were Angli-
can—showed much interest in proselytizing among their slaves, and
few slaves—most of whom were African born—showed much interest
in the rather stiff, formalistic, and hierarchical religion that their masters practiced. Instead, the slaves' spiritual lives took shape largely
beyond the slaveholders' reach and notice, and they were composed
of those traditions that could be maintained in the face of forced separations or rearranged among Africans from different ethnic groups. The
process was facilitated by sensibilities that West and Central Africans
broadly shared, not simply among themselves, but also with Europeans
of humble background who staffed the slavers and other Atlantic trading vessels, labored as indentured servants, or supervised the scattered
holdings of wealthy planters: that is, the white folk with whom African
slaves of the late seventeenth and early eighteenth centuries likely had
protracted contact. Together, they imagined a world in which secular
and sacred, natural and supernatural knew no discrete boundaries, in
which the living, the dead, and the gods resided in close connection,
in which spirits were omnipresent and magical powers could be exercised, and in which past, present, and future were related cyclically.[54]

The itinerant ministers who sparked the Great Awakening initially
preached a harsh Calvinism that bore little resemblance to the
worldview of West Africans. But the itinerants themselves came from
relatively poor and obscure backgrounds, had little schooling or formal
training, attacked the established clergy, and invited all ranks and races
to hear a message that heaped scorn on worldly vanities and proclaimed
the dignity and self-worth of even the most downtrodden. More important, the new evangelical denominations that they represented, especially the Methodists and Baptists, emphasized the experience of spiritual rebirth and personal communion with Christ, challenged the ways
of the landed elite, questioned the morality of slaveholding, and welcomed black people—slave and free—as members. The evangelical
movement in the South swept with particular force through those areas

in which whites and blacks had been in most intensive contact, and it allowed blacks exceptional initiative and participation. In some places, black evangelicals converted their masters, established churches before their white counterparts did, and preached both to mixed and predominantly white congregations; more generally, they introduced other slaves and free blacks to the Christian faith as they understood it, doubtless filtering it through an African cosmology that, in one form or another, still held sway.[55]

By the end of the eighteenth century, black Methodists, and especially Baptists, had gained a significant foothold in urban areas of Virginia, South Carolina, and Georgia, and had begun to fan out into the adjacent countryside. Independent black churches sprouted either on their own or as offshoots of biracial congregations, and there is evidence of a growing millennial fervor among them, owing in large part to the revolutionary upheavals touching many corners of the Atlantic world. But there remained substantial resistance to the spread of black Christianity, from slaves and slaveholders alike, and the aborted revolts, first of Gabriel and then allegedly of Denmark Vesey, each showing the imprint of evangelical activity, brought down the heel of official repression on black churches and preachers. When the Second Great Awakening inspired renewed interest in spreading the gospel among the slaves in the 1830s and 1840s, white ministers, evangelical planters, and plantation missions spearheaded the effort and slave converts generally joined churches controlled by white masters.[56]

On the eve of the Civil War, according to necessarily rough estimates, between 15 and 25 percent of adult slaves were aligned with Christian denominations, the great majority of whom—particularly in the rural districts—were Baptists. But this may simultaneously understate the number whose spiritual sensibilities and activities were influenced by Christianity and exaggerate the social and cultural impact of the denominational faiths. In an extraordinary survey of his slaves conducted in the mid-1830s, an evangelical planter from Fluvanna County, Virginia, who had already constructed a chapel on his estate and manumitted several Christian slaves, was probably shocked to discover that a decisive majority (about 60 percent) rejected his overtures and disclaimed his religion. A variety of observers who witnessed black worship either during slavery or immediately afterward made a related point: they found intense and often moving displays of spiritual energy

that showed the trappings of Christianity with little of what they regarded as its substance. "Their notions of the Supreme Being; of the
character and offices of Christ and of the Holy Ghost; of a future state;
and of what constitutes holiness of life," complained the Reverend
Charles Colcock Jones, who had more than a fleeting interest in the
matter, "are indefinite and confused. Some . . . have heard of Jesus
Christ; but who he is and what he has done for a ruined world, they
cannot tell." A foreign traveler less cerebrally described services as "a
jumble of Protestantism, Romanism, and Fetishism."[57]

The slaves did, for the most part, reject the bases of Christian funda-
mentalism. That is to say, they rejected the notion of original sin and
most everything else in Christian theology positing a radical alienation
of the individual from the divine or a radical disjuncture between earth
and heaven, natural and supernatural. They embraced, on the other
hand, those elements of Christian faith and practice that could be interpreted as invoking the palpable presence of God in the world, the
communal expression of religiosity, and the personal experience of
spiritual power. "They seem," one European visitor recorded, "to see
God bending over them like the sky, to feel his presence on them and
around them, like the storm and sunshine. . . . Many of them have
strange inward experiences, and believe that God gives them special
revelations." The slaves' attraction to Baptism—especially to the Ar-
minian variant—was therefore not simply because the denomination
permitted considerable local autonomy and an untutored ministry; it
was also because West African and Baptist worldviews resonated with
one another. Central to both was the idea of rebirth, of symbolic death,
visions and spiritual journeys, and of the sudden emergence of a new
soul. Although conversion narratives compiled from the recollections
of ex-slaves lack many specifically Christian features, the Baptist adherence to adult baptism, total immersion, and the laying-on of hands
provided a broad and compelling framework.[58]

Yet whether they called themselves Baptists, Methodists, Presbyteri-
ans, or even Catholics, slaves assimilated Christianity to deeper and
more traditional folk beliefs. As a contributor to the *Southern Christian
Advocate* lamented, "Instead of giving up their visionary religionism,
embracing simple truth . . . our missionaries find them endeavoring to
incorporate their superstitious rites with a purer system of instruction,
producing thereby a hybrid, crude, undefinable medley of truth and

falsehood." A white minister similarly thought that the "dreams, visions, trances, and voices" described by slaves during conversion had "a striking resemblance to some form or type which has been handed down for generations," and went on to charge that "*Antinomianism* is not uncommon, and at times, in its worst form." Had they been exposed to it, the slaves may well have felt a spiritual kinship to the antinomian tradition, with its emphasis on justification by faith, its millennialist outlook, and its implicit challenge to the authority of established institutions.[59] As it happened, the slaves were drawn in scripture less to the harsh moral injunctions of the Old Testament than to the "stories, parables, prophecies, and visions" of the Old and New Testaments, and to notions of collective deliverance and personal redemption in this world from their sufferings and misfortunes. Theirs was what might be called a premillennialist orientation with a rather vague messianic aspect: They seem to have imagined a divine intervention that would end their collective oppression, punish their oppressors, and allow them to build a new order of freedom. And their deliverer was often represented as a figure showing the marks not only of several Biblical characters—most notably Moses and Jesus—but also of the specific social and political context in which they found themselves; a figure who would not so much bring total destruction to the world of their enslavement as lead them out of it. Thus a black Mississippian claimed to have "heard in slave days of one Jesus, but thought, from the way his fellow slaves spoke of Him, that He was a great planter in some other State, who was to buy all the coloured people one day and set them free." Eventually that messianic figure, and chiefly after his death, would be Abraham Lincoln.[60]

The millennialist and messianic threads that can be detected in what some scholars have termed the slaves' "sacred cosmos" were woven through and reinforced by an intensely communal style of worship. The slaves who belonged to biracial churches often outnumbered the white members, sometimes overwhelmingly, and when they attended Sunday services they might have heard a black preacher or exhorter— under the watchful eye of the presiding white minister—lead in the singing of hymns and spirituals and perhaps offer a short sermon. But the spiritual activities of their own creation were most likely to be found in the sites and settings that they controlled with limited interference from their masters: in the chapels and praise houses built on the very largest plantations and at what the slaves called "brush arbor" or "hush arbor" meetings. There the slaves met more frequently, with the proceedings conducted by one of their number. Anna Carter, a northern white missionary writing from Hilton Head, South Carolina, in 1864, seemed to recognize the distinction between the more and less formal convocations. "There has been no preaching here for some months," she told an official of the American Missionary Association, but "the people are faithful to sustain their own meetings in their own way. They have prayer meeting every evening, and at dawn Sunday morning. Then this summer they held meetings in rotation on the three different plantations." It did, in fact, appear to be a common practice in the black belt, when the slaveholders did not stand in the way, for the meetings "to change from plantation to plantation getting around in some 6 or 8 weeks." When the slaveholders did not yield, the slaves had to improvise. "We had our own church in the brick yard way out on the field," recalled Elizabeth Rose Hite, who was born on a Louisiana sugar plantation. "We hid behind the bricks and had church every night [even though] we was only supposed to have church on Sunday." Other slaves assembled secretly in their cabins or deep in the woods and, relying on folk wisdom, turned an iron kettle or wash pot upside down to muffle the sound of their prayers and singing and thereby avoid attracting the notice of owners, overseers, or patrollers.[61]

The churches, chapels, praise houses, and brush arbor meetings were not simply collections of individual slaves; they were collections of households and kin, and initiation into membership served as the principal ritual by which the slaves marked and consecrated the boundaries of their communities. Scattered evidence suggests that the initiation process itself often involved younger following older, husbands following wives, children following parents, and kin following kin into communion so that the congregation regularly mapped relations of power and influence as the slaves might have understood them. Moaning that "there is not one [slave] family in a thousand in which family prayer is observed morning and evening," a white minister in Georgia nonetheless acknowledged how kinship became reconfigured: "A general meeting of all members of the church as well as of worldly members for prayer in the evening on plantations . . . takes the place of family worship—the plantation is considered one large family."[62]

It should not be surprising, therefore, that sacred and secular leaders were usually one and the same, that they included folk practitioners as well as preachers and women as well as men, and that they normally had an organic relationship to their congregants. The correspondent to the *Southern Cultivator* who found that "on almost every plantation of Negroes there is always one among them . . . to [whom] they look as an oracle," added that "this same oracle . . . [is] most generally a *preacher*." By the late antebellum period, conjurers and sorcerers, some female, who at one time "wielded a fearful amount of spiritual influence among their followers," had lost ground to those more conversant with the culture of the gospel, though in some places—especially where West African and Caribbean currents made themselves strongly felt—they continued to maintain a tenacious hold. Other slave women also numbered among the spiritual leaders, and one white observer thought that "at some of their religious meetings" the women were "as free to lead as the men." Slave congregations may well have provided exceptional room for women to speak and exercise devotional authority. But as Christian sensibilities and practices became more widespead, those opportunities probably narrowed and women would more likely have achieved prominence and respect in the role of "spiritual guides" or "spiritual mothers," preparing young slaves for their entry into the religious community and then assisting "seekers" in their spiritual "travels." [63]

Black preachers who had acquired local reputations and whose demeanor proved acceptable to whites were occasionally brought in, either by slaveholders or biracial churches, to conduct services of a Sunday. But most of the religious leaders were homegrown, living and working among their congregations. Frederick Law Olmsted discovered that on "almost every large plantation and in every neighborhood of small ones . . . there is one man who has come to be considered the head or pastor of the local church." Often mature in years, frequently demonstrating a variety of skills and talents, probably familiar with the ways of white owners while being closely linked to other slaves through kinship, they were generally natural leaders who "felt the call" and knew that preaching was their road to power, prestige, and service. Most of the preachers remained illiterate or semiliterate, but many struggled to avail themselves of opportunities offered by sympathetic white missionaries or fellow slaves to learn how to read and write. For some, it was a collective undertaking. "We slaves were allowed night farms," former slave Byrd Day remembered, but "in order that I might study the Bible, the other slaves on the place worked my patch for me. So I studied the book and read it to them." The Reverend Jacob Nelson, who was considered by the slaves on a Louisiana sugar plantation to be "the best preacher," set a particularly high standard: he spoke five languages and attracted "the educated white folks . . . to hear [him] preach." More commonly, the preachers were distinguished by what one white traveler termed "a remarkable memory of words, phrases, and forms; [and] a curious form of poetic talent."[64]

Such abilities served them and their congregations well. Whatever the specific setting or denominational affiliation, slave worship was characterized by intense emotion channeled into the making of a communal spirituality and identity. And the preachers, who were particularly adept at the call-and-response pattern of prayer and song that harked back to West Africa—and who may have first displayed their talents on work gangs in the fields—became the crucial facilitators. James L. Smith, a slave in Northumberland County, Virginia, was "learning the shoe-maker's trade" when he "became deeply interested in my soul's salvation," "united with the church," and "commenced holding meetings among my people," sometimes traveling as far as ten miles to do so. Being "very zealous," Smith conducted meetings at which "we continued to sing and pray . . . all night." "The singing," he emphasized, "was accompanied by a certain ecstasy of motion, clapping of hands, tossing of heads, which would continue without cessation about half an hour; one would lead off in a recitative style, others joining in the chorus." Soon, "the old house . . . rang with their jubilant shouts and shook in all its joints." If the preacher was literate, "a chapter of the Bible" might be read and a hymn "given out and sung"; if he could not read, a "brief exhortation . . . on some remembered passage . . . of the Scriptures" would be substituted, followed by "a hymn from memory and prayer." The singing would then begin again and, in some places, might lead into a "shout" or "ring shout," among the most West African of the slaves' religious ceremonies.[65]

The various houses of slave worship not only pulsed with a communal spirit and religiosity but also vibrated with the more somber chords of collective deliberation and discipline. For these, too, were the sites of the slaves' "councils" and "courts," where members of the community gathered to discuss local events, resolve disputes, and dispense justice.

Commenting on the many quarrels, depredations, and "domestic dis-agreements" that he believed erupted regularly among plantation slaves, the Reverend Charles Colcock Jones noted that "the Sabbath is considered a very suitable day for the settlement of their difficulties." A northern missionary, working among the contrabands at Fortress Monroe, Virginia, in September 1861, was more impressed by the pro-ceedings he found. Having "observe[d] the intellectual status of a con-siderable number of brethren at a church meeting," he "was surprised at their understanding and wisdom in regard to church order and pro-priety, and tone of discipline." "High ground was taken in regard to the Sabbath, the temperance cause, and other matters of Christian mo-rality," he noted, and "in discipline stress was laid on the propriety and duty of private admonition . . . before public censure." Each slave community appears to have devised its own customs and rituals, some displaying the traditions of West Africa, some the forms of evangelical denominations, some the imprint of American republicanism, and some a complex combination of each. A white Methodist missionary in coastal South Carolina during the 1830s who learned with distress that the slaves had "organized societies among themselves," all "under Bap-tist influence," considered their practices as to penance "very corrupt." "They had three degrees of punishment . . . [according] to the mag-nitude of the crime," he sneered. "If the crime was of the first magni-tude, the perpetrator had to pick up a quart of benne seed . . . poured on the ground by the priest; if of the second, a quart of rice; and if of the third a quart of corn." But "it was also a rule among them never to divulge the secret of stealing: and if it should be divulged . . . that one had to go to the low seat or pick up the benne seed." The mission-ary did not appreciate the slaves' ethical distinctions. The slaves made no mind; they were too busy defining and carrying out their political responsibilities.[66]

❖

The slaves' political struggles to contest and transform the relations of domination under which they lived were evident from the very establishment of slavery on the North American mainland, but in the first decades of the nineteenth century they took place in a new and contradictory context. On the one hand, a slave society of unprecedented size, wealth, and stability was being created in the southern states thanks to the cotton boom and to the aggressive designs of slave-holding settlers and their political representatives. The antebellum South would boast by far the largest slave population in the Western Hemisphere and its slaveholding planters would rank as the richest and politically most powerful of Americans. On the other hand, the revolutionary movements that began to sweep the Atlantic world during the last third of the eighteenth century toppled or weakened slave regimes in a variety of European colonies and provided a language of natural rights and republicanism that confounded the principles on which systems of slave labor customarily were based and that the slaves could appropriate for their own ends. Although the geographical expansion of the United States soon eliminated potential allies and quasi-safe havens for the slaves in Spanish Florida and French Louisiana, the concurrent abolition of slavery in the northern states made for the possibility of others. By the 1850s, the slaves were therefore subject to the power of masters who proclaimed slavery a positive good and a reflection of inherent inequalities, yet they could at the same time know that the institution was under national and international attack and that folk like them might aid, or even lead, a successful assault against it.[67]

It is difficult, if not impossible, to discover how far or to what extent the political currents of the Atlantic world extended into the slave quarters of the antebellum South; but it is clear that those currents, at very crucial moments, were both encountered and influenced by enslaved peoples of the South, the Caribbean, and other parts of the Americas. The slaves were, after all, among the most international of travelers not only because of their forced diaspora, but also because they subsequently manned transoceanic commercial vessels, accompanied and occasionally fought with imperial and colonial armies, worked in growing port cities, and traversed ever-shifting borders owing to the almost constant state of warfare among European powers of the eighteenth and early nineteenth centuries. Indeed, the Atlantic might usefully be imagined as a large political, as well as cultural, "contact zone" in which Africans and African Americans mingled regularly with each other and with sailors, soldiers, servants, and other plebeians from Britain, France, Spain, and the Netherlands—and in which all were simultaneously transmitters and receivers of news and ideas carried chiefly through increasingly dense networks of maritime communication. Consider only some notable connections associated with the revolutions in the North American colonies and in St. Domingue: the thousands of American slaves taken by loyalist masters to the British Caribbean; the hundreds of blacks from the French West Indies—including future leaders of the Haitian Revolution—recruited to participate with French troops in the American War for Independence; and, most spectacular and consequential of all, the thousands of refugees, free and slave, from the great slave revolt in St. Domingue who came disproportionately to the United States and flooded the ports of Baltimore, Norfolk, Wilmington, Charleston, and New Orleans during the 1790s, on the eve of the large migrations from the seaboard South into the interior.[68]

The repercussions can only be glimpsed, yet they are enough to suggest that the political sensibilities of slaves and free blacks, especially though not exclusively in coastal and urban areas, were deeply affected. They may be seen in the Richmond of slave blacksmith Gabriel around the tumultuous year 1800, when fellow slaves in an extended perimeter appear to have imbibed an artisan republicanism and to have become conversant with the revolutionary impulse in France and the role of Quakers and Methodists in the antislavery struggle. They may be seen in the Charleston of the well-traveled and multilingual free black carpenter Denmark Vesey during the early 1820s, as the city's slaves, many with skills and mobility, drew upon the Bible, newspaper accounts of local politics, and awareness of events in Haiti to assess and communicate—in subterranean discourse—their prospects for freedom. And they may be seen in David Walker, a North Carolina free black who spent most of his life in the South and whose fiery *Appeal . . . to the Coloured Citizens of the World* of 1829 wove threads of natural rights, anticapitalism, Christian millennialism, and pan-Africanism into an indictment of slavery and white power. Published when Walker was in Boston, this tract seems then to have circulated among blacks at least in several southern cities.[69]

The political knowledge and sophistication to be found in a Gabriel, a Denmark Vesey, or a David Walker surely remained a rarity among slaves, particularly among those who lived on plantations and farms. But there is good reason to think that, over time, growing numbers learned basic lessons of the new national politics: that black people did not live as slaves in the northern states, that some white and black Americans in those states spoke and organized against slavery, and that a conflict over the question of slavery brewed. The lessons were most readily available to slaves in the urban and upper South, where proximity to the free states together with concentrations of free blacks and white immigrants made for a more edifying environment. Working on the sensible assumption that an enemy of my enemy must be my friend, Frederick Douglass first became interested in the abolitionists after hearing slaveholders vilify them, but his horizons were expanded by two sympathetic Irish dockworkers who told him that he "ought to run away, and go to the north; that [he] should find friends there, and that [he] would be as free as anybody." Hired out to a navy yard in the District of Columbia shortly before he fell into the hands of a slave trader, Charles Ball had his eyes opened by a free black sailor living in nearby Philadelphia who told him "of the liberty enjoyed there by black people." Tom, a slave in Montgomery County, Virginia, found out about public affairs "from poor people in the neighborhood" and "by hearing the newspapers read." The sources of information exploited by James Curry, who lived on the border of North Carolina and Virginia before his successful flight north, are not apparent; what is apparent is that he "knew there were free states" and "had heard of England, and that *there* there were no slaves."[70]

It was not long before lessons such as these became more widely disseminated. For as the cotton economy expanded and pulled thousands of slaves southwestward, so too did it facilitate the spread of their political impressions and experiences. Traveling in Louisiana in the winter of 1853–1854, Frederick Law Olmsted thus came upon an elderly slave who had been born and raised in Virginia and who crowed about the "right good" Quakers he had seen in his journeys as a blacksmith before being sold south. "This shows how knowledge of the abolition agitation must be carried among the slaves to the most remote districts," Olmsted concluded. Louisiana and Gulf Coast slaves could have learned about abolitionist agitation of a different sort from the descendants of slaves pushed northwestward: of those who arrived in New Orleans, Mobile, and Pensacola in the 1790s and 1800s with owners fleeing the revolution in St. Domingue, and who made their presence felt in an aborted conspiracy in Pointe Coupée in 1795 and in the largest of America's nineteenth-century slave revolts in St. John the Baptist Parish in 1811.[71]

Most slaves, whether in the upper or lower South, continued to receive intelligence through their customary networks of communication—the "grapevine way," as one put it—yet the advent of mass party politics and the related advances in the circulation of print media, beginning in the 1820s and 1830s, increased the volume and the opportunities. Slaves could now become familiar with the language and issues of local and national politics not only from the casual conversations of neighborhood whites, but also from the lips of politicians speaking at campaign stops, court days, and barbecues that they attended, from the mushrooming number of newspapers that political parties sponsored and literate slaves might get hold of, and from political tracts and broadsides that could be produced cheaply and sent through the mails. The former slave and postwar political leader Robert Smalls remembered hearing of Frederick Douglass as a boy when one of three literate field hands on his master's Ladies Island plantation in South Carolina, recently arrived from Charleston, read them a copy of Douglass's speeches that he had managed to pick up. Solomon Northup commented on "the extravagant hopes" that word of the Mexican War "excited" among his fellow slaves in Bayou Boeuf, Louisiana, provoking in one instance a plot "among a number of slaves . . . to fight their way against all opposition, to the . . . territory of Mexico." Even an ex-slave from interior Marshall County, Mississippi, who claimed that "we slaves knew very little about what was going on outside our plantations," nonetheless noted that "it was impossible to keep the news of John Brown's attack on Harper's Ferry from spreading."[72]

And yet the slaves' acquaintance with the politics and political culture of the South and the nation expanded at the very time that their room for political maneuvering seemed to narrow. Following a series of events that shook their confidence, if not the foundations of their society—the Virginia slavery debates, the Nat Turner insurrection, the publication of David Walker's *Appeal* and William Lloyd Garrison's *Liberator*, and the abolition of slavery in the British West Indies—the slaveholders of the antebellum South launched an aggressive campaign to secure their property and seize the political offensive. In the

1830s and 1840s, they moved on several fronts to hedge in the world
of their slaves and to fend off potential adversaries from within and
without. They toughened slave codes, made private manumissions
more difficult, and restricted the privileges of free blacks and slave
preachers. The younger and upwardly mobile of the slaveholders took
command of the Democratic party and used their leverage in it to
defeat the last vestiges of Indian and maroon resistance in the southeast, to impose the gag rule in Congress and censorship of the mails
in southern post offices, to annex Texas and wage war against Mexico,
and to begin agitating for imperial ambitions in the Caribbean and
Central America and for reopening the African slave trade. Their view
of emancipation in the French and British Caribbean as an utter failure
steeled rather than softened their stand against gradualist solutions to
the slavery question at home. And although the expansion of electoral
politics during the Jacksonian period yielded in part to pressure from
nonslaveholders, it politically incorporated white southerners who
might otherwise have opposed the slaveholders' projects.[73]

Thus, although the slaves were well aware of social divisions among
southern whites and of tensions between different groups of them,
potential political allies were in exceptionally short supply. Most of
the white nonslaveholders were small land- and propertyowners who,
so far as the slaves could see, either did the slaveholders' bidding,
hoped to join their ranks, or vented their frustrations on black people.
Poorer white folk, with little property and few skills, were another
matter. Some were hired for odd jobs on plantations and farms, and ex-
slaves recalled working side by side with them and perhaps engaging in
conviviality of several sorts; a few ex-slaves expressed sympathy for
the predicaments of the hardest pressed and noted conditions and humiliations that they may have shared. But the slaveholders tried to see
to it that there were few sites in the countryside where such conviviality could have more than limited duration or where a deeper sense of
mutuality could be nourished, and the poor whites who were not connected to respectable kin or dependent on the good offices of the prop-
ertied were, like outsiders in general, eyed with suspicion. Nowhere
in the South could they claim the numbers or autonomy to mount a
substantial challenge to slaveholding interests, and nowhere could they
find the voices and institutions to articulate what that challenge would

be. The few nonconformists among them or the elite were harassed, marginalized, silenced, or ruthlessly driven out.[74]

The most important and reliable allies the slaves had, and the most nagging irritants the slaveholders had to suffer, were nineteenth-century America's best examples of maroon societies: the free black communities of the northern states. Located chiefly in urban areas and composed heavily of fugitive slaves and their children, they occupied a precarious place on the political landscape while fashioning their own institutions and doing the main work of sustaining abolitionism. Indeed, the most significant contribution that the slaves may have made to the national struggle over slavery in the years after the Nat Turner rebellion was in the form of runaways—usually numbering over one thousand each year—who added to the size of these communities, troubled the consciences of otherwise indifferent northern whites, and provoked a direct political crisis in the relations between the slave and free states. Subscribing to antislavery newspapers, joining black abolition societies, collaborating on autobiographical accounts of their enslavement and escape, attending conventions that pressed for black civil and political rights, and organizing to resist enforcement of the Fugitive Slave Law, a good many of the runaways became schooled in modern politics. Ultimately, they would return to the South during the Civil War and Reconstruction as shock troops of political revolution.[75]

The runaways testified to and amplified the vibrancy of communication networks among the slaves and between the slaves and the fugitive communities of the North. So too did the political weapon that slaves who remained behind came to wield with potent effect: the weapon of rumor. A proposition for belief, a truth claim passed along chiefly by word of mouth, rumor surely had much to recommend as a discursive practice for slaves, as it did for other highly repressed social groups. Its source is cloaked in anonymity; it normally flows through established channels of everyday life; and it is open to continuous improvisation and embellishment, thereby activating and energizing (in effect politicizing) those who become involved in its circuits. Rumor seems especially to thrive when events of vital importance are taking place, enabling the articulation of aspirations and anxieties that cannot otherwise be expressed, and thus it may be regarded as a form of

popular political discourse, a discourse of expectation and anticipation.[76]

Yet in societies such as the antebellum South, in which neither master nor slave could acknowledge even the political character of the
contests between them, rumor was perhaps more than a means for
expressing anxieties and aspirations; it may have been a necessary device in each of their hands and hence a veritable field of political struggle in its own right. Nowhere was this more apparent than at times
of great social and political stress, when reports of behaviors and
speech acts eventually produced insurrectionary panics. The sequence
of events generally followed a similar course: word of suspicious movements or activity among the slaves or of a provocative remark issued
by one or more of them; the extraction from a suspect, often by coercion, of a "plot" involving violence and violation against the white
population, or the confirmation of such a "plot" by a trusted slave; the
implication of white instigators or co-conspirators, usually outsiders to
the community or transgressors of local norms; and the mobilization
of white "citizens" along with a choreographed investigation in which
some of the accused would be absolved of guilt while the remainder
would suffer summary punishments. Scholars, not unreasonably, have
then asked either whether the plot was "real," or, assuming it must
obviously have been the concoction of fevered white imaginations,
what it might tell us about white society. But it may be equally useful
to see at work the circulation of multiple rumors among more parties
and participants, including the slaves: to see, that is, a process whereby
the slaves too interpreted the meaning of events and then tested those
interpretations in various ways. In the Texas Republic of the early
1840s, when the question of annexation to the United States or of
British support for independence in exchange for emancipation sparked
heated debate, "the citizens of several of the eastern counties" became
alarmed at the "conduct of the slaves" who "might be seen at all hours
of the night coming in and going out of town, and going from one
plantation to another." A decade before in Virginia, as rumors of further unrest floated wildly in the aftermath of Nat Turner's rebellion,
one prominent white politician, fearing the encouragement they might
afford the slaves, claimed "that the blacks themselves have in some
instances had the address to put reports into circulation in order to

enjoy the spectacle resulting from the unaccountable panic of the whites."[77]

Difficult as it is to determine the content of the rumors and interpretations that passed through the quarters at any particular point, there was, certainly by the first decades of the nineteenth century, evidence that the slaves had begun fashioning their own understandings of the Atlantic's revolutionary political tide. In the 1820s, black preachers in Edgecombe County, North Carolina, apparently convinced their congregations that "the national government had set them free . . . and that they were being unjustly held in servitude." Just before the presidential election of 1836, according to the recollections of a fugitive slave from the same state, "there came a report from a neighboring plantation, that, if Van Buren was elected, he was going to give all the slaves their freedom." The rumor "spread rapidly among the slaves," prompting great "rejoicing" and "one old man, who was a Christian" to advise that "all we had got to do, was, as Moses commanded the children of Israel . . . 'to stand still and see the salvation of God.'" Four years later, in the telling of Emily Burke, who lived on a large plantation in Georgia, the slaves "were all bold enough to assert publicly that 'when William Henry Harrison became President of the United States, they should have their freedom.'" The Georgia politician Howell Cobb found during the campaign of 1844, when the Liberty party selected a presidential candidate, that the "negroes are already saying to each other that great men are trying to set them free and will succeed."[78]

Not surprisingly, rumors of slave insurrection bubbled very widely and intensely during the fall of 1856 as the Republican party fielded its first contestant for presidential office; but rumors flew as well among many slaves that their liberation was at hand. Insisting that stories of the plots were "greatly exaggerated" and that he had "no idea that there was any organized plan for an insurrection," a white Tennessean could nonetheless admit that "the negroes hearing so much of Fremont began to think that if he was elected that they would all be free." William Webb, who moved between Kentucky and Mississippi during his time in bondage, dated the slaves' awareness of "another Nation wishing for [them] to be free" to Fremont's campaign and described secret meetings and discussions over an extended territory. "They would make speeches among themselves, to the best of their knowledge about what steps they would take," Webb recalled. "Some would speak and say, 'wait for the next four years.' They said they felt as if the next President would set the colored people free."[79]

The slaveholders had good cause for concern, for these versions of what has been called "naive monarchism"—the notion that the ruler had proclaimed some great change in the lives of his subjects but that his wishes were being thwarted by unfaithful subordinates—were common to the history of slave and peasant rebellions in the West, especially once the age of revolution commenced and an ever-widening group of servile laborers learned that they might have friends and allies in positions of power. Virtually every plot or revolt from at least 1790 on was surrounded by rumors among the slaves that amelioration or freedom had been decreed by the king, the imperial parliament, or the colonial office only to be withheld by the local regime. Indeed, this can be seen in one form or another in St. Domingue in 1791, in Barbados in 1816, in Demerara in 1823, and in Jamaica in 1831, not to mention in Charleston, South Carolina, in 1822, where at least some of the slaves in Denmark Vesey's circle appear to have believed that the state legislature—which had recently debated the question of private manumissions—"had made us free."[80]

Between the 1830s and the secession crisis of 1860–1861, the prospects for a successful slave revolt in the southern states, despite the reverberations of sectional conflict, were remote in ways that most slaves surely grasped. The white population was substantial and well armed, the slaveholders were becoming more militant and self-conscious in defense of their interests, and a consensus was being achieved among white social classes at least on the centrality of slavery to the preservation of social order. The many rumors of slave conspiracies that surfaced during these years, taken simply as indications of slave unrest and of contention between slaves and masters, were thus all the more remarkable. But by invoking the will and authority of a presidential candidacy, a political party, or a governmental body in support of their own aspirations, whether attached to rumors of conspiracy or not, the slaves were practicing the politics of those traditionally denied admission to a society's official political arenas. Unable to advance political demands through argument or merit or by rallying their numbers, unable even to represent themselves as political actors because they stood outside of formal politics, the slaves instead projected a terrain of struggle in which their aspirations could be advanced and in which they might imagine powerful allies. If this did not propel a frontal assault on the institution of slavery, it enabled them to create a fledgling political community, founded on shared perceptions, under-standings, and expectations. And it would inspire them to act when those imagined allies tried to crush a rebellion launched by their owners.[81]

❖ 2 ❖

"THE CHOKED VOICE OF A RACE
AT LAST UNLOOSED"

> Got a canoe and a sail, and started for Fort Monroe. . . . That was
> before General Butler had allowed we was contraband. I went to him
> and asked him to let me enlist, but he said *it wasn't a black man's war*.
> I told him it *would* be a black man's war before they got through.
>
> Harry Jarvis, ex–Virginia slave

The Civil War began in an Atlantic world that appeared to have lowered the curtain on its revolutionary age. More than a decade earlier, the revolutions of 1848 in continental Europe and the Chartist movement in Britain had been roundly defeated, and with them the political projects of both liberal-minded bourgeoisies and nascent working classes nearly six decades in the making. Although the last vestiges of peasant servility west of Russia and of colonial slavery south of Cuba had been eradicated before the political tide had fully turned in various metropolitan centers, those emancipations carried little of the optimism and humanitarianism that had previously been in evidence. Instead, they bowed before political necessity and came with a host of state-sponsored compensations for the landed classes, who in turn were about to ride a wave of expanding staple production and technological innovation. Even former champions of abolitionism had begun to express disenchantment with the results of freed labor and raised few objections to the importation of indentured workers, most notably from the East Indies and China, to help restaff sugar estates stretching from Jamaica and Martinique, to Trinidad, Guyana, and Surinam, to the Peruvian coast. The new Latin American republics that had proclaimed their independence in the name of Enlightenment ideals in the early nineteenth century, dealing substantial blows to the institution of slavery along the way, were now securely in the political hands of landed oligarchs and under the economic thumbs of European powers. And the black nation of Haiti, perhaps the most remarkable of the age of revolution's early products, had been cordoned into diplomatic and economic isolation, there to stagnate into rural impoverishment and political authoritarianism.[1]

The conservative winds of the 1850s were felt in the United States as well. The heady political reforms of the Jacksonian era, which eliminated property-owning requirements for voting and officeholding and made most public positions elective rather than appointive, eventually found their limits on the newly "naturalized" distinctions of race and gender, and on the new circumstances of industrialism. Claims for civil and political inclusion by female suffragists and northern free blacks were either ignored or utterly rejected during the 1840s, and the massive influx of poor and propertyless Irish Catholics in the late 1840s and early 1850s provoked a powerful nativist movement, especially in the Northeast, that sought to impose political disabilities on what was a growing section of the urban working class.[2]

In the South, the political winds blew more ominously still. Responding to the antislavery campaign and the prospect of four million emancipated black workers in their midst, slaveholders and their representatives struck back in increasingly reactionary ways. Within the South, some called for the reenslavement of free blacks and the reopening of the African slave trade, while others argued that slavery served as the proper status for all poor people regardless of race. Nationally, southern members of Congress won a stronger fugitive slave law, effectively rewarding northern justices for returning runaways and further eroding the already precarious position of northern blacks. A southern-dominated Supreme Court, in the *Dred Scott* case, denied the rights of citizenship to all black people and opened the way for the expansion of slavery westward. And by 1860, a rising chorus, concentrated in the Democratic party, demanded federal protection for slavery in the western territories.[3]

It appeared, in short, that the boundaries of the official political community had been stretched as far as they would go, North and South. There was neither enough of a popular will nor enough of a well-developed vocabulary to make the case for enfranchising those traditionally regarded as socially or economically dependent. If anything, popular support grew for delineating and patrolling the boundaries more tightly, and for disfranchising those who had managed to slip inside of them. Indeed, the Republican party, committed as it was to excluding slavery from the western territories, derived no small amount of energy from those intent on excluding blacks and Catholics from the body politic too. Southern slaveholders could, therefore, have expected sympathy from a great many northerners had they accepted a gradualist—and compensated—solution to the issue of slavery, even if that solution was long-term and entailed the denial to former slaves and their heirs of meaningful civil and political rights. But by the 1850s most slaveholders thought they had learned from the experience of the British and French West Indies that emancipation was a failure, whether gradual or not; and many, fortified by the sway of King Cotton, believed that the winds of history might now be blowing in their direction even if it required rebelling against the presumed authority of the national government and risking civil war.[4]

The slaves, however, perhaps alone among America's social groups, seemed to have sensed very different possibilities. They sensed the prospects of emancipation and a new order of life that might go along with it, and thus felt empowered to turn one rebellion into two: to turn a rebellion of their masters against the authority of the federal government into a rebellion of their own against the authority of their masters. It was not the sort of rebellion that slaveholders had customarily feared and that historians customarily chronicle—sudden, massive, and direct violence against the white population. It was rather a rebellion that proved difficult to detect and even more difficult to staunch, a rebellion many months in duration. It began by unsettling the policies and institutions of the Union and Confederacy alike, and then initiated a social and political transformation. The rebellion not only weakened the project of the Confederacy and strengthened that of the Union; it also helped create unprecedented spaces for slaves to meet one another and educate themselves, and unprecedented opportunities for the making of new black leaders. It simultaneously reenergized and redirected the course of the federal government, placing emancipation on the table of official deliberation and turning the army of Union into one of liberation. Ultimately, the rebellion inspired the most sweeping revolution of the nineteenth century, and shifted the social and political course of the Atlantic world.

❖

As the decade of the 1850s came to a close, and especially in the months surrounding the national election of 1860, many slaves and many slave-holders interpreted the meaning of political events in remarkably similar ways. They believed that the Republican party was actively hostile to the institution of slavery and would, if successful in gaining control of the federal government, move decisively against it. Despite the repeated assurances of Republican leaders that the Constitution would be upheld and slavery respected in the states where it existed, most slaveholders and their nonslaveholding allies saw the "black" Republicans as intent on subverting the southern social order from within and without. This perception became a powerful and persuasive argument for disunion, whether by separate or cooperative state action.[5]

In part because the slaveholders' apprehensions traveled with particular speed and vibrancy, the slaves also came to attribute revolutionary intentions to the Republican party, although they looked on them with anticipation rather than apprehension. Indeed, the rumors and expectations regarding Republican policy had earned astonishing currency in the slave quarters. They could be detected not only in the border South, in port cities, or along major thoroughfares like the Mississippi River, but also as far into the interior as political meetings, court circuits, weekly newspapers, and the mails might go. From western South Carolina, central Georgia, northern Alabama, and northeast Texas—from plantation and nonplantation districts alike—came reports that the slaves knew of the presidential campaign, had learned of Lincoln's election, and imagined that he "is soon going to free them all." In early September 1860, a local editor complained that "every political speech . . . delivered in Macon [Georgia] had attracted a number of negroes, who, without entering the Hall, have managed to linger around and hear what the orators say." The slaves evinced such an "interest in politics" that fall in nearby Columbus that the mayor ordered city police to chase them away from "the meetings and discussions of different political parties." Booker T. Washington, who "was awakened" early one morning "by my mother kneeling over her children and fervently praying that Lincoln and his armies might be successful," puzzled at "how the slaves throughout the South, completely ignorant as were the masses so far as books and newspapers were concerned, . . . [kept] themselves so accurately and completely informed about the great National questions that were agitating the country." "During the campaign when Lincoln was first a candidate for the presidency," Washington recalled, "the slaves on our far-off plantation, miles from any railroad or large city or daily newspaper, knew what the issues involved were," and "even the most ignorant . . . on the remote plantations felt in their hearts . . . that the freedom of the slaves would be the one great result of the war, if the Northern armies conquered." Reminding himself of "the many late-at-night whispered discussions that I heard my mother and the other slaves on the plantation indulge in," he then acknowledged that "they kept themselves informed of events by what was termed the 'grapevine' telegraph."[6]

The outbreak of hostilities between the federal government and the rebellious slaveholding states at once fueled the circulation of news and rumor and seemed to confirm early predictions of the Lincoln administration's designs. Excited discussions and prognostications among slaveholders, local troop musters and movements, speeches and ceremonial rituals, and dire warnings to all white southerners as to the consequences of Yankee domination during the spring and summer of 1861 all suggested to the slaves that a great struggle had commenced between their owners and their owners' enemies. And who could doubt what was at stake? According to Kate Stone, "the general impression" in the vicinity of her plantation in Madison Parish, Louisiana, "has been that the Negroes looked for a great upheaval of some kind" on the Fourth of July. "In some way they have gotten a confused idea of Lincoln's Congress meeting and of the war," she recorded the next day. "[T]hey think it is all to help them, and they expected for 'something to turn up.'" Elizabeth Rose Hite, who was enslaved on a sugar plantation not very far away, explained that she came to such a conclusion when one of the house servants and then her mother discovered that the master "was afraid of the yankees," that he said "the yankees would kill them and take all the slaves and free them."[7]

Near Natchez, Mississippi, the slave George Braxton told how the worries of one slaveholder could influence the expectations of slaves in an entire neighborhood. "Thomas Turner used to be the mail and messenger servant of the Surzette place," Braxton testified. "[H]e used to come over to our place often and . . . he told me once during the war that the Union soldiers were going to gain the day, that he heard his mistress say as much, and that if they did we would be free." Susie King Taylor, growing up in coastal Georgia and having put her cleverly acquired literacy to effective use even before the Civil War began, remembered that the warnings spread by white folk only encouraged her to consult more reliable sources. "The white people would tell their colored people not to go to the Yankees," Taylor wrote, "for they would harness them to carts and make them pull the carts around, in place of horses." Already skeptical because she had been reading on the sly about the Yankees, Taylor was fully disabused by a conversation with her grandmother, who regularly went to church and sang freedom hymns. South Carolina planter and diarist Mary Chesnut did not bother to "speak of the war" to her slaves, since "on that subject they do not believe a word you say," but her friend William Henry Trescott took no chances as to the comprehension of his. Complaining that "the black waiters are all ears now," and concerned "to keep what we have to say dark," he resorted to speaking French in his slaves' presence. The Virginia-born black educator Robert Russa Moton later maintained that the slaves devised strategies similar to Trescott's although to the opposite ends, constructing their own codes and vocabularies of political communication: "If a slave coming back from town greeted a fellow servant with the declaration, 'Good-mornin, Sam, yo' look mighty greasy this mornin,' that meant that he had picked up some fresh information about the prospects for freedom which would be divulged later on."[8]

As the Confederacy organized and mobilized to defend its newly proclaimed independence and the foundation of slavery on which it rested, new opportunities were opened for slaves to become better acquainted with each other and with the course of political events. Although few Confederates imagined, at the earliest stages, that slaves could be armed without dooming the vitals of their own cause, there could be little doubt that slave labor would be necessary for the prosecution of the war: for the building of fortifications, the operation of war-related industries, the transportation of supplies and equipment, and the general service of army life, not to mention the production of food crops to sustain soldiers and civilians. Through a combination of donation, hiring, and, eventually, impressment, hundreds—and, in some cases, thousands—of slaves and free blacks were assembled at military and industrial sites across the South. In states like Virginia, Confederate engineers and civilian contractors availed themselves of well-established networks of black hiring; elsewhere they accumulated their labor forces more haphazardly, often from small squads of field hands taken from plantations and farms over a considerable area. Torn away from their families and friends and exposed to hardships and dangers of several sorts, these laborers rarely welcomed the assignments. But they could also mingle with African Americans with a variety of experiences, exchange ideas and information, and learn more about the wider world. Those who returned after what were commonly short stints usually brought a good deal of new knowledge with them—about the war, about the perspectives and aspirations of other slaves, and about the prospects for freedom.[9]

The growing expectations of an impending change in their circumstances led some slaves, as early as the fall of 1860, to engage in activities that their masters saw as threatening and rebellious. In Spartanburg County, South Carolina, at least two slaves stood accused of "talking about being set free" and readying themselves to fight if necessary. In northern Alabama, a vigilance committee reported that slaves were "making preparations to aid [Lincoln] when he makes his appearance." And in New Castle, Kentucky, some sixty slaves apparently marched through town "singing political songs and shouting for Lincoln." More serious conspiracies, though of limited size, may well have been hatched in Mississippi, Louisiana, and Arkansas in anticipation of the arrival of northern troops.[10] In the end, however, the slaves' expectations led many of them to a form of rebellion that neither the Confederates nor the Yankees had quite imagined.

◈

The slaves' rebellion drew, as servile rebellions normally do, on well-established practices of everyday resistance to their masters' power—on the experience, wisdom, trust, and discipline gained from political skirmishes taking place over years and, perhaps, decades. It drew on the resources they had accumulated, on the concessions they had obtained, on the relations and obligations they had fashioned. And, in the first instance, it drew on the individual and collective intelligence—about local geography, temporary safe havens, and desired destinations—that made flight from plantations and farms possible. For the slaves' rebellion properly started not with acts of vengeance against their owners, but rather with small-scale and often clandestine departures for Union lines and the freedom they believed they might find there. The slave rebels, that is, initially assumed the guise of fugitives.[11]

Whatever the slaves believed they might find, the last thing the Lincoln administration hoped to make of its military outposts was a magnet for fugitives from slavery. Indeed, looking to crush the slaveholders' rebellion in the "insurrectionary states" without provoking either a revolt of their slaves or the defection of Unionist slaveholders in the border, Lincoln, with the strong support of Congress, promised to respect "established institutions" when his armies marched south. Yet well before a major campaign could be launched, it became clear that such respect was easier to tender than enforce, especially when those "institutions" were being used in aid of the slaveholders' rebellion. For in late May 1861, very soon after General Benjamin F. Butler and his force of Massachusetts volunteers occupied Fortress Monroe in southeastern Virginia, not very far from where the first African slaves were purchased in North America nearly 250 years earlier, the first wartime slave fugitives made their appearance before Union troops.

The fugitives encountered one of the least likely of allies in the upper echelons of the Union army. An old Democrat, Butler had supported the presidential candidacy of John C. Breckinridge in 1860, and later, when marching his troops from Annapolis to Washington, D.C., had assured the governor of Maryland that he would protect slave property and cooperate in the suppression of any slave uprising. But Butler also knew that the Confederates were already employing slaves to construct batteries in the surrounding tidewater, and sensibly asked whether "they [shall] be allowed the use of this property against the United States, and we not be allowed its use in aid of the United States." He thus declared the fugitives to be "contrabands of war" and put them to work behind his lines. It was not the last time that Butler would initiate policies that disturbed slavery, nor the last time that such initiatives would flow from unlikely sources.[12]

Within days, word of Butler's tentative welcome seems to have spread among the slaves in the vicinity, and the number of fugitives—some from plantations and farms, some from Confederate encampments—consequently multiplied. By the time of the Battle of Bull Run, and well before Congress effectively ratified Butler's policy with the First Confiscation Act, nearly a thousand slaves had made their way to Union lines and an uncertain fate. One was Harry Jarvis. Born into slavery in Northampton County, Virginia, sometime around 1830, Jarvis labored for a master he described as "the meanest man on all the Eastern shore" who became even more brutal "after the war come." Finally, after being shot at, Jarvis "took to the woods" for three weeks, where he survived thanks to "friends who kept me informed how things was going on, and brought me food." Then, upon learning that his master "gave a big party for his birthday," and knowing "they'd all be a drinking and carousing night and day," he "took the opportunity to slip down to the shore in the night, got a canoe and a sail, and started for Fort Monroe," about "thirty-five miles across the bay." By Jarvis's reckoning "that was before General Butler had allowed we was contraband," though certainly not before he had determined to his own satisfaction what the war was about. "I went to him [Butler] and asked him to let me enlist," Jarvis audaciously claimed, "but he said *it wasn't a black man's war.*" Jarvis held his ground: "I told him it *would* be a black man's war before they got through."[13]

Jarvis's experience highlighted the dangers and difficulties that early fugitives faced, their reliance on the assistance and intelligence of slaves remaining behind, and how their political sensibilities could move well in advance of those held by Union army officers. It suggested, too, the persisting vulnerabilities of fugitive slaves even after they made it to Union lines. Like others who reached Fortress Monroe at this stage of the war, Jarvis was set to work and, by his lights, "was getting on very well, till one day I see a man given up to his master that come for him." The contraband policy, quite simply, did not challenge the legal basis of slavery, and the First Confiscation Act, passed in August of 1861, applied only to property used directly "in aiding, abetting, or promoting" the rebellion. Otherwise, the Fugitive Slave Law remained in force. The arrival of women and children accompanying able-bodied male fugitives had already complicated and confused the logic of Butler's actions. "I am in the utmost doubt what to do with this species of property," he wrote his superior in the very late spring. Jarvis thereby concluded that Fortress Monroe "was not the place for me," and "hired on to a ship going to Cuba, and then on one a going to Africa, and was gone near two years." By the time he "landed in Boston," Jarvis found that his prediction had been confirmed, "that it had got to be a black man's war for sure," and he enlisted in the Fifty-fifth Massachusetts Infantry on December 21, 1863.[14]

It is tempting to see the contraband policy as the first of several federal steps leading inexorably to the Emancipation Proclamation, but this was by no means the case. A product of immediate military and political necessity and provoked from unexpected quarters, the policy tried to hew a very fine line on the slavery question with no clear end in view. Secretary of War Simon Cameron could therefore tell General Butler in early August 1861 that receiving all fugitives would "best protect . . . the substantial rights of loyal masters" since "upon the return of peace, Congress will doubtless provide . . . for just compensation," while ordering him "neither [to] authorize nor permit any interference by the troops under your command with the servants of peaceful citizens . . . nor encourage such servants to leave the lawful service of their masters." Lower piedmont and tidewater Virginia, after all, leaned toward secession and the owners of fugitives at Fortress Monroe more likely than not were rebels.[15]

But matters were different in other parts of the upper South. Hoping to avoid the messy issues surrounding the institution of slavery and to attract slaveholders to the Union side, military commanders in Missouri, Kentucky, Tennessee, and Maryland moved in the fall of 1861— with the blessing of Democratic general-in-chief George B. McClellan—to exclude fugitive slaves from their lines entirely. As General Henry W. Halleck, who at the time headed the Department of Missouri, put it, "our fellow-citizens" must be shown that "we come . . . [not] to oppress and to plunder" but "merely to crush out rebellion and to restore to them peace and the benefits of the Constitution and the Union." Slaves in those areas continued to make their way to federal posts and, by exchanging labor, information, or goods, gain admission. Yet the limited opportunities and generally inhospitable environment that greeted them meant that the social profile of wartime fugitives remained very similar to that of their antebellum counterparts: overwhelmingly young men fleeing as individuals or in small groups. At an army post near Jackson, Tennessee, nearly 90 percent of the fugitives arriving between September 1862 and May 1863 were male, and nearly two-thirds of them were under the age of twenty-six.[16]

The volume and character of slave fugitives changed as the federal government became less solicitous of the interests of slaveholders and the Union army moved deeper into Confederate territory. Yielding to the outcry of abolitionists and the disgust of Yankee soldiers—not to mention the tenacity of the runaways—the Congress moved first, in March 1862, to prohibit military personnel from surrendering fugitives to their owners and then, four months later, with the Second Confisca-tion Act, declared all slaves held by rebel masters "forever free of their servitude" once they came "under the control of the Government of the United States." Union lines thereby became liberation zones so long as Confederate manuevers did not shrink or collapse them, though in truth circumstances left fewer and fewer alternatives. The occupa-tion of the Port Royal area of coastal South Carolina in November 1861 and the invasion of the lower Mississippi Valley in the winter and spring of 1862 brought federal forces not only into the crescent of the rebellion, but also into some of the most densely populated plantation districts to be found in the slave states. The pool of potential contrabands there was further enlarged by the flight of many planters to the interior of South Carolina, Mississippi, Alabama, Louisiana, and east Texas who found it exceptionally difficult to carry most of their slaves off with them. "With the advance of the forty-five thousand troops or more in Grant's command," a chaplain in the Army of the Tennessee could later write, "the cotton plantations were abandoned by their owners and the Negroes . . . flocked in vast numbers—an army in themselves—to the camps of the Yankees." It was, he gasped, "like the oncoming of cities."[17]

The numbers quickly pressed upon the space and resources of hast-ily constructed contraband camps. At one in Lake Providence, Louisi-ana, in the winter and early spring of 1863, fugitives arrived at a rate of one hundred per day and, according to a northern observer on the scene, "would do so [in even larger] numbers . . . but for the close vigilance of Masters and overseers." They came, no longer principally as individuals or in small "squads" but as groups, often linked by kinship, representing much of the slave labor force of entire plantations and farms. When John Eaton, general superintendent of contrabands in the Mississippi Valley, surveyed the camp at Grand Junction, Tennessee, in late April 1863, he found a population of just over 1,700. The adults, composing just under half of those present (48 percent), were overwhelmingly field hands (83 percent) and fairly evenly divided between men and women (43 percent men, 57 percent women); about half in each case (50 percent of the men, 45 percent of the women) were reported as being married.[18]

Marked by conditions that should have deterred all but the hardiest and most determined of souls, the contraband camps and colonies nonetheless became more than mere collecting points for slaves who had rebelled against the authority of their masters. They also became the first great cultural and political meeting grounds that the war produced. With between several hundred and several thousand contrabands at any one time, the camps brought slaves together in greater concentrations than had ever existed in the South. Only the largest sugar and rice plantations could rival the numbers to be discovered in the smaller ones. And with an assortment of missionaries, educators, and entrepreneurs from the northern states soon descending on them, they offered the settings for the initial encounters between nineteenth-century America's worlds of slavery and freedom.[19]

Galvanized by Benjamin Butler's contraband policy, the federal encampments in southeastern Virginia served as the first of these settings. By the early fall of 1861, the American Missionary Association (AMA), an educational and evangelical organization with a strong antislavery record, already had agents at work providing aid to the fugitives. With fitting symbolism that could hardly have been lost on the blacks in attendance, the first of its many Sabbath schools opened on September 15 at the home of the slaveholding former president John Tyler, not far from Fortress Monroe and now under federal occupation. Not long after, the AMA founded other schools in Norfolk, Portsmouth, Newport News, and on plantations in the immediate environs, including one owned by the arch-secessionist former governor of Virginia, Henry A. Wise. In Hampton, a section of the county courthouse was appropriated for such purposes, prompting the Reverend L. C. Lockwood, who played a leading role in the AMA's efforts in Virginia, to remark on the inversions that now seemed righted: "[O]nce a place of injustice, under the name of justice, [the courthouse] was thus converted to the holy purposes of education and religion among a despised and persecuted race." Other northern relief and philanthropic organizations eventually joined the AMA in its endeavors, and similar beachheads were soon forged elsewhere in the occupied South, most notably on the South Carolina sea islands south of Charleston.[20]

The missionaries and reformers, charged as many were with evangelical fervor, sought not only to strike fatal blows against the institution of slavery but also to reshape the character and morals of the institution's direct victims. Assuming, for the most part, that the slaves had emerged from an experience of degradation and cultural barbarism, they expected to teach essential lessons in the proper conduct of faith, family, health, and livelihood as well as in the rudiments of reading and writing. They queried the contrabands about their material conditions, their understandings of marriage and parental responsibility, their notions of property and liberty, their ideas of honesty and propriety, their religious beliefs, and their disposition to labor. Some accosted them with regular injunctions as to the need for thrift, industry, and self-discipline, showed disgust with their folk customs and practices, and warned repeatedly that freedom did not mean idleness. In these attitudes and condescensions, contrabands well may have glimpsed the harbingers of future disappointments and struggles with their apparent allies. Moses Battle, a slave in Tennessee, politely but firmly chided one northern philanthropist who announced that blacks would not work unless compelled to do so. "Don't know what for, sir, anybody think that," Battle shook his head. "The colored folks, what been keeping up the country. When they had to work all day for the masters, they work all night and Sundays for themselves. Now when its all day to themselves don't know what for they lie down and starve."[21]

But the more sensitive and humane of the northerners quickly recognized that the situation was far more complex, that the fugitive slaves had well-developed aspirations, mores, relations, and senses of obligation; and the more politically conscious and idealistic of these northerners hoped to enlist the former slaves in a larger project of reshaping the republic. The contraband camps thus came to reverberate with political as much as moral and pedagogical instruction. Speeches could be heard outlining federal policies and objectives, denigrating the power and authority of rebel slaveholders, and adumbrating black prospects in a postemancipation world. General Joseph Mansfield, who became commander of the post at Newport News, Virginia, in 1862, put his own interpretation on recent developments when speaking to the contrabands and "asserted the freedom of every colored man within the lines of our army, and their right in common with other citizens, to go where they please and receive just compensation for their labor." Months later, at a large contraband camp in Corinth, Mississippi, General Lorenzo Thomas, then recruiting black troops in the Mississippi Valley, took the occasion of a visit to address the now freedpeople "briefly and pertinently telling them . . . that the President had sent him out here so far to tell them that they were free and to tell all the soldiers they must receive them, treat them kindly, provide work for them, feed them if hungry, clothe them if naked and to make soldiers of the strong and healthy men so that they might fight for the liberty of their wives and children and against the rebellion." Political information and opinion flowed, too, through less official channels and at times in a manner that proved very difficult to monitor. Noting the doings of a "Mr. L.," an aspiring army chaplain, the superintendent of contrabands at Fortress Monroe complained: "His preaching is reported to be more of a political cast discussing the war, acts of Congress and the Pres[i]d[en]t, plans of colonization, the rights of the slaves &c, keeping them in a constant state of excitement."[22]

The contrabands-turned-freedpeople were hardly passive recipients of the lessons, doctrines, and discourses fashioned by various northerners, but they fled slavery (or refused to flee with enslavers) with different accumulations of belongings, resources, and sensibilities. Northerners themselves sometimes came to recognize as much, increasingly struck as they were by the many fugitives who simply did not conform to the image that the antislavery literature and movement had suggested. They noted that some of the fugitives arrived with goods regarded as their own property, that some seemed to hold fairly complex "notions of liberty," that some espoused "remarkably correct" views "of the leading doctrines of the Bible," that many understood "compensation received for work as a general thing," and that a good number were not only "shrewd in their small way" but "a great deal shrewder and smarter" than poor southern whites. Commenting that he "scarcely ever met a Negro who has not been able to support himself" and that "when they are not [astute at making money] it is an exception to the rule," Union Navy Rear Admiral David D. Porter, who became acquainted with slave and freed communities in the lower Mississippi Valley, in the end believed that the "character of the Negroe depends very much on the Plantation from which he had been taken."[23]

Porter could only see the "the policy of the owners" as the chief determinant, yet he grasped a significant point nonetheless. Some of the fugitives had experienced slavery in communities with deeply planted and long-defended kinship networks and with hard-won privileges related to the organization of work, the allocation of provision grounds, and the disposition of produce; some had experienced slavery in communities that were stretched very thin and subject to almost constant rearrangement; and some had experienced slavery in a series of contexts. At all events, those experiences framed the ways they received the messages of northern officials and reformers, tried to fend off abuse and exploitation, and, where possible, began carving out small worlds of freedom amid a universe of battle.

The manifestations became evident in the tensions and struggles that erupted when able-bodied slaves and contrabands were pressed to work on plantations in Union-occupied areas of the lower South. There what became known as the contract lease or labor system (initiated by General Benjamin Butler, who had been transferred to New Orleans) reflected an assortment of motives, high and low: an opportunity for antislavery zealots to demonstrate the superiority of free labor and "tutor" the ex-slaves in the ways of the marketplace; an outlet for the opportunism and greed of northern entrepreneurs, loyalist masters, and federal bureaucrats who saw potential windfalls in the wartime cotton market; and an occasion for Union officials to ease the strain imposed on their resources and personnel by the swelling numbers of fugitives. Accordingly, estates owned by loyal slaveholders or abandoned by their rebel counterparts and subsequently leased to northern investors would be staffed with black laborers and operated under federal guidelines, which effectively turned them into halfway houses between slavery and freedom. Small monthly wages would be paid on the basis of age and gender, subsistence and medical attention would be provided to sick and elderly family members, and corporal punishment would be prohibited. At the same time, the mobility of the laborers would be strictly regulated, wages would be docked for a variety of infractions, and the Union army promised to enforce work discipline if necessary. The system eventually extended throughout the Mississippi Valley and encompassed hundreds of agricultural units and tens of thousands of African Americans.[24]

The results, for the most part, were sad and disconcerting. Loyalists and lessees alike often took the first chance to violate the guidelines, cheat the laborers out of their already meager rewards, and cash in as quickly as possible; the federal government seemed to be assuming the responsibility for maintaining or restoring the shaken plantation system. It is not surprising that former slaves began to wonder who their friends really were or that some later historians would wonder if slavery had not been reinstituted in a different guise. But it would be a mistake to see the wartime labor system merely as an example of white cupidity, black victimization, and the ineffable limits of the federal vision of freedom. It was also a testing ground, a new terrain of mobilization and struggle, as gains made under slavery came to be shared and defended, and demands for change came to be aired in a public fashion that would have proved suicidal under the slave regime. Where slaves resisted becoming refugees well behind Confederate lines and remained on abandoned estates, they commonly had a jump on reordering plantation life more as they thought fit. They tried to reconstitute their families, rearrange work details, and plant crops that would enrich their diets rather than their owners. When "new masters" then arrived on the scene, holding leases or outright titles, they battled mightily over the allocation of labor, over the crop mix, and over the disposition of the harvest. Edward Philbrick, the Boston engineer who supervised the Coffin Point plantation on St. Helena Island, South Carolina, in 1862 and believed that raising cotton was "the most Eligible Employment" for the black laborers there, learned quickly that the laborers felt otherwise. Within weeks of his arrival, "a little rebellion" surfaced. "Two men," another observer recorded, "refuse to work the four hours a day they are required to give to cotton, but insist upon cultivating their own corn patch only."[25]

Where contrabands were hired out to lessees or loyal planters, they tried to use their previous achievements—not to mention their brief political educations in contraband camps—to demand conditions worthy, in their view, of free people. A Union provost marshal in Carrollton, Louisiana, noting local labor troubles, thought that "the planters and overseers do not sufficiently appreciate or regard the change that has taken place, especially in respect to this institution of slavery." "The negroes come back to the plantations, with altogether different feelings, with those of former times," he explained. "[T]hey have obtained in the camps, and wherever they have been . . . a spirit of independence—a feeling that they are no longer slaves, but hired laborers; and demand to be treated as such." Some planters, the provost marshal claimed, "seem to have recognized this feeling and have caused it to be respected," specifying significantly that "they have given [the laborers] . . . Land to plant, and a portion of time each week to work on it," along with "reasonable tasks, and an opportunity to work and get extra pay." Thomas W. Knox, a correspondent for a New York newspaper who leased plantations in Louisiana, similarly discovered that the freedpeople he hired not only had well-developed ideas of what free labor should mean but also were very reluctant to dispense fully with what they had compelled slaveowners to provide. "All expected to labor in their new condition, but they expected compensation for their labor and did not look for punishment," Knox wrote. "They expected, further, that their families would not be separated, and that they could be allowed to acquire property for themselves." Yet "when we came to the distribution of goods, many of the negroes changed their views [and] urged that the clothing and everything else we had purchased should be issued as 'presents,' and that they should be paid for their labor in addition." Perceptive as his profession encouraged him to be, Knox saw the distinctive economic logic of the freedpeople: "Whatever little advantages the old system might have, they wished to retain and engraft upon their new life. To be compensated for labor was a condition of freedom they joyfully accepted. To receive 'presents' was an apparent advantage of slavery which they did not wish to set aside."[26]

The laborers on Knox's plantations likely had experience, as slaves, in receiving pay for their "overwork," in cultivating provision grounds, in marketing their produce, and in acquiring some personal property that customary practices, and perhaps proximity to the Mississippi River, may have afforded. Many other contrabands-turned-contract laborers had much more to learn about the nature of compensation and the rules of the marketplace. And as women increasingly became the backbone of the agricultural workforce in occupied areas, largely because the Union army began recruiting great numbers of adult males, they may have been further disadvantaged in their negotiations since it had been more common for slave men to earn cash and trade goods. But whatever their experiences in slavery, it became apparent during the war that freedpeople widely shared the desire to obtain land and use it as a basis for securely planting their families and kinship networks. "The chief object of ambition among the refugees," the American Freedmen's Inquiry Commission declared in 1864 after conducting an extensive inquiry, "is to own property, especially to possess land, if it be only a few acres, in their own State."[27]

Although the federal policy of leasing abandoned plantations to northern entrepreneurs already hinted that the consequences of the Confiscation Acts might not be terribly advantageous to the former slaves, there were many questions still to be settled, and wartime dislocations did provide opportunities for African Americans in several different settings to gain access to land and make early forays in community-building. In these, both the sensibilities of slaves and the new influences of freedom became evident. In the lower Mississippi Valley a relatively small number of black men succeeded in leasing land from the government, but many more appear to have worked out subleasing arrangements with northern planters. In either case, the undertaking usually required the pooling of resources. Thomas Knox probably exaggerated when he claimed that "during 1863 many negroes cultivated small lots of ground on their own account," though not when he suggested that "two, three, or a half-dozen negroes would unite their labor, and divide the returns." This could be seen in St. John the Baptist Parish, Louisiana, late that year when four freedmen, aided possibly by eight additional family members, rented a farm of roughly one hundred acres for five years at $500 per year, as well as on a government "home farm" near Desoto Landing, where freedmen took charge of cultivating four tracts of land ranging in size from ten to 175 acres, with "the profits to be divided according to the amount of stock and force each one produces in the said tillage of the tract." By mid-1864, a federal provost marshal, surveying a district that stretched from Lake Providence, Louisiana, to Natchez, Mississippi, could enumerate 180 "FREEDMEN LESSEES" supporting a total of 1,280 freed hands and dependents on 5,870 improved acres, and this, he added, did "not include many small pieces of ground being cultivated by one or two freedmen, who have no claims to their land."[28]

John Eaton subsequently identified "the independent Negro cultivator" as "without doubt the most successful . . . of all elements in the Valley," and on the holdings of the freed lessees as well as on plantations operated by northern or loyal southern whites where the labor force was "mostly made up of the original hands," new signs of community and collective self-improvement could already be glimpsed: the public beginnings of churches, of mutual-aid and protective associations, and especially of schools. The freedpeople in these circumstances impressed a variety of observers with their industry, self-respect, interest in managing their own affairs, and tremendous desire for learning to read and write. "They are anxious," one noted pointedly, "to have their children *well* educated." White teachers sent into the interior plantation districts of Louisiana discovered that local blacks had already established schools and "had educational matters well in hand." One former slave organized a plantation school at Tigerville by gathering books from the children's libraries of neighboring estate owners; others marshaled their meager resources and located black teachers.[29]

Easily the most prominent example of wartime black self-management in the Mississippi Valley—or anywhere else for that matter— was to be found at Davis Bend, the site of plantations owned by Confederate president Jefferson Davis, his brother Joseph, the fireater John A. Quitman, and several other wealthy Mississippians. It was an appropriate location for such an undertaking in more ways than one. Much earlier, Joseph Davis, influenced by the British utopian socialist Robert Owen, had begun to create what he regarded as a model slave community, winning a good deal of local attention and, he may have thought, the appreciation of his more than two hundred bondpeople. The Union invasion of April 1862 thus made for a rude awakening, for as Joseph fled, the slaves not only chose to remain behind on the premises but also took the first opportunity to sack his mansion. A year later, as Union forces laid siege to Vicksburg, General Ulysses S. Grant decided to initiate a second experiment at the Bend, turning it into "a Negro paradise" of a different sort by leasing the land to "companies" of freedpeople. Appropriating the system previously established by Joseph Davis, though now deployed under very different conditions, the black denizens elected their own sheriffs together with judges for a court in which "all petty cases were tried." By early 1864, the independent black settlement numbered three thousand and was beginning to produce cotton, profits, and leaders of several types who would achieve prominence during and after Reconstruction.[30]

As was true at Davis Bend, many of the freedpeople on the Union-occupied coast of South Carolina continued to cultivate land they had tended as slaves, and for a short time it appeared that they might have the opportunity to obtain legal title to some of it. Those who came forward to stake their claims usually did so in resource-pooling groups and generally sought to build on the kinship networks and practices of land use that had sustained them in slavery. Thus, the sixteen black "heads of household" who wished to preempt tracts of twenty acres each on the Port Royal Island plantation of J. F. Chaplain included Ben Stevens and his two sons Ben Jr. and Robert (with adjoining plots), and Joseph Green and his son Joseph Jr. (with nearly adjoining ones). To their "almost unbearable" disappointment, they soon discovered that federal officials and northern speculators had very different views of land use, and only a few freedpeople succeeded in either leasing or purchasing it. But the signs of self-activity and self-governance were also there for close observers to see. On some of the coastal islands, according to the sympathetic Union brigadier general Rufus Saxton, the freedpeople had established "civil government, with constitutions and laws for the regulation of their internal affairs," and in villages like Mitchelville, on Hilton Head—named for General Ormsby M. Mitchel, who advocated an ambitious plan for black settlement before succumbing to yellow fever—the more than three thousand inhabitants and refugees eventually elected their own mayor and town council, and took charge of schooling and the dispensation of justice.[31]

Where it occurred, the leasing and sale of land privileged the position of black men as "heads" of their households and centers of their community, reflecting the northern gender norms that came to be inscribed in wartime policy and legislation and that would give powerful shape to the political lives of former slaves from this time forth. But it was not at all clear that the work of reconstituting and transforming slave communities within Union lines had not from the first been more equally shared by women and men; and once the full-scale mobilization of black soldiers commenced in 1863, the responsibilities and burdens fell disproportionately on those the northerners regarded as dependents: women, children, the elderly, and the infirm. Under the circumstances, the work went on rather remarkably. Especially in Union-occupied areas of the upper South, where the pressure of northern speculators was little felt, contraband camps and the immediately surrounding countryside became nascent freed villages in which black women and men constructed shelters, farmed land on their own account, built churches and schools, and ran stores. "We have already staked out the outlines of an African village of grand proportions," the Reverend Horace James wrote from Roanoke Island, where slaves had fled from the surrounding districts of North Carolina and Virginia, highlighting "the zeal with which the freedmen set upon the work of clearing up their little acre of land . . . and preparing it for their rude loghouse." Union Village in Suffolk, Virginia, "contained 1500 freedmen, 170 small tenements and a school-house all built by themselves" before a "change of our military lines"—an ever-present danger—broke it up. To these could be added the camps and villages near Little Rock, Arkansas; in Clarksville and Pulaski, Tennessee; in Yorktown, Alexandria, and Hampton, Virginia; and on the estate of Confederate General Robert E. Lee, overlooking the Potomac River.[32]

Indeed, of the many symbolic inversions that rebellions-turned-revolutions inevitably produce, few could be more politically compelling than the sights to be seen in parts of the Union-occupied South. For the slaves had not simply fashioned their own interpretation of the sectional conflict and the Civil War, and in great numbers rebelled against their owners at the first opportunity; as the war unfolded, they also began to make a new world of freedom on the grounds that the lords of slavery and leaders of the Confederacy had ruled and then fled: on the plantations of Robert E. Lee, of Henry Wise, of John Tyler, of Jefferson Davis, and of the once-haughty rice planters of South Carolina who rended the Union.

❖

By the middle of 1864, as Abraham Lincoln pessimistically contemplated his reelection prospects, nearly 400,000 slaves had rebelled against their masters and gained a presumptive freedom within Union lines. Their numbers were greatest in the border South and Mississippi

Valley states where northern armies had long been conducting operations, and, to a lesser extent, along the Atlantic coast, where small federal outposts had long been attracting fugitives. Although precise figures are impossible to obtain, a reasonable estimate would include between one-tenth and one-quarter of the slave populations of Tennessee, Missouri, Louisiana, Kentucky, Arkansas, Mississippi, Virginia, and the Carolinas.[33] Conversely, the decided majority of blacks most everywhere in the Confederacy—and especially in much of the Deep South—remained on plantations and farms in presumptive slavery. Yet the boundaries of experience separating the minority and the majority were anything but tightly drawn. In parts of the South, owing to shifting troop movements, the boundaries were regularly traversed; more generally the rebellion-by-flight of some slaves and the opportunities that it created came to exert an increasingly powerful influence on the day-to-day lives and struggles of virtually all others. Haphazardly and unevenly as the process developed, the relation of master and slave behind Confederate lines was being renegotiated in ways far more fundamental than those envisioned by southern white reformers in the churches and state assemblies—who sought to encode the obligations of Christian trusteeship by recognizing slave marriages and family relations and repealing restrictions on slave literacy and preaching. As a consequence, by the middle of 1864 if not before, the status quo antebellum was probably beyond resurrection no matter what the outcome of the Civil War.[34]

For a great many slaves, the course of the war made flight from slavery exceptionally difficult. Substantial sections of interior Virginia, North and South Carolina, and Mississippi; almost all of Georgia, Alabama, Florida, and Texas; and sections of Tennessee and Louisiana remained in Confederate hands at least until the war's last months. Rebel troops and cavalry traveled the roads, home guards and "partisan rangers" occasionally patrolled localities, and considerable distances might separate slave plantations and farms from Union army posts. Only the young, the swift, and the resourceful could hope to complete the journey, and even then they would likely leave family and friends behind. When Union army soldier Robert A. Tyson recorded that a "squad of negroes . . . had come 75 miles" to his camp at Madisonville, Louisiana, in early 1864, he added that "they numbered about 12 stout hearted robust fellows." For other slaves, proximity to Union lines

brought hazards and risks together with attractions. Threats of summary retaliation from owners, fears of possible separation from kin,
and worries about the political disposition of the Yankees all faced
those wishing to defect. An Arkansas master warned his slaves that
"if them Yankees . . . get this far . . . you all ain't going to get free
by them because I going to line you on the bank of Bois d'Arc creek
and free you with my shotgun!" More than a few of his counterparts
shot fugitives or brought severe punishment on loved ones who had
to stay behind.[35]

Slaves did not have to believe the tales told by their masters to view
Union army posts or contraband camps with critical eyes; they only
had to rely on their own intelligence networks to learn that fugitives
could be denied entrance, surrendered to demanding owners, impressed into military service, contracted to profit-hungry lessees, physically abused and sexually violated by Yankee soldiers, and generally
treated with contempt. It was political sophistication, not misplaced
fidelity, that discouraged the slave Moses, an elder and community
leader on a large Mississippi Valley plantation, from following the example of his "name-sake of the Bible" and bringing his people "out
of bondage." "They call me doubting Moses, and I have my own opinions," he told a Union navy officer, explaining that "some of our bucks
run away and enlisted board a gun-boat, and expected to be treated
just like white men [but] they put those bucks to shovel coal and working before a hot fire, and didn't even give them good hog and hominy."
"If I had my way," Moses could insist, "I'd be on the Canada side:
the colored man is safe there, and make no mistake."[36]

In many places, therefore, the presence of Yankee troops acted less
as an irresistible magnet for rebellious slaves, or as a rapid solvent of
slavery, than as a corrosive element that weakened the chattel institution's supports and rearranged its balances of power and negotiation.
Hardeman County, Tennessee, had been under federal occupation for
about seven months when the Emancipation Proclamation was signed,
but planter John Houston Bills had yet to see the "trouble" that he
and other slaveholders had "anticipated." Then, in early March 1863,
he noted that "14 of T. A. Parrans Negroes run away to camps,"
though it was not until May that Tom, "a man of 35 or 40 years of
age," whom Bills assumed "would be the last . . . to go," became "the
first to leave me." In June, Bills complained of a "stampede" to the

Yankees and of "Negroes all going off with returning troops [and] some com[ing] back to urge others to go," while acknowledging that most of the "servants" on his two plantations could still be found "at home." By year's end, only twenty-one of his eighty slaves had departed. But life on the Bills's plantations was also governed by a very different logic and routine. The "people" were "working only as they see fit." Some were disposed "to serve the federals rather than work on the farm," and two carried "a stolen hog to their camp." Others tended chiefly to their "own" crops. As summer turned into fall, Bills described the "affairs at the plantation[s] in a wretched condition" even though the "negroes [were] not in mutiny," and could only sigh at his predicament: "The institution of slavery is worthless to us as it now exists but we cannot drive off our people."[37]

Mutiny more nearly characterized the conditions in Plaquemines Parish, Louisiana, during the summer and fall of 1862. In August, the slaves on Woodland plantation told their overseer that "they would not work any more unless they got paid," and although they finally agreed to go on for another week without pay, shortly thereafter Woodland, together with a number of surrounding sugar estates, adopted a wage system. Only the large Magnolia plantation seemed to hold the line by promising laborers engaged in a slowdown a "handsome present" when the crops were harvested. But in fact the plantation's troubles had only begun. Within a month, the Magnolia slaves had demanded a month's pay, and they commenced another slowdown when the demand was rejected. Not long after, all the women went on strike and refused to return to the fields despite the urgings of a federal army officer brought in to encourage cooperation; a week later they were joined by the men. By the end of October, the only work that the hands had completed was a chilling sight to the plantation managers: they had erected a gallows in the quarters, claiming to have been told that they "must drive [the managers] off the plantation[,] hang their master &c and that then they will be free." With this, Magnolia's absentee owner apparently had enough. He promised compensation once the crop was gathered and sold, and the slaves went back to work.[38]

Just as the Magnolia slaves appear to have done, those on a plantation below New Orleans drew on forms of organization and discipline forged under slavery to redefine the rules and rights of wartime labor.

Objecting to a newly hired overseer who "was in the habit of wielding the whip pretty freely and of using abusive language to the negro women," a "delegation of field hands" approached the master one morning and "very respectfully stated their objections." He would have none of it, told them he could hire whomever he pleased, and sent them off. They promptly "went to their cabins, packed up their bundles, and started on the road to Fort Jackson [where] . . . they knew they could get employment." They had not gone far before the master reconsidered. "He called them back [and] told them they should have any overseer they wanted." Some miles away in Pointe Coupée Parish, the absentee planter William Dix, who customarily gave his slaves most of the responsibility for managing his estate, took the path of least resistance in 1863 so as "to keep his hands at home on the plantation." He "told us all," one of the slaves later reported, "that if we would stay there and cultivate and take care of the place, we might have all we could make from cultivating it for division among ourselves."[39]

Such contests and accommodations between masters and slaves transpired throughout those regions of the Confederate South that felt the direct effects of the Union invasion and the fugitives' rebellion, and after 1863 they increasingly yielded the sort of arrangements that seemed to acknowledge the passing of an old order and the emergence of a new one. In Giles County, Tennessee, one planter began to divide the harvest with the laborers remaining on his place, while another soon agreed to pay his black workers ten dollars a month. Not far off, in Rutherford County, landowners interested in "securing the services of there [sic] slaves—or," as a local unionist put it, "to conciliate & prevent them from running away," offered ten cents a pound "for all the cotton they may produce & take care of & support them as they have done before." Others offered seventy dollars per year along with customary provisions, and a few told "their slaves to go on as usual and they will see they are as well off as those employed by the Government or others." Near Huntsville, Alabama, Alfred Scruggs, "turned loose" by his master in 1862, "rented about forty acres of land from Mrs. Patteson" in 1863 and the next year "farmed on Mr. Ed Spotswoods place." Even in Kentucky, where slavery remained legal until December 1865, some slaveholders began to provide crop shares and other inducements to dissuade slave men from enlisting in the Union army. One slave there continued bargaining well after he had departed for the Yankees and supposedly consented to return if he received additional "privileges and advantages."[40]

Farther into the Confederate interior, the dislocations of warfare and the prospects available to fugitives from slavery had less of a direct effect on the daily operations of farms and plantations, and there may well have been slaves who knew little if anything about the war and who could later maintain that "things was just about the same all the time till just before freedom." Yet most everywhere behind rebel lines, slaves struggled to keep themselves informed of military and political developments, passed and debated rumors as to their fortunes, and in a variety of ways eroded the customary manifestations of masterly authority. In the hills of western Virginia, according to Booker T. Washington, slaves not only "watched . . . every success of the Federal armies and every defeat of the Confederate forces . . . with the keenest and most intense interest," but also often "got knowledge of the results of great battles before the white people," owing to the clever machinations of the bondman assigned to pick up the mail. A former slave who lived in a remote section of east-central Texas similarly explained that "during them times just like today nearly everybody knows what going on" and that slaves using passes or slipping "out after dark" helped "news travel pretty fast." George Washington Albright, who would serve in the Mississippi state senate in the 1870s, told of a far more elaborate and well-organized network of communication in Marshall County that sped word of the Emancipation Proclamation while "the plantation owners tried to keep the news from us." "That was my first job in the fight for the rights of my people," he remembered, "to tell the slaves that they were free, to keep them informed and in readiness to assist the Union armies whenever the opportunity came." Fifteen years old at the time, Albright claimed to have become "a runner for what we called the 4-Ls—Lincoln's Legal Loyal League" and to have "traveled about the plantations within a certain range and got together small meetings in the cabins."[41]

The South Carolina planter and politician James Henry Hammond was certain that he could see the disconcerting results of such communication networks "on all the negro faces" on his Redcliffe plantation in late June of 1863. He observed a "gradual thickening ever since the Richmond battles of last year and more especially since the last repulse at Charleston." But while he thought that "they seem utterly subdued as if by blasted hopes," he could take little comfort in the "peculiar furtive glance with which they regard me and a hanging off from me that I do not like." "I have no doubt that they have all along been well apprised with the Abolition version of what is going on," Hammond admitted to himself, and "the roar of a single cannon of the Federals would make them frantic-savage cutthroats and incendiaries." Several months later, near the town of Charlotte though still quite far from the fighting, a North Carolina planter made a worried request for help in obtaining a military exemption for his brother so that "order and discipline" might better be maintained "in the neighborhood." There was, he reported, "a disposition among the negroes to be more sulky and not so bidable."[42]

Complaints of sulkiness, demoralization, insolence, and outright insubordination among their slaves resounded in the diaries and letters of slaveholders remaining at home or refugeed at other sites, and testified to what could be considered a "second front" opened by slaves within the Confederacy. Well aware that the military assault on their owners depleted slavery's customary police apparatus, they seemed to be testing more regularly than ever the boundaries of power and authority. The many confrontations and skirmishes manifested themselves locally in violent encounters, small-scale desertions, and complex renegotiations of expectations and responsibilities; even more consequentially, they required armed force to contain and thus provoked a political crisis that weakened the Confederate war effort. Indeed, the imperatives of controlling a restive slave population strained relations both between state and Confederate leaders and between slaveholding and nonslaveholding whites, while taxing the already overburdened military resources at the Confederacy's disposal. The "twenty nigger law," which provided service exemptions to those who owned twenty or more slaves and thereby brought loud protests from white commonfolk in the ranks, was only the most conspicuous example of how the "second front" came to eat at the vitals of the slaveholders' republic.[43]

There is scattered evidence that by the fourth year of the Civil War there was cooperation between slaves and poor southern whites who had lost faith in the Confederacy. But perhaps more important was the slaves' knowledge of the political as well as physical geography of their localities, and the assistance this knowledge would ultimately render to Union soldiers. When two Yankees escaped from a Confederate prison camp in Columbia, South Carolina, and found their way to a large plantation in the Pickens district, the slaves there not only treated them kindly, gave them provisions, and gathered information as to the whereabouts of Sherman's army, but also were able to advise them "to stop at the home of John W. Wilson, a strong Union man." Most everywhere the Yankees went, they encountered slaves such as these ready to provide information about the local terrain, the movement of Confederate troops, the location of useful supplies, and the presence of rebels and political sympathizers alike—sometimes at great personal risk.[44]

It was no doubt a bitter scene for the slaveholders, who had tried for so long to convince themselves of their slaves' loyalty. But perhaps nothing revealed the limits of that apparent loyalty more painfully than did the sensibilities of a slave like W. B. Allen. Born and raised on a cotton plantation in Russell County, Alabama, Allen was known to his masters as a "praying boy," and late in the war, "when the South was about to be whipped and General Wilson was headed our way," was asked "to pray to God to hold the Northern armies back." Unlike many other slaves, Allen "didn't have any love for the Yankees," but had to tell his "white folks straight from the shoulder that I could not pray along those lines":

> I told them flat-footedly that, while I loved them and would do any reasonable praying for them, I could not pray against my conscience: that I not only wanted to be free, but I wanted to see all the Negroes freed! I then told them that God was using the Yankees to scourge the slaveholders, just as He had, centuries before, "used" the heathens and outcasts to chastise His chosen people—the Children of Israel.[45]

By the middle of 1864, the status quo antebellum was beyond resurrection not only because a rebellion of slaveholders against the authority of the federal government had provoked a rebellion of slaves against the authority of their masters, but also because the rebellion of slaves had turned into a revolution that challenged many of the relations, institutions, and practices on which the American republic had rested. Nothing more clearly embodied and carried forward that revolution than did the mobilization of black troops into the Union armed forces. Pressed from the outset of hostilities by abolitionists black and white and eventually embraced by a Republican administration anxious to take charge of both the war and the slavery question, black recruitment turned thousands of African Americans—more than 80 percent of whom had been slaves in 1861—into soldiers, and thousands of African-American soldiers into political actors who buried slavery, secured the defeat of the Confederacy, and nourished the debate over the meaning of freedom. In the end, black recruitment played the central role in linking emancipation with the redefinition of civil and political society in the United States.

Before the Civil War the character of the military and of military service reflected the peculiarities of territorial geography, the imperatives of divided sovereignties, and the sensibilities of republicanism. Although the Constitution and then the Congress made provision for a national standing army, the suspicions of state-rights proponents and the relative absence of threatening neighbors combined to keep that army, by comparative standards, remarkably small and limited in political clout. During the 1850s it boasted a fighting force of fewer than twenty thousand men scattered, for the most part, among outposts in the trans-Mississippi West, together with a tiny staff housed in Washington, D.C. The state militias served as the vehicles of mobilization, and they sought to embrace the ideals of local control and the citizen-soldier. Most everywhere, white adult males (those regarded as independent household heads) were eligible for duty and expected to turn out for irregular musters, presided over by their elected officers—who were commissioned by the governors and ordinarily came from the ranks of the politically and socially prominent. Most everywhere, too, blacks, whether slave or free, were excluded from participation. Anticipating the Supreme Court's *Dred Scott* decision, the Congress in 1792 had resolutely barred blacks from serving in the militias, effectively registering their subaltern status and depriving them of claims to full citizenship at the state or national levels.[46]

Given President Lincoln's initial war aims, the authority he delegated to the states in raising a volunteer army, and the general climate of public opinion, it is not surprising that early efforts to contest prevailing military policy and win approval merely for the enrollment of northern free blacks met with swift rebuffs. From New England to the upper Midwest, state and local officials and regimental commanders rejected offers of service tendered by black leaders and prospective recruits, and their actions were quickly sustained by the national administration. "This Department has no intention to call into the service of the Government any colored soldiers," the Secretary of War bluntly asserted.[47] But if advocates of black enlistment found a cold reception in the North, they discovered new opportunities in the Union-occupied South and the militarized border, as abolition-minded officers and politicians encountered rebels in flight from slavery. Acting on their own initiative in 1862, generals David Hunter in South Carolina and John W. Phelps in Louisiana, along with Senator James H. Lane in Kansas, began forming and drilling black outfits. Phelps, who aptly noted that "the enfranchisement of the people of Europe has been, and is still going on, through the instrumentality of military service," thought that "by this means our slaves might be raised in the scale of civilization and prepared for freedom" while "the necessity for retrenching our liberties" might be prevented. "It is evident," he wrote, "that a considerable army of whites would give stringency to our government, while an army, partly of blacks, would naturally operate in favor of freedom."[48]

These initiatives were not welcomed at the time. Hunter soon disbanded his regiment, Phelps found himself drummed out of the army, and Lane's troops would suffer an assortment of indignities during the war and after. Yet a process had commenced that, owing to a shortage of Union manpower and an excess of fugitive slaves within Union lines, soon proved irresistible. In the late summer of 1862, the War Department, in a surprise move, authorized the establishment of a black regiment in coastal South Carolina and by late fall the First South Carolina Volunteers, composed of former slaves under the command of the New England abolitionist Thomas Wentworth Higginson, had taken shape. But full-scale mobilization fittingly came with the Emancipation Proclamation of January 1, 1863, which both declared "all persons held as slaves" in the rebellious states "henceforward" free and provided for receiving "such persons, of suitable condition . . . into the armed service of the United States." Only then did the federal government permit northern governors to begin enrolling black men living in their states, and, according to the best estimate, nearly three-quarters of all those between the ages of eighteen and forty-five (32,671) came forward. By far the greatest number of black soldiers, however, came to be recruited in the slave states and especially in the slave states of the Confederacy. Totaling 140,313, they composed by the last year of the war well over 10 percent of the Union army, and in some departments close to half of it. "Emancipation had thus two ulterior objects," W. E. B. Du Bois wrote. "It was designed to make easier the replacement of unwilling Northern white soldiers with black soldiers; and it sought to put behind the war a new push toward Northern victory by the mighty impact of a great moral ideal."[49]

African Americans showed great enthusiasm for the opportunity to help crush the rebels and guarantee the end of slavery, but recruitment in the slave states posed more than a few problems. In rebellious areas long occupied by federal troops, recruiters often had to vie with loyal planters and northern lessees for access to able-bodied male laborers, while in the slave states that had refused to join the Confederacy recruiters' activities were constrained by federal policy.[50] Elsewhere recruiters combed the countryside, sometimes with raiding parties, in an effort to entice or carry off potential enlistees whose kin might then suffer retribution from enraged masters. Success thereby required a mix of accommodations and coercions: accommodations to the relations and networks built by slave communities, and coercions against both masters and slaves who tried to resist. When General David Hunter began to organize a regiment of Sea Island blacks in early 1862, he sought the counsel of the black Baptist preacher Abram Murchison, who was based in Savannah but known to have great influence among the slaves on Hilton Head Island. Murchison responded with alacrity and quickly called a meeting at which he delivered a speech on the political issues of the war and then invited each man to step forward as a volunteer. Within a week, Hunter had the core of his later-to-be-disbanded unit.[51]

Few recruiters could as easily avail themselves of the good offices of local black leaders, but many learned how best to approach and attract those eligible for military service. If possible, they set up headquarters in a public building, house, or barn and sent small parties out to visit farms and plantations within a radius of twenty or thirty miles.

They often found greatest access to rural blacks on Sunday (the customary free day) and gained greatest leverage with them by including black soldiers in their recruiting parties. General Edward A. Wild, an abolitionist and early advocate of black recruitment who had been involved in mobilizing the Fifty-fourth and Fifty-fifth Massachusetts regiments, hired some northern blacks to help start recruiting his "African Brigade" in coastal North Carolina. Then, in the winter of 1863–1864, he took northern black troops on expeditions into the Carolina backcountry both to liberate slaves and enlist additional soldiers. It was not long before the African Brigade was ready for the field, and Wild may well have discovered what other commanders of black troops generally did: that effective recruiting demanded attention not only to the concerns and sensibilities of the recruits, but also to the needs and vulnerabilities of their families. The Union army officers who arrived at a plantation in St. Bernard Parish, Louisiana, in the late summer of 1863 seemed particularly cognizant of this. They first collected up the hands, "told them that now was the time to decide about being free or being slaves for life," and explained "that they could take their families to N[ew] O[rleans] & they would be supported at Govt expense." One officer "then called up the women &c and made them a speech—Telling them that they were as free as he himself although their skin was a little darker than his . . . [and] might work as much or as little as they pleased." Eventually, the officers "selected 71" and managed to "t[ake] them off."[52]

The operator of the St. Bernard Parish estate—either a Unionist sugar planter or recent lessee—was away at the time of the recruitment and roared in protest shortly after he returned. His voice, and those of similarly disgruntled loyal planters, were apparently heard, for the federal government soon moved to placate them. Planters and farmers who could not claim federal protection lacked such avenues of appeal and had few alternatives to striking bargains with their laborers to fend off the lures of recruitment, though even that strategy had limits for both parties. When manpower needs outpaced the flow of black volunteers, the army simply resorted to impressment, occasionally staffed press gangs with black soldiers, and often showed little respect for the circumstances of either employers or recruits. An engineer working for the Union army at a fort in Florida reported that the black men under his supervision had "been attacked in the night by Major Strong of the 1st So. Ca. Vol. with an armed guard and five of them have been siezed and carried away by force." "My men," he could complain, "have not been drafted . . . [but] kidnapped . . . and that by men who proclaim to be their peculiar friends." The coercive power of the state had begun to make itself felt in a great many quarters.[53]

Indeed, black recruitment simultaneously destroyed many of the petty sovereignties and parochialisms characteristic of slavery and invested the federal government with new forms of authority. Black regiments, like their white counterparts, were typically organized in specific locations and originally carried the emblems of them: the First South Carolina Volunteers, the First Louisiana Native Guards, the First Arkansas Volunteers of African Descent, and so forth. From the outset, however, these units drew recruits from a much wider range of settings and conditions. The First Kansas Colored Volunteers filled principally with fugitive slaves out of Arkansas and Missouri. The Fifty-fifth Massachusetts included recruits born in at least sixteen different states and three foreign countries. The Fifty-seventh U.S. Colored Infantry, raised in Arkansas, showed enlistees born in twelve other states, Tennessee chief among them. And the Twenty-third U.S. Colored Infantry, raised in Virginia, boasted men born in nine other southern states, three northern states, the District of Columbia, and the British colony of Jamaica. More than three in ten of the blacks who served in Tennessee units came from plantations and farms in Alabama, Kentucky, Georgia, and Arkansas. By the late spring of 1863, control over the recruitment and organization of black soldiers had been centralized in the Bureau of Colored Troops under the auspices of the adjutant general. Thereafter, blacks were mustered directly into federal service.[54]

To the extent that it redefined the relationship between African-American men and the federal government, military recruitment—tied as it was to emancipation—must therefore be seen as integral to the building of a new nation-state. But the political contours of that nation-state were still to be determined, and black soldiers played a crucial part in testing and reshaping them. They had enrolled in an institution that showed many of the marks of the racism and civic subordination to which blacks had been subjected in antebellum America. Their units were segregated from those of white troops. Their combat roles and status were initially in question. They were, with few exceptions, denied the opportunity to become commissioned officers. They were paid at far lower rates than their white counterparts. And they were often treated with contempt by white officers and enlistees alike. Many northern governors had come to embrace black recruitment chiefly because it eased the conscription quotas and casualties inflicted on the white populations of their states; they scarcely imagined a newly inclusive civil and political order in the making.[55]

There was more than a little at stake in the experience of these deeply inscribed patterns of discrimination. The Confederate Congress, effectively acknowledging that fugitive slaves armed and turned against their owners were indeed slaves in rebellion, prescribed summary punishments for black soldiers and their commanding officers (regarded as the instigators) captured in battle. Within Union encampments, the inequities in pay, the constraints on promotion, and the relegation of many to the menial labor that whites were reluctant to perform not only proved extremely galling to large numbers of black soldiers but also jeopardized both the immediate welfare of their wives and children as well as their longer-term prospects for achieving economic independence. "There are men in this regiment," one black sergeant claimed, "who have respectable families that have been torn to pieces and driven to beggary." Charlie Davenport, having grown up in slavery in Adams County, Mississippi, remembered bitterly that when his father joined a Yankee company in Vicksburg "they put a pick in his hand instead of a gun [and] made him dig a big ditch." "He worked a heap harder for his Uncle Sam than he'd ever done for the master," scoffed Davenport, who himself "stayed on the plantation and put in a crop."[56]

Black soldiers, especially those recruited early amid optimistic expectations, struggled against these many badges of inferiority, and their greatest success came in establishing something of a juridical basis of equality in the ranks. Their best known and organized actions focused on the issue of discriminatory pay (seven dollars per month for black privates as opposed to sixteen dollars per month for white privates), itself rooted in the notion that blacks would serve chiefly as military laborers rather than as combat troops. By refusing any pay until the wage scales were equitably adjusted (while avoiding, save in one instance, mutiny or resignation), they captured the attention and sympathy of the northern public and, in June of 1864, obtained a substantial measure of congressional redress. Less well recognized, though also of considerable importance, was the agitation to gain federal protection against the Confederacy's policy of treating black soldiers as rebellious slaves. It achieved first fruits in the spring of 1863 with War Department General Orders No. 100, which provided black troops with belligerent status, required that they be regarded as public enemies, and promised severe retaliation should they be enslaved and sold. Some months later, after reports of atrocities at Milliken's Bend, Battery Wagner, and Port Hudson provoked a stronger storm of protest, President Lincoln pledged to enforce the General Orders by either executing or placing at hard labor a rebel soldier for each violation. The murder and mistreatment of black troops at the hands of Confederates did not stop, but northern opinion was galvanized and the federal government acted to declare that military service liberated all slaves (even those in the loyal states) and lent black and white combatants an officially identical status.[57]

The efforts to challenge discriminatory practices in the Union army based on race and previous condition of servitude were led, as might be expected, by northern black troops and their allies in public life, who were more familiar with the practices and discourses of institutional politics and more likely to link the wartime goal of emancipation with that of racial equality. Yet soldiers who had been slaves on the eve of the Civil War made their political presence felt from the very first and over time gained growing knowledge and sophistication in the politics of war and nation. Indeed, the military served as a great political crucible for African-American men: it took thousands in the South and North with varied experiences of subjection and struggle and melded them into an increasingly well-disciplined and self-conscious army of liberation and unification. A white missionary in the South Carolina sea islands was simply "astonished" at the "effect" that only a few months of "soldiering" had. "Some who left here a month ago to join the 2nd Regt. S.C. Vols. cringing, dumpish, slow," he marveled, "are now here as a picket guard and are ready to look you in your face—are wide awake and active."[58]

It was not that slave recruits failed to display political acumen. The abolitionist Thomas Wentworth Higginson, who commanded some of them and had feared the effects of the plantation, almost immediately thought that "the general aim and probable consequences of this war are better understood in [his] regiment than in any white regiment."

It was instead that they widely lacked the skills and experience to conduct politics by the standards of free society in mid-nineteenth-century America and necessarily suffered from the ignorance and dependency that slavery was meant to enforce. Few could read or write; few knew much about the workings of official political institutions; few had conceived of their own aspirations in relation to those of other social groups; none had framed petitions or other public resolutions; and none had engaged in open political debate.[59]

The wartime military, by its very nature, thus provided the sort of basic political educations that enslaved people had found almost impossible to come by. In it they could meet former slaves from the loyal as well as the rebel South, free people of color from the southern and northern states (perhaps even from the West Indies), and white officers who had spent years in the antislavery movement or had fled as political refugees from failed revolutions in Europe. In it they could follow the progress of the war, become conversant with the course of federal policy, and discuss their previous experiences and future prospects. In it they could discover forms of authority and loyalty other than those prescribed by their masters or by their small communities. And in it, mixing secular and spiritual concerns, they could obtain the rudiments of literacy. "Generally there was one of three things the negro soldiers could be found doing when at leisure," the historian and former Yankee soldier Joseph T. Wilson observed. "[D]iscussing religion, cleaning his musket and accoutrements, or trying to read."[60]

As in other instances of rapid change and innovation, military necessity opened opportunities for black schooling. Illiterate soldiers and noncommissioned officers simply slowed the most routine tasks of army life and thereby forced literate commanders to assume still more duties and responsibilities. But as in other instances, black initiative turned the opportunities to far greater effect. Eager to learn their letters, often to read the Bible and sign their names, they flocked to regimental schools, begged for them when they did not exist, and, where necessary and possible, collectively organized and financed their own instruction. "So ardent were they," a colonel in one regiment exclaimed, "that they formed squads and hired teachers, paying them out of their pittance of $7 per month, or out of the bounty paid to them by the state to which they were accredited." In Vicksburg, Mississippi, a northern missionary insisted that she had "*never* seen such zeal on the part of pupils nor such advancement as I see here" in the black Twelfth Louisiana. In Tennessee, at least half of the black regiments had their chaplains or company officers giving classes. In the South Carolina sea islands, according to a sergeant in the Fifty-fifth Massachusetts, "evening schools have been established" and the soldiers, keenly aware of "the disadvantage of being dependent upon others to do their writing and reading of letters[,] . . . are now applying themselves assiduously with spelling book, pen, ink, and paper." An observer in Port Hudson, Louisiana, reported a black soldier walking "with his gun upon his shoulder, and hanging from his bayonet by a bit of cord was a Webster's spelling book," while a foreign traveler later noted that the quest for literacy embraced settings and teachers of many types. Black troops not only "carried [lesson] books with them when the army marched," he recorded, but they frequently "gathered round the bivouac fires at night eager over their spelling books, hearing each other spell, or listening to one of their number who had got on far enough to be able to read to them from the Bible." When the smoke of battle cleared, "these spelling books and Bibles were often found upon the bodies of the dead."[61]

We must be careful not to exaggerate the effects of these educational endeavors on overall literacy rates within the ranks. Although reliable figures are unavailable, it appears that reading and writing skills could be claimed at war's end by perhaps one-quarter of the privates and nearly all of the noncommissioned officers in northern (mostly free black) regiments, and by substantially fewer in regiments (mostly slave) raised in the Mississippi Valley and Deep South. Fighting rather than schooling was, after all, the chief object of these units and even the best-laid projects could quickly be disrupted or dissolved. Which makes some of the achievements all the more remarkable and consequential. A correspondent with the Fifty-sixth and Sixtieth U.S. Colored Infantries, stationed in Helena, Arkansas, in late 1864, told the editor of the *Christian Recorder,* with evident pride, that a school had been "established in each regiment" and that "many" of the men had "made such rapid progress as to be able to read and write well enough to sign their names on the payroll." The commander of the Sixty-second U.S. Colored Infantry, raised in the bloody slave state of Missouri, could be more precise and so had reason to describe the "progress" of his men in "acquiring the rudiments of a common education" as "under the circumstances truly wonderful." "Out of four hundred and thirty one men," he boasted to the outfit, "ninety nine have learned to read, write and cipher, and are studying geography; two hundred read and write understandingly; two hundred and eighty four can read; three hundred and thirty seven can spell in words of two syllables, and are learning to read; not more than ten have failed to learn the alphabet."[62]

However much black struggles for literacy and against discrimination within the ranks helped transform their political consciousness and prospects in Civil War America, it was undoubtedly their efforts on the battlefield that proved most consequential. For it was in the face of military stalemate and of grave doubts about their potential military contributions that the federal government embarked on the mass recruitment of African-American men. And it was only military victory that could secure the freedom that many black soldiers and their families had tentatively attained. The rapidly circulating reports of black bearing under Confederate fire, of tenacious fighting under the riskiest of circumstances, of remarkable fortitude and courage in the heat of battle, and of tremendous casualties and savage retribution sustained at the hands of their former masters simultaneously bolstered the élan of black troops and challenged the racial attitudes of white northerners. "There are about 500 Nigroes here drilling for Soldiers and they do first rate," a white Union army private stationed in Brashear City, Louisiana, in the late spring of 1863 wrote his niece. "[T]hey will make tip top soldiers better than white ones ever dared to be . . . for they will fight like the Devil."[63]

The élan and consciousness of black troops, their growing sense of themselves as the saviors of the Union and the liberators of their people, their view of military service as a personally and collectively transfiguring experience, and the very powerful effect that this political process had on white colleagues and observers can be glimpsed at many poignant moments, from a number of different perspectives. When Colonel R. D. Mussey, the commander of a U.S. Colored Infantry outfit posted in Nashville, Tennessee, was invited by local Unionists to attend their Fourth of July celebration in 1864 but without his unit, he promptly declined while reminding his presumed hosts that the Declaration of Independence proclaimed all men created equal "and until you . . . learn this fundamental truth, till you can invite all the defenders of the country . . . be they black or be they white, your celebrations of our National Anniversary are mocking farces." Instead, the black troops in Nashville commemorated the event by decorating their own headquarters with a large transparency bearing the names of Fort Pillow, Petersburg, Olustee, and Milliken's Bend—some of the by then well-known markers of black heroism in the cause of the nation.[64]

Colonel Thomas J. Morgan told a more elaborate story. Ordered in November 1863 to organize the Fourteenth U.S. Colored Infantry in Gallatin, Tennessee, he discovered "several hundred negro men in camp." "They were a motley crowd—old, young, middle aged," he recalled. "Some wore the U.S. uniform, but most of them had on the clothes in which they had left the plantations, or had worn during periods of hard service as army laborers." Within a short time, however, the changes in their presentation and disposition, not to mention their political condition, were readily noticeable. Acting as pickets, the soldiers stopped anyone without proper permits from passing through the lines and sent them to headquarters under guard, so "many proud slaveholders found themselves marched through the street, guarded by those who three months before had been slaves." Morgan noted that "the negroes often laugh over these changed relations," but he took care to add that white southerners rarely "had reason to complain of any unkind or uncivil treatment from a colored soldier." By February 1864, the regiment had moved on to Chattanooga, the headquarters of the Army of the Cumberland, where the troops almost daily paraded before as many as two thousand "officers, soldiers, and citizens from the North" and could attend "regular school[s] . . . established in every company." While there, he believed, the regiment, along with two others Morgan formed, served "as an object lesson to the army and helped revolutionize public opinion." Three hundred of the soldiers under his command later fell on one day during the Battle of Nashville, but through the awful carnage he could see rays of hope: "Colored soldiers had again fought side by side with white troops; they had mingled together in the charge; they had supported each other; they had assisted each other from the field when wounded, and they lay side by side in death. The survivors rejoiced together over a hard fought field." With this, Morgan thought, "a new chapter in the history of liberty had been written."[65]

For George Thomas, born and raised a slave in Nelson County,

Kentucky, joining the Twelfth U.S. Colored Heavy Artillery in the fall of 1864 proved to be a combination of liberation and revelation. "While living in Nelson County I indeed thought it was right that all colored people should be slaves, and I was far from being the only one having the same opinion," he informed the *Weekly Anglo-African* more than a year and a half later. "There were five or six colored people in the county who could read, and they were disliked very much by the white people," but while this and other of the slaveholders' "cruel practices were not strange to me, neither did I think the masters cruel." Well after the war broke out, probably owing to Kentucky's peculiar stance in the conflict, he went to Louisville, enrolled in the Union army, and "by the providence of God [was] partly released from ignorance by learning to read; then I saw that slavery was contrary to the law of God and debasing to man." "My only sorrow," Thomas felt, "is that I did not enlist sooner."[66]

Thomas's apparent political ignorance and naivete as a slave had its counterpoint in Prince Lambkin, a corporal in the First South Carolina Volunteers. During one December evening of singing and speech-making in camp in 1862, Lambkin, a former Florida slave "just arrived from Fernandina" who apparently had "a previous reputation among them," delivered what his commander Thomas Wentworth Higginson considered "the most eloquent" of addresses. Indeed, Higginson, outsider that he was, remarked on Lambkin's "very interesting" and, to him, undoubtedly surprising, "historical references." "He reminded them," Higginson reported, "that he had predicted this war ever since Fremont's time, to which some of the crowd assented; he gave a very intelligent account of the presidential campaign, and then described most impressively the secret anxiety of the slaves in Florida to know all about President Lincoln's election, and how they all refused to work on the fourth of March, expecting their freedom to date from that day." But Higginson was most stunned when Lambkin "brought out one of the few really impressive appeals for the American flag I have ever heard." "Our masters," Lambkin exhorted his comrades-in-arms, "they have lived under the flag, they got their wealth under it, and everything beautiful for their children. Under it they have grind us up, and put us in their pocket for money. But the first minute they think that old flag mean freedom for we colored people, they pull it right down and run up the rag of their own. But we'll never desert the old flag, boys, never; we have lived under it for *eighteen hundred sixty-two years,* and we'll die for it now."[67]

Years later, the Methodist minister James L. Smith, a slave in the northern neck of Virginia until his escape to the free states, lent deeper, though chastened, perspective to what Prince Lambkin already grasped in reflecting on the political meaning of what black soldiers did during the Civil War. "Many of the colored people deserve much of this country for what they did and suffered in the great national struggle," Smith wrote in 1881. "When the Rebels appeared in their strength, and defeat followed defeat in quick succession, while the government was bleeding at every pore, and there appeared to be no help or power to save the Union, then our colored soldiers came onto its timely aid and fought like brave men."[68]

❖

The black military role in support of the Union made possible a revolution in American civil and political society that was barely on the horizon of official imagination as late as the middle of 1864. The Emancipation Proclamation may well have committed the federal government, if victorious, to abolishing slavery in the Confederacy, and the institution itself may already have unraveled beyond the point of restoration, but there was still much talk of an armistice to end hostilities, of compensation to slaveholders for the loss of their slaves, of gradualist solutions to emancipation in the border states, and of challenges to the constitutionality of many war measures. At the same time, there was precious little to suggest that the spirit of *Dred Scott* would not prevail in putative freedom as it had come to prevail in slavery—that black people, free and freed, would not be consigned to a legally subordinate status designed by the states and accepted by the nation.[69]

The harbingers of such an outcome were to be seen in efforts to build new political regimes in the border and Union-occupied South, radical as most appeared in other respects. With the exception of Kentucky, where the old rural slaveholding order remained stubbornly entrenched, all of the slave states that had remained in the Union underwent a process of self-reconstruction during the latter phases of the war that promised dramatic shifts in the balances of power. First in newly established West Virginia, and then in Maryland and Missouri, coalitions of social groups tied to urban centers, free labor, and the Republican party availed themselves of the dislocations and military supports of wartime to seize control of the state governments and rewrite state constitutions to consolidate their political ascendancy. Everywhere they succeeded in abolishing slavery (and, save for West Virginia, without compensation), undermining the traditional political props of rural oligarchs, establishing public school systems, protecting the productive property of smallholders, and ending imprisonment for debt—which is to say, in toppling the old slaveholding elites and empowering those groups in the free population previously marginalized. Without exception, however, the regimes hoped to encode these changes by restricting the political privileges of former Confederates through tough franchise qualifications rather than by enhancing the rights and cultivating the allegiance of former slaves and free blacks. Like the Jacksonians before them, their vision of democracy had no place either for black people or "aristocrats."[70]

Unionists in the Confederate South, though more likely to encompass a faction of planters, followed a similar course in response to the occupation of federal troops and the advent of Lincoln's "Ten Percent Plan" encouraging political loyalism.[71] In Arkansas, based chiefly in the nonplantation districts, they managed to assemble a constitutional convention in January 1864 and draft a document that abolished slavery, declared secession null and void, repudiated the Confederate debt, limited the use of indentures, expanded the number of elective offices, and bolstered the power of the legislature; before adjourning, they also selected a provisional governor. Two months later, their work was ratified in a lightly attended election, and a new state government was thereby organized on a very insecure basis. Tennessee Unionists, found principally in the mountainous east, seemed better situated. Federal troops had taken Nashville in 1862 and, with the avid assistance of war governor Andrew Johnson, soon moved to make rebels "feel the burden of their own deeds." Nashville's mayor and city council were ousted after refusing to swear oaths of allegiance; prominent secessionists in surrounding areas were arrested, imprisoned, and exposed to raids on their properties; and Union sympathizers were protected and then armed to combat Confederate guerrillas. In early January 1865, a hastily organized convention of "unconditional" Unionists, few of whom had prior political experience, fashioned a constitutional amend-

ment that not only ended slavery but also equated secession with treason, voided acts of the Confederate state government, increased the
legislative representation of the eastern counties, and provided the
General Assembly with the power to determine voter qualifications.
A ratification election the next month, restricted to like-minded voters
who could take an "ironclad" oath of loyalty to the federal government, rendered an overwhelming endorsement and ushered in Tennessee's brief period of Republican rule. But as was true in Arkansas,
the new government sought to solidify its power by punishing and
disfranchising Confederates instead of rewarding and enfranchising
African Americans, who in fact were prodded to find homes elsewhere.
This despite the roughly twenty-five thousand blacks from both states
who enlisted and fought in the Union army.[72]

Prospects for the extension of civil and political rights to at least
some blacks seemed more propitious in Louisiana, owing to the substantial number of free people of color in New Orleans and its rural
environs who were wealthy, cosmopolitan, savvy, and like their forebears in St. Domingue, initially eager to use a revolutionary moment
to press their own agenda. And in contrast to the other slave states that
experienced wartime Reconstruction, in Louisiana the issue became a
subject of public recognition and debate. By the spring of 1864, as
federal officials made preparations for state elections and a constitutional convention under the auspices of Lincoln's Ten Percent Plan,
free black leaders had already petitioned the military governor and
sent a delegation to President Lincoln in a quest for "the rights of
franchise and of citizenship in this country." They had some cause for
optimism. General Nathaniel P. Banks, who had replaced Benjamin
Butler over a year earlier as commander of the Department of the
Gulf, seemed receptive to the idea of qualified black suffrage and Lincoln quietly offered his encouragement. Banks may in fact have considered permitting a few people of color to participate in the February
1864 election for governor and other state officials, though in the end
thought better of it.[73]

The results of the Louisiana constitutional convention therefore
proved all the more disappointing. The delegates, elected in March by
white male voters who took Lincoln's loyalty oath in nineteen of forty-
eight parishes, reflected the social and political fault lines running
through the state's unionism: they were representatives of conservative

sugar planters who hoped to gain compensation for their slaves and salvage what they could of the old order, and of white workingmen, immigrants, retailers, professionals, and northern officials residing primarily in New Orleans and anxious to construct a new state in their varied interests. Although a minority of radicals controlled many of the convention's committees and may have favored some form of black suffrage, they made little headway. The majority not only took steps to shift power and influence to New Orleans at the expense of the countryside, to set a minimum wage and nine-hour day on public works, and to establish a progressive income tax and system of public schools; they also asked Congress to compensate loyal slaveowners for the losses exacted by emancipation. Nothing was done to define or support the freedom of the state's black population, and only concerted pressure from Banks and the newly installed governor coaxed the delegates to approve clauses in the constitution providing blacks with access to public schools and permitting the legislature to act if it chose on the question of black suffrage.[74]

If in Civil War Louisiana the idea of black suffrage meant, at best, some form of "partial suffrage," much the same could be said for the national administration. Lincoln won little support in his own cabinet for the idea of enfranchising "the very intelligent" people of color, "especially those who have fought gallantly in our ranks," and so made sure that this "suggestion" did not become "public." Even the Wade-Davis bill, the harsher alternative to Lincoln's Ten Percent Plan that Radical Republicans easily pushed through Congress in July 1864, failed to address the question of black political rights, and when Josiah Grinnell in the House and Charles Sumner in the Senate tried to attach such amendments, they were voted down "by large majorities." Republican and assistant secretary of war Charles A. Dana, who regarded blacks as "a great deal more [docile and easily led] than other laboring men" and feared the consequences of "a great negro democracy," told the American Freedmen's Inquiry Commission in January 1864 that he "would not give the negroes [in the southern states] suffrage, except with certain qualifications." He preferred "to have a property qualification," the so-called "English method," which, Dana believed, "is universal in all countries where there is a desire to restrict the exercise of political rights."[75]

The issue of black suffrage would, at this stage, have to be carried by blacks themselves. Energized by the federal assaults on slavery and the thousands of black troops fighting to save the Union, they launched a movement to recast the American body politic. The potential contours first became apparent in Louisiana, where the *gens de couleur* had for the most part come to recognize that their own political ambitions could not be advanced without the mass support of freedmen. By the time the new constitution of 1864 had been ratified and the new state legislature had met, they were advocating broad suffrage rights for "the most loyal citizens of the United States . . . [as] an act of justice." But the movement became far wider in scope when 150 black leaders, representing seventeen states and the District of Columbia, opened "the most truly national black convention" that had ever been held, in Syracuse, New York, on October 4, 1864.[76]

Nine years had passed since the last National Convention of Colored Men, and so too had much of the political gloom and divisiveness that enveloped it. The question of emigration, increasingly at the fractious center of debate among northern black leaders during the reactionary 1850s, was now pushed to the margins as the prospects for achieving a meaningful place of equality in American society appeared to brighten. The convention delegates could at once allow the emigrationist Henry Highland Garnet to share the presiding platform with the integrationist John Mercer Langston while denouncing colonization at home or abroad. Drawing up a "Declaration of Wrongs and Rights," they went on to demand the "immediate and unconditional" abolition of slavery; to extend a "hand of fellowship to the freedmen of the South" and exhort them to follow a course toward frugality, education, and the accumulation of property; to insist that they were entitled to a "fair share" of lands through confiscation, conquest, or other means; and to recommend that "colored men from all sections of the country" settle on the lands opened by the Homestead Act of 1862. Most of all, citing the "unquestioned patriotism and loyalty of colored men" who, "without pay, without bounty, without prospect of promotion, without protection of the government, vindicated their manhood," they asked to be granted the "full measure of citizenship" and created the National Equal Rights League to further press their "just claims."[77]

Among the delegates in Syracuse were five from the State of Tennessee, where a movement for political equality had been growing in Nashville and Memphis since the time of federal occupation. As early as July 4, 1863, Nashville blacks gathered to hear a slave read the Declaration of Independence and speak on the rights of his people to the enjoyment of liberty, and for the remainder of the war both cities experienced an assortment of demonstrations celebrating the Emancipation Proclamation, the abolition of slavery in the British West Indies, and the Union Republican ticket headed by Abraham Lincoln and Andrew Johnson. The processions were organized by African Americans who generally had been free in 1860 and were literate, had craft and transport skills, preached the gospel, had attained a measure of economic independence, or served in the federal army; and they presented a portrait of the emerging urban black community and its political allies. With black retailers serving as marshals and black regiments in the lead, they often included ministers, military employees, benevolent societies, artisans, and schoolchildren each parading as a group under the appropriate banner, and they rallied around demands for civic equality and the suffrage. Some of the men in Nashville went on to enact the part of political citizens, attending Union party rallies and helping to disrupt conservative meetings during the fall presidential campaign of 1864; ultimately they cast almost 3,500 ballots at a mock polling place in November.[78]

But Tennessee had been exempted from the jurisdiction of the Emancipation Proclamation and free blacks there could hardly imagine a secure future without close ties to slaves and former slaves in the countryside. Thus, in early January 1865, sixty-two "colored citizens of Nashville" petitioned white Unionists then meeting in constitutional convention "to abolish the last vestige of slavery by the express words of your organic law" and to extend the franchise that had been exercised until 1835 by "free colored men" at all elections "without question." Fearing that masters "will certainly make every effort to bring [their slaves] back to bondage after the reorganization of the State government" and insisting that "freedom is the natural right of all men," the petitioners explained that they "knew the burdens of citizenship, and are ready to bear them" and that they saw in the sacrifice of "near 200,000 of our brethren . . . in the ranks of the Union army" the basis for both action and confidence. "If we are called on to do military duty against the rebel armies in the field, why should we be denied the privilege of voting against rebel citizens at the ballot-box?"[79]

On the very day that Nashville's "colored citizens" signed their petition, a convention opened in New Orleans the likes of which had never occurred either in Louisiana or in any other state of the Confederate South. Inspired by the national meeting in Syracuse and following organizational assemblies designed to choose "the ablest from among them," nearly one hundred black men gathered to establish the Equal Rights League of Louisiana and to demand the vote. It was about as impressive a deliberative body as could be found in mid-nineteenth-century America, dominated as it was by the prominent freeborn of the Crescent City and determined from the outset that "every question might be put to the house in English and French." Presiding over it was a man who seemed to embody the political experiences and sensibilities that only a revolution could produce: James H. Ingraham. Born a slave and freed at the age of six, Ingraham, a carpenter by trade able to read and write, became a captain in the Union army, a hero at the battle of Port Hudson, and a delegate to the National Convention of Colored Men at Syracuse. "He was," according to the Belgian-born editor of the *New Orleans Tribune*, "the Mirabeau of the men of color in Louisiana, Mirabeau before his alliance with the court."[80]

The French Revolutionary allusions were apposite in more ways than one, for the convention proved as distinguished by its actions as by its members. It not only created the structure for an Equal Rights League composed of chapters in many localities as well as New Orleans, but it also made the case for civil and political rights based on a notion of national citizenship that was still to be constructed constitutionally. On the convention's fourth day, the delegates prepared to protest the practice of segregation on railroad cars in New Orleans, modified months before to make an exception for black soldiers, and urged that "no distinction be made between citizens and soldiers." "We must claim the right of riding for every one of us and claim it unconditionally," one delegate, himself in the military, instructed. "[W]e must take this matter in hand as free citizens in general [for] . . . it behooves Louisiana—who raised the first colored troops—to step forward." Amplifying James Ingraham's supportive insistence that "we must ask our rights as men" and "take a bold and general position," another delegate took care to tie the destinies of "the black man" and the "light colored one" and discourage action "confin[ed] . . . to some particular classes." In the end, marking the "difference between 'citizens of the United States' (as we are recognized by Attorney General Bates), and 'citizens of Louisiana' (that we are not according to the laws now in force)," the convention resolved to petition the commanding general in the city and to have the petition "embrace 'all the citizens of the United States.' "[81]

The distinction between state and national citizenship was even more forcefully, though divisively, confronted over the question of the suffrage. Owing to the agitation and disappointments of the previous year, the delegates easily united around a petition demanding the electoral franchise on the same basis that whites enjoyed it. But when a committee of the convention favored submitting the petition to the state legislature, Ingraham immediately mobilized opposition. Reminding the delegates that the legislature "has treated with contempt every bill which was in favor of us," Ingraham instead advised that the petition be sent to the U.S. Congress, which in his view, "alone has [the] power . . . to grant us a general suffrage." "If we are not citizens," he asked, "why make soldiers of us? That Legislature has been only elected by the whites. It is not before them, but before the world, that we have to lay our claims." The delegates registered their agreement. When put to a vote of the whole, Ingraham's argument decisively prevailed.[82]

As the convention adjourned, the *New Orleans Tribune,* designated as the official organ of the Louisiana Equal Rights League, proclaimed the inauguration of "a new era." And although the paper may have exaggerated the diversity of representation to be found in the hall, the political landscape and significance it imagined in the event were very nearly as important. Having earlier reasoned that the free and the freed, "equally rejected and deprived of their rights[,] cannot well be estranged from one another," and prescribed a relationship in which "the emancipated will find in the old freemen friends ready to guide them . . . [while] the freemen will find in the recently liberated slaves the arms to uphold them," the *Tribune* saw a genuine beginning:

> It was the first political move ever made by the colored people of the state acting in a body . . . [and] the first time that delegates of the country parishes . . . came to this city to act upon political matters, in community with the delegates of the Crescent City. . . . There were seated side by side the rich and the poor, the literate and educated man and the country laborer hardly re-

> leased from bondage, distinguished only by the natural gifts of
> mind. . . . [A]ll classes were represented and united in a common
> thought: the actual liberation from social and political bondage.

"We must come out of the revolution," the *Tribune* implored, "not
only as emancipationists, but as true republicans."[83]

For African Americans seeking to extend the revolutionary consequences of the Civil War, there was much to recommend in appropriating the dominant discourse of republicanism and fastening it directly
to the experience of military service in defense of the nation. Those
entitled to political rights in the antebellum United States were regarded as capable of exercising the responsibilities of citizenship,
achieving personal and economic independence, and displaying civic
virtue—which is to say, of being and behaving like men as the world
of the nineteenth century imagined them to be. Those showing the
marks of dependency or of loyalties based on submission were, as
Irish immigrants well knew, automatically held in serious suspicion
and subject to scrutiny and qualification; those legally subordinate,
economically impoverished, and culturally represented variously as ef-
feminate, childlike, and savage were generally beyond the pale. Since
the Constitution failed to provide a clear definition of citizenship and
since the Supreme Court had determined that black people were not
to be eligible for it in any event, black leaders first constructed a concept of citizenship for which they qualified by linking the natural rights
theory of the Declaration of Independence with their participation as
combat troops in the Union army, and then laid claims to the franchise
by emphasizing the manly character and demeanor that the circumstances of war enabled them to reveal.

In so doing, they made a significant contribution to the fashioning
of a new foundation for national identity while at the same time legitimating the political distinctions that would long make them vulnerable
to reaction. Yet in embracing the gendered language and boundaries
of mainstream discourse and practice, they also lent powerful political
meaning to the roles that the Civil War was already delineating: that
black men had become both the liberators of their people and the protectors of black women and children. There were, to be sure, few
alternative strategies for African Americans struggling for official em-

powerment at the local, state, and national levels. But there would be unsettling consequences as well.

❖

Neither the prospects nor the consequences were as yet apparent in the countryside where, as the Union armies marched in late 1864 and early 1865, the impending defeat of the Confederacy and the abolition of slavery were interpreted less with the language of republicanism than with the imagery and metaphors of deliverance and millennialism, and where the political projects for the near future had less to do with ballots, courts, and legislatures than with land, kin, and communities. Only months into the war, a contraband told an anxious prayer meeting near Fortress Monroe that although "we have been in the furnace of affliction and are still," he felt sure "that what God begins he will bring to an end" and counseled "faith, patience, and perseverance." But "as the great day [of emancipation] drew near," spirits seemed to lift and voices long muffled and disguised could be heard with a new clarity. "[T]here was more singing in the slave quarters than usual," Booker T. Washington remembered, and "it was bolder, had more ring, and lasted later into the night . . . [And] now they gradually threw off the mask, and were not afraid to let it be known that the 'freedom' in their songs meant freedom of the body in this world." As the war drew to a close, the beleaguered sugar planter William J. Minor could complain about the "religious fanaticism" among the hands in the vicinity of his Terrebonne Parish estate. They "collect from all parts of the country," attend "meetings from eight or nine o'clock until morning," and listen to the sermons of "designing preachers . . . who have been dead for twenty years," Minor fretted. "One feller preached that he was the servant of Christ &, as such, was not required to work except for him & that the same doctrine applied to them that joined his church, and that the Lord put them in possession of my houses & none but the Lord could put them out." "Very bad doctrine," the planter exclaimed.[84]

More generally, rural blacks, who understood the world both in highly personal and in spiritual terms, tended to see acts of divine intervention manifest in the figures of new earthly hosts. "[The ne-

groes] almost adore the persons who have brought them deliverance,"
the Reverend Horace James, federal superintendent of Negro affairs
in North Carolina, observed in January 1865, "but Abraham Lincoln
is to them the chiefest among ten thousand. . . . They mingle his name
with their prayers and praises evermore." Writing from Savannah,
Georgia, on Christmas Day 1864, General William Tecumseh Sherman
similarly remarked, though with obvious amusement, that "the negroes
. . . flock to me old and young, they pray and shout and mix up my
name with that of Moses and Simon and other Scriptural ones as well
as Abum Linkum, the great Messiah of 'Du Jubilee!'" But it was in
coastal South Carolina—with its large and deeply rooted slave population, its proximity to the cultural currents of the Atlantic, and its early
wartime occupation by northern soldiers, political officials, and missionaries—that the actors and symbols of national and international
politics seemed to be most closely assimilated to folk religious and
political sensibilities and that the complex strands of a new political
consciousness could best be glimpsed.[85]

The teacher Elizabeth Hyde Botume was one of a number of northern observers who saw this process at work. "The 'rice people' always
spoke of the President as 'Uncle Sam' and 'Papa Lincum,'" she wrote,
and "they gave him credit for all the wonderful things that have been
done since the world began." She then went on to describe what happened when she tried to teach a group of black adolescent boys about
the Ten Commandments and how "they were given by God to Moses."
"I thought they understood," she noted, until "I asked who wrote the
commandments?" The answers included "Uncle Sam" and "General
Saxby [Saxton]." A short time later, Botume watched a white visitor
ask a group of black schoolchildren, "Who is Jesus Christ?" "For a
moment, the whole school seemed paralyzed," she reported. "Then
one small boy shouted out, 'General Saxby, sar,'" only to be upraided
by "an older boy [who] sprang up, and, giving him a vigorous thrust
in the back, exclaimed, 'Not so boy! Him's Massa Linkum.'" "Talk
of Lincum—talk of Lincum; no man seen Lincum; Lincum walk as
Jesus walk," a freedman could tell a captain in the Union army, who
later remarked on "what ideas they get from the Bible."[86]

Such apparent confusions inclined more than a few northern missionaries to conclude, as the captain surely did, that while "the people
are a *religious* people" they knew "little of practical religion," that "one

of the pressing wants of the freedmen is *good religious instruction"* in the *"plain gospel truth."* The Philadelphian Laura Towne, commenting on the freedpeople who spoke of "Pa Linkum," appeared to have a deeper sense of the cultural appropriation taking place. "You know they call their elders in the church—or the particular one who converted and received them in—their spiritual father, and he has the most absolute power over them," she explained to one of her correspondents in the spring of 1865. "These fathers are addressed with fear and awe as 'Pa Marcus,' 'Pa Demas,' etc." She could therefore respond with less than the usual puzzlement when one freedman told her, "Lincoln died for we, Christ died for we, and me believe him de same mans."[87]

The folk religion and politics of the South Carolina freedpeople were not simply being enriched by the assimilations and appropriations; they were also being transformed, as appropriations gave way to symbolic and institutional reconfigurations that sketched the outlines of new collective histories, associations, and aspirations. On January 1, 1864, in what the African Methodist Episcopal minister James Lynch called "one of the greatest demonstrations ever held on southern soil," more than four thousand freedmen, women, and children paraded through the low-country town of Beaufort, once the watering hole of wealthy local rice planters, to celebrate the Emancipation Proclamation. Their procession, with the Colonel Thomas Wentworth Higginson as marshal, included units of black soldiers and sailors, "colored laborers and mechanics" from several quartermaster's departments, the general superintendents of labor and instruction, the schools of Beaufort and the vicinity, missionaries and pastors from the various churches, and contingents of freedmen from most of the coastal islands. It took them an hour to reach the meeting ground, where Lynch read the Proclamation, black leaders presented swords to General Rufus Saxton and Higginson, and a great barbecue commenced: all under a banner "which bore the historic names of 'Washington, Adams, Lincoln, John Brown, Toussaint L'Ouverture, and [Robert Gould] Shaw.'"[88]

The next year, just days before the U.S. Congress passed the Thirteenth Amendment and a few months before the Confederacy surrendered, an equally large Emancipation Day celebration, like the previous one "organized exclusively by and largely patronized by" the freedpeople, was fuller still iconographically. For just behind the black musicians of the 102d U.S. Colored Infantry, who stepped out in the lead, came a "wagon drawn by eight white horses, . . . festooned with evergreens, and draped with Union flags," which carried "twelve little girls and a colored woman representing the Goddess of Liberty." Moving slowly toward the library building, they were received by "General Saxton and other friends." Then, "after the close of General Saxton's speech," the "Goddess of Liberty struck up" the spiritual "In That New Jerusalem," which Elizabeth Hyde Botume described, in a way more prescient than she probably realized, as "the Marseillaise of the slaves":

> In that New Jerusalem
>   In that New Jerusalem,
> In that New, in that New Jerusalem,
>   We must fight for liberty
>   We must fight for liberty
> We must fight, we must fight
>   For liberty
> I am not afraid to die, etc.
> We shall wear a starry crown, etc.

"The words are simple enough," Botume gasped, but when "chanted by 3,000 people" the "effect was electrical." It was, as Thomas Wentworth Higginson exclaimed on first hearing the spirituals, like "the choked voice of a race at last unloosed."[89]

What had therefore begun as rebellions against the authority of slave masters became not only a revolutionary assault against the institution of slavery and a revolutionary challenge to prevailing notions of civil and political society, but also a moment of political redefinition and transformation for people of African descent in the South—slave, free, and freed. The experiences and struggles of slavery had clearly given shape to the many rebellions that erupted and to the ways in which rebellious slaves would try to carve out relations and expectations of freedom. Yet the rebellions themselves were made possible by widely shared understandings and interpretations of political events, and as they unfolded and disturbed the policies of Union and Confederate officials alike, they created grounds on which the understandings and interpretations could be enriched, embellished, and refined. In contra-band camps and army units, on leased and abandoned plantations and farms, new senses of collective experience and identity emerged, new projects were embraced and new possibilities glimpsed, new leaders came forth and new educations were obtained. A new relationship be-tween their grassroots aspirations and a nation-state was being imag-ined. In the history of slavery and freedom in the Atlantic world, there never had been nor ever would be anything quite like it.

3

OF RUMORS AND REVELATIONS

And you shall . . . proclaim liberty throughout the land to all its inhabitants; it shall be a jubilee for you, when each of you shall return to his property and each of you shall return to his family.

Leviticus 25:10–12

The Confederate armies surrendered over a period of nearly two months in the spring of 1865, but in many of the cities and towns of the rebellious South the meaning of the war and of the peace to come received special commemoration on the Fourth of July. Thirteen years before, Frederick Douglass had told a large audience in Rochester, New York, that to the American slave the Fourth signified "the gross injustice and cruelty to which he is the constant victim," and exposed the "thin veil" of "bombast, fraud, deception, impiety, and hypocrisy" used "to cover up crimes which would disgrace a nation of savages." Now, thousands of freedpeople claimed access to the public spaces they had previously been denied and celebrated both the restoration of the Union and the birth of what they imagined to be a new republic. Their processions often included contingents of black troops, members of local black benevolent societies, black representatives of urban trades, and hundreds of black schoolchildren, and they marched through the main streets, past the homes of once prominent white officials, to public squares and reviewing stands where U.S. flags flew triumphantly and the voices of nascent black leaders, from the North and the South and from military and civilian life, rang out.[1]

The crowds, swelled by "many persons [traveling] in from the country, ten or fifteen miles around" to what one participant called "the first anniversary of liberty," were said to number anywhere from the few hundred in Columbia, Tennessee, to the thirty thousand stretched over a route of three miles in Louisville, Kentucky. David Swain, the conservative president of the University of North Carolina, sullenly contrasted two scenes that could be witnessed that day in the state capitol of Raleigh. On the one hand, some local whites summoned a speaker from Chapel Hill to address what turned out to be "a thin audience, without the ordinary accompaniment of dinner, wine or toasts." "The negroes, on the other hand, with flaunting banners . . . were prominent in the principal streets, had speeches, songs, religious observances, a plentiful and luxurious dinner, and cast their white brothers entirely in the shade." And, as if to emphasize the utter inversion of political order that it all appeared to embody, Swain added that "the gentler sex *shone* conspicuously."[2]

The ceremonies varied in their particulars yet almost everywhere seemed to symbolize the materials of a reconstituted nation. The speakers' platforms usually held an assortment of Union army officers— some of whom may have commanded black regiments—perhaps a number of northern white missionaries and reformers, a visiting member of the Republican administration, and where possible a black spokesman who had been freeborn or had escaped from slavery and served the war effort in some capacity: the Reverend James D. Lynch, John Mercer Langston, the Reverend Henry McNeal Turner, and Martin Delany among the most prominent. Both the Declaration of Independence and the Emancipation Proclamation were customarily read, the deceased President Abraham Lincoln movingly remembered, a spirit of reconciliation urged, and new stories of the nation's trials, institutions, and place in the world told. When Henry McNeal Turner addressed a crowd of 3,500 on Roanoke Island, "he reviewed the history of the country from the discovery by Columbus, . . . spoke on slavery from its inaugurating until it was destroyed by the proclamation of our lamented president, [and] concluded by paying the nation's flag a glorious tribute." "The extremities of color, white and black,"

Turner predicted, "had made it the world's theater . . . and as soon as God would knock down the wall of prejudice between whites and blacks, sectional divisions would crumble into dust throughout the entire globe." Then the gathering of free and freed may have been asked to pray for and work toward "a 4th of July in this country," as a sergeant in the Twenty-seventh U.S. Colored Troops put it, when "all of our race . . . would be able to dwell under the bright and genial rays of universal liberty, enjoying the right of suffrage, and the rights and immunities accorded to others."[3]

The political visions and agendas adumbrated on the Fourth reflected the work of mobilization that had commenced in wartime and subsequently swept through much of the urban South during the early months of 1865. In those cities and adjacent areas occupied by the Union army before the surrender—New Orleans, Mobile, Norfolk, Wilmington, the coastal districts south of Charleston, Nashville, and Memphis—political organization was most advanced, with the institutional harbingers of the Republican party (Union Leagues and Equal Rights Leagues) in evidence. Elsewhere, mass meetings and smaller gatherings served to proclaim a new black political presence: that is, to establish a collective public life, air grievances, and express aspirations. They issued calls for assembly, introduced leaders from near and far, explained the role of black troops in the abolition of slavery and the defeat of the slaveholders' rebellion, protested abusive and discriminatory treatment at the hands of federal officials and former Confederates alike, and in many cases pressed for entrance into American civil and political society. On the evening of May 31, at the Union Street Methodist Church, the "colored men" of Petersburg, Virginia, passed a set of resolutions "demanding an equality of rights under law" as "true and loyal citizens of the United States." Citing their military contribution from the Revolution to the recent liberation of Richmond, they denied that "our color, former enslavement, . . . [or] our comparative ignorance . . . is a just cause for our proscription nor disfranchisement, as the word white or slave is not found in the Constitution of the United States . . . [and] as we can compare favorably with a large number of our white fellow citizens."[4]

By year's end, such activities were to be found even in fairly remote towns of the former slave South. During December 1865 John Mercer Langston traveled through Missouri and spoke variously at town halls, churches, and, in Jefferson City, at the state house of representatives. To audiences of "colored men and women who listened with breathless attention," Langston reviewed the conduct of blacks in all of the country's wars, argued for black citizenship by reason of nativity and previous political participation in some of the states, insisted that the Constitution made no distinctions based on race, advocated "impartial suffrage," and advised those in attendance to fulfill contracts and acquire character, education, money, and property. Few better captured the significance and drama of these—and many similar—moments than the *Daily Courier* of Hannibal, where Langston spoke on a Saturday evening. "Right here, where five years ago it was dangerous to breathe even softly antislavery utterances, where public demonstrations in favor of freedom were altogether tabooed, . . . right here in the great Hall of the city—with open doors—with full publicity of the fact," the paper marveled, "a former slave addressed his fellow former slaves, now citizens, on the great subjects . . . that now claim the attention of all American citizens."[5]

The political initiatives that erupted in the urban South were fed both by the flow of black migrants during and immediately after the war and by the institutional networks that free people of color and slaves had built there over the course of many years. Reversing a demographic trend of the last antebellum decades, the black population of many southern towns and cities increased dramatically between 1860 and 1870, and especially in the first year after the surrender, as rural freedpeople tested their new mobility and sought out the advantages that urban places appeared to offer: more diverse opportunities for employment, denser concentrations of other black folk, less surveillance from former slaveowners, and the presence of federal troops. In Richmond, Norfolk, Wilmington, Charlotte, and Raleigh the black population doubled; in Portsmouth, Knoxville, and Nashville it roughly tripled; in Vicksburg and Chattanooga it quadrupled; and in Atlanta and Little Rock it grew more than fivefold. Smaller towns and county seats could see even more spectacular changes, as did Edgefield Courthouse, South Carolina, where the handful of blacks resident in 1860 mushroomed to more than five hundred ten years later. This despite the growing efforts of federal officials to stem the tide and send new black urban dwellers back into the countryside.[6]

Rural migrants came to suffer many hardships and disappointments, but, particularly in the upper South, they found a far better developed social and cultural infrastructure than anything they had known on the plantations and farms. For in urban areas, African Americans—slave and free—had moved about more easily, often hired their own time, faced fewer restraints, and grounded their communities more concretely in residential zones, in schools, in benevolent and mutual aid societies, and, most importantly, in churches, which commonly embraced educational and associational activities as well. Such institutions "honeycombed" the larger cities, and during the last two decades of the antebellum era the number of black churches grew impressively despite an increasingly hostile political atmosphere. By the time of the Civil War, Baltimore could boast fifteen black churches, Louisville nine, Savannah five, Nashville and Macon four, Memphis and Mobile two, and Raleigh one. Not surprisingly, these churches frequently provided the settings for the first political meetings of the postemancipation period and their ministers—together with other urban blacks (free and freed) who had acquired craft skills, literacy, and possibly experience in the Union army—frequently emerged as the early political leaders.[7]

Nowhere was the influence of these early leaders more apparent than at the freedmen's conventions that assembled in most of the former Confederate states in the summer and fall of 1865. There the leaders, joining hands with northern blacks, some of whom were returning to states from which they had escaped as slaves, played the part of America's true Jacobins, pressing to create a new and enlarged political nation: one shorn of historical distinctions based on race and servitude, inclusive and equitable as to standing before the law and suffrage, concerned with public education and the general welfare, and based on a redefined and expanded notion of the "citizen." "We have met here," the Reverend James D. Lynch told the Tennessee freedmen's convention that August in Nashville, "to impress upon the white men of Tennessee, of the United States, and of the world that we are part and parcel of the American Republic."[8]

Despite the tones of moderation and conciliation that characterized both their proceedings and resolutions, the conventions exuded a "jacobinical" spirit throughout. Organized from the bases of wartime freedom and political activism, and usually placed in the state's capitol or biggest city, they were meant to anticipate, coincide with, or respond to the state constitutional conventions, which were held under the auspices of President Andrew Johnson's policies and were selected only by the white voters who qualified. They thereby cast immediate doubt on the legitimacy of the "constitutional" assemblages while presenting themselves as the political consciences of—if not the protoconstitutional alternatives to—the Presidential Reconstruction process. In the freedmen's conventions of North and South Carolina, counties were permitted the same number of delegates as they had representatives in the lower houses of their respective state legislatures, and one delegate-elect, himself an African Methodist Episcopal minister and chaplain for the Thirty-second U.S. Colored Troops, insisted that "the great question with us is" whether "traitors to our country [shall] hold the balance of power again." Virtually all of the conventions not only passed resolutions but also sent addresses, memorials, and petitions to the state constitutional conventions, the state legislatures, and the national Congress, and several established state branches of the National Equal Rights League to mobilize supporters and pursue their objectives.[9]

The moving forces at all of the freedmen's conventions were men who had been free before the war, lived in the major cities of the states or came there during the Union occupation, had achieved literacy and perhaps more than the rudiments of an education, plied urban trades or even more likely worked as teachers, physicians, lawyers, and especially as ministers, and could be regarded as mulattoes. Their numbers and power were most pronounced in South Carolina, where Charleston, like New Orleans, claimed a cosmopolitan and prosperous free colored community; nearly half of the convention's delegates resided in that seaboard city. But elsewhere they also predominated among the conventions' elected officers, headed most of the committees, drafted the resolutions and addresses, did much of the speaking on the floor, and generally controlled the agenda and proceedings. They had had the greatest exposure to America's public political culture and the greatest opportunities to gain oratorical skills and some knowledge of parliamentary rules. And they had the means and experience to make their way in a multiracial postemancipation world. "There are three things which we want," the Reverend James W. Hood, the Pennsylvania-born president of North Carolina's convention, proclaimed in an opening address that would have won approval in the other state assemblies. "First, *the right to testify in courts of justice.* . . . Secondly, *representation in the jury box. . . .* Third and finally, *the black man should have the right to carry his ballot to the ballot box.*"[10]

Highly self-conscious of the historical occasion and parallels, the conventions' leaders took care to invoke the language and traditions of the country's founding, together with the African-American role in helping to save the Union. In Virginia, noting that "in the darkest hour of American history . . . we remained loyal to the Government of the United States . . . [and] gladly came forth to fight her battles and to protect the flag that enslaved us," they could resolve "that any attempt to reconstruct the states . . . without giving to American citizens of African descent all the rights and immunities accorded to white citizens . . . is an act of gross injustice." In South Carolina, they asked "for no special privileges or favors . . . only for *even-handed Justice.*" "We simply desire," they announced, "that we shall be recognized as men . . . that the same laws which govern white men shall direct colored men . . . that we be dealt with as others, in equity and justice." Charleston's Zion Church, where the convention met, was likened to Boston's Faneuil Hall, and Major Martin Delany, who attended as an honorary member, was introduced as "the Patrick Henry of his race in this, the second revolution for the rights of the colored man." With similar referents, a meeting to select convention delegates in one North Carolina county maintained that "representation and taxation should go hand in hand" and objected to being taxed "for the support and expense of the Government, and at the same time" being denied "the right of representation." In more than one instance, a freedmen's convention issued a "Declaration of Wrongs and Rights," delineating grievances as well as "inalienable rights."[11]

Far more than the Louisiana Equal Rights Convention of the previous January, however, the freedmen's conventions had "the rich and the poor, the literate and educated man and the country laborer hardly released from bondage" sitting "side by side." In each case, convention organizers sought balanced, statewide representation and in no instance did the former free people of color define particularistic interests or seek a separate political peace with any group of southern whites. Their prominence, in numbers and influence, more clearly reflected their cultural attainments, institutional supports, and proximity to the meetings at a time when transportation and communication networks could function slowly and unevenly and former slaveholders could move quickly to intimidate local black leaders. Nonetheless, the rural districts, where the overwhelming majority of freedpeople lived, registered an impressive presence and showed the beginnings of grassroots mobilization. Delegates from plantation counties outnumbered their urban counterparts at some of the conventions, and many were chosen by local meetings and country churches at which candidates presented their claims to sizable audiences and sparked a spirited discussion. Even in South Carolina, where urban leadership was especially pronounced, more than 40 percent of the delegates represented the countryside.[12]

The North Carolina Freedmen's Convention, held in Raleigh's African Methodist Church, may have been the most stunning of the lot. With well over one hundred delegates representing at least thirty-four of the state's ninety counties, it best encompassed the social character of the South's African-American population at the moment of emancipation. For while the convention's leadership came disproportionately from the ranks of the formerly free, some by way of the Union army's early occupation of coastal districts, more than two-thirds of those in attendance lived in rural counties, and the great majority of them had only recently been slaves. The northern journalist Sidney Andrews, who observed the proceedings closely, thought that "scarcely a quarter . . . can read and write," and he allowed that many "were obliged to leave their homes in the night, are asking safe-conduct papers from military authorities, and will even then quietly return home in the night." Dressed "in the very cheapest homespun," "awed by the very atmosphere of a city," the delegates, in Andrews's telling, spoke "a language that no Northern white man can understand." And although few came from the more heavily white central and western sections of the state, popular enthusiasm for the convention was sufficiently high in the east that some delegates, "certified only by local organizations, church societies, etc.," arrived without "regular credentials." "The difficulty of the occasion" was resolved by turning "the affair into a general mass Convention of those who had credentials from any organized body of freedmen."[13]

Andrews probably exaggerated the humble circumstances of many of the rural delegates. At least half, it appears, practiced a skilled trade, taught, or served as a minister; perhaps half had achieved basic literacy; and nearly half seem to have owned some property. This may help explain why so little of the convention's time—not only in North

Carolina but also in the other states, where similar social profiles could be detected among the delegates—was devoted to the immediate concerns of plantation hands: land and rural labor relations. Still, the range of participants and the imagined community good were remarkably broad. Andrews insisted that "the men who, by virtue of some education, some travel, and some association with Northern people, aspired to rule matters for their own interest and aggrandizement, were very quietly shelved on the second day" of the meeting; and the resolutions and address eventually adopted showed that even if the rural members "for the most part sat mute," their presence surely was felt. The convention pressed the "subject of equal political rights before the law," recommended education and self-improvement, expressed faith in the "government and Union that their fathers fought to defend," and "hailed" emancipation, the Freedmen's Bureau, federal recognition of the independence of Haiti and Liberia, the admission of a black lawyer to the bar of the Supreme Court, the establishment of schools for freed children, the efforts of Republicans to secure black rights through the action of Congress, and the progress of republican liberty. The delegates also chided former masters for "denying freedom, withholding compensation, and driving hands off without pay," "urged suitable measures to prevent unscrupulous and avaricious employers from unjust practices" and to help reunite families broken apart by slavery or war, and created the North Carolina Equal Rights League, with provision for subleagues in every county. "Here we have toiled and suffered; our parents, wives, and children are buried here," they asserted in concluding their address, "and in this land we will remain unless forcibly driven away." They then sent the address, through Provisional Governor William W. Holden, to the state constitutional convention, a body similar in size though very different in composition that was deliberating, as it happened, several blocks away.[14]

The North Carolina freedmen's convention seemed to be heeding the advice of several of its prominent leaders in following "a moderate conservative course in demanding . . . equal rights." But there was nothing either conservative or moderate about the course being followed at roughly the same time by the Friends of Universal Suffrage in Louisiana. Closely associated with the radical wing of the state's fledgling Republican party, the organization both sought the extension of the franchise to black men and opposed the readmission of Louisiana to the Union under the racially restrictive constitution of 1864. When Governor J. Madison Wells, who courted the support of former rebels, called for congressional elections in November 1865, the Friends and the Republicans not only refused to field a candidate; they insisted, reflecting the position of party radicals at the national level, that the state be remanded to "territorial" status and chose instead to hold their own election for "territorial delegate" to Congress. Their candidate was Henry Clay Warmoth, a lawyer and former Union army officer from Illinois, and their methods were frankly provocative. They began in September by conducting a registration of the "loyal disfranchised citizens" designed "to make a sure and authentic account" of their prospective voters and "to show the number of citizens that are excluded from the polls by the unjust laws of Louisiana." They went on to designate "election places" and appoint "commissioners of election" from among those "who can read or write" though without regard to color. In the end, they would submit the returns to Congress, rather than to the state authorities, "Congress being the sole and absolute judge of the qualifications of its members."[15]

Most of the work of registration took place in New Orleans and the immediately surrounding districts. But organizers did make their way into the sugar parishes of lower Louisiana and, according to federal officials, "embarrassed plantation labor" by encouraging freedmen to attend meetings and registration sessions. When "one Manuel Bijou, a colored man" acting as "commissioner of registration," opened an office in the small town of McDonoughville in October, an army provost marshal complained that "the negroes . . . left the plantations en masse" and assembled there "to vote." Despite later instances of "intimidation in the country parishes," the election itself brought nearly twenty thousand freedmen to the "polls," more than one-quarter of them in the rural areas outside New Orleans and Baton Rouge, and sent Warmoth off, credentials in hand, to lay his claim before the Congress.[16]

In an important sense, the political project of the Friends of Universal Suffrage in Louisiana was no different from that of the freedmen's conventions meeting in other former Confederate states. Together they sought to help define the meanings and set the terms of both emancipation and national unification: meanings and terms that no social group had ever articulated, let alone supported, before the explosion of the

Civil War. Invoking their understandings of the country's founding principles, celebrating the part of black people in the defeat of treason, and mindful of the dangers that former masters and rebels posed, they quite simply envisioned a nation that did not yet exist. It was a nation based on a concept of citizenship that owed its vitals to birth and loyalty rather than race, servitude, and other particularisms, and whose rights, limits, and obligations would be prescribed and protected by a federal government chosen and sustained by all adult men. It was a nation in which opportunities for education, self-improvement, property ownership, and public life would be generally available. And it was a nation in which the scales of justice and equity would be color-blind and the notion of legal equality would reign supreme.

But the political project could not be carried by the mobilizations of urban blacks, even in alliance with some formidable friends in Congress and the Republican party. Their numbers were too few, their influence too constricted, and their challenges to the balances of power and authority in the South and the nation too threatening. However moderate and conciliatory their demeanor might be, their requests usually met with fierce and dismissive resistance. The North Carolina freedmen's convention did not decide to stage its own congressional or legislative elections or to assume the mantle of constitutional authority. The delegates chose instead to submit quietly to the state constitutional convention, for its consideration, an address that Sidney Andrews regarded "as one of the most remarkable documents that the time has brought forth." Andrews did not in fact "see how they could have presented their claims with more dignity, with a more just appreciation of the state of affairs, or in a manner which should appeal more forcibly either to the reason or the sentiments of those whom they address." Yet although the address was received by the constitutional convention and referred to a special committee of five—itself no small acknowledgment of the new state of affairs—the subsequent report could only describe "the freedmen" as "ignorant of the operations of civil government, improvident of the future, careless of the restraints of public opinion, and without any real appreciation of the duties and obligations imposed by the change in his relations to society," and could only "deplore the premature introduction of any schemes that may disturb the [still] kindly feelings [between the two races], or inflame the inherent social prejudice that exists against the colored race."[17]

Neither there nor in any other southern state did the constitutional conventions or state legislatures under Presidential Reconstruction make any substantial moves to include freedpeople in the arenas of civil and political society customarily occupied by whites. They not only ignored Andrew Johnson's rather unobtrusive recommendation to contemplate a black suffrage highly qualified by literacy and prop-ertyholding requirements, but also went on both to fashion "Black Codes" that effectively inscribed a separate legal and social status for free and freed blacks and to send newly selected delegations to take seats in the Thirty-ninth Congress.[18] It was clear, in short, that the fate of the political project constructed chiefly by African Americans based in southern and northern cities would depend on the dispositions of their far more numerous counterparts in the countryside, who had their own political projects and who engaged in distinctive forms of political struggle.

❖

Even more than the region's cities and towns, the rural South of 1865 was a liminal political world. Both the foundation of social relations (slavery) and the most recent structure of order and governance (the Confederacy) had almost simultaneously been destroyed, but no new social or political system had either quickly emerged or been imposed to replace them. Former masters and their supporters had been defeated militarily and faced the prospect of further punishment owing to their treasonous actions, but most retained control of valuable resources and remained armed. Former slaves had been liberated from bondage and looked to the possibility of further rewards for their part in crushing the rebellion, but far more had been decided about what they left be-hind than about what they could expect. The outlines of federal policies regarding free labor and new governments at the state and local levels had been sketched since Union soldiers first stepped onto Confederate soil, but they were designed principally to hasten the war's end rather than to define the subsequent peace, and, at all events, they were very much contested. Only the army of occupation held official political authority in most areas, but the troops were dispersed quite unevenly across the southern countryside and local commanders had considerable latitude in carrying out their still-ambiguous and ever-shifting assignments.

Thus the ostensible paradox. Because so few individuals in the former Confederate states could claim secure standing in official political society, much of day-to-day life there became politicized. With the old rules apparently obsolete and the new ones ill-prescribed, almost every act seemed to bear on the more general struggle over socially meaningful power: finding a different place of work or residence, reuniting immediate family and other kin, wrestling over the terms of labor and leisure, constructing and negotiating relations within households, hunting or fishing for subsistence, exercising control over children and others regarded as dependents, and taking complaints to a federal official. Because so much was at stake in such an unstable and explosive environment, because so much was left to be done and so little could be explicitly acknowledged, the pursuit of what would be a revolutionary settlement often involved the elaboration and intensification of customary political practices. The great issues of land, labor, power, and authority would be contested in good measure by means of personal confrontations, community skirmishes, and subterranean discourse.

What circulated through the rural South during the summer and fall of 1865, therefore, were not processions and petitions demanding "equal rights" but mutually reinforcing rumors of a world turned wholly upside down either by federal government fiat or armed black insurrection. Some quickly thought, or feared, that the day of reckoning could arrive at any time; most looked to the Christmas season, and particularly to Christmas or New Year's Day. Expectations varied as to what would, in fact, occur. A good many freedpeople seemed to hold the rather vague belief that there would be "some great change in the condition of affairs," that "something very important is going to happen," or that there would be "some great enhancement of their condition."[19] Growing numbers of whites, on the other hand, warned of a race war, "a negro Jubilee insurection," when the ex-slaves, reenacting the "horrors of Jamaica and St. Domingo," would attempt to murder or drive off their former masters.[20] But of widest currency were the ideas that "a general division of property will take place," that "the Government is going to take the Planters land and other property from them and give it to the colored people," or, failing that, that the blacks would carry out the deed themselves.[21]

Like rumors of slave or peasant rebellions and emancipations that erupted intermittently in many rural societies, those associated with the confiscation and redistribution of rebel land in the South have some murky and mysterious features. It is not entirely clear when and where the rumors first surfaced, how widely they circulated, or whether some of them, and the undeniably growing outcries they encouraged, ever had much substance. If the reports of alarmed southern whites and concerned federal officials together provide some indication, word of general property division and black-inspired violence began to circulate along the coast of North and South Carolina by the early summer of 1865, and then spread quite rapidly, especially through those areas where freedpeople could be found in the largest numbers. By November, both the expectations of blacks and the apprehensions of whites had been raised in the plantation districts of Virginia, North Carolina, Georgia, Alabama, and Texas, and more widely still in the Mississippi Valley states of Louisiana, Mississippi, Arkansas, and Tenneseee. One Freedmen's Bureau official familiar with Mississippi, Arkansas, Tennessee, and Alabama reckoned that "a majority of the colored population . . . positively believed that the government would take the plantations, with their old masters who had been in rebel service, cut them up into forty acre parcels, and give them to the colored people."[22]

Sam McAllum, a Mississippi ex-slave, appeared to be one of the believers. "There were a heap of talk about the Yankees a-giving every Nigger forty acres and a mule," he later told a white interviewer. "I don't know how us come to hear about it. It just kind of got around. I picked out my mule. All of us did." McAllum's story reflected, at least in part, the vagaries and personal distancing that usually characterize the traveling of rumors, and that undoubtedly offered him a greater sense of comfort and security as he related it to a potentially hostile listener. Yet ex-slaves like McAllum and ex-slaveowners as well had good cause to lend such rumors more than a little credibility.[23] By the time the Civil War ended—owing to congressional legislation, military fields orders, and wartime planter flight—the federal government controlled nearly 900,000 acres of southern land with authority to set it apart for eventual acquisition by "loyal refugees and freedmen." Much of that land lay in the fertile areas of the southeastern sea-board and the lower Mississippi Valley, and a good bit of it, chiefly in the low country of South Carolina and Georgia, was already occupied by freedpeople who expected to obtain formal title. Although President Andrew Johnson, in his Amnesty Proclamation of May 29, 1865, made provision for the restoration of this property to its former owners, the "land question," like other issues of social and economic reorganization in the South, remained very much alive. "We are but at the beginning of the war," a worried North Carolina conservative wrote that July.[24]

Indeed, the rumors of federally sponsored property redistribution thrived, as rumors often do, on the mix of hopes and fears that the war had unleashed and on the great contention that soon went into the making of federal policy.[25] Observers pointed not only to the influence of sympathetic Union soldiers and government agents who wished to break the slaveocracy even in the face of executive resistance, but also to the dire warnings of Confederate planters who had tried to rally support against the Yankee invaders. A Methodist missionary working in the Department of the South claimed that the blacks had "gained this impression, *first*, from the *Planters themselves* whom they often overheard in conversation, during the war, saying to each other, 'If the Yankees *conquer* they *will divide our lands among the Niggers.*'" In early 1863, a group of Louisiana planters blamed "designing persons" among the occupying forces for leading "many of the negroes . . . [to] believe that the plantations and everything on them belong to them." And in a few areas, slaves had either seized and cultivated plantations abandoned by their masters or leased them from federal authorities. General Rufus Saxton, briefly the Freedmen's Bureau assistant commissioner for South Carolina, Georgia, and Florida, thus summarized:

> Previous to the termination of the war the negroes had heard from those in rebellion that it was the purpose of our government to divide up the southern plantations among them, and that was one of the reasons the rebels urged among their own people to excite them to greater activity. . . . Our own acts of Congress and particularly the one creating the Freedmen's Bureau, which was extensively circulated among them, further strengthened

them in this dearest wish of their heart—that they were to have homesteads.[26]

The rapidity and scope with which rumors about federal policies, with attendant embellishments, circulated among southern blacks astonished northern officials who knew little or nothing about the networks of communication that slaves had built out of years of struggle, experience, and accumulated trust. "It was a wonder to me," remarked Lieutenant George O. Sanderson, who served in North Carolina. "It seemed to pass, as intelligence will, in the strangest manner, from one to another quickly . . . with unaccountable speed." Former masters were more familiar with the slaves' "grapevine telegraph" and had often come to mistrust those who regularly traversed the countryside and moved from the quarters to the big house, the courthouse, the tavern, the marketplace, and then back to the quarters: house servants, coachmen, boatmen, artisans, and hired slaves, some of whom had acquired the rudiments of literacy. But the Civil War and early Reconstruction both brought these communications networks to more public light and helped to extend, deepen, and institutionalize them.[27]

The combination of Confederate mobilization and Union invasion pushed and pulled thousands of slaves to social sites at which rumors, news, and debate about the politics of war flew in a manner impossible to control. The slave William I. Johnson, taken by his owner into Robert E. Lee's Army of Northern Virginia in 1863, first "learned from another slave that Lincoln had freed all of us." A year later, in camp near Fredricksburg, he seized an opportunity to talk with some recently captured Yankee prisoners who "explained to us about slavery and freedom . . . and told us if we got a chance to steal away from camp and got over to the Yankee side we would be free." Along with four other slaves, Johnson soon fled and ended up in a Union quartermaster's corps. Such fugitives could then have met the likes of George H. Hepworth, a white lieutenant in the black Fourth Louisiana Native Guards, who believed that "the *best* thing to do was to enlist all able-bodied men, confiscate every plantation in the department, and, dividing the land into twenty acre lots, give each black family one such lot, and let them try the experiment of free labor for themselves."[28]

At war's end, the flow of black migration and the organizational activities linked to the initial phases of Presidential Reconstruction together multiplied and amplified these lines of communication. Indeed, as federal policymakers and their subordinates increasingly locked horns over the questions of land, labor, and political rights, they appear to have fueled, rather than stifled, the freedpeople's expectations. When thousands of rural ex-slaves flocked, at least temporarily, to towns and cities, they could have joined urban blacks at processions and mass meetings and heard the speeches of federal representatives and local black leaders with the sensibilities of George Hepworth. In Savannah, Georgia, they could have heard General Rufus Saxton promise to "aid you in getting 40 acre farms as homes." In Pulaski, Tennessee, they might have heard what was derisively described as an "impudent [and] . . . incendiary speech of a Capt. Rexford," which seems to have lent some in the black audience "an idea that they are to be vested with a sort of proprietary interest in the lands and houses of the white people from whom they contract to work." And in Hampton, Virginia, they would have been assured by the fiery lawyer and Union League organizer Calvin Pepper that "they could *all* have lands, and their rights should be secured to them." Near the South Carolina capital of Columbia, the planter E. B. Hayward thus grumbled about the "extravagant expectations" that members of the "radical party of the north" had nourished.[29]

As many of the black migrants later departed from urban areas, they opened only some of the proliferating channels through which these "extravagant expectations" could move across the countryside. Returning contrabands and other refugees, especially from districts in which wartime labor experiments hinted at more general land reform, opened additional ones. Union army officers in the interior of South Carolina, noting the "general discontent . . . on the part of the negroes" around their posts, attributed it to the arrival of "many freedmen" who had been "absent on the coast," where early federal occupation and Sherman's Field Orders No. 15 (reserving land for black settlement) had begun to reorganize the plantation system. "They lead them to believe that they are to have land, on the first of January," Lieutenant Colonel F. H. Whittier wrote from Sumter, and although he did "all in my power to do away with the expectation . . . I no sooner get back than there is another story started."[30]

More important in disseminating ideas about the freedpeople's prospects, and in raising their expectations, were black Union soldiers.

Nearly 85,000 of them served in the army of occupation—accounting for more than one-third of the total federal occupying force by the fall of 1865—and over half were in Mississippi, Louisiana, Tennessee, and Kentucky, from which many of the reports regarding land redistribution and possible black insurrection emanated. Planters and other white southern leaders came to groan incessantly about what they viewed as the "demoralizing" influence of the "colored troops" on the free black labor force, particularly by encouraging belief in property division. "The Negro Soldiery here," a Panola, Mississippi, landowner charged, "are constantly telling our negroes that for the next year, the Government will give them land, provisions, and Stock and all things necessary to carry on business for themselves." "Strange to say," he added with evident befuddlement, "the negroes believe such stories in spite of facts to the contrary told them by their employers." Near Aiken, South Carolina, the planter Henry William Ravenel, assuming that "the negro troops . . . learnt their lessons well from their abolition instructors," confided to his diary that "they boast of keeping down the white man and elevating the negro, and thus spread the seed of discontent among the blacks." Returning from a tour of the southeastern states, General Ulysses S. Grant blamed some agents of the Freedmen's Bureau as well as "colored troops" for "imbuing" the "late slave . . . with the idea that the property of his late master should by right belong to him." Even Carl Schurz, who reported to President Johnson on conditions in the South and generally praised the discipline and demeanor of the black troops, nonetheless acknowledged that they "are sometimes found to put queer notions into the heads of negroes working on the plantations."[31]

The presence of black troops and of black veterans mustered out of service helped to advance the local organization of rural freed communities. The Reverend Horace James, federal superintendent of Negro affairs in North Carolina, marveled in January 1865 that blacks "form societies, leagues, combinations, meetings, with little of routine or record, but much of speech making and sage counsel." Within months, countless meetings, some large and some small, had assembled elsewhere—in rural churches, county seats, campgrounds, plantations, and less accessible locations—where discussion ranged widely and, at times, promoted and validated rumors of land redistribution. In June, the Freedmen's Bureau superintendent of the eastern district of Arkansas expressed irritation at black preachers who spent their "time teaching the people that they should, *of right,* own every foot of soil" instead of instructing them in "sound practical truths." At the end of September, twenty members of the Wilkes County, Georgia, grand jury told a Freedmen's Bureau official that a recent meeting of nearly three thousand blacks, "of which much the larger proportion were Males . . . [and] sworn to secrecy," supplied many with the belief "that there will be a general division among them of the lands and property of the county." And in early November, a series of meetings in Terrebone Parish, Louisiana, from which whites were excluded, appeared to raise the idea that "some great change in the condition of affairs was expected to take place before the 1st of January."[32]

For growing numbers of rural freedpeople, these incipient forums of mobilization framed the issues of early Reconstruction and, in the words of a Union officer in Georgetown, South Carolina, "strengthened . . . the impression that lands are to be given." When two candidates vied for selection to the North Carolina freedmen's convention before a late September gathering of blacks in the town of Tarboro, one "took the ground that there would be no division of Land, and that they only would get land who made money to buy it." "He did not receive a single vote out of an assembly of probably 1500 persons," the local Freedmen's Bureau agent recorded "as another sign of the times." But "the other took the opposite ground and was unanimously elected." Small wonder that federal authorities often had difficulty trying to convince rural blacks that no property division would occur. One such emissary in Amite County, Mississippi, who provided the freedpeople with "all the necessary instructions and advice they needed" and thought "they seemed at the time to be very well satisfied," later learned "that a great many of them said they did not believe what I told them. . . . They are still hopeful that something is going to turn up about Christmas."[33]

The planters were, of course, quick to see any nonsubmissive behavior on the part of the freedpeople, or any interventions on the part of federal agents, as harbingers of grander and more insidious designs; and blacks themselves, at mass meetings and conventions, frequently took pains to dispute any suggestion that they planned an armed rising. "[W]e pray you do not believe the falshood our enemies has got up for some purpose that we intend an insurrection," the "colorde peple" of Claiborne County, Mississippi, implored the state's governor in December 1865. "[W]e have [no s]uch thought now."[34] Yet the rumors of land redistribution must not then be dismissed as mere "illusions" entertained by ex-slaves or as mere creations of frightened white imaginations. The rumors derived powerful credibility from federal actions, spread widely among African Americans in the southern countryside, and despite (or, better, because of) reversals in federal policy, percolated through a myriad of meetings and encounters. Given the freedpeople's exclusions from the official arenas of political negotiation and the risks they faced in publicly expressing their aspirations and wills, the rumors could have served them as vital points of political contact, conversation, and identification; as safer ways in which to introduce themselves as political actors; and as potent means for shaping—and advancing—the terrain of political debate. The rumors, the "extravagant ideas" of what freedom might bring, that is, played a significant role in defining the political communities of rural blacks newly emerged from bondage.[35]

Whatever many planters preferred to believe, rural freedpeople did not need tutors or outside agitators to nurture their desire for, or sense of entitlement to, the land. They neither had to be apprised of the advantages that proprietorship would hold nor reminded that their long-endured and uncompensated toil and suffering built both the South's great fortunes and the nation's prosperity. "Our wives, our children, our husbands, has been sold over and over again to purchase the lands we now locates on," the Virginia freedman Bayley Wyat declared in explaining why "we has a right to [that] land. . . . [D]idn't we clear the land and raise de crops. . . . And den didn't dem large cities in de North grow up on de cotton and de sugars and de rice dat we made?" Wyat and others who shared his views demonstrated that slaves had become familiar with and could appropriate a powerful, if contested, national political discourse that exalted manual labor and associated freedom with economic independence. The federal commander of the district of West Tennessee managed to convey more of this argument even as he dismissed the hope for rebel expatriation and land partition as a species of the "agrarian idea" and "chimerical in the extreme": "Says the newly emancipated black, toil was the chief misery of my former condition. I am now free. . . . And if I am compelled to work for wages to support me wherefore is my condition bettered?"[36]

Yet the former slaves' expectations of property division revealed more complex aspirations and sets of beliefs. And they shed considerable light on the ways in which African Americans drew on the political sensibilities and rituals they had forged under slavery to give shape and substance to the course of emancipation and early Reconstruction: on shared understandings of power and process that the general social relations of slavery had encouraged; on the discrete, and often very different settings and circumstances in which those relations took hold; and on the new formulations and projects that the military destruction of slavery had made possible.

The expectations of land redistribution expressed almost universally held notions of just compensation for the travails of enslavement, of what was rightfully due those who tilled the soil, and of what could provide meaningful security in a postemancipation world. In this, the ex-slaves closely resembled subject rural folk in many societies, for in one form or another the "land question" charged social struggles in all servile and semiservile labor systems and surfaced in connection with almost all servile emancipations.[37] But the expectations also reflected the freedpeople's intensely personal and spiritual conception of the world, and the logic of the millennial deliverance narratives that many had constructed as slaves. Thus, more than a few remembered learning of their liberation from bondage when "Marse Linkum" came riding through their locales, conflated the figures of Lincoln, Rufus Saxton, and William Sherman with Moses and Jesus, and called emancipation the "day of Jubilo," singing in many parts of the South,

> Old master's gone away and the darkies stayed at home;
> Must be now that Kingdom's come and the year for jubilee.

Rich in the stories, characters, images, and allegories of the Bible as their community religious experiences came to be, could they not have known, too, that the Biblical "jubilee" joined freedom with the restitution of the land to its rightful claimants?[38]

Freedpeople in south Georgia may well have been signifying such an understanding when they proclaimed "that 'Head man' will come before next Christmas and will make them 'more free' and 'distribute the lands' to them." Others, in Mississippi, heard ("from the voice of the Angels probably," as one local agent chortled, perhaps acknowledging the echoes of the millennial Book of Revelation) "that a Great Document has been received by the 'Freedmens Bureau' sealed with four seals . . . to be broken on the 1st day of January 1866," the third anniversary of the Emancipation Proclamation. "This wonderful paper [is thought] to contain [the freedmen's] final orders from the Yankee Government which they believe is omnipotent." Thomas Wentworth Higginson, the Massachusetts abolitionist who commanded black troops in wartime South Carolina and listened attentively to their spirituals, tellingly insisted that "the Apocalypse . . . with the books of Moses, constituted their Bible; all that lay between, even the narratives of the life of Jesus, they hardly cared to read or hear."[39]

The mythic and millennial aspects of these expectations had both deep symbolic meanings and concrete political uses. By investing the government, often in the person of the President, with the authority and intent to carry out the injunctions of the "jubilee," the freedpeople not only rejected their former owners' pretensions to sovereign power, but also provided a standard of justice and equity against which the policies and actions of federal officials were to be judged. A Mississippi planter conceded as much when he wrote Andrew Johnson, with considerable exasperation, that local blacks thought "that they will own all and we will have to emigrate elsewhere . . . [and] all will come by you and from you." Efforts to dissuade them simply failed because "some of the negroes dont believe a word of it—and say the *President* will do more for us." A Freedmen's Bureau agent in northern Louisiana made a related point in trying to explain, with more equanimity and some amusement, why "the illusion . . . [of] a general division of property . . . [was] very natural for their simple minds": "Inasmuch as the Government has made them free they consider that a share of the property which their past services have acquired justly belongs to them; and imagining that the Government regards the subject in the same light, they adhere to the fallacy very tenaciously." So tenaciously, in fact, that the freedpeople might suspect the motives and veracity of federal authorities who sought to disabuse them of such a "fallacy." In the tradition of invoking the just and good ruler betrayed by unfaithful subordinates, "a large number of Freedmen" in southern Mississippi announced "that the late President Lincoln intended . . . to divide the lands of their former owners among them; that in some way his intention has been defeated and that they are being cheated out of their rights."[40]

It was not by accident, then, that many of the ex-slaves looked to the Christmas season for the dispensation of their just rewards, for at no other time of the year had the slaveowners' claims to sovereign authority been more ritualistically displayed and contested. Largely suspending work and loosening the reins of supervision for the Christmas to New Year's interlude, the masters, by handing out gifts and providing meals and parties for their black, as well as white, "families," sought to present themselves as powerful and benevolent patriarchs who ruled their small domains of acres and dependents. And listening at times to the slaves serenade them with joyful cries of "Christmas gif', Christmas gif'," they undoubtedly congratulated themselves on their generosity and imagined that the loyalties and labors of their charges would be suitably encouraged. But they authored only part of the script. In the quarters, the slaves found the gifts and festivities provided for them a much less important feature of the holidays than the accompanying opportunities to provide for themselves and to choreograph a rather different version of the occasion.[41]

The slaves were thus able to move relatively freely to visit family and friends on neighboring plantations and farms, where they staged their own rites of community, put on their own dances and celebrations, and partook of the spirit—and the spirits—of the season. So unruly could the frolicking appear that more than a few slaveowners nervously warned of the need for greater vigilance. Not surprisingly, a substantial portion of the antebellum slave insurrection panics happened during the Christmas interlude, all the more so after Jamaican slaves set a terrifying example by launching the largest rebellion in the history of the British West Indies on December 27, 1831. In 1856, as the Republican party first competed for national power, slave unrest was widespread and numerous "plots" were said to have been uncovered, with apprehensions rising notably during Christmas week.[42] When the Civil War broke out, these apprehensions only intensified. In December 1862, planters in the Union-occupied sugar-growing districts around New Orleans dreaded an impending slave revolt, and two of them, in St. John the Baptist Parish, charged fitfully that "three carts loaded with Slaves arrived at Boutte Station, Shrieking threats, singing and inciting to insurrection, and mentioning Christmas as the time set for the emancipation of the slaves." "As far as the memory of man can go, there has existed among the negro population a tradition which has caused us many sleepless nights," a planter in St. Charles Parish wrote one day earlier. "They imagine that they are to be freed by Christmas. Vague reports are spread about that they intend, taking whatever weapons they can find, to come in vast numbers and force the federal government to give them their freedom."[43]

In their preoccupation with the potential consequences of revelry in the quarters, worried slaveholders tacitly admitted the limits of their paternalist sway while supplying lurid visions of social inversion that the slaves preferred to enact symbolically and metaphorically, eventually lending further substance to rumors of a momentous change in the making. Like dependent classes in other preindustrial societies, the slaves used holidays such as Christmas not only to strengthen the threads binding their communities, but also to ridicule the pretensions of their betters and conjure up a world in which relations of subordination might be negated or inverted.[44] The most ritualized manifestations of these symbolic inversions and appropriations of white prerogatives were to be found in the yuletide "Jonkonnu" of eastern North Carolina and southern Virginia. But elsewhere in the South, albeit less elaborately and agonistically, the slaves mocked the structure of plantation authority, transgressed the customary spatial boundaries of slave life, enacted rites of reciprocity rather than submission, and tossed satirical jabs at their masters through song, play, folktales, and dance. The slaveholders may well have been amused, and the festivities undoubtedly provided a relatively safe release for accumulated social tensions, not to mention a chance for the slaves to engage in rivalries of their own. Yet in these special ways, the slaves also forged collective sensibilities of their self-worth, of their masters' false claims to rule, and of the possibilities of constructing the world in an altogether different fashion.[45]

If the freedpeople saw in the rumors of a Christmas property division the hand of a truly just and sovereign authority acting against the pretenders and usurpers, they imagined in the results less a wholesale inversion—when masters would become slaves and slaves masters—than a rearrangement or reconstitution of social relations. And although representations of the process could be rather vague, expectations and claims seemed to derive significantly from the concrete experiences of enslavement. Many African Americans in plantation districts, and especially in areas long settled and relatively stable, therefore anticipated obtaining control, not just of any land, but of the estates on which they had lived and labored. Their attachment to their "old homes" or the "old range" was, as white observers widely commented, deep and powerful. It expressed not only a sense of place and of "right to the cattle and hogs that they have raised and taken care of, and the [crops] that they have raised," but also a commitment to maintaining and reinforcing the networks of kinship, friendship, and customary practice that had sustained them under slavery and informed the sense of right itself.[46] J. W. Alvord, a Freedmen's Bureau official who toured Virginia, North Carolina, and much of the lower South in 1865, found the blacks to "be a remarkably permanent people. They love to stay in one place, where they have always lived, where they were born and where their children are buried. Their local associations are very strong." "Tell Lincoln that we want land," a black church elder implored a northerner who visited Port Royal, South Carolina, in 1864. "[T]his very land that is rich with the sweat of we face and the blood of we back. We born here, we parents' graves here; this here our home." Along the coast of South Carolina, where slave communities had especially extended generational roots, the freedpeople might even reject opportunities to preempt or take title to tracts of land if doing so necessitated relocation.[47]

The interrelation of land, kinship, and years of community labor helps explain why expectations of land redistribution were far less common in regions of the South in which farms and small plantations predominated. There the slaves were more closely tied to the organization and rhythms of white households. It was more likely that they had to work in the fields alongside their owners; it was less likely that they could live with all members of their immediate families, tend customary garden plots, and engage in the day-to-day activities that made for a dense culture of the quarters and encouraged identification with the parcels of land on which they resided. For them, the immediate postwar period was given over chiefly to the tasks of reuniting and reconstituting their own households and kinship groups, which had been scattered over the neighboring countryside, if not over far greater distances.[48]

Observers attested to the many related struggles in which such freedpeople engaged when they reported that "nearly all the negroes in this country have changed homes," that some would only sign labor contracts offering provisions to "non-workers on [the] place," and that "there has not been one solitary exception when they have failed to lay claim to and contend for their children." Moses Scott, a freedman residing in eastern Mississippi in 1865, kept up an extended correspondence with his wife in Virginia as they tried to find suitable conditions for resettlement. By December, Scott believed that they "can do well here," urged his wife to "come out and bring all your children and tell Neverson and William to come," and closed the letter by giving "my love to cousin Randall Quarles" and asking to be remembered "to father, my brothers, and all my friends." There was, in short, good reason why a former small slaveholder in western North Carolina wrote that "the idea with the negroes is that they are not free until they leave their masters."[49]

As one moved from non- and small plantation regions back into the plantation belt, rumors of an impending property division could be heard once again. But in the more recently settled or socially volatile districts, and in those where few holdings had been abandoned by the owners during the war, the rumors may well have been interpreted as a government promise less to partition particular estates, than to provide opportunities for the acquisition of homesteads, farm implements, and draft animals under favorable terms. Asking "what is the good of freedom if one has nothing to go on?" some freedpeople searched for the chance to set up on small tracts or patches where they could "become householders themselves." And according to one disgruntled white North Carolinian, "they believe that the Government will wink at the attempt to assert . . . their ideas, and will maintain them in their claim of equality."[50]

Other freedpeople began to pool resources accumulated by years of extra work, hiring out, and selling the eggs, poultry, and vegetables raised on their provision grounds in hopes of buying or leasing land that was, or would be, confiscated. In July 1865, Thomas W. Conway, the sympathetic Freedmen's Bureau assistant commissioner in Louisiana, wrote of receiving "many applications from freedmen, some who have $10–15,000, some $3–5,000, and some who have nothing but are anxious to work and give a share of the crop for advances." A month later, "a portion of the freedmen of Lenoir County [North Carolina] . . . being desirous of embracing every facility which the U.S. government offers to provide for ourselves the comforts of a permanent home," formed "a society to purchase homes by joint stock," pledging to raise $10,000 in monthly installments by January 1, 1868. In this, they and other ex-slaves may have been influenced by black soldiers who, in squads, companies, and even regiments, took their savings and applied "for such portions of land as they consider themselves able to purchase and cultivate." Thus, when an "intelligent" Mississippi freedman, exemplifying the "great eagerness of the blacks . . . [to] have homes of their own," was told that "the whites intend to compel you to hire out to them," he shot back, "what if we shall compel them to lease us lands?"[51]

The agitation and rumors as to land distribution were principally rural affairs, and they dramatized the political gulf between the mobilizations of countryside and town. Yet that gulf was gradually being bridged in 1865, not simply as rural freedpeople first migrated to urban areas and then, in many cases, returned, but also as federal officials, black leaders, and black soldiers well attuned to the official political culture moved into the country districts to assemble the freedpeople and apprise them of their rights and prospects. For in so doing, they simultaneously enunciated and embodied the end of the old order, while providing a new language and new categories in which aspirations for land could be expressed. Already, such voices as the *New Orleans Tribune* had outlined the arguments in terms familiar to national politics and political discourse. Proclaiming that the inauguration of freedom required that masters as well as slaves be "dispense[d] with," the *Tribune*, which had embraced equal rights and excoriated wartime federal policies that served to restore the plantation system, called too for the confiscation and redistribution of rebel-owned property. "There is . . . no true republican government, unless the land and wealth in general, are distributed among the great mass of the inhabitants . . . no more room in our society for an oligarch of slaveholders or property holders," the paper lectured. "The Louisiana landowner['s] . . . hands are red with a treason unparalleled in the world's history. . . . His lands are forfeited, his slaves are free. . . . Sooner or later this division of property must come about. . . . The land tillers are entitled by a paramount right to the possession of the soil they have so long cultivated."[52]

The editors of the *Tribune*, by the fall of 1865, thought that some, "and especially the most active," of the freedmen in the "country parishes" had read at least a few issues of the paper.[53] Early political lessons were to be received, as well, from white and black allies who aided the ex-slaves in defending claims to the lands they occupied, in resisting the coercions of their former masters, and in finding avenues to secure independence. Albeit slowly and unevenly, rural freedpeople learned how to compose and frame petitions, to best articulate their expectations, and to represent their goals in relation to the larger political struggles sweeping the South and the nation.

Among the most extraordinary of the students were Henry Bram, Ishmael Moultrie, and Yates Simpson, constituted as a "committee in behalf of the people" of Edisto Island, South Carolina.[54] In late October 1865, having learned "with deep sorrow and Painful hearts" that the lands they cultivated under the provisions of Sherman's Special Field Orders No. 15 would soon be restored to the white owners, the committee wrote to President Andrew Johnson and Freedmen's Bureau Commissioner Oliver Otis Howard to ask that the decision be reconsidered. They began by attributing their emancipatory jubilee to divine authority carried "through our Late and Beloved President (Lincoln) proclamation and the war," and prayed that Johnson might be guided "in making Your decisions" by "that wisdom that Cometh from above to settle these great and Important Questions." Echoing peasant appeals to a sovereign, they then suggested that the new President's policy reversals must be the result not of motives they believed unjust, but of "the many perplexing and trying questions that burden your mind."

The committee rested their claims to the land, in part, on the traditional ground of unrequited labor performed by a kin-based community over many generations: "[W]e are at the mercy of those who are combined to prevent us from getting land enough to lay our Fathers bones upon. We have property in Horses, cattle, carriages, & articles of furniture. . . . Here is w[h]ere we have toiled nearly all our lives as slaves and were treated like dumb Driven cattle. This is our home, we have made These lands what they are." Yet significantly, the committee also couched their grievances in language and constructions that spoke both to the direct experiences of their people and to what the President might find compelling. They took their understandings of the war and its results and of the political predilections of Johnson, whose hostility to the Confederacy and the southern landed aristocracy was well known, and used them to make their case:

> Here is where secession was born and Nurtured. . . . we were the only true and Loyal people that were found in possession of these Lands. We have always been ready to strike for Liberty and humanity yea to fight if needs be To preserve this glorious union. Shall not we who Are freedman and have always been true to this union have the same rights as those enjoyed by Others? Have we forfieted our rights of property In land?—If not then! are not our rights as A free people and good citizens of these United States To be considered before the rights of those who were Found in rebellion against this good and just Government (and now being conquered) come (as they seem) with penitent hearts and beg forgiveness For past offenses and also ask if thier lands Cannot be restored to them are these rebellious Spirits to be reinstated in thier *possessions* And we who have been abused and oppressed For many long years not to be allowed the Privilige of purchasing land But to be subject To the will of these large Land owners? God fobid, Land monopoly is injurious to the advancement of the course of freedom, and if Government Does not make some provision by which we as Freedmen can obtain A Homestead, We have Not bettered our condition. . . . We pray that God will direct your heart in Making provision for us as freedmen which will tend to united these states together stronger Than ever before.[55]

The Edisto Islanders may well have been hitching their particular aspirations for land to the national project being devised and advanced by Radical Republicans and their black allies, still chiefly to be found in southern and northern cities. But perhaps there as elsewhere in the plantation South, the inverse was more properly the case: that they were seeking to protect and consecrate their own project of community building by placing it under the jurisdiction of an earthly sovereign power that they themselves had helped to sustain. This was, after all, the logic of federal policies and promises now being revoked. Nine months earlier, having arrived in Savannah, Georgia, with hundreds of poor black refugees accompanying (and burdening) his army, an exasperated General William Tecumseh Sherman felt the heat of additional pressure. Suspicions had been aroused in Washington that Sherman "manifested an almost *criminal* dislike to the negro" and sought "to repulse him with contempt" rather than "carry out the wishes of the Government in regard to him." When the visiting secretary of war Edwin M. Stanton "shared these thoughts" and "seemed desirous of coming into contact with the negroes to confer with them," Sherman convened an extraordinary meeting, in his room, with Stanton and twenty black leaders for the purpose of consultation and action.[56]

All of the twenty blacks who attended were "class-leaders, deacons, and divines" in black churches. Nineteen of the twenty had been born and raised in Georgia or the Carolinas, three-quarters had been slaves, and more than half had spent at least a portion of their lives in the countryside. "To express their common sentiments upon the matters of inquiry," the group selected the sixty-seven-year-old Garrison Frazier, born in Granville County, North Carolina, enslaved until "he bought himself and wife" in 1857, and a Baptist minister for thirty-five years. Frazier, who understood slavery as "receiving by *irresistible power* the work of another man" and freedom as "placing us where we could reap the fruit of our labor, take care of ourselves and assist the government in maintaining our freedom," believed that "the way we can best take care of ourselves is to have land, and turn it by our own labor." And he stated a preference "to live by ourselves . . . rather [than] scattered among the whites . . . for there is a prejudice against us in the South that will take years to get over." The Reverend James D. Lynch, freeborn in Baltimore and having spent much of his life in the North, quickly objected. The former slaves, he thought, "should not be separated" from the whites "but live together." His was the lone voice, however. "All the other persons present, being questioned one by one, answer[ed] that they agree with Brother Frazier." Four days later, hoping to meet "the pressing necessities of the case," Sherman issued Special Field Orders No. 15, "reserv[ing] and set[ting] apart for the settlement of the negroes . . . the islands from Charleston south, the abandoned rice-fields along the rivers for thirty miles back from the sea, and the country bordering the Saint John's River, Florida," to be subdivided "so that each family shall have a plot of not more than forty acres of tillable ground."[57] It was a vision of righteous policy and social organization that the rumors of land redistribution would later generalize.

❖

By the fall of 1865, white southerners had good reason to doubt that the federal government would continue to spearhead a program of property confiscation and redistribution. Thaddeus Stevens's early September speech calling for the provision of a forty-acre farm to each black household may have been widely circulated, and some federal officials did try mightily to keep hold, and facilitate the division, of lands that had previously been abandoned or confiscated. But these radicals were fighting a rearguard battle and losing ground steadily as Andrew Johnson simultaneously hastened the restoration of rebel-owned estates and reprimanded, overrode, or dismissed those who sought to stand in the way.[58] What southern whites increasingly claimed to fear was a move by disappointed freedpeople to take matters into their own hands by the only means left available: concerted violence.

This has come to be known as the "Christmas Insurrection Scare of 1865," and its resemblance to earlier slave insurrection panics (not to mention similar panics in other highly oppressive societies) was not fortuitous. It came at a time of heightened tensions and anxieties, of political division and social unrest; it inflated episodic resistance and discontent into full-blown conspiracies; it implicated outsiders; and it served to inspire greater vigilance among whites and greater repression against blacks.[59] But whereas previous panics tended to be localized and somewhat brief, the 1865 scare proved more protracted and far more extended in scope. And together with the rumors of property redistribution that circulated among freedpeople, it came to be a weapon of direct struggle over the balances of power in the countryside.

To some northern observers at the time, as well as to many scholars of a later day, white anxieties about black insurrection seemed the product of a peculiarly irrational psychology. A federal army commander at Baton Rouge, Louisiana, captured the political irony of this apparent mindset when he scoffed, in December of 1865, that "those men and women of this community who profess to believe that the negroes evidence should not be taken in a 'court of justice' because unreliable—will listen with hair erect & protruding eye balls to the whispered mutterings of any old crone who tells them of secreted arms and intended violence."[60] In important respects, however, the apprehensions followed quite logically from both the social relations and cultural choreography of slavery and the political process and consequences of emancipation.

Even more than other systems of unfreedom, slavery rested on the principle of the absolute authority—the petty sovereignty as it were—of the master and the utter dependence of the slave. Difficult, indeed impossible, as this principle was to maintain in practice, it nonetheless required personal disciplinary power sanctioned by the state together with various rituals of domination, appropriation, and submission that incorporated both coercion and ostensible consent. The slave's recalcitrance could be explained by the ignorance, inferiority, and backwardness that were said to justify enslavement; resistance to, or rejection of, the master's authority, if acknowledged, had to be treated summarily, for there was perilously little middle ground to be occupied. Outsiders and intermediaries, whomever they might be, were particularly to be feared.[61]

The prospects of abolition would therefore have been chilling under any circumstances. Yet while in most other slave and servile societies emancipation had gradualist features and left former owners in full control of the countryside during the transition, in the American South it came in a sweeping and forceful fashion, without even the masters' grudging participation and agreement, and it created something of a power vacuum filled in part by the military arm of a federal government committed to, if nothing else, contract rather than coercion as the new basis of social relations.[62] As a consequence, ex-slaveholders who, in the words of the traveler J. T. Trowbridge, scarcely comprehended "[t]he first principles of a free-labor system" and believed "some compulsory system . . . indispensable," faced the postwar "labor question" with uncertainty and an assortment of disabilities and challenges to their customary prerogatives.[63] That many blacks quickly

asserted their new freedoms by moving about, attending to family responsibilities, seeking to provide for themselves, and refusing to work
as before proved troublesome enough. More galling was their ability
and desire to enlist in their daily skirmishes the counsel and assistance
of Union army personnel and Freedmen's Bureau agents.

A Tennessee merchant and land speculator expressed some of the
meaning of this altered circuit of negotiation when he informed President Andrew Johnson of the "terror which [the Freedmen's Bureau]
holds over our people—by listening to and sustaining the negro in
evy [*sic*] frivolous and malicious complaint—[it] amounts to a practical
denial of the rights of the white man." "The effect of [Yankee] occupation is to make the negroes insolent and idle and protect them in their
meanness," the conservative North Carolinian David Schenck similarly
recorded in his diary. "[E]very complaint which he lodges against his
employer or former master subjects such person to the annoyance and
disgrace of going before the Yankee commander to answer said negro's
charge, and there to have no more dignity and respect than is shown
the negro." A white Virginian, explaining to the northern journalist
John R. Dennett why the "jurisdiction of the military authorities" was
"very distasteful to the former masters," told of an army captain who
"sent out more than ten miles and made a gentleman and his wife
come and appear before him to answer some charge one of their own
niggers made against them." "I tell you, sir," the Virginian snorted,
"it's mighty humiliating."[64]

Such humiliations provoked the old masters to countless acts of
personal violence against their former slaves—acts that Freedmen's
Bureau agents attempted to track under the apposite rubric of "outrages." But as rumors of federal land redistribution further inflated the
freedpeople's expectations and assertiveness, white landowners not
only charged that a black insurrection brewed; they also began to use
the alleged threat of insurrection to dismantle the freedpeople's means
of resistance and to legitimate their own efforts to readjust the balances
of local power. An episode in the Alabama black belt revealed how
quickly, and under what circumstances, the dynamic could be set in
motion. In the early fall of 1865, a freedman came into the office of
Freedmen's Bureau agent Captain Andrew Geddes in Tuskegee wishing "to get a few arms and permission for himself and 2 or 3 others"
to go "down to Pike County" and give "aid to their friends and rela-

tives" who "were being treated very cruely and unjustly by the white citizens." Geddes was not sympathetic. He denied the request and threatened the freedman with arrest, whereupon the freedman "seemed to go off satisfied." Soon thereafter, however, "a committee of citizens" told Geddes that it had "been *reported* to them that an 'insurrection' was on foot among the negroes and that application had been made for arms &c." Despite Geddes's denials, the committee remained "quite excited and appeared to seriously apprehend an immediate rising of the negroes armed and equipped and crying for *vengeance*." They decided to alert Lewis Parsons, the native Alabamian who had been appointed the state's provisional governor by President Johnson.[65]

Growing numbers of planters and other white landowners brought their fears of insurrection to the attention of federal officials and, especially, to governors appointed or elected under the auspices of Presidential Reconstruction. They were most likely to do so in states where blacks formed clear or near population majorities, and where some federal officials, together with newly installed post-Confederate officeholders, were regarded as sympathetic to their concerns—Mississippi, Louisiana, Alabama, Georgia, and South Carolina being the prime examples. They called for the withdrawal of black troops, who were represented as the chief instigators, and for the authority to raise local militia companies so as to maintain order and generally "overawe the colored population." A group of "white citizens of Caddo and Bossier parishes, many of whom are planters," wrote to Louisiana Governor J. Madison Wells in October of "a prevailing idea among the colored people that after January 1 there is to be a general distribution of property . . . [instilled] principally by the colored troops, who have been for some months stationed among us." They insisted that "great apprehension pervades the countryside," and asked Wells for such help as arms and ammunition and permission to organize the militia "under officers of our selection."[66]

The governors, in turn, contacted the commanders of military departments, the assistant commissioners of the Freedmen's Bureau, and, if necessary, President Johnson to win official support for the suppression of a potential outbreak. In this, the governors served less as the President's state representatives than as the planters' national brokers, testing the boundaries of federal policy while presenting the planters' case in a way the President might view as a demonstration of public responsibility. Most vocal and persuasive among them was Mississippi's William L. Sharkey, a former Whig who had opposed secession but was closely identified with the planting interest. As early as August, Sharkey wrote Johnson that "the negroes are bold in their threats" and "there is a . . . widespread opinion amongst the people . . . that about Christmas they intend a general rising for the purpose of taking the property." To "begin preparation for such an emergency and to suppress crime," he thereby "called for volunteer companies of militia in each county" and asked for control of the "state arms" and the power "to organize the whole of the militia." Sharkey later warned Freedmen's Bureau Commissioner Oliver Otis Howard that black troops were expected to lead a revolt in the winter if the distribution of property was not carried out, and suggested that they be expeditiously removed from the state. Other governors added their voices, including Governor Parsons of Alabama who forwarded a resolution of the state constitutional convention recommending the formation of "one or more companies of militia, in each county, as soon as practicable, to aid in repressing disorder and preserv[ing] the public peace."[67]

Federal officials in the former Confederate states generally responded to these alarms with studied skepticism. Samuel Thomas, the Freedmen's Bureau assistant commissioner in Mississippi, for one, disputed many of Sharkey's complaints and thought that "all such reports originated among the old women around log-cabin fires [and] . . . People who . . . have an ulterior motive."[68] Nevertheless, by November the bureau had begun to send agents into the rural districts with instructions to "disabuse" the freedpeople of "the false impression that the lands of their former owners are to be divided out among them on or about Christmas next" and "urge them at once to make contracts for 1866." In the less "extravagant" political economy of freedom that most federal authorities had come to preach, the blacks heard that "you must labor for what you get like other people," that "idleness and vagrancy" would not be tolerated, that property had to be purchased, and that any attempt "to take property from anyone . . . would be punished with utmost severity."[69]

Initially, however, army commanders blocked the mobilization of the militias, and Johnson was given good reason to sustain the commanders' actions. In Louisiana, General E. R. S. Canby found that local militia companies "indulged in the gratification of private vengeance and worked against the policy of the Government," while from Mississippi Carl Schurz pleaded that "General Slocum's order . . . prohibiting the organization of the militia in this state . . . be openly approved." Schurz had met Governor Sharkey, and although he believed Sharkey to be "a good, clever gentleman, and probably a first class lawyer," he doubted whether Sharkey could be trusted. "He is continually surrounded by a set of old secessionists whom he considers it his duty to conciliate," Schurz cautioned. Johnson thus stunned many federal officials in the South, and aroused suspicion and mistrust in much of the North, by agreeing to countenance—and then by welcoming—what proved to be the official rearming of ex-Confederates and the revitalization of slave patrols. Indeed, shortly after approving Sharkey's actions, Johnson advised neighboring provisional governor Parsons to raise "in each county an armed mounted *posse comitatus* organized under your militia law," noting that "a similar organization by me in Tennessee when military governor worked well."[70]

Johnson's decision followed from a more general aim to restore self-government quickly in the South through policies that might stimulate a show of loyalty, moderation, and proper conduct. But as with other concessions to what has been termed "self-reconstruction," the organization of militia companies only stimulated white defiance toward the federal government and retribution against the freedpeople. If anything, it blurred the lines between "legal" and "extra-legal" coercion, and gave the green light to vigilantes who, like the "Black patroles" around Tuskegee, Alabama, traversed the countryside "whipping and otherwise male [*sic*] treating the Freedmen."[71] Deploying the threat of insurrection as shield and sword, the planters and their allies launched a campaign to disarm, disperse, and intimidate rural blacks, intending to reassign them to the "tender mercies" of white landowners. Any black assembly, any sign of economic independence, any attempt to ignore or reject the conventions of racial subordination became an invitation to harassment or summary punishment. Away from their posts, even black soldiers fell vulnerable. In Summit, Mississippi, "in broad daylight," two whites accosted a member of "'D' Co. 66 USC Infantry" on a five-day pass, and in a ritual of humiliation "cut off his coat buttons and the fastenings for shoulder scales and gave him an hour to leave town." A few days earlier, in Copiah County, a "religious meeting composed mostly of colored soldiers . . . was broken up by a company of militia because the preacher was a freedman, and not licensed to preach the gospel." The scourge came, too, on freedpeople walking the roads, camping in the woods, operating small makeshift enterprises, and cultivating abandoned or rented land. As a "party" of whites in Sumter County, Georgia, proclaimed, "they would make their own laws . . . and if the negroes failed to hire and contract upon their terms before Christmas, or at that time, they would make the woods stink with their carcasses." "Our negroes have . . . a tall fall ahead of them," predicted a white Mississippian, who looked on with approbation. "They will learn that freedom and independence are different things."[72]

Federal authorities and other northern observers largely mocked the reports of freedmen secreting arms, holding nightly meetings, and drilling in military fashion that rural whites cited to mobilize and legitimate their raiding. A Freedmen's Bureau agent in South Carolina dismissed such "stories" as "not worthy of serious consideration" after one investigation turned up "30 or 40 men, women, and children" engaged in "a frolic imitating the soldiers." Another in Leon County, Florida, having been warned by local "citizens" of "an immense collection of colored people [to be] assembled at the plantation of Mr. F. R. Cotton . . . on Christmas day for the purpose of concocting measures detrimental to the well being of the country" instead discovered "some 30 persons . . . the rest of the people of that plantation were off gunning and fishing" who "said they were going to have preaching there."[73]

Yet exaggerated as they normally were, these "false alarms" also spotlighted the early political activity of black communities and the developing contests for power that emancipation had unleashed. For just as white landowners turned rumors of land distribution into harbingers of insurrection so as to reassert their local prerogatives, the freedpeople used the rumors of land redistribution to bolster their own bargaining positions. When, during the summer of 1865, a planter in northeastern Mississippi "broached the matter of hiring to his negroes [by proposing] to give something to eat and keep some till Christmas," they showed their "exalted ideas" by rebuffing him and demanding "in addition a part of the crop." In mid-September, the overseer on William Alexander Graham's Leper plantation in York District, South Carolina, finding it difficult to maintain order, charged that "your hands say they will git one half of your crop let them work or not and you cant drive them off for this land dont Bee long to you." A group of Arkansas landowners, who were wrestling with black laborers on their estates later that fall, could see "an unusual stir . . . to exist among the negroes and a great deal of passing to and fro at night and congregating at certain out of the way places." In this, they "apprehended" a "great danger and considerable probability of an outbreak" since the laborers had "an idea amongst them that they are to have homes and farms of their own allotted to them after the present year" and "many are known to have firearms in their possession." While traveling through east-central North Carolina, the journalist Sidney Andrews, discounting the "charge that the blacks are pretty generally organizing and . . . drilling semi-weekly," nonetheless learned "that negroes hold weekly meetings in some neighborhoods."[74]

More widely, the freedpeople refused to enter into labor agreements for 1866 despite the prodding of planters and Freedmen's Bureau agents alike. Some, associating the terms of contracts with the compulsions of servitude, feared "that if they hire to their former masters for the coming year, they will be held for 5 years and if they attempt to leave they will be punished." Many others saw no reason to accept the small remuneration, open-ended responsibilities, and close supervision commonly offered when the new year might bring the opportunity to farm on their own account. The "Negroes . . . are not inclined to make any contracts until after Christmas," a landowner in Madison County, Tennessee, recorded in October 1865, in a typical complaint. "They seem to expect something to take place about that time, a division of lands or something of the kind."[75]

Whether or not they genuinely anticipated a federally sponsored division of property, the freedpeople often sought to utilize the breathing space and maneuvering room that such a rumor afforded. This is what John Dennett came to recognize as he conversed with a group of blacks on a large estate near Marion Village, South Carolina, in late October. Inquiring about their work, Dennett learned that they "didn't plant cotton . . . just done broke corn" and "don't know" if they would "make cotton this next year." "We's waiting till January come. Then we can know," one of the men piped. "We hear this and that, this an that," an older freedman added, "and we told [Major G——] we'd hold on till January." As several men and women came "out of the neighboring cabins or were standing in the door-ways," Dennett remarked "that Major G—— had made you a very fair offer" and asked "why not sign the agreement now?" "I ain't going to bind myself," a young fellow answered, "not till I can see better." Dennett then brought up "the subject of a division of lands" since "such an opinion is universally prevalent in the lower districts of the state," and although the freedpeople "seemed disinclined to speak plainly," they finally said, "with some hesitation," that "they'd been told so." Dennett replied that "it was very unlikely that any land would be given away by the Government," but while "they listened to what I said," they "appeared to receive it with dissatisfaction and incredulity." "We're going to wait anyhow," interjected another freedman. "We don't know where we'll be next year, nor what they'll do with us. They tell what they'll do at Columbia, and they tell another thing over to headquarters, and I go for waiting anyhow."[76]

❖

The wait eventually ended. When January arrived, the freedpeople on Major G——'s estate probably accepted terms to work there or reached agreement with a neighboring planter, and soon commenced to plant cotton as well as corn. In so doing, they joined the great mass of rural blacks who, during the first two months of 1866, reluctantly but steadily signed labor contracts to cultivate the land as agricultural laborers. They had few alternatives. All that the Christmas season had brought them were further rounds of harassment, floggings, and late-night searches. Little wonder that a federal agent in Lowndes County, Alabama, just after the new year could find "a great deal of timidity on the part of the freedmen." No gift of land was offered, and no black insurrectionary plot, small or large, had been hatched.[77]

What was a bitter pill for the freedpeople, however, was a source of relief, if not of emboldenment, for many southern whites who accepted and spread the rumors of upheaval, and perhaps embraced them in their battles for local power. Indeed, those who had urged defiance instead of conciliation as the best means to combat an even more revolutionary settlement of the Civil War could see some vindication in the tumultuous course of the "Christmas insurrection scare." For rather than provoking the strong fist of the federal government, the strategy seemed to bring many of the desired results. President Johnson redoubled his efforts to restore confiscated and abandoned lands to former owners; military commanders removed black soldiers from trouble spots, to some extent for the soldiers' own safety; and Freedmen's Bureau officials went to considerable lengths to dispel rumors of impending property division and pressure freedpeople into contracting for the coming year. At the same time, southern legislatures elected under the auspices of revised state constitutions began to restrict black opportunities for either economic independence or civic equality. Before the end of 1865, South Carolina and Mississippi (the two states with black majorities in their population) had enacted draconian "Black Codes" and Alabama legislators had fashioned a series of bills that the Freedmen's Bureau Assistant Commissioner Wager Swayne "could only pronounce the revival of slavery."[78]

On the local level, planters availed themselves of the atmosphere created by the rumors of insurrection and by Johnson's "self-reconstruction" policies to put their counteroffensive on a firmer basis. Meeting in many black-belt counties, they agreed to enforce contracts, punish "vagrants," limit competition for laborers, prohibit the renting or selling of land to blacks, and provide for regular policing. "No system can secure success," one such gathering in Bennettsville, South Carolina, resolved in December of 1865, "if the discipline and management of the freedmen is entirely taken out of the hands of the planters." By early 1866, prospects for their "success" may have seemed promising. A host of federal authorities sympathetic to the freedpeople—including Rufus Saxton and Thomas W. Conway—had been removed from their posts, numerous black regiments had been sent out of the South, and about half of the land held by the federal government at the end of the Civil War had been relinquished. During the fall of 1865 the War Department moved to disband all black regiments raised in the North (which is to say, those with soldiers possessing the longest experience of freedom), and between the summer and winter, as pressure from southern landowners and political leaders mounted, the overall black representation in the army of occupation was reduced by about 20 percent. Within a year, only a few thousand black troops remained in the South; the last of them departed by October of 1867, as Radical Reconstruction took shape on the ground.[79]

Yet if it appeared that ex-masters and ex-Confederates were regaining on the field of peace much of what they had lost on the field of battle, appearances could be deceiving. For the rumors of land redistribution and the related struggles that such rumors promoted were not, in the end, without notable effect. By widely holding off from signing contracts until the new year—often as a consequence of collective decision-making—the freedpeople created a temporary labor shortage and weakened the landowners' attempts to tie them down and dictate the terms. They began "changing homes" and seeking better arrangements. Some blacks, as on the Virginia peninsula, "were willing to work for fair wages for the certain length of time, but were unwilling to hire themselves for one year, choosing to change about for any slight difference in wages."[80]

Most others yielded to annual agreements while pressing for higher monthly pay or larger shares of the crop, and for greater control over their labor time. A Freedmen's Bureau agent outside of New Orleans reported that so "many of the old year's hands have left and gone up river" and so "many have returned from above . . . that fully 2/3 of the plantation hands . . . are people who are but imperfectly acquainted with their employers" and demanding hikes in pay. Near Salisbury, North Carolina, freedpeople, whose "minds are set on a landed interest," refused "to make any contract for labor for 1866 by which they are not secured a 'patch' of their own, or a share of the crop." Even in Lowndes County, Alabama, where blacks initially showed "a great deal of timidity" and "planters made a strong combination to hire no negro away from home," it was discovered that "the freedmen stood it out until the planters gave way and they finally hired at random, at a little higher wages than they were generally paid elsewhere." Delay in contracting, observed an army officer in Orangeburg, South Carolina, "proved to be beneficial to many because planters anxious to secure their services gave them better pay after New Years than they would have given before Christmas."[81]

More consequential were the effects to be seen on national politics, as Presidential Reconstruction increasingly fell into disarray. It was not destined to be so. Andrew Johnson and his policies initially enjoyed wide support in the North, among Republicans and Democrats alike, reflecting confidence in his leadership and a spirit of magnanimity toward the mass of defeated Confederates in most quarters. And it took quite a lot for that support to be badly shaken. Johnson's Amnesty Proclamation of late May, his determination to pardon most former rebels and restore their property, and the ambiguous signals he sent on the question of black suffrage caused consternation and alarm chiefly among the ranks of abolitionists and Radical Republicans. Most northern states, after all, still denied the electoral franchise to black men and most northerners endorsed, at best, qualified suffrage for those in the South. The disposition of southern constitutional conventions on the matters of slavery and secession, later described in Congress as "nothing more than an unwilling admission of an unwelcome truth," and the subsequent refusal of state legislatures to accord freedpeople more than the most limited place in civil society, then raised wider doubts about the wisdom of the President's course.[82] But perhaps nothing troubled and incensed more northerners, or pushed more moderate and conservative Republicans toward disenchantment if not outright opposition, than did the epidemic of violence against blacks and white Unionists that exploded amid the rumors of federal land reform and Christmas insurrection. Reported extensively in the antislavery and Republican press and on lecture circuits that drew growing audiences, the violence seemed most directly to threaten the results of the war and rupture the boundaries of northern tolerance. "The most favorable opportunity was afforded" to the southern people, the *Cincinnati Daily Gazette* editorialized in early December. "Conventions were authorized; Constitutions were adopted; legislatures were convened and congressmen were elected. . . . But the spirit in which this was responded to was a rebellious one. It showed very clearly that the people were not in a condition to be safely entrusted with the privileges which it was desired to show."[83]

A great turning point of Reconstruction thus arrived. Congress, out of session for nearly a year, was to convene the first week of December and determine whether the eighty-four congressmen-elect and senators-elect from the formerly rebellious states—a delegation that included prominent ex-Confederates—would be granted the seats that their predecessors had duly resigned in the winter of 1860–1861. Only a month earlier, Massachusetts senator Charles Sumner, who understood the political stakes as plainly as anyone, was fretting as to "how Congress will stand," and in his message to Congress of December 4, Andrew Johnson recommended that the southern states "resume their places in the two branches of the National Legislature" once the Thirteenth Amendment had been officially ratified (to occur within days). But what Sumner called the "brutality and cruelty" visited upon "Unionists . . . and the poor freedmen," together with the likely alliance between returning southerners and northern Democrats, had already led the dominant Republicans of the Thirty-ninth Congress to heed the advice of their House Speaker Schuyler Colfax and reject that of the President: "Let us rather make haste slowly and we can hope that the foundations of our Government, when thus reconstructed on the basis of indisputable loyalty, will be as eternal as the stars." They refused to admit the southern claimants, formed the Joint Committee on Reconstruction, and began in earnest to contest Johnson's policies and authority.[84]

Had the Congress done otherwise, Reconstruction would have been, in the words of the *New York Times*, "for all practical purposes completely and irreversibly consummated." Freedpeople would have been consigned to the direct jurisdiction of state and local governments that, while accepting the abolition of slavery, had only grudgingly disavowed secession, repudiated war debts that could not in any event have been repaid, and at most witnessed political reforms that shifted the locus of power to smaller planters and landowners at the expense of the old black-belt aristocracy. Almost everywhere—and especially in the Deep South—the political leaders and officeholders were still former slaveholders who aided the Confederacy even if they had opposed secession; unlike the governments organized under Lincoln's wartime Ten Percent Plan, not one of those organized under Johnson's auspices attempted either to penalize rebels or reward Unionists. Nowhere would freedmen or freedwomen have been able to represent their own interests more than marginally in public life. Recognizing the most limited meanings of emancipation, state constitutional conventions and then legislatures under Presidential Reconstruction did make provision for blacks to marry, enter into other contracts, own some property, and gain highly circumscribed access to the courts. But no state gave even fleeting consideration to any form of black suffrage. If the rebellious states had "resume[d] their places in the National Legislature" when the Thirty-ninth Congress assembled, therefore, the Union would have been restored under a Constitution that may have given white southerners greater political power than they had previously enjoyed, and the old masters would have been placed in a position to supervise the transition from slavery to new social relations that they could have designed with little federal interference, much like their counterparts in other postemancipation societies.[85]

Instead, the expectations of land and the accompanying contests over the relations of freedom that swirled through the southern countryside in the summer and fall of 1865 helped expose the dangers that an overly hasty course of sectional reconciliation entailed. Far more, perhaps, than the pressure of Congressional Radicals and urban-based black leaders, they undermined Presidential Reconstruction, rendered untenable a southern world as ex-slaveholders would have made it, and opened the way for wholly different possibilities. The political momentum now shifted not only to Congress, but also to those in Congress who saw the Declaration of Independence rather than the old Constitution as the guiding light of Reconstruction policy. Through the Joint Committee on Reconstruction, empowered to "receive all papers which may be offered relative to the late so-called confederate States of America," they began to gather testimony on the temper of white southerners and the circumstances of black, much of it derived from the explosive atmosphere surrounding the Christmas insurrection scare several months before. By the early spring they had concluded that a new polity and constitutional compact had to be constructed.[86] In effect, the convulsions erupting through the rural South in 1865 carried forth the Jacobin vision of Radical Republicans and urban blacks: turning the defeat of the slaveholders' rebellion into the birth pangs of a new political nation.

PART II

To Build a New Jerusalem

4

RECONSTRUCTING THE
BODY POLITIC

I am convinced that the freedman's community is no desirable field of
operation for the political demagogue.

Lt. Jno. W. Jordan

In March 1867, nearly two years after the Confederate armies had
begun to surrender and more than a year after Congress had refused
to seat representatives from the former Confederate states, the mark
of Radicalism was indelibly inscribed into the cornerstone of the reconstructed American republic. It did not herald the draconian policies—
imprisonments and executions, massive disfranchisement, or confiscation of landed estates—that some Republicans had advocated and
many Rebels had initially feared. And it required a combination of
white southern arrogance and vindictiveness, presidential intransi-
gence, and mounting African-American agitation before it could be set.
But with the Military Reconstruction Acts, Congress gave the federal
government unprecedented power to reorganize the ex-Confederate
South politically, imposed political disabilities on leaders of the rebellion, and, most stunning of all, extended the elective franchise to southern black males, the great majority of whom had been slaves. Never
before in history, and nowhere during the Age of Revolution, had so
large a group of legally dependent people been enfranchised.[1]

Yet the triumphalism that swept through Radical Republican quarters was tempered by real trepidation. Black enfranchisement provided the Republican party with an opportunity to establish a mass base in the South and thus to secure its hold over the national government once the ex-Confederate states were readmitted to the Union. But to whose benefit would the black vote, in the end, redound? In the absence of significant land reform, almost all prospective black voters still depended on white landowners for their livelihoods. Would they not then be vulnerable to a host of coercive tactics designed to control their political activities or render them inert? Would they not quickly succumb to the direct power and influence of former slaveholders and local Democratic bosses? Now that the federal ratio had been abolished (by the Fourteenth Amendment) and blacks were counted the same as whites for the purpose of congressional apportionment, would black enfranchisement not effectively give former Rebels even more political muscle than they had been able to flex before the Civil War?

Such fears had been expressed since the question of black political rights first gained a substantial hearing. They were eminently sensible and reflected both conditions in the South as northerners saw them and the logic of republican political thought that resonated throughout the nation. The political community, many Americans believed, ought to encompass only those citizens capable of achieving economic independence: citizens who owned property, plied skills, and did not do the bidding of others. Those who occupied circumstances of legal, customary, or economic dependency, however, could threaten the vitals of a republic, courting the machinations of "demagogues" and tyrants. Charles Sumner, the Republican senator from Massachusetts who championed "political equality without distinction of color," thus greeted the passage of the Reconstruction Acts by demanding "further guarantees," chief among them being tougher "precautions . . . against Rebel agency," "public schools . . . for the equal good of all," and homesteads for the freedmen "so that at least every head of a family may have a piece of land."[2]

Congress, even at the high tide of Radicalism, would not provide these "further guarantees." But the freedmen responded to the Reconstruction Acts in a manner that generally confounded both the fears of Republicans and the logic of republicanism. They registered to vote in great numbers, aligned overwhelmingly with the Republican party, widely resisted the overtures and threats of white Democrats, marched to the polls in legions, and helped to write new state constitutions that dramatically reconstructed the body politic of what had been a slave society. In the process, they began to build—with an assortment of tensions and conflicts—new political relations, institutions, and aspirations within their own communities. How former slaves accomplished these tasks remains one of the most remarkable, though yet relatively unexplored, chapters in American history.

❖

When Congress passed the Military Reconstruction Acts, David Medlock was one of the well-established leaders of African Americans in Limestone County, Texas. A former slave now over forty years of age, Medlock had been in the county since at least the 1840s when he had been brought from Georgia by his master and set to work on what would become one of several large plantations along the banks of the Navasota River. Owning little or no property and soon to be called a "laborer" by the federal census taker, he nonetheless appears to have acquired the rudiments of literacy and preached the gospel, skills and activities that no doubt contributed to his local influence and prestige. His political independence and concern for the welfare of the county's freedpeople were surely critical too, for although his former owner had been an ardent secessionist and supporter of the Confederate cause and may well have remained his employer, Medlock helped to organize a chapter of the Union League and played a leading role in establishing the local Republican party. In a letter to the league's state president, he therefore described himself "[A]s a Colerd man and one who Feals and Intrest In our cause and Future Happiness and Success."

Medlock worked to mobilize a community that was already multigenerational and bound together by extended ties of kinship and personal acquaintance. Joining Medlock in the Union League were his brothers John and Nacy as well as Dick Johnson, who grew up on an adjacent plantation and was probably related to the Medlock clan. Indeed, Medlocks headed numerous black households in postemancipation Limestone County, forming part of a family base of support that eventually catapulted David Medlock to a seat in the Texas state house of representatives. "It must be remembered," a historian of black Limestone County would write in the 1930s, "that the slaves . . . were more or less related . . . and unto this day . . . most of the Negroes in this section call each other cousin and trace back as far as their elders can remember family ties."[3]

Medlock was one of the very few African Americans during the postbellum era who won election to state or county office from a white majority district. In his, whites outnumbered blacks by a nearly two-to-one margin.[4] But in other respects his example offers an important perspective on the process and dimensions of grassroots politicization in many parts of the rural postemancipation South. For African Americans built their new political communities—as they had done under slavery—from many of the basic materials of everyday life: from the ties and obligations of kinship, from the experiences and struggles of labor, from the traditions and skills of leadership, and from the spiritual energies and resources of religion.

They began by attempting to assemble their immediate families and close kin, to lend those relations civil legitimacy, and to find circumstances in which those relations could establish meaningful and useful foundations. Where slaves had lived on large and relatively stable plantations and where, upon emancipation, agents of the federal Freedmen's Bureau were readily accessible, these efforts could proceed expeditiously. Everywhere else, freedpeople faced formidable undertakings. The most vivid examples are of black men and women wandering tens or even hundreds of miles across the southern states in search of parents, spouses, and children who had been separated from them by sale and forced migration. But perhaps far more common—though often no less poignant or arduous—were the moves that took place within the boundaries of a county or two and that involved joining husbands or wives, registering marriages, collecting children and other dependent kin, finding suitable arrangements for life and labor, and fending off the many coercive interventions of landowners and employers. Insofar as slaves had been chained to their owners as individuals and denied official recognition of their marriages and families, these may be regarded as among the first political acts that simultaneously rejected the legacy of enslavement and celebrated the vitals of freedom.[5]

Reconstituted freed families played crucial parts in the early quests for landed independence. They both helped to defend claims to property that had been abandoned or confiscated during the Civil War as well as attempted to generate the resources necessary to lease or purchase substantial-sized tracts. In many of the southern states, kinship held together and financed an assortment of "societies," "associations," and "joint-stock companies" that formed with astonishing rapidity after emancipation and aimed to settle anywhere from a few dozen to a few hundred freedpeople on lands sufficient to sustain them. When the Freedmen's Bureau assistant commissioner in Louisiana made over fifty thousand acres of land on sixty-eight abandoned plantations available to freedpeople in September 1865, the applicants included seventy-three cooperative groups composed of 584 men, 458 women, and 644 children. Black families in Wilkes County, Georgia, managed to raise seven thousand dollars by November of 1865 with the intention of acquiring land in the still thinly populated southwestern part of the state. One year later, in nearby Greene County, "a colony of 124 families and 620 in number," led by "headman" Charles Martin, petitioned the bureau for transportation to Arkansas, where they hoped "to set up on Government lands" designated by the Homestead Act of 1866.[6]

Impressive as they were, and certainly more numerous than has generally been allowed—indeed "heads of familys" in Alabama, Georgia, and the Carolinas were already looking into the possibility of emigrating to Liberia, initiating what would later grow into a mass movement—these land acquisition and colonization projects were hampered from the first by capital scarcity and white hostility. Few even got the opportunity to make a go of it. And as the prospects for more general land reform dimmed, community-building necessarily focused on the arrangements that could be forged on white-owned plantations and farms. But here, too, reconstituted families and their extended kinship networks struggled to form a social foundation in what were otherwise a great variety of settings and crop cultures. The nearly sixty freedpeople who contracted to work W. R. Capehart's large estate in Edenton, North Carolina, in 1867 thus included Gabriel Capehart and his wife; Jackson Capehart, his wife Adeline, and five of their children; Edmund Capehart, his wife, and one child; Bristow Capehart and his wife; Isaac Capehart and his wife; Edward Williams, his wife, and five children; Miles Williams and his wife; Jim Bolin, his wife, and five children; and Andrew Bolin and Anthony Bolin, both single and in their twenties. In Russell County, Alabama, the planter Edgar Dawson employed almost fifty freedpeople in 1870, among whom were six families of Dawsons and three families of Terrells.[7]

The labor force working land owned by George W. Swepson and R. Y. McAden in Perquimans County, North Carolina, in 1867 was composed chiefly of six single men, though all came from Alamance County and counted in their number Jerry Ruffin, Osborn Ruffin, George Freeland, and Lindsey Freeland. In the tobacco-growing areas of southside Virginia, a Freedmen's Bureau agent, commenting in early 1866 on the "mania for renting," added significantly that "when one rents a place, he gets all of his 'kinfolks' to join him that he possibly can." Even where freedpeople found themselves in the decided minority and where plantation agriculture had established only a limited foothold, a similar process and pattern could be detected. Johnson County lay on the edge of Georgia's wiregrass and piney woods regions and African Americans made up only three in ten of the inhabitants. Yet by the early 1870s, the tax records revealed a lacework of kinship connecting the small-scale labor arrangements in the county's militia districts: in district 1202, for example, fourteen adult males surnamed Wright worked for eight different employers, thirteen surnamed Walters worked for ten different employers, nine surnamed Hurt worked for five different employers, five surnamed Smith worked for four different employers, another four surnamed Hicks worked for four different employers, and four surnamed Arline worked for three different employers. Contemporary observers who failed or refused to recognize the centrality of kinship to the aspirations of the freedpeople therefore mistook the geographical mobility that attended emancipation or the completion of a crop year for mere wanderlust. J. C. Caruthers, who managed a plantation in Yazoo County, Mississippi, suggested otherwise. "Freedmen through the country have been unusually quiet the past week though a great many of them were changing homes," he told his uncle in early January 1866. "Wyatt and family including Manda and Ed left in my absence and went to Vaughns, Nath and his were already there. John has married one of Dick Swayzes women and settled at Bells . . . The others are contracting to stay with me."[8]

In reconstituting their kinship networks on a more proximate and stable basis, freedpeople not only tried to provide loved ones with protection and subsistence but also acknowledged the fundamental threads of economic and political solidarity that they had woven and had learned to rely on as slaves. Whether they had lived on plantations or farms, whether they had labored in cotton, tobacco, rice, sugar-growing, or general farming districts, the kin (and fictive-kin) relations they painstakingly constructed and reconstructed served as the central weapons in their struggles to limit utter dependence and exploitation. And so, amid the myriad contracts and other labor agreements that were to be found in the immediate postemancipation South, black family networks represented a foundational link. In them, freedpeople saw the best opportunity to guarantee that freedom would build on their prior achievements and expectations.

Most commonly—and owing in part to the role of the Freedmen's Bureau and other northern officials—the relation between kinship and labor involved agreements between landowners and black nuclear families, with the families usually represented by the designated male head. But there were arrangements, too, featuring collections of black families, groups of family heads representing other family members, or "headmen" representing family-based work gangs. From DeWitt County, Texas, where blacks composed less than 30 percent of the population, a Freedmen's Bureau agent wrote that "as a class the freedpeople are working for a portion of the crops and mostly on small farms, which they cultivate with the help of their families." A planter in Beech Branch, South Carolina, made a "contract between myself and each of the following 'freedmen' viz July, Cassius, Toby, and Frank who are the 'heads' or 'leaders' of parties of labor." Frances Butler Leigh's two Sea Island rice plantations were studies in contrast: on St. Simon's Island the contracting process had her "in the office without once leaving my chair . . . for six mortal hours . . . while the people poured in and poured out, each with long explanations, objections, and demonstrations"; on Butler's Island, "there were only fifty . . . and at the head of the fifty was Bram, with eight of his family at work under him."[9]

As these rather diverse examples suggest, kinship infused the contest over the reorganization of agricultural labor widely and quickly. This can be observed most clearly in the appearance of work groups—referred to variously as "companies," "clubs," and, even more commonly, "squads"—that accompanied the efforts of landowners to maintain antebellum patterns of control under the new conditions of emancipation. Some historians have, in fact, come to speak of a "squad system" representing an intermediate stage on the road from gang labor to family-based tenancy and sharecropping, but it appears to have been less a "system" than a loose set of arrangements linking the struggles that flared during slavery with the more decentralized land tenure forms familiar to the 1870s and 1880s. Numbering somewhere between two and ten, and usually embracing "members of the same kinship network and friends," squads and companies were probably integral to postbellum gang labor from the first; then, where possible, they may have taken on an increasingly "self-regulating" character, replete with their own leaders and forms of discipline, due in part to the prevalance and complexities of share wage payments.[10]

William A. Graham Jr., looking after one of his father's North Carolina plantations, testified to the early emergence and resilience of such labor groupings. Writing in September 1866 of his intention to employ their overseer, Mr. Reel, "for another year," he announced emphatically that he would "have no more working in squads." But just over a year later, as he completed one crop cycle and began to prepare for the next, Graham revealed that he had failed to hold the line. "The negroes," he explained to his father, "are anxious to work in different companies [and] I told them . . . [that] if they would divide themselves into three parties . . . you would consent to it." The northern abolitionist Charles Stearns, who purchased a plantation outside of Augusta, Georgia, and who supplied his laborers land to work in twenty-five-acre parcels "in the way they preferred," found that "many united together in small squads, admitting none but near relations." Traveling through the Tennessee Valley area of northern Alabama in late 1870, the British journalist Robert Somers took note of squad organization there and similarly pointed to the centrality of kinship. "A strong family group," he observed, "who can attach other labour and bring odd hands to work at proper seasons, makes a choice, if not always attainable, nucleus of a 'squad.'" But Somers also remarked on the connections between the old order and the new: "The negroes toiled in gangs or squads when slaves, and they toil necessarily, though under much less control of the planter still."[11]

It appears that the squads consisted chiefly of men, and while this may further substantiate the links between "gangs" and "squads" it points as well to the recrafting of social relations and gender roles within black households. The earliest indications of the phenomenon come from southern landowners and federal officials, who complained frequently that black women (and married black women in particular) refused to work, were lazy and troublesome, wished to live off their husbands and employers, and seemed more interested in "playing the lady" much in the manner of their former white mistresses. As a Freedmen's Bureau agent in Columbia, Texas, grumbled, black women had "become almost useless as field hands," preferring instead to go into town and "spend [their] husbands' earnings in fineries which are no use to them." Others placed the blame on black husbands who "object[ed] to their wives performing labor in the fields and would not enter into contracts . . . which required them to do so." Together, these observers described a virtual "withdrawal" of freedwomen and children from field labor. What they failed to see was a process of reorganization and renegotiation designed to limit the discretionary power of employers, better protect vulnerable family members, and redeploy the labor force to the advantage of freed households—a process initiated by emancipation in every former slave society of the Western Hemisphere.[12]

There can be little doubt that black women, and especially those attached by kinship to able-bodied black men, performed less field labor immediately after emancipation than they did as slaves. But freedwomen "withdrew" not so much from field labor in general as from *full-time* field labor under the supervision of white employers and managers. They sought to avoid work environments that left them most exposed to the direct exploitation and abuse of white men and struggled instead to devote more of their energies to the immediate needs of their families and households. They therefore increasingly entered into labor contracts, where possible, as members of families for whom the male head negotiated the terms.[13]

The specific objectives and arrangements varied widely as to crop cultures and customary practices. During the postwar period, in the rice-growing districts of South Carolina, where task labor and slave petty provisioning had become deeply entrenched, there rapidly emerged a system (bearing some resemblance to forms of labor organization in the postemancipation Caribbean) under which freedpeople exchanged two or three days of plantation task work each week for small plots of land that they could cultivate independently. Much of the responsibility for tending to rice and other subsistence crops on these plots fell, in turn, to freedwomen and children while freedmen chiefly performed the tasks and then, for the remainder of the week, sought out wage-paying jobs in the rural or urban vicinity. Freed families in the cotton belt usually had less leverage in formally marking distinctions between the time and work owed to their employers and that reserved to themselves, but they too quickly pressed to associate those distinctions with gender-based norms and divisons of labor. A Burke County, Georgia, planter complained in January 1866 that his former slaves only agreed "to stay with me . . . upon the condition that I feed and clothe them and the non-workers on my place, and give them the privilege to continue to raise their hogs and poultry" and "to work their *own* crops on my place with my stock." Where labor requirements and rhythms were more seasonal and urban settings close by, as they were in some mixed-farming sections of the upper South, the logistics of household, gender, and labor could become complex. A Freedmen's Bureau agent in Lexington, Virginia, consequently found that black men "in many cases" had gone to work in the country while renting "rooms in town for their wives and children," the women hating "the restraint that a life of service in the country imposes."[14]

It may be tempting to see in these developments the construction of patriarchal relations of power and gendered "spheres" of activity in which black women as well as black men had a genuine investment. There were, after all, a good many anticipatory customs and practices to be discerned well before emancipation. Yet it would be a mistake to imagine that rural black gender roles and norms took shape speedily, fell into neat categories, and gained wide and easy acceptance. The picture is rather one of shifting boundaries, and of potentially explosive tensions and conflicts. In reports of "domestic quarrels," of "complaints that the freedmen do not exercise proper control over their families," and of freedwomen being "seized with the idea of living indolently and independent of the authority of their liege lords," we sense the strains and discontents. A landowner in the Georgia black belt went so far as to insist that his greatest "difficulty" in making contracts consisted "in disagreements between husbands and wives."[15]

Many of the earliest collective activities and formal organizations to be undertaken by the freedpeople—those evident well in advance of the franchise—were therefore held together by sinews of kinship, concerned with issues bearing directly on labor and households, and marked by ambiguity as to gender distinctions. In important respects, these reflected the infrastructure and social divisions of slave political life now given the possibility of more public display.

The most conspicuous and dramatic examples of these activities and organizations could be seen in areas that had fallen under federal occupation sometime before the war's end and witnessed the eruption of intense social struggles owing to disputes over land claims and labor obligations: most notably along the south Atlantic coast but also where black troops and returning black veterans helped inspire local confidence and spark a rapid mobilization. These ranged from the colonies of freed families established in early 1865 on Sapelo and St. Catherine's Islands under the leadership of northern free black Tunis G. Campbell (which, proclaiming "separatism for strength," quickly framed a government, founded a militia, and opened schools); to the "committees" formed by freed communities on Edisto Island, South Carolina, or at Trent River settlement in North Carolina in efforts to resist the effects of land restorations; to the prospective freeholders on several of the Sea Islands who battled not only former slave and plantation owners, but also federal troops seeking to dispossess them. Even more widely in evidence were "associations" and "companies" of black laborers who met, marched, and drilled in pursuit of their aspirations, much to the consternation—some of it bordering on apoplectic—of white employers and observers.[16]

It has been easy to dismiss or ignore these associations in part because of the extravagant charges made by local whites and in part because, upon investigation, the charges usually proved to be groundless. Landowners complained about "armed organizations" of blacks "drilling late at night" with the "avowed intention" of "having lands or blood," of "threatening the landed proprietors and others with confiscation," of "plundering and robbing the white people," or of commencing "a general massacre of the white population." Federal officials, in turn, often uncovered scarcely more than "frolicks," wooden muskets, and community meetings.[17] A report by a U.S. army officer regarding alleged disturbances in the district of Charleston, South Carolina, however, offers a more intriguing perspective. "The rumor of intended risings among the freedmen and of their banding together and organizing military companies proves upon investigation to be without foundation," he wrote in January 1867. At the same time, however, he conceded "that they have been and are holding meetings at various points for the purpose of consulting together on their condition and arranging their plans and terms for labor during the year." In the Abbeville district to the northwest, planters complained to federal officials through Governor James L. Orr of three hundred "armed" freedmen who had been meeting every other week since September 1, 1867, at Morrow's Old Field "for the purpose of drilling and . . . preparing to fight for land," and, as a consequence, "absent[ed] themselves from their farms and farm work." They had, it seems, selected their own officers, taken to wearing old army uniforms, "and usually spen[t] the entire day drilling, firing &c." Closer scrutiny confirmed that three hundred had been assembling regularly and about seventy-five had been drilling under the command of Captain Edward Brown and Lieutenant Aaron Johnson, both former slaves, but added that the "company" had "sticks in place of guns" and had organized "for no other purpose than to establish among them a uniform rate of prices for next year" and to "arrest and punish . . . all that let themselves to planters for less."[18]

In North Carolina, the conservative governor Jonathan Worth fretted in late 1866 about "mass meetings" being held in his home county of Edgecombe at which "the negroes . . . drill and go through all the military evolutions." Insisting that "the real design" was to slaughter the whites, the governor nonetheless noted that "the ostensible purpose of these meetings are [*sic*] a strike for higher wages." A similar portrait of local mobilization emerges from the descriptions of observers in many plantation-belt counties stretching from Virginia to Texas.[19]

Governor Worth "supposed" that the drilling and "military evolutions" were "directed by some who have served in the Federal Army," and it appears almost certain that the mobilization of freed laborers took on military aspects in areas closely in contact with federal (and especially with black) troops, perhaps as early as the fall of 1865 when harvest settlements, preparations for a new crop year, and rumors of federal land redistribution combined to inspire collective discussions and activities.[20] Yet these were hardly exercises in simple mimicry, for the quasi-militarization of organizational and work life had both practical and symbolic importance: It acknowledged and responded to the dangers of collective action in the postemancipation South. This was a world in which social relations had always been based on the use and threat of personal violence and in which any challenge to white authority could be treated summarily. By drilling, marching, and posting sentinels, freedpeople reminded each other of the risks they faced while offering protection in their numbers, warning systems, and weapons of self-defense.

Equally significant, the drilling, the adoption of military titles by leaders, and the display of other types of military paraphernalia helped forge solidarities across plantations and farms that necessarily transcended ties of kinship, while investing the process with special political meaning. The "companies" and "associations," carrying "arms" (whether rifles, gunstocks, corn stalks, or wooden sticks) under the "command" of "captains" and "lieutenants," lent visibility, order, and seriousness to the early efforts to define new forms of community. At the same time, they celebrated the very organizations that had crushed their haughty former owners and served as the foundation of claims to citizenship: for, by nineteenth-century standards, participation in the military and militia most clearly defied the representations of what it meant to be a slave or abject dependent, marginalized in or excluded from the arenas of civil and political life.[21]

Although the drilling companies appear to have been composed chiefly if not exclusively of black males, the early collective actions of freed laborers were not directed and carried out only by men. Precisely because the issues involved normally bore immediately on the welfare of families, households, kin networks, and emerging communities, the boundaries of participation were by no means tightly drawn. Black women could be found at meetings where the "plans and terms for labor during the year" were being discussed, including those at which drills were conducted; by many accounts they quickly earned reputations for truculence and militancy, often in the very areas where the drilling associations were prevalent. What seems instead to have been the case was that communities as a whole were being mobilized, while collective action and militancy took a variety of forms, some of it gender specific. Hence, whereas black men increasingly used the institutional expressions of "organized" politics to demonstrate their unity and resolve and to maintain discipline, black women more likely relied on verbal abuse and defiant language, physical confrontations and attacks, and quasi-ritualized shaming and harassment, all of which had long been a part of their resistance to enslavement.[22]

Whether manifest in confrontation and militancy or in efforts at self-protection and regulation, the building blocks of collective behavior—of politics—among freedpeople almost anywhere in the early postemancipation South were kinship and shared experience. When about eighty freedmen on the Orange Grove plantation in Plaquemines Parish, Louisiana, stopped work and demanded higher wages in the late winter of 1867, they informed a federal official "in a body" that "they were born and raised on the plantation and would fight before they would leave." Around the same time, "the people of Carsneck," Georgia, met "in conference" and petitioned the Freedmen's Bureau for supplies of corn, bacon, and salt, pledging to "morgage our crops for the said amount" and signing as "S. Wilson and family," "S. Monroe and family," "Mrs Rose Lord and family," "A. Monroe," "Miss J. Lord," "N. Winn and family," "Mrs F. Andrews and family," "D. Gibbons and family," "J. Jackson and family," "R. Anderson and family," "W. T. Goldin," and "L. Griffin."[23]

The freedpeople who held a series of "arbitrations" on the Crescent plantation in Rapides Parish, Louisiana, in March 1866 included a core of families present since at least the mid-1850s when the estate had been consolidated through marriage and inheritance. Although it is not entirely clear when the practice was initially established—perhaps before emancipation, resembling as it did the "plantation councils" and other forms of internal slave governance glimpsed opaquely and fleetingly across the Deep South—in 1866 it surely was a mechanism for punishing those who had transgressed the community's self-determined rules and norms. A rotating group of "arbitrators," selected in part by the parties in conflict, heard the allegations and then assessed an assortment of small fines for such infractions as "breaking the peace of the quarter," "using immoral and improper language," "fighting," and "whipping." While the arbitrators seem only to have been men, those disciplined included females and males, and the judge in one proceeding could become the judged in the next. Here, that is, in quite mundane fashion, the political lives and experiences of slaves became foundations for the developing politics of freedpeople.[24]

By the summer of 1867, complaints of "armed organizations among the freedmen," of late-hour drilling, and of threatening "assemblages" had grown both in volume and geographical scope. The entire plantation South appeared to pulse with militant and quasi-military activity. But now, in the months after the passage of the Reconstruction Acts, investigation revealed a more formal process of politicization, and one tied directly to the extension of the elective franchise and the organizational initiatives of the Republican party. From Virginia to Georgia, from the Carolinas to the Mississippi Valley and Texas, the freedpeople showed "a remarkable interest in all political information," were "fast becoming thoroughly informed upon their civil and political rights," and, most consequentially, were avidly "organizing clubs and leagues throughout the counties." Of these, none was more important to the former slaves or more emblematic of the developing character of local politics in the postemancipation South than the often vilified and widely misunderstood body known as the Union League.[25]

Emerging out of a network of organizations formed in the northern states in 1862 and 1863 to rally public support for the Lincoln administration and the war effort, the Union League embraced early the practices of both popular and patrician politics. Bound by secrecy, requiring oaths and rituals much in the manner of the Masons, and winning a mass base through local councils across the Midwest and Northeast, the league also took hold among loyalist elites meeting in stately clubs and townhomes in Philadelphia, New York, and Boston. In May 1863, a national convention defined goals, drew up a constitution, and elected officers, and councils were soon being established in Union-occupied areas of the Confederate South to advance the cause. Once the war ended, the league continued its educational and agitational projects and spread most rapidly among white Unionists in southern hill and mountain districts, where membership could climb into the thousands. But committed as the league was "to protect, strengthen, and defend all loyal men without regard to sect, condition, or race," it began as well to sponsor political events and open a few councils for the still unfranchised African Americans—chiefly in larger cities like Richmond, Norfolk, Petersburg, Wilmington, Raleigh, Savannah, Tallahassee, Macon, and Nashville.[26]

With the provision for a black franchise and voter registration encoded in the Reconstruction Acts, league organizers quickly fanned out from these urban areas into the smaller towns and surrounding countryside, and particularly into the plantation belt. Indeed, full-scale preparations had been under way since at least January 1867 when the Republican National Committee determined to organize the South through the auspices of the Union Republican Congressional Committee, which in turn leaned heavily on Union League speakers and activists to reach black communities. They included northern Radicals with experience in the military and Freedmen's Bureau, southern white Unionists who had already helped establish leagues in the hill country, and African Americans who had served in the army, attended early freedmen's conventions, or preached the gospel to the emerging black congregations of the postbellum South. Ministers of the African Methodist Episcopal (AME) Church played an especially vital role because the church establishment lent its support, because they could mix spiritual and political messages in a fashion that resonated powerfully in the rural districts, and because their religious affiliations offered some cover in intensely hostile environments. "Where visions of the 'halter' rise up before me," the Reverend James D. Lynch, who recruited in Mississippi, explained, "I commence as a preacher and end as a political speaker."[27]

Like many other organizers, Lynch would begin his work in a substantial town, such as Vicksburg or Jackson, where concentrations of black folk could be found and Union army detachments could provide some measure of security. A public meeting would be called, probably for a Saturday when the local population customarily swelled with blacks from the nearby rural districts. Hands employed on more distant plantations, for their part, might defray the expenses of their "best man," who was then dispatched as their representative. On the appointed day, the organizer, perhaps with other federal officials at his side, would unfurl the flag, apprise the freedpeople of their new rights and privileges, and then speak at length on the objectives of both the Republican party and the Union League. Interested listeners would, in the end, adjourn to a more secluded location, learn the rituals, become initiated, and establish a council. With beachheads thereby created (Lynch formed leagues "twice at Vicksburg and once in" Jackson), the organizer would move out toward county seats and other smaller, rural towns (Canton and Brandon, Mississippi, in Lynch's case), and eventually go to "work back in the counties."[28]

It was arduous and extremely dangerous work, for as organizers trekked out to where the mass of freedpeople resided, they fell vulnerable to swift and deadly retaliation at the hands of white landowners and vigilantes. Having organized the Mount Olive Union League Council in Nottoway County, Virginia, in July of 1867, the Reverend John Givens reported that a "colored speaker was killed three weeks ago" in neighboring Lunenberg County. But Givens determined to "go there and speak where they have cowed the black man," hoping "by the help of God" to "give them a dose of my radical Republican pills and neutralize the corrosive acidity of their negro hate." Those less courageous or less fortified by their beliefs than Givens might sensibly seek to enlist the aid of a sympathetic officer from the army of occupation in their travels; at all events, organizers looked to be inconspicuous in their movements, often depending on information transmitted orally, and selected sites that might allow for unobtrusive assemblages: semi-isolated cabins, local schoolhouses, crossroads stores, and especially rural churches. When league activist C. D. Morris was summoned by blacks in a section of east Texas never previously "invaded by a 'Radical,'" he took Captain Welch with him and met "some 200 colored men and women . . . at a log church, and not a white man to be seen."[29]

Traveling the hinterlands between Macon and Augusta, Georgia, on his own, AME minister and Union League organizer John Costin simply trusted "in the Lord," confident that "he has been with me." But Costin's work, if not his faith, was probably typical. During the course of a campaign, he claimed to have addressed sixty-five meetings. Some were fairly large, on occasion with a "vast audience" present, in county towns like Penfield, Woodville, Lexington, Crawfordville, and Sanderville; many others were more modest in size and often held after dark, taking place variously in small villages, "sometimes in the cabins, sometimes on the plantations, and wherever the chance occurred, in the churches after preaching." Throughout, Costin made sure to read "them the registration and civil rights acts, . . . explain[ing] and comment[ing] upon each section and impress[ing] upon the people the importance of registering as well as furnishing all the information I could." For some of the freedpeople in attendance, who may have walked as far as twenty-five miles to get there, it was the first time they had ever heard their rights explained to them. Keenly attentive to the circumstances and conditions in the localities, Costin managed to establish not only Union Leagues but also "Union Republican clubs, Educational and Temperance Societies in nearly every place of any prominence where I have been."[30]

The formation of a Union League council officially required the presence of at least nine loyal men, each twenty-one years of age or older, who were, upon initiation, to elect a president and other officers from among those regarded as "prudent, vigilant, energetic, and loyal," and as "possess[ing] the confidence of their fellow citizens." They were expected to hold meetings weekly, to follow the ceremony, and to "enlist all loyal talent in their neighborhood." The president was to assume the chair, rap the gavel, call the council to order, and allow the marshal to "drape the altar" with an assortment of icons symbolizing the interdependence of nationalism, political democracy, religious faith, and manual labor: the flag of the Union, the Bible, the Declaration of Independence and the Constitution, a sword, a ballot box, a censer of incense, a sickle, a shuttle, and an anvil. The roll was then to be called, the minutes of the previous meeting read, reports of committees heard, prospective members examined and elected (a three-fourths vote was needed), new members initiated and instructed in their obligations, and new business—including "speaking," which councils were encouraged to have "whenever they can"—taken up. Such councils, with "distinctive names" and "regularly numbered," would, it was hoped, sprout in each of a county's several election precincts.[31]

The experience and operations of local councils depended to some extent on the training and ability of the organizer, but perhaps even more on the social and political conditions in the specific counties and precincts. In hilly Rutherford County, North Carolina, where only one in five inhabitants was black and where the Whig party had been dominant before the Civil War, the Union League seemed to function—at least initially—in an unusually open and relaxed manner. One Saturday a month at noon, the courthouse bell in the village of Rutherfordton would be rung to announce a meeting and summon "every citizen who wished to come." Membership in the league was not concealed and some men who had served in the Confederate army belonged. The league might also assume a fairly public posture in those locales where African Americans composed an overwhelming proportion of the population and where even exasperated landowners could do little more than grouse. In the densely black sections of Chatham County, Georgia, along the Ogeechee River not far from Savannah, Union Leaguers would "sound a horn as a signal to assemble" after the day's labor and then march with "fife, drum, and American flag" to a local church and hold a meeting. In Edgecombe County, North Carolina, where nearly seven in ten of the inhabitants were black, a "grand procession" involving about 2,500 freedmen at the county seat of Tarrboro in May 1867 had the "county Union League at the front followed by Leagues from Martin and Pitt counties."[32]

Yet where blacks made up between one-third and two-thirds of the population—and where, not incidentally, the great majority of Union League councils was to be found—the situation was rather different. Here, most league members were black and they encountered a substantial and largely antagonistic population of whites. Whether they met weekly, biweekly, or monthly (and there was considerable variation), they relied on word of mouth rather than bells, horns, or posters; they usually assembled at night; and they generally favored sites that would attract as little adverse attention as possible, often posting armed sentinels outside. Some league councils either organized their own drilling companies or linked with companies that already existed. One observer in the South Carolina piedmont district of Abbeville fretfully reported that local leagues with "their Captains, and other Officers," were meeting "with their Guns . . . in secret places, but do not meet twice in the same place." Recognizing the dangers, the freedman Caleb, who worked for a particularly hostile landowner in Maury County, Tennessee, where blacks formed just under half of the population, chose another course: he went to his employer in April 1867 "and wholy denyed having any thing to do with the Un[i]on League," insisting that he "has not joined it nor never will."[33]

Given the freedpeople's economic dependence on white landowners, Caleb's action made a good deal of sense, and more than a few Union League organizers acknowledged the "unbounded influence one white man [could] wield," especially in localities far from towns. Thus, the success the Union League had in rapidly mobilizing significant numbers of black plantation and farm laborers is all the more remarkable.

Although it would be an exaggeration to claim that virtually every
eligible black adult male joined the league, there is no question that
the organization spread very quickly through much of the plantation
South, and that local councils soon amassed sizable memberships. In
Texas, league councils were planted in virtually every county in the
east-central plantation belt, and although some commenced with few
more than the requisite number of members, most appear to have
grown substantially. Near Austin, the first meeting of a council drew
only ten souls. But the next meeting drew twelve, the next drew
twenty, and before long council meetings drew sixty. The trajectory
of the Fairfield Council in Freestone County was more impressive:
organized with over one hundred members, it could boast three hundred members within a month and, according to a league activist, was
still "increasing rapidly." The league council in Walker County met
once a month and attendance generally ranged from 200 to 250, but
the council claimed three times as many members and a "special meeting [could] bring out 600 or 700." Miles away in North Carolina, the
black membership of one council exploded from 13 to 106 in just five
months. And in the Alabama piedmont a league organizer reported,
even more spectacularly, that he took in about one hundred new members per week. In the cotton districts, councils eventually initiated between fifty and five hundred members.[34]

The Union League spread rapidly through the plantation belt because of its association with the military defeat of the Confederacy,
the abolition of slavery, the Republican party, and the expansion of
civil and political rights for African Americans. But the league could
also build on the organizational struggles and structures that freed
communities already had established, or accommodate the less formal
networks and practices that had deeper roots in slavery. Institutionally
hierarchical, with national and state councils, the league was at the
same time intensely local in its composition and orientation. And although it embraced election precincts as the foundation of mobilization, it proved quite adaptable to the basic units of black social and
cultural life: church congregations, laborers' associations, drilling companies, fraternal lodges, mutual aid societies, and plantation arbitration
boards. The Reverend Henry McNeal Turner, AME minister and Republican party leader in Georgia, acknowledged as much when, in the
summer of 1867, he and a collection of black activists representing forty

counties in the state determined to educate "in our country churches, societies, leagues, clubs, balls, picnics, and all other gatherings."[35]

Most important, the unit of local league organization comfortably meshed with the perimeters of reconstituted kinship groups that could span a number of plantations and farms. In the black belt, the proliferation of league councils may indeed have been defined more by the geography of black kinship clans than by the official boundaries of state and county politics. Consider the Leasburg league in tobacco-growing Caswell County, North Carolina, where blacks made up about 70 percent of the population. Sometime in 1868, the league had twenty-nine members, all of whom were former slaves and all but four of whom lived in Leasburg township. At the center of activity was the Yancey family. Frank Yancey, a blacksmith in his mid- to late forties, served as the president and Felix Yancey, a house servant about twenty years of age, served as the marshal. Felix, in turn, lived in the household of yet another league member, Daniel Yancey, a blacksmith around eighty years of age (who may well have been Frank's father), as did William Yancey, a twenty-year-old farm laborer, who also belonged to the league. Frank's household included league member Watt Johnson, a sixty-odd-year-old blacksmith who probably worked with Frank and was likely related to two other league members: David Johnson, the assistant secretary, and Armistead Johnson—ages thirty-six and fifty-four, respectively, and both employed in a tobacco factory. Two Cunninghams, two Numans, two Curries, and three Leas filled out most of the remaining membership. In Limestone County, Texas, where fewer than one inhabitant in five was black, at least three league councils could be found operating. One was the bailiwick of David Medlock and his clan; a second was located in the black Methodist community of Springfield; and the third, based in the small county seat of Groesbeck, appears to have been dominated by the Trammels, another large and influential black family in the county.[36]

The Union League sprang to life through the plantation districts because its goal of mobilizing black support for the national government and the Republican party fed on and nourished the sensibilities and customs that organizers found in many African-American communities. League councils served as crucial political schools, educating newly enfranchised blacks in the ways of the official political culture. New members not only were instructed in the league's history, in the "duties of American citizenship," and in the role of the Republican party in advancing their freedom, but also learned about "parliamentary law and debating," about courts, juries, and militia service, about the conduct of elections and of various political offices, and about important events near and far. With meetings often devoted, in part, to the reading aloud of newspapers, pamphlets, and government decrees, freedmen gained a growing political literacy even if most could neither read nor write. One federal official in southside Virginia, impressed at the rapid progress of local blacks, found that "instead of obtaining information from public speakers" they preferred to "*secur*[e] for their own use *all* kinds of public documents and in small squads are advising themselves through some of the more intelligent colored people who read and explain to them the subject matters of such papers &c. as they may have." But the league was by no means simply pedantic and hierarchical in its function and culture. Rural blacks could certainly appreciate the organization's secrecy, acquainted as some already were with "secret societies" and as all undoubtedly were with the temper of their former owners. They surely did not have to be reminded about the importance of solidarity and mutual loyalty. "No earthly motive will ever induce them to betray one another," the northern planter Charles Stearns observed of the Georgia freedpeople he had come to know, comparing them to "free-masons." "They *dare* not tell of each other, even if so disposed." The league's initiation ritual, in which inductees took a sacred pledge while forming a circle "with clasped and uplifted hands," in fact bore resemblance to the ring shout and other forms of spiritual communion in their religious worship.[37]

Even the most didactic of league exercises might be assimilated to the cultural and spiritual styles of rural black audiences. The "dialogue" was thus regarded as a central educational device for league and party organizers alike, and it was said to have been in the "hands of every Radical who could read." Presented as a conversation between "a white Republican and a colored citizen," it was a series of pat questions and answers designed to acquaint the new voter with his political duties and cement his allegiance to the Republican party: exalting the party's role in protecting freedpeople and advancing their rights while identifying the Democrats with slavery and the rebellion. Critics derisively referred to it as the "League Catechism" because blacks apparently "were drilled in its principles" and subjected to an almost religious indoctrination. But blacks themselves infused it with a different sort of community and spiritual vibrancy, reminiscent instead of the call-and-response rhythms that traditionally went into the making of spirituals, sermons, prayer, and the general celebration of religious faith. When the Reverend Henry McNeal Turner prepared local black leaders for their work, he and Tunis G. Campbell faced each other across the room and "read over the dialogues," Turner acting "as the freedman and Mr. Campbell as the true Republican, I asking and he answering in a suitable voice." The effect was electric. "When Campbell would read some of those pointed replies," Turner marveled, "the whole house would ring with shouts, and shake with spasmodic motions and peculiar gestures of the audience." A white South Carolinian, commenting on the "disorder" that could prevail at league meetings, noted a similar phenomenon: "At their gatherings all have something to say, and all are up at once. They have a free flow of language, and their older men exhibit a practical, get-at-the-facts disposition. . . . While they are speaking, their orators are subjected to all kinds of interruptions—questions, impertinences, points of order, etc."[38]

League councils sought in other ways to tie their own official objectives to the political practices and concerns of rural black communities. Reflecting the provisions of the elective franchise and the gender conventions of mainstream political culture, formal membership in the Union League was restricted to males, twenty-one years of age and older, and the available records and minutes of local councils reveal no exceptions. To this extent, the league seems to have been in tune with the social division of politics detected among rural African Americans. But the record also suggests that "membership" did not fully define the range of participation, and that the league depended on a much wider level of mobilization and involvement. In many locales, women and children, as well as men, took part in league processions, in organizing assemblages, in league-sponsored public meetings and speakings, and even in the business of the councils. There is scattered evidence of black women engaged in the selection of officers, the drafting of bylaws, and the give-and-take of council discussion and debate; in some cases they may have formed auxiliaries. At all events, they had a genuine visibility designed to symbolize the nature and depth of league support and to bring sanction against those who resisted the call, violated the pledge, or strayed from the fold.[39]

Indeed, league councils quickly constituted themselves as vehicles not only of Republican electoral mobilization, but also of community development, defense, and self-determination. In Harnett County, North Carolina, they formed a procession "with fife and drum and flag and banner" and demanded the return of "any colored children in the county bound to white men." In Oktibbeha County, Mississippi, they organized a cooperative store, accepting "corn and other products . . . in lieu of money," and, when a local black man suffered arrest, "the whole League" armed and marched to the county seat. In Randolph County, Alabama, and San Jacinto County, Texas, they worked to establish local schools so that, as one activist put it, "every colored man [now] beleaves in the Leage." In the Fairfield District of South Carolina, they gathered on land some freedmen had leased, established their own court, and advised freedpeople to carry their complaints there rather than to the district court. And, in the neighborhood of Perote, in Bullock County, Alabama, they similarly "resisted the processes of civil law," and instead formed a code of laws, opened a court, and selected a sheriff and deputy to govern their community, provoking complaints of "insurrection" and the eventual arrest of their leader.[40]

The league may well have had its widest early influence on labor relations, building as it often did on previous struggles and less formal associations. "[T]he is a grate menny Womens and Childrens and boys going about working for people and dont know how to make a Bargain and they is not theyr Rights by a grate dail," a council leader in Lincoln County, North Carolina, told Governor William Holden, "and we want to know if Some of the Best men of our Ligue Could Stand as garddeans for all such people in our Reach not let them make a Bargain them selfs but some of us go and make it for them and see that they git the money &c." Here and elsewhere in the plantation South, league councils enabled and encouraged freedpeople to negotiate better contracts, contest the abuses of their employers, engage in strikes and boycotts, claim their just wages and shares of the crop, and generally alter the balances of power on the land. Small wonder that league organizers were commonly accused of "promising the freedmen a division of stock land & money of the country" and of promoting agrarian rebellion.[41]

The mass recruitment of rural freedmen into the Union League beginning in 1867 thus simultaneously enlarged the organization and changed its character. Most Unionist whites from nonplantation districts, who initially composed the social base and who were far more interested in punishing ex-Confederates than in empowering ex-slaves, reeled at the prospect of joining hands in membership with African Americans. Large numbers, it appears, quickly withdrew from the league entirely, while many others chose to maintain virtually segregated councils. And if willingness to work with freedmen seemed relatively limited among native southern whites in regions where whites predominated, it was almost nonexistent in regions where blacks predominated. League councils in the plantation districts generally counted few whites among their members, and these tended to fit the label of "carpetbaggers": northerners who had come South during and immediately after the Civil War (in the Union army, in the Freedmen's Bureau, as teachers and missionaries, or as planters)—and who, for a variety of reasons, saw the league as a means to satisfy political sympathies and personal ambitions. Not surprisingly, they often emerged as early leaders, offering a host of useful services for still inexperienced and largely illiterate black folk and, in return, received some deference and gratitude in the form of council officerships and political loyalty.[42] The deference and gratitude usually proved short-lived, but to the extent that the rank-and-file of the councils in the plantation districts was heavily black, the league helped to encourage social and political aspirations and forms of collective struggle that national and local white leaders neither envisioned nor approved. The days of reckoning would be painful and politically disastrous.

Yet at the same time, we should not ignore or underestimate the extraordinary sites of interracial cooperation that the league also provided and that, once destroyed, would take many more decades to replicate anywhere in the United States. Some, commonly small in size, were to be found in plantation areas like Colorado County, Texas; some were to be found in mountainous areas like Blount County, Tennessee. Most, however, existed in the piedmont and hill South, where blacks composed between 10 and 30 percent of the population, where farms rather than plantations ruled the landscape, and where dissenting political traditions had set roots. Here the white majority had not necessarily bowed to the will of the secessionist slaveocracy or easily supported the Confederacy, but here too enclaves of African Americans were of sufficient size and organizational potential to tip the new balances of local power. So here the possibility of political experimentation was most auspicious.[43]

Surry County, at the foothills of the Appalachian Mountains in north-central North Carolina, was one such site. Chiefly a grain-growing county of small to modest farms, Surry sat on the edge of the slaveholders' regime. In 1860, fewer than one inhabitant in seven was black, fewer than one white household head in nine owned slaves, and fewer than one slaveholder in three owned more than five slaves. County voters had traditionally cast their ballots for the Whig party and, in the late winter of 1861, overwhelmingly rejected secession. They then showed the Confederacy only lukewarm allegiance and may have supplied some troops to the Union army and some support for the Unionist Heroes of America. In April of 1867, twenty-six of them established the Hamburg lodge of the Union League.[44]

The original members of the lodge were white and residents primarily of Mount Airy township. Their leader, John M. Brower, was a wealthy manufacturer, but almost all of the rest were yeoman farmers and tradesmen who had been born in either North Carolina or Virginia. By the fall of 1867, their ranks had swelled to 168, and while many of the new members were related to the founders and to each other, they were as a group even more humble in their circumstances. Roughly one in three owned no land, and, of those who did own land, roughly half owned less than five hundred dollars' worth. On the face of it, that is, they seemed typical of white southerners who were known to scorn wealthy slaveholders and poor slaves alike. But in May, at their third meeting, they received a petition from three African Americans to "join our council" and they appointed a committee to "investigate the character of the colored men." Two weeks later, after hearing favorable reports on these and a few others, the Hamburg lodge elected and initiated thirteen black men. Two meetings later, in early June, they admitted twenty-nine additional black members and by the fall they could count 106 black men, composing more than one-third of the entire lodge membership.[45]

We do not know why the first few black men submitted their petitions for admission to the lodge, except to presume that they had been invited by one of the white leaders or had reason to expect that their petitions would win a serious, if not a favorable, hearing. What we do know is that most of those African Americans who became members of the lodge resided in Mount Airy township, most if not all had been slaves (though few if any had been owned by white members of the lodge), and most were now propertyless farm tenants and laborers. Only one in ten claimed a trade and just over one in ten owned any land. Yet more than poverty, proximity, and an experience of enslavement tied these men together. They also appear to have been part of a dense network of kinship. For among the thirteen initial inductees, there were at least three members of the Banner family—Isaac, Joe, and Sam—and they eventually were joined by at least eight others, all living and working at close range, perhaps on two or three adjacent farms, in Mount Airy township. Black members of the lodge came to include as well six Gwyns, five Hills, five Whitlocks, four Hammocks, and four Tuckers. Virtually every member, it seems, could find some close kin in the council, suggesting that the local black community had been substantially reconstituted by the spring of 1867.[46]

Although a distinct minority of the lodge's members, African Americans were by no means marginal to the business and concerns of the organization. Only one week after the first black members were initiated, "a proposition was made in open council and unanimously adopted that the officers" seek the appointment of John M. Marshall as the local Freedmen's Bureau agent since it "is very much desired by the Unionists of both races." "It is a position that is very useful to the colored people—and can be mad[e] so to the Loyal element of the whole county," the lodge's white president explained, for "the Freedmen have been neglected by the former Comr. . . . [who] is their enemy both politically and socially and have been in the interest of their former masters instead of the freedmen." Soon black members would be serving on lodge committees and speaking to the lodge on the "state of affairs in [the] country." By the late summer, two were elected to lodge office, one as marshal and one as sentinel. With remarkable speed, a new political culture was taking shape and a new basis for political mobilization was being laid.[47]

◈

Among the diverse activities that Union League councils across the former Confederate South pursued in 1867, few commanded more immediate attention than those required to implement the provisions and goals of the Reconstruction Acts. Within months, the Republican party had to be organized in the states and counties, delegates had to be nominated and elected to serve in state constitutional conventions, new state constitutions enfranchising black men and investing state governments with new structures and responsibilities had to be written and ratified, and the general congressional expectations for readmission to the Union had to be fulfilled. First and foremost, the outlines of a new body politic had to be drawn and legitimated through a process of voter registration. Members of the Hamburg lodge devoted much of their meeting time between May and October 1867 to advancing the cause of the league in Surry County, discussing the prospects of the Union Republican party, choosing representatives for countywide conventions, instructing those representatives as to the will of the lodge, and recommending "men suitable for registration officers" to the appropriate federal authorities.[48]

To those who have demonstrated that the American system of voter registration stands as the greatest barrier to popular electoral participation, the history of registration must seem surprising and ironic. Until the advent of Military Reconstruction, the franchise was one of the clearest symbols of political federalism. It was wholly within the province of individual states and the rules governing its exercise were, at once, varied and loose. State legislatures determined the official qualifications of voters for elective offices at the national, state, and local levels—age, gender, race, propertyholding, and residency—and although most of them had established white adult male suffrage by 1840, there was nothing approaching uniformity. As late as 1860, black men could vote in some of the New England states and in New York, and white men had fewer hurdles to jump in some places (generally the newer states of the West) than in others (generally the slave states of the South and the manufacturing states of the Northeast), all the more so after the Know Nothing movement imposed literacy and toughened naturalization requirements in parts of New England and the Middle Atlantic during the 1850s. The conduct of elections showed even more variation, whether regarding the timing of the contests, the location of polls, or the duration and method of polling. At the same time, there was no formal procedure for enforcing franchise qualifications and conditions. The polls were rather staffed by local representatives of the political parties, and often by the candidates and their managers as well, who evidently presumed that personal familiarity in a still small-scale environment would be sufficient to determine whether prospective voters satisfied the legislated standards.[49]

The Reconstruction Acts radically altered the traditions and presumptions both because they enfranchised large numbers of former slaves against the wishes of their former owners, and because they disfranchised some white southerners for their participation in the rebellion. The commanders of each of the newly prescribed military districts were therefore instructed to register those who, under sworn oath, could meet the now congressionally mandated qualifications: Voters had to be males "of whatever race, color, or previous condition," who were at least twenty-one years of age, citizens of the United States, residents of their respective states for a year, not subject to exclusions for disloyalty as defined by the Fourteenth Amendment, and willing to "faithfully support the Constitution and obey the law of the United States." To that end, the states were to be divided into registration districts and three-member boards of registrars, chosen from among the "loyal officers and persons" available, assigned to complete the registration by September 1, 1867, and superintend subsequent elections to facilitate the writing and ratification of new state constitutions.[50]

The project was daunting, owing in good part to what one Republican newspaper termed "practical difficulties." Some were logistical and bureaucratic. Registrars not only had to cover sizable territories on foot or horseback; they also had to enroll prospective voters who might not yet have taken surnames, did not know or could not reliably establish their correct ages, or might falsely swear to their past loyalty. Federal officials urged utmost caution to prevent those disqualified under the law from registering and voting, and suggested that corroborating testimony be obtained wherever possible. But the greatest difficulties were of a political nature. Understaffed as most already were, military district commanders had a tough time securing the requisite number of registrars, for in many parts of the former Confederacy few "loyal persons" able to read and write could be identified. Even then, registrars often encountered a thicket of interference, especially in the interior districts where government representatives had never regularly been stationed. Hostile white landowners, complaining that the new political opportunities "demoralized" labor and courted upheaval, struggled to maintain the freedpeople in ignorance, to prevent them from attending political meetings, and to confuse them about the meaning and objectives of registration. "There is good reason to believe," one Freedmen's Bureau agent reported, that "the colored people living on farms remote from the towns . . . are still ignorant of their political status, their former masters and employers having taken no pains to enlighten them, and much to keep them ignorant on this front." Others found that interested freedmen had been threatened with personal violence or dismissal, or had been warned that registration would bring reenslavement, military impressment, higher taxes, or "another war upon the country."[51]

For the most part, however, the military district commanders took their responsibilities seriously and moved quickly and aggressively to get the job done. They carved out registration districts, solicited recommendations from Freedmen's Bureau agents for eligible registrars, widely came to insist that one of the three local registrars be black, ordered registrars to travel out to plantations and farms, made adjustments in the routine—sometimes prolonging the registration period or sending black registrars in advance—to enroll as many black voters as possible, and rarely put up with mischief from irritated whites. In Mississippi, General E. O. C. Ord, who had reservations about black suffrage, nonetheless acted with dispatch. Within days of his arrival in the state, he ordered four of his subordinates to devise a comprehensive plan for registration and then appointed more than two-thirds of the registrars from the ranks of former Union soldiers living there. He went on to instruct the registrars to divide their districts into precincts, send out handbills to inform residents when and where they would appear, explain to freedmen the meaning of the franchise and the "true object of registration," offer advice about responding to harassment, and spend long enough in each precinct to permit a full registration of qualified voters. Ord had no patience for those who tried to obstruct the process, sending one abusive east Mississippi yeoman to federal prison "for a ninety-day period of reflection." In the Third Military District, which included Georgia, Florida, and Alabama, commanding general John Pope offered further incentives: he paid registrars about twenty-six cents for each voter registered. Never again would the federal government or its agents so proceed to ensure American citizens of their right to vote.[52]

Yet the success of the undertaking would have been far more limited were it not for the enthusiastic and multifaceted response of the freedpeople themselves. They mobilized their ranks, streamed to places of registration (often defying the wishes of their employers), helped identify suitable black registrars, challenged the misinformation and indifference of hostile white registrars, and worked to educate and protect freedmen who did not understand the process or feared the consequences of their involvement. That the Republican party and Union League were organizing simultaneously served to give registration added energy and direction. From Hillsboro, North Carolina, to Bolivar, Tennessee, to Jefferson County, Mississippi, to St. Martin Parish, Louisiana, and on to Brenham, Texas, the grumbling of planters was much the same: "Registration is going on here—negroes all enrolling"; "250 Black men in town for voting certificates—such a crowd as never before witnessed . . . all my Employees registered"; "The negro men have all went to Fayette to register their names so they can vote, it is a disgrace to civilized people"; "All our men went to town this morning to have themselves registered as voters, I took up work again at 2 o'clock." Even some federal officials could express annoyance. Citing inclement weather that disrupted work and imperiled the crops, one moaned that "unfortunately the registration of voters commenced at this critical period and the freedmen flocked to town from all parts of the county and also from other counties where registration had not commenced. It has taken all my authority and exertions to arrest this temporary demoralization of the laborers."[53]

Hackneyed as the planters' complaints came to sound, the process and pulse of registration in fact varied across the South according to the nature and level of local politicization. In tidewater Northumberland County, Virginia, "meetings for Registration" were "held under the auspices of the Union League," and the freedmen drew praise for their "orderly and quiet behavior." In the Marion District of South Carolina, however, African Americans invited a trusted Freedmen's Bureau agent to address them at their schoolhouse in late April and took care to surround the whole place with "armed sentinels." The Georgia Education Association, established by an early state freedmen's convention, joined forces with the Republican party and the Loyal League in the spring of 1867 to further the ends of registration, forming grassroots clubs to spread the message and bolster resolve. In Charles City County, Virginia, blacks apparently received the news of the right of suffrage "without demonstration," and in biracial meetings "interrupted" the speakers with "numerous queries," while in Coweta County, Georgia, only "the colored citizens" held a meeting as to their political rights and duties and invited "gentlemen from abroad to address them." White Unionists in Natchitoches, Louisiana, "formed a club previous to the commencement of the Registering Committee" and "sent out notices to the freedmen to come and join." The next Saturday evening, about one hundred responded, "walking quietly in procession and regular order . . . with sticks and clubs and one thing or another," but "from a distance" they "looked like 50,000" with "dust rising like a cloud," provoking some locals to shut up "doors, blinds &c" for fear that "the niggers were coming to take the town."[54]

In many interior districts of the Deep South, however, where few federal troops had been stationed and suspicions born of intense localism abounded, military officers and registrars commonly had to work through more traditional channels of communication and interpretation. Visiting estates situated miles from market towns, rail lines, or navigable waterways, they might gather up freed laborers still dimly aware of the great changes in motion but find it necessary to converse, either directly or indirectly, through recognized community leaders. One Freedmen's Bureau agent, checking on the progress of registration in a particularly isolated section of the Mississippi Delta, could therefore report that "the head man is [usually] put forward as spokesman for the party, and the others carefully refrain from taking any part in the conversation. But they usually act by his advice, or often his example."[55]

Under circumstances such as these, it was "difficult," as the agent commented, to know "the nature and degree of information possessed by the freedmen." A few observers, insisting that "our new found brethren had no idea what registration meant," described scenes they regarded as "ludicrous." "Quite a number brought along bags and baskets 'to put it in,' and in nearly every instance there was a great rush for fear we would not have registration 'enough to go around,'" a correspondent for the *New York Herald* chuckled from South Carolina.

"Some thought it was something to eat; others thought it was something to wear." No doubt there was confusion in many quarters—and for good reason. Registration had never before been attached to the formal political process. But we must also be alert to the ways in which freed communities assimilated this, and other aspects of the official political culture, to their own aspirations and understandings of empowerment. And nothing was more widespread than the association of registration with land. Where mobilizations had been going on since 1865 or 1866, registration could therefore be viewed as an opportunity to press forward on the land question in new, and more directly available, political arenas. In Halifax County, North Carolina, "two meetings of the colored citizens took place" in early May 1867, and at the one "addressed by colored speakers only," the audience was "advised that a division of lands must be had, and that pure republicans, either colored or yankee must be voted for." Coastal Georgia, influenced since late in the war by Sherman's Field Orders and by the Radicals Aaron A. Bradley and Tunis G. Campbell, similarly saw the freedpeople "much agitated in reference to the question of confiscation, many . . . expecting a division of lands."[56]

Elsewhere, the construction freedpeople placed on registration harked back to the rumors that circulated during the summer and fall of 1865. Remarking on the information that freed plantation laborers had obtained as to "their duties and responsibilities as citizens," a federal agent in Grenada, Mississippi, noted that "some had the impression that the certificate of Registration entitled them to a portion of Government lands." In eastern Arkansas, a newspaper found that "scarcely a grown up man or woman of African extraction . . . but believes that he or she will very shortly be placed . . . in possession of the comfortable homes and broad acres of his or her white master or mistress." The very correspondent who poked fun at South Carolina African Americans for imagining that registration was something to eat, wear, or carry away went on to admit that "quite a number thought it was a distribution of confiscated land under a new name." From Farmville in Virginia's southside, a Freedmen's Bureau official made the general point in a lengthy and revealing comment and contrast. "The opinion *generally* entertained by the reflecting freedmen," he wrote, "is that the property held by their employees has been forfeited to the Government by the treason of its owners, and it is liable to be confiscated whenever Congress demands it," especially "if the owners of the property *use* the power which it gives them to make *political slaves* of the poor." Small wonder that some federal officials came to gripe about the "bad use" local black leaders had made of their educational efforts, or that some freedpeople fell victim to land-related swindles, in one case purchasing stakes to mark off their plots.[57]

If registration permitted black community leaders to translate formal political policies and practices into terms that best resonated with their own ideas and goals, it also helped bring some of those leaders into clearer public—and historical—light. In much of the ex-Confederate South, federal officials determined to appoint black registrars and, to that end, sought to identify black men "in whom both races have confidence and who have the most influence over their own people." Nominations and recommendations came from Freedmen's Bureau agents, Union League councils, Republican party county conventions, church congregations, mass meetings, white native Republicans, and individual black aspirants themselves. But the most extensive and revealing lists—with a total of 1,004 names—were compiled by the Freedmen's Bureau assistant commissioners for Virginia and North Carolina.

Although these lists of "prominent freedmen" likely excluded black men known to be politically militant or to have otherwise antagonized resident whites, they offer a glimpse of certain black leaders at a crucial point in the transition from the politics of slaves to the politics of freedpeople, and indeed of those more closely tied to the former than the latter. For generally speaking, the designated individuals resembled the figure of the plantation or community elder during the antebellum period. Most had been slaves; almost all had been born in their respective states, with a great many relatively long-time residents of their respective counties; and most were at least thirty-five years of age. As a group, that is, they were men of mature age who were in a position to be at the intersection, if not at the head of, dense kinship networks and to have exercised local influence for quite some time. Given the tasks at hand, a significant number had acquired the skills of formal literacy. But few had participated in early freedmen's conventions and few would take an active part in the new political culture they were helping to usher in: few would organize Union Leagues or Republican party clubs, few would serve as delegates to the upcoming state constitutional conventions, and few would run for or serve in state or local office.[58]

It is true, of course, that these "prominent freedmen" may have reflected official, as opposed to grassroots, conceptions of influence and leadership, identified as they ultimately were by representatives of the Freedmen's Bureau. Yet evidence suggests that officials often discerned or yielded to popular wishes and sensibilities. Robert Jarvis appeared on the Freedmen's Bureau list for Surry County, North Carolina. Age thirty-six, he seems to have been born in North Carolina and lived in the county for years. But Jarvis's name had been forwarded by the Hamburg lodge of the Union League even though he was not a member of the organization. When blacks in Lauderdale County, Alabama, gathered at the Florence AME Church in April 1867 to nominate a registrar, they were addressed by James T. Rapier, who had been freeborn in the county in 1837, educated in Tennessee and Canada, and in attendance at a Tennessee freedmen's convention in 1865 before returning to Alabama. A committee of five, however, chose Rapier's father—John H. Rapier Sr.—to fill the post. Fifty-nine years of age, John H. had been in the area since 1819, obtained his freedom in 1829, and although a barber by trade with a white clientele, he appears to have maintained complex connections to the slaves of Lauderdale County. Alabama's bureau assistant commissioner, Wager Swayne, received nominations from other local black meetings, as well as from white and black correspondents. The "colored council" of a Union League in Lawrence County, with the support of white "union men," selected Alf Peters, "a highly respected and trustworthy man and a minister of the Baptist church, which is far the most numerous and clannish sect in this district," whose "influence among his people is far above any man of color in the county." A "convention of colored men" in Morgan County chose former slave Henry Sims, who was "about as worthy a man as could be" found. And a bureau agent endorsed the appointment of George Houston "as the best man [in Sumter County] for the place." Houston, the agent wrote, "has more influence and intelligence, has worked harder and collected more money to establish the colored school in Livingston than any other man, and is loyal in every sense of the word."[59]

As political appointments unavoidably will, these provoked no small amount of squabbling and discord; and they quickly hinted at the sort of internecine struggles that would eat at the Republican party in the southern states. Some white Unionists from the hills and mountains rankled at the prospect of any black registrars. Emerging party factions already began to battle for patronage and support among black constituents. And freed communities started to show their own complex fissures and rivalries. But for all of this, the registration process proved to be a stunning success. By the early fall of 1867, the rolls of eligible voters had been compiled and they included an astonishingly large proportion of eligible black men: over 90 percent everywhere except Mississippi, where about 83 percent registered. Even more consequentially, black voters now composed a very substantial proportion, if not a majority, of the total electorate in all of the states subject to Reconstruction, and especially in the counties and parishes of the black belt where slaveholding planters had long ruled. The contours of a new body politic were increasingly in evidence. Or, as a wealthy Alabamian with more atmospheric than corporeal sensibilities groaned, "the political horizon is *darkening*."[60]

◈

The enfranchisement and registration of black men initiated a competition for black votes that could have enabled the old leaders and former masters to reestablish—and perhaps considerably enlarge—their own power bases. Black voters had no previous experience in the electoral arena and perilously few had managed to escape dependence on white employers. By mixing paternalist appeals with a range of incentives and penalties at their disposal, local elites and landowners might, in the short run, have hedged the worst that could come from the state constitutional conventions and then, in the long run, have harnessed the fruits of black voting strength while eliminating federal interference in the political process. They might have secured home rule on terms acceptable to the great majority of northerners and looked to recapture a meaningful share of power at the national level.

Yet the prospect of campaigning for black votes was by no means alluring. Former Confederates almost universally rejected the principle of black suffrage, and few accepted the constitutional legitimacy of Reconstruction. Democrats, especially those who operated farms or smaller plantations or who lived in white majority counties, appeared most resistant: they either lacked the affinity for paternalist rhetoric, the leeway for incentives, or the need for black political support. And so they and their representatives counseled either nonparticipation in the elections leading to constitutional conventions or active rejection of the conventions themselves. But there were others who took a different view. Persuaded that black suffrage was a fait accompli and that more severe punishments could still be visited on the South, they thought that by cooperating with the dictates of the Reconstruction Acts they might be able to forge a biracial coalition under their control and attract the resources necessary to rebuild the region. Some were former Whigs in search of a new political home; others were wealthy Democrats attracted by the idea of a new conservative alignment; a few, like Albert Gallatin Brown of Mississippi and Joseph E. Brown of Georgia, had been ardent secessionists. Most resided in black majority districts and imagined that the "old allegiances" could be reactivated. "We can control and direct the negroes if we act discretely," the South Carolina planter and political leader Wade Hampton insisted, "and in my judgment the highest duty of every Southern man is to secure the good will and confidence of the negro."[61]

In the spring and summer of 1867, as registration coincided with the developing campaign for state constitutional conventions, "cooperationists" sought to pursue such a strategy. Few believed that the task would be easy, and many acknowledged what they might be up against. "The most respectable citizens" of Warrenton, Virginia, put the matter bluntly. "We must educate the nigger ourselves and give them southern ideas and get rid of the Yankee influence," they declared, conceding that "the freedmen are all awake to their new rights." A planter residing near Stateburg, South Carolina, made the same point with more delicacy. "I am very politic in all I do and say with a view toward acquiring as strong a personal influence over [the negroes] as possible," he told a North Carolinian, for with it "likely that they will outnumber the whites at the ballot box in this state, it behooves all who have the opportunity to bend their minds in a right direction as far as possible." To that end, cooperationists sponsored meetings or addressed those convened under other auspices, and by their lights reached out a hand of friendship and reconciliation. They spoke of their kindly feelings toward black people, of the loyalty and devotion many had previously cultivated among slaves, of their commitment to recognizing black political rights, and of their concern for black interests. They, in turn, warned black audiences of the mischief Radicals would cause and invited blacks to accept their leadership as the best means to secure racial peace and regional progress. Some even found a conservatively inclined black man to stand by their side or to make a speech ratifying their opinions.[62]

For their work, cooperationists attracted a smattering of support and encouraged the formation of a handful of black "conservative" clubs, chiefly in urban areas where social stratification among African Americans was most complex and the largest concentrations of antebellum free blacks were found. Indeed, the cooperationists made some efforts to pry the freeborn and formerly manumitted away from the mass of freed blacks with flattering appeals to their superior skills and intelligence. More generally, however, they managed to stir confusion and apprehension, because they almost invariably coupled the promise of benefits with direct threats. Federal officials and other northerners were at times beseiged by freedmen seeking their advice and instruction. One, in Tupelo, Mississippi, reported that "many of them do not understand the difference between Republican and conservative" and "had been imposed on by white people." Another, in Sterling, Texas, discovered that "the Freedmen all want to know if they are to vote this fall, and who to vote for." "The planters," he soon learned, "have already begun to poison their minds—telling them that if the Freedmen vote for the planters, the Cotton tax will come off &c &c, and that if the Freedmen do not vote the way the planters want them to, they will all be discharged from work."[63]

It was not long before the most optimistic of cooperationists had to admit impending failure. By late summer, freedmen had not only registered to vote but also overwhelmingly showed their intention to support new constitutional conventions and align with the Republican party. In part, cooperationists proved to be their own worst enemies. They spoke to blacks with condescension, offered blacks no direct access to or share of power, and effectively refused to see that a new framework for political discourse had already been established. Even black conservatives, who desired a "spirit of harmony" between the races and believed Radicalism "unfavorable" to this "aim," resolved "that our right to vote involves the right to hold office" and "that our interests and rights as free men require also that we should have the right to sit on juries." But far more important in defeating the designs of the cooperationists was the role of the Union League and Republican party in organizing freed communities at the grassroots, educating freedmen about the exercise of their new political rights, providing local black leaders with positions of authority and empowerment, and combating the confusion and apprehension that cooperationists often sowed.[64]

Whatever the differences and divisions in their ranks, Republicans alike embraced a vision of civil and political society that was altogether new in the South, and they had no match in mobilizing black mass support. With beachheads established in the larger cities and towns well before the passage of the Reconstruction Acts, the party moved into high gear in April and May 1867. Hundreds of public meetings took place in both countryside and town, at which the party platform was read, the claims of conservatives and cooperationists contested, an organizational structure put in place, debate encouraged, and resolutions adopted. Although the party targeted eligible voters, its activities often became communitywide affairs, embracing the styles of public celebration that first surfaced during the last months of the war and the first months of freedom. In heavily black eastern North Carolina, a mass meeting in New Bern in late April, attended by the Radical senator from Massachusetts Henry Wilson, brought a great turnout from the "colored population." "Their various societies—religious, civic, and political—assembled at the different headquarters, and then," according to one observer, "marched through the streets of the city, headed by a band of music, gathering accessions to their ranks." Soon, the procession "entered the park, headed by the 'Abraham Lincoln League,' accompanied by their excellent brass band, and bearing several beautiful banners with appropriate mottoes and inscriptions [including] 'Good Will to Man' and 'Equal Rights in the Law,'" and as Senator Wilson approached, "the children of the freedmen's schools . . . sang a beautiful chorus." Within weeks, meetings on a smaller scale would be reported in neighboring Pasquotank, Green, and Jones counties, and as far west as piedmont Alamance and Person counties. "Negroes are holding meetings in all the towns organizing under the

auspices of the Republican party (so-called) and demanding complete
political equality," the conservative David Schenck grumbled from
Lincolnton in late May.[65]

Elsewhere the net of participation was cast broadly too. In Beaufort,
South Carolina, what was described as the "largest political meeting"
ever held in the state convened on April 15 and, according to one
observer, "every man and woman appeared to understand, if by inspiration, the great political issues of the day." "They were thoroughly
radical and scouted the idea of any 'best friends,'" he noted with obvious reference to the entreaties of cooperationists, demanding instead
through resolutions crafted by black leaders "that all excepting those
belonging to the judiciary shall be elected directly by the people, . . .
that public schools shall be sustained by the state, and that no distinction be made on account of color." In the Virginia tobacco belt, a
Freedmen's Bureau official who complained that "political candidates
are disturbing the agricultural interests" illustrated by alluding to the
"almost daily meetings" to "which men, women & children flock indis-
criminately." An irritated landowner in Maury County, Tennessee,
made the same point more prosaically one Tuesday that July: "the
negroes Male and Female has gone to hear Hughs . . . near Col Pil-
lows."[66]

The meetings not only acquainted African Americans with the policies of the Republican party; as in Beaufort, they also identified and
elevated a grassroots leadership, articulated issues of special concern
to local black constituents, alerted audiences about the deceptions to
which they might be subjected, and framed the meaning of political
discipline. An assemblage in Prince Edward County, Virginia, thank-
ing God and Congress "for the emancipation act and the military bill,"
declared it the "duty of all to have their children fairly educated" and
resolved to "support no candidate for office not openly in favor of
equal civil and political rights"—specifically urging "that colored citizens not allow themselves to be bribed into voting against their interests." In nearby Bedford County, a meeting of "loyal colored people"
presided over by two of their number organized a Union Republican
party, invited the sympathy and cooperation of all blacks, and "dis-
countenance[d]" those who would not sustain and protect "the rights
of our race." Addressing another Republican mass meeting at New
Bern later in the year, Abraham H. Galloway, a runaway slave who

had returned to North Carolina during the Civil War and had been active in state and local politics ever since, thundered "that the Conservatives were no friends but open enemies," and that "he could not see where the people would be doing themselves justice other than [by] sustaining the Republican party, and voting for the convention." "The proposition of the Republican party," Galloway proclaimed, "is to allow every man in the nation to be his own *master.*"[67]

When, therefore, state Republican parties held conventions in the summer of 1867 to formalize their organizations, fill out their executive committees, ratify platforms, and prepare for the upcoming constitutional conventions, the black presence was fully in evidence. In Alabama, 100 of 150 delegates, 4 of 23 executive committee members, and the convention's vice president—James T. Rapier—were black. In Texas, blacks composed a clear majority of the almost six hundred delegates and many were "plantation hands," reflecting the work of the Union Leagues that spring. At a July convention in South Carolina, African Americans took up 64 of 80 delegate positions and the body's presidency (R. H. Gleaves was elected). In Georgia, Florida, and North Carolina, blacks accounted for at least half of the party's convention delegates. And in Virginia, throngs of freedmen backed by community support turned an August convention set for the Richmond's First African Baptist Church into a raucous open-air gathering in Capitol Square. Only in Arkansas, where the convention met very early and where the population away from the river counties was mostly white, did blacks fail to register significant numerical strength.[68]

Local Republican clubs and Union Leagues—which at times overlapped or were one and the same—linked the state parties to grassroots constituents and especially to the networks of kinship and community institutions that simultaneously provided sustenance to the ranks and imposed sanctions against those who might abstain or defect. This proved all the more necessary as cooperationists, finding their hand of friendship largely rejected by the freedmen, joined other white conservatives in harassing black employees who attended Republican political meetings and evicting those who continued to do so. A Freedmen's Bureau agent in Woodville, Mississippi, issued a typical report in late summer about the "many contracts . . . annulled by planters since the organization of the Union Republican club," dissatisfied as they claimed to be "with the freedmen for neglecting their work."

From Eufaula, Alabama, another official similarly described a deterioration in the "feeling between the races" and attributed it, "in great degree, to the heated political contest . . . in the subdistrict." "It has been the opinion of many white men up to this time that they could control the politics and . . . the votes of the colored men, especially those in their employment," he explained, but "seeing that the colored men are determined to think and act and vote as they please, the whites are losing some of their 'tender regard' for, and 'strong attachment' to their 'former slaves.'"[69]

Through Union Leagues and party clubs, freedpeople moved on a number of fronts to meet the challenge. They sought advice from sympathetic northerners, searched for suitable candidates to represent them in the constitutional conventions, debated the relative merits of announced contenders, brought complaints about coercion to bureau agents and military officers, requested easier and more extended access to voting places, planned marches to the polls on the days of election, and brought pressure of their own against black men who dragged their feet or bowed to their employers' dictates. Even skeptics could be "surprised and delighted" by the "comparative ease with which [the freedmen's] new-born politicians" came to comprehend "seemingly abstruse political problems." "At first it seemed nothing but folly to attempt to explain politics to them," the northern planter and abolitionist Charles Stearns admitted, "but I soon saw . . . they were keen-eyed in their political vision, fully justifying the buoyant expectations of those who had conferred on them political privileges." The Mississippi Delta planter and future moderate Republican governor James Lusk Alcorn pinpointed the source of both the "forebearance" and "keen-eyed political vision." "[T]he Loyal League is upon you," he told other planters, and "even a brief experience with the workings of that voting machine will satisfy you, as it has me, that all which our people claim for the influence of the 'old master' on the freedmen is neither more or less than *nonsense*." "The general fact," Alcorn sighed, is that "in the presence of the Loyal League" the "'old master' . . . has passed from fact to poetry."[70]

By the time of the elections, white Democrats and conservatives had for the most part abandoned the field, especially in the plantation districts and the Deep South more generally, while the freedmen turned out in great force. "They came," a Rapides Parish, Louisiana, newspaper marveled, "from every portion of the parish and none were left home . . . all were on hand eager and panting from freedom's boon." African Americans appear to have had the least trouble in the upper South where, in states like Virginia, nearly 90 percent of those registered to vote cast ballots. Intimidation and coercion were more pronounced in the cotton states and particularly in counties where blacks composed a substantial, but not a majority, portion of the population. Even so, at least 75 percent (in Georgia), and more commonly at least 80 percent (in Alabama, Mississippi, Louisiana, and Texas) of eligible black voters came to the polls, and virtually all supported the constitutional conventions and the Republican candidates hoping to serve as delegates. In some places, the election was said to have "passed off quietly"; in others, federal detachments were summoned to provide added protection. But most everywhere it was clear that black voters made their preparations well in advance and arrived at the polls in groups, at a predetermined hour, sometimes armed or marching in military fashion, always ready to impress white and black onlookers with their numbers, solidarity, and resolve. "When I began to receive votes, on the first day," an election supervisor in Clarke County, Alabama, wrote, "there must have been present, near one thousand freedmen, many as far as thirty miles from their home, all eager to vote and return."[71]

The results simultaneously revealed the dawning of a new day in southern society and politics as well as the dangers that would inevitably shadow what Military Reconstruction had made possible. In every state, constitutional conventions won the overwhelming support of those who voted and Republican delegates won a vast majority of available seats. Recorded opposition was most substantial in Virginia, North Carolina, Texas, and Arkansas, but in none of these states did it exceed 40 percent of the total vote; in South Carolina, Georgia, Alabama, Mississippi, and Louisiana it was scarcely detectable. Of the thousand-odd delegates who would consequently gather in the state capitols of the former slave and Confederate South to restructure their respective governments, few had previously exercised political power and authority. More than one-quarter of the delegates were African American. Yet, the lopsided returns could not disguise a deeper dilemma. Most eligible white voters had simply refused to validate the proceedings. They withheld their votes and in so doing announced what black southerners had always known: that political struggle would not and could not be confined to the officially designated arenas. A Freedmen's Bureau agent in Virginia put it a different way. "Whether the political adherence of the colored man be regarded as right or wrong this right has been exercised by them freely in the face of menacing threats," he said, and "the present election has proven that the colored man will neither sell nor barter away his vote either by compromise or duress." Unfortunately, "this adherence to what they believed was right has cost many of them their situations."[72]

❖

The scenes were no longer wholly without precedent. They had been glimpsed in New Orleans in 1865, in Macon in 1866, and, since early 1867, at local Union League councils, mass meetings, and Republican party conventions across the former slave states. "Black men and white men sat side by side," an astonished British traveler recorded, "the galleries . . . thronged with woolly heads; and a negro . . . on his feet addressing" the assembly. It was rather the settings and occasions that marked their dramatic and revolutionary character. The last time southern state capitols had hosted constitutional conventions, the rebellion had just been defeated and President Andrew Johnson's requirements for readmission to the Union were struggling to gain acceptance. But the delegates in attendance then, as had been true since the Union itself was established, simultaneously embodied and reinforced the notion that the body politic was to include only those whose civic standing could not be compromised by the stigmas of dependency associated with race, gender, and servitude. They were white adult men, most claiming at least modest wealth and political experience, who, while conceding the end of slavery and the uselessness of secession, refused to admit any black men to the franchise and sought to relegate all black people to an officially subordinate status.[73]

The delegates who gathered in Richmond, Raleigh, Charleston, Atlanta, Tallahassee, Montgomery, Jackson, New Orleans, Austin, and Little Rock during the last months of 1867 and the first of 1868 not only composed "the first official assembl[ies] in the United States where black men participated with whites"; they also set out to do something that no other society in the world, let alone state in the South or the

Union, had so much as attempted. They would inscribe into fundamental law the enfranchisement and full civil standing of a very large social group—one making up nearly half of the population and much more of the labor force, and held for over two centuries in the condition of slavery—thereby reconstructing the body politic of the South and potentially reordering the politics and society of the nation. "Never heretofore in America," the conservative North Carolina planter William Alexander Graham revealingly wrote in October 1867, "has the elective franchise been extended to new classes of voters, except through the agency of conventions chosen by those who had enjoyed it exclusively before."[74]

And never heretofore had the "new classes of voters" been directly involved in the proceedings that extended the elective franchise. The African-American delegates were, it is true, distributed unevenly across the state conventions, and nowhere were they "typical" of the constituents who elected them. Predictably, they served in largest and most influential numbers in the states that combined high black to white population ratios, early Union occupation and efforts at political mobilization, and weak bases of white Unionism (South Carolina, Louisiana, Virginia, and Florida); the fewest served in the states where blacks made up decided population minorities, Union occupation was late in coming, and significant pockets of white Republican support were to be found (Alabama, Arkansas, North Carolina, and Texas). In general, they were disproportionately mulatto, free before the Civil War, able to read and write, and independent. A good many, that is, were ministers, craftsmen, teachers, and petty property owners. But outside of lower Louisiana and South Carolina, where educated free people of color from the vicinities of New Orleans and Charleston held sway, the delegates did more closely approximate their grassroots supporters. Most had been slaves, lived and worked in the countryside, and had emerged as local leaders through their activities in the Union army, in postemancipation reorganization, in the Union League, and in the Republican party. In South Carolina, where plantation agriculture covered almost the entire state, African-American delegates represented all but three of the counties. In Georgia, they represented the northeastern and southwestern ends of the cotton belt, fanning out from bases in Augusta and Macon. In Virginia, they chiefly represented the counties of the tidewater and piedmont tobacco belt, while in North

Carolina, they represented counties along the seaboard around Wilmington and in the northeast. In Alabama, they represented counties both in the central and Tennessee Valley plantation belts, and in Mississippi they represented primarily the lower river counties in the environs of Natchez, Vicksburg, and Jackson. On average, they represented counties in which roughly 60 percent of the residents were black. And everywhere, the majority of delegates, black and white, owed their positions, as William Alexander Graham implied, to the votes of men who had never before enjoyed the elective franchise.[75]

As in the Republican party, the black convention delegates found themselves part of complex and, at times unwieldy, political coalitions. Outside of South Carolina, Louisiana, and Florida, they composed distinct minorities of the total delegations either because they lacked suitable candidates to advance, deferred to trusted whites, or bowed to pressure from white Republican leaders fearful of "overloading" conventions with blacks. Where blacks did not stand for convention seats, black voters generally preferred Yankees (carpetbaggers) to represent them, explaining "that they do not feel they can place reliance in any one belonging to the place." And if they lived in the plantation belt, they had the best opportunity to do just this, choosing from whites who had been among them as Union soldiers, Freedmen's Bureau agents, or nouveau planters. Responding to the enthusiatic appeals of blacks in Yazoo County, Mississippi, where he had leased a plantation and had his employees tear down the old slave jail and build a schoolhouse in its stead, the northern-born army veteran Albert T. Morgan "consented" to join "a ticket with a freedman, a blacksmith named William Leonard, and Charles Clark, an ex-Union officer, who had been 'trying' to plant in that neighborhood." Morgan's ticket swept to victory. Northern whites, who made up about 15 percent of all convention delegates, overwhelmingly gained election from black majority counties or districts.[76]

Beyond the plantation belt, black voters faced thornier problems. Candidates from their own communities had almost no chance to be selected as delegates, even if they possessed the requisite skills, because, as an observer in northern Alabama put it, "our white people did not like to vote for a negro," and few sympathetic northerners were to be found. Where Union Leagues had established interracial councils, blacks could influence the nomination of native white (scalawag) candidates and imagine that their specific interests would be duly recognized and defended. The Hamburg lodge of Surry County, North Carolina, supported two of its white members for the constitutional convention and instructed the county Republican convention "to lay down a platform of principles for the candidate[s] to act upon." Both were elected. But in much of the nonplantation South, white aspirants had no experience working politically with blacks and instead saw themselves representing the concerns of numerically dominant white farmers and tradesmen. They would come to form a delegate voting bloc whose idea of Reconstruction revolved around protecting the position of white petty proprietors, weakening the power of traditional black-belt elites, and punishing ex-rebel enemies in their midst. Some were explicitly hostile to black suffrage and officeholding. Not surprisingly, on election day black turnout in these locales was sometimes low.[77]

White delegates from the plantation belt, whether carpetbaggers or scalawags, could for the most part be entrusted to uphold the freedmen's new political rights. Their candidacies had been ratified by county conventions with heavy black participation and their political futures quite simply depended on black votes. Yet aside from a small core of Radicals who struggled for political democracy and racial equality through economic and educational reforms, most were attuned primarily to the goals of party formation and economic modernization—to securing for the Republican party a majority base of support, rebuilding the economic infrastructure of the region, and attracting the capital necessary to reconfigure the South in the image of the North. In a nation in which racial subordination remained the customary practice and in which capital felt most comfortable where labor was properly managed, such an agenda imposed real limits on what might be done to advance the prospects and power of black laboring communities.[78]

Despite the many obstacles and pitfalls, however, black delegates made their presence felt. Almost to a man, they were committed to constructing a political and civil society in the South in which the lines of exclusion based on race or previous condition would be eliminated, in which popular control over governance would be expanded, and in which the state would help promote the welfare and aspirations of its ordinary citizens. In this, they reflected the sensibilities of nineteenth-century radicalism as well as the objectives of the earlier freedmen's conventions; and they pressed the goals most vigorously and effectively in South Carolina, Louisiana, and Virginia, where their numbers were large and their leaders experienced and articulate in the language of constitutionalism. They supported, in coalition with white Radicals, the abolition of property qualifications and the reduction of residency requirements for voting and officeholding, the destruction (where they existed) of bastions of oligarchical rule, and the multiplication of elective offices, especially at the local level. "Manhood and not property or color," a black Virginia delegate declared, invoking the gender categories that had come to define the boundaries of political culture in the Atlantic's age of revolution, "is the foundation upon which suffrage should be based."[79] In league with most carpetbag and scalawag delegates, they demanded, as well, the creation of state-financed systems of public schools open to all children. And they led the fight against racial distinctions and discrimination in public life. In South Carolina, Virginia, and especially Louisiana, where educated, urban, and generally freeborn leaders among the substantial African American delegations had long felt stung and aggrieved by segregation and exclusion, the greatest strides were made toward equal access and mandated integration. In most other states, black delegates generally failed to outlaw public discrimination but successfully fended off mandated segregation even when, as in the case of public schools, they accepted its inevitability.[80]

The black voices most commonly heard at the state constitutional conventions, whether in Louisiana and South Carolina or Alabama and Arkansas, were those of delegates who had been free before the war, formally educated (often in the North), and trained in the crafts or professions. An urban and civic universalist perspective was, therefore, unavoidably privileged, and the goals of a nascent black bourgeoisie were at times fronted. Yet with rare exception, these delegates had come to see their destinies as inextricably linked to those of the rural masses, some because they had escaped from slavery, some because they saw no real possibility for a meaningful separate peace with any group of southern whites, and most because the process of mobilization had increasingly acquainted them with the political sensibilities and styles of the freedpeople. Many had been engaged in starting up newspapers, organizing Union League councils and Republican party clubs, addressing mass meetings, and attending precinct and county conventions where the concerns of rural folk were aired and intense debates could flare among them over issues of land, labor, and community development. Indeed, the Union League had probably attained the height of its influence in the South when the constitutional conventions met, and some of its most accomplished state and local leaders, white and black, were among the delegates.[81]

Thus, although they were formal deliberative bodies, the conventions could not easily distance themselves from the pulse and character of political activism at the grassroots, especially where a substantial black institutional infrastructure was already in evidence. The gathering in Richmond, Virginia, was particularly striking, for here, in the former capital of the Confederacy and at the state capitol building recently occupied by the Confederate Congress, the delegates sat amid a throng of black bodies. Young and old, male and female, many having left work, they "crowded" into the capitol's galleries, "swarmed" in the rotunda, and "massed" outside, ever interjecting their views, prodding and empowering their representatives, lambasting their foes, and continuing discussion of the day's issues far into the night. They debated the disfranchisement of leading rebels, the confiscation of rebel estates, the structure of taxation, the integration of public facilities, and the future of viva voce voting, and then rose or shouted to register their preferences with all—men, women, and children—apparently participating. The conservative *Richmond Enquirer* groaned that "the negro [delegates] have come here with their heads full of the wildest notions as to the power of the convention and what should be done by it."[82]

With white delegates chairing most of the committees (and virtually all of the important ones) at Virginia's and other state constitutional conventions, black delegates sometimes had a difficult time getting proposals of interest to rural laborers a general hearing, let alone enacting them. But almost everywhere, they brought such proposals into the proceedings. They called, variously, for mechanics' and laborers' liens to protect the wages of rural and urban workers alike, for aid to black laborers and tenant farmers, for the maintenance of common hunting and fishing rights on unenclosed land, for the implementation of progressive taxation, and, perhaps most important, for increasing the availability of land for black homesteads. To be sure, "confiscation" rarely entered into the official convention debates. If anything, it was summoned by black delegates only to be discountenanced and dismissed. The issue had, however, reverberated through state party conventions and local meetings in the weeks before the conventions met, dividing leaders and supporters while at the same time reminding delegates-to-be of the strong expectations among the rank-and-file. In places like Richmond it could resound right outside the convention hall. As a consequence, other, more "judicious," avenues of land redistribution were actively pursued. Some delegates called on the national Congress "for a grant of one million dollars to be appropriated for the purchase of lands"; far more widespread was the strategy of boosting real estate taxes and requiring the state governments to sell in small tracts land seized for nonpayment. The African-American-dominated convention in South Carolina succeeded in establishing a state land commission to carry out just such a policy, and the conventions in Louisiana, Mississippi, and Virginia took more modest steps in a similar direction. But even in Arkansas, William H. Grey, one of only eight black delegates in attendance, tried to nurture support for the "land question."[83]

Black delegates pushed at the boundaries of nineteenth-century politics and political culture further still. Since the advent of their suffrage campaign in the northern states during the 1830s and 1840s, African-American men had made their case for the franchise by fully embracing the gendered constructs that the democratic revolutions of the late eighteenth and early nineteenth centuries had prescribed. Political rights, it was said, could be justly and safely claimed only by those groups of people who had—owing to self-possession, property ownership, and direct power over others—the independence necessary to resist worldly manipulations and tyrannies. They were, in short, "privileges" of "manhood." Insofar as it denied both the legal status and cultural representation of enslavement and race, manhood thus offered blacks a vehicle for political inclusion that would be hardest to contest, all the more so after the valiant military service of nearly 200,000 of them during the Civil War. And from the mid-1860s, the demand grew for enfranchising black men as a reward for their demonstrated loyalty, bravery, and martial bearing. But when the constitutional conventions met to implement the provisions of the Military Reconstruction Acts, a new dynamic of discourse was injected. For the delegates had to determine not only the basis on which recently enslaved people would be admitted to the political arena (whether there would be, for example, literacy, property, or gender—as opposed to racial—qualifications), but also the basis on which, and the extent to which, recently rebellious people might be cast out.

The result was, in many instances, a wide-ranging and searching debate on the nature and compass of political rights. And as if to acknowledge that the Reconstruction Acts at least implicitly challenged the categories of inclusion by extending the franchise to the most historically dependent of men, black delegates raised possibilities that conservatives had warned against and even the most radical of white allies had rejected. Some insisted, therefore, contrary to the prevailing wisdom, that political rights were "natural" or "inherent," and a few went on to accept or to advocate the argument's logical extension: women's suffrage. The fiery Thomas Bayne, an escaped slave and the leading black radical at Virginia's convention, was one who made the connection. "In speaking of the right of women to vote," he announced on the floor, "I thought it an inherent right, and that women were wrongfully deprived of it." Bayne by no means denied patriarchal prerogatives or disclaimed domestic ideology, adding that "women's right is [also] a right to stay home . . . to raise and bear children, and to train them for their future duties in life." But in South Carolina, the northern-born free black William J. Whipper, who represented the low-country district of Beaufort, spoke even more fully and forcefully in moving that the word "male" be struck out of the new constitution's franchise provision. Conceding that "this body will not show themselves so liberal and progressive to act favorably upon this subject at the present time," Whipper nonetheless proclaimed his belief "in universal suffrage" and predicted that "the time will come when every man and woman in this country will have the right to vote."[84]

Whipper's motion was rejected; no vote was recorded. And there is no reason to think that either he or Bayne expressed a powerful tendency among African-American delegates. Indeed, the delegates' democratic instincts and general reluctance to exclude large categories of people from the franchise had rather different and more dangerous consequences: many of them bridled at the efforts of white Radicals to impose severe political disabilities on former Confederates. In Georgia, Florida, Texas, and the Carolinas, black delegates ultimately helped to defeat such efforts, and in Louisiana, Mississippi, and Virginia they struggled among themselves before largely adopting them. Perhaps the delegates understood the franchise, as some of their grassroots constituents undoubtedly did, as a collective as well as an individual possession, effectively enfranchising African-American women as well as the men who would formally cast the ballots. But most of them also likely saw the franchise as a way, simultaneously, to recognize the official political leadership of men, put blacks on a plane of legal equality with whites, and empower black communities more generally. Neither interpretation would resolve the tensions and contradictions that Whipper and Bayne had identified, nor fully smooth the transition from the politics of slavery to the politics of freedom.[85]

Yet the questions and tensions related to the franchise not only underscored how the constitutional conventions had reshaped the body politic of the South; they also suggested that the meanings and effects of the constitutions varied considerably across states. It is easy enough to see in the convention proceedings and the documents they produced limitations and lost opportunities, especially concerning the fate of the freedpeople. None of them moved to effect significant land reform and few offered substantial protection for the black civil and political rights officially established. Save for South Carolina and Louisiana, most of the attention was in fact fixed on achieving political and economic modernization for the sake of Republican party power. White delegates, in turn, struggled over the appropriate balances and, more than anything else, over how much political punishment of the rebels would be necessary. In some states, like Georgia, where delegates preferred to lure upcountry yeomen rather than disfranchise black belt planters, the political prospects of outvoted and outmaneuvered African Americans could accordingly be sacrificed.[86]

But there could be no mistaking the expectations that the constitutional conventions raised among black men and women in the southern countryside. They did not, as a Freedmen's Bureau agent grumbled in the midst of Mississippi's convention, "labor as faithfully as they should both for their interest and that of their employers." They insisted "on having [Saturday] to themselves" and commonly left "work to attend political meetings and speakings of various kinds and at different places," sometimes "travelling the distance of from 2 to 25 miles," sometimes holding "private club meetings," all "contrary to the wishes of their employer." In other states and districts, they "determined not to enter into contracts" until they had learned whether any "further provision" would be made for them. Almost everywhere, some freedpeople believed that lands were soon to be "divided among them," while some whites, sensing the anticipation and exuberance, warned of "conspiracies" and the "banding" of "secret negro societies" to advance "the work of disfranchisement or confiscation." Complaining in March 1868 that black workers outside of Columbia, South Carolina, were still refusing to sign contracts or rent land and were waiting instead for "imaginary assistance," another bureau agent noted that "reports come to the colored people there from the convention now sitting in Charleston that the Government intends supplying them not only with subsistence for the year, but with land and animals to work it." Although he "made every effort to disabuse their minds of the foolish idea," they thought the convention "has power enough to do almost anything." The former Confederacy had seen nothing quite like this since the fall and early winter of 1865.[87]

There also could be no mistaking the possibilities that the new constitutions opened up for the majority of freedpeople living in the plantation belt. Simply by enfranchising African-American men and prescribing that all county offices be subject to election, they created an unprecedented basis for local democracy. In the seaboard states of Virginia and North Carolina, such a prescription alone obliterated decades of customary practice and entrenched elite rule. But even where the tide of democratization had much earlier strengthened the leverage of ordinary voters, the advent of the black franchise transformed the very substance of democratization itself. Few captured the sweep of change more clearly than a local black leader in the South Carolina piedmont who thundered to an enthusiastic crowd of his followers: "Now is the black man's day—the whites have had their way long enough—now is *our time*."[88]

❖ 5 ❖

"A SOCIETY TURNED BOTTOMSIDE UP"

[Democrats] do not care so much about Congress admitting negroes to
their halls . . . but they do not want the negroes over them at home.

Henry McNeal Turner, 1871

The gallery of the U.S. Senate was crowded with spectators waiting
expectantly but uneasily to witness "the novel sight." Two days earlier,
the State of Mississippi had been officially restored to the Union, and
now its Republican senator-elect Hiram R. Revels sat on a sofa behind
Massachusetts senator Charles Sumner as prospective colleagues debated his qualifications for a seat in the chamber. A freeborn mulatto
from North Carolina, Revels had been ordained in the African Methodist Episcopal Church and had preached in many of the border states
before moving in 1865 to Mississippi, where he worked for the
Freedmen's Bureau, served as an alderman in Natchez, and gained
election to the first state senate chosen under the auspices of the Radical
constitution. Hostile Democrats thus insisted that, owing to the *Dred
Scott* decision, Revels had not been a citizen for nine years as required
by the Constitution.

But Sumner, among others, responded to such arguments with thun-
derous contempt, and when debate finally closed at five o'clock on the

afternoon of February 25, 1870, forty-eight of the fifty-six senators present, in a strict party vote, ordered Revels sworn in. Amid "a general buzz in the galleries, a rising up and a bending forward," Revels then advanced toward the clerk's desk "with a modest yet firm step," took the oath of office, and walked to the seat directly behind Tennessee senator William G. Brownlow, which he then occupied, becoming the first African American to serve in either chamber of the U.S. Congress. The seat had been vacant since January 1861, when Mississippi had seceded from the Union and its claimant, Jefferson Davis, had resigned from the Senate to lend his support to the slaveholders' rebellion. "Within a brief decade," wrote the black historian George Washington Williams—himself in attendance for the event—"Mississippi sent to succeed the arch traitor a *Negro*, a representative of the race that Mr. Davis intended to be the cornerstone of" the Confederacy.[1]

Hiram Revels's accession to the Senate may have served as a particularly dramatic symbol of the social and political revolution sweeping the country, but in state capitals like Jackson, Mississippi, the changing of the guard was far more arresting and consequential. For there, the legislature that elevated Revels, once the arena of slaveholding planters and their white allies, was now wholly dominated by the party that had waged war on the Confederacy, thirty-six of whose members (31 of 83 in the house, 5 of 26 in the senate) were black and well enough organized to agree unanimously on presenting Revels's name to the Republican Legislative Caucus and then to carry the vote of every Republican in joint session.[2] The scenes in Montgomery, Little Rock, Austin, Tallahassee, New Orleans, Atlanta, and Raleigh were similarly striking. Everywhere the nascent Republican party claimed the majority of seats in the newly constituted state legislatures, and everywhere except Tennessee black men were among their numbers.[3]

Then there was South Carolina, the home of militant proslavery theory, of nullification, of secessionist radicalism, and of the haughtiest slaveholding class to be found in the southern states, where in 1868 75 of 124 seats in the house and 10 of 31 seats in the senate—fully 55 percent of the entire legislature in the state capital of Columbia—were occupied not simply by Republicans but also by black Republicans who formerly had no political standing in the state. "The body is almost literally a Black Parliament," the northern journalist James S. Pike would scoff a few years later. "The Speaker is black, the Clerk is black, the door-keepers are black, the little pages are black, the chairman of the Ways and Means is black, and the chaplain is coal black. . . . [I]t must be remembered, also, that these men, with not more than a half dozen exceptions have been themselves slaves, and that their ancestors were slaves for generations." Reflecting on the "orators and statesmen" who had once walked the aisles, and on the "white community" of "wealth, culture, and refinement" that now lay "prostrate in the dust," Pike could only see "the spectacle of a society suddenly turned bottomside up."[4]

Yet nowhere was "the spectacle" more compellingly in view than in the many small county seats that dotted the rural districts where former slaves composed the majority of the population. Once virtual appendages of the surrounding plantations where slaveholding clans and their clients resolved disputes, reinforced their local rule, and enacted hierarchies of class, gender, and kinship, these courthouse towns experienced political transitions and inversions of an immediacy and magnitude unprecedented in the region, nation, or hemisphere. Here, where the most pivotal social relations were to be mediated and enforced, those long subject to almost unbridled personal domination could now hold the official levers of power: as jurors, magistrates, county commissioners, tax assessors, constables, and even sheriffs. Whatever their disgust and discomfort at the idea of black men representing their counties and parishes in the Congress or the legislatures, the old rulers were absolutely aghast at the prospect of losing their grip on local power. "There is not half so much interest on the part of democrats in this State about Congress as there is about the Legislature, or ordinaries or sheriffs," explained Georgia's black Republican leader Henry McNeal Turner. "They do not care so much about Congress admitting negroes to their halls . . . but they do not want the negroes over them at home." The Georgia planter, politician, and former Confederate Howell Cobb made the same point more threateningly. "I am very conservative as to the Legislature—which sits in Atlanta and can tolerate my driver voting for his own color then," he wrote, "but when it comes to the home-municipal government—all the blacks who vote against my ticket shall walk the plank."[5] Never before—and rarely again—in the history of the United States would such a substantial section of the working class have the opportunity to contest the power of their superiors in the formal institutions of governance that affected their lives most directly. It proved to be a turbulent and telling experiment in the meaning of democracy.

⟡

During Reconstruction, black men held political office in every state of the former Confederacy. More than one hundred won election or appointment to posts having jurisdiction over entire states, ranging from superintendent of education, assistant commissioner of agriculture, superintendent of the deaf and dumb asylum, and member of the state land commission to treasurer, secretary of state, state supreme court justice, and lieutenant governor. One African American even sat briefly as the governor of Louisiana. A great many more—almost eight hundred—served in the state legislatures. But by far the largest number of black officeholders were to be found at the local level: in counties, cities, smaller municipalities, and militia districts. Although a precise figure is almost impossible to obtain, blacks clearly filled over 1,100 elective or appointive local offices, and they may well have filled as many as 1,400 or 1,500, about 80 percent of which were in rural and small-town settings.[6]

The geography of local black officeholding was shaped by demography, state politics, and the experience of local mobilization. Which is to say that black officeholders were most commonly and widely in evidence where state Republican governments ruled the longest, where black populations were densest, and where organization by the Union League and Republican party had provided direction to leaders and constituents alike. Not surprisingly, this meant the Deep South and particularly the states of South Carolina, Alabama, Mississippi, and Louisiana, though black men also held a significant number of offices in North Carolina and Texas. In Virginia and Tennessee, relatively few blacks held local office and those who did resided chiefly in the urban areas of Richmond, Petersburg, Norfolk, Nashville, Memphis, Knoxville, and Chattanooga. Within individual states, moreover, blacks had their best opportunities to hold local office in counties where at least 40 percent of the population was black, and their best opportunities to hold a number of offices where at least 60 percent of the population was black. Thus, the bases of black officeholding stretched from the cotton plantation counties of east-central Texas; through the

Red River counties and parishes of east Texas and Louisiana; up the Mississippi River counties and parishes of Louisiana, Arkansas, and Mississippi; across much of north-central Mississippi; through the Tennessee Valley, central black belt, and southwest of Alabama; along the northern tier of counties in Florida and the coastal counties of Georgia; through all but northwestern South Carolina; and into coastal and north-central North Carolina. In all, in more than two hundred counties in the former Confederacy at least one black man held local office during Reconstruction, and in more than eighty, at least three did so.

At one time and place or another, a black man occupied virtually every office available at the local level. Black men served as coroners, surveyors, treasurers, tax assessors and collectors, jailors, solicitors, registers of deeds, clerks of court, police officers and marshals, firefighters, and even mayors. But the greatest number (roughly two-thirds of the total), especially in the plantation districts of the Deep South, served as members of county and municipal governing boards, as magistrates and justices of the peace, as election officials and registrars, and as sheriffs and their deputies. In some locales, blacks came to dominate the county governments by claiming majorities on the governing boards and perhaps two-thirds of the remaining offices including sheriff, and whites, according to one disgruntled informant, could at best "try to secure the elections for certain negroes who they thought would make fairly honest officers." In other locales, a black officeholder or two helped more numerous white Republican allies wrest the reins of local power from the hands of the old landed elite. In still others, black officeholders formed part of a contentious, two-party mix.[7]

Wherever black men vied for and assumed local office, the stakes were high. Although sheriffs, magistrates, county commissioners, and registrars might appear to be less consequential officeholders, they in fact represented the formal linchpins of the postemancipation South's emerging political order. For with the petty sovereignties of masters destroyed by the abolition of slavery, local officials became the arbiters and enforcers of social relations and constellations of power still being determined. They established county and municipal regulations; took care of roads and bridges; levied taxes, imposts, and fines; controlled appropriations; designated militia districts and townships; and oversaw boundary disputes. They issued warrants, made arrests, kept armaments, enforced vagrancy statutes, and carried out foreclosures. They assessed property values and collected taxes. They heard civil and criminal cases, selected jurors, and meted out punishments. They created school districts, helped allocate funds, and apprenticed minors and orphans. And they supervised the electoral process from registration to balloting to the counting of votes. They therefore had much to say about the settlement of contract disputes, the resolution of personal injuries, the use of public and private land, the prerogatives of employers and the obligations of employees, the condition of educational and charitable institutions, the fortunes of political parties, and the overall balances of local power: much to say, that is, about the essentials of everyday life for former slaves and their prospects for building stable, just communities.[8]

Elevating black—or for that matter white Republican—officeholders demanded the mobilization of entire communities. In no other way could African Americans successfully overcome the obstacles of inexperience, illiteracy, economic vulnerability, and widespread harassment to secure their objectives in the novel arena of formal politics. When blacks in Wilson County, Tennessee, "voted solid" to elect their candidate as magistrate over four white candidates, making him "the first negro ever elected to any [local] office," another black leader drew an important lesson. The result, he observed, "thoroughly demonstrated . . . the absolute necessity of organization."[9]

Effective organization invariably required an institutional structure tied directly to the conduct of elections and the hierarchy of party politics, and this customarily meant Union Leagues (or their equivalents) and Republican clubs. Through these vehicles eligible voters could be identified and educated, candidates for office could be nominated or advanced for appointment, local grievances could be aired and issues debated, campaigns could be charted, preparations could be made for balloting, and—perhaps most important—some level of protection could be afforded to leaders and the rank-and-file by raising veils of secrecy and either incorporating or establishing paramilitary companies. In Jefferson County, Georgia, where about three-quarters of the population was black, members of a club resembling the Union League pledged not only to ensure the acceptance of their votes at polling places but also to resist the legal or economic harassment of their comrades even if it required battering down the county jail or seizing some of a landlord's property. To many freedmen, the Union League and other semisecret political orders such as the Lone Star Society in Virginia or the Grant Rangers in Georgia were necessary to all public political projects. Requesting authority "to establish Leagues," blacks in Rusk and Panola counties, Texas, told the state Union League president that "there is no better way than that agency to organize the Republican party." [10]

Local activists served as the pivots around which these institutions revolved. Usually in their late twenties and early thirties, often previously enslaved, and grounded by birth or kinship, they boasted one or more attributes that set them apart from most rural freedpeople and that proved indispensable to the life of their new political communities. The great majority had attained functional literacy and many possessed special skills as craftsmen, farmers, squad leaders, teachers, and ministers. Some had joined or aided the Union army during the Civil War; some had accumulated small amounts of real or personal property; and some had attended early freedmen's conventions. Almost all combined strong provincial attachments with an emerging worldliness, and almost all displayed an independence of mind and spirit. Together they struggled to build not just a new political citizenry but a new political culture. Remarking on the progress made along the coast of South Carolina, where mobilization began well before the war had ended, Elizabeth Hyde Botume noted by 1869 that once a black man had joined a political club, "these duties became more absorbing than all else. Every boy considered himself a man at eighteen and every man had some office in his neighborhood which was to him of vast importance even if only that of doorkeeper in their small meetings." [11]

Profiles of these activists suggest less a representative "type" than a social division of politics attuned to the demands and dangers of electioneering in the rural postemancipation South. Thomas M. Allen, an ex-slave shoemaker and Baptist preacher, organized first a Union League chapter and then a Grant Ranger club in Jasper County, Georgia, and "the colored people came to [him] for instructions." It was no wonder. Having attended a freedmen's convention in 1866, Allen also took the *New York Tribune* and other papers, and therefore "found out a great deal" and could tell "them whatever I thought was right." "I said to them that I thought they had been freed by the Yankees and the Union men," Allen explained, "and I thought they ought to vote with them." Mississippi-born George Washington Albright could not match Allen's skills as a tradesman and minister, but by the age of twenty he had acquired substantial experience and tools of his own. A former slave, Albright had learned to read and write and subsequently served as a messenger for the clandestine Lincoln's Loyal League during the war. Thereafter he enrolled in a freedmen's school, became a teacher, and helped organize a black volunteer militia "to keep the common people on top and fight off the . . . attacks of the landlords and former slaveowners." [12]

Jack Johnson, a stone mason and farmer from Laurens County, South Carolina, who "took a great propriety in counseling the people which way to vote," was the only black man in his neighborhood to own a mule, and so "would go 'way off to speeches, and come back and tell the news how the speeches were." In Coosa County, Alabama, Smith Whatley managed to gain a measure of independence by renting land, and, partly as a result, became "the regular one" to distribute ballots. Bully Jack, from Noxubee County, Mississippi, built on his reputation under slavery as "a most powerful physical man, a great foot racer, and an uncommon good worker," to emerge as "a sort of leading man in the neighborhood" after emancipation, going so far as to "form himself into a court, or a judge of a court, and h[o]ld negro courts about." Abram Colby of Greene County, Georgia, combined good fortune, an assortment of skills, and family support with sheer courage in the face of violent intimidation to represent the interests of local freedpeople with whom he was closely connected. Born and raised in the county, Colby had been freed by his owner and father in 1851 and worked variously as a barber, laborer, and minister. Soon after the war, he sought redress from the Freedmen's Bureau for injustices done to the county's African Americans, and, although illiterate, he was able to depend on his son, who had been sent to school, to read and write for him. Pressured by local whites who "said I had influence with the negroes of other counties and had carried the negroes against them," Colby was initially offered $5,000 to become a turncoat. "I told them," Colby testified, "I would not do it if they give me all the county was worth." [13]

Black Republicans relied on men such as these not only to chair meetings, address constituents, do the rounds of campaigning, and rally the faithful, but also to enable eligible blacks to carry out the basic task of voting. It was not an easy assignment, for polling practices of the day left illiterate and economically dependent voters vulnerable to harassment and effective disfranchisement. Polls were sometimes placed at inaccessible locations or on the land of hostile planters. Election supervisors could ask unwarranted questions, make confusing demands, or open and close the polls at will. Members of opposition parties attempted to bribe voters or hand them the wrong tickets. Employers congregated at voting boxes and threatened their employees, while other white landowners and their allies jostled, abused, and assaulted blacks seeking to cast ballots.[14] The problems were especially pronounced—and often intractable—where African Americans composed a minority of the population. In an early election in Crenshaw County, Alabama (20 percent black), the sitting white sheriff summoned men "known for their violence and recklessness in dealing with freedmen" to "crowd around the polling-window and occup[y] all the space behind the ropes, so that every voter had to run the gauntlet of their jeers and threats." "For some time," according to one report, "they made every colored man take off his hat and bow, before they could pass" and then assisted employers who watched to see whether their hands had voted.[15]

Union League and Republican party activists therefore had to prepare carefully for election day lest their other efforts be nullified. They had to petition military commanders and Republican governors to appoint favorable (and dismiss hostile) election officials and to designate suitable polling sites, particularly if Democrats still controlled county governing boards. They had to get their voters to the polls, at times over a distance of many miles, and make sure that those voters received the correct tickets. They had to minimize the opportunities for bribery, manipulation, and intimidation. And they had to oversee the counting of ballots. Voting required, in essence, a military operation. Activists often called a meeting of fellow leaguers or club members the night before an election to provide instructions and materials. The chairman of the Tunica County, Mississippi, Republican executive committee had men come to the town of Hernando from all over the county on the day before the election and distribute tickets to those political clubs meeting that night. At times groups of black voters might spend the night before an election on a safe plantation or in the woods, perhaps sending a small party ahead to check for possible traps or ambushes, and then move out at first light to arrive at the polls well before their opponents or "rebel spies" could gather. Henry Frazer, who organized for the Republican party in Barbour County, Alabama, claimed that he went out with as many as "450 men and camped at the side of the road" before going into the town of Eufaula at eight in the morning where they would "stand in a body until they got a chance to vote."[16]

At all events, it was imperative that black voters traveled to the polling sites collectively and in large numbers, for those who arrived individually or in small, unorganized groups could most readily be, as one east Texan put it, "browbeaten . . . intimidated [or] driven from the polls." Most often, they would mobilize and march "in a solid column"—as they had been preparing to do for weeks—sometimes wearing similar attire or emblems, frequently carrying "flags and banners," sticks and corn stalks, projecting a martial spirit and demeanor. When necessary or possible, they might be accompanied by armed guards on foot or horseback, or, in some places, details of state militia. Once at the polls, they might then form a line between their ticket distributor and the ballot box, making it difficult for hostile parties to intercede. Facing particularly intense harassment during the fall of 1868, Abram Colby of Greene County, Georgia, organized his followers into companies and, on election day in November, marched company after company to the polls. He succeeded in carrying the local contest for the Republicans.[17]

Protecting black Republican voters from white intimidation was only the most obvious goal of such martial organization and display, however. There was also the need to prod the timid and punish the apathetic or disloyal within their own communities. Activists learned early that elections could only be carried by securing overwhelming allegiance to the Republican party and then by ensuring that the eligible voters overcame fear or inertia to cast ballots. Political parades and torchlight processions during election campaigns and on the eve of polling—often with black men dressed in their club uniforms, beating drums, "hallooing, hooping," and, on occasion, riding full gallop through the streets—thereby served several purposes: to inspire enthusiasm, advertise numbers and resolve, and coax the participation of those who might otherwise abstain. Where coaxing proved insufficient, more coercive tactics could be deployed. Union League members in a North Carolina county, upon learning of three or four black men who "didn't mean to vote," threatened to "whip them" and "made them go." In another county, "some few colored men who declined voting" were, in the words of a white conservative, "bitterly perse-cut[ed]." One suffered insults, the destruction of his fences and crops, and "other outrages." [18]

Especially harsh reprisals could be brought against blacks who aligned with conservatives and Democrats, for they were generally regarded not merely as opponents but as "traitors." As black Mississippian Robert Gleed put it, "[W]e don't believe they have a right to acquiesce with a party who refuse to recognize their right to participate in public affairs." In the rural hinterlands of Portsmouth, Virginia, black Republicans attacked "colored conservatives" at a prayer meeting and beat two of them badly. In southside Virginia's Campbell County, a black man who betrayed the Union League was tied up by his heels and suspended from a tree for several hours until he agreed to take an oath of loyalty. Two "conservative negroes" in Lincoln County, North Carolina, had their houses stoned and doors broken down, and one, who had previously belonged to the Union League, was told that "joining the conservative club was a commission of per-jury" and was threatened with incarceration; he relented and "went back to the society." The other "continued his connection with the conservative club" and the night after the election had his house sur-rounded by black leaguers who, in a further ritual of community intim-idation—"with tin pans and horns, guns and pistols"—cried that "they had come to ride him on a rail, that he had voted himself back into slavery." Such disciplinary compass and persistence were not un-usual. Monday, the foreman of a South Carolina rice plantation who, along with several other blacks, voted Democratic at a recent election, acknowledged that every one of them "had been punished." One saw his colt killed, one was "bombarded in his cabin," and one had his rice crop lifted. Monday himself lost a cow. "Ef I didn' vote de 'Publi-can ticket," he informed his Democratic employer, "I couldn' make dese niggers work. I couldn't do nothin' 'tall wid 'em." [19]

Monday's troubles with the rice workers in his charge suggested that effective imposition of political discipline depended on strong community backing. Indeed, violent retribution was only one of sev-eral sanctions—and not necessarily the last or most effective—that could be directed against those who, in the eyes of kin and neighbors, either faltered in or betrayed their political responsibilities. Young and old, male and female served on the court of local opinion and helped carry out the punishments. Family members might be cast out, friends might be shunned or subjected to public humiliation, and preachers might be driven from the pulpit. One black man living outside Augusta, Georgia, went so far as to insist that he would cut the throat of any son "willing to be a Democrat." But in a kin-oriented world in which subsistence was precarious and white patrons quixotic, social isolation could be a devastating, and potentially lethal, sentence in its own right. Speaking of an "intelligent colored man that was on our ticket," a white Mississippi Democrat found that the man "was ostracized to such an extent that he got back among the negroes in a hurry." "[I]t was," he reckoned, "positively dangerous for any negro to pronounce himself a democrat in my county." [20]

Women, the hubs around which kin and community networks ordinarily grew, were particularly well placed to influence mobilization and discipline, together with conduct in the political arenas that officially denied them direct participation. Here we can see how dependent the electoral sphere was on other spheres of political and social life, and how the social division of black politics overlaid the very boundaries of those spheres. For women not only attended rallies and meetings and often registered their sentiments; they also became so deeply involved in the creation and expression of partisan loyalties that the vote could itself be regarded as something of a household and family property. Some gathered and transmitted necessary intelligence; some taught rural schools; and some helped to defend public assemblies from attack. Where possible, a good many more accompanied voting-age men to the ballot box, providing added cover, showing the depth of community support, and steeling the nerves of those in the male ranks. Commenting on what he considered the absurdity of "unlettered blacks" going up and "voting on questions of state interest," a Tennessee planter could scowl that on election day he stayed home while his "negroes went to the polls." To make matters worse, the "negro women went, too," leaving his wife as "her own cook and chambermaid." [21]

Yet it was as enforcers that black women may well have made their most powerful and distinctive contribution to the developing political culture of their communities. Manipulating gender conventions and the expectations of courtship and sexual favor, they both shamed reluctant menfolk into performing their political duties and wreaked the most intimate and humiliating vengeance on those who strayed from the fold. The northern planter and politician Albert T. Morgan, who worked closely with freedpeople in Yazoo County, Mississippi, told of a particularly revealing episode during the election campaign of 1868 when Grant and Colfax badges became "the cause of domestic troubles almost without number." "[I]f a freedman, having obtained one, lacked the courage to wear it at home or on the plantation in the presence of 'ole marsa and missus' or of 'the overseer,'" Morgan remembered, "his wife would often take it from him and bravely wear it upon her own breast." And if "the husband refused to surrender it" or "hid it from her or locked it up," she might walk "as many as twenty or thirty miles" to "buy, beg, or borrow one, and thus equipped return and wear it openly, in defiance of husband, master, mistress, or overseer." [22]

Black men who voted the Democratic ticket or in other ways chose to support the Democratic party suffered even more summary rebukes from women, who were best able to sever ties of family and community where they seemed most firmly knotted. In many places, such a male turncoat could not "get any countenance from a colored sweetheart," and, if married, might be denied bed, board, and field labor—might, in fact, be outright abandoned. A black Democrat in Opelika, Alabama, testified "about 30 or 40 colored women" who "belonged to a club" and went "around and talk[ed] to the Democratic men." "I know women today," he insisted, "who are away from their husbands because they voted the Democratic ticket." As a crowning, raucous act, black women could well spark and head up local crowds organized to assault and drive a traitor into exile. "The negroes are as intolerant of opposition as the whites," a conservative white South Carolinian observed at the end of Reconstruction, ostracizing, expelling, and even killing "all of their own" who "would turn democrats." And, by his lights, the "women are worse than the men, refusing to talk to or marry a renegade, and aiding in mobbing him." [23]

It was, therefore, a significant measure of the success achieved by grassroots mobilization—in educative, protective, and disciplinary forms—that during the early phases of Congressional Reconstruction black Democrats were so few. They were most likely to be found in cities and smaller towns working as barbers, waiters, and personal servants: that is, physically cut off from the mass of freedpeople and engaged in occupations wholly reliant on white patrons. "As a general thing," Mississippi carpetbagger and governor Adelbert Ames claimed, "it is only where a negro has been working with the same man for a very long space of time—a relation found to exist chiefly in the villages—that he votes as his employer desires." This seems to have been true in Warren County, North Carolina, for when the local newspaper listed the names of blacks who supported the conservatives in 1868, more than half of the thirty-one resided in the county seat of Warrenton. The remainder could be found scattered across three other militia districts.[24]

In the countryside, Democrats might attract the allegiance of black voters in counties and districts where whites formed decisive population majorities and the Democratic party was well organized, or in locales remote from railroads where freedpeople fell "almost entirely under the influence of the whites." There they might also attract the votes of blacks who, owing to special circumstances, were inordinately dependent on powerful white landowners: blacks who continued to live on the estates of longtime former owners; blacks who had been left land and other property at their old master's death; blacks who were accustomed to seeking and receiving assistance from whites in times of need; and blacks who could not pry themselves free of extreme economic subordination. A planter in Claiborne County, Mississippi, describing the harassment to which black Democrats were subjected, bluntly drove home the point. "I have five or six negroes on a plantation that I venture to say will vote side by side with me always, because they are released from that intimidation that formerly existed. . . . They are dependent on me for every morsel they eat."[25]

Even so, black allegiance to the Democratic party proved extremely thin, extracted principally by bribery or (more likely) threats from men less vulnerable to retaliation from black Republicans. In most instances, white pressure would discourage blacks from voting altogether rather than prompt them to vote the Democratic ticket. Only a handful of blacks supported the Democrats "to keep on the good side of white people, to keep from being interfered with," explained William Ford, a north Alabama freedmen—but because of black intimidation "when they can't vote for a republican they don't vote at all." Appearing before a congressional committee, a Freedmen's Bureau agent who served at three different posts in rural Mississippi between August 1867 and December 1868 put the matter succinctly. Asked if any black men aligned with the Democrats from instinct, he replied: "Only from the instinct of self-preservation."[26]

❖

The community support necessary to conduct electoral politics found its institutional anchors not in the clubs and committees attached to the Republican party, but in black religious congregations. This was most readily apparent in the urban South, where various African churches had been organized longest and where the postemancipation withdrawal from white denominations occurred with breathtaking speed. Even before the Civil War had ended, black Baptist and Methodist churches in Union-occupied cities provided the settings for political assemblies, and by the late summer of 1865 they were hosting the first state freedmen's conventions: at the African Methodist Episcopal (AME) churches in Nashville and Raleigh, the Zion Church in Charleston, and the AME Zion Church in Mobile. Soon they would be the sites of Union League meetings and Republican party convocations.[27]

In the countryside, the process of church formation—and reconstitution—was more complex and protracted, though in the end perhaps even more consequential. On the one hand, organized Christianity had made fewer and generally less even inroads among rural slaves. Northern observers and missionaries (black and white) in the early postemancipation South seemed almost unanimous both in recognizing the freedpeople's intense faith and spirituality and in disparaging the substance of what was depicted as their religious practice. "Ignorance," "infidelity," "heathenism," and especially "superstition" were the terms most frequently used to describe the freedpeople's customs of worship and their understandings of the Bible and Christian doctrine, and to explain the great challenges that missionaries faced. Charles Stearns, the northerner who took up a plantation in Columbia County, Georgia, was typically scornful. "A more melancholy misnomer than that of the Christian religion, as applied to the heathenish observances of the plantation blacks, cannot be conceived," he recorded. But Stearns and others clearly identified an African-American religious culture that assimilated Christianity to a larger body of folk beliefs, and did so in ways that varied from place to place.[28]

At the same time, even those rural freedpeople who claimed church membership usually had belonged to biracial churches presided over by whites and in most instances lacked the opportunities and resources to construct churches of their own quickly. Separation, particularly among black Baptists, therefore occurred on a congregation by congregation basis and might take several years to complete. In the rural districts of central Georgia, blacks had only a handful of church structures by 1867 and not a single one in at least three entire counties. In the Mississippi Delta county of Issaquena, it was 1875 before blacks (who outnumbered whites by nearly nine to one) succeeded in establishing the Pleasant Green Church on Dunbar Ridge, their very first. Small wonder that black laborers often sought to use their limited bargaining leverage to persuade employers to build—or permit to have built—houses of worship on their plantations. And small wonder that chapels such as these were, at best, plainly framed and rudely furnished cabins, with leaky roofs, glassless windows, and crude flooring.[29]

During the earliest years of freedom, rural congregations for the most part improvised as well as they could, gathering and holding services in the old quarters, in dilapidated plantation sheds, in abandoned crossroads or village shacks, or in clearings in the woods. Freedpeople on one Louisiana estate met to worship in half of a double cabin so that, in the words of a visitor, "you had your choice—you could visit the family or go to church." In the eastern section of Lincoln County, North Carolina, they assembled "near the river, in a rough building made of old field pine poles, and with an earthen floor." In this, they built directly on the experiences of slave folk religion, which grew in small praise houses and brush arbors and defied rigid denominational categories. Too impoverished to support a full-time minister, most congregations relied on circuit riders and itinerants who arrived for preaching once or twice a month, and, more regularly, on elders and exhorters from their own ranks who led meetings on Sunday and perhaps on one or two evenings during the week. They also may have worshipped on occasion with other congregations nearby, even those of different denominations, and attended large interdenominational camp meetings that could draw hundreds of the black faithful from miles around.[30]

Yet if rural black congregations often lacked the visible structure and clear denominational orientation that we commonly associate with "the church," they were bound unmistakably to the localized lattices of kinship, work, and obligation. Composed chiefly of interconnected families laboring on a single plantation or on adjacent plantations and farms—and sometimes dominated by one or two extended clans— they were, in effect, the very embodiments of reconstituted African-American communities. Indeed, denominational affiliations and rivalries were as likely to be reflections of specific kinship networks as of doctrinal differences. Commenting on the difficulties of attracting freedpeople to his services in Port Royal, South Carolina, the American Missionary Association minister Augustine Roots noted that "their ties to the old places and old associations are strong," and "the watchmen and elders" would call those who strayed to account, in one case "scolding" a plantation foreman "for being absent from 'the church' to attend service." Identifying "a strong sectarian Baptist current which sets against other brethren in Christ," Roots concluded "that the colored people understand the doctrine of *close communion* perfectly well."[31]

Given the still skeletal associational life—fraternal and benevolent societies—to be found in much of the postemancipation rural South, the churches and congregations became virtual community centers, assuming a range of vital functions. Almost invariably they established Sunday schools and welcomed other educational activities, disseminated news and information, helped resolve disputes among members, defined collective norms, and brought sanctions against their transgressors. They offered, as best as circumstances allowed, assistance to congregants suffering illness or special hardship and proper burials to the deceased. And they provided unique forums for discussion, debate, and the fashioning of sacred and secular opinion that lent influence and authority to women as well as men. There were, to be sure, congregations in which women were "allowed no part in the church meetings," and few if any in which women were permitted formally to preach. But females normally composed the majority (and often the sizeable majority) of congregants, and there is a good deal of evidence for what one scholar has called "dual-sex politics": a structure of power that could institutionalize a base for women who, owing to age, spiritual maturity, and community service, had earned special deference and respect. A black male Baptist acknowledged as much in complaining about the "church mothers," "gospel mothers," and "old sheppards"—veritable "officials" of the congregations who were "quite outside of the New Testament arrangement." They "claim to be under the special influence of the spirit and exercise an authority, greater in many cases than that of the ministers," he groused, and "woe to that disciple who is so unfortunate as to be out of their favor." [32]

Congregations and churches, therefore, had an unrivaled ability to mobilize community sentiment and action and to unify rural African Americans across district and county lines. To this extent, they were by definition political institutions, and most everywhere they devoted organizational resources to partisan ends. In them newspapers, proclamations, contracts, and legal documents were read aloud for the edification of illiterate congregants; in them local, state, and national issues bearing on their future were considered and argued over; in them local Union Leagues often conducted business; in them Republican party activists and returning black veterans came to speak; and in them the bonds of political solidarity could be forged. Some ministers and congregations sought to steer clear of electoral politics in an effort to cultivate peaceful relations with whites, but this was not a choice that most thought possible to make. The AME Church officially regarded politics as indispensable to preserving and expanding the domain of freedom, as an "imperative duty"; and it eagerly placed the time and talents of its organizers in the service of the Republican party. Baptists left the initiative to individual congregations, which without much exception determined to enter the fray. [33]

But congregational embrace of electoral politics expressed a deeper popular sensibility that drew no clear distinction between the sacred and the secular, the spiritual and the political. The churches did not simply open their doors to the world of politics; they assimilated politics into their very rhythms of worship and community life. Nothing better testified to such an integrated worldview than the tirades of white landowners and politicians about the "religious fanaticism" of the freedpeople. Like the Louisiana sugar planter William J. Minor, they complained about "the designing preachers" who attracted freedpeople "from all parts of the country" to twice-weekly meetings that lasted "until morning"—meetings where the "women become hysterical" and the laborers generally grew "demoralized." A white lawyer from Barnwell, South Carolina, claimed that "the great mass of our plantation hands" relished preaching, funerals, and political speeches in no special order. "They are of a very religious turn of mind, . . . a superstitious people, and believe strongly in the spiritual world," he observed, and then added immediately that "they are organized into leagues" and that "those leagues are opened by prayer, for the preachers are generally there, and they are counseled as they love their immortal souls to vote no other than the straight republican ticket."[34]

The prominent place that black ministers and exhorters occupied in local social and political life exemplified this sensibility and set of interconnections. For the very qualities that lent individuals spiritual authority in their communities also tended to thrust them forth as leaders in the secular arenas of politics. Working principally as farmers, croppers, and laborers, rarely having the benefits of formal education and training, they often showed independence of mind, special fluency of speech, a facility for conducting call-and-response communication, a folk wisdom, and an ability to resolve conflict. Most could also read and write, and probably enjoyed rich local kinship ties. Thus, former South Carolina governor James L. Orr thought that "the native leaders" in his home county of Anderson "constitute the leaders of the colored race," and although he could not "say that the political leaders have been preachers," he did believe, significantly, that "most of the preachers are politicians." At the same time, black preachers needed to reflect as well as shape popular sentiments, and missteps in one arena would likely compromise their standing in another. When a preacher in Madison County, Mississippi, voted Democrat, the congregants "had no more to do with him; turned him off," and "would not hear him preach or do anything else any more for us."[35]

The encapsulation of spiritual and political energies by congregations and churches, and the intensive mobilization it allowed, had a very tangible logic: the reconstitution of black communities was increasingly seen to require institutional power at the local level. By the time Congressional Reconstruction had enfranchised black men in the former Confederate states, freedpeople had obtained a substantial—and unsettling—education in the workings of local "democracy."

They had passed, in effect, from slavery to a form of subjecthood that offered limited standing in civil and political society. No longer bound to owners as individuals and, at least in theory, able to make contracts, form families, own property, and sue in court, freedpeople nonetheless encountered a new system of group dependency legislated in the main by former slaveholders acting under the reconciliation program of President Andrew Johnson. An assortment of laws enacted by state assemblies and local governing bodies—laws familiar to most rural societies in the wake of servile emancipations—hedged in the prospects of freed laborers and left them few avenues of redress that their employers did not control. Vagrancy ordinances, apprenticeship laws, antienticement statutes, stiff licensing fees, heavy taxes, the eradication of common-use rights on unenclosed land, and the multiplication of designated "crimes" against property constructed a distinct status of black subservience and a legal apparatus that denied freedpeople access to economic independence. Citing the "rules and regulations" issued by the "high and mighty police juries of the country parishes," which demanded that "negroes must do this" and "negroes must do that," the radical *New Orleans Tribune* thus saw in the late summer of 1865 "an entering wedge to divide the population of the state into two classes with separate interests, rights, and privileges." Where the Freedmen's Bureau managed to establish offices and "Freedmen's Courts," former slaves might challenge the prerogatives of white landowners and find a modicum of justice; elsewhere they met planters and their clients, many of them ex-rebels, who held the local offices and judgeships and sat on the local juries.[36]

The consequences threatened the integrity of freed households, families, and kinship networks and therefore the basic relations necessary to placing freedom on a stable foundation. County courts, governing boards, magistrates, grand and trial juries, and sheriffs—all elected by white men who had their political rights restored or had received pardons from the President—reflected the concerns (and usually the direct interests) of landowners and employers. They bound out black children designated as "orphans" (generally to former masters), failed to prosecute acts of personal violence, ruled for employers in contract disputes, taxed dogs and confiscated firearms, debarred testimony by African Americans against white people in legal proceedings, imposed excessive fines and jail terms for minor infractions, arrested freedpeople who

refused to work for white employers, and harassed those who sought
to supplement their subsistence. "Justices of the Peace attach and seize
property of freedmen *that under the state law is exempt*," charged a
Freedmen's Bureau agent in Huntsville, Texas, while "sheriffs serve
writs, make arrests, [and] seize crops for rent." In Avoyelles Parish,
Louisiana, a freedwoman and three of her husband's relatives were
indicted in early 1867 "for going into a field and picking from the
ground a few walnuts," and although a lawyer induced the husband
to give him a note for $150 to mount a defense, the prospects for
acquittal were dim. "If this is to be settled according to the manner
of disposing of such cases in this parish heretofore," a federal official
predicted, "these parties will certainly be sent to prison, perhaps to
the penitentiary."[37]

Rural blacks who sought to protect themselves and their families
and gain legal remedy discovered a host of onerous hurdles, unless
they had the support of a white patron. There were burdensome lawyers' fees and court costs, hostile judges, unsympathetic juries, and the
likelihood of further white retaliation. A "Committee of Freedmen"
in the cotton belt of eastern Georgia, complaining that they can "obtain
very little justice . . . as the civil courts are now managed," poignantly
explained that while white men, "mostly rebels," regularly drove them
off without pay as soon as their crops were laid by, they were "too
poor" to hire a lawyer and unable "to incur the expense" of traveling
to Augusta (forty-five miles distant) to place their grievances before
the Freedmen's Bureau. In central Alabama, freedmen had been persuaded to withdraw lawsuits entered against their employers for nonpayment of wages because they lacked money sufficient to "carry it
through." One Freedmen's Bureau agent, struggling to assist similarly
aggrieved black laborers in Wilkinson County, Georgia, found it "impossible to procure anything like justice," and acknowledged the delight of those "who believe blacks dont have rights whites are bound
to respect."[38]

The spirit of *Dred Scott* did indeed prevail in the South of Presidential Reconstruction and would surely have defined the postemancipation landscape were it not for the advent of Radicalism and the accompanying mobilizations of freedpeople. Together, they pushed the spirit
into retreat and summoned new forces and possibilities that could

hardly have been to the liking of those who had no respect for the rights of black folk.

❖

White conservatives of the time and their apologists of a later day had a term for it: "Negro rule." It captured in the most direct way their view that the dreaded revolution of the middle period came neither with the military defeat of the Confederacy nor with the abolition of slavery but with the enfranchisement of the freedmen and their participation in state and local government. Nothing seemed more menacing or illegitimate, nothing more vindictive or humiliating, than the installation in positions of official political power of former slaves, of abject and "ignorant" dependents belonging to an "inferior race." In an inversion that even Christmas revelry never conjured, the ruled had become the rulers and the rulers the ruled.

So deeply did this image of inversion and usurpation leave an imprint on the story of Reconstruction that serious historians still feel the need to address and expunge it. And they have certainly mounted an impressive rebuttal. Outside of South Carolina, they show, blacks never dominated either the executive, legislative, or judicial branches of any southern state, and in South Carolina, the executive and judiciary always remained under white control. Statewide, African Americans were most likely to be found in "ceremonial" positions (lieutenant governor or secretary of state), and they rarely chaired important legislative committees. On the local level, the best that blacks could generally hope for was a significant share of county and parish offices, and then usually the ones offering the least police authority or access to entrenched wealth. The prospects for using state power to carry through a social revolution faltering in Congress were, in short, virtually nonexistent, and most black officeholders appeared to pursue relatively moderate objectives.[39]

Yet we must not to allow the racist fears and condescension that the term "Negro rule" embodied to blind us to the context in which it acquired meaning. For in a manner that only one other revolution before the twentieth century approached (that in St. Domingue), Radical Reconstruction occasioned a massive transfer of power at the state and local levels. Whereas during the period from disunion through Presidential Reconstruction there effectively occurred a *shift within* the slaveholding elite, from younger planters-on-the-make who had aligned with the secessionist faction of the Democratic party to older, more established planters who had aligned with the Whig party, during Radical Reconstruction there was a *shift away* from the former slave-holding elite toward a collection of groups who had been outsiders to the formal arenas of southern politics. They included white northerners who had served in the U.S. Army and Freedmen's Bureau, had taken up planting or merchandising, or had engaged in teaching and mission-ary work; white southerners who had been Unionists or unenthusiastic Confederates, had been nonslaveholders and small slaveholders, or had lived beyond the immediate orbit of the planter class; black northern-ers, some having escaped from slavery, who had acquired education and skills, had joined the Union military effort, or had served as minis-ters and missionaries for the AME Church; and black southerners who either had been free before the Civil War or had gained their freedom as a result of it. Together, they were substantially less wealthy, less experienced politically, and less committed to perpetuating the old plantation order. And together, they usually owed their positions to black votes.[40]

The emergence of genuine bases of black power was, therefore, only the most spectacular of these transitions, but it was also unexampled. It occurred not on the periphery, but in the very heart of what had been the Old Regime, and it simultaneously staunched the efforts of local elites to enforce new forms of black submission while enabling freedmen and women to negotiate the terms of freedom from new circumstances of strength. Black power, which took shape in en-claves—generally a county or a number of adjacent counties scattered across the plantation districts of the Deep South—always showed the marks of particular conditions, experiences, and leaders. At the same time, it revealed a widespread impulse to use the instruments of official politics to achieve community reconstitution and self-governance, and to imagine the electoral process as a vehicle of community definition and empowerment. Not the destruction of established institutions or the redistribution of private property but the pursuit of simple justice proved to be its predominant device. Ostensibly modest in design, in the postemancipation rural South this agenda was both radical and consequential.

Few enclaves of black power more clearly displayed the marks of local history or the revolutionary repercussions of the moment than the one in McIntosh County, Georgia. At the southern end of the antebellum rice kingdom and home to some of the Old South's wealthiest planter aristocrats, the county's staple-crop economy unraveled during and immediately after the Civil War and, by the spring of 1868, experienced a drastic recomposition of its political power structure. In place of the grandees, their kinsmen, and white clients, black men now served as county clerk, county ordinary, justice of the peace, constable, city marshal, and election registrar, and represented the county in the general assembly and state senate. Before long they would also serve as sheriff, deputy sheriff, coroner, election manager, and city alderman, not to mention as jurors and bailiffs. A dense and generationally rooted black population that outnumbered whites by a factor of nearly three, the departure of planter families in the face of wartime federal incursions, and the effects of Sherman's Special Field Orders No. 15 (which had set aside land for blacks) made possible this stunning transition; a remarkable and energetic leader from afar proved to be the lightning rod.[41]

Tunis G. Campbell was one of many northern black men who brought considerable talents and resources to the task of reconstructing the ex-slave South, but few built such a formidable local following or invited such intense controversy. Born in New Jersey in 1812 and educated at a white Episcopal school in neighboring New York, Campbell became active in both the antislavery and black convention movements, converted to Methodism, and worked for more than a decade as a hotel steward. Too old to enlist for active military service, he set out for Union-occupied Port Royal, South Carolina, in the summer of 1863 with the endorsement of Secretary of War Edwin Stanton and more than three thousand dollars of his own money, hoping to assist in educating the freedpeople and promoting a biracial democracy. Commissioned in the spring of 1865 as the superintendent of the Georgia Sea Islands and already convinced of the need for "separatism for strength," Campbell then established freed colonies on St. Catherine's and Sapelo Islands with their own governments, militia companies, and schools, and, when it became necessary, helped mobilize settlers to fend off the restoration of their lands to the original white owners. But federal harassment eventually persuaded Campbell to abandon the islands and to seek a new base on the mainland of McIntosh County, where he and many of his followers could be found when Congress initiated Radical Reconstruction.[42]

Campbell had a keen understanding of the essentials of political power and the aspirations of freed communities. Advancing $1,000, he leased a 1,250 acre plantation from a Union sympathizer and divided it among black families who would control the plots and pay an annual rent in kind. He wrote a constitution and organized the BelleVille Farmers Association to function much like a local government with elected officials. And he gained appointment as an election registrar, thereby enrolling and educating prospective black voters in McIntosh and two adjoining counties; the potential of the fivefold registration advantage that blacks subsequently enjoyed was not lost on him. By the summer of 1867, a Freedmen's Bureau agent found the colony in "a most promising condition" economically and the hundred-odd denizens preparing to erect a schoolhouse. In November, Campbell was selected as a delegate to the state constitutional convention, and the following April Campbell's son was elected to the statehouse while Campbell himself won election as state senator and local justice of the peace. The rice planter Frances Butler Leigh saw in these results the "most absolute control" that Campbell exercised over McIntosh County blacks.[43]

Although Campbell's control was hardly absolute, he did come to wield enormous influence. Not only as leader of the BelleVille colony, as election registrar, and as justice of the peace, but also as an elder in the AME Zion Church, he could play the roles most closely attuned to the needs of rural freedpeople and speak a language that resonated with their political sensibilities. Frequently calling county blacks together to answer questions about labor relations, counsel them about contracting, encourage them to "save their money so that they may buy homes," and instruct them as to their political duties, he seemed to mix practical advice and "good republican doctrine" with a spiritual cadence and fervor. Equally impervious to bribery or intimidation, Campbell thereby won deep and abiding personal support (one federal official claimed that his followers "almost worship him") and used it to build a political machine and grassroots organization, replete with a citizens' militia company that strongly resembled a chapter of the Union League. While Republican prospects in the State of Georgia and most black initiatives at the local level there either began to flounder or meet strong conservative resistance, black power in McIntosh County continued to grow and become more firmly entrenched.[44]

Nowhere were the implications more evident or irritating to white planters than in Campbell's justice's court. With two black constables to assist him, and eventually a black sheriff and deputy sheriff to lend added muscle, Campbell provided black laborers with new leverage in their relations with white employers. Showing no patience for the mistreatment, insults, swindles, and personal abuse to which the freedpeople were customarily subjected, he had the accused arrested, brought before his bench, and, if found guilty, fined. Not surprisingly, local planters became indignant and charged that Campbell "administered justice with a high hand and happy disregard of the law." "[H]e is tyrannical overbearing and determines questions not upon principles of law but by his individual prejudice and caprice," one scowled; and his "teachings" are "calculate[d] to destroy the efficiency of labor in this section and inaugurate a reign of terror." For their part, freedpeople often left the plantations "en masse" to attend Campbell's court and associated political meetings and, by one account, commonly returned with "a disposition to refuse to enter into contracts, or if already made to violate them." It would not be long before McIntosh County whites launched a series of vindictive, and ultimately successful, strikes against Campbell. But it would be years before black political power in the county was fully dislodged, and never would there be a return to the old order. During the early twentieth century there was an atmosphere of moderation in race relations and an economic landscape in which three of four black families owned their homes.[45]

Mississippi presented a very different political map, for if McIntosh County was an exception to the local experience of Reconstruction in most of Georgia, it had many more analogues in the Magnolia state. No former Confederate state gave rise to as many enclaves of black political power or to as many local black officeholders. Home of Jefferson Davis, the rich Natchez "nabobs," and many of the largest cotton plantations to be found in the antebellum South, Mississippi seemed to epitomize Black Reconstruction as much as it did the cotton kingdom of slavery times. Stretching from Wilkinson and Adams counties in the south to De Soto and Panola counties in the north, the bases of black political strength ran principally along the Mississippi River and through the Yazoo-Mississippi Delta, but also spread into the northeast sections of the state to include Monroe, Oktibbeha, Pontotoc, and Chickasaw counties. In counties such as these, blacks may have come to hold two-thirds of the offices.[46]

Unlike coastal Georgia and South Carolina, black political achievements in Mississippi did not benefit from the effects of either generationally rooted slave communities or war-related land reform: the social and economic development of Mississippi was a product of the four antebellum decades (and of the interregional slave trade) and the federal government had fewer than fifty thousand acres of rebel-owned land under its control at war's end. Yet the early appearance of Yankee troops, the early experiments with free labor in the lower Mississippi Valley, the importance of black troops in the early army of occupation, and the work of effective Union League organizers simultaneously hastened political mobilization in the river counties and put an unusually large contingent of carpetbaggers on the scene. This, together with a substantial number of counties boasting heavy black population majorities (26 of 74 counties were at least 60 percent black), helped bring the radical faction of the Republican party to statewide power under the leadership of Union army general Adelbert Ames. And Ames initially used his executive and military authority to notable effect: appointing blacks to local office, demanding that they be regarded as "competent jurors," and using troops to protect black voting rights.[47]

Panola County, situated in the northwestern corner of the state only a few miles from the banks of the Mississippi River, seemed to exemplify the process of local political revolution. Blacks accounted for six of ten county residents, and for even greater majorities in most of the election precincts. A garrison of black troops had been stationed there in the late summer and fall of 1865 and they appear to have emboldened freedpeople before being removed. And a trio of determined white Republicans, two of whom hailed from Massachusetts and had purchased a large plantation, helped establish an active Union League and advance the cause of voter registration. But the first stunning signs of change were to be seen in the jury box, where black men made their initial appearance during the November term of 1869. Soon thereafter, it became the "custom" for jurors to be equally divided between the races. When local elections were finally held in 1871 (the ratification of the Radical constitution having been delayed), blacks then began to turn their numerical advantages to good effect. They immediately succeeded in claiming two of five seats on the governing board of supervisors, at least three positions as magistrate and two as constable, and both of the county's seats in the state legislature. Two years later, after another round of elections, they claimed three of five seats on the board of supervisors.[48]

Other river and Delta counties and a few counties on the Alabama border to the east experienced much the same political results during the early 1870s. In Claiborne County, amid a Republican sweep, three of five supervisors, several justices of the peace and constables, and the sheriff were black. In Madison County, grand and petit juries were "mostly composed" of blacks and a local white complained that "they had a board of supervisors there . . . not one of whom could write his name." In Monroe County, blacks served as magistrates, treasurer, state legislators, and sheriff while dominating the board of supervisors, with one of their number—a former slave and preacher—chosen as board president. In Issaquena County, blacks eventually held all five seats on the board of supervisors. And in Warren County, with Vicksburg the county seat, blacks would hold the office of sheriff, circuit clerk, treasurer, and justice of the peace and briefly control four of five supervisory seats. When a correspondent for the *Christian Recorder* arrived in Greenville, Mississippi, in May 1871, he marveled that "there were two juries empanelled with about two-thirds colored men" and noted that "the courthouse yard was crowded with the descendants of Africa." Four years later, a visitor to Leflore County found that nine of eleven justices of the peace were "negroes" and "white property-holders are compelled to appear and submit to their judgment on questions of law, upon which sometimes great interest depends." Looking back on this period in Bolivar County, a white state senator recalled that "the twelve jurors were often negroes, with a negro clerk of court, negro lawyers in the courtroom, and all witnesses negro with the court deputies [and] almost every justice of the peace of the county negroes." A total of thirteen counties, composing about one-third of Mississippi's black population, elected black sheriffs.[49]

With the levers of local office in their grasp, black Republicans, with the support of some of their white allies, moved to adjust the balances of power and shift important resources toward their communities. They generally raised taxes—in some cases forcing plantation land onto the market—initiated beneficial building projects, established and aided charitable institutions, and provided for the educational opportunities envisioned at the Radical constitutional convention by constructing "colored" schools, hiring teachers, increasing salaries, and purchasing basic supplies. Even a white critic of "Negro rule" had to concede that many of these efforts were "extraordinarily successful." Most of all, they curtailed the arbitrary and coercive power of white landowners, bringing perpetrators to heel and lending substance to the notion of civil equality. Appointed a justice of the peace in Adams County by General Ames in April 1869, the former slave John R. Lynch discovered that his duties were even more critical than he had supposed. With original jurisdiction in petty civil cases and in criminal cases below the grade of felony, he could sit as a committing magistrate, examine witnesses, and decide whether testimony sufficed to bind the accused over to a grand jury and fix bail. Little wonder that some of Lynch's constituents "magnified" his position far beyond its official description and determined to seize on the smallest offense to "come to law." "To them," Lynch observed, "this was something that was entirely new, and they were anxious to avail themselves of such a glorious privilege"—and the expected sympathy that would flow from "a colored man . . . in charge of the office." [50]

The winds of political revolution did not seem to sweep through Warren County, North Carolina, as turbulently as they did through Warren County, Mississippi. Federal armies had not marched through eastern North Carolina and voters there never elevated a black man to the office of sheriff. But the cotton, tobacco, and grain-growing county had been one of the most rabidly secessionist in the state during the late winter of 1861 and the potential consequences of Radical Reconstruction were not lost on the conservative *Warrenton Indicator*. The editors reeled, in 1868, at the spectacle of "depraved adventurers and ignorant negroes" taking seats at the state constitutional convention "once occupied by the most illustrious citizens," rejected the principle of black suffrage, and fretted at the prospect of black judges and increased taxes on real and personal property. They could hardly have greeted the resulting black political accession with much relief. Beginning in the summer of 1868, well over fifty black men came to serve regularly in several capacities that contributed to the protection, edification, and vitality of their families and communities: as election registrars and judges, justices of the peace, and school committeemen. A smaller number would serve as tax assessors and list-takers, coroners, and county commissioners. But from the late 1860s through the 1870s, the greatest number (over three hundred) would serve on superior and inferior court juries, generally composing between one-third and one-half of the jurors during any given term. There, they deliberated on civil and criminal actions and oversaw probate, guardianships, and the apprenticing of orphans—of no small importance in a state where former slaveholders had been especially notorious for using apprenticeship to regain control of black children and undermine the integrity of black family life.[51]

A large black majority and the organizing work of the Union League clearly enabled freedmen to wield institutional political power in Warren County, as in many other counties of eastern North Carolina. So, too, did the state constitution of 1868, which lent county townships "corporate powers for the necessary purposes of local government" (including taxation) and permitted eligible voters in them to elect justices of the peace (who also constituted a board of trustees) and school committeemen. "All the old courts have been abrogated or essentially changed by the new state constitution," a Freedmen's Bureau agent reported in July of 1868, "and now with colored men as magistrates in every precinct of these counties, and a fair proportion of colored men on every jury we may hope for justice." Black officials struggled to find resources to build schoolhouses and provide instruction for at least four months of the year, to give aggrieved laborers means of legal redress, and to offer some manner of social service and assistance to freed communities. Although it is difficult to know just how much justice they secured, they did establish a base of political strength that withstood the full onslaught of the state's redeemer Democrats and may have contributed to noteworthy economic gains by the end of the nineteenth century. In 1870, fewer than 80 of the nearly 2,500 black household heads in Warren County owned real property and fewer still owned farmland; by 1900, blacks owned 33,212 acres or more than one-sixth of the county's farmland and almost one-third of all black farm operators were owners rather than tenants.[52]

The examples can be multiplied a good many times over. In Edge-field County, South Carolina, well-organized and armed black Republicans, benefiting from Union League activity and their party's command of the governorship and legislature, gained control of the county courthouse despite the opposition of Democratic clubs and agricultural societies. Led by the charismatic former slave and Union army sergeant Prince Rivers (a man, according to Thomas Wentworth Higginson, who made "Toussaint perfectly intelligible"), they challenged the power of local landowners and advanced the cause of African-American community development. By 1872, white planters felt the squeeze of higher taxes and complained that they could not get a fair hearing in the trial justices' courts; two years later, black schoolchildren outnumbered whites by a ratio of two to one, while black and white teachers received identical pay. At the other end of the Deep South, in Washington County, Texas, black power was hitched to a biracial and multiethnic Republican party that took the reins of county government in 1870 and held them for over a decade. Although blacks routinely yielded the offices of sheriff, district judge, and county judge to their white allies, they did claim most of the nominations for state legislature and eventually served as clerks of court, treasurers, deputies, and justices of the peace. Perhaps more consequentially, they were heavily represented on grand and petit juries. Together, they helped promote black access to local offices (by accepting black sureties on bonds) and gave black defendants meaningful protection.[53]

Even where black representation in office was limited, the advent of Republican rule on the local level—especially when black votes proved crucial in elections—could make an immense difference to freed inhabitants. "Since the resumption of the civil supremacy and the removal of the old county and state officers, much of the most difficult labor of this office has become a thing of the past," a Freedmen's Bureau agent stationed in northern Alabama found. "Colored complaints in cases of trespass, assault, debt &c. are now referred directly to the civil officers who, where sufficient cause of action appear, commence proceeding at once." The Vermont carpetbagger Marshall Twitchell, who presided over the organization of Red River Parish, Louisiana, in the early 1870s from a post in the state senate and a plantation near the new parish seat of Coushatta, made a similar point in waxing exuberant over his own achievements: "For the first time since the war, the laborer felt a degree of confidence that he would get the profits of his labor." The significance of black political power resided not only in the array of officials who would attend to the pressing concerns and grievances of freedpeople, but also in the effective institutionalization of what had been informal mechanisms for resolving disputes, thereby lending voice to those who remained formally disfranchised. Without strict regard to age or gender, rural blacks crowded county courthouse grounds or made their way to the sites of magistrates' courts—sites that may have included farms, plantations, churches, schoolhouses, or crossroads—and simultaneously witnessed and influenced the proceedings. They rendered their support, their opinions, and their judgments so that elected officers and jurors could serve as leaders, mediators, and vehicles of neighborhood sentiment.[54]

At all events, Radical Reconstruction gave tremendous stimulus to the development of black associational life, extending the already dense civic sphere found in the cities and larger towns into the countryside. Mutual aid and benevolent societies that, of necessity, had been clandestine now came to public light while new ones were launched. In Front Royal, Virginia, freedpeople started up a "Union Relief Association" to tend to the sick and bury the dead. In Rowan County, North Carolina, they organized a savings bank and pooled resources to purchase land for use as a cemetery. In Baldwin County, Georgia, where federal troops had been stationed and a Loyal League had been active, they established a welfare society, an "axe club" to assist in firefighting (and perhaps to act in the community's defense), and a farmers' club to aid tenants and freeholders. In Pontotoc County, Mississippi, they founded a mutual aid society, "the purpose of which," according to a less-than-sympathetic local observer, "was the betterment of the freedmen and the establishment of their rights." Even in nonplantation districts, the pulse of organizational activity was in evidence. In Cass County, Georgia, where blacks composed less than one-third of the population, "colored men" formed a "Mechanic and Labroing [*sic*] Men association" in 1869, which met monthly "to unit the labroing [*sic*] men in the county," assess their economic prospects, and collect dues "tell we can make some good amount to due some good with." "We wants to pays land as soon as we can to give homes to our poor peoples," one of the leaders explained, "for maney ar be dout homes and land to worke and cheated out what maney Workes for."[55]

Writing from the Virginia piedmont county of Orange on the last day of 1868, a Freedmen's Bureau agent accordingly reflected on the changes he could observe among the freedpeople since the war. In 1865, he remembered, they were "abject and fearful in the presence of the master class" and "joyous and affectionate in the presence of representatives of the [federal] government." They were "unsettled and working for small or no remuneration," knew "little about saving or spending money," and, by his lights, were "largely ignorant and superstitious" and gave "family relations" slight regard. Now, however, the picture was wholly different. The freedpeople were "much less abject and more settled, ambitious and industrious." They will "generally resist if attacked." They "receive higher wages and take better care of themselves." Some had "purchased homes and most aspired to" do so. Families had been "gathered together and relations between husband and wife and parent and child are," the agent thought, "better understood." "Many schools and Sabbath schools" had been organized in the county and, as a consequence, "large numbers of adults have learned to read." And, to round out the impressive accomplishments, "various societies for the promotion of temperance, charity, schools, and politics have been established." In all of this, the agent saw "honest pride and manly integrity" and a wonderful advance "toward civilization and enlightenment."[56]

The South Carolina planter Henry W. Ravenel more likely saw a further descent into barbarism when he tersely recorded on May 14, 1870 that all his hands "have gone from here" into the nearby town of Aiken for a celebration "with processions, drums, and a barbecue." For what the freedpeople commemorated on that day was the ratification of the Fifteenth Amendment—officially prohibiting the denial of "the right to vote" on the grounds of "race, color [or] previous condition of servitude" but doubtless imagined by most in attendance as a constitutional conferral of "certain rights." The crowd was large and enthusiastic as the procession formed and proceeded to an assembly point across from the new residence of the black Republican leader Robert Elliott, who after the amendment was read, spoke for about three hours. Yet a low-country newspaper correspondent also took care to note the many "organizations" in evidence from Aiken and the surrounding towns and counties: colored fire companies, benevolent associations, brass bands, military outfits, and cavalry—as well as a host of "prominent persons" from Hamburg, Edgefield, Columbia, and Augusta. It was a picture of black political and civil community constructed in the whirl of revolution and gathering momentum for challenges to come.[57]

❖

Extraordinary as they were, black political achievements were from the outset tempered by tensions, frustrations, and obdurate hurdles that only grew over time. Rural blacks had to struggle not simply to organize their supporters, nominate candidates, and win elections, but also to assume, hold, and wield the powers of office. In large part this was because of the enormous pressures brought to bear by white Democrats through formal and paramilitary means, but it was due, as well, to deepening conflicts among southern Republicans and a battle for the soul and apparatus of the party. A unified Republican party with a shared set of objectives and sense of purpose may have been able to defeat the counterrevolutionary moves of the Democrats; an increasingly fractious party at odds with itself was almost fatally exposed.

The product of war and emancipation, black affiliation with the Republican party was unique and contradictory. On the one hand, no other group of working people in the nation's history has ever become so closely aligned with a political party; on the other, the Republican party's program and leadership was never determined by black constituents—it never became "their" party. The consequences were to be felt at all levels of political life, yet nowhere more intensely than in the counties and municipalities as the faith, hope, and guarded optimism that accompanied the advent of Radical Reconstruction widely soured. In some cases the disenchantment could set in with remarkable speed. In the early spring of 1867, a black Union League leader in Tennessee sang the praises of Republican governor William G. Brownlow, who had labored "unceasingly for the elevation and education of the colored race" and made it possible for them to "cast [their] votes," "inherit and transmit property," "sue and be sued in courts," "make and enforce contracts," and "testify in the courts of the country." But little more than a year later, a local black organizer and officeholder asked what Brownlow and other "home Radicals," had "done for us" and suggested that "we have got nothing to expect from him" in the way of either patronage or policy. "What is the use of talking about ecolity before the Law there is noone," a former slave from Fayette County told Brownlow's Republican successor in 1869, "you have been telling us that we are allowd to hold office I do not see noone of my collor in office and you says that we are allowd to sit on the juree bench but that is not so." Writing pseudonymously, a black South Carolinian complained just as bitterly in 1872 about the white Republicans who made "loud and big promises to the freedmen till they got elected to office, then did not one single thing," who refused to support the nomination of "a colored man" for major office, who "removed a number of black trial justices," and who "disarmed a number of black militia companies in the upcountry." "The first duty of any race of people," he thundered, "is to see to their own interests specially."[58]

Looking after "their own interests" was, however, a difficult endeavor. Early on, local Republican organizations were headed disproportionately by northern and southern whites, and black leaders and constituents alike widely accepted those claims to authority and office. In large part, this reflected the party's role in advancing the cause of black civil and political rights and the belief that white party members could be counted as true allies. But it also represented an act of deference to those better educated and experienced in the workings of electoral politics, as well as a desire to appear politically "responsible." In plantation districts, blacks would ordinarily find places on county executive committees, help fill delegations to state party conventions, and receive nominations for a seat or two on the county governing board, for a few (usually less consequential) county offices, and perhaps for a seat or two in the state house of representatives. Nominations for the more visible and prominent posts—Congress, the state senate, judgeships, the majority of governing board seats, sheriff, tax assessor and collector—generally were tendered to whites. In nonplantation districts, where Republicans were far more dependent on white votes, blacks rarely received nominations for public office and, at best, could hope for influence within local party circles.[59]

The problem was at least twofold. With scant exception, white Republicans neither clearly understood nor entirely supported the aspirations and objectives of the black rank-and-file. Nor were they prepared to accord local black leaders the status of full partners in the political project. And given their social profiles and locations, this should not be surprising. Although white Republicans may well have been outsiders to the formal arenas of southern politics, they were similarly outsiders (and likely antagonists) to the informal arenas of black politics. Where black voters formed majorities, white Republican leaders were either northerners who had served in the Union army or had taken up plantations, southerners who had been paternalist slaveholders and supporters of the Whig party, or local merchants who wished to pry black laborers loose from their traditional economic dependence on white landowners. Where black voters found themselves in the minority (and often the distinct minority), white Republicans were southerners who owned property but had little sympathy for the Confederacy and a good deal of interest in empowering those regions (white majority) and social groups (white yeomen and former nonslaveholders) that had regularly fought and lost the internal political battles of the antebellum period. Under the best of circumstances, white Republicans embraced the ideals of civil and political equality, pressed to see the freedpeople treated justly by their white employers and neighbors, came to their assistance in a variety of ways, and perhaps imagined an identity of economic and political interest between them. In most instances, they viewed themselves as the freedpeople's political tutors and hoped that black votes would compose a stable foundation for the power and livelihood of the Republican party and leaders like themselves—that is, if they did not seek to marginalize black constituents and interests entirely.[60]

But there was an even deeper dilemma. Either the Republican party failed to attract a significant bloc of white voters or, when it did, those voters would rarely support black candidates and specifically black demands. In the black belt, white Republicans were generally so sparse in number that they could often be identified in name by the party faithful who registered similar assessments from county to county and state to state: "There are only 43 white men of this county who call themselves Republicans"; "the only white man of this vicinity" who supported Grant; "they are all rebels here except a few white men and the Negroes"; "there is no white Republican in either of those Townships." The Republican Central Club of Ward 12 in the Red River parish of Natchitoches (60 percent black) claimed nearly one hundred members, but fewer than ten were white. In Greene County,

Georgia, where black voters outnumbered whites by more than two to one, Abram Colby reckoned that when he ran for the state legislature he received the votes of only four white men.[61]

Although Colby could win an election without the aid of white votes, his experience not only illuminated the highly limited basis of white Republicanism in black-majority districts; it also suggested the more widely precarious nature of the support that was to be found anywhere, for Colby polled less than half of the identifiable white Republican votes in his county. Black Republican leaders and office seekers quickly discovered, to their dismay, that white allegiance to the Republican party was often thinly tendered and readily shaken, and that black interests and aspirants could easily be sacrificed. This was especially true in white-majority areas, where white votes were crucial to party prospects and sympathy for black civil and political equality was regarded as a great political liability. Perhaps the most glaring example was the expulsion—with strong moderate Republican support—of duly elected black legislators from the Georgia General Assembly in 1868. But there were many others. Republicans in a Bertie County, North Carolina, township nominated Jordan H. Parker and George Bishop—a black and white man, respectively—for magistrate in 1869, confident that each was loyal to the party. They erred. A few days later, Bishop announced that "he would not surve with Parker," and when black Republicans dug in their heels and stood behind Parker, Bishop bolted and ran as a Democrat. "If the white Republicans are such good men," a disgruntled black leader in east-central Texas complained, "why will they not vote for a colored man[?]" What a Houston newspaper observed in 1870 was far more generally fitting: "Not a colored man in Texas has a good office that was not conferred upon him by the votes of his own people."[62]

It was not very long before black Republicans in many parts of the rural Deep South—but particularly in those states where the party controlled the governorships and legislatures into the early 1870s—began to push for a larger share of offices and patronage and more influence in party affairs. "All the colored men wanted and demanded," Mississippi leader John R. Lynch maintained, "was a voice in the government under which they lived and to the support of which they contributed, and a small but fair and reasonable proportion of the positions that were at the disposal of the voters of the state and of the administration." Greene Lewis of Perry County, Alabama, who served as a justice of the peace, a state legislator, and a convention delegate several times over, was more militant and direct. "We are done begging and pleading for our rights," he exclaimed in 1874. "Hereafter we intend to demand them and press [for] them on every occasion."[63]

Black assertiveness varied in its particulars but was similar in its essentials. It looked toward local political power and independence and began to construct a new political identity. Black laborers called white party leaders to account. They moved to control the county and district party machinery. They rejected white office-seekers and substituted black ones. They nominated all-black electoral slates. Much less frequently, they arranged deals with cooperative Democrats. In Yazoo, Mississippi, the carpetbagger Albert T. Morgan found the freedpeople, "whose sterling good sense and practical knowledge of affairs in some measure made up for their lack of school training," no less hesitant about deferring to "colored men from the North" than to white northerners, and claimed that "unless the Northern colored man could make his argument . . . the freedman who aspired for leadership was likely to carry off the prize." A white Republican who had moved recently to Mecklenburg County in Virginia's southside discovered the party there to be "headed by negroes." A district nominating convention in the Alabama black belt in 1869 saw "the negroes . . . arrayed against both carpetbaggers and scalawags." In a speech at the courthouse in Washington County, Texas, in 1871, radical Matthew Gaines "openly denounced many of [the] leading white Republicans and advocated the establishment of a *black man's party,* and a general ousting of *scallawags* and *carpetbaggers.*" In Leflore County, Mississippi, during the mid-1870s, according to the testimony of Republican planter Thomas Walton, "the negroes have their clubs" and they "have generally acted in such a way as to leave me to believe that they did not want my presence there." When county conventions met, Walton "observed that the negroes . . . very strongly resisted white influence," and "it produced an impression . . . that these meetings meant nothing but the organization of one race against another." "The truth is," he concluded, "a white man, especially a southern white man, belonging to the republican party, does not seem any more acceptable as one of their counselors or advisers than those who belong to the opposition."[64]

Writing in early 1877, a conservative South Carolinian who thought ill of the "negro's capacity for government" nonetheless acknowledged blacks' political acumen when he reported perceptively that whereas "on national questions the negroes . . . implicitly follow the dictation of northern republicans," in "home matters they are more indepen- dent." For several years they had "displayed great dissatisfaction with their white leaders," so that those who had not been "discarded" had to use "money and official patronage to retain their influence." "The negroes have been accused of being easily led by demagogues," he noted, "but they really rule the demagogues, not the demagogues them. Let the politicians do anything which is distasteful, and oppo- nents spring up in every quarter." On his travels through Louisiana in 1875, the northern journalist Charles Nordhoff similarly found that the "negroes are becoming a nuisance to their corrupt white allies" and "begin to grasp after all the offices." "They are ready to give judgeships to the whites," he explained, "but the legislature, the sher- iffs' places, the police-juries (county supervisors)—all the places where the money is spent or appropriated—they demand in those par- ishes where they are in the majority." [65]

There were tangible results, notably in those states where Radical Reconstruction did not come to a quick end. The combination of black militance in the plantation districts and white retreat in many of the nonplantation districts turned the southern Republican party blacker and blacker over time. Fewer whites were to be found at rallies and conventions and more black claimants won nominations and offices. Indeed, the incidence of black officeholding appears to have grown during the 1870s, peaking on the state and local levels around 1874. But at the same time, the party became a weaker and weaker vehicle for achieving and maintaining power, as factionalism intensified and many white Republican leaders pursued new avenues to broaden their base and appease their opponents. Struggles over the dispensation of state and federal patronage were in part to blame, and they knew no neat racial boundaries. Even more damaging, however, were various "reform" initiatives that responded to—or themselves advanced— charges of "corruption" and "financial mismanagement" and looked to ally moderates in both parties in the interests of property, tax relief, and economic retrenchment. [66]

Thus, as blacks increased their grassroots leverage in the Republican party, white party leaders proved less able or willing to see that leverage have significant consequence for policy and power. But black and committed white Republicans also found that, without strong party support and a meaningful threat of force in their favor, the winning of elections (and appointments) and the putative right to hold office did not necessarily or easily translate into actually holding and wielding the instruments of office. The snares and obstacles to be encountered were so numerous, formidable, and institutionalized as to try the forbearance and courage of even the most determined local leader; and they suggest how difficult it was to dislodge the old guard and govern in the name of the new. Where military commanders did not or could not remove sitting officeholders before the installation of those elected under the provisions of the Radical state constitutions, Republican claimants might find the entrance to the courthouse blocked, Democratic incumbents refusing to relinquish their offices, or no one available to administer their oaths. Where Democrats or moderate Republicans filled a share of the posts, black officeholders in particular might find that they would not carry out directives or serve warrants. And where federal troops were not readily at hand, white community opinion might be sufficiently hostile and organized as to reject the authority or even force a Republican officeholder out.[67]

The carpetbagger Charles Stearns felt the wrath of the white community. Elected judge of ordinary in Columbia County, Georgia, "by a majority of over 1,200 voters" in the spring of 1868, he set out for the county seat in September to take up his important duties: selecting jurors, designating election precincts, choosing election managers, and disbursing county funds. He was not welcomed. A raucous mob had assembled and greeted Stearns with hisses and threats, crying out that he was "elected by nigger votes and the niggers had no right to vote." Although the mob eventually dispersed, Stearns could get no protection from the sheriff and another crowd soon dragged him out. Fearing for his life, Stearns left town and resigned. Around the same time in neighboring Alabama, several newly elected Republicans experienced similar harassment and "Riotness." One traveled to the seat of Washington County to assume the offices of probate judge and circuit court clerk but discovered "a black flag flying before the Court House door" along with "about 50 or 60 men assembled all armed with revolvers." Another probate judge was "assaulted and assailed in his office" and complained of "a virtual rebellion" against the authority of the state government in the county of Butler. In Choctaw County, the Republican sheriff managed to take office in the summer of 1868, but owing to "the hostile actions" and "malicious threats" made against him found it impossible to execute the law.[68]

Intimidation and obstruction could assume other, less blatant though not much less effective, forms. When the registration board of Hinds County, Mississippi, met in June 1868 they found their work "greatly retarded and incommoded" by a committee of three who claimed a right to witness the manner in which the board's business was transacted "and to interrogate the members as to their knowledge of the official duties imposed on them." The frustrations of James Syms, an African American appointed judge of the district court of McIntosh County, Georgia, began when his solicitor "refused to swear in under him." But they became almost intractable when the local "bar met and refused to take cases before his court," thereby preventing "him from being able to do anything." Even a context of black power proved no guarantee that the affairs of government would be duly administered. And in many cases, appeals to federal military authorities for assistance only served to confirm the political and logistical dilemmas. Forwarding a plea "for any available force" from the Republican sheriff of Warren County, Georgia, who felt stymied in carrying out the legal actions of the courts, Governor Rufus Bullock received a reprimand in return. If the situation in Warren County qualified as an "emergency," commanding general George Meade told Bullock, then troops would have to be sent "not only into every county in this state, but in all the five states comprising this department."[69]

Yet some of the most troublesome obstacles in the path of local Republican, and especially black Republican, power were embedded in the very framework of governance. Indeed, they were explicitly intended to obstruct the "unsponsored" political ascent of poor working folk after property qualifications for voting and officeholding had been eliminated: county officer bonds. Every southern state required county officers to post bond before they could take their oaths, receive their commissions, and begin to carry out their duties. Although the provisions varied from state to state, locality to locality, and office to office, the most important offices everywhere carried the most substantial bonds while even lesser offices called for bonds well beyond the means of ordinary propertyholders, let alone laborers. Sheriffs had to post between $5,000 and $90,000; tax assessors and collectors had to post as much as double the tax revenues owed the state by their counties; and lowly clerks of court might have to post up to a few thousand dollars. Prospective officeholders could, of course, call on men of means to stand as security, but such sureties generally had to own unencumbered real estate and live within the immediate jurisdiction of the offices for which they stood.[70]

Bond posting requirements thereby turned large landowners into a local electoral jury of ultimate resort, giving them the opportunity either to rein in the choices of county voter majorities or dispense with them entirely. This proved particularly daunting to Republicans in the plantation districts, where few white propertyholders supported the party and few black supporters held real property, but it dogged black elected and appointed officials almost everywhere owing to the poverty of their constituents and the hostility of most white southerners to black officeholding. In North Carolina, Republican governor William W. Holden learned of numerous sheriffs, commissioners, clerks, constables, coroners, and magistrates in the eastern part of the state—many of them black—who failed to qualify on this account in 1868 and 1869. "I wase Elected Coroner of Hertford County . . . and afford my siceurity of the Best Colard men in the County and men of Property," one explained. "But the Commishers would not take them and i think the Reason is becase that i am a Colard man for all the white men that offerd thair Bonds wase all taken." In Glynn County, Georgia, Democrats who worried about the "influence" of Hosea Sherman, the newly elected black tax collector, first threatened Sherman's sureties and then "nixt him on acct of taking insufficient security bond." Small wonder that a Republican observer, having finished a tour of southwest Georgia, urged Governor Bullock to commission "our new officers . . . immediately" since "many of them will be unable to give bonds as required by law oweing to the combination of Democrats to prevent men of means from going on the bonds."[71]

The rejection or subversion of bonds, sporadically employed in the earliest years of Radical Reconstruction, appears to have emerged as part of a concerted strategy to deny blacks (and other Republicans) local offices and return them to white control. Outlining the road to the White-Line campaign of violence in Mississippi in 1875, E. H. Stiles, a Republican lawyer in the river town of Port Gibson, explained that hostile whites first attempted to intimidate Republican voters, then organized a taxpayer's league and began to persecute Republican officials, and then quickly moved to harass individual bondsmen and pressure the board of supervisors to reject bonds that were submitted. Stiles himself "had to go out in various parts of the county" to make what he described as a "very good bond" for the newly elected sheriff in 1874 but discovered upon returning to Port Gibson that "some of the most responsible men . . . said that they would have to go off that bond." Only when such tactics did not prove uniformly successful did White-Liners determine to carry the next elections "at all hazards."[72]

At the very least, the need to make acceptable bonds could either limit the independence of black officials and the constituents they represented or enable Democrats to hedge the manuevering room of Republican officeholders more generally. When the former slave J. J. Evans was elected sheriff of the Mississippi Delta county of De Soto in 1873, he had to post a $75,000 bond. A longtime county resident later assumed that Evans's six sureties, two or more of whom were carpetbaggers, "really administered his affairs and ran his office." But exaggerated and racist as this assumption undoubtedly was, it nonetheless identified a kernel of truth: Evans was in some measure beholden to his bondsmen and dependent on their continued good graces. In Fort Bend County, Texas, where eight of ten inhabitants were black, such a recognition framed contests for local power. Soon after the advent of Radical Reconstruction, county Union League president Walter Burton won an election to become sheriff and found that although "he could give the Bond required by law," it was "rejected on the grounds that the parties on the Bond was not worth anything." Somehow Burton managed to qualify and serve in office until 1874, but his successor, Henry Ferguson, also African American, had no supporters with resources to stand as sureties. Ferguson's only option was to cut a deal with a number of Fort Bend whites, including the wealthiest man in the county. They would make Ferguson's bond if Ferguson agreed to accept two "reputable" whites as deputies. "As it now stands," Albert T. Morgan sighed in the midst of his own frustrating bond experience in Yazoo County, Mississippi, "not more than a handful of landowners may defeat the will of a majority of two thousand out of three thousand voters, and where they combine as they have here, secure entire control of the offices." A "society turned bottomside up" was, it seems, far easier to imagine than achieve.[73]

❖

Bonding requirements fell under the authority of the state legislatures, and in Louisiana at least, Republicans in that body moved quickly to allow prospective officeholders to seek sureties outside of their official jurisdictions. In this way, as in many others, access to local power could be heavily dependent on control over the levers of state government. And in this way, as in many others, the limits to what freedpeople in the rural districts could accomplish became ever more apparent. Legislative Republicans clearly sought to undermine the patron-client politics long practiced by parish planters and extend the party's hold over areas where most of the state's population resided. But rather than dispensing with or scaling down the bond requirements, they instead effectively shifted the patronage to Republican bankers and brokers who lived chiefly in New Orleans and who likely had reservations about the development of black power in the countryside.[74]

The centralization that Radical state constitutions generally made possible and that many of the Republican regimes for a time pursued must, of course, be regarded as a political revolution, given the conditions that had previously prevailed: conditions that enabled slaveholders to claim the status of sovereigns, plantations to dominate the social and economic life of much of the South, and big landowners during Presidential Reconstruction to use state and county governments to reinvigorate their direct control over black laborers. With the overwhelming support of black voters and the influence of black legislators, these regimes widely commenced a transformation of civil society and political economy in the former Confederate states, undoing the worlds that slaveholders had made and ex-slaveholders initially tried to remake. They repealed the vestiges of antebellum slave codes and post-emancipation black codes, ended corporal punishment, and modified the penalties for crimes against property. They adjusted the burdens of a tax structure that had rested "lightly upon the large land holders and heavily upon the laboring man and the poor." They dramatically expanded the public sector and social services, especially in the area of education. And they moved against laws and traditions of racial exclusion and discrimination in public life. They also slowed, and in some cases halted, a veritable flood of local legislation designed to hedge or defeat black struggles to escape dependence on white land-holders: laws prohibiting the "enticement" of laborers, the violation of contracts, the grazing of livestock and hunting of game on unen-closed land, and the sale of agricultural produce after dark.[75]

Where African Americans attained substantial representation in Re-construction legislatures, moreover, they could develop an agenda, shape Republican party policy, and help advance contests for power at the local level. In South Carolina, blacks not only held a majority of the seats, but also came to control most of the committees and thereby pressed potentially far-reaching legislation in the areas of civil rights, labor relations, and landownership. The newly created state Land Commission, which in the words of Union League president Francis L. Cardozo "proposes to give the poor people the opportunity to become owners of the soil they cultivate," stood alone in the former Confederacy in directly addressing the explosive issue of land reform.[76] Mississippi blacks never dominated their state's legislature to such an extent, yet at the height of their power they claimed 55 of 115 seats in the house, 9 of 37 seats in the senate, and the speakership of the house. Accordingly, they moved to restructure the mechanisms of county law enforcement, pushed through an act that one carpetbagger described as "equally strong as Sumner's civil rights bill," and sup-ported tax packages that soon put about one-fifth of the state's land area in public hands for delinquency, purportedly to be sold in small tracts. Most strikingly, they succeeded in electing Blanche K. Bruce, a former slave, teacher, editor, and local officeholder, as well as Hiram Revels, to the U.S. Senate.[77]

Even then, the direct aspirations and grievances of rural laborers rarely took center stage, and legislative efforts meant to address them often failed to pass. In part, this owed to the subordination of state parties in the South to the interests and objectives of the national Re-publican organization (which were clearly shifting away from those of "producers"). Far more important, however, were the divisions pro-voked—under the most auspicious of circumstances—not only among southern Republicans generally but also among black Republicans in particular. Although the black legislative delegation in South Carolina achieved impressive unity on issues relating to civil rights, that unity dissipated when the issues were "economic" and "political." A variety of bills designed to protect farm and plantation laborers against eviction, fraud, and extra-economic coercion either died in committee, were gutted by compromise, or went down to defeat before the entire assembly with the aid of black votes, many cast by the freeborn mulattoes who had a disproportionate voice in policy-making. In Louisiana, where African Americans composed as much as one-third of the legislature and well-educated, freeborn mulattoes wielded even greater power, the results were much the same. Republican legislators quickly enacted a law penalizing employers for discharging or pressuring laborers for political purposes, but most of the bills advanced by black parish representatives that would have aided the struggles of plantation workers met a different fate. A bill to establish an eight-hour day was buried in committee; one to repeal plantation trespass statutes failed to come up for a vote; one to permit laborers to sue employers who lived in other parishes for nonpayment was defeated in the senate; and one to allow laborers provisional seizure of their employers' property in contract disputes was defeated in the house.[78]

It may well have been that the social and cultural distance between many of these legislators and their constituents largely accounts for what, to rural black laboring people, must have been seen as law-making limits and failures. The sensibilities of freeborn mulattoes clearly resonated with the rhythms and relations of urban public life and with petit bourgeois notions of respectability, and in no southern state did as many as half of the legislators claim agricultural occupations; in most of the states, well under one-third did.[79] Yet we should not make too much of this. In no popular movement—even the most effective—do the social profiles of leaders and elected representatives match those of the rank-and-file. And many of the black artisans, ministers, and teachers who won seats in the legislatures were closely tied to their rural supporters through residence, experience, and kinship. More relevant was the underrepresentation of African Americans as a group in almost all of the state Republican legislative delegations, and especially on the important legislative committees. They simply did not have the numbers or leverage to shape the agenda and enact laws in the face of the ignorance, indifference, or hostility of their white Republican colleagues (not to mention their white Democratic opponents). Outside of South Carolina, and to some extent even there, the best that they could hope to do was to construct bills that would enhance the ability of the Republican party to maintain power, offer some protection to their constituents against personal and political coercion, and advance the development of their localities through minimally controversial measures: incorporating municipalities, securing ferry privileges, changing district boundaries, and aiding benevolent societies.[80]

It was not, therefore, in state legislatures but rather in "colored mens'" and "colored labor" conventions that the concerns, expectations, and wishes of rural black folk found the best venues for public articulation. With antecedents in the antebellum North and the immediate postemancipation South, these conventions assembled chiefly on a statewide basis, and served as political mouthpieces and pressure groups, urging Congress and Republican legislatures to action while attempting to stimulate further organization on the local level. Already in the spring of 1867, soon after the passage of the Reconstruction Acts, their militance set them apart from the freedmen's conventions of 1865–1866. No longer were they simply petitioning for their rights; they were demanding to exercise them: to hold office, sit on juries, and use all public accommodations. In at least one case, they threatened confiscation for white landowners who fired black workers for political reasons. But it was in 1869, responding to a set of disappointments in state and national politics, that they began to take decidedly new shape by gathering large numbers of rural delegates and placing the experience of laborers and laboring communities at the center of their proceedings.[81]

One of the largest of these conventions met in October in Macon, the heart of Georgia's cotton belt. With nearly 250 delegates representing as many as eighty counties, it reported on conditions and "outrages" throughout the state and resulted in the formation of a mechanics' and laborers' association. The convention's leaders included local Union League president Jefferson Long, Republican party activist Henry McNeal Turner, McIntosh County political boss Tunis G. Campbell, and several grassroots organizers from the surrounding plantation districts: Philip Joiner of Dougherty County, Abraham Smith of Muscogee County, and George H. Clower of Monroe County. Several of them had been expelled from seats in the Georgia legislature and all were closely in touch with the struggles of black workers in town and country. Creating more than ten committees, urging "the heads of families in every neighborhood" to "unite themselves together for the purpose of establishing schools," and emphasizing the importance of having black preachers, lawyers, doctors, and editors, the delegates directly addressed the interests and aspirations of rural freedpeople. They demanded higher wages for field hands and recommended the establishment of cooperatives for the purchase of supplies and land, the "withdrawal of women from field labor whenever possible," the formation of clubs for self-defense among plantation workers, and the welcoming of "any immigrants who may choose to cast their lot among us as laborers . . . whatever nativity they may be." [82]

Shortly thereafter, an even larger convention assembled in Columbia, South Carolina. Although prominent black "politicians" were much in evidence, so too were Union League and state militia officers, and of the three hundred delegates representing all of the counties, most were farmers and agricultural laborers. They elected as convention president the freeborn lawyer and editor Robert B. Elliott, who represented rural Edgefield County in the statehouse and had helped to organize the Republican party in the country districts. And the concerns of black rural workers came to the fore. Indeed, the convention's chief product was a memorial itemizing legislation "of benefit to agricultural laborers," which came to some effect: it provided them with a "preferred lien" for wages on the employer's land; appointed a commissioner of contracts in each county and an officer to draw up jury lists, seeing to it that "the laboring classes . . . have a fair representation"; gave their lawsuits for wages precedence on court calendars; directed that land sold under execution be divided into tracts of fifty acres or less; and established a nine-hour day for skilled labor. [83]

Similar, though smaller, gatherings took place in Virginia and Texas before the year was out, and in early 1871 ninety-eight delegates from forty-two counties, a majority of whom were "farmers and farm laborers," met in the statehouse in Montgomery to form the Labor Union of Alabama. With the "interest" of rural workers "more largely represented than any other class of labor," the convention heard reports on wages, schools, and churches. But much of the time during three days of organization, discussion, and debate was given over to the question of emigration. It was not the first occasion on which the matter arose in such a public forum. Strong resolutions favoring emigration had been introduced at the labor convention in Macon in 1869, and an emigration meeting had taken place in Nashville at about the same time. But in Montgomery both the committee on homesteads and the committee on "the condition of the colored people of Alabama" presented emigration as the logical answer to the predicament that blacks had come to endure. Believing that "the present condition of our people, as a mass, is infinitely worse than that of any other class of laborers in any country known to us," that they were "huddled" in a market that depresses "wages down to starving rates," and that "under existing circumstances it will be impossible for us to procure homes advantageously," they saw emigration, preferably to Kansas or to some other territory "in the broad and free West," as a "panacea." There, they imagined, "we will be able to sit under our own vine and fig tree," far from the "midnight hauntings" of the Ku Klux Klan. There, "we can produce abundantly more with the same labor than we can here" and "not be compelled to plant one kind of crop." And there, we "can enjoy [our] political opinions without being murdered" and hold "religious meetings" without the "danger of being fired into" by "men who are opposed to our moral and political advancement."[84]

The convention's delegates "unanimously" adopted the reports and resolved to appoint a committee to "proceed to Washington city, to memorialize Congress and also visit Kansas" to gather information "as to the location of a colony, prices of lands, implements for farming, etc. and the best route of travel, and means of transportation." One year later, when the labor union met again, the delegates heard from a committee spokesman, who had made the journey the previous summer, that "it is within the reach of every man, no matter how poor to have a home in Kansas." Although the assessment was greeted favorably, prevailing sentiment seemed to suggest that they "rest here a while longer," trusting "in God, the President, and Congress, to give us what is most needed here—personal security to the laboring masses—the suppression of violence, disorder, and ku-kluxism—the protection which the Constitution and the laws of the United States guarantee," and hoping that they might "secure homesteads . . . here."[85] Reconstruction was, after all, still alive in the state and the nation. But most of the delegates, and likely most of the black folk at home, undoubtedly feared that, for them, the revolution had already run its course.

6

OF PARAMILITARY POLITICS

The cruelties of property and privilege are always more ferocious than the revenges of poverty and oppression. For the one aims at perpetuating resented injustice, the other is merely a momentary passion soon appeased.

C. L. R. James

When the U.S. Congress conducted an investigation of the Ku Klux Klan in the early 1870s, more than a few of the reputed leaders testified that the organization was a necessary response to the alarming activities and tactics of the Union League. They complained of secret oaths, clandestine meetings, accumulations of arms, nocturnal drilling, threatening mobilizations, and a general flaunting of civilities among former slaves across the plantation South. In so doing, they helped construct a discourse, later embraced by apologists for slavery and white supremacy, that not only justified vigilantism but also demonized Radical Reconstruction for its political illegitimacies. The enfranchisement of ignorant and dependent freedmen by vengeful outsiders, the Klansmen insisted, marked a basic corruption of the body politic and a challenge to order as it was widely understood. Unfit to act as "self-reliant electors," the ordinarily "quiet, peaceable, and content" ex-slaves were "stirred up" and pressed into military-style leagues where they "voted en masse" and could be empowered to rule over communities in which they had no rightful claims as members. "Self-protection and self-defense" therefore required the rejection of formal political practices and the resort to personal coercion and force of arms.[1]

It has been common for serious historians since at least the 1960s to dismiss such charges against the Union League as self-serving cant and yet accept the notion that rampant vigilante violence was a suspension or defiance of "normal" political conduct. This was, after all, a revolutionary moment very much tied to the nation's most profound experience of violence. But we may gain a better and deeper appreciation of the developing struggle by doing just the reverse: by accepting many of the representations of the place and role of the Union League while questioning the view that vigilantism was something of an abberration in the course of political events. For if emancipation destroyed the petty sovereignties of former masters and if Reconstruction brought about a redefinition of the electoral arena, the exercise of political power nonetheless demanded ready and effective access to the means of violence.

African Americans hoped otherwise. In perhaps the most revolutionary of moments in an era of revolutionary change, they eagerly embraced the elective franchise and sought mightily to make its peaceful use the bedrock of a new political world. No people in the South were more committed to enacting and enlivening the rites of democracy. But their own experience as slaves and unfranchised freedpeople had taught them hard and searing lessons. Better than anyone in the former Confederacy or the nation—then and since—they understood that the rites of democracy had been built on rituals of violence and suppression directed against them. Better than anyone, they understood that the South's "politics" simultaneously embraced the rites and the rituals. And so they understood that whatever success they might achieve would depend on their ability to do battle of a different sort. Paramilitary organization had been fundamental to the social and political order of slavery; it remained fundamental to the social and political order of freedom.

◈

Ku Klux Klan leaders and sympathizers who blamed the Union League for their resort to vigilantism were at least right about the chronology.

Union League mobilizations generally preceded the appearance of the Klan. But the character and activities of the league itself reflected a well-established climate of paramilitarism that assumed both official and unofficial forms. Already during the summer and fall of 1865, despite the presence of a Union army of occupation, bands of white "regulators," "scouts," and cavalrymen rode the countryside disciplining and disarming freedpeople who looked to harvest their crops, make new labor and family arrangements, and perhaps await a federally sponsored land redistribution. Planters in the Deep South, warning of a possible black insurrection, increasingly pressured provisional governors and President Johnson to reinvigorate state militias and received a favorable hearing. And local white political leaders, anticipating the eventual withdrawal of federal troops, made plans to call out the militia "as regularly as necessary" and to authorize "volunteer companies" to "patrol and police" their neighborhoods. Black-code "justice" and paramilitary units composed the twin pillars of postemancipation society as the old slaveholders would have made it.[2]

Federal measures voiding the black codes and then disbanding the provisional militias of Johnsonian Reconstruction derailed this project and drove underground the use of organized force against African Americans. It was in this context that the phenomenon of the Ku Klux Klan erupted in much of the former Confederate South, and "phenomenon" may indeed be the best descriptive term. With apparent beginnings in middle Tennessee in the spring of 1866—a state, not coincidentally, already under Republican rule—the Klan was less a formal organization than a rubric embracing a variety of secret vigilante and paramilitary outfits showing the marks of their local settings. Alongside or incorporated with what members and observers may have called the Ku Klux Klan (or more likely "Ku Klux"), North Carolina fielded the White Brotherhood, the Invisible Empire, and the Constitutional Union Guard; Louisiana gave rise to the Knights of the White Camelia, the Swamp Fox Rangers, the Innocents, the Seymour Knights, and the Hancock Guards; and Mississippi could claim the Washington Brothers, the Knights of the Black Cross, Heggie's Scouts, and the Robinsons Clubs. In many instances, the Ku Klux came to be a general signifier for any vigilante band operating in disguise, and those who suffered attack came to speak of being "ku kluxed."[3]

This may help explain the variations in leadership, social composition, rituals, zones of engagement, goals, and activities that make it impossible to identify a typical or representative Klan experience and that have contributed to interpretive disagreements. Klans could be found in white and black majority districts. They could be organized and led by planters, by merchants, by the sons of large landowners, or by hardscrabble yeomen. They could establish networks across county and state lines or confine themselves to single neighborhoods. They could be sources of white unity or reflections of division and tension. They could boast elaborate costumes or use little more than threadbare masking. Their rites of initiation (of members) and humiliation (of victims) could be highly gendered and sexualized, or not. Klans could be involved chiefly in labor discipline, or in moral regulation, or in political intimidation and assassination, or they could engage in all of these. They could become more violent and less controllable over time, or they could maintain their original hierarchies and behaviors.[4]

Yet it would be a mistake to exaggerate the differences and variations. In an important sense, they remind us of the locally inflected compass of political conflict in the rural South. They also should not obscure what is especially meaningful about the foundation and trajectory of the Klan's growth. Loosely constituted as it may have been, the Ku Klux Klan (and allied organizations) almost everywhere built on traditions of enforcing domination and submission, on grids of kinship and political patronage, and on generational legacies of military defeat. In late 1867 and 1868, they spread across the South with great speed, in response not so much to black enfranchisement as to the mass mobilization of freedpeople by the Union League and the Republican party and to the failure of Democrats and Conservatives to attract or compel substantial black support. Acknowledging that there was no "uniformity of understanding" about the Klan and that "every county seemed to be independent in its organization," one North Carolinian who briefly joined up nonetheless explained that he "first heard of [the Klan] in 1868 [when] the republican party was gaining great numbers to its ranks through the instrumentality of the League, Red Strings, and Heroes of America," and that the Klan "was gotten up as a counteracting movement."[5]

From the first, the Klan proved particularly attractive to young, white men who had served in the Confederate army. All of the founders in Pulaski, Tennessee, were youthful Confederate veterans, and most everywhere former Confederate officers, cavalrymen, and privates sparked organization and composed the bulk of membership. Klan dens and other vigilante outfits often became magnets for returning soldiers and, at times, they virtually mirrored the remainders of specific Confederate companies. Powell Clayton, the Republican governor of Arkansas who effectively combated the Klan, complained in retrospect about the Confederates being paroled or allowed to desert without surrendering their arms, ammunition, and horses. To this extent, the Klan not only came to embody the anger and displacement of a defeated soldiery and to capitalize on the intensely shared experiences of battlefields and prison camps; it also may be regarded as a guerilla movement bent on continuing the struggle or avenging the consequences of the official surrender.[6]

But the very associations between the Klan and the Confederate army suggest a deeper historical and political context, for Confederate mobilization itself was enabled by longstanding and locally based paramilitary institutions. Militias were perhaps most important because state governments required the enrollment of all able-bodied white men while leaving much of the organizational initiative to counties and neighborhoods, where volunteer companies could elect their own officers, make their own by-laws, and then secure recognition by the legislature. The militias, in turn, were closely connected with slave patrols—for a time through formal control, and more generally by way of personnel and jurisdiction—which policed the African-American population, instructed all white men in their responsibilities as citizens in a slave society, and could be enlisted as something of a posse by the state in the event of emergency. A martial spirit and military presence thus suffused the community life of the antebellum South.[7]

And the political life. The militia served simultaneously as an index of local wealth and power, a means of establishing patronage networks, and a launching pad for political careers. Companies were usually formed by slaveholding planters who could supply the troops with uniforms and equipment, expect election as captain, amass a following of kin and other white men, and perhaps aspire to higher rank in the county regiment or statewide system. Muster days, which often brought out a large audience of free and slave alike, provided opportunities to display martial masculinity and personal loyalty and to mix politicking and militarized festivity. Politicians customarily saw musters as crucial campaign venues not only because of the crowds in attendance, but also because officers had the influence to deliver the support of their men. Muster grounds commonly doubled as sites for politicking and polling, and it was by no means unusual for militia companies to assemble and march to the polls on election days. Political parties were, in many respects, collections of militia-based patron-client networks, and partisan conflict was not easily distinguishable from the struggle between various planter patrons for place and preferment. There was, at once, a politicization of the military and a militarization of politics, and it was not merely a way of demonstrating the relationship between the franchise and the symbol of masculine citizenship; it was also an acknowledgment that electoral activity and policing, that the ballot and the militia company or patrol, were two sides of the coin of local politics. Not incidentally, the "beat"—the geographical unit of militia companies and patrols—also came to be accepted as the geographical unit of polling and civil administration in what has rightly been called "the militant" antebellum South.[8]

The Reconstruction Klan was widely viewed, especially by African Americans, as a reconstitution of the old patrol system. And there can be little doubt that Klans showed many important features of both the patrols and the militia.[9] There were, of course, the links to the Confederate army and to the policing of the countryside on horseback. But there were powerful resonances in organization, membership, and direction as well. Klan "dens," "lodges," and "camps" were often between the size of patrols and militia companies (that is to say, somewhere between five and fifty members) and based in militia districts or beats. The leaders generally had held rank in the army (and probably in the militia) and were connected to families of local prominence. Indeed, kinship ties that were socially vertical seemed to be much in evidence. A raiding party of nine in Clarke County, Alabama, included two Odoms, two Barnes, and two Goodloes, most of whom had served in the Suggsville Grays during the war, with property holdings ranging from nothing to $3,500 in real estate. A confessed Klansman in nearby Rutherford County was a farmer and butcher roughly twenty-one years of age, but his father was described as a "very respectable farmer" and his second cousin, who had served in the state legislature, was a den chief in neighboring Cleveland County. "The captain of the [Ku Klux] in my immediate neighborhood is Charles M. Doss," explained a resident of Noxubee County, Mississippi, who fought for the Confederacy, and the privates included "William Doss, his son John Doss, his brother James Doss" together with Jasper Featherston, Doctor Featherston, Neil Featherston, Scott Williams, Taylor Williams, Max Williams, John Williams, Thomas Cockerell, Dent Cockerell, John McMorris, Joe McMorris, William McMorris, Madison Brooks, Harding Brooks, Jehu Kirksey, and Cicero Kirksey.[10]

Observers commonly drew distinctions between those who carried out vigilante actions and those who directed them, although the distinctions were by no means fixed. On occasion, the shock troops were young men who had acquired reputations as roving toughs and could be called upon for specific assignments. But for the most part, they belonged to local dens and likely saw their participation as an outlet for violence, a means of demonstrating their loyalties, and an opportunity to complete a social and political rite of passage. In Pontotoc County, Mississippi, where several dens operated, at least one was "composed mostly of young men and boys who sought to bring themselves in favor with the people."[11]

They also sought favor with local leaders, who tended to be older, socially established, and almost invariably active in the Democratic or Conservative party. In St. Mary Parish, Louisiana, the Knights of the White Camelia was launched by Daniel Dennett, who had edited the *Franklin Planters' Banner* since the 1840s, and attorney Alcibiades De-Blanc, who had been a colonel in the Confederate army, a member of the state legislature, a signatory at the Louisiana secession convention, and a leader of a parish vigilance committee in 1859. Elsewhere, those who headed up Klans, particularly at the county level, were usually from the "best families," and had either sponsored officeholders, held office, or had recently been ousted from office. In Fayette County, Texas, described in 1871 as "totally under Ku Klux domination," the district judge was apparently the "grand cyclops" and the sheriff, clerk, and magistrates his "subordinates." But in Jefferson County, further to the east, complaints of a "secret organization of Rebels . . . who hold regular nightly meetings" identified participants with the "Armstrong-Likens clique" which "*had* run the county."[12]

The Klan and kindred organizations, therefore, seem to have combined elements of private armies controlled by rural bosses, fascist-style squads, and "shadow governments." Albion W. Tourgee, the carpetbagger and novelist who organized for the Union League and then served as a judge in North Carolina, captured the social and political dynamic that the Klan embodied when explaining what he regarded as the "fatal mistake" of northern Reconstruction policy. "Every family [at the South] has its clientage, its followers, who rally to its lead," he remarked through the fictionalized voice of Comfort Servosse,

> but this fact seems to have been dimly recognized, though not at all understood or appreciated, by those who originated the Reconstruction Acts. They seem to have supposed, that, if this class were deprived of actual position, they would thereby be shorn of political influence. . . . [But] the dead leader has always more followers than his living peer. Every henchman of those lordlings at whom this blow was aimed felt it far more keenly than he would if it had lighted on his own cheek. The king of every village was dethroned; the magnate of every crossroads was degraded. Henceforth each and every one of their satellites was bound to eternal hostility toward these measures and to all that might result therefrom.[13]

❖

There are no better markers of African-American political struggle and advance in the immediate postemancipation period than the vigilantism of the Ku Klux Klan. Like previous paramilitary outfits, Klans sought to enforce the general subordination of former slaves and to punish whites and blacks who challenged or threatened a variety of racially defined hierarchies. But Klans were particularly involved in combating the social and political repercussions of Radical Reconstruction, and their targets make up a roster of the individuals, institutions, and developments that made those repercussions tangible. Klansmen attacked and murdered local leaders and organizers. They intimidated and coerced Republican party supporters and voters. They tried to force out objectionable officeholders and election registrars. They harassed and abused black men and women who had gained measures of personal and economic independence. They disturbed white landowners who rented or sold land to black laborers, white merchants who bought crops from and sold goods to black customers, and white employers who enticed black workers with higher wages. They burned down black churches and schoolhouses and drove off repugnant teachers and ministers. Most of all, they set out to destroy the Union League.[14]

The league drew the attention and wrath of the Klans in part because it effectively mobilized newly enfranchised black voters and tried to protect members through means that included secrecy and armed self-defense. But the league also advanced the wider African-American struggle to reconstitute communities on a more stable and self-governing basis. At a time when the infrastructure of black associational life in the rural areas was still weakly elaborated, the league served as a particularly important vehicle for gathering people together, debating issues and making decisions, negotiating labor contracts, and caring for the sick and vulnerable. As Klansmen and other white vigilantes seemed to recognize, the league stood at a crossroads, and in some places at the vital center, of black community life.

Klan assaults took a variety of forms but all were meant to obliterate the solidarities that the league helped to build and maintain. There were spectacles of intimidation that warned of the Klan's numbers, might, and violent intent: some of them bellicose "promenades," with weapons and disguises, in the darkened streets of rural towns; many more involving rounds of "armed bands" in the dead of the night that invaded farmsteads, displayed firearms, and promised vengeance against all who opposed them. Klans were especially concerned with ferreting out and forcefully dispersing league assemblies and related activities. The organizer of a "coloured council" in Calhoun County, Alabama, told a leading Republican that "the entire citizens hear are anty League and they sware . . . that not be another meeting and have the freedmen all allarmed." A newly established league in Freestone County, Texas, was quickly warned not to hold meetings in the county. And members of a "League Society" based on the Burgwyn plantation in eastern North Carolina found that as they returned from a "Flag Raising" in the town of Halifax, vigilantes "form[ed] a line a Cross public Road with gun and pistle to prevent us from going home."[15]

Mere support or sympathy for local leagues was sufficient to invite harassment and corporal punishment from neighborhood vigilantes. But Klans devoted great—and at times protracted—energy to paralyzing or eradicating the league's leadership. For these were men (and in a few cases women) who possessed influence, skills, resourcefulness, and considerable courage in the face of danger.[16] In mid-1867, traveling Union League organizer George T. Ruby came upon a black community in Brazos County, Texas, that was already constructing its own institutions despite an atmosphere of white hostility. Within a month, a predominately black league had been established with minister George Brooks at the helm, and it soon succeeded in electing Stephen Curtis, a former slave, to the Radical constitutional convention in Austin. Mindful of the tense situation in the county, Brooks was at pains to avoid directly antagonizing anyone, but neither would he allow white intimidation to go uncontested. When in June 1868 a disguised party of fifteen white men swept through their village, he rallied blacks to fight back and then commenced arming and drilling them. Less than two months later, despite working with the Freedmen's Bureau agent in the county seat of Millican to reach an accord prohibiting any "armed band, organization, or secret society not authorized by law," Brooks was murdered.[17]

A shoemaker by trade, George Flemister was an officer in a forty-member Union League council in Morgan County, Georgia. Although the Klan had broken up their organization once, Flemister helped put "it together again," making it possible for Republicans to gain election to most offices in the county. When a black plantation laborer named Charles Clarke was jailed while a dubious rape charge against him was being adjudicated, Flemister rounded up an armed guard of leaguers—with the encouragement of the Republican mayor of the county seat—to protect Clarke from an expected lynching. They stood their ground for a few days with pistols and a shotgun until they "could get no powder and shot" and the mayor mistakenly thought that Clarke would be safe. That night, a party of fifty whites with "long gowns and dough faces, and some great sharp things upon their heads," marched into town, forced the jailer to give up the keys, shot Clarke to pieces, and plundered Flemister's shoe shop. Before leaving, they posted a notice on the jailhouse door naming Flemister as one of the "leading men" marked for execution. Flemister had seen enough. He quickly packed his tools and headed for the relative safety of Atlanta.[18]

Wyatt Outlaw was as formidable an adversary as the old guard was ever to find. The son of a slave mother and a white father (himself a

Unionist) in Alamance County, North Carolina, Outlaw had learned the skills of carpentry, opened a shop in the county seat of Graham after the Civil War, and served as a delegate to a state freedmen's convention in 1866. Soon thereafter, he organized a Union League chapter with a substantial membership of railroad workers (some of whom may have been white) and an orientation toward community development and political power. Under Outlaw's direction, the league helped to establish a black school and an AME Zion church, aligned with the moderate wing of the state Republican party, and enabled the Republicans to take control of the town and county governments in 1868. Outlaw was rewarded by newly elected governor William W. Holden with appointments to the state council of the Union League and to the post of town commissioner (he was elected to a second term). When the White Brotherhood began to menace his followers, Outlaw organized a small police patrol to defend Graham while at the same time discouraging individual blacks from arming themselves and perhaps provoking mass violence. But it was Outlaw's political acumen, determination, and ties to white Republicans that represented the provocation. On the night of February 26, 1870, more than one hundred members of the Brotherhood took Outlaw from his bed and, with mounted guards posted, marched him into the central square of Graham. There, they hanged him from a large oak tree across from the county courthouse where Republican officeholders and the carpetbagger judge Albion Tourgee sought to carry out their duties. "Beware you guilty both white and black," read the note pinned to Outlaw's lifeless and mutilated body.[19]

We can indeed glimpse in the profiles of the Klan's many brave and unfortunate victims, both in the Union League and out, much of what political leadership and resistance meant for African Americans in the rural South. "Information has been made to us that you are the leader of the negros in your neighborhood, and that you and them are arrayed against the K.K.K. and the whites generally," Ben Turner of Northampton County, North Carolina, was told in an anonymous message warning him "to cease from your course or you will be dealt with severely by thee." Like Outlaw, Flemister, and Brooks—or like Dick Malone and Jerry Brown of Noxubee County, Mississippi; Joshua Terrill of Maury County, Tennessee; Washington Eager of Washington County, Georgia; Ben Brown of Sumter County, Alabama; and Jack

Dupree of Monroe County, Mississippi—Turner undoubtedly had
won the "confidence" of the people, was a "thorough republican and
took an active interest in the success of its principles," "had a right
smart wit" and would "speak his mind," and "was a sort of teacher . . .
[and] a fore-light man among them." Perhaps he could "read and write
and put it down himself," had served in the "Federal army," had urged
blacks to "arm themselves" and "resist the visits of these Klans," or
"had charge of a squad of men working some man's plantation." Perhaps, too, he was known to stand up to his employer and defend the
interests and claimed rights of fellow black workers. Or perhaps he had
even managed to accumulate sufficient resources to rent or purchase a
parcel of land and "work for himself" or "form partnerships." Most
likely, he had exhibited the "moral courage and firmness" to defy white
demands for submissiveness and convince the fearful to follow. So it
was that in the face of such assertions of independence, fortitude, and
"manhood," the Klan not only brutalized and murdered but also often
enacted rituals of degradation or emasculation.[20]

The politically symbolic and practical elements of Klan vigilantism
were similarly evident in attacks on black churches and, especially,
schoolhouses. Aside from Union League meetings, no institutions or
organizational forums proved more vulnerable, and this was in part
because churches and schoolhouses often served as the locations of
league meetings. But they represented as well the wider aspirations,
networks, and solidarities that the Klan moved to destroy. Between
February and June 1871 alone, just a few months after the Klan had
made its first show of local strength, twenty-six schools were burned
in Monroe County, Mississippi, with many of the teachers forced to
seek refuge in the county seat of Aberdeen. "There is an eternal ha-
tred," reported a Tennessee legislative committee investigating the Ku
Klux Klan in 1868, "existing against all men that voted the Republican
ticket, or who belong to the Loyal League, or [are] engaged in teaching
schools, and giving instruction to the humbler class of their fellow
men."[21]

Schools, like churches (and there was much overlap between the
two), were sites of African-American initiative and empowerment, and,
unlike most churches, of interracial cooperation and alliance. During
the Civil War, northern religious denominations and charitable organizations began to establish schools for ex-slaves in areas of Union occu-

pation—generally staffed by abolitionist women and men—and once the war ended these efforts spread over the South, principally under the auspices of the American Missionary Association. But they built on a base of "educational activism during slavery," and they tapped an intense thirst for education among those who had been held in bondage. Observers marveled at the enormous enthusiasm and commitment among male and female, young and old, parent and child; and by early 1866 hundreds of day and evening schools, Sabbath schools, "native" schools, and plantation schools were in operation. The Freedmen's Bureau school inspector estimated "the whole number of pupils" in the former slave states at more than 90,000 and believed that "much more is being done."[22]

The task was daunting. The missionary associations, aid societies, and Freedmen's Bureau provided some assistance, but outside of the cities and larger towns and away from the densest plantation areas, the burdens of establishing and running schools fell chiefly to the freedpeople themselves. They had to pool their meager resources, rent or purchase a tract of land (or prevail upon their employer to provide a parcel for them), build a schoolhouse, and hire a teacher. Those who lived in nonplantation districts had a particularly difficult time "owing to the great scarcity of freedpeople" and the distances that separated them. But even where plantations—and therefore large concentrations of black folk—were to be found, and even after Republican Reconstruction governments began funding public schools, poverty and the rhythms of household labor threw up enormous obstacles for any educational project. Most remarkable, therefore, were the lengths to which many freedmen and women would go "to secure the advantages of education" for themselves and especially for their children. They moved to more promising locales, walked miles to attend classes, and sacrificed sleep and sustenance. "They are anxious to learn," a less than sympathetic white North Carolinian conceded, "and will deny themselves of any comfort to send their children to school."[23]

Freedpeople clamored for schooling because they viewed it simultaneously as a rejection of their enslaved past and as a means of power and self-respect in the postemancipation world. Literacy would permit them to negotiate the new relations of production and exchange, involving as they now did contracts, store accounts, mortgages, and promissory notes. It would allow them to fend off the duplicities of "unprincipaled employers" and merchandisers and to make use of the judicial system. It would expand their political horizons and better equip them to exercise the new rights of citizenship. And it would enable them to read the Bible. Freedpeople could be seen "during the intervals of toil" holding "some fragment of a spelling book in their hands, earnestly studying." One Scottish traveler who visited a night school in Montgomery, Alabama, noticed "a perfectly black man of about fifty years of age studying a big Bible that lay on the desk before him" and discovered that "he is a labourer on a farm a good way out of town" who comes "every night as punctual as the clock," usually "without his supper that he may be here in time."[24]

Impressive as such individual exertions were, book learning was likely to be a family and collective undertaking, and one in which familiar hierarchies of authority could be disrupted or inverted. When the "colored citizens" of Oak Hill in Granville County, North Carolina, petitioned the local Freedmen's Bureau agent to see about furnishing a teacher for the "log school house" they expected to put up, they signed as heads of twenty-two families, at least four of whom were women. Black women seem indeed to have played a particularly active part in advancing the cause of education by helping to form school committees, raise the necessary funds, ready the buildings, and find and board the teachers. They seem, as well, to have seized every available opportunity to gain literacy and then, like many school-age children, to have become teachers in their own rights. A federal official in Georgia, who was impressed with the freedpeople's "desire for education," noted in mid-1867 that "many are learning from each other," and the "children which have been in school for the past two years have become the private tutors of their parents and other adults."[25]

But the schoolhouse was an educational center in an even broader sense. It was not only a place where freedmen, women, and children could learn to read, write, and cipher; it was also a place where they could be taught about the course of Reconstruction, the substance of their rights, the goals of the Republican party, and the importance of voting. Local leaders, Union army officers, and Freedmen's Bureau agents might address community assemblies there, and teachers usually saw their educational role as extending well beyond book learning. Klans assumed an almost inextricable connection between the schoolhouse and the Union League or Republican party because much of what went on there appeared to aid the ends of partisan mobilization. Small wonder that African Americans in Craven County, North Carolina, who gathered to organize a "free school" could "resolve that the system of universal education is necessary to the permanence of republican institutions."[26]

Indeed, Klans widely assumed that schoolteaching was a mere cover for more overt political objectives and that schoolteachers were chiefly concerned with emboldening the freedpeople, turning them against white employers, and currying their favor for the Republican party. "There was a Carpetbagger from Connecticut teaching a Negro school between Greensboro and Newburn," a vigilante in the western Alabama black belt recalled. "He pretended to be teaching, but he was organizing the Negroes in some kind of League and was drilling them every Saturday." A black Union League president nearby, complaining that local whites were "badly opposed to order and peace and welfare of the colored people," told the governor that "several men of the most pernicious character" had accosted their "peaceful teacher." "Cursing him," they vowed to "fix him well . . . the first time they found him in the league, or reading newspaper or in the act of giving instruction to colored people in regard to equality of race, or privilege acquired by from the damned *radical party*." Both of these teachers, white northerners, escaped with threats; others who stood their ground were generally whipped and driven off. Black teachers—women and men—fared even worse. They could expect to be humiliated and whipped or murdered.[27]

As early as 1867, African Americans composed about one-third of the teachers to be found in the fledgling freedmen's schools, and their proportion grew over the course of Reconstruction. This, in good measure, reflected a mix of attainment and intimidation: the increasing literacy of former slaves and the declining willingness of northern whites to venture into the South. But it also reflected the role of local schools as vehicles of black political power and patronage. For as the state Reconstruction governments began to create public school systems, county superintendents and school boards gained the authority to impose new taxes, establish schools, and employ teachers. And where black voters formed majorities and were able to cast ballots, the results could be startling. In Republican-dominated Panola County, Mississippi, black school enrollment exploded from 55 to 750 and then to 1,884 while the number of black schools more than quadrupled; in 1873, the superintendent could count forty-three African-American teachers, most native to the county, who "by close application had fitted themselves for teachers of the lower grades."[28]

When, therefore, vigilantes burned schoolhouses, assaulted teachers, and harassed appointed or elected school officials, they struck at a newly constituted political hub, and one that could align the balances of local power in several ways. E. H. Adams of Colorado County, Texas, embodied the interconnections as schoolteacher, Union League leader, and militia officer. Attacked by a white man wielding a hatchet in the summer of 1871, he explained that "the people do not know how to appreciate a colored man here that has any part at a learning . . . they said they wanted to get Rid of me and did not want no d——d nigger School Teacher and Capt about them." Klansmen and other vigilantes, that is, marked the broad parameters of Reconstruction's paramilitary politics.[29]

❖

The geography of Klan activity was, in essence, a map of political struggle in the Reconstruction South. Klan-style vigilantism surfaced at some point almost anywhere that a substantial Republican constituency—and especially a black Republican constituency—was to be found: from Virginia to Florida, South Carolina to Texas, Arkansas to Kentucky. Reports of "outrages" and "depredations" emanated from areas that were heavily black (eastern North Carolina, west-central Alabama), heavily white (east Tennessee, northwest Georgia), and racially mixed (eastern Mississippi, northwest South Carolina, east-central Texas). But whether the eruptions were brief or prolonged and whether they achieved their objectives depended on the nature and effectiveness of black resistance and, by extension, the readiness of the state Republican governments to respond with necessary force.[30]

Spectacles of intimidation notwithstanding, Klansmen could ride few places without some fear of resistance or retaliation. They might be fired on by intended victims, frustrated by pickets stationed outside Union League meetings, confronted by guards defending targeted leaders and structures, ambushed by armed bands, or challenged by federal troops. Outside the town of Carthage, Mississippi, in June 1868, a raiding party of fifteen disguised white vigilantes was foiled because "the colored men were in too great a force to be attacked safely." In Maury County, Tennessee, that same year, blacks, having "promised to stand by each other if we were attacked," came to the aid of local leader Pleasant Hillman after his "doors were broken down" by the Ku Klux Klan. They struck back "with muskets and revolvers" and, "in this way kept them off and defended ourselves . . . until daylight when they left." In 1869 in Sumter County, South Carolina, threats against a local storekeeper who "trad[ed] with Negroes" prompted the blacks to organize "at once" and vow to "burn all the dwellings and cotton houses in the township" if that store was destroyed. A Republican newspaper in Greensboro, North Carolina, in 1869 went so far as to recommend that the party become "one vast vigilance committee" and "avenge the blood that has been shed before it is yet cold in the earth."[31]

Union Leagues and Republican party clubs had, in some places, already begun to mount a response to Klan violence, at times bringing pressure against suspected Klan leaders. Black members of a Pickens County, Alabama, Union League boycotted a white landowner thought to be "head of the Ku Klux." They were so effective that, in his words, he "could not hire a darkey at any price." In a number of locales scattered across the plantation districts, they appear to have taken even more direct and destructive action by torching the mills, barns, and houses of former slaveholders. But the leagues and clubs more likely moved to put themselves on a paramilitary footing, if they had not embraced rituals of armed self-defense from the outset. Black Union Leaguers in Darlington County, South Carolina, fearing Klan violence, gathered weapons, took control of a town, and threatened to burn it down in the event of attack. Near Macon, Mississippi, the combination of local outrages and the very bloody Meridian riot led blacks to organize "secretly" and ready themselves to "meet the mob." "There will be no more 'Meridians' in Mississippi," a white ally of theirs declared. "Next time an effort of this kind is made there will be killing on both sides." The tenor of conflict and mobilization in Granville County, North Carolina, in the fall of 1868 was such that a prominent Democrat offered Union League members a bargain: "if we would stop the leagues he would stop the Ku Klux."[32]

There were social and demographic boundaries to the work of the

Klan. Vigilantism was generally sporadic and organized offensives were uncommon in areas where the black population outnumbered the white by at least twofold. The coast of South Carolina and Georgia and the river counties of Mississippi did not see any outbreaks; there, African Americans composed at least two-thirds of the population. But the effect of numbers cannot easily be distinguished from that of early mobilization. Where freedpeople were concentrated on large plantations and had begun to construct political institutions during or immediately after the war—often owing to the presence of Union troops, black and white—they presented formidable obstacles to raiding parties and other forms of vigilante terrorism. Tunis G. Campbell, who built a base of power in coastal McIntosh County, Georgia, made the point in describing the widespread atmosphere of intimidation together with his varied fortunes in campaigning for a seat in the state senate. "At one place in Liberty County [68 percent black] they swore they would shoot me down on sight," he told a congressional investigating committee, "but the negro people began to swear too, and as they outnumbered the others three to one, the others left." Matters were rather different in neighboring Tatnall County, also in the senatorial district, where three of four denizens were white: "I could not go [there]; I found they had too many guns for me."[33]

A foundation of political experience and armed strength could compensate for shortfalls in numbers. In the Lower Cape Fear region of North Carolina, blacks composed just under half of the population, although they accounted for nearly 60 percent in New Hanover County where the town of Wilmington was located. Whites had a long tradition of militia activity, with a full regiment available in New Hanover, while federal troops (there since the very last months of the war) had been reduced to a token number. As the election to ratify the new Radical constitution and fill state and county offices under it approached in April 1868, the Klan, headed up by a member of the local gentry who had commanded a Confederate cavalry unit and served as a militia staff officer, threatened a reign of intimidation. But blacks, especially in Wilmington, had been active in the Union League, perhaps as early as the summer of 1865, and were prepared to meet force with force. On the night of Saturday, April 18, unexpected by the Conservatives or the Klansmen, they commenced patrolling the streets with guns and fence rails. Four "tempestuous" nights later, they had ended the career of the Ku Klux Klan in Wilmington. When the votes were counted, the constitution won ratification and the Republicans took four of the seven Cape Fear counties and carried Wilmington by a margin of two to one.[34]

If the streets of Wilmington required four tempestuous nights to secure against the Klan—and larger urban areas were generally inhospitable to Klan vigilantism—the countryside proved far more difficult to police and defend. In the cotton-growing interior, even in black majority districts, African Americans were likely to be found in relatively small groups on plantations and farms, all the more so as gang labor gave way to tenancy and sharecropping, while the combination of their poverty and previous rounds of white raiding left them without horses or adequate weaponry.[35] It is indeed remarkable that Union Leagues and other political clubs did as well as they did, given the rather inauspicious moment at which Klan violence first erupted. By the spring and summer of 1868, federal troops in the former Confederate states numbered fewer than 20,000 on fewer than one hundred posts, the Freedmen's Bureau was being phased out, and the new Republican governments were, at best, in the very early stages of organization with no authority to establish and call out a militia.[36]

If anyone still harbored doubts, Klan violence demonstrated that political power in the Reconstruction South grew out of the barrel of a gun. Not surprisingly, the governors who first and best grasped this truth were hardened veterans of the civil wars that had recently raged between and within the states. Republican William G. Brownlow, the "fighting parson," hailed from the Unionist stronghold of east Tennessee and became the state's governor in early 1865 under the provisions of Lincoln's Ten Percent Plan. But Confederate strength in middle and western Tennessee left him with a shaky foundation once the war ended, so as he faced the critical state elections of August 1867 (Tennessee had already been readmitted to the Union) he pressed successfully for black suffrage and mobilized a state guard composed chiefly of fellow east Tennessee Unionists. Democrats groaned about the "Brownlow Malisha," and for good reason; the troops not only encouraged the expansion of Union Leagues among freedmen but also secured Brownlow's reelection and Republican control of the legislature. Just over a year later, after Klan activity had flared for several months, that legislature empowered Brownlow to raise a new militia and impose martial law in affected counties. Thus armed, Brownlow kept the Klan in check and the Republicans in charge until his departure for the U.S. Senate resulted in the installation of a successor more interested in making amends with the opposition.[37]

Like Tennessee, neighboring Arkansas had a white population majority, a solid base of Unionist sentiment in the mountains of the northwest, and a Republican party that looked to punish former Confederates. But Arkansas had been remanded to military rule by the Reconstruction Acts of 1867, and in the spring of 1868 eligible voters put Republicans in command of the general assembly and the carpetbagger Powell Clayton in the governor's chair. A native of Pennsylvania and a civil engineer by training, Clayton had been out in Kansas during the 1850s and commanded a Union cavalry regiment in Arkansas during the war, where he saw a good deal of action against Confederate guerillas. After the surrender, he settled in Arkansas and bought a plantation, but run-ins with ex-Confederate neighbors led him into politics; he first helped to organize the state Republican party and then accepted the party's nomination for governor. By the time of Clayton's inauguration in July, Klan activity was sufficiently pronounced in the southern and eastern sections of the state that he wasted no time in responding: with the approval of the legislature, he began mobilizing a state militia and, as intimidation of Republican voters and local officials intensified and a Republican congressman fell victim to a Klan ambush, he declared martial law in ten counties. Armed skirmishes between militiamen and Klansmen, together with arrests, trials, and a few executions, followed. By early 1869, the Klan had pretty well "ceased to exist" in Arkansas.[38]

Both Robert K. Scott in South Carolina and Edmund J. Davis in Texas similarly oversaw the creation of state militias and put them to use. Scott, a Union army general and Freedmen's Bureau assistant commissioner, was particularly focused on the Klan-infested upcountry and sent in well-armed black troops, helping to secure his reelection in 1870. Davis, a Texas Unionist who had organized a loyalist cavalry during the war, declared martial law in at least two counties, and statewide, his forces made over 4,500 arrests in eighteen months. In a move that befitted the peculiar political culture of Louisiana, the carpetbagger and ex–Union army officer Henry Clay Warmoth not only asked the legislature to authorize a militia bill shortly after he was inaugurated as governor in the summer of 1868, but also quickly established in and around New Orleans the Metropolitan Police Force, which effectively served as his private army.[39]

Yet Warmoth proved reluctant to equip and deploy militia units in other parts of the state, fearing that the appearance of predominantly black troops would both alienate moderate whites and incite further violence. His concerns reflected the contradictions of paramilitary politics in the Reconstruction South. While Republican governors generally recognized the need for an active militia to protect their constituents, most hoped to expand their power base by attracting white support. Although militia service was, in principle, open to all able-bodied men, few whites came forward, leaving the governors with militias that were overwhelmingly black, and therefore emblems of the illegitimacies that repelled whites.[40]

In North Carolina, the contradictions bedeviled the regime of Governor Holden. No novice to the world of political violence, Holden moved to organize a state militia soon after his election in 1868. But hoping for a peaceful resolution and refusing to authorize the use of armed blacks (at least outside the coastal areas), he responded to escalating Klan terrorism in the piedmont (where black and white populations were roughly in balance) by issuing proclamations, appealing for order, and requesting federal assistance. It took two years and the brutal assassinations of Wyatt Outlaw and Republican state senator John W. Stephens before Holden finally called in the troops—in this case white troops recruited from western North Carolina and eastern Tennessee. By then it was too little, too late. Despite scores of arrests, the Democrats gained majorities in ten of the counties that had experienced Klan violence and won control of the state legislature; they then added insult to injury, making Holden the first governor in American history to suffer impeachment, conviction, and removal from office.[41]

Elsewhere, much less was done. In Mississippi, the Whig-turned-Republican governor and Delta planter James L. Alcorn agreed in 1870 to organize a militia but the legislature, dominated by moderate white Republicans, refused appropriations for weapons and equipment. In Alabama, the Republican legislature provided enabling legislation, but as Klan terrorism exploded in the Tennessee Valley and the western black belt, the scalawag governor William H. Smith refused to act. In Georgia, white Republican conservatism and Democratic power in the assembly combined to preclude any action.[42]

The accession of Republican Ulysses S. Grant to the presidency in March of 1869 offered some welcome possibilities to those governors who stood ready to deploy state militia units. Previously, the Johnson administration had refused requests for arms, and governors were left scrambling to equip their troops. Arkansas's Powell Clayton first tried to borrow guns from various northern states and then, when this failed, sent an emissary to New York to purchase rifles and ammunition. Unfortunately, a contingent of well-prepared Klansmen intercepted the shipment between Memphis and Little Rock. Florida's carpetbag governor Harrison Reed chose to go personally to New York to procure arms soon after the legislature passed a militia law in August 1868, but the result was even more embarrassing. Under the nose of a federal detachment, Klansmen boarded the train carrying the armaments to Tallahassee and destroyed them. Grant, on the other hand, proved more receptive than Johnson and made substantial supplies of weapons available to Governors Holden and Scott in the Carolinas.[43]

Even more consequentially, the national government itself finally moved in earnest against the Klan and masked vigilantism generally in 1870–1871, when Congress passed the Enforcement Acts, making various kinds of political harassment and terrorism federal offenses. Arrests and indictments quickly ensued, primarily in the Carolinas, Mississippi, and Alabama, and although few convictions were ever obtained, they appear to have broken the back of the Klan's operations. But the damage was already enormous and impossible to repair. Beginning with the fall elections of 1868, vigilante violence played havoc with Republican voters and set back party mobilization. Louisiana experienced the most dramatic consequences, as the Knights of the White Camelia and the Klan had almost free rein outside of New Orleans and the adjacent parishes of the southeast. Republican majorities that had put the party in control of the legislative and executive branches of government in the spring evaporated. Caddo Parish in the northwest was not at all unusual. In April 1868, according to a congressional investigating committee, the 2,987 Republicans "carried the parish"; "in the fall they gave Grant one vote." "Cowed and frightened" was how one white Republican described the spirit of his mostly black fellow constituents. Georgia, with no militia and a timid party organization, also saw a precipitous decline in Republican voting strength and the delivery of the state's electoral votes to the Democrats. But even where the Republicans managed to withstand the onslaught, they were weakened and their vulnerabilities exposed.[44]

Chief among those vulnerabilities was the failure to provide more than sporadic protection to the party's leaders and followers. With federal troops in diminishing supply and governors reluctant to activate militias, local supporters had to rely on their own devices and resources, which could obstruct but rarely derail Klan terrorism. Assassinations of prominent figures were particularly frightening and demoralizing, suggesting as they did that no one could move about safely. The victims of Klan murders and assaults included Republican congressmen, state legislators, former delegates to constitutional conventions, and county officeholders: not least armed sheriffs and constables, magistrates, and solicitors.[45] But undoubtedly most devastating were the relentless attacks upon grassroots leaders and the structures of black mobilization. Although the toll is impossible to calculate with any precision, it must have run into the many hundreds, if not thousands. These were the organizers, the registrars, the teachers, the ministers, the petty property owners, the skilled, the literate, and, of course, the officers of Union Leagues and political clubs—murdered, whipped, humiliated, threatened, and driven off. In some places—especially in North Carolina, Georgia, Alabama, and Texas—the leagues and associated infrastructures of political life were almost wholly destroyed, thereby depriving African Americans not only of effective means of struggle and empowerment, but also of their best mechanisms for collective defense and retaliation.[46]

Across the South, however, the destruction was by no means total. Advances on the local and state levels were still being made, most notably in the black-majority districts of South Carolina, Mississippi, and Louisiana, while black political power along the southeast Atlantic coast and the lower Mississippi Valley remained well entrenched. As the federal government arrested and indicted reputed Klansmen, the Republican regimes in the Deep South, outside of Georgia, still stood, however shakily. Yet rather than undermining the base of terrorism, the federal offensive against the Klan ironically expanded it. For by moving chiefly against those who embraced the tactics of conspiracy and disguise while simultaneously reducing its own troop strength, the federal government enabled southern Democrats to pursue their counterrevolutionary activities much more openly and brazenly. Unable or unwilling to grasp the essentials of paramilitary politics, national Republican leaders thus set a disastrous course for their allies in the South at the very moment they seemed to bring the most deadly of the vigilantes to heel.

❖

Klan-style paramilitarism always existed alongside other forms of political violence and coercion and cannot be easily dissociated from them. They included personal intimidation, threats of dismissal from employment, harassment of Republican party voters and supporters, manipulation of ballots and returns, and what contemporaries (and later historians) called "riots." Together they came to compose the materials of various "plans" for ridding the former Confederate states of Republican rule and black power: the Georgia plan of 1870, the Alabama plan of 1874, the Mississippi plan of 1875, or the South Carolina plan of 1876. Each, with its own peculiar mix, meant the use of violence, fraud, and intimidation to achieve the political end of "redemption." But what appear to be mere variations on a theme were rather increasingly organized and tenacious battles. For if the Klan managed to weaken the institutional bases of rural black politics, it was generally too diffuse and uncoordinated to dislodge Republican regimes and reclaim political supremacy in more than limited areas. That work would be left to the rifle clubs, the White Leagues, and the Red Shirts—the true paramilitary wings of the Democratic party. They would not only have to overawe, outmuscle, and outgun the Republicans through most of the individual states and often across state lines; they would also have to destroy the African-American capacity for armed resistance.

The Klan's effectiveness depended on a wider political climate that gave latitude to local vigilantes and allowed for explosions of very public violence. Louisiana and Georgia, which alone among the reconstructed states supported Democrat Horatio Seymour for the presidency in 1868, had at least seven bloody riots together with Klan raiding that summer and fall.[47] The term "riot," which came into wide use at this time, quite accurately captures the course and ferocity of these eruptions, claiming as they did numerous lives, often over several days, in an expanding perimeter of activity. But "riot" suggests, as well, a disturbance that falls outside the ordinary course of political conduct, and so by invoking or embracing it we may miss what such disturbances can reveal about the changing dynamics and choreography of what was indeed ordinary politics in the postemancipation South. Simultaneously harking back to forms of struggle prevalent under slavery while illuminating new sites of tension and conflict that came with freedom and the franchise, the "riots" demonstrated in convulsive ways something far more generally applicable: that the ballot box registered not so much the balances of public opinion as the results of paramilitary battles for position.

Consider the Camilla riot in southwest Georgia, which captured the greatest attention but shared many features of the others. In late August 1868, Republicans in the state's Second Congressional District, most of whom were black, met in the town of Albany and nominated William P. Pierce, a former Union army officer, failed planter, and Freedmen's Bureau agent, for Congress. It would not be an easy campaign. Although the party had claimed the governorship and formal control of the legislature in elections the previous spring and although black voters outnumbered whites in the district by a margin of roughly two to one, the atmosphere quickly became ominous. In early September, moderate white Republicans joined with Democrats to expel thirty-two duly elected African Americans from their seats in the state house and senate, and as Pierce began his canvass it appeared that the district's Democrats had become emboldened. A "speaking" in the town of Americus on September 15 brought menacing harassment from local whites and Pierce barely escaped violence. But he did not interrupt plans for a similar event in Camilla on Saturday, September 19.[48]

News of the rally—which would feature Pierce, several other white Republicans, and Philip Joiner, a former slave, local Loyal League president, and recently expelled state legislator—circulated through the neighboring counties. So, too, did rumors of a possible attack by armed whites who, it was said, proclaimed that "this is our country and we intend to protect it or die." Freedpeople did have ample cause for alarm. Camilla, the seat of relatively poor, white-majority Mitchell County in an otherwise black majority section of the state, crackled

with tension. Gunfire had broken out there during the April 1868 elections, and many of the blacks had resolved that they would "not dare
. . . go to town entirely unarmed as they did at that time." The white
Republican leaders tried to quell these fears when the Dougherty
County contingent gathered on their plantations on Friday night the
18th; and as the group moved out on Saturday morning for the twenty-
odd mile trek to Camilla, most heeded the advice to leave their weapons behind and avoid a provocation.[49]

The procession was led by a wagonload of musicians playing fifes
and drums. Moving southward, it attracted the attention of growing
numbers of freedmen, women, and children, who left the fields and
joined the ranks. Others, departing Mitchell County plantations and
farms in small groups, converged as well. Perhaps half of the men
toted firearms of some kind for protection and effect (most only had
birdshot for ammunition), while many of the others carried walking sticks. Collecting at China Grove, a short distance from Camilla,
they numbered between two and three hundred. In several important
respects—finding safe havens the night before, marching in quasi-
military fashion, sounding fife and drum, welcoming the participation
of the entire community—they displayed practices associated with
Union Leagues, Republican political clubs, and drilling companies, and
expressed their intent to claim the full rights of citizenship.[50]

But to the whites of Camilla, such a procession could only constitute
a "mob," with no civil or political standing, and mean "war, revolution, insurrection, or riot of some sort." Once spotted on Saturday
morning, it thereby sparked another round of rumors, these warning
of an "armed body of negroes" heading toward the town. Although
evidence suggests that local Democrats had been busy for at least two
days accumulating weapons and preparing to respond with force, the
rumors clearly sped the mobilization of the town's "citizens," who
appointed a committee to ride out with the sheriff and "meet the approaching crowd." A tense exchange followed, with the Republican
leaders explaining that they only wished "to go peaceably into Camilla
and hold a political meeting," and the sheriff warning them not to
enter the town with arms. It was not hard for the seasoned leaders to
see the risks of accommodating the sheriff and stacking their weapons,
though they briefly looked into shifting the meeting's site to a nearby
plantation. But when the plantation owner refused them, fearing that

"the people would be down on him," they determined to continue as planned, with their arms, and have speeches at the Camilla courthouse, as was their "right." For his part, the sheriff returned to town and effectively deputized the entire white male population.[51]

Two of the white Republican leaders riding in a buggy entered Camilla's courthouse square first. Some fifty yards back of them, the procession followed in what the sheriff described as a martial demeanor: "side drums and fifes going on, some commanding them in military order, they marching four deep" with "about twenty mounted negroes" who "seemed to act as outriders." But with their walking sticks and birdshot, the marchers could be no match for the "squads" of heavily armed whites waiting on the south and west sides of the square, confirming, it seemed, the rumors that had circulated earlier. Suddenly, a local drunkard, waving a double-barreled shotgun, ran out to the wagon and, significantly, demanded that the drumming (associated both with a citizens' militia and slave communication) cease. A moment later he fired, and the "squads" of white townsmen immediately joined in. Freedmen who had guns briefly returned the volleys and then, with the others, commenced a desperate flight for safety. The sheriff and his "deputies" followed them into the woods and swamps with deadly purpose, some looking for "that d——d Phil Joiner." Joiner escaped, but eleven days later he reported that "the mobing crowd is still going through Baker County and every Colored man that is farming to his self or supporting the nominee of grant and Colfax he either have to leave his home or be killed."[52]

Prospects for black retaliation briefly ran very high. As word of the shooting spread through Dougherty County that Saturday evening, agitated freedmen in Albany sought out the local Freedmen's Bureau agent. Some talked of going immediately to Camilla to rescue and protect those who remained at risk. A few hours later, African Methodist minister Robert Crumley heatedly reminded his congregants that he had advised those bound for Camilla the night before not to go with fewer than 150 well-armed men, and then suggested traveling there en masse the next day to "burn the earth about the place." The Freedmen's Bureau agent managed to discourage such a course by promising a full investigation and urging his superiors in Atlanta to send federal troops. The investigation showed Camilla to be a massacre that had left at least nine African Americans dead and many more wounded. But all that came out of Atlanta was a proclamation by Republican governor Rufus Bullock urging civil authorities to keep the peace and safeguard the rights of the people. Election day proved to be remarkably quiet in southwest Georgia because the contest was over well before. Only two Republicans bothered to cast ballots in Camilla, and the turnout was so low elsewhere in the district that the Democrats, despite being greatly outnumbered among eligible voters, registered an official victory. There would be resurgences of local black power in the future, but this was the beginning of the end for Republican rule in Georgia.[53]

Even more emblematic of the developing dimensions of Reconstruction's paramilitary politics was yet another "riot" and massacre—one of the very bloodiest in American history—which took place in Colfax, Louisiana, on Easter Sunday 1873. Whereas Camilla revolved principally around the question of whether black Republicans would be able to exercise their political rights and claim the use of public space for political purposes in relative peace, Colfax exploded out of the complex struggle for state and local power that the dynamic of Reconstruction was increasingly producing, a struggle that (it became clearer and clearer) would be decided in favor of the side with the greatest firepower at its disposal. Latifundist in character, the cast at Colfax included rural bosses, rival claimants, and private armies all connected to a larger drama being played out in New Orleans over who would hold the reins of authority in the state.[54]

Located in the heart of the Red River Valley, Colfax was born of the Republican party's effort to reclaim the Louisiana countryside after the violent political debacle in the fall of 1868. For as the Warmoth legislature drove to centralize power and loosen the Democrats' hold on the rural districts, it created nine new parishes whose officials were initially to be appointed by the Republican governor. One of these, carved out of Rapides and Winn, was the bailiwick of scalawag William Calhoun, who owned five plantations and had won a seat in the state assembly. Named Grant Parish in honor of the new president, it was evenly divided racially, with blacks numerically dominant along the river bottoms and whites in the hilly pine woods back of them. Fittingly, the parish seat, named in turn for Grant's vice president Schuyler Colfax, was not a town but one of Calhoun's plantations, with a stable serving as the courthouse.[55]

It did not take long for Grant Parish to become entwined in the bitter battles of the state's Republican party or for Calhoun to begin losing influence among the local party faithful. The most substantial challenge came from a group of black radicals who bridled at Governor Warmoth's attempts (with, it seems, Calhoun's approval) to attract white votes by appointing moderate-to-conservative Republicans to important parish offices. Two of the blacks were ex-slaves from the parish who had previously been allied with Calhoun; but four had served in the Union army and became acquainted while stationed at Ship Island, Mississippi, soon after the war. The most formidable of them was William Ward, an ex-slave from Virginia who plied the skills of carpentry, rose to the rank of sergeant, and, after leaving the army, followed one of his buddies to Grant Parish. Undoubtedly owing to his military experience, Ward quickly received commission as the captain of a state militia unit there.[56]

Ward took his militia duties seriously. When one of his white allies was assassinated by disgruntled conservative opponents, Ward used his militia company not only to arrest the murderers, but also to round up other conservatives suspected of violating the recently enacted federal Enforcement Acts. So independent and forceful was his behavior that the Warmoth administration, fearing the political fallout, ordered the company to disband. Ward refused to comply and continued to drill his men, helping to strengthen the radicals' grip on local power and to unite black Republican support for a ticket he headed up in the 1872 parish and state elections.[57]

The elections threw the entire state into crisis, for the fraud and intimidation were so great that they produced the first example of Reconstruction's paramilitary conundrum in the Deep South: dual governments. The regular Republicans had been opposed by a Fusionist ticket made up of conservative Republicans and Democrats, and both sides claimed to have won control of the governorship and the legislature. Only federal authority and troops could break the deadlock, but in the meantime outgoing Governor Warmoth issued commissions to the Fusionist claimants in Grant Parish, who took office in January of 1873. For a while, rival legislatures deliberated in New Orleans, but after the Metropolitan Police thwarted a Fusionist coup attempt in late February, the Republicans gained recognition as the rulers of Louisiana. When their governor, William Pitt Kellogg, hesitated to endorse the commissions that Warmoth had issued, Ward (who now represented the parish in the legislature) and his followers made their move. Toward the end of March, catching the Fusionists off guard, they seized possession of the courthouse.[58]

Rumors began to spread almost immediately that allies of the ousted claimants intended to retake the courthouse and hang Ward and the other radicals. As a consequence, when an armed party of roughly fifteen, headed up by planter and reputed Klan leader James Hadnot, did approach Colfax on April 1, they found it well defended and were forced to retreat. Skirmishing over the next few days, coupled with the murder of a black farmer by another armed white band, further polarized the situation and led black men, women, and children from the surrounding countryside to flee into Colfax for protection. By Monday, April 7, about four hundred of them were camped out at the courthouse. But such alarm notwithstanding, the skirmishing also demonstrated that on their own, Grant Parish conservatives lacked the numbers and firepower to dislodge the radicals. They therefore called for "reinforcements," and a "veritable army" of vigilantes (many former members of the Klan or the Knights of the White Camelia) from Winn, Rapides, Natchitoches, and Catahoula parishes rapidly assembled in Grant "to suppress negro domination."[59]

In the eyes of the conservatives, the blacks defending Colfax "assumed a semi-military character," with elected officers, mounted guards, pickets, constant drilling, and weapons that included shotguns and Enfield rifles. And there can be little question that the signs of militia and related organizational experience were very much in evidence. The blacks began to build an earthwork around the courthouse, fashioned crude artillery out of pipe, and, led by the women, scoured the countryside at night for provisions. But the truth was that only eighty of their number had arms and, looking out on a white paramilitary force of roughly three hundred replete with cannon, their prospects for holding off an attack were dim. Ward knew that they, too, needed reinforcements, and on April 9, with a few other leaders, he slipped out of Colfax and headed for New Orleans hoping to summon state and federal troops. Levin Allen, another Union army veteran, was left to hold the now entirely black fort, as the few white Republicans remaining in Colfax hastily departed.[60]

Once the Civil War began, slaves rebelled against the authority of their masters and headed to Union lines, increasingly with family members and the goods they had struggled to obtain. These men, women, and children from the "upcountry" arrived at the federal encampment in New Bern, North Carolina, in early 1863. (*Harper's Weekly*, February 21, 1863, p. 116)

After the Emancipation Proclamation, growing numbers of slave men, who had rebelled by flight against their masters, enlisted in the Union army to fight against slavery and the Confederacy. These black troops under the command of General Edward A. Wild, known as the "African Brigade," liberated slaves in North Carolina. (*Harper's Weekly*, January 23, 1864, p. 52)

Slaves who made it to federal lines and contraband camps during the war and, owing to gender and age, did not serve in the Union army, created new sites of freedom, some of which endured into the postwar period. This "Freedmen's Village" was constructed in Hampton, Virginia. (*Harper's Weekly*, September 30, 1865, p. 613)

At the Trent River Settlement, a freed village in eastern North Carolina, Union generals John B. Steedman and James S. Fullerton confer with freedpeople in their church. (*Harper's Weekly*, June 9, 1866, p. 361)

Although Radical Reconstruction extended the franchise to African-American men, the conduct of politics involved the mobilization and participation of entire communities, without regard to gender or age. Here black men, women, and children listen to an aspiring candidate for office. (*Harper's Weekly*, July 25, 1868, p. 468)

For African Americans during Reconstruction, the practice of electoral politics often required martial organization and armed self-defense. These black voters in Lincoln County, Georgia, guns in hand, ford a creek on their way to the polls. (Charles Stearns, *The Black Man of the South and the Rebels*, New York, 1872, p. 419)

Suffrage made it possible for African Americans, especially in the plantation districts, to elect black officeholders and other local officials, like this member of the police force. (*Scribner's Monthly*, June 1874, p. 157)

Freed adults as well as children eagerly seized the opportunity to educate themselves during Reconstruction, and black women played a particularly important role in the establishment and maintenance of new local schools. (*Harper's Weekly*, May 21, 1870, p. 336)

White vigilantes, many of them ex-Confederate soldiers, harassed, disarmed, and murdered members of freed families who sought to achieve economic independence or to exercise their civil and political rights. (*Harper's Weekly*, February 24, 1872, p. 160)

White paramilitary violence aimed to destroy the developing infrastructure of black political life (such as Union Leagues, Republican clubs, schools, and churches) and the political leadership most effective in mobilizing the black vote for the Republican party. (*Harper's Weekly*, August 8, 1868, p. 512)

In 1875 and 1876, rifle clubs and White League paramilitary units connected with the Democratic party helped topple the last Republican governments in Mississippi, South Carolina, and Louisiana. The violent intimidation of black leaders and voters played a central role. (*Harper's Weekly*, October 21, 1876, p. 848)

CONVENTION!

To the Freedmen of North Louisiana:

FELLOW-CITIZENS: In order that we may unite in a common band of brotherly love and union, I, as President of the Negro Union Co-Operative Aid Association, appeal to the Freedmen without regard to sex, religion or politics, to immediately assemble in their respective religious bodies, and all other societies as may choose, to send Delegates to a Convention which will meet in Shreveport, at 12 m., on

Thursday, Dec'r 5, 1878.

To the discouraged we have but one remark to make: Join with us and try by one mighty effort to elevate ourselves morally and socially, and to aid each other in getting lands and homes, that we may not give all we make every year to stay on somebody's plantation. The foregoing is presented to you as a plan for coming together in council to devise a general plan whereby we may become united as a race.

APPORTIONMENT FOR DELEGATES:

Any organized Religious Body, one delegate; any Benevolent Society, one delegate; any Secret Organization, one delegate; any Plantation with 50 persons, one delegate; any organization composed exclusively of Negro people, one delegate. Each delegate is requested to come prepared to pay the sum of two dollars towards paying the expenses of the Convention.

OFFICERS AND DIRECTORS.

R I Cromwell, President; E Allen, Vice President; O Morris, Secretary; J Cleaveland, Treasurer; P James, Ass't Treasurer; H Human, Agt. J Alexander, E Johnson, Aaron Williams, J M Mitchell, R L Cook, Chas. Wilson, S High, H Adams, President Liberia Council.

After the collapse of Reconstruction, rural blacks interested in finding "lands and homes" of their own began to direct their political energies toward building an emigration movement, either to the west or to Liberia. One group, the Negro Union Cooperative Aid Association, made an inclusive convention appeal and organized the apportionment of delegates according to the institutional bases of African-American life. (Papers of the American Colonization Society, courtesy of the Library of Congress)

In the early phases of what became known as the "exoduster" movement, black emigrants from the rural districts of the Gulf states arrived in St. Louis on their way to Kansas. (*Frank Leslie's Popular Monthly*, January 1880, p. 48)

Black families from Phillips County, Arkansas, on their way to Liberia. (*Frank Leslie's Illustrated Newspaper*, n.d.)

Alienated by Republican party failures to address their concerns and offer a fair distribution of political offices, some blacks voted the Democratic party ticket. The rewards, they believed, would be a measure of social peace and perhaps a share of local power. (*Harper's Weekly*, December 8, 1877, p. 972)

By the end of Reconstruction, African Americans in the rural as well as urban South were constructing an increasingly rich associational life of churches, lodges, and educational institutions, which also served as important political networks. This fraternal organization in Helena, Arkansas, around 1880 included two former state legislators. (Courtesy of A. H. Miller Collection, University of Arkansas at Little Rock Archives and Special Collections)

Most important was the emergence of the White League, and of the "White-Line" movement more generally, in Louisiana and Mississippi. Committed to drawing the racial "line" in politics and inviting "all white men without regard to former party affiliations" to "unite," the league was first organized in Opelousas in late April and then spread very rapidly. It clearly built on foundations established by the Klan and the Knights of the White Camelia—a Union army commander regarded the league as a "second edition of the White Camelia campaign of 1868"—but was even more directly aligned with the Democratic party. Indeed, leagues were often little more than local Democratic clubs converted into paramilitary companies. "If the democratic party is arrayed against the negro and the republicans," the *Opelousas Courier* proclaimed, "it becomes a White League, and no one can object to its efficient organization."[63]

White Leaguers surely recognized that the federal government was losing interest in interfering in southern politics and sustaining Republican regimes by military means. But they also responded to the growing assertiveness of African Americans within the Republican party, which showed itself in the rising incidence of black officeholding. Charges that blacks had first drawn the color line by refusing to vote Democratic and by demanding a greater share of the spoils from white Republican leaders, that "to oppose republicanism is to oppose negroism," clearly aided the campaign for white unity. Yet they simultaneously acknowledged that the struggle for black empowerment remained alive and would not easily be turned back. During the early 1870s there were in fact major increases in the number of blacks serving as state legislators and county officers, especially in Mississippi, Louisiana, South Carolina, and Alabama, with the high point reached in 1874. And many of these black leaders represented localities in which the Klan had been unable to launch an effective assault. The White League, therefore, sought to topple Republican rule by moving in force against both the leaders in the state capitals and, more importantly, the local bastions of black political power.[64]

Easily the boldest and most ambitious of the early operations was a well-orchestrated conspiracy on the part of the Crescent City White League—"a veritable who's who of New Orleans respectability"—to oust Louisiana governor Kellogg and the rest of the Republican state government in mid-September. Culminating in the "Battle of Ca-

Even in the face of segregation and meager resources, African Americans struggled to educate their children and, by extension, to empower themselves. These teachers and students attended a public school in Yazoo City, Mississippi, in 1908. (From Richard J. Powell and Jock Reynold, *To Conserve a Legacy: American Art from Historically Black Colleges and Universities*, Cambridge, Mass., 1999, p. 84; courtesy of Tuskegee University)

On Easter Sunday morning, April 1.
sheriff and one-time "respectable" Repub.
Nash came to deliver the ultimatum. He .
courthouse and promised the blacks safe passaṛ
would surrender their arms. Skeptical of such pro.
it was his duty to defend the courthouse, and dei
until aid arrived with Ward from New Orleans; Nash
minutes to evacuate the women and children. When the s
menced shortly after noon, Allen's crew managed, remarka.
the white army at bay for nearly two hours. Then the white
fire with their cannon and charged the black defenses. Some
blacks, in panic, headed toward the woods as the whites tried tᴄ
them down; others retreated to the courthouse, which was soon s
ablaze, and those who sought to escape the flames faced a hail of bullets. As the gunfire quieted, about forty of the blacks were left as "prisoners." Nash told them they would be released on good behavior the
next morning. But some of the younger members of the force thought
differently. That night, they took the prisoners out to a cottonfield
and shot them down. When state and federal officials finally came on
the scene two days later, the battle of Colfax was long over and more
than one hundred African Americans lay dead.[61]

By the mid-1920s, divisions of Marcus Garvey's Universal Negro Improvement Association could be found in many parts of the South, especially in small towns and rural areas. This division was organized in Decatur, Georgia. (Courtesy of Skip Mason Archives)

Colfax was to be a turning point, though for a time it was unclear which way events would turn. Initially, the Republicans were restored to parish office and federal authorities moved against the white aggressors, indicting ninety-eight of them for violations of the Enforcement Acts. But only nine could be arrested and brought to trial in New Orleans, and by the summer of 1874 most of them had been acquitted while a member of the Supreme Court sitting in on the proceedings declared sections of the Enforcement Acts to be unconstitutional—a position upheld by the entire court two years later in the famed *Cruikshank* case. What could, therefore, have been a red or yellow light in the face of paramilitarism turned into a green one. As the Colfax "prisoners" returned home to a jubilant white parish welcome in July, the consequences were already very much apparent.[62]

nal Street," when nearly nine thousand White League troopers routed a much smaller combined force of Metropolitan Police and black state militia, it fell short of its ultimate goal only because of the last-minute intervention of federal troops. But by that time, leagues had done substantial damage in the Louisiana countryside, crippling or overthrowing Republican officials in at least eight parishes, including Red River Parish where the sheriff, tax collector, a registrar, a justice of the peace, a Republican attorney, and several black Radical supporters were murdered near the seat of Coushatta in late August. By that time, too, White-Line counterparts in Vicksburg, Mississippi, had demonstrated how paramilitary mobilization and "very definite intimidation" could bring electoral success even where black voters held decided numerical sway.[65]

If anything still held back a full-scale white paramilitary offensive, it was removed when, in the November elections of 1874, congressional Democrats won control of the House of Representatives for the first time since southern slaveholders had rebelled against the national government. In Vicksburg, White-Liners seemed to commemorate the event by moving quickly to complete the work they had begun in the summer. This time, they focused on the county, rather than the municipal, government, which was almost wholly dominated by black Republicans, including the sheriff Peter Crosby, a native Mississippian who had served in the Union army during the war. Meeting in early December, they demanded the resignations of all the black officials and pressured Crosby to yield under what he regarded as threat of assassination. Crosby then headed to the state capital for help. Republican governor Adelbert Ames, of the party's radical faction, turned a sympathetic ear. He ordered the "riotous and disorderly persons" who had "expelled from office the legally elected sheriff" to "disperse and retire peaceably" and "submit to the legally constituted authorities." He also instructed a Warren County militia company to "cooperate" with Crosby's effort to "regain office" and "suppress the mob," and suggested that Crosby should summon a posse for further assistance.[66]

Ames's orders did little to change the behavior or temper of the Vicksburg whites, but Crosby's call for a posse revealed a strong foundation of loyalty and organizational readiness among African Americans in the surrounding countryside. With dispatch, owing to the churches, political clubs, and other institutions of black community life, a major mobilization took place. As several hundred blacks marched in three columns toward Vicksburg, even Crosby feared the consequences and tried to turn some of them back. It was too late. Whites opened fire and, despite some brief standoffs, the blacks were forced to flee. For another ten days, some of the young white participants, joined by reinforcements from across the river in Louisiana, stayed on "the war path." When the smoke cleared, at least twenty-nine African Americans had been killed and a great many more had been wounded and terrorized. The seat of county government remained in the hands of the White-Liners. And Peter Crosby, briefly held prisoner, was compelled to resign yet again.[67]

Ames called the state legislature into special session and together they succeeded in convincing Grant to send a company of federal troops to quell the disturbances in Vicksburg and reinstall Crosby as sheriff. But Crosby's days in office were numbered and so too, it appeared, were those of Republicans over much of the state. For the several-month White-Line campaign in Vicksburg and Warren County amounted to a "rehearsal for redemption" in Mississippi. Torchlight processions, paramilitary drilling, the disruption of Republican political meetings, the harassment of black workers, the intimidation and assassination of black leaders, the driving off of local officeholders, and the disabling of armed black resistance—all of which made their appearance in Vicksburg in 1874—were to come into concerted use in 1875 in counties that previously had "safe" Republican majorities. "Riots" at Friar's Point and especially at Clinton, a few short miles from the state capital, gained the greatest notice and seemed to epitomize the "Mississippi plan," but they did not differ in their essentials from the events that unfolded in Yazoo, Amite, Monroe, Noxubee, Claiborne, Chickasaw, De Soto, Holmes, Madison, and Panola counties.[68]

Ostensibly, Mississippi Democrats resolved to "win" the 1875 state and local elections "at all hazards," and they did devote considerable energy to ensuring a large turnout of white voters. But in the black-majority counties the important work would be completed well before the polls ever opened—if they did ever open. By the end of August, Democrats had widely organized to "overawe the negroes and exhibit to them the ocular proof of our power." In eastern Monroe County (more than 60 percent black), they had formed a committee of twenty, with five from each district, and moved on several fronts: meeting secretly, raising funds, selecting the "enemy's" vulnerable points, and training military companies of "60 or 70 men each." There, and in many other such counties, they planned to pressure their black employees, hold torchlight parades at the county seat, wear red or gray shirts (harking back to the Confederacy), amass rifles and cannon, and break up Republican political assemblies by heckling speakers, demanding a "division of time," and making a general show of force. The intent was to "deter [the negroes] as much as possible from holding meetings and from organizing other clubs," that is, to destroy their ability to mount a campaign, defend their ranks, and contest for power.[69]

The Clinton riot of early September erupted during one of these assemblies at which, not incidentally, at least five or six hundred black men arrived in "clubs," some mounted on horses, led by the aptly named Oliver Cromwell in a plumed hat and cavalry saber, and marched "around the place for about an hour and a half." It eventuated in "detached squads of white men . . . scouting through the country murdering and driving the colored people from their lands," in utter defiance of the Republican sheriff's attempts to summon a posse and bring the squads to heel. Republicans in Hinds County would not again gather in large numbers that fall, and many of the clubs were simply abandoned. In Oktibbeha County (almost two-thirds black), Democrats "made it a point" to whip the leaders of "negro drum companies" and disperse their meetings. In Lowndes County (three-quarters black), the former slave, Union League organizer, state senator, and candidate for sheriff Robert Gleed was forced to flee "for fear of his life" as "young [white] men went along" with "cannon and pistols and one thing and another . . . very much like an army." Whites in almost "every neighborhood" of Copiah County (half black), according to the weary Republican sheriff, had "formed themselves into military organizations," "purchased and armed themselves with army guns and bayonets and cannon," and ordered African Americans seeking to assemble "back to their homes." In many parts of the county, the sheriff added, the blacks "even had their pocket knives taken from them." Armed "democratics" in Madison County (more than 70 percent black) were similarly brazen; they challenged Republican clubs marching to their meeting grounds, tried to have some of the members arrested, and, on one occasion, fired into the house of Bailers Fairfax, a local black leader who, together with several other blacks, had "rented the Kinch Kearney Plantation for the year."[70]

Cotton-producing Amite County, on Mississippi's southern border with Louisiana, has not assumed a prominent place in the historical telling of Reconstruction. It was not the home of well-known political leaders nor was it the scene of a major riot or massacre. Yet in many ways it exemplified the paramilitary politics of the state's "redemption." With African Americans accounting for more than six in ten of the county's inhabitants, the Republican party had a substantial potential base of support and, owing to effective mobilization, it succeeded in winning control of the local government in the early 1870s. By 1875, Republicans dominated the board of supervisors, four of five of whose members were black, and claimed the sheriff's office with a white yeoman farmer who had initially been appointed by the military governor in 1869 and then was elected by a more than 650-vote margin in 1873. Amite was, in short, quite securely in Republican hands by the standards of conventional electoral politics, and former slaves had succeeded in gaining and exercising significant power.[71]

But there was never anything conventional about the electoral politics practiced in Amite County during Reconstruction, and in 1875 White-Line Democrats set out on a "campaign of intimidation . . . through military organization" and resolved that the sheriff "and other county officers should be tarred and feathered and taken beyond the borders of the county." They began making visits at night to the "houses of prominent negroes" and the "officers of negro clubs," and warning that elected Republicans would "not be allowed to live and hold the place." In this, they sent "parties" who "were not known to the negroes" but instead came from a "neighborhood seven, eight, or ten miles away." Using armed pickets, paramilitary companies, and reinforcements from Louisiana, they created further "difficulties" for black Republicans by preventing them from attending a local nominating convention and disrupting other political gatherings. Before the end of September, the sheriff worried that Amite was "approaching a similar to worse condition than that of Clinton."[72]

African Americans were not about to abandon the field, however, and none of them seemed more determined to fight back than William DeShields. A farm laborer who had accumulated a little personal property and learned how to read and write, DeShields had emerged as a leader in the county's third district and was sufficiently effective to be regarded by white Democrats as "a very bad negro." He had won a seat on the board of supervisors and, in the face of White-Line harassment, wanted to "organize a Republican club" with two hundred other black laborers and get gubernatorial permission to "drill" as something of a state militia unit. "We dont intend any harm by this application," he told the governor in making the request; "we want to keep even with our 'beloved democrats.'" Fearful of what would undoubtedly be considered a provocation, the sheriff advised DeShields against pursuing such a course; we do not know how the governor responded. On a dark Sunday night shortly thereafter, "a party of white men" rode to DeShields's house, called him out, and shot him dead. "I imagine in this state of things there is something similar to Mexico. A Mexican state of society," a white Mississippian who sympathized with the Republicans later explained to a congressional committee. "[A]nyone who can get fifteen or twenty desperate fellows at his heels can do as he pleases; and that is about the way it is down there in the lower part of Amite County."[73]

DeShields may well have heard that Governor Ames had begun to mobilize the state militia after the Clinton riot and the Grant administration's refusal to lend additional military assistance. He may not have heard that Ames's effort was half-hearted and exceedingly delimited from the first, and had already been abandoned when DeShields asked for the "privilege to organize and drill." By the time of the election, Democratic clubs held complete sway in the Amite County countryside, firing their guns, ransacking the dwellings of black folk at will, and running many of them off. According to one estimate, at least five hundred black men were to be found "laying out" in the woods to escape the terror. When the votes were "counted," the strong local Republican majority had evaporated and the Democrats claimed victory. They celebrated the next night by forcing the sheriff out of the county.[74]

Amite County was not simply Mississippi writ small. But when the "campaign of 1875" came to a close, the county seemed very much a variation on a process that had enabled Democrats to wrest control of the state legislature and conquer local Republican strongholds. Sheriffs and other Republican officeholders had been driven out or debilitated—some before the election, some during, and some after—in at least ten plantation counties. Paramilitary squads terrorized rural districts, county seats, and other polling places, sometimes with the help of counterparts from Louisiana and Alabama, on election eve and election day in most places where an organized Republican constituency was still to be detected; where quiet seemed to prevail, it was most likely the result of coercive operations concluded earlier on. Months later, after "only a partial and cursory examination of the innumerable cases" of election law violations, the foreman of a federal grand jury in the northern district of Mississippi could conclude that the "fraud, intimidation, and violence perpetuated" in 1875 were "without a parallel in the annals of history."[75]

Ames was not scheduled to stand for reelection in 1875, but when the new Democratic state legislature convened in January 1876, its members moved against him much like Democratic legislators in North Carolina had moved against William Holden a few years before. Threatened with impeachment, he resigned in late March and left Mississippi for good. Ames's carpetbag ally Albert T. Morgan, the sheriff of Yazoo County who was himself forced to flee the previous September, pronounced the epitaph, though it was one to which the governor would surely have assented. "When the general arming of the whites first became known to me . . . I counseled [the colored men] against irregular arming, advising all to rely upon the law and its officers," Morgan informed a congressional investigating committee. "I hoped by steadfastly pursuing this course, by offering no pretext for violence, we might pass the ordeal I saw approaching." "I was," he sighed, conceding his mistake, "unused to guerilla warfare."[76]

It is fitting that the last major battle of Reconstruction took place in South Carolina, where the slaveholders' rebellion began, and more fitting still that the once haughty Carolina planters, who had achieved a remarkable unity against the antislavery challenge, faced the most formidable struggle anywhere in the former Confederacy to reclaim state and local power. They had, first, to mend divisions over matters of strategy within their own ranks, and then, to defeat well-organized and armed freedpeople, who would prove quite resistant to their blandishments and threats. It was here that the paramilitary politics of redemption reached their greatest intensity.

By the mid-1870s, it appeared that conservatives in South Carolina had many of the same opportunities as their counterparts in Mississippi, Louisiana, and Florida. The state Republican party was racked by internal tensions and federal troop strength was limited. But given South Carolina's substantial black majority and extended experience of black political mobilization, the party was much better positioned to withstand attack and retain power. Black Republicans were so well entrenched in the low country that vigilante violence proved of little consequence there and the best that conservatives could hope for was some sort of coalition with moderate or disgruntled Republicans that would enable them to exert influence and trim the sails of Radicalism. In the upcountry, on the other hand, the balance of forces was more evenly split and the white landed elite rough and aggressive: the heirs, as it were, of the eighteenth-century regulators rather than of the coastal aristocrats. Here the Klan had ridden to notable effect; here it was possible to imagine an end to "negro rule"; and here the "shotgun" and "straight-out" policies that paved the way to redemption were hatched and nourished.[77]

It was in 1874, around the time the White League surfaced in Louisiana and Mississippi, that a paramilitary network of rifle and sabre clubs began to take form in the South Carolina upcountry, and especially in areas such as Edgefield County, across the Savannah River from Georgia. The organizers were substantial landowners already prominent in local agricultural societies, Granges, and conservative political clubs, and they built on a foundation of activity established by the Klan, the Confederate army, and the antebellum militia. The young Ben Tillman, later to serve as the state's governor and U.S. senator, helped to form one of these—the Sweetwater Sabre Club in Edgefield—and by 1876 Republican governor Daniel Chamberlain was estimating that almost three hundred rifle clubs with at least 14,000 members were at work throughout the state. By that point, too, the rifle clubs were propelling the gubernatorial campaign of General Wade Hampton, the wealthy planter and Confederate war hero, in a reconstituted "Red Shirt" paramilitary movement.[78]

The rifle clubs and then Red Shirts did not simply confront the Republican party's numerical advantages. In early 1869, both as a response to Klan violence and as an effort to ensure his reelection the next year, Governor Robert K. Scott signed a legislative bill creating a new state militia. Although whites as well as blacks were eligible to enroll, the refusal of most South Carolina white men to serve with black men, and the refusal of Scott to commission all-white militia companies, effectively laid the basis for a black militia. And black men, with wide community support, greeted the prospect with great enthusiasm. By the fall of 1870, nearly 100,000 may have joined, and in this they were assisted by an African-American network of political and paramilitary organizations. Indeed, it appears that marching companies, Union Leagues, and Republican clubs—many already practiced in drilling and protecting freedpeople in the exercise of their rights— often presented themselves and were accepted as units into the ranks. At other times, a black officer might be met by black people from all parts of a county, who would quickly form militia companies and elect or appoint officers. Mustering would likely begin before arms and ammunition were furnished by the state, but the black militiamen soon made a powerful impression. Describing the "show" put on by the "negro militia" in August 1870, a white resident of Laurensville complained that "our darkies were dressed in black coats and white pantaloons, those from Cross Hill in Red coats and white pants—Clinton men in yellow coats and white pants" with "four men" parading "up and down on horseback through the streets."[79]

Black militia companies made an important difference in the 1870 election, coming as it did amid a wave of Klan terrorism, and although their official standing and relationship with the state government proved to be complex, they became central to black political life in many South Carolina localities. In Newberry County, according to a disgruntled white observer, freedpeople "never had any political gatherings or any celebrations, except these companies appeared with their arms," and their performances (if we may overlook his obvious hostility and exaggeration) combined overt repudiations of submissiveness with symbolic representations of the new links between sites of community activity and the institutions of state authority. Thus: "They marched through the streets frequently, and shoved everybody off the sidewalks who came into contact with them. . . . Their celebrations generally occurred in a grove not far from the town; and they generally closed their celebrations by marching into the courthouse square and occupying the courthouse steps, from which harangues were delivered to them." There and elsewhere, the militia could simultaneously be a vehicle for and an acknowledgment of local leadership and empow-

erment. In Edgefield County, four black state legislators had remarkably similar profiles. All had been slaves. All possessed skills (carpenter, teacher, shoemaker, barber). All had acquired literacy. All were
ministers or deacons in the Baptist church. All owned real estate. All
had held positions in the Union League, Republican party, or county
government. And all served as officers in the state militia.[80]

The close connection between black political power and militia organization in Edgefield County may help explain the determination
and ferocity of the white counterattack, given over as it came to be
with the forays of rifle clubs and the rejection of compromise or fusion
arrangements with any Republicans. Certainly by the mid-1870s, politics in Edgefield was chiefly a paramilitary undertaking, and as early as
1874 armed whites sought direct confrontations with black militiamen.
Edward "Ned" Tennent and his company were the first of the targets.
A former slave, Union League official, and soon-to-be-elected county
commissioner, Tennent was despised both for his fearless and ostenta-
tious demeanor (he adorned his hat with an ostrich plume) and for his
effective work as a militia captain. To celebrate the Fourth of July that
year, he had drilled his men in Meriwether Township to the playing of
fife and drum; hours later, young members of the Sweetwater Sabre
Club fired into his dwelling on a local plantation as "a warning [to]
frighten him or precipitate trouble of some kind and bring on a conflict." Shaken though uninjured, Tennent had his drummer sound the
"long roll," and by morning about two hundred militiamen had assembled, sparking rumors of black vengeance that hastened the massing
of sixty or seventy members of the sabre club. Only the quick action
of a federal army officer defused the impending confrontation, but it
would not be long before Tennent was again pursued, this time for
allegedly torching the residence of the prominent Edgefield planter and
Democratic political leader General Matthew C. Butler.[81]

What Ben Tillman called the "Ned Tennent riot" set the stage for
a far more serious and politically consequential paramilitary encounter
precisely two years later in the nearby town of Hamburg. With an
overwhelmingly black population and a local government wholly under black control, Hamburg represented just the sort of enclave that
most whites found threatening and rifle clubs wished to destroy. One
white leader, boasting in the spring of 1876 that "the democrats had
made it up in their minds [to kill] a certain number of niggers, leading

men . . . so they could carry the majority," reportedly added that "if they could be successful in killing those they wanted to kill in Hamburg, they would certainly carry the county." It would not necessarily be easy to do. Hamburg had experienced and savvy leadership, chiefly in the person of Prince Rivers, a former slave and Union army veteran who had been active in the Union League and elected or appointed to a variety of posts, including state legislator and major general in the state militia. By 1876, Rivers owned real and personal property and was serving as a local trial justice. The town also had a recently revitalized militia unit under the command of Dock Adams, another Union army veteran and "boss carpenter," who had come over from Georgia where he previously organized a militia company and ran for local office. Although Adams spoke of the oppression that blacks suffered in Georgia as the explanation for his move to South Carolina, he may too have been "implicated" but never charged in an "insurrection of negroes" in Georgia's Jefferson County. At all events, Adams was tough, independent, and militant, drilling his men with "thumb-loading rifles" once or twice a week rather than once a month as the law required.[82]

On July 4, 1876, the hundredth anniversary of American independence, Adams and his company were parading on the main street of Hamburg when they had an altercation with two young white men, from locally prominent families, riding in a buggy. The young men demanded the right of way; Adams initially refused, then relented. Both parties filed complaints before Prince Rivers. Hoping to keep the peace and apparently having his own differences with the truculent Adams, Rivers scheduled a hearing for July 8. He could hardly have welcomed the result. The white plaintiffs not only retained Matthew Butler as their lawyer but also arrived in Hamburg with armed members of local rifle clubs, including Ben Tillman's. Butler did not intend to bargain or abide by legal procedures. In bellicose fashion, he simply insisted that Adams's company give up their arms and apologize for their behavior on the Fourth. Recognizing the danger, even Rivers suggested that the militiamen turn over their weapons, but Adams and his men instead took refuge in their "armory" in town. As more rifle clubs appeared on the scene, Butler hastened across the river to Augusta for artillery and additional reinforcements. The shooting commenced in the early evening and raged for almost five hours. A black town marshal and militia lieutenant were gunned down, and as the rifle clubs' volleys intensified, some of the blacks began to flee. Adams managed to escape, but others were wounded and about thirty were captured. Before dawn, five of the black prisoners regarded as particularly obnoxious were executed with bullets to the head; the rest were ordered to run and then fired on. "We are going to start at Hamburgh, and we are going to clean out the government offices, from Chamberlain down to the last one in South Carolina," one of the white paramilitary men taunted. "By God we are going to take your guns [and] . . . the United States Government hain't got anything to do with it . . . the Constitution is played out, and every man can do just as he pleases."[83]

Hamburg polarized the state along partisan lines and thereby bolstered the position of the "straightout" Democrats in the upcountry, who continued their offensive against organized and armed black Republicans. In mid-September, after some skirmishing, rifle clubs surrounded a militia unit in a swamp near Ellenton in Aiken County, shooting and killing numbers of black men before a detachment of federal troops arrived. These and other white paramilitary bands went on to harass black militia officers and presidents of political clubs in the vicinity, insisting that the groups be broken up and the meetings cease on pain of death. "A perfect reign of terror," in the words of a federal official, spread through the surrounding districts, as the rifle clubs rode "day and night," forcing a great many black men to lie "out of doors and away from their homes." The "Colored citizens of Laurens county," having witnessed the assassination of white ally and militia officer Joe Crews, complained to Governor Chamberlain that they were now "under intimidation and without the least protection whatever with our lives in jeopardy every day." A Republican trial justice in Barnwell County described the "condition of affairs" as "truly deplorable," with "armed bands of mounted men," none "other than the Rifle Clubs," "raiding about the country every night threatening the colored people."[84]

And yet we must not underestimate the extent and tenacity of black resistance. White toughs did, to their misfortune, in the village of Cainhoy, a short distance from Charleston. Attempting to intimidate a Republican speaker at a "joint discussion" in mid-October, they found themselves outgunned as well as outnumbered by a black crowd that included several militia companies. When the smoke cleared, five whites lay dead and as many as fifty had been wounded. Most in evidence along the coast, such militance was nonetheless to be found at various points in the interior. As rifle club activity intensified in Barnwell County, a "company of negroes," acting on their own authority, appropriated arms issued during Governor Scott's administration and "threaten[ed] to destroy the town" of Blackville. In Darlington County, a "negro militia company consisting," according to a local Democrat, "of the worst elements in this section," continued to drill and cause "a great deal of trouble," coming in one instance to the aid of a favored trial justice. Sporadically, there were acts of arson and sabotage, ambushes and assaults.[85]

More consequentially, black mobilization and resistance influenced the strategies of South Carolina Democrats in the campaign of 1876 and then confounded some of their efforts. Upcountry "straightouts" had followed events in Mississippi closely and hoped that the "Mississippi plan" of 1875 might serve as their guide. But owing to black numbers and organizational strength, it proved well-nigh impossible to embrace a White-Line solution. They would rather need to combine paramilitary violence and intimidation with some attempt to attract black votes. Gubernatorial candidate Wade Hampton—the voice of "force without violence"—took the lead in this, assuring "the colored people that their rights are fixed and immovable" and appealing for their support at the polls. But even advocates of the "shotgun" policy recognized that overturning black majorities would require more subtle work as well: concentrating on "selected negroes," forming "affiliated Democratic clubs," and protecting "all who will come in and behave themselves." Edgefield County's Martin Gary who, in a Machiavellian turn of mind said he preferred murdering a Radical to threatening one ("a dead Radical is very harmless—a threatened Radical . . . is often very troublesome, sometimes dangerous, always vindictive"), still expected every Democrat to control at least one black vote.[86]

It was not without effect. Martin Delany, the northern free black, Union army officer, and disgruntled Republican, campaigned enthusiastically for the Democrats in the fall, while a mounted guard of roughly five hundred, led by ex-slave Richard Mack of Orangeburg County, appears to have marched with Hampton across much of the state. On the local level, there was further activity, with enclaves of black support detected in Charleston, Columbia, and in Barnwell and

Abbeville counties, if not in some other rural districts. According to one estimate, as many as eighteen black Democratic clubs with nearly seven hundred members may have been formed in Barnwell.[87]

Yet given the climate of paramilitary intimidation and the fissures rupturing the Republican party along class, race, and factional lines, it is remarkable how few African Americans defected to the Democrats. In part, this was because Hampton's promises of good will and protection had, to say the least, a hollow ring. An "independent" black Republican with sympathies for conservatism and reform saw the Democrats "frame a ticket discarding my race" and could only conclude that they had "made up [their] minds that this is the white man's land and must forever remain so." Far more important, however, were the community solidarities that managed to survive the onslaughts since emancipation and both anchored loyalties and brought sanctions against those who thought to stray. The Barnwell County Democratic Executive Committee conceded as much when instructing party clubs "to operate on the individual negro and carefully avoid attempting to influence him in masses." "Just as much as your party has vim, ours has got vim," an African-American constable from Aiken County told a congressional committee in explaining why he refused to join the Democratic party when approached. "Just as certain as I was to go and join your democratic club I wouldn't be safe. I wouldn't know but they might kill me."[88]

Most striking indeed about the reports of conflict and turmoil within African-American political communities at this moment was less the indication of real struggle over party allegiance (under whatever circumstances) than the evidence of harsh treatment meted out to the few who chose to align with the Democrats. In urban and rural areas, in low country and upcountry alike, black Democrats were mobbed, shot at, beaten, verbally abused, and warned off by black Republicans. The harassment became a community undertaking, with black women— widely regarded as among the most loyal and vociferous Republicans—often assuming the lead. Even where Democrats might find some fertile grounds of support among African-American men (as in Abbeville County), they generally met stiff opposition from African-American women. Not for nothing did white Democrats go out of their way to emphasize the "protection" they were ready to offer black allies. And not surprisingly, those allies tended to have longstanding dependent relations with (usually wealthy) whites and thus were less vulnerable to the punishments that black communities might impose. The most generous estimate suggests that a mere five thousand blacks statewide cast ballots for Wade Hampton in 1876 (less than 5 percent of those eligible to vote), and we cannot know how many of them did so voluntarily.[89]

In the end, despite the work of the rifle clubs, it took massive fraud on election day for the Democrats to claim victory for Hampton and a majority in the legislature. In Edgefield and Aiken counties, home to the architects of the "shotgun policy," black Republicans managed to vote in substantial numbers and Democrats had to report returns that, in sum, exceeded the entire voting age population of the counties. The claims were viably contested by Republicans, who believed that, without the fraudulent results, Chamberlain had been reelected and they still controlled the legislature. By mid-December, two governors had been inaugurated and two legislatures attempted to rule the state.[90]

✦

The paramilitary politics of the Reconstruction South had previously produced dual state governments in Louisiana (1872), Texas (1873), and Arkansas (1874), but in 1876–1877 they also provoked a national crisis of governance. Not only were the state returns contested in both South Carolina and Louisiana, but there, as well as in Florida, the electoral college returns were contested too, leaving the outcome of the Presidential race—and control of the executive branch—in doubt. As Republicans and Democrats struggled to reach an accord before Grant's term expired in early March, tensions and threats that harked back to the winter of 1860–1861 seemed to abound. Yet through all of this, what appeared to be taking shape was less a "compromise" than a shared political sensibility in northern ruling circles that questioned the legitimacies of popular democracy. That sensibility had always been in evidence among conservatives and had spread during the 1850s, only to be pressed to the margins by the revolutionary mobilizations of the 1860s. It now expressed itself as weariness with the issues of Reconstruction, as skepticism about the capabilities of freedpeople, as concerns about the expansion of federal powers, as revulsion over political corruption, and, especially, as exasperation with the "annual autumnal outbreaks" in the Deep South and the consequent use of federal troops to maintain Republican regimes there.

It required elaborate fictions and willful ignorance for critics to argue, as some did, that the military had no business rejecting the popular will in the South. For if detachments of federal troops at the statehouses in Columbia, South Carolina, and New Orleans, Louisiana, alone enabled Republicans to hang onto the last threads of power, their Democratic rivals made no effort to conceal their own dependence on superior force of arms. In Louisiana, Democratic gubernatorial claimant and former Confederate brigadier general Francis T. Nicholls quickly demonstrated his understanding of political necessities. He designated local White League units as the legal state militia, commandeered the state arsenal, and took control of the New Orleans police. In South Carolina, Wade Hampton's allies succeeded in garrisoning the state capitol with as many as six thousand Red Shirts, while rifle clubs drove out Republican officeholders in upcountry counties. Although the Democrats, in both cases, avoided a direct resort to violence, fearing further federal intervention, the threat of violence hung palpably in the air (Hampton reportedly boasted that he held Governor Chamberlain's life in his hands). And as efforts to resolve the national crisis proceeded, these large-scale paramilitary deployments made Nicholls and Hampton the de facto governors of their states.[91]

But it was not, in fact, the continued use of federal troops per se that repelled most northern critics of Reconstruction. It was rather the use of federal troops to empower certain groups over others. The problem of American political life, as the editors of *The Nation* saw it in the spring of 1877, was that the very notion of "majority government" had been transformed in such a way as to threaten the fate of the republic. At one time, it had meant "a majority of taxpayers, or a majority containing a fair representation of the intelligence, sagacity, and social and political experience of the population," and this had allowed the "establishment of universal suffrage by the abolition of the property qualification" to come "easily." But now, in the "great cities" as well as in the Reconstruction South, "political power" was being severed from "intelligence and property," and the "rule of a mere numerical majority" was being "made visible." Had this "severance" existed at the time of the nation's founding, "the republican form would assuredly never have been adopted," for the men who "formed the bulk of earlier settlers" never would have "lodged [power] in the hands of a proletariat." "Every man of character and patriotism and conscience" would feel obliged to "resist" such a "state of things" even by "force." Thus, far from "condemning the people of South Carolina and Louisiana" for their "determination to overthrow [Ring rule] by hook or by crook," *The Nation* felt "indebted to them" despite "their occasional resorts to violence."[92]

The withdrawal of federal troops from the statehouses of South Carolina and Louisiana in April of 1877 did not therefore mark the end of their role in protecting the rights and property of American citizens; it only marked the end of their role, at least for nearly another century, in protecting the rights and property of African Americans and other working people. If anything, the collapse of Reconstruction and the defeat of Radicalism nationwide ushered in a new era of state-organized violence in defense of private property and respectable prop-ertyholders at all levels of government: the deployment of federal troops in labor disputes and to secure the trans-Mississippi West for white settlement; the professionalization of state militias and the Na-tional Guard; the expansion and retraining of urban police forces. Unlike their Republican predecessors, Democratic governors in the redeemed South would not hesitate to use (now white) state militia companies—if local paramilitary outfits did not suffice—to maintain "order" in black-majority districts.[93]

African Americans in the countryside were not vanquished politi-cally with the ending of Reconstruction. There remained significant enclaves, owing to numbers and organizational strength, where blacks could still exercise their electoral muscle and place their representatives in the seats of local and state governments, if not in Congress. In some of these, they negotiated complex power-sharing agreements with rival Democrats who had failed to dislodge them. Elsewhere, the struggle to realize or redefine their goals of community reconstitution and self-governance took a variety of forms outside of the electoral arena, most combining the old with the new in ways that would chart the course of political activity for decades to come. But it also seemed dishearten-ingly familiar. From the birth of the American republic until the spring of 1861, blacks as slaves and free people had conducted their politics in a context of official hostility and repression, where the apparatus of the state was in the hands of those who denied or ignored their claims and aspirations. Then, for nearly two remarkable and revolutionary decades, they not only gained a dramatically new standing in civil and political life; they also had an access to state power that few other working people had ever or would ever enjoy. Now the state was again controlled by their avowed enemies or by those who were indifferent to them.

Yet if this appeared to be merely another example of a revolution gone backward, appearances could be deceiving. The revolution that African Americans, the "jacobins of the country," had played such a signal role in advancing had substantially weakened the old guard, and the Redeemers, well-armed and enthusiastic as they may have been, were in fact a motley and rather fractious crew. Dominated by land-owners who had been Democrats, they nonetheless included merchants, townsmen, and manufacturers, a good many of whom had previously been Whigs. They did not have a unified vision of the redeemed South's future, and the restoration of "home rule" did not bring with it a return to the national power they had once shared. The consequences would be felt by all southerners in the last depression-ridden decades of the nineteenth century, and for African Americans the economic hardships would be accompanied by the old fists of exploitation and oppression. But there would be new possibilities as well.[94]

PART III

The Unvanquished

7

THE EDUCATION OF
HENRY ADAMS

I have conversed with colored men here from Mississippi, Alabama, Arkansas, and Georgia . . . [and I told them I] was working for my race to get them to leave the Southern States . . . for God says . . . that he has a place and a land for all his people, and our race had better go to it.

Henry Adams, 1880

In November 1878, Henry Adams, a self-described "laborer" and grassroots organizer, joined with thirteen officers and members of the Shreveport-based Negro Union Cooperative Aid Association in calling upon the "Freedmen of North Louisiana" to meet in convention. They had just suffered through tumultuous state and local elections in which Democrats sought forcibly to complete the work of Redemption in the densely black northern and northeastern parishes, and they wished "to devise a general plan whereby we may become united as a race." Adams had been active in promoting mass emigration to Liberia or to some other part of the United States while many of the others favored resettlement within the South, but all of them hoped the convention would contribute to "one mighty effort to elevate ourselves morally and socially, and aid each other in getting lands and homes, that we may not give all we make every year to stay on somebody's plantation." Significantly, they "appeal[ed] to the Freedmen without regard to sex religion or politics, to immediately assemble in their respective religious bodies, and all other societies" to choose delegates according to the following plan of "apportionment": "Any organized religious body, one delegate; any Benevolent Society, one delegate; any Secret organization, one delegate; any Plantation with 50 persons, one delegate; any organization composed exclusively of Negro people, one delegate."[1]

The convention call simultaneously expressed aspirations held by most African Americans in the southern countryside and identified the social bases and parameters of their politics. It thus draws our attention to a field of political activity that can easily be overlooked, though only at great peril. Indeed, by the late 1870s emigrationist sentiment had not only gained a wide hearing but had also constituted a substantial movement among black laborers, chiefly in the cotton South—a movement that belies the notion that Redemption set black politics into full-scale retreat. What we can see, instead, is a reconstitution of the relationship between the electoral and other arenas of political practice, and the emergence of projects and conflicts that would shape the social and political landscape for the next three decades.[2]

Henry Adams's education suggests how this might have been so, mapping as it did many of the intellectual and political thoroughfares that eventuated in what may be called grassroots emigrationism. Born a slave in rural Newton County, Georgia, in 1843, Adams and his family were taken some seven years later to the Louisiana parish of De Soto, bordering northeast Texas, where they worked on plantations until learning of emancipation in June 1865. Owing perhaps to his being hired out during the last few years of slavery and to the influence of his father, who preached the gospel in the face of white intimidation, Adams brought into freedom some personal property together with an extremely independent disposition. "I feared God but not man," he claimed to have told a local planter who had warned him of the inveterate hostility of poor white folk. And refusing to sign a labor contract, he took to the roads of De Soto and neighboring Caddo Parish, usually heading to and from Shreveport.[3]

Harassed, robbed, and beaten as he tried to fashion a livelihood and having witnessed an array of other "outrages" inflicted on freedpeople, Adams decided to join the U.S. Army in September 1866. For the next three years, he served in three units and rose to the rank of quartermaster-sergeant, all the while imbibing powerful and enduring lessons. Like many of the African Americans who enlisted in the Union armed forces during the Civil War, Adams learned how to read and write. "I knowed the letters and figures when I seed them," he later recalled, "but I could not put them together under no circumstances" until taught by a white woman at Fort Jackson, on the outskirts of New Orleans. At the same time, he had occasion to travel across Louisiana, on the roads and waterways, visiting plantations and farms and riding the steamboats, where he not only saw many of the everyday brutalities of black life but also suffered personal indignities and discrimination despite wearing the emblems of federal authority. So it was that Adams and "a parcel of we men that was in the Army" came to bridle at "the way our people had been treated during the time we was in service" and apparently determined "to organize ourselves" after being discharged.[4]

Forming a secret committee, Adams said he attracted as many as five hundred followers in a quest to "look into affairs and see the true condition of our race, to see whether it was possible we could stay under a people who had held us under bondage." To that end, "one hundred or one hundred and fifty" of them "worked our way from place to place and State to State," at their own expense, "amongst our people in the fields, everywhere, to see what sort of living our people lived." Splitting rails and managing plantations for W. C. Hambleton and Company to earn his bread, Adams spent much of his time in the environs of Shreveport (where he owned a town lot with his cousin, purchased with his army bounty), using his skills and experience to help freedpeople negotiate contracts, settle accounts, and "get what was due them." But he also seems to have moved along the Mississippi and Red River valleys of Louisiana and "conversed with colored men here from Mississippi, Alabama, Arkansas, and Georgia." Reports filtering in from other committee members, although suggesting more favorable conditions in Virginia, Missouri, Kentucky, and Tennessee, generally comported "with what we saw and what we had seen in the part where we lived . . . it was very bad."

Thus, when Louisiana's White League burst on the scene in the spring and summer of 1874 and "said this is a white man's government, and the colored men should not hold any offices," Adams and his comrades called a meeting in Shreveport and organized a Colonization Council. Believing "it was utterly impossible to live with the whites of Louisiana," they sent a petition to President Ulysses S. Grant that September, asking "to be removed to a territory where they could live" and voicing a willingness "to be sent to Liberia, if no better place could be given them." Three years later, another meeting of the council adopted "a preamble and set of resolutions," addressed this time to President Rutherford B. Hayes, that also requested the appropriation of "some territory in which we may colonize our race" or the "means whereby we can colonize in Liberia or some other country," if protection "of the rights guaranteed to us by the Constitution" could not be afforded them in the South. They explained that "the colored people of the South had been debarred from . . . the right to *vote hold office* and the privilege of *education* without molestation," and that they "have been *oppressed, murdered,* and *disfranchised* on account of our race and color." They expressed the fear that the "*blood of the martyrs of freedom*" had "been *shed* in *vain*" during the Civil War, since "after twelve years we find the colored race of the South in a worst Condition . . . [and] a worse state of Slavery . . . than they were before those Constitutional guarantees were extended." They likened their grievances to "the passage in Lamentation Chapt. 5 of the Holy Scriptures" and doubted that they could "live in the South in peace, harmony, and happiness." And they saw in "the exodus of Our people to some country where they can make themselves a name and nation" the "only hope and preservation of our race." But now several hundred supporters had their names attached to the document and perhaps as many as five thousand attended the meeting, representing—according to Adams—"69,000 colored people of the South."[5]

By the time that Henry Adams helped form the Colonization Council in 1874, emigrationist sentiment had found a popular base in the southern states, although its lineage was complex and contradictory. Surfacing in the late eighteenth century, and receiving more powerful expression in the 1830s and then the 1850s, black emigrationism—customarily represented as involving migration out of the United States—originally won support principally from the ranks of educated, urban, and entrepreneurial free men of color in the North who chafed under the hardening racism and political vulnerabilities they increasingly encountered. While their interest in the project ebbed and flowed, many embraced what could be regarded as an early, civilizationist, variant of pan-Africanism: They searched for a site in Africa, Latin America, or the Caribbean where they might have the opportunity to enjoy freedom, to prosper, and to uplift the black masses by converting them to Christianity and petty bourgeois values. Never building a substantial movement, they nonetheless gave important shape to antebellum black political discourse and generally displayed sharp antagonism to the goals of the white-dominated American Colonization Society (seeking to rid the nation of its free black population in part as an incentive to gradual emancipation), which did succeed in settling nearly eleven thousand African Americans (nearly all from the slave states) in Liberia by the outbreak of the Civil War.[6]

It is, therefore, ironic that the work of the American Colonization Society may have had the most immediate influence on the rapid emergence of interest in emigration in the postemancipation South and, even more, that freed blacks seem to have adjusted the society's goals to their own purposes. As early as the fall of 1865, the society began receiving applications for passage to Liberia, and by the fall of 1866 it reported that "never perhaps in the history of the American Colonization Society . . . have calls upon it for help to Liberia been more numerous or pressing." Eager parties resided in cities, towns, and villages as well as in rural districts, but overwhelmingly in Virginia, the Carolinas, Georgia, and Tennessee, the states that together contributed seven in ten of those who migrated to Liberia under the society's auspices before the rupture of the Union. By the late winter of 1868, applications for transportation had come in from Lynchburg, Williamsburg, Abingdon, Christiansburg, and Albemarle County, Virginia; Charleston, Columbia, Mars Bluff, Newberry, Winnsboro, Mullins Depot, Ridge, and Edgefield, South Carolina; Halifax and Bertie counties, North Carolina; Augusta, Macon, Columbus, Sparta, Savannah, Marion, LaGrange, Ringgold, and Carroll County, Georgia; and Knoxville, Nashville, Philadelphia, and Dover Court House, Tennessee. Between 1865 and 1868, 2,232 blacks actually emigrated, for an annual average of 558, more than twice the annual average for the entire period from 1820 to 1861.[7]

Although blacks with skills and some level of literacy—"of that independent class," as one observer saw it—appear to have figured prominently among the first groups of postemancipation applicants, the emigration idea also spread early among poor laboring folk in the countryside. For them, the appeal had little to do with the "civilizationist" impulse to be found among associates of the American Colonization Society or the more privileged and educated of their race who wished to become "missionaries to the millions of Africa."[8] The attraction rather derived from its resonance with an array of practices, contests, institutions, and goals that they had struggled for under slavery and imagined as vital to their freedom: with rebellions aimed at escape from bondage, with nascent black churches, benevolent societies, and brush arbor meetings, with large plantations that sank deep generational roots, and, of course, with the aspirations for land subsequent to emancipation. That resonance was in evidence among the black ministers who met with General William T. Sherman in Savannah in January 1865, in the rumors of federal land redistribution that circulated in the summer and fall of 1865, and in the various "colonies" and "joint stock" companies that looked "to select and locate lands for their settlement."[9]

For growing numbers of rural blacks, therefore, interest in emigration arose as one of several strategies designed to create or reconstitute freed communities on a stable foundation—and at arm's length from whites. One local black organizer near Lynchburg, Virginia, said as much when explaining to the American Colonization Society in June 1866 that he "had got up heigh as eighty to go [to Liberia] but some have heard that they are to get some land and a hundred dollars." That, he conceded, put "a stumbling block in my progress." Around the same time, a society agent in coastal Georgia doubted whether blacks, in their "present condition," could be "induced to leave this country," since "the idea has been put into their heads" that they "are to have the southern country as their own, and that the white people must retire." Not surprisingly, emigration seemed to have had little appeal in much of the postemancipation Caribbean where, owing to the availability of vacant land, claims on provision grounds, and the resources accumulated by many slaves through the marketing of provision crops, these strategies took shape chiefly in free village movements and the establishment of peasant freeholds. Only from Barbados, where ex-slaves had few alternatives to wage labor on the sugar estates, did a contingent move to Liberia.[10]

Not surprisingly, too, "the extreme change in the status of the Freedmen" occasioned by the advent of Radical Reconstruction and "their sudden elevation . . . to the privileges of citizenship" further trimmed the sails of African emigrationism in the South and reduced the number of emigrants by two-thirds over the next four years.[11] But emigrationist sentiment by no means evaporated. It still gained a hearing and, broadly conceived to include black-organized migration to other parts of the South and the United States, found a secure place on a dynamic continuum of black political activity, capable of being quickly asserted. Disappointments about Republican party policies and conduct, the rapid collapse of some Reconstruction regimes, and the toll of paramilitary violence all served to stimulate or resuscitate interest. And in the late 1860s and early 1870s, the prospect of emigration was already gaining serious consideration at several "colored men's" and "colored labor" conventions.[12]

Henry Adams, who later told U.S. Senate investigators that he "never had anything to do with politics any more than going to vote," demonstrated quite well how permeable and interconnected the boundaries between electoral and other forms of local politics could be. Thus, once he left the army, Adams not only formed the secret committee and ministered to the needs of black laborers in Caddo Parish; he also became involved in partisan politics, organizing Republican clubs, serving as an election supervisor, and providing instructions to black voters. For these reasons, Adams was "considered a leading man with the people there," and, in the spring of 1874, was dismissed from his job managing plantations. Even after establishing the Colonization Council and beginning to travel to Texas, Arkansas, and Mississippi in its interests—earning his keep as a laborer and "faith doctor"— he continued to canvass for the Radicals on northern Louisiana plantations, preside over a Republican club in Shreveport, and supervise balloting. And although Adams eventually testified that "we never lost all hopes in the world till 1877," 1878 found the Colonization Council advising black men to vote "as long as we stay here in the Country" and found Adams taking "an active part in the campaign and [trying] to help carry the election for the Republicans." Small wonder that, in 1880, a local planter could describe Adams as "a sort of politician" who had "a good deal to do with politics in the county."[13]

Thus, when grassroots emigrationism began to erupt in the mid-to late 1870s, it could take advantage of networks and forums made possible by more than a decade of political mobilization. Consider the case of Samuel L. Perry. An ex-slave who lived in Lenoir County, North Carolina, Perry became aware of emigration as early as 1872 because "old Hemer Bergen," elected a magistrate "three or four times[,] . . . was always talking about going to Liberia or to the West." Perry then sent for "some circulars or pamphlets . . . giving a description of government lands and railroads that could be got cheap" in Nebraska, and, on Sunday evenings, he and others of the "laboring class of our people" would "meet and talk about it." "We . . . thought that if we could get out West somewhere we could go in a colony," Perry mused. By 1877, after organizing as "complete[ly] as any secret society" and holding "mass meetings," a petition "signed by nearly every colored voter, preacher, and politician in [that] part of the state" was delivered to the legislature asking that Congress be memorialized "to set us apart a territory in the West." Perry vehemently opposed emigration to Liberia, believing "we had a right to stay in this country," but he would play a central role in bringing several thousand North Carolina blacks to Indiana in 1879–1880.[14]

As Perry's experience suggests, information about the prospects for emigration could spread across the rural districts through a number of channels, with word of mouth and personal contact assuming great importance (as befits a powerful oral culture). Lectures sponsored by emigrant aid and colonization societies galvanized black audiences, such as the one in Duplin County, North Carolina, which "got . . . in a fever about Liberia" after William Coppinger of the American Colonization Society spoke in the village of Warsaw in June 1878. Travelers and migrants themselves brought news from Norfolk, Savannah, New Orleans, and other places that had long been ports of departure and perhaps had been sites for celebrations of Liberian independence, or they alerted communities along major thoroughfares of their own intentions. One official could thereby comment on the "considerable excitement" raised among freedpeople living near the railroad in Opelika, Alabama, when "a party of emigrants" passed through on the way to Liberia. That excitement could then be transmitted further on the well-established grapevine. "As one of the effects of slavery," the Louisiana carpetbagger Marshall Twitchell noted, "the negroes had a perfect network of trails between different plantations, which they could follow without the least danger of interception." Indeed, if the sources of incoming correspondence to the American Colonization Society provide meaningful clues, the circuits of communication produced clusters of interest and activity, often straddling state lines: in northeast North Carolina and southeast Virginia, in southwest Georgia and southeast Alabama, in northwest Mississippi, east-central Arkansas, and west Tennessee, and in northwest Louisiana and northeast Texas.[15]

But the very volume of correspondence to the American Colonization Society from rural blacks (which could be counted in the hundreds of letters in the late 1870s and early 1880s) should caution us against exaggerating the persistence of a traditional oral culture and underestimating the new communicative salience of the written and printed word. By the end of Reconstruction, owing to their many struggles for schooling and literacy, somewhere between 20 and 30 percent of African Americans over the age of ten in the former Confederate states could read and write, and the significance of print media to them was showing signs of steady advance.[16] Between 1865 and 1880, more than fifty newspapers edited, and at times owned, by African Americans commenced publication, a number that grew rapidly in the 1880s and 1890s. Alabama led the way with fourteen black papers started during the first decade and a half of freedom, while Georgia, South Carolina, North Carolina, Mississippi, Louisiana, and Tennessee boasted several each. Most were based in the larger cities and towns, had limited circulations, and, because of various constraints, rarely maintained operations for more than a year or two. But most were also partisan in their concerns, with editors who wore multiple political hats. Mississippi's black editors included senators Hiram Revels (the *Southwestern Advocate*) and Blanche K. Bruce (the *Floreyville Star*), secretary of state and Union League organizer James D. Lynch (the *Vicksburg Colored Citizen*), and speaker of the state house I. D. Shadd (the *Greenville Herald*). As a result, the papers found their way to black audiences in the surrounding rural districts, often being read aloud by literate local leaders at churches, schools, Union League and Republican club meetings, and other community gatherings, creating the basis for a more substantial readership. Before the century was out, black newspapers in Mississippi had been published in more than thirty-seven different locations.[17]

These and other newspapers, some printed by religious denominations, together with handbills, circulars, and pamphlets, came to play
a prominent role both in sparking and disseminating emigrationist sentiment. They advertised mobilizations, destinations, methods of transportation, developments near and far, and public debates. "I noticed
a publication in the N.O. Picayune of March 13 clipped from the N.Y.
Herald that there were many of our Cold friends from different portions of the States manifesting a desire to emigrate to Liberia," the
president of a committee of fifteen in St. Mary Parish, Louisiana, wrote
in the spring of 1878, displaying his own sophistication. A Baptist minister in Phillips County, Arkansas, who wished to go to the "New
African Republics," for his part worried when he "heard it rumered
and in fact stated in our county paper that the Gaboors of Western
Africa had declared war against the Liberians and would drive them
out." Another minister, looking after black migrants to Kansas in 1879,
discovered that they learned of the "exodus" through "the usual
method of communication among our people"—the church papers.[18]

Yet no printed source appeared to be as centrally involved, over so
extensive an area, as the *African Repository,* journal of the American
Colonization Society. Most of the correspondents, whether in the Carolinas, Mississippi, or Arkansas, had gotten hold of the *Repository,* had
heard tell of the *Repository,* or asked to be sent copies of the *Repository.*
"I saw in the African Repository your statement concerning the emigration to Africa and I want to Know something about it," went a
typical letter. "Please send me a map of Liberia and African Repository," went another. There was, it seems, a circuit by which the *Repository* made its way to fairly remote sections of the countryside, and
collective discussion and distribution were likely crucial to the flow.
"I have Read the Circle to my Col. friends & also ishes [*sic*] them out
to them & all are in favor to hear & to Read them," a "laborern Man"
in Chickasaw County, Mississippi, haltingly told the Colonization Society's secretary. In Edgefield County, South Carolina, a local leader
"had the pleasure of laying your letter before the ordiance" at church
and then "distributed those papers among them in Different Portion
of the County." Indeed, we can see in this process the extension and
vitality of a new popular culture of belief and verification tied more
closely to the printed or written, rather than the spoken, word. "I have
got here some near fifty head of people And Can get some near A

hundred providing I can hear the true Documents of the Condition of the said republic of Liberia," a correspondent from New Bern, North Carolina, explained to the Colonization Society in requesting "some of your papers And Book or two"—"they wants to hear it read."[19]

Correspondence such as this was usually the work of local organizers, and it highlights their contributions to the making of the emigration movement. Some of them had achieved a measure of prominence during Reconstruction, serving in the state legislature or in county office, like the Reverend Isaac Alston of Warrenton, North Carolina, a state senator for eight years who was "determined to go to Liberia" and supposedly "could move half of Warren County." Most had less public visibility but nonetheless claimed important attributes. Generally literate, possessing at least some knowledge of the world beyond their localities, and possibly situated at the intersection of kinship networks, they provided resources for and had won the confidence of rural black communities in their capacities as teachers, ministers, negotiators, and intermediaries. Thus, the peripatetic Henry Adams not only had acquired literacy and worldliness in the army and secret committee, but also had kin in De Soto, Bossier, Tensas, and Bienville parishes. Along the coast of Georgia, "a negro Baptist preacher" named Jonathan E. Francis created such "a great upster" with his "mad lectures about Africa" that local whites offered to secure him admission to a doctor of divinity program at the University of Georgia if he would stop giving them. Less dramatically, others "went forth among the people" to discuss emigrating, delivered sermons, circulated papers, and wrote off for "infermission." "I am re cuested to rit with a most hastey," began Eli Morrow of eastern Mississippi, in a letter to the American Colonization Society that asked "to no Sumpting" and to be sent copies of the *African Repository*.[20]

Morrow wrote on behalf of "a but 300 pepel" in the "foth and fift be[a]t of Munro and Chickasaw Countey" who had been talking about the matter of emigration for at least a short time. We do not know whether public meetings took place there; but we do know that they occurred in a good many locations in the Deep South. By November 1877, blacks in Harrison County, Texas, had been "holding meetings weekly and debating . . . emigration to Liberia," and, as a consequence, "have seemingly gon wild on the subject." Even earlier, "the colored people" in and around Concord, North Carolina, were "widawake on the question of going to liberia" owing to meetings held at the county courthouse. Tunica County, Mississippi, saw a "Libria meeting" in 1878 at which each participant pledged "to Save all the money that tha Could." And in the summer of 1879, while the black population of Warren County, North Carolina, was summoned to "a meeting of Colonization" at the Warrenton courthouse "for the purpose of appointing someone to go to Liberia and examine that country," blacks in Washington County, Texas, gathered in the interest of migration to Kansas.[21]

Some of these meetings gave birth to local organizations devoted specifically to the cause of emigration: the Liberia Exodus Association of Pinesville, Florida; the Pilgrem Travelers of Robertson County, Texas; the Liberian Exodus Arkansas Colony of Phillips County; and emigrant aid clubs in the vicinity of Blacksville, South Carolina, to name only a few. "We understand that there is a Society at Washington, D.C. known as the American Colonization Society," C. L. Paine wrote in June 1877 in his capacity as the "corresponding secretary" of the Corinth (Mississippi) National Colonization Society. Paine wished "to ascertain" the American Colonization Society's "existence" for the sake of "co-operation."[22]

Both the public meetings and the local organizations relied on a rural political infrastructure that linked African Americans on scattered plantations and farms, and provided vehicles for the exchange of information and ideas. Plantation councils, militia district clubs, crossroads schoolhouses, and neighborhood protective and benevolent associations, which since the advent of freedom had served the ends of labor negotiation, partisan politics, and community self-help, also spread the emigrationist message. In the early 1870s, Daniel Parker leased land on the Widow Crane's place in Madison Parish, Louisiana. Required to pay a hefty ten dollars per acre, he and other tenants formed "a club to get a reduction in rent," and, although in his mid-twenties, Parker had earned sufficient trust and respect from the club members to be "made president." But the club apparently took up a variety of subjects of interest to the tenants on the Crane estate, and Parker eventually "was accused of teaching the people to leave the South." Blacks who lived and worked near the village of LaGrange in Lenoir County, North Carolina, customarily gathered fortnightly at a schoolhouse to discuss conditions and prospects; on one occasion, they invited their neighbor Samuel Perry to make a brief speech about "going to Kansas" and then spent the next several sessions debating it. When John W. H. Lee of Clarke County, in southeastern Mississippi, began "working among my race" for the goal of finding "a Country of our own," he quite naturally called "a colored meeting in my beat" at which "we elected President and Vice and a Secretary."[23]

Yet no institution proved more pivotal to the political infrastructure that advanced the cause of grassroots emigrationism than did the church. Blacks turned to the church not only for their spiritual needs but also as the center of their "civilization," a minister from Thomas County, Georgia, later explained: "Here [the Negro] learns the price of cotton or the date of the next circus; here is given the latest fashion plates or the announcement for candidates for justice of the peace." And here, blacks bound together by faith, geography, livelihood, and kinship likely first heard about Liberia, Kansas, or Indiana. Asked by a U.S. Senate committee if "the colored people had some peculiar way of communicating with each other," the Reverend B. F. Watson of Missouri answered that it was "generally done through their churches." F. R. Guernsey, reporting in 1879 on the "Negro exodus" from the lower South, found the "immediate cause" in the "distribution among negro preachers" of "alluring circulars" issued by railroad companies. "'Going to Kansas' was diligently preached in hundreds of little churches on the plantations," Guernsey observed, "until . . . the movement actually began in earnest."[24]

Church and ministerial opinion was hardly uniform—and certainly not overwhelmingly favorable—on the emigration question. The African Methodist Episcopal Church, in particular, was a locus for heated debate and bitter division, while local ministers, whether Methodist or Baptist, could easily balk: after all, they risked losing their congregations unless they were prepared to lead the migration. But especially in the countryside, where denominational fissures were less pronounced and less intrusive, the churches became, at the very least, primary sites of agitation. A Caddo Parish, Louisiana, landowner, having witnessed eleven of his laboring families leave what they called the "Liberia Plantation" for Kansas in December 1879, could therefore complain that they "have a church on the plantation that is also used as a school-house . . . [and] some preachers come to that place from thirty miles away . . . [and] preach whenever they please." When a large number of blacks in Warren County, North Carolina, decided to meet "for the purpos of organising our selfs for homes in Liberia," they chose the "Looly Hill Baptis Church" and commenced their proceedings with a hymn and a reading from the Book of Ezekiel. Bud Steven, a "leader of my race" in a settlement near Edgefield Court House, South Carolina, first requested information about Liberia from the American Colonization Society, and then presented it to "a large gathering of the colored people" at church. Reeling from the political bulldozing that exploded across northern Louisiana in the late 1870s, blacks in Madison Parish took a more clandestine approach. They established "a secret organization known as the Colored Men's Protective Union" and "held their little meetings quietly in the churches." After much debate, "they seemed to understand the situation better than their leaders," and resolved to "get away" in "squads . . . as soon as they could," variously to Ohio, Indiana, Kansas, and Arkansas.[25]

Henry Adams and his fellow activists in the Negro Union Cooperative Aid Association had therefore become well acquainted with the political infrastructure that rural blacks had built when they issued their convention call in November 1878. Asking the freedpeople to assemble and select delegates who directly represented not geographical areas or party clubs, but religious bodies, benevolent societies, secret organizations, large plantations, and "any organization composed exclusively of Negro people," the association pinpointed the institutional foundations of their grassroots politics.

❖

Percolating for more than a decade after emancipation, emigrationist sentiment and activity seemed to build rapidly after 1875 and then reach peak intensity in 1879 and 1880. Scores of letters of inquiry and application flooded into the office of the American Colonization Society; thousands of African Americans lined the Mississippi River and the railroads leading to St. Louis, Kansas, Washington, D.C., and Indiana; and black conventions gathered in North Carolina, Tennessee, Louisiana, Arkansas, Virginia, and Texas to consider the question. So widespread and disruptive did this movement appear that the U.S. Senate felt compelled, in the winter and spring of 1880, to investigate "The Causes of the Removal of the Negroes from the Southern States to the Northern States." That investigation yielded three large volumes of testimony and assessment.[26]

It has been common for historians to treat the Kansas/Indiana (western) and Liberia "exodus" movements as somewhat discrete phenomena—in part because the western drew far more contemporary attention than the Liberian—and largely to discount or ignore the political significance of each.[27] But this may be a serious mistake, for there is good reason to treat them as manifestations of a more general and remarkably widespread impulse. They certainly shared many features, one of which was their very breadth. Interest in migration, either to Liberia or to other parts of the United States, could be detected in all of the former slave states and in most sections of those states: in the upper South as well as the lower, and in nonplantation as well as plantation districts.[28] At the same time, the greatest ferment—again in all instances—was to be found in areas that displayed similar characteristics. They tended to be cotton-growing areas with large and numerically dominant black populations that had experienced political mobilizations and in many cases substantial political gains during Reconstruction, but that also saw explosions of paramilitary violence and then concerted attacks on black rights and protections once Redemption was achieved. Which is to say that emigrationism seems to have been most evident and powerful in places where freedpeople labored on cotton plantations, had made major efforts—with at least some success—to organize themselves and create stable communities, but then suffered, or were threatened by, serious reversals. In these regards the eastern and central counties of North Carolina, the piedmont of South Carolina, southwestern Georgia and northern Florida, east-central Mississippi and Texas, the cotton parishes of northern Louisiana, and the delta counties of Arkansas, Mississippi, and Tennessee figured most prominently.[29]

Observers and participants alike debated the governing logic of emigrationism. Hostile and unnerved Democrats, in Congress and the South, variously blamed the opportunism of northern Republicans, railroad and land companies, and their black minions. Most others weighed the relative importance of economic exploitation, political outrages, educational disadvantages, and legal disabilities.[30] And there was a strong argument to be made for each of these factors. Red Shirt and White League violence had just exploded in South Carolina and

Louisiana, while bloody paramilitary forays had earlier beset Georgia, Texas, North Carolina, Alabama, and Mississippi; redeemed state legislatures most everywhere, though especially in the Carolinas, Georgia, Alabama, and Mississippi, had begun to undermine the power of black voters, augment the economic leverage of planters and landlords, and drastically cut newly implemented social services; Louisiana had called a constitutional convention to undo the work of Radical Reconstruction; and many blacks, particularly in the states most recently redeemed, feared that a Democratic victory in the national elections of 1880 might result in peonage or reenslavement.[31]

But the voices of the "exodusters" and emigration-minded African Americans, along with those of white southerners well acquainted with them, rarely made such distinctions. Indeed, rather than emphasizing one cause or another, they normally mentioned a host of them in describing a world besieged by threats, coercion, vulnerabilities, insecurities, and limited prospects for themselves, their families, and their children. This was very much the spirit and message of the petition that Henry Adams and the Colonization Council signed and sent to President Hayes in September 1877. John Henri Burch, a black journalist and former state representative from Baton Rouge who sympathized with the movement, similarly explained, "I suppose the causes of the exodus may be grouped under the head of a fear on their part of class legislation" and "of interference with their educational privileges; the uncertainty of their obtaining means for themselves and their families; the interference with their religious and personal rights, together with fear of disfranchisement." "These people are generally landless and homeless," Burch added, "and they have not the satisfaction, even when they acquire homes, of knowing that they will be secure in the possession of them in every respect."[32]

A group of emigrants to Indiana from North Carolina claimed "that though nominally free their condition [has been] one of servility and gradually growing worse; their wages barely sufficient to supply the coarsest food . . . the laws administered so as to discriminate against them . . . [and] the public schools were curtailed." Other migrants from Texas, Tennessee, and Mississippi who arrived in Kansas complained "that they [had been] defrauded out of their rights, denied school facilities, and interfered with in their politics." A black leader in Washington County, Texas, writing to the editor of the local newspaper, specified more fully still the reasons why African Americans there "seriously considered emigrating": their former masters now controlled all departments of the state government; whites regarded emancipation as wholesale robbery and therefore enacted laws that deprived blacks of civil rights and would eventually reduce them to peonage; blacks would likely soon lose all opportunities for education; and high rents for land coupled with oppressive landlord and tenant laws prevented blacks from purchasing small farms. "[W]e wants to be a People," two longtime leaders in Chickasaw County, Mississippi, told the American Colonization Society; "we cant be it heare and find that we ar compell to leve this Cuntry."[33]

"[W]e wants to be a People." Henry Adams and the Colonization Council had spoken, too, of becoming "united as a race" and of finding some "country" where they could "make themselves a name and a nation," reflecting no doubt sensibilities that were widely current. And there is to be seen in the letters, petitions, and testimonies about emigration the articulation of a deep sense of identity among those who simultaneously shared African descent and suffered white oppression, of an incipient popular nationalism, and of a desire for social separatism. Some of this, especially among the better educated and more economically independent, showed the marks of a pan-Africanist consciousness that had taken hold in quarters of the antebellum North and upper South. A few prospective emigrants thus hoped to leave the "oppressive soils of the Western Continents" and return to "the rich Progressive . . . Eastern continent of Africa," "to their natif land where god First place our fourfathers," "to our Fathers Land From whence we came," and "where we Can be a nation of People." "For the sake of our children," a member of the Liberia Exodus Arkansas Colony wrote, "we desire to emigrate . . . that they may grow up more useful men and women than they can in this country" and "help civilize Africa." Around the same time in Lyon County, Kentucky, William Mohr was "trying to get up a exodus movement" in "this Little Christian Community" to "the ancestral Land of our forefathers." They wished, he stated pointedly, "to Establish for them selves and for the rising and future generation A free and independent government."[34]

Yet for most of the rural blacks who talked of it, the notion of becoming a "race," a "people," a "race of people," or a "nation" seemed to be more modest in objective and more localized in bearing.

It seemed to mean having the opportunity to create communities in which collections of families could find and farm land independently, in which authority would emanate chiefly from within their own ranks and according to their own rules, in which their institutions could have room to develop, in which they could venture forth without fear and meet others on a basis of mutual respect, and in which such conditions could be reproduced generationally. And both Kansas and Liberia were imagined as the kind of place where this could happen. Kansas, in particular, assumed mythic and millennial dimensions, in good part because of the state's militant antislavery heritage ("they know that this is the land of freedom," as one observer put it), and "exodus fever" came to rage intensely during the winter and spring of 1879.[35]

To an extent, the dynamic of Kansas exodus activity harked back to the summer and fall of 1865, when rumors spread of a federally sponsored redistribution of land and freedpeople thereby insinuated themselves into the early political struggles over the fate of the post-emancipation South. Now, as Louisiana's redeemers arranged for a constitutional convention designed to undermine black civil and political rights, a great many black laborers in the lower Mississippi Valley, north Louisiana, and Texas again chose to act. In Congress that January, the sympathetic senator from Minnesota, William Windom, had introduced a resolution suggesting the promotion "of a partial migration of colored persons from those States and congressional districts where they are not allowed to freely and peacefully exercise and enjoy their constitutional rights as American citizens, into such States as may desire to receive them and will protect them in said rights, or into such Territory or Territories of the United States as may be provided for their use and occupation." Reported widely in the press and through other channels, the "Windom Resolution" appears to have been reinterpreted at the grassroots as an invitation to Kansas (what other state would be more likely to receive and protect them?) with the sanction of the federal government. Indeed, rumors quickly circulated that a steamboat or through train would come and transport all who wished to go, and biblical analogies were easy to embrace.[36]

Some of the migrants, therefore, compared themselves to "de chilun ob Israel when dey was led out o' bondage by Moses," and may have had "a vague idea" that Kansas was "flowing with milk and honey," that "they would be given 40 acres of land and a mule and farming utensils necessary to cultivate it," and that "the government was interested in the movement." A correspondent for the *International Review* thought that "many" blacks left their "homes in the lower Mississippi Valley under the stimulus of a sort of religious exaltation," regarding Kansas as "a modern Canaan and the God-appointed home of the negro race," and expecting that "once arrived . . . they would find agents of the General Government standing ready to bestow upon each of them a mule, 160 acres of land, and rations for a year."[37]

But if some of those who caught the Kansas fever could envision the hands of the good Lord and the benevolent state enacting the justice that had failed to materialize at the time of emancipation, most now looked only for the opportunity to rebuild their communities principally with their own resources, "to go where they can buy land on time and work it out," aided perhaps by the federal government and sympathetic northerners. A "society" of African Americans in York County, South Carolina, having heard that "we can get Land for home" in Kansas, thus took pains to insist that "we do not say that we wants Lands giveing to us for us to have without paying for it." J. W. Wheeler, who, with fellow blacks, talked with and assisted numbers of exodusters, made much the same point. Acknowledging that "in some way they received the impression that Kansas was a good place to go," he quickly added that "many of them hoot at the idea of being given anything. They have no expectation of receiving 'forty acres of land and a mule,' or anything of the sort."[38]

Yet despite its distinctive aspects and trajectory, the Kansas exodus movement erupted precisely in those areas that had already been touched by emigrationism, in areas where Henry Adams and the Colonization Council had already been organizing, in areas that had already learned of the American Colonization Society's project. And so we must see Kansas and Liberia in close connection and recognize that the favored destination of interested southern blacks could shift and often depended on the circumstances of local social and political life. It often depended, that is, on the disposition of an influential leader, the ventures of friends and kin, the circulation of particular stories and printed sources, or the appearance of an organizational emissary. In many instances—the Shreveport petition of September 1877 again comes to mind—the options could be conceived interchangeably. William Benson, a "Farmer by trade" and a "Deacon of the Baptist

church" in north Georgia's Cherokee County, wished "to go some
where where I can do some good and enjoy some Liberty of government and schools among my own people." Initially he "had decided
to go to California"; then he "reseived a book of the African Repository" and, being "very much pleased In the emigration of our race,"
set his sights on Liberia.[39]

In Enterprise, Mississippi, A. B. Coleman saw his people "driven
about . . . like the wild Tartars . . . without any settlement" and "hoped
the day is not far distant when every tub shall have to stand on its
own bottom and justice will be meted out to everyone without regard
to color or former condition of servitude." Liberia, he believed, might
best suit them, but since "the majority are too poor, barely able to go
fifty miles away from home and pay their fare," he glimpsed some
promise in the "great influx West" that seemed to be under way. The
"500 head of people in our clubs" in Falls County, Texas, had greater
resources and prospects according to local spokesman A. G. Randolph.
"Sufing [sic] here in this State," they possibly could "meet the cost"
of travel to Liberia, "where we can be a nation of People," so long
as the American Colonization Society sent a ship to pick them up in
Galveston rather than New York. Yet when Randolph delineated the
meaning of their becoming "a nation of People," his words resonated
with the aspirations of black laborers seeking refuge elsewhere: "not
be subject to any class of men north or south."[40]

Fittingly, it was Henry Adams who perhaps best exemplified both
the range and nature of black sensibilities on the emigration question.
Mixing the religious and the secular, the biblical and the constitutional,
injecting millennial themes, Adams bristled at the economic and political oppression his people suffered and predicted that "the God of high
heaven will put a curse should we continue to live with our former
masters" without "the same rights as he has ordained that we shall
enjoy in our own native soil." "For God says in His Holy Word,"
Adams counseled, "that he has a place and a land for all his people,
and our race had better go to it." Partial though he was to Liberia and
proclaiming that "the colored people are determined on a nationality,"
Adams nonetheless entertained a variety of alternatives from early on,
worked with those involved in the Kansas movement, and always distinguished the objective from the specific site of its realization. Hence,
in the spring and summer of 1879, acknowledging that "some of us

are still trying to procure a ship and in it go to Liberia" while "others are trying to go to Kansas," he held several "migration meetings of those wishing to go to Liberia" and then planned to set off on "a tour through the western states and territories." Some members of his race, Adams discovered, desired "going to Kansas in order to make money with the intention of going from there to Liberia." At all events, however different the routes, the goal was much the same. Remarking on the "Kansas fever," Adams made the more generally applicable point: "It is not that we think the soil climate or temperature of Kansas is more congenial to us—But it is the idea the thought that pervades our breast 'that at last we will be free,' free from oppression, free from tyranny, free from bulldozing, murderous southern whites."[41]

The general character and meaning of grassroots emigrationism come into even sharper relief if we consider who wished to go and how they wished to do it. For what emerges most strikingly is the broad similarity in pattern and process across localities and regardless of the specific destination in view. These were not, to begin with, movements of individuals or of individual families, however many such examples are to be found. Nor were these movements of proletarians recently jettisoned from the land or denied access to agricultural means of production, although some had been driven off by particular farm or estate owners. Rather, these were collective undertakings by rural black laborers joined together, in the main, by a combination of kinship, work relations, political experience, and religious belief.[42]

Groups of prospective emigrants could range in size from a handful to several hundred; more likely they numbered between twenty and one hundred. But, small or large, the groups were organized around family networks: from the "little squads of two or three families," seen near Delta, Louisiana, by a correspondent of P. B. S. Pinchback's *Weekly Louisianian*, "with their effects wending their way to Kansas," or the four Yorkville, South Carolina, families who "expect to move to Liberia in May 1878," to the "fifty Families in Granville County," North Carolina, or the "150 heads of family" in Pinesville, Florida, who hoped to book passage to Liberia.[43] And although it is difficult, if not impossible, to trace the many complex lines, these families were, in turn, often linked to one another by marriage and blood relations. Thus, the party of twenty-eight African Americans in Edgecombe County, North Carolina, that was making preparations to emigrate sometime in 1879 consisted of Cary and Manerva Bellamy, their two children, and daughter-in-law; Henry and Mary Ann Bellamy and their four children; Charles and Jane Taylor and their three children; and Moses and Chanie Taylor and their four children, along with Albert and Susan Phillips, Jerry and Manerva Sherrod, Ann Tilery, and Manerva Whitaker, some or all of whom may have been related to the Taylors and Bellamys. Nine such families in St. Helena Parish, Louisiana, included three Morgans, two Wilsons, and two Tabors, while a list of adult males from Aiken County, South Carolina, "interested in going to Liberia" showed five Browns, six Williams, and four Johnsons among them.[44]

These families and kin groups formed the foundation of communities that were also defined by work, occupation, and land tenure. Overwhelmingly, the emigrants and prospective emigrants farmed, and, for the most part, did so as tenants, sharecroppers, and wage hands. The larger of the parties might well have included mechanics, carpenters, blacksmiths, brickmasons, coopers, and, perhaps, a landowner or two; many of the smaller parties included a teacher and minister.[45] But throughout, the greatest number were landless farming folk. In some cases—as with the "renters at Rose Dale" in Pasquotank County, North Carolina, who planned to travel to Liberia, or the "60 families" who one day up and left Mare's estate in Madison Parish, Louisiana, and boarded a Mississippi steamboat for St. Louis—they lived and cultivated the soil on a single plantation. In other cases, they worked on neighboring plantations and farms, possibly in the immediate vicinity of a village, hamlet, or crossroads, and had been brought together by mutual ties and responsibilities, weekly socializing, political activism, and, most commonly, the church.[46]

For these were communities of laboring families who tended to worship together as well. The Rose Dale renters were Methodists, as were the Morgans, Wilsons, Tabors, and their clan in St. Helena Parish. The Bellamys, Taylors, Phillips, and Sherrods of Edgecombe County, on the other hand, were Baptists, as were the 1,011 prospective emigrants in nearby Warren County in 1879. The roughly "100 familys" in Perquimans County, North Carolina, who wished to depart for Liberia in late 1877 were represented by their "preacher belonging to Zion Convention." At times the parties divided denominationally— almost always between Baptists and Methodists—but the social and cultural lines were never rigidly drawn. Indeed, in the rural South, where ministers often had to preach in more than one church and where circuit riders arrived irregularly, worship services, much like "protracted meetings," could be interdenominational affairs.[47]

But we must not overemphasize the cohesiveness and cooperation that all this may imply. When the Negro Union Cooperative Aid Association, in calling for a convention, appealed to the freedpeople "without regard to sex religion or politics," it both expressed a broadly inclusive idea of political engagement and acknowledged that inclusiveness by no means guaranteed harmony, hoping as the organization did to "unite" as a "race." Although emigrationism did embody a powerful community-based impulse, it also revealed divisions and struggles within those communities, thereby allowing us to glimpse power relations and dynamics of decision-making at a critical moment in the post-Reconstruction period.

Most apparent was the significance of gender and age. For if these were movements of family and kin, the lines of authority and public representation flowed from male household heads and then, perhaps, from older patriarchs regarded as leaders of more extended clans. Local black correspondents with organizations like the American Colonization Society were almost invariably adult males, and they often spoke of, or listed, only the "heads of familys" composing their groups. An African-American man from Craven County, North Carolina, therefore introduced all the members of a Liberian emigration association that he helped to form in 1878 as he introduced himself, folding the identities of wives and children into those of husbands and fathers. "William Hayes," he wrote, "is a man of Family and is good standing and belong to the Baptis church at New Berne and his occupation is farming. He have 5 in family his age is 36 year and his wife is 32 year." Officials of local emigration or colonization societies, too, were exclusively male, as were those selected as society delegates to larger public meetings.[48]

Black men such as Hayes surely saw in emigrationism a means to protect themselves from political harassment and persecution, and their wives and children from exploitation of various kinds. But they un-

doubtedly also saw in emigration the prospect of asserting and protecting their own prerogatives from the challenges and invasions that
white landowners had been pressing since the time of emancipation
and that had fed black political mobilization from early on. "I seen on
some plantations . . . where white men would drive colored women
out in the fields to work when their husbands would be absent from
their homes and would tell colored men that their wives and children
could not live on their places unless they work in the fields," Henry
Adams reported, sketching some of the vectors of this contest. "The
colored men would tell them they wanted their children to attend
school; and whenever they wanted their wives to work they would
tell them themselves." Suggesting that in emigrationism the struggle
for black "home rule" could be quite literal, Adams summarized: "If
he could not rule his domestic affairs on that place he would leave it
and go somewhere else."[49]

And yet it was not only the call for freedpeople to assemble "without
regard to sex religion or politics" that hints at the play of more complex
gender dynamics. G. W. Hayden of Phillips County, Arkansas, who
wished "when I die to be in my farther lan" of Liberia, nonetheless
complained that his "Wife objects going with me" and whenever "I
am a bout Ready she Brings some thing in my way." Other observers,
however, claimed that women, not men, drove emigrationist sentiment.
Conversing with exodusters who arrived in St. Louis, one found that
"a great many of these women rose up and said that if their husbands
did not leave, they would." "They seemed," he noted, "more determined and spoke more freely than the men," who "seemed more reti-
cent to tell the whole story than the women did." There were, of
course, good reasons why black women could more safely express
anger and outrage at injustice and discrimination than could black men:
their civic subordination and exclusion from the official arenas of politics. But such speech postures cannot be understood apart from a grassroots politics that focused on constructing and defending the integrity of a household economy and the kin relations sustaining it. To
this extent, black women and men shared an interest in any project
designed to limit the power of white landowners and employers; if
anything, given their responsibility for many of the activities that
maintained and nurtured household and community life—producing
market and food crops, cultivating garden plots and caring for live-

stock, preparing food and making clothing, educating the children, and carrying out many of the obligations of kinship and friendship—black women may have had a more intense interest. Insofar as emigration threatened to disrupt this already beleaguered world and set of relations, they very likely would oppose it. Hayden's wife had learned that "her adopted Farther and Morther" wanted to stay in Arkansas. But if emigration could be imagined as a means to reproduce and strengthen this world and these relations, then black women would probably favor it and work mightily to extend its social embrace.[50]

The black journalist John Henri Burch, insisting that "the women have had more to do with [the exodus] than all the politics and men in the country," appeared to recognize as much. "These women, since Reconstruction, have followed their husbands and brothers and all who had a vote, from morning till night, around the parishes demanding that they should vote the Republican ticket," Burch explained, placing the gender politics of the emigration movement in deeper perspective. He knew that black women had "been very active since 1868 in all political movements," that "they form a large number in all political assemblages," and that they had a great "interest in all that pertains to politics so far as their husbands and fathers and brothers were concerned." Their partisan loyalties, Burch went on to point out, had "always been placed . . . on the ground that it was only through the Republican party and principles of that party that they could secure homes for themselves and educational advantages for their children, and protection in all the rights accorded them by the Constitution of the nation." But now that the women "have seen their Republican government swept away from under them," they "turned their attention to this emigration." Henry Adams and the Negro Union Cooperative Aid Association, in asking the freedpeople to gather on their plantations and in their societies "without regard to sex religion or politics," appeared to grasp this as well.[51]

There were other points of struggle and disputation defining the politics of black emigrationism. The best known of them involved major national race leaders, many residing in the northern states or the District of Columbia, who looked with critical eyes on the Kansas and, especially, the Liberia movements. Frederick Douglass, long hostile to colonization and emigration, leveled one of the harshest indictments, portraying the exodus as "an abandonment of the great and paramount principle of protection to person and property in every state of the union," a "disheartening surrender" that "leaves the whole question of equal rights on the soil of the South open to settlement." Conceding the oppressive conditions that southern blacks routinely faced, he nevertheless emphasized the gains that had been made since emancipation and insisted that the South was "the best locality for the Negro" both "on the grounds of his political power" and "as a field of labor." "The colored race is a remarkably home-loving race," Douglass maintained, appropriating the language of paternalism, and he saw the "real cause" of the exodus in the machinations of "political tricksters, land speculators, defeated office-seekers, [and] Northern malignants."[52]

Opposition, at least to mass emigration, came too from the likes of Bishop Daniel A. Payne of the African Methodist Episcopal (AME) Church and from the former U.S. senator Blanche K. Bruce, not to mention from blacks who had settled in Kansas during the previous decade and feared the consequences of an influx of their poor, propertyless southern brothers and sisters. But their views did not go uncontested, and debate raged in the black press, in black organizations, and at black conventions. The AME Church suffered sharp divisions, as annual conferences north of the Potomac and east of the Mississippi tended to denounce the movements, and as the pages of the AME's *Christian Recorder* crackled with controversy. The most notable exchange involved Bishop Payne and Henry McNeal Turner, the freeborn South Carolinian who tilted between electoral politics and emigrationism in Reconstruction Georgia and then became an AME bishop in his own right.[53] The National Conference of Colored Men, meeting in Nashville in May 1879 and including delegates from seventeen states and the District of Columbia, therefore sought to walk a careful line. The official address cast emigration as "evidence of a healthy growth of manly independence" and endorsed the recently organized National Emigration Aid Society, while recommending a "national educational system," the pursuit of "strict morality, temperate habits, and the practice of economy" among black youth, and the enforcement of all rights "accorded the other nationalities of our country."[54]

More significant, however, were the rifts created among African Americans in the South, for they reveal the struggle for a new politics that began to take shape during the latter phases of Reconstruction, as well as the developing tensions between the needs and aspirations of local leaders and those of the grassroots communities they claimed to represent. The most vocal opposition to emigrationism within the South came from black leaders who had an established base, had essentially become "professional" politicians, were literate and owned some property, and had shown enough interest in reaching accommodations with white Democrats that they could imagine political futures after Redemption: such figures as P. B. S. Pinchback and David Young in Louisiana, Jeremiah Haralson in Alabama, William A. Pledger in Georgia, and Robert Smalls in South Carolina.[55] North Carolina boasted a particularly sizable contingent, many of whom resided in the Second Congressional District, a bastion of black electoral power and of emigrationist sensibility. Led by James Harris and James O'Hara—themselves political rivals—the group included William Mabson, George T. Wassom, George Price, Osborne Hunter, and AME Zion bishop James W. Hood. Painting a more benign picture of race relations in the "old north state" and believing that black grievances ought to be redressed there, they blamed "self-constituted negro leaders" living in Washington, D.C., and "knowing . . . little about the real condition of the colored masses" for controlling the exodus movement.[56]

Many blacks who organized for the Republican party, served in the state legislature, held county office, or pastored a church—those, in sum, who occupied official positions of local leadership—knew firsthand of the oppressions their people suffered and usually turned a sympathetic ear to emigrationist ideas. But their very leadership stature often caused them to hesitate in practice. Some were reluctant to endorse emigration; some cautioned against the dangers that emigration would entail; and some came on board only after the movement was well advanced. As a consequence, emigration both exposed and contributed to a growing chasm in some places between black leaders brought to the fore by Reconstruction party politics—those, at times, referred to as "representative colored men"—and the black leaders who remained very closely tied to the daily lives and concerns of rural workers. From the outset, Henry Adams held "colored politicians" in sufficient suspicion that he had them excluded from Colonization Council meetings and claimed that the council was composed "entirely of laboring people." "We had a terrible struggle with our own selves," Adams sighed, alluding to the opposition of "ministers" as well as "politicians." In Lenoir County, North Carolina, Samuel L. Perry similarly avoided those he called "the big professional negroes, the rich men," and instead "got among the workingmen" in the cause of emigration West.[57]

Indeed, more than a few of the "established" leaders found themselves in wrangles they did not anticipate. Louis Stubblefield of the Mississippi Delta county of Bolivar, who owned substantial real estate, sat on the county board of supervisors, and described himself as something of a political boss, discovered his constituents to be aflame with emigration fever in 1878. It seemed that "a colored man from Helena [Arkansas] by the name of Doctor Collins" had come across the river and "got it into the minds of the people there that they could go to Liberia." Within a short time, "nearly half of the county" had been organized and even people Stubblefield knew well "were ready to throw down everything they had in the world and go off and leave it." Alarmed, Stubblefield summoned "the best men in the county" and urged them "to fall in and join these clubs . . . in order we might have a combination against this thing." They apparently succeeded, in part by discrediting Collins; but the "next thing" they knew "this Kansas movement . . . sprang up." Once again, Stubblefield and his allies "got into that" and managed—though not without a major effort—"to keep our people at home."[58]

Not all of Stubblefield's counterparts did as well in keeping these movements in check or their reputations intact. Witnessing the ranks of prospective exodusters swell in Washington County, Texas, C. P. Hicks, said to have "more influence over the masses" than "any of the leading colored men here," called "a large meeting" with the intention of dissuading them. Standing before the crowd that subsequently assembled at the county seat of Brenham, Hicks read a letter from Kansas governor St. John informing "them that Kansas had no free land etc." As might be expected, the message "fell like a wet blanket on the hopes of a large class of freedmen." But rather than accepting Hicks's word and simply showing their disappointment, they turned their skepticism and hostility on Hicks himself. Many of the freedpeople charged that the letter must be a "forgery"; others believed that the Kansas governor had written it in response to Hicks's "misrepresentations." Stunned, a white Republican in attendance drew a powerful lesson. Regardless of Hicks's prior standing in the community, "the very moment he or other leaders throw themselves against the popular wishes and tide of sentiment of their people—right then their influence begins to ebb."[59]

William Murrell Jr. experienced much the same phenomenon in Madison Parish, Louisiana. A former slave, Methodist minister, newspaper editor, and two-term state legislator, Murrell carried substantial authority among the parish's large black population. When, however, he initially opposed the Kansas exodus and "tried to reason" with those clamoring to migrate, he "found out one thing that was very peculiar—one thing that I would not have believed if I had not seen it." "Those who had been leading the colored people in political matters could not lead them any more when it came to this matter," Murrell had come to realize; "the colored people would not pay any attention to them whatever." It was not, as some thought, that emigrationism was a leaderless, almost spontaneous, movement of desperate and destitute African Americans—that, in the words of one participant, "every black man is his own Moses now." It was that a different group of leaders had asserted themselves, and that the relations between leaders and led were being renegotiated.[60]

It is likely that large numbers of African Americans in the former Confederate South became aware of emigrationist ideas and agitation at some point in the 1870s and early 1880s, and that many more local movements were hatched, especially in the cotton districts, than congressional investigations and the records of the American Colonization Society allow us even to glimpse. Without further intensive research, we cannot fully map the spread of emigrationist activity, nor can we explain why it may have taken hold in one community and not in another. But it also seems clear that emigrationism made limited, if any, headway in some sections of the rural South, and a closer look suggests that this reflected the nature and tenor of local struggles rather than significant differences in social goals.

The low country of South Carolina might well have become a cauldron of emigrationist sentiment given powerful circumstances of cultural life. Georgetown and Savannah had been points of departure for Liberian emigrants since the 1820s (and Charleston became one immediately after the Civil War), American Colonization Society officials lectured there on several occasions, and Liberian independence had been commemorated since the mid-1850s. Equally compelling, the region as a whole contained a dense black population that greatly outnumbered the white and showed more of the influences of West Africa than was the case most anywhere else in the South: in their forms of social organization, spirituality, material culture, dress, and language, notably the prevalence of Gullah dialect. Yet little of the interest in Liberia and emigration that surfaced in the cities appears to have seeped out into the countryside.[61]

In part, this was because the very conditions that sustained West African resonances among rural blacks in the low country also nourished a profound rootedness. By the time of the Civil War, most of the slaves there resided on large, relatively stable, multigenerational plantations that had earlier imported thousands of Africans. The quasi-absenteeism of the planters, the elaboration of intricate black kinship networks, and the demands of rice and long-staple cotton cultivation created a discrete cultural milieu and gave special shape to the slaves' many battles. The emergence of the task system, of family provision grounds, of slave petty marketing—all of which offered measures of control, security, and experience in a new world of production and exchange—represented some of their most visible achievements, and consequently made attachments to persons and place almost inextricable.[62]

At all events, therefore, the transition from slavery to freedom in the low country would have assumed a distinctive character. But the explosion of sectional tensions opened a series of unforeseen opportunities. Early Union occupation, the flight of many coastal planters, the recruitment of slaves into military service, Sherman's Field Orders No. 15, and then the advent of the elective franchise enabled freedpeople to reconstitute and mobilize their communities speedily and to build them in familiar soil that they might now claim for their own. Although much of the "Sherman reserve" was soon officially restored, the old planters faced formidable and often intractable challenges in reasserting their power. By the 1870s, freedpeople had managed to forge a patchwork of land and labor arrangements that—like peasantries in much of the postemancipation Caribbean—combined, in various ways, household production with work on the rice and cotton estates. Small landowners, cash renters, and squatters, who at least supplemented their subsistence with stints on the plantations, could be found alongside laboring families who helped to establish what became known as the "two-day system": exchanging, in yearly contracts, between two and three-and-a-half days of task work on the plantations for a parcel of land that they could farm for themselves. Unlike their counterparts in the Caribbean, however, freedpeople in the low country had, for a crucial period, the added advantage of political muscle at the state and local levels. With their leaders and neighbors serving as county officers, trial justices, and jurors, and with Republican allies holding sway in the capital, the maneuvering room for the planters was decidedly limited.[63]

The planters nonetheless tried to do what they could to regain the upper hand, and they were aided in their efforts by the economic depression of the 1870s, which pressed upon the resources of low-country blacks and made available wage laborers from other areas. Despite the strictures of the Republican legislature, they also began compensating workers in checks, or scrip, rather than cash, redeemable only at the plantation store. A drought and the mounting Red Shirt campaign of Wade Hampton in 1876 seemed to offer inducements for an even wider counteroffensive, and in the spring of that year planters commenced by cutting task payments by nearly one-third. But if they believed that the balances had now clearly tilted in their favor, they were badly mistaken. In May, day laborers on E. B. Heyward's New Port plantation on the Combahee River ceased work, demanding an increase in wages and payment in cash, and, fittingly, at a meeting in front of the plantation store, elected officers and drafted a letter to Republican governor Daniel Chamberlain. They appear to have been helped by the black former state legislator Alexander P. Holmes, who had been teaching school on the property since February and subsequently received appointment as a trial justice. The strike then spread rapidly along the Combahee and Ashepoo rivers, following well-established lines of communication, and drew in contract as well as day laborers. Soon, squads of black strikers, some numbering in the hundreds, marched from plantation to plantation—with horns, drums, and clubs—pressuring those still in the fields to join their ranks; more than a few of the recalcitrant suffered the personal harassment and rough justice that customarily befell those regarded as political traitors. Unable to enlist the support of either local officials or the governor in the restoration of "order" (Chamberlain in fact expressed some sympathy for the strikers), most of the planters were compelled to yield.[64]

But not all of them did, and in August, as harvest approached, labor troubles erupted once again, this time revealing even more fully the dynamics of power in the region. Angry rice workers, hoping, perhaps, to take advantage of the local momentum now swung in their direction, pressed for harvest wage increases as well as an end to the checks system, and, initiating another strike, blocked the marketing of already harvested rice while attacking blacks who remained on the job. Rumors circulated that rice barns might become targets for arson, and planters complained of incessant "rioting" on their estates. "It was at first pretended," one of them reported, "that the strike was against the checks system . . . [but] laborers have repeatedly been driven from the fields whose owners have invariably paid cash only; cotton plantations are visited as well as rice; all classes of workmen are compelled to demand higher wages." Only a "strong hand," he believed, could "put down" the unrest, yet it was unclear where such a hand could be found. State militia units were composed of low-country blacks who either sympathized with the strike or actively participated in it. When a local rifle club attempted to step in and arrest the purported ringleaders, the tables were turned by incensed strikers. "The most unfortunate phase of the case," a rice grandee fretted, "is the bitter feeling exhibited at any attempted interference on the part of whites."[65]

The "strong hand" required was that of influence not of force, and as the state attorney general told the governor, "it is no use to send any one down there who is unknown to these people for they would not respect him but would say he was sent there by the 'rebels' or 'Democrats.'" They sent Robert Smalls. A former slave, constitutional convention delegate, state legislator, and now congressman representing the low country, Smalls was a man of "great influence" surely capable of stopping the "troubles." But as a recognized "politician," even he had to walk a careful line. If he were thought to be "interfering" with them, the strikers would give him no truck; in that case, some apparently threatened "to tie him up and give him 150 lashes on his big fat ass." Smalls understood what was required. He refused to call out the militia, as the attorney general had suggested, claiming that he found neither "rioters" nor any evidence that there had been a "riot." Instead, he quickly determined that the checks system, which he called a "hardship," was the "cause" of the strike and recommended its "abolition" as the means to "restore quiet satisfaction among the laborers." By that afternoon, the planters had agreed to "pay cash once a week." Smalls also managed to obtain safe passage for the besieged rifle club. And he asked the strikers warranted for arrest to step forward, which they did, having "objected" to being arrested by "white men." Together they went to the office of the local trial justice, himself a rice planter appointed in a conciliatory move by Chamberlain, but he was not in. So, "without guard," Smalls and the arrested strikers walked fourteen miles to the town of Beaufort—Smalls's bailiwick—where the crowd on the streets apparently "applauded them and publicly announced that they should not go to jail." The next morning, a black trial justice dismissed the charges and released the strikers. It was, to say the least, an unusual episode in the annals of American labor history.[66]

This would not be Smalls's last mission to the rice districts that year. Labor disturbances continued well into the fall. Yet the planters' defeat was already plain, and they could hardly take much solace in the Redemption of the state by Wade Hampton and the Red Shirts some months later. There would, of course, be little further sympathy in the state capital for the struggles of rural workers, and there would be a new and "reliable" militia available for dispatch. But black power remained entrenched in the low country, and the once mighty rice and long-staple cotton kingdoms continued to crumble. By the turn of the century, much of the area was dominated by black-owned truck farms rather than white-owned plantations, although the outlines of this social landscape were earlier in evidence. "Day labor is becoming scarce owing to the improvement in the condition of the laborers," a black newspaper correspondent wrote in the summer of 1880, shortly after the Senate committee had finished its investigation of the recent exodus, and "colored men who ten years ago worked as field hands for 50¢ a day now own their own lands and earn a comfortable support from them."[67]

The sugar parishes of lower Louisiana also served as a counterpoint to the spread of emigrationist sentiment and activity—an especially dramatic one given the exoduster eruption just to the north and the decades during which Liberian emigrants departed from the docks of

nearby New Orleans—though not for want of unrest. Labor disturbances exploded regularly in the 1860s and 1870s. But freedpeople there
had more success in making and then defending their gains than was
true in many of the cotton-growing areas; thus collective action, as in
the rice districts, continued to focus on achieving social and community
goals where they were. A white Caddo Parish observer seemed to
acknowledge this when, at the "height" of the "exodus fever," he
thought that as many as ten thousand blacks might be "induced" to go
"from these parishes to the sugar plantations" rather than to Kansas.[68]

Like the South Carolina low country, the parishes of southern Louisiana had a distinctive historical experience and character. Having long
been appendages of St. Domingue, they showed the complex cultural
and political marks of French and Spanish colonialism and the indirect
effects of the Haitian Revolution, as many of the refugees—slave and
free alike—ended up there. It was only at this point, in the late eighteenth and early nineteenth centuries, that sugar production really took
hold, organized increasingly around large, capital-intensive plantations
and slaves with a variety of skills and claims. Indeed, although gang
(rather than task) labor prevailed on the sugar estates, the slaves widely
came to cultivate provision grounds, raise domestic livestock, receive
pay for extra work, and engage in petty trading. And there is reason
to believe that, at least in some cases, institutions of community regulation, built around family and kinship groups, emerged.[69]

But, again as in the low country, the Civil War offered new possibilities. The arrival of the Union army in 1862 simultaneously undermined slavery and destabilized the plantations as many slaveowners
fled and a complex free-labor regime assumed ever-shifting forms.
Hundreds of blacks did then suffer the exploitation of profit-hungry
northern lessees, but they and others who found themselves in the
liminal world of the occupied South pressed for advantage: they sought
to increase their compensations and recast the conditions of their work,
to limit their responsibilities in the cane fields and expand them in
their provision grounds, and all in an intense atmosphere of political
contention. As the war neared its end and sugar production collapsed,
growing numbers of black labor "companies" rented or leased sections
of estates under federal control, and following the surrender, they and
other freed groups and associations—some benefiting from soldiers'
bounties and many likely the embodiments of prewar networks of com-

munity life—hoped to purchase parcels of the almost sixty thousand acres of abandoned land briefly made available. Small wonder that when President Johnson initiated his restoration policy and freedpeople learned that 1866 would bring them contracts rather than proprietorships, they gathered to consider their prospects and spread rumors of an impending division of land.[70]

The postemancipation sugar economy was therefore able to rise from the ashes of wartime destruction and disarray, and it did so chiefly from a foundation of plantations and gang labor. But the ascent was uneven, rather than phoenixlike, and, owing to labor shortages and Republican party mobilization, freedpeople wielded bargaining leverage that put an upward pressure on wages and enabled them to reconstitute kinship ties and secure time and resources for household-based production on the periphery of the estates. The planters, in turn, began an extended search for alternative sources of labor, especially harvest labor, and when the panic of 1873 led them to cut wages, a firestorm of protest broke out.[71]

What one hostile newspaper called a "war" in Terrebonne Parish involved at least two hundred sugar plantation workers who met at the Zion Church, formed an "association," paraded through the town of Houma "headed by fife and drum," and looked to spread their strike by a mix of persuasion and intimidation. It was, in the view of the *New Orleans Daily Picayune*, "a fair example of the manner in which a large number of negroes in the State expect to conduct themselves under the prevailing system of Republican government." And there can be little doubt that the grids of political power gave important shape to the course of struggle. Black state legislator William H. Keyes, who had previously served as Terrebonne Parish sheriff, addressed an early meeting of the strikers, lending his support (and perhaps urging them to more radical action), and although the then-sitting black sheriff would form a posse and Republican governor Kellogg eventually sent a small contingent of troops, both acted with caution and restraint. Keyes then helped to quell tensions and, after twelve of the strike leaders were arrested, joined with black state senator and former justice of the peace and parish tax collector Thomas A. Cage in posting bond to secure their release.[72]

Yet if the Terrebonne Parish strikers battled to resist the wage cuts and other exploitive features of the developing gang labor system, most notably the planters' practice of withholding half of their monthly pay until year's end, their aspirations for land and community independence remained powerful. So too, apparently, did their organizational sensibilities, which had found expression in the labor "companies" of the war and early postemancipation period. Thus, when the two hundred workers initially met at Zion Church, they bound "themselves not to work for any planter for less than $20 per month, rations, etc., the payments to be made monthly in cash." But their first "object" was "to form sub-associations and rent lands to work by themselves."[73]

Although the strike did not succeed in reversing the wage reductions, neither did it signal a downward trajectory of loss and defeat. Indeed, the remainder of the decade saw modest economic gains both for the core of regular plantation laborers (working for the entire crop season) who generally lived in family units in the old quarters and had access to provision grounds, and for the jobbers and short-term laborers, who tended to be young, single, and highly mobile men. Wages crept back upward and some planters were compelled to pay cash on a weekly basis during harvest and distribute a greater portion of the monthly allotments. By the end of the decade, according to the best recent estimate, the annual gross earnings of black sugar workers may have been double those of tenants and sharecroppers in the cotton districts, and a significant number began to accumulate some personal property; a few even purchased tiny plots of marginal land and resided in small settlements at the back of the estates.[74]

Nor was the political turmoil of the 1870s nearly as destructive in the sugar parishes as in the northern sections of the state or in the cotton South more generally. While paramilitary violence and political harassment were certainly in evidence, they tended to be more limited and episodic in their reach—flaring intensely in the neighboring parishes of St. Mary and Iberia, though only sporadically elsewhere. This reflected, in part, the economic leverage of sugar workers, as many planters feared that political coercion would only worsen the labor shortage, and in part, the presence of some Republican planters (who wanted tariffs on imported sugar). But we must not overlook the social organization of the sugar plantations themselves. Unlike the cotton districts, where centralized management and gang labor steadily gave way to decentralized tenancy and sharecropping, the sugar estates remained, as they had been before emancipation, large-scale units worked by gangs of laborers who dwelled in close proximity to one another, often in the former slave quarters. As a consequence, there was a substantial, and geographically concentrated, basis from which blacks could construct a political and associational infrastructure and fend off intimidation and attacks of several sorts. Whatever the evolution of tenancy and sharecropping may say about the struggles and achievements of freedpeople on cotton plantations and farms, it usually left them and their community institutions far more vulnerable. Political clubs and leagues could more easily be destroyed, leaders more readily assassinated or driven out, and voters more directly harassed when they lived scattered across the countryside than when they lived together in large numbers.[75]

Redemption was, of course, a decidedly unwelcome turn of events for African Americans in the sugar parishes, as elsewhere. But it did not come with the explosiveness or bloodshed of the other parishes and it did not dislodge local black power or marginalize the Republican party. Blacks there continued to vote, hold parish office, and represent their constituents in the state assembly. And the Republican party continued to attract most of their support. This, together with the economic advances of the 1870s, may help explain why emigrationism made such little progress in the region. It may also help explain why, as exodus fever still burned in the lower Mississippi Valley and Texas in early 1880, sugar workers set out on a different course: they struck.[76]

The strike of 1880 began in mid-March on two plantations in St. Charles Parish, in response to price increases rather than wage cuts, and it quickly spread first, and most prominently, across the line to St. John the Baptist Parish and eventually, though more haphazardly, to Ascension, St. James, St. Bernard, Jefferson, and Plaquemines. The now-Democratic governor Louis A. Wiltz immediately ordered in state militia companies, and white officials in St. Charles cooperated in having fourteen blacks regarded as "ringleaders" arrested for trespassing. One justice of the peace there told a crowd of strikers that they would get nothing by "riot" and that "the great arm of the great wheel of agriculture is the nigger. Next is the mule." But matters were different in St. John's, where black sheriff John Webre seemed "unwilling or unable to make arrests," where one justice of the peace "joined the strikers," and where black state senator Henry Demas could serve as a mediator. A former slave and Union army veteran,

Demas had previously been elected constable and state representative, emerging—much in the manner of Robert Smalls—as a parish political "boss." Although he also owned a small sugar property that was affected by the action, Demas sympathized with the strikers so long as they did not coerce other workers, and he managed to secure pardons for those arrested in St. Charles.[77]

Yet the unrest persisted, and in it we can detect important indicators of a social and political consciousness that sugar workers seemed to share with blacks in much of the rural South. The strikers, to be sure, did not create a unified movement either in St. John's or any of the other parishes, and it appears that day laborers were the driving force. But they had marched from plantation to plantation insisting that "the colored people are a nation and must stand together," and quickly drew up a "constitution" that bound them by oath to hold out for "a dollar a day" and promised a "severe thrashing" for any who strayed. One observer thought the constitution was the basis for a "visionary government." Even as they sought the support of Henry Demas, "believing our request is just and consistent and that the rewards for our toils should keep pace with the demands of the cost of living," some predicted that "when the U.S. Gov't saw the fields going to waste because of the strike it would take them away from the planters and parcel them out among the strikers"—or urged the blacks to go to Kansas "if they did not get their $1 a day." Indeed, news of a visit by former president Grant to lower Louisiana seemed to reenergize the strikers. They now "expected," a reporter on the scene noted significantly, "that one of three things will happen: that the Government will divide out the land among them; that the Governor will send them to Kansas; or that Grant will come up and make the planters pay the extra wages demanded."[78]

Grant did not come; the militia did. The arrival of another set of state troops conducting "war like movements," and the arrest and jailing of the strike leaders, effectively ended the agitation in St. John's. But disturbances continued in surrounding parishes well into the spring, and just over a year later an "association of laborers" in Ascension Parish whose "object" was "better wages" was thought to be "ripe for a strike." They had already established thirteen branches, each based at a plantation, a schoolhouse, or a church, and met to adopt a "constitution." After extended and at times heated discussion, they chose instead to organize the Workingmen's Protective and Mutual Aid Association of Donaldsonville in hopes of enforcing contracts and protecting laborers from the "rapacity" of storekeepers. It would not be long before the Knights of Labor would find this, and other parishes in the sugar country, to be fertile terrain for activity.[79]

✦

Just as the 1880 sugar strikes erupted, the *New Orleans Daily Picayune* took occasion to compare them to the recent "negro exodus." Both were "phases" of the "labor problem." The *Picayune* was attempting to discount the notion that they were manifestations of race antagonism, "outbreak[s] of blacks against whites," and further "illustration of the tyranny and injustice with which Southern whites treat Southern blacks." But we might well take the suggestion seriously and construe it broadly because, whatever their guise, emigrationist movements failed, at least in the short run, to produce much physical movement. Although contemporary estimates of black migration to Kansas in 1879–1880 ranged as high as 60,000, the most careful recent study puts that number somewhere between 20,000 and 25,000, fewer than half of whom came from the states of Alabama, Mississippi, Louisiana, Texas, and Arkansas. Another 1,500, mostly from North Carolina, may have made their way to Indiana, though a substantial body of them either returned to North Carolina or moved on to other states. Even this seems large when compared to Liberian emigration. Between 1877 and 1880, 388 blacks made the voyage to West Africa, most of whom left the Carolinas and Arkansas, for an annual average of just under one hundred; if we are to take the entire post–Civil War period into account, the total is less than 4,000 (3,812), or 238 annually.[80]

There were, of course, a great many obstacles to emigration, and the most formidable were imposed not by hesitant or hostile black leaders, but by the very system of social and political relations that black laborers sought to escape. Not surprisingly, the fists of white harassment were widely in evidence, especially where prospective emigrants worked for small planters and landowners who had limited resources and who had aligned with the White-Line faction of the Democratic party. In eastern North Carolina, a black laborer complained that when "our native white people . . . found that we wantes to go and meanes to go" to Liberia, they cut "us off of a great maney thang which we would have goten." White employers in Edgefield County, South Carolina, moved on several fronts. They "resolved to pay no money to colored laborers but to give them orders on merchants"; they warned blacks that the American Colonization Society "intends to carry them off to Cuba and sell them"; and they "threatened to strip [families] of their entire crops if they attempt to leave."[81]

Miles distant, in Phillips County, Arkansas, where "the Ku Klux are so numerous" that "our lives are in jeopardy every hour," one party of African Americans "trying to Emigrate to Liberia" discovered that when "our southern (white) Brethren learned of the exodus," they helped render "everything so gloomy that none can go." Further southwest, "in the country regions" of east-central Texas, "leading colored men suspected" of encouraging migration to Kansas were "arrested on the slightest pretext and put under bonds." One December Sunday in 1879, "a body of armed men" searching for one such leader surrounded a church in Sabine County and leveled "their guns over the congregation" in which they expected to find him. "Since these Southern white people found out we were trying to get away from here," Henry Adams wrote from northern Louisiana, they "have shut down on the cotton and taken all the cotton and corn and everything else . . . and the majority of our race is now living from hand to mouth."[82]

At no time were coercive tactics more fully deployed than during the early weeks of the 1879 Kansas exodus in the lower Mississippi Valley. As hundreds of laboring families began to leave their plantations and farms and head toward the banks of the Mississippi River, hoping to board a northbound steamboat, local landowners, merchants, and political officials tried to stem the flow by means of persuasion, intimidation, paramilitary violence, and the instruments of state power. Gatherings of exodusters were broken up; leaders were arrested for failure to pay their debts or fulfill their labor contracts; and armed bands traversed the rural districts to scatter parties on the roads and disperse exoduster encampments on the riverbanks. Most effectively, steamboat companies were threatened with boycotts and boat captains with vigilantism if they stopped to pick up black passengers. The companies buckled under the pressure and left emigrants stranded. Only the efforts of Radical Republican Thomas W. Conway to charter his own steamers forced the companies to relent, though by then the movement's momentum had been lost.[83]

And yet overall, such a strategy offered limited rewards, owing chiefly to the failure of southern whites to unify around it. Poorer white landowners reliant on the labor of their households and neighbors, together with white tenants, sharecroppers, and wage hands, often welcomed the departure of African Americans whose services they did not need or with whom they may have vied for employment; if nothing else, they did not readily enlist in the campaign of containment. Hardy Hogan Helper of Davie County, North Carolina, looking to establish a colony in Liberia, thus believed he could "meet all the opposition that may come from planters, storekeepers [and] politicians" because he had won the support of "the women of all shades and condition . . . as well as the entire class of poore white men."[84]

Wealthier planters, on the other hand, while hardly averse to strong-arm measures, had the means and flexibility to take a longer view. In some rapidly developing areas, like Washington County, Texas, they could encourage black emigration and seek instead to attract a different labor force. In other places, like the heavily black Mississippi Delta, they could make concessionary gestures of several sorts. In April 1879, the conservative *New Orleans Times* went so far as to admit that "the negroes are leaving the state because there exists among them a sense of insecurity" and to blame these "not altogether unreasonable . . . apprehensions" on "the conduct of a class of irresponsible younger men . . . who seem to emulate the name of bulldozers." The paper even advised planters to consider selling tenants "their 40 acres, on a long term arrangement, thus binding them to the land." One, Colonel Edmund Richardson of Hinds County, Mississippi, reputed by his agent to be the "largest planter in the world," had already promised to lower rents and provision charges. And early in May, at the behest of the governor of Mississippi, a biracial Mississippi Valley Labor Convention assembled in Vicksburg. Acknowledging an array of grievances that had led to the exodus, the delegates (who were, for the most part, planters and moderate-to-conservative black leaders) affirmed an identity of interest between landowners and laborers and called for the protection of black rights, fair elections, reform of the credit system, and efforts to dispel false rumors about Kansas.[85]

Few took much comfort in the convention's proceedings or in the

assurances of some prominent planters. "We wanted," in the words
of William Murrell Jr., "less promises and more practical operations."
But whether they dreamed of Kansas or Liberia, whether they lived
along the Mississippi River or in the Carolina cotton belt, the most
intractable barriers that prospective emigrants faced were the very material conditions of their own existence: their poverty, their want of
resources, their economic dependence, and their subjection to the agricultural calendar. Those who wished to relocate to Liberia had the
most severe problems, for the cost of transportation alone proved almost prohibitive. While the American Colonization Society had, until
1874, offered emigrants both ship's passage and land titles in Liberia
as incentives, the financial panic and subsequent depression made anything but partial subsidies impossible; the society was even forced to
sell its sailing vessel, the *Golconda,* and to discourage more forcefully
than ever anything that resembled "an indiscriminate and general exodus." A great many of the African Americans corresponding with the
society inquired as to the costs involved, asked for assistance of various
types, and tried to coordinate departure dates with the task of getting
in order the affairs of numerous laboring families.[86] It was not easy.
Invariably, prospective emigrants had to await the disposition of the
harvest before receiving their pay, and then only had a few short weeks
before the first ship would set sail for West Africa. The next voyage
usually occurred in late spring, by which time most laborers had entered yearly contracts and planted their crops.[87]

Some black communities struggled heroically for years, often to
little avail. In 1878, "the colard People" of Tunica County, Mississippi,
according to their leader L. G. Goodwin, "Call a Libria meeting and
Each one of them was sworn to Save all the Money tha Could on the
Enters for Libria." Unfortunately, they "all fail to save anouth" that
year "to Comply with the Neads for Travling." The next year, they
did a bit better: "all com Near it . . . than Ever But could not make
it." So, in very late December 1879, Goodwin called a "Libria meeting"
and "Each one of the member Comm up with his money and all of
them wish to know what would the hole fare." Goodwin then took
"Each family as tha was and make a Calcularshon," but discovered
that they "all Could not start Because tha diden have anouth." "Some,"
it seems, "had $25 som $50 som $75 som $100 and so on." They would,
as a result, have to use "whar money tha have" to buy "a good lot

of supplies" and try "to mak it agin," although they recognized that "the times have just got so that the Black people" were not "making any money." "You must Bar with us," Goodwin told William Coppinger of the American Colonization Society, with remarkable faith and determination, reminding him that "the children of Israel was 40 years getting out of the Williness and 25 or 35 are non to long for us to do good if apend on god houre maker."[88]

Kansas and Indiana surely seemed—and were—more reachable. The rails, the rivers, or the roads could be traveled, and the distances were not nearly as great or as complicated to navigate. Even so, the burdens were not inconsiderable. Except for those exodusters who, most likely in the early months of 1879, imagined that the federal government would provide transportation and farms, migrants had to amass resources sufficient both for the journey and for sustaining themselves once they arrived. And as those who ultimately made the trip learned, neither land nor employment were easy to come by: at least in a way that allowed for the reconstitution of whole communities. Tracts of "cheap" land sizable enough in acreage fell well beyond the financial reach of most rural black folk, and organizations such as the Kansas Freedmen's Relief Association, which tried to facilitate the establishment of landed "colonies," refused to permit more than a few families to settle in one neighborhood. Kansans, in the words of the relief association's general superintendent, "do not run their farms in the same way as the people of the South." They had small holdings and could offer work only to individual adults or, perhaps, to a single family. The exodusters, by contrast, seemed to the Kansans "clannish" and extremely reluctant "to live isolated . . . like the white man."[89]

As chapters in "migration history," therefore, these movements do not seem terribly significant. Yet we must not allow the unimpressive demographic figures to obscure the importance of emigrationism as a social and political phenomenon, and one that would have widespread and enduring repercussions. For the narrow migration figures tell us little about the thousands of black southerners who learned about Liberia and other possible destinations, discussed the prospects of resettlement, organized clubs and associations toward that end, debated the question at public meetings, and made formal inquiry, if not application, to the American Colonization Society and the federal government. In 1879, the corresponding secretary of the American Colonization Society, who did not favor mass emigration, estimated that as many as half a million African Americans might be "considering the expediency of emigrating to Liberia." Nor do the figures tell us much about how widely the "Kansas fever" spread or about the thousands who tried to leave their places of employment, waited unsuccessfully for steamboats and trains, or made it only so far as Memphis or St. Louis. Indeed, a northern observer on the scene wrote that the exodus assumed many of the characteristics of a "labor strike."[90]

Emigrationist activity may generally have lacked the organization and discipline to be found in a "labor strike," but, as the *New Orleans Daily Picayune* implied, it was closely entangled with the "labor problem" in the rural areas. And it very much disturbed the social and political landscape of the southern states just at the moment when white Democrats had finished the work of toppling the Reconstruction governments and begun the work of rolling back the gains that freed African Americans had made. Some of the effects were localized, though hardly unimportant: the reduction of rents and the clearing of debts at plantation stores in a few Delta counties and parishes; the provision of multiyear leases in parts of east-central Texas; the renegotiation of labor contracts in sections of the South Carolina piedmont; and increased financial support for black schools in districts of North Carolina. On one northern Louisiana plantation, the new owner, taking keen note of the unrest, "improved the general appearance of the whole place." The hands responded by renaming the estate "Kansas." Nearby, another plantation had become known as "Liberia." Two years later, the black-owned *New Orleans Weekly Louisianian,* which had voiced serious reservations about the exodus, nonetheless had to concede that emigrationism helped "teach [labor's] value [and] compel respect for its rights."[91]

Other repercussions of the emigration movements were much more encompassing, and nowhere was this more apparent than in Louisiana. There, just as the Kansas exodus commenced in earnest during the spring of 1879, delegates assembled at a state constitutional convention, called by the Democrats, with the intention of officially restricting black civil and political rights. Indeed, fears about the convention's designs had been racing through black communities in Louisiana since the enabling legislation had been passed in January, fueling the exodus itself. Enough Republicans cast ballots in the election for delegates to send thirty-two of the party faithful—most of them black—to the convention; and as the tremors of the exodus were felt more powerfully, enough Democrats bolted from the hard-line camp to defeat the poll tax recommended by the convention's committee on the franchise. It was no small victory, sustaining as it did precious breathing room for continued black electoral activism.[92]

But emigrationism also helped to widen and transform, as well as sustain, political activism. Injecting the term "exodus" into the political vocabulary of the post-Reconstruction South, it offered new forms of collective struggle both to fend off oppression and to create social spaces for African-American community life. Perhaps the most dramatic example occurred in late 1881 in Edgefield County, South Carolina, where a statewide attack on common grazing rights seemed to reignite resentments over "political serfdom, high rent, and the tenantry system" that had sparked interest in Liberia several years before. That fall new emigration societies were organized, the largest by a Baptist preacher and a former school commissioner near the village of Trenton, and by the last week in December as many as five thousand blacks, intending "to migrate in a body and settle all in a community," headed toward Arkansas. Hearing that some of the county's largest plantations had thereby been left without a single laborer, a northern journalist saw the just desserts being served up: "The planters . . . who have been conspicuous for years for their zeal in maintaining red-shirted rifle clubs to terrify the blacks in political campaigns, find at last that there is a Nemesis in human affairs." Not long after, blacks in neighboring Lexington County sent an agent to Arkansas "to see whether they will better their condition by pulling up stakes and moving there." By 1886, another "colored exodus" west took hundreds of blacks workers from the cotton fields of North Carolina, Georgia, Alabama, northern Mississippi, and west Tennessee, leaving white landowners indignant at the "demoralization which always accompanies a movement of this kind."[93]

These movements are largely to be distinguished from the increasingly important migrations of individuals and individual families in search of seasonal employment, higher wages, and more promising circumstances—migrations that took them from countryside to town, from the southeast to the southwest, from the hills into the Delta, from agriculture to coal and phosphate mines, tobacco factories, and turpentine camps.[94] But not entirely so. These short- and long-distance migrants sought to cobble together livelihoods, accumulate petty resources, protect small properties or favorable tenures, educate their children, and more generally, crawl out from under the thumbs of white employers, perhaps making, in the words of one black newspaper, "their oppressors and spoilators see the error of their way." In Mississippi, a "negro exodus" in the mid-1880s from the "hill country" to the "river bottoms" resulted in twenty or thirty wagons and teams departing some days, "often going in trains or squads like caravans," simultaneously improving "the conditions of negroes in the upland country" and creating by their sheer numbers what one newspaper correspondent called "an Africa in America." In the process, they would establish new sites and terrains of struggle in the dawning age of Jim Crow. All along, several hundred letters a year continued to flow into the office of the American Colonization Society from interested, and at times desperate, black southerners.[95]

It is with this in mind that we may consider what on the surface appear to be Henry Adams's extravagant estimates of the following he helped attract. When speaking of the number of African Americans enrolled by the Colonization Council, he made claims that varied wildly but were always very substantial: 69,000 at one point, 29,000 at another, 33,000 at yet another, all the way up to the 98,000 he cited in testimony before the U.S. Senate committee in 1880. He scarcely retreated to conservatism in referring to the "Kansas fever" of 1879, which by his lights, "aroused the colored people to mania" and led them to depart "in vast number." "[T]here will Be a Bout 250000 will leave the South by the time of the nx President election," he predicted. In at least one instance, a petition that he helped submit to the American Colonization Society was said to contain "over 3000 names."[96]

And yet, what Adams may have lacked in the bureaucratic skills of precision he seems to have made up for in political acumen. His Senate testimony and Colonization Society correspondence proved him a keen observer as well as a dedicated participant, and we therefore must take the fruits of his education most seriously. For in his years of traveling and organizing, speaking and listening, he learned about the aspirations and heartaches of a great many rural African Americans and about their paths to acquaintance with emigrationism. With good reason he had come to believe that the movement he was so instrumental in building had mass appeal in the post-Reconstruction South. When last heard from in 1884, Adams was still engaged in the Liberia project, though this time with a view to business connections emanating out of New Orleans, to which he had fled after the violent Louisiana state elections of 1878. But he left behind the outlines of a different political world: a world of Booker T. Washington, Marcus Garvey, and the Great Migration.

❖ 8 ❖

OF BALLOTS AND BIRACIALISM

We ask but an equal chance before the law, no more, *no less*. . . . We
do not seek your society, we only ask you as Christians, as servants
of the Master to help us safely anchor our little boat in some quiet
haven.

Huntsville (Alabama) Gazette

When the Civil War ended, Virginia seemed as ready as any state
of the former Confederacy to hatch a vigorous emigration movement.
During the four antebellum decades, almost 3,600 black Virginians had
emigrated to Liberia, roughly one-third of the total number of Liberian
emigrants sponsored by the American Colonization Society and well
over twice the number emigrating from nearest state rival North Carolina. After a war-related interruption, interest surfaced again very
quickly. In 1865 alone, 172 more black Virginians left for Liberia (about
double the annual antebellum average), the port city of Norfolk resumed its place as an important point of departure, and applications
for passage over the next few years suggested organizational activity
in several locations around the state. But then the momentum not only
stalled, as was true most everywhere with the advent of Radical Reconstruction; it appeared to dissipate. Although Norfolk remained a port
of call for Colonization Society vessels and the neighboring counties
of eastern North Carolina experienced an intensifying mobilization,

emigrationist sentiment in Virginia through the 1870s was remarkably delimited, revealing itself only in some of the other cities and towns—Portsmouth, Hampton, Richmond, Petersburg, and Lynchburg—and rarely, if ever, in the rural districts.[1]

The failure of emigrationism to establish much of a foothold in postemancipation Virginia owed in part to opportunities made available to freedpeople by a process of agricultural diversification that preceded and accompanied the transition from slavery. The increasing importance of truck and grain farming, most notably in the tidewater and older tobacco areas, was encouraging white landholders to sell off small plots to freed families as a means of accumulating liquid capital and harnessing a now more seasonal labor force. Although the plots were insufficient to provide a basis for social and economic independence, they did compose foundations for community reconstitution and, in some cases, enabled further acquisitions. A British traveler along the Virginia coast in the late 1870s thus remarked on the "large black proprietary" he found owning their "small patches of land and their own cottages," while Grangers in nearby Nottoway County complained a few years earlier about the "mistaken policy pursued by our farmers and landowners in squatting and colonizing large numbers of colored people on their lands." By the early twentieth century, Virginia boasted the greatest number and highest proportion of black landowners of any state in the old Confederacy. Yet the tenor of politics and political activity likely proved even more consequential. For just as emigrationism began to pulse in the post-Reconstruction cotton South, Virginia was swept by an unprecedented electoral insurgency that rallied whites as well as blacks: the Readjuster movement.[2]

The Readjuster movement became the most spectacular and successful example of challenges to Democratic party rule that erupted, in one form or another, in every southern state during the late 1870s and 1880s. At times the projects of disgruntled Democratic office seekers, but more commonly the products of disenchantment with Democratic policies that favored wealthy elites in town and country alike, they reflected social disruptions in evidence throughout the industrializing nation and gave the lie to Redemption-era celebrations of white solidarity. Almost everywhere, these challenges of Independents, third parties, and revitalized Republicans exposed deep divisions among white southerners that had been exacerbated rather than repaired by the defeat of Radical Reconstruction: divisions that set whites in non-plantation districts against those in the plantation belt, and yeoman farmers in the nonplantation districts against big landowners and merchants who lived among them. Almost everywhere, too, the challenges offered precious political breathing space to African Americans because they depended on the direct appeal for black votes.[3]

Blacks thereby preserved the electoral arena as a significant site of struggle, although its dynamics were now shaped by hostile state power on the one hand and widespread social and political instability on the other. Redemption meant, first and foremost, that white Democrats would control the state governments, and they wasted little time in targeting the vehicles of black civil and political empowerment. Rejecting the legitimacy of the Reconstruction order, many called for conventions to write still another round of new state constitutions, and in seven of the states—Tennessee, Arkansas, Texas, North Carolina, Alabama, Georgia, and Louisiana—they managed to do just that. But opposition arose in a number of quarters, not least among enfranchised African Americans who helped doom such efforts in South Carolina and Mississippi and defeat the conventions' most threatening work in Louisiana, Texas, and Arkansas. In the world of the Fifteenth Amendment, it was not entirely clear how such ends might be achieved without inviting federal interference.[4]

What followed, therefore, was a rather haphazard attack, carried out chiefly by the Democratic-controlled legislatures, in which black power was variously weakened, hedged, contained, and rendered vulnerable. Most of the states gerrymandered congressional, legislative, and judicial districts either to dilute black voting strength or mitigate its effects. A few states enacted registration laws that gave discretionary authority to state-appointed registrars and demanded complicated information from prospective voters. Several states made the payment of a poll tax (at times cumulative) a prerequisite for voting. North Carolina went so far as to make county government legislatively appointed rather than locally elected (so as to "redeem" the black-majority eastern counties); South Carolina passed, first, a restrictive registration law and then an "eight-box" election ballot law designed to confuse the poor and illiterate; Virginia disqualified eligible voters convicted of petty theft.[5]

Yet if the Democratic attacks were haphazard, they were not without effect. Indeed, they must be regarded less as precursors or preludes to the era of Jim Crow than as centrally a part of the advent of Jim Crow itself: of the construction of state-sponsored and sanctioned social and racial hierarchies in search of formulas and constituencies of support. Coming on top of the paramilitary terrorism that had dismantled Republican regimes, these measures helped erode black voter turnout in many places, shifted some black support from Republicans to Democrats, contributed to a dramatic decline in black officeholding, especially in rural areas, and left only a few bastions of black power relatively intact. Already in 1880, fewer than half of the eligible black voters in Georgia and Mississippi bothered to go to the polls, just over half did in Louisiana and Alabama, and in five of the southern states (most in the Deep South) more than 20 percent of the black voters cast ballots for the Democrats.[6]

But the formulas and constituencies of support for Jim Crow were not easily or quickly found, and in an atmosphere of contention over policy and power, black communities remained politically mobilized and alert to new openings, arrangements, and alliances. Some of these could involve horse-trading with local planters and some the manipulation of white paternalism. Some could involve staying the Republican course or dividing among themselves over which course to take. The most daring and risky involved coalitions of various types with white independents or white adherents of third parties who could not hope to dislodge the Democrats without black electoral support. For the first time, the meaning of political biracialism would be confronted and determined by native southerners. It was during the 1880s, not the 1890s, that the prospects and limits of such a venture would become painfully apparent.

❖

Virginia may have given rise to the most spectacular example of post-Reconstruction insurgent politics because it experienced the least spectacular example of Reconstruction politics. Alone among the former Confederate states, Virginia did not produce a Republican regime in the late 1860s and early 1870s despite having been remanded to military rule in 1867. When the state submitted its new constitution to Congress and gained readmission to the Union in January 1870, those calling themselves "Conservatives" effectively controlled the governorship and the legislature, with 138 of 180 seats in the lower house of delegates and 36 of 49 seats in the senate. But this was not because the Republican party was stillborn or because freedpeople had failed to respond effectively to emancipation and the advent of the elective franchise.[7]

If anything, popular mobilization had proceeded very rapidly. Within months of the war's end, mass meetings of freedpeople had taken place in Richmond, Norfolk, and Petersburg, as well as in smaller towns and villages in the countryside; a state freedmen's convention had assembled in Alexandria; protests against racial discrimination had been organized in Richmond and demands for civil and political equality had been voiced from many points east of the Blue Ridge; Union Leagues began appearing in black-majority sections of the coast and piedmont; and the Republican party was preparing to hold a state convention.[8] Following passage of the Reconstruction Acts, newly eligible black voters registered in impressive numbers. The problem was that the Radical Republicans, most of whom were black, may have been too well organized and determined to press their agenda given the peculiar circumstances of Virginia politics. For Conservatives and moderate Republicans were alike connected principally with urban, banking, and railroad, rather than landed, interests and they had a powerful ally in military district commander General John Schofield. When the Radicals came to dominate the state Republican party and then the constitutional convention, producing a document that disqualified anyone who had voluntarily supported the Confederacy from holding political office, their opponents reacted with dispatch and effect. Schofield delayed the ratification election and moderate white Republicans formed a development-oriented electoral alliance with Conservatives. With the blessing of President Grant, the disqualification provisions were separated out from the rest of the new state constitution in the ensuing referendum and went down to defeat. With high voter turnout generally in this white-majority state, the Radicals lost the gubernatorial and legislative contests.[9]

But they were hardly vanquished. Especially in the black-majority counties of the tidewater and tobacco-growing southside, they sank substantial roots and, during the 1870s, closely contested or regularly carried state and national elections. Almost seventy African Americans came to serve in the legislature, all but eleven in the lower house, representing twenty-nine counties, most of which were rural with blacks making up at least 60 percent of the inhabitants. Although Conservative policies—imposing a poll tax, abolishing some local offices, reducing the size of the house of delegates—further threatened the Republicans' social base and prospects, there were also hidden political benefits from the Conservatives' immediate ascendancy to state power. Quite simply, the Virginia countryside was not overrun with the paramilitary violence that had destroyed Republican party rule, eliminated effective black leaders, and often left the black institutional infrastructure a shambles in much of the cotton South. It could have turned out otherwise. Harassment, intimidation, and personal violence were widely in evidence in the state in the early postwar years, and the Norfolk riot of 1866 demonstrated that a combustible mix was no less present there than in any other place where African Americans were prepared to assert their claims for citizenship and equality. But because Radical Reconstruction was short-circuited, neither the Klan nor White League–style units really organized in Virginia, and political struggles were conducted in an atmosphere of relative calm and security.[10]

Together with the distinctive features of Virginia's postemancipation economy, these circumstances had striking implications for the development of local black leadership and black civic and political life more generally. We may glimpse some of these by looking more closely at the African Americans who won election to the legislature before 1880, for as a group they were not only skilled and literate but also acquiring property and establishing themselves as formidable political actors. Almost all were either farmers, craftsmen, ministers, teachers, or retailers (some plying a combination of two or three occupations), and nearly 80 percent either owned land before entering the legislature, purchased land while they were in the legislature, or became landowners after they left. To an extent, this reflected the legacy of Virginia's Revolutionary-era manumissions, which gave rise to a free black population scattered chiefly across the rural tidewater, working as farm hands, artisans, tenants, laborers, boatmen, or domestic servants, usually maintaining connections with local slave communities, and in some cases accumulating small parcels of land. At least 40 percent of the legislators were freeborn, and some entered the post-emancipation world with real property. But more had been slaves who commenced buying land only after 1865.[11]

Nearly half of the legislators served at least two terms or would hold at least one additional political office. They had been launched, that is, on political careers, and their experience is suggestive of a phenomenon that appears to have become widespread: the rise in the rural black counties of a generation of leaders, with skills, property, kinship ties, and links to a number of social institutions, who for years would be the fulcrums around which local politics pivoted. Mecklenburg County's Ross Hamilton exemplified the type. Born a slave in the late 1830s, Hamilton learned the carpentry trade and, after the war, opened a store in the small town of Boydton. He soon began to purchase both land and livestock. With the aid of his son and two other freedmen who belonged to small kin groups, Hamilton mobilized support for the Republican party and then began a stint in the legislature that lasted, with some interruption, until 1890. No other African American in Virginia served more legislative terms in the nineteenth century than did Hamilton, and along the way he headed up something of a black courthouse ring in the county. A complex alliance with a wealthy white, Democratic landowner offered Hamilton financial assistance and protection, but even more consequential were his involvements with the black Baptist church, the Boydton Academic and Bible Institute, and two secret black benevolent societies. Together, they enabled Hamilton to weather challenges to his local power and steer a remarkably independent political course.[12]

Although Hamilton's legislative longevity may have been unusual, the development of his local political power base was not. In the eastern shore county of Northampton, there was Peter Carter, a former slave who had managed to gain literacy and then ran off to the Union army during the Civil War. Thereafter, he entered Hampton Institute and returned to the eastern shore, becoming involved in Republican politics. Elected to the legislature in 1871 and serving until gerrymandered from his seat in 1879, Carter earned a reputation as an impressive speaker, a tireless organizer, and a tough-minded politician especially interested in controlling the federal patronage. He also purchased several tracts of land in Northampton, the largest encompassing 150 acres.

Carter was, one observer claimed in 1881, "omnipotent with the colored people on this shore."[13]

Cumberland County's Reuben Turner Coleman never sat in the Virginia legislature, but he became the "patriarch" of an extended and influential local clan. Apparently born a slave, though of mixed parentage, Coleman received an education of sorts and, more importantly, financial resources from his white father. As early as 1866, at the age of twenty-two, he bought 366 acres of land in the county and was soon selling liquor, operating a tavern, and expanding his holdings. Appointed and then elected justice of the peace, he served for eighteen years while presiding over a growing family enterprise and while his brother-in-law, the shoemaker and preacher Shed Dungee, eventually recognized as a "pioneer in the promotion of school and church" in Cumberland, won election to the house of delegates.[14]

When Henry D. Smith became Greenesville County's representative to the house of delegates in 1879, it seemed an acknowledgment of his community standing and power. An ex-slave who lacked any formal education, Smith acquired the rudiments of literacy and, in the years after 1865, enough real estate to make him the county's largest black property owner. His purchase of "Merry Oaks" must have been particularly satisfying: it had been the farm and residence of his old master. In the process, owing to successful farming and distilling operations, he seems to have emerged as an important political broker, serving, among other things, as a surety for Republican officeholders; on one occasion, he even posted a $10,000 bond for the white Republican postmaster at the county seat of Emporia.[15]

Slave-born Caesar Perkins of Buckingham County, who served terms in the house of delegates sixteen years apart, used his skills as a brick mason, farmer, and minister to take his place as a "leader in all movements for the welfare of his race for a period of forty-five years." Louisa County's John W. Poindexter, born free and elected to the legislature in 1875, benefited from the "large group of Poindexters" who lived close by as well as from his work as a schoolteacher and his position as a landowner. And Ballard T. Edwards, part of an old free black family in Chesterfield County, gained the rewards of state and local office (a term in the legislature, and terms as justice of the peace and overseer of the poor) after building a base by teaching a freedmen's school, instructing apprentices in the bricklaying trade, serving as clerk in a Baptist church, and buying several lots in the town of Manchester.[16]

Black political leaders such as these contributed to and benefited from the growth of an increasingly dense civic and associational life, a social and political infrastructure and set of networks, that marked the postemancipation period in the rural areas. It bore resemblance to trends evident in urban centers and was quite unlike most of the rural districts of the Deep South, where poverty and vigilante violence left something more skeletal. By the early 1880s in Hanover County (50 percent black), one might have identified seventeen black churches, most with their own ministers, together with an assortment of "colored societies," which provided aid in times of sickness, death, and economic hardship: the Star, the True Reformers, the Young Sons of Abraham, the Rising Sons of Zion, the Working Sons of Hope, the Farmers' Benevolent Society, the United Sons and Daughters of Jacob, the Benevolent Sons and Daughters of Zion, and the United Sons and Daughters of Love, each with twenty or more members. Other counties had lodges of the Odd Fellows and Masons and, perhaps, a volunteer black militia company. "Next to churches in importance come the secret and beneficial organizations, which are of considerable influence," W. E. B. Du Bois wrote in his 1897 study of the tobacco processing and marketing town of Farmville in Prince Edward County, noting that the oldest of them "had been in existence . . . for over twenty years."[17]

But there can be little doubt that over the course of the 1870s, black Republicans became increasingly restive. Their party was hardly moribund; a strong press had been established in Richmond, Norfolk, Petersburg, and Alexandria, and major organizational efforts were undertaken, especially during presidential election years. Party representation, particularly black representation, in the legislature had, however, been in decline, and white leaders appeared more interested in federal spoils than in attending to the concerns of the party's overwhelmingly black constituents. Like their counterparts in every southern state, black Republicans in Virginia complained about being denied their fair share of offices, and they surely had a point. The evidence suggests that in the rural counties blacks might sit as justices of the peace or constables in a few of the districts or as overseers of the poor, but rarely on the county board of supervisors or in offices with greater power and responsibility, such as sheriff, treasurer, or commissioner of revenue. While legislative gerrymandering did create the black Fourth Congressional District where, according to one observer, black Republicans outnumbered whites by a margin of sixteen to one, the whites—aided, it seems, by blacks who tendered support in return for "inferior" positions—succeeded in preventing any African American from winning the party's congressional nomination. Bitter struggles within the party were becoming more and more widespread, and by 1877 the disarray was so pronounced that the Republicans failed to put forward a candidate for governor.[18]

Opportunities beckoned, however, because disarray and struggle seemed even more pronounced among the Conservatives. For them, the unrest focused on the issue of paying the state debt. Accumulating since the antebellum period, when the Virginia legislature had approved the borrowing of millions of dollars to build railroads and other internal improvements, the debt had reached the considerable sum of $30 million even before the Civil War. By 1870, it had grown much larger, approaching $46 million, and now, in the aftermath of Confederate defeat, threatened to bankrupt the state. Party leaders and constituents therefore wrestled over whether the debt would be repaid (with interest) in full, adjusted (scaled down), or repudiated. More than the principle of fiscal responsibility was at stake; the battle was about the balances of power in Virginia and who would shoulder the burdens of settlement.[19]

Virginia was by no means alone in facing the problem of how, or whether, to pay its debt. Most of the other southern states had a similar reckoning to make, and their politics were all agitated by it. Yet outside of Virginia, the circumstances and dynamics were different, both because a sizable portion of their debts had been contracted by Reconstruction Republican regimes and because big landed interests figured centrally in the Democratic coalitions that had redeemed the states. Looking to slash taxes and social services and to put an end to state-sponsored economic development, large and small white landowners generally joined hands to favor a downward readjustment of the debt, and in much of the lower South they succeeded without significant resistance. More of a contest erupted in Tennessee, Arkansas, and Louisiana before the forces of readjustment prevailed. But in Virginia, Republicans could not be blamed for raising taxes and running up the debt and the Conservatives, dominated as they were by urban mercantile, banking, and railroad interests, had more reason to do right by the state's creditors. With the Funding Act of 1871, they tried to do just that.[20]

The "Funder" Conservatives (as they came to be known) would have had a difficult time under the best of circumstances paying off the creditors without imposing a belt-tightening regimen on various social groups in the state. But the panic of 1873 and the ensuing economic depression required draconian measures just to make the interest payments, and in an attempt to protect the fiscal "honor" of the state— not to mention the lines of capital that would promote further development—the Funders moved to boost taxes on real and personal property and cut social services, most notably state aid to the public schools established by the Republican constitution of 1868. In so doing, they provoked a broad front of opposition, located primarily in the rural areas, and ranging from old planters in the east (who bridled at the increased taxes on their landholdings) to white yeoman farmers in the west (who objected both to the property taxes and to the attacks on public schools) to African Americans most everywhere (who absorbed the brunt of many Conservative policies, and were especially riled by the further threats to their schools). By the mid-1870s, the Funders came under growing reform pressure from within the ranks of their own party, and that pressure soon found new organizational bases. The Grange, led by substantial white landowners and boasting a membership of nearly twenty thousand statewide, began to mobilize against debt repayment and talked of running a candidate for governor. In 1877, twenty-two "independents," almost all of whom favored some type of debt adjustment, won seats in the Virginia legislature. And in early 1879, 175 delegates who called themselves "Readjusters" met in Richmond and formed a political party aimed at wresting state power.[21]

In important respects, Virginia may be seen as an example of a struggle enveloping postwar America and threatening the positions of the established political parties. The struggle was over the course the country would follow and who would chart it. Already in the early 1870s it was being waged most aggressively and effectively by the industrial and financial interests, principally of the urban Northeast and Middle Atlantic, who had emerged strengthened and energized by the Civil War. They were exerting more and more control over both the Republican and Democratic parties, and the results of their work were evident in policies—deflation, hard money, the creation of privately owned national banks, protectionism—that privileged their aspirations. At times the struggle took on a regional cast, since the industrialists and financiers were most closely associated with the Northeast and their opponents with the South and West. While this is a great oversimplification, opposition would be increasingly prominent in the states—more rural and agricultural—of the South and trans-Mississippi West, where it either tried to reclaim control of the Democratic or Republican parties, or set out on an independent and insurgent path.[22]

Virginia may also be seen as an example of the strains besetting Democratic parties across the post-Reconstruction South. For once the Democrats had driven the Republicans from power and demonized them as a black man's party that no respectable white man could join, they had to keep the peace among a diverse collection of whites, some with antagonistic interests or political genealogies, in turbulent social and economic times.[23] Disappointed Democratic office seekers might therefore choose to bolt the party and run as "independents" in congressional races or on the county and parish levels, as they did in virtually all of the states across the upper and lower South. Other white dissidents, most notably in Alabama, Texas, and Arkansas, mobilized against the policies of the dominant faction of the Democratic party and aligned with the Greenback-Labor party nationally in the name of inflation, a government-controlled money supply, and the needs of small producers. At all events, they invoked the new language of "anti-monopoly" in denouncing the general concentration of wealth and power, the machinations of merchants and commercial interests, and what they called "ring rule." With rare exception, they had to seek the support of black voters.[24]

When the Readjusters assembled in Richmond to organize their party in February 1879, a handful of African Americans, all apparently from the counties of New Kent and Halifax, were among those in attendance. They had responded to the convention call, which invited "the people of Virginia without distinction of color," and at least one of them rose to address the gathering. Insisting that he was a Republican but also an "ardent" Readjuster, he told the new party members that most blacks in his district were Readjusters too and ready to join with them. "We are for peace," he proclaimed, "and we accept the overture made toward us." The overture was a rather cautious one, however, suggesting that the Readjusters, like other independent movements of the era, imagined at their inception pressing forward in the interests of white dissidents alone. Indeed, it was not until months later in this legislative election year that further overtures were made, and not until very late in the fall campaign that real cooperation with black Republicans was proposed.[25]

Those prospects brightened dramatically in the immediate aftermath of the election, for unlike other contemporary independent movements, the Readjusters stood on the threshold of controlling the state government. The Conservatives still claimed the governorship, but owing to impressive gains in the white-majority counties of the west and valley, the Readjusters took charge of both the house and the senate by gaining the support of thirteen black Republicans who had won seats as well (eleven in the house and two in the senate) and consequently held the balance of power. Even the planter Readjusters from the eastern sections of the state recognized that blacks would have to be lured into their party's caucus, and that necessity and wisdom would at least require "dividing to the colored readjusters of the General Assembly some of the offices." It fell to William Mahone, chairman of the party executive committee and leader of the movement, to cut the deal.[26]

Mahone seemed a most unlikely insurgent leader. A civil engineer trained at the Virginia Military Institute, a Confederate major general who had served under Robert E. Lee, a lifelong Democrat "of the straitest sect," and the president of three railroad companies attempting to consolidate a small-scale empire, he seemed every bit the Funder. And for a time, he effectively was. But jealous competitors and the economic depression of the 1870s combined to undermine his plans, and in an effort to reclaim his losses and exact revenge, Mahone ran for the Conservative gubernatorial nomination in 1877 as an anti-Funder. If principle and opportunism mixed freely in his attack on the Funders for their undemocratic and unconstitutional assault on the school system, Mahone did find a formula to attract popular support.

When his bid for the nomination failed, he—like more than a few other disgruntled Democratic aspirants in the South—turned toward insurgency.[27]

Engineer and railroad man that he was, Mahone's political ambitions and organizational energies had no rivals among his insurgent counterparts. Not only was he able to harness the widespread discontent with Funder rule; he was also ready to build strong political bridges. As soon as the election of 1879 was over, his intelligence networks were vibrating with information as to how he might "*at once* organize *all* readjusters without regard to color." In the process, he learned what it would take to convince the black legislators that "we are their friends" and win their cooperation: a "share" of the "patronage of the state," "something in the way of office," abolition of the whipping post, "repeal of poll tax payments as [a] prerequisite for suffrage," and provision "for the public schools." In December, Mahone chose to meet personally with the thirteen black members of the assembly and assure them that he would see these issues addressed. Some, including Ross Hamilton, had already expressed support for him; the remainder now came on board. For the moment, the alliance was sealed, the Readjusters had a majority in the legislature, and Mahone was catapulted to the U.S. Senate.[28]

There was, among African Americans in Virginia and elsewhere, no shortage of skepticism as to what the election and the alliance would bring them, a sense that they offered no more than "a faint ray of hope to our people for bettering their condition." The benefits to be expected, one black newspaper observed, rested on "political pledges," which, like "pie crusts," were easily broken. Signs of "good faith" were admittedly early in evidence, as the Readjusters quickly selected a black man to serve as doorkeeper of the house of delegates. But whether black Virginians would get "redress of their grievances and a proper recognition of their political rights" in return for their votes remained to be seen. For some time thereafter, the jury was very much out, and the alliance seemed tentative. So long as the Conservatives held onto the governor's chair, the Readjusters' legislative achievements were likely to fall victim to executive veto, and so long as the Republican party resisted coalition or "fusion" with Independents, blacks in Virginia—as in other southern states—would face difficult decisions. Would they turn their backs on the party that had defended their rights and still sent some of the spoils of federal patronage their way, thus aligning with a new organization run by white men who, in the main, regarded themselves as Democrats? Or would they maintain their allegiance to the "straight-out" Republicans, who rejected debt readjustment and had no chance of gaining state power? "Our colored voters are readjusters on all state questions," one of Mahone's correspondents wrote in explaining the dilemma, "but in national matters republicanism is part of their religion." Most of them, accordingly, rejected Mahone's slate of unpledged presidential electors in 1880, and cast their ballots, as they had in the past, for the Republican nominee.[29]

Much work, in short, was still to be done before the biracialism of the Readjuster movement could be tested. "If the Readjuster party would win the next Governor, legislature, and state offices," Mahone asserted only days after his 1880 defeat, "they must prepare *now* for the contest." To that end, he gave especially "careful attention" to the "black belt," attempting simultaneously to pry African Americans loose from the Republican party organization and to ensure that they would have the opportunity to go to the polls on election day. His hand was surely to be found in the call for a "general convention of colored citizens" to meet in his hometown of Petersburg in March 1881 for the purpose of charting a "new political course" and acting in concert "with the most liberal party in Virginia." So well did Readjuster sympathizers define the terrain of the convention proceedings that a small group of "straight-out" Republican bolters nonetheless counseled blacks against supporting "any man who refuses to vote for abolition of the whipping post, the payment of the capitation tax, and is not for the maintenance of free schools." When the entire party then gathered in June to nominate a state ticket, more than one hundred African Americans took seats as delegates.[30]

That Mahone's vote enabled Republicans to control the closely divided U.S. Senate and that the Readjuster party platform (reflecting the resolutions passed at the black convention) squarely advocated increased appropriations for schools, an end to the poll tax, and a state government responsive "to all classes of the citizenry," as well as debt readjustment, helped ease many black Virginians into the Readjuster camp. "I don't propose to carry the war to Africa," the party's gubernatorial candidate, and former Democrat, William Cameron could tell the convention, "but to carry Africa into the war." Yet a full-scale electoral mobilization depended, in the final analysis, less on Mahone's organizational wizardry—impressive as it was—than on the political infrastructure that African Americans had long been constructing. Mahone seemed to acknowledge this when he instructed local loyalists to supply him with the names of the "most active and well-informed colored men in your county who would be suitable to organize clubs" and with a "list of the colored churches in your county and the full name of all colored preachers and the Post Office address of each." "We want," Mahone explained to them, "the men of influence with the colored people." His voluminous correspondence revealed, chiefly for the black-majority counties, a dense landscape of institutions and activism. Mahone compiled the names of scores of local black leaders, many of whom, like James H. Shields and James Hatten Jr., in Accomac County, were "old and shrewd in politics" and experienced in organizational work for the Republican party, or, like the "influential Republican" minister R. G. Tate in Mitchell's Station, were able to carry "200 votes" since "nearly every Negro in the district is a church member." Only from the overwhelmingly white western counties was Mahone told that he need not "pay any attention to the colored vote" because "they have no colored leaders and are entirely under the control of the whites."[31]

The Readjusters embraced the quasi-military methods of mobilization that had long been part of local political culture and that the Union League and Republican party had adopted throughout the rural South during Reconstruction. With the information he had accumulated, Mahone called for the designation of a white and a black "lieutenant" to oversee activities in every county election precinct, and then a "squad captain" for every ten voters, of each race, thought to be likely Readjusters. He also selected black "canvassers" who would move through the counties, addressing local meetings, coordinating events, and exerting influence. Together, they would try to rally local communities, identify both the faithful and the "doubtful," determine whose poll taxes were "delinquent," and eventually march their squads to the polling places and distribute Readjuster ballots. In Louisa County, there would be 13 black lieutenants and 178 squad captains; in King and Queen County, 6 black lieutenants and 99 squad captains; in Southampton County, 11 black lieutenants and 175 squad captains.[32]

It was a sprawling, daunting operation. And an expensive one. The

most formidable and consequential financial challenge, generally regarded as "the prerequisite to Readjuster success," was the need to
pay the poll taxes of a great many eligible black voters, sympathetic to
the cause, who had fallen into delinquency and faced disfranchisement.
Mahone grasped the problem early on in the campaign and when local
organizers responded to his request for an assessment, the magnitude
became all too apparent. In many of the black belt counties of the
tidewater and Southside, more than 20 percent—and in some instances
more than 40 percent—of the African Americans who supported the
Readjusters had failed to pay their poll tax. In Amelia County (71
percent black), 254 of 997 had failed to pay. In Halifax County (61
percent black), it was 929 of 2,981; in Northampton County (58 percent
black), 455 of 975; and in Hanover County (50 percent black), a whop-
ping 1,168 of 1,843. "The great majority at each precinct," one organizer glumly reported, "are colored men whose cap[itation] taxes in
order to secure a Readjuster victory will have to be paid for them."
But there were further logistical snares. Even if the taxes could be
paid, the receipts had to be collected and then distributed to the voters
so that they could be presented to the polling officials, together with
Readjuster tickets, on election day. It was, to say the least, a tall order
for the party and for the local operatives.[33]

Money to pay the poll taxes of poor black—and white—Readjusters, however, represented only a portion of the funds necessary to run
an insurgent campaign in Virginia of the early 1880s. For as robust
and centralized as Mahone's developing political machine appeared to
be, the county and precinct level organizers supplied the crucial horse-
power, and their services often came at a price. At a time when African
Americans were increasingly disenchanted with the "straight-out" Republican party while at the same time remaining skeptical as to the
intentions of the Readjusters, cash could be a powerful source of political allegiance. It was neither just crass opportunism nor a sign of
indifference or vulnerability. It was a manifestation of power and assertiveness. The work of canvassing and community mobilization, as
Washington Flood of Amherst County discovered, often imposed an
assortment of financial burdens. In order to turn his considerable energies "to get[ting] out the vote," Flood not only had to leave his job
on the railroad, but also had to pay "his own expenses." A Readjuster
in Amelia County learned that he could "secure the services of two

influential and competent colored men to organize clubs provided they can be paid something for their time." Other black activists regarded cash payments as an early form of political patronage, an indication of the party's commitment to fulfill its pledges, or an important acknowledgment of their local prestige. "The colored leaders here," according to one correspondent, "say they will work with either side that will pay them."[34]

Mahone was well aware that the "question of carrying [a] county" could be "a mere matter of dollars and cents applied to capitation and colored canvassers," and that both Funder and Republican opponents intended to enter the fray, "coining" (as a black minister put it) African-American voters. Such was the dilemma of white insurgent leaders across the South. But Mahone and the Readjusters came to occupy a singular position. Owing to his alignment with the Senate Republicans and, especially, to the assassin's bullet that ended the life of James Garfield and put Chester A. Arthur in the Presidency, Mahone had, by the fall of 1881, rich veins of patronage at his disposal. For unlike Garfield, who had supported the straight-out faction of the state Republican parties and detested debt readjustment, Arthur looked to bolster southern independent movements—in Virginia and elsewhere—as a strategy to break the hold of redeemer Democrats. The timing could not have been better. Although the resources that subsequently flowed through federal patronage networks and from wealthy northeastern Republicans were hardly unlimited, they enabled Mahone to take on the challenge of the poll tax and begin rewarding "lieutenants," "squad captains," "canvassers," ministers, and other black men with political talent and influence.[35]

The efforts paid off mightily. By election day, African Americans, especially in Virginia's black belt, had overwhelmingly embraced the Readjusters. In many places local organizers had come to expect more than 90 percent of the eligible black voters to cast ballots for Readjuster candidates, and although turnout rates varied (largely because of persisting poll-tax delinquency), the results confirmed their optimism. The Readjusters carried all but five of the counties that had majorities of black voting-age males and they gained firm control of the state government. The governorship and both houses of the legislature were now in Readjuster hands, with fifteen African Americans (three in the senate and twelve in the house) to be found in their delegation. While blacks contributed about two-thirds of the total Readjuster vote, thirty-three of the white-majority counties, most in the Shenandoah Valley and mountain west where small farms rather than large estates predominated, also sided with the insurgents. It was just the sort of coalition—joining freed blacks with yeoman whites—that Radical Republicans had imagined but failed to build during Reconstruction across the former Confederate South.[36]

For those who had hoped that the Readjusters might usher in "a new era," might "give effect to the 100,000 colored votes in the state," might "redeem" their campaign pledges, the next several months must have been encouraging if not astonishing. Party legislators struck quickly at the state debt, repudiating one-third of it and reducing the interest rate on the remainder, but they also moved on a number of fronts to further reward their constituents and strengthen their social base. They slashed taxes on real estate while hiking them on railroads and other corporate property. They chartered labor unions and fraternal organizations. They enacted a mechanics' lien law. And they sought to regulate tobacco warehouses and railroad companies and to undermine the power of courthouse cliques. Most of all, with black lawmakers playing leading roles, they provided for repeal of the poll tax, abolished the whipping post, and dramatically increased funding for schools and other social services, thereby addressing the needs and concerns of their humble followers in town and country alike. Black Virginians would see rapid growth in the number of schools open to them and in the enrollment of black students: in the short period between 1879 and 1883, the black schools multiplied from 675 to 1,715, and the students enrolled increased from 35,768 to 90,948. They would see black teachers replacing white ones in those schools and racial discrepancies in teacher salaries outlawed. And they would see the legislature—again encouraged by black representatives—appropriate funds for a black state college and an asylum for the black insane, both to be located in Petersburg.[37]

Power shifted markedly on the local level as well. Petersburg stood as the most dramatic and visible example, with the Readjusters electing the mayor, a majority of city councilmen, and an assortment of officers (members of the board of supervisors, justices of the peace, and constables) in surrounding Dinwiddie County. Impressive gains were also registered in Richmond and Lynchburg, owing in good part to mobilizations among black and white factory workers. But the changes in the rural and small-town tidewater and southside can be regarded as equally, if not more, breathtaking. By the spring of 1883, the Readjusters had come to occupy offices—often most of the offices—in virtually all of the black-majority counties. "We have made a clean sweep," one activist in Powhatan County gleefully told William Mahone. "[W]e hold every office in the county; not a Funder on guard." In Greenesville County, where Funders had held all but two of the offices, the Readjusters pushed them out of all but six. In Brunswick County, Readjusters first became sheriff, treasurer, commissioner of revenue, and board supervisors, and then elected ten additional magistrates. In Amelia County, where Readjusters and Funders had previously divided the offices, the Readjusters took charge countywide. And although most of the Readjuster claimants were white, blacks were to be found, in small numbers, as magistrates, constables, members of the board of supervisors, and overseers of the poor, and in greater numbers as jurors and election officials. The new atmosphere could be chilling for those who imagined that business would go on as usual. When a white conservative refused to serve on a jury with a black man in one county, the Readjuster judge slapped him with a $250 fine and ten days imprisonment for contempt. "This changed the mind of the haughty Virginian," a black newspaper correspondent chuckled, "and he signified his willingness to serve, whereupon the penalties were removed."[38]

But the Readjusters' power and influence did not depend only on the direct results of elections. There was the state and federal patronage to dispense, and Mahone and Cameron used it aggressively to create a political infrastructure of loyalty and support. Postmasterships and clerkships were particularly prized because there were so many to fill and because they were so central to the dynamics of local politics. Few appointees could so readily control, both to the benefit of their party and the detriment of their opponents, the flow of essential information: the distribution of newspapers, broadsides, money, and private communications. Few, also, could so effectively represent the party at the grassroots, gathering political intelligence and helping sympathetic voters get to the polls. Savvy as he was, Mahone seemed to take special relish in removing Democratic incumbents and installing Readjuster replacements. Equally significant, he and Cameron deployed the patronage to meet the demands of African-American organizers and constituents for the political recognition that party nominations for elective office frequently denied them. "[W]e have caried our county in the faver of the reajester party," one who used all his "influrance" wrote to Mahone, and while he did not "ask for no ofice in the state," he did ask to be given "the door keeper place." Black Readjusters like him won appointment as clerks and postmasters, as policemen, inspectors, and watchmen, as state prison guards and doorkeepers, as state college professors and asylum physicians, as workers in federal shipyards and other departments in and out of Virginia, as schoolteachers and principals. In Richmond and Petersburg, amid great controversy, they took seats on local school boards previously occupied by white Democrats. "My office looks like Africa," remarked the federal revenue collector in Danville, "because I have so many colored people in it."[39]

When the black editor of the newly established *Petersburg Lancet* complained in the summer of 1882 that "we have not received our proportion of the patronage," he hinted that the Readjuster mobilizations might well spark, rather than contain, new rounds of black militancy. Already there were reports of "colored citizens" in the southside pressing school boards to "elect colored teachers in all our colored schools" and of dissatisfaction with the scarcity of black candidates on Readjuster electoral tickets. Yet as the editor looked around, he could not help but see "steps" in the right "direction." "We can see changes," he wrote, "that never were wrought before." Whether they marked "a complete 'giving way' to an irresistible sentiment against Bourbonism" remained to be seen.[40]

❖

Political biracialism—meant to suggest both direct and indirect cooperation between whites and blacks—was by no means confined to Readjuster Virginia or to other areas of insurgent activity in the South. In one form or another, it characterized African-American participation in electoral politics most everywhere in the decade after Reconstruction. It signified enduring strengths as well as new weaknesses, coexisting in many places with interest in emigrationism. And it revealed a crucial contradiction that has often been overlooked. With some exception, biracialism tended to offer African Americans better chances to hold offices and exercise measures of official power at the grassroots in association with Democrats than it did with independent or insurgent movements. This contradiction was fundamental to the nature of insurgency in this period, and it accentuated divisions in black political communities previously held in check.

Despite the paramilitary violence that destroyed Republican rule in much of the Deep South, bases of substantial black political activity and power managed to survive, albeit in more vulnerable forms. Either they had successfully resisted vigilantism (as in the case of low-country South Carolina and Georgia), or their overwhelming ratios of blacks to whites enabled them to make some recovery from the onslaught (as in the Mississippi Delta), or their unusual social and political makeups provided some maneuvering room (as in the sugar parishes of Louisiana, with the smattering of Republican planters). On occasion, more than one of these circumstances was in evidence. At all events, African Americans in these areas could no longer depend on allies dominating the statehouses and governorships, and their opponents, while outnumbered, had new weapons to deploy. The result was an arrangement that came to be known as "fusion."

Fusion represented a concession to black numbers and organizational strength locally in the context of superior Democratic power statewide. And it had less to do with fusing together than with dividing up. Although many variations could be found, white Democrats and black Republicans generally agreed to support a single ticket, rather than to nominate separate ones, in which candidates from each party would receive some of the offices. Where blacks were particularly well entrenched, as in South Carolina low-country counties like Beaufort, they could effectively shape the terms and claim the greater number and most consequential of the offices. More commonly, white Democrats shaped the terms and blacks had to accept much less, not to mention Democratic vetting of their candidates. In the Delta counties of Mississippi, black Republicans could expect two of five seats on the board of supervisors, one or two seats in the lower house of the legislature, the offices of clerk and assessor, and perhaps half of the constables and magistrates. The Democrats, in turn, took the remaining three seats on the board of supervisors, the seat in the state senate and perhaps one in the lower house, the offices of sheriff, treasurer, district attorney, and chancery clerk, and at least half of the constables and magistrates. Which is to say that the Democrats would hold the majority, as well as the main police and financial, power. Across the river in Arkansas, Democrats might name the county judge, county clerk, tax assessor, and state senator while the Republicans chose the sheriff, circuit clerk, and state representatives. Republicans in the southern Louisiana parishes of Iberville and St. John the Baptist accepted a Democratic proposal to keep the offices of sheriff and clerk of court but surrender seats in the state assembly and the offices of district judge and coroner. In North Carolina, where the Democratic legislature could appoint most of the local officeholders, persisting black strength in the eastern counties—gerrymandered into the "Black Second" congressional district—brought at least some rewards; and in one of them, blacks had long supported Democratic nominees for sheriff, clerk of the superior court, and treasurer in return for access to other local offices, including magistrate, county commissioner, and register of deeds.[41]

Concerned as many were that this "two-sided arrangement" would not last, that Democrats would eventually want "the whole loaf," African Americans could nonetheless find advantages in fusion. First and foremost, it offered an alternative to the paramilitary politics that had cut down their leaders and ravaged their community institutions—an alternative that nonetheless did not fully yield to Democratic domination. It encouraged Democrats to seek black votes with political appeals and patronage, while requiring them to concede a share of power to those who did not come around. It helped blacks send representatives to state legislatures for more than a decade after Reconstruction—99 from Mississippi, 75 from South Carolina, 79 from North Carolina, 30 from Louisiana, 56 from Arkansas, 13 from Tennessee, 49 from Texas—and thereby maintain some influence over political appointments and public policy. And it left them with a hand, attenuated though it was, in the administration of county affairs and local justice. In the late 1870s and throughout the 1880s, blacks could be found in scattered plantation districts serving as county clerks, tax assessors, coroners, constables, justices of peace, and jurors. Before the Democrats took charge of the North Carolina legislature, Warren County blacks usually made up between one-quarter and one-half of the jurors selected during any court term. By the end of the decade that had changed substantially, but black jurors were still being chosen.[42]

At the same time, fusion clearly altered the dynamics of local politics, limiting the grassroots mobilizations that had marked the Reconstruction period, empowering black political bosses and brokers who had learned to work with white Democrats and who had chief responsibility for negotiating the deals, and loosening black allegiance to the Republican party. Some of these bosses and brokers achieved considerable prominence and—like Mississippi's John Lynch and Blanche K. Bruce, South Carolina's Robert Smalls, and North Carolina's John Hyman—gained election to numerous offices, including the U.S. Congress. Most others, scorned as the "colored politicians" by Henry Adams and his followers, operated chiefly in the counties and legislative districts from relatively secure home bases. They often owned real estate, may have become financially involved in small-scale local enterprises, and likely had strong connections to the institutions of black associational life. They also struggled among themselves and with rival claimants. Indeed, as the organizational structure and discipline of the Republican party weakened in some of these areas amid factional disputes and disenchantment, Democrats had a better opportunity to exploit the divisions and conflicts among rural blacks through the auspices of either established or aspiring bosses.[43]

Those divisions and conflicts had many sources and were ever-present. They grew out of the contention among different kinship groups, religious congregations and denominations, and social leaders; out of the construction of new hierarchies of gender, status, and service; out of the involvement of a range of "outsiders" in community life; out of the process of social and cultural differentiation tied to working arrangements, tenures, and accumulations of petty property and productive resources; out of the establishment of benevolent societies and educational institutions. At all times, they threatened to explode into the arenas of electoral politics, and in some instances they did. But the mobilizations of Reconstruction, carried on by the Union Leagues and Republican clubs and embracing women and children as well as enfranchised men, contained them to a remarkable extent through the creation of new political solidarities and the harassment of those who would, with their grievances, think to break ranks. Thus, neither promises of protection nor the use of coercion enabled Democrats to attract the support of more than a few African Americans who were not already cut off from the mass of rural freedpeople.[44]

Sobered and depleted by the circumstances leading to Redemption, the ranks were more likely to fracture or break thereafter. One black newspaper in the Deep South voiced an increasingly widespread view when it declared in 1880 that the Republican party could no longer be regarded as a "fair representation of the party of Lincoln, Sumner, Greeley, and Chase and the other great leaders," and suggested that no "sensible colored man" could "conscientiously give it his aid and support." Explaining why one hundred blacks in his precinct of Copiah County, Mississippi, voted the Democratic ticket in 1883, a former black Republican noted that, like him, "a great many had been Republicans and as there was no Republican ticket in the field they desired to vote for such men as they thought best to fill the offices" and "bring about peace and harmony among the colored people." Democrats in Granville, Tennessee, told their governor in 1884 that a contingent of blacks had carried "a large Cleveland Hendricks & Bate flag" on election day and that fewer black votes had gone to the Republicans and more had gone to them. Hearing what he termed the "odd" result of an election in Opelika, Alabama, when the Democratic candidate had won "a majority of the black vote," a northern traveler learned that "the Democrats managed to capture a whole colored church, minister and all, by a moderate subscription to the church fund." "What are the colored people to do?" a former black Republican leader in East Carroll Parish, Louisiana, asked. "Abandoned by their white leaders, left as it were to the mercy of the Bulldozers; edged on by their late-professed white friends. Cannot they also become Conservative?"[45] There were, in short, a good many reasons why local black leaders left standing in the post-Reconstruction period (or those who emerged as leaders at this stage) might be receptive to Democratic overtures (bribes very much included), and why the ranks might follow along rather than run such leaders off.

Even so, the great majority of African Americans managed to remain loyal to the Republican party and, if they thought to stray or "fuse," looked to the insurgent campaigns and parties instead of to the Democrats. In most places, Democratic appeals for black votes testified both to the persistence of Republican electoral vitality and to the new threats posed by insurgency. It was not that the insurgents directly addressed the needs and concerns of rural blacks (or urban blacks, for that matter) or offered a partnership in any meaningful sense; their bases of support were chiefly to be found among hard-pressed small farm owners and tenants in white-majority hill country districts. But, as was true in Virginia, struggling whites and poor blacks had some grievances and interests in common, and, if the insurgents were to "throw off the yoke" of Democratic rule, they needed all the help they could get.[46]

The insurgents had their best chance of establishing formal or informal coalitions in those states—Georgia, Alabama, South Carolina, Mississippi, Louisiana, and Texas—where, in the late 1870s and early 1880s, Republican organizations had effectively abandoned hope of winning elections. And, whether affiliated with the Greenback-Labor party or regarding themselves simply as "independents," they constructed platforms designed, at least in part, to resonate favorably with the Republicans' black rank-and-file. In Georgia and Alabama, they called for an end to election fraud and the poll tax, increased funding for public schools, and the abolition of convict leasing. In South Carolina, they attacked the recently enacted stock law and eight-box election law, which together were sparking an "exodus" of black tenants and croppers from the piedmont. Everywhere, they advanced a slogan that all those who contested Democratic power could eagerly embrace: "a free ballot and a fair count."[47]

That the insurgents hoped to expand their base among disgruntled hill-country Democrats with the votes of disenchanted Republicans there and in the black belt was both promising and problematic. On the one hand, these had long been the foundations of opposition to the politics and culture of the planter class, and in most of the states only a coalition such as this could defeat the Democrats. On the other hand, hill-country whites and African Americans occupied very different social positions and had almost no experience working together toward shared social and political goals. If anything, they regarded one another with suspicion and hostility, and even those who had become convinced of the wisdom of cooperation usually had rather incompatible ideas of what cooperation should entail.

The prospects for advancing the cause of an insurgent biracialism were perhaps best within hill-country districts where the black minority had built and maintained institutions of political and associational life: where, that is, blacks continued to vote and engage in public political activity but had no hope of gaining power either on their own or with a little help. Insurgency thus offered a potential meeting ground where mutual benefits could be obtained and the most explosive issues avoided. White Independents and Greenbackers could find votes that they desperately needed, while African Americans could find some protection for their civil and political rights. Both could find opportunities to work together in county committees and conventions and on campaigns. But blacks would not likely test the limits of the white commitment to coalition—the whites' understandings of biracialism— by pressing for offices and other potential signifiers of their contribution and equal standing. In the hilly sections of north Alabama and Georgia, black Republicans gave substantial, and at times overwhelming, electoral support to white insurgents, often supplying the margin of victory when it occurred. One Democratic newspaper in the Georgia hill country, in accounting for the defeat of the party's nominee in a congressional race in 1878, conceded that "we did not count on the negro vote going solid, but . . . nine-tenths of them voted the Independent ticket." Rewards occasionally came in modest but notable ways, in nominations for a minor office or a seat in the state legislature, in support for black schools, or in the selection of black jurors.[48]

Matters were more complex in the plantation belt where the bulk of the black vote was to be found, for there African Americans simultaneously had more options and faced more dangers. In Mississippi, blacks in the Delta counties lent scant support to white insurgents, wedded as they appear to have been to the fusion arrangements that provided at least a genuine share of local power, but in counties where fusion did not operate or where the racial demography was more evenly balanced, they showed the insurgents much more favor. In Copiah County—and in most of the counties carried by Greenbackers and Independents in the early 1880s—the majority of insurgent votes came from the blacks. In other plantation areas, black Republicans might wholly reject both coalition with white insurgents and fusion with white Democrats; in still others they might struggle over which one of several courses to follow. Grant Parish, Louisiana, scene of the bloody Colfax massacre of 1873, experienced one such struggle. Mindful of the consequences of militancy, parish blacks (who composed about half of the population) looked for a way to maintain the peace yet also protect their civil and political rights. Most initially favored an alliance with white Independents from the hilly section of the parish who wished to break the hold that the Democratic elite of planters and merchants had over the local government. But as the 1880s wore on, a growing number—led by the black parish Republican party president, Charles Thomas—pressed for an accommodation with the Democrats that would enable them to negotiate with their employers and have a role in the administration of justice in the ward where most of them lived.[49]

Once a radical, Thomas had come to believe that white Independents had no intention of really sharing power with African Americans and that neither the Independents nor the Democrats would tolerate any black challenge to prevailing social relations in the parish. The political landscape remained treacherous, all the more so given the fissures within the white South. Although paramilitary politics had subsided in much of the countryside after the Republicans were driven from state power, "election disorders," as one federal investigator put it, erupted continually. Fraud, corruption, intimidation, and small-scale violence—generally known as "bulldozing"—much of it now carried out by Democratic officials, emerged as a basic feature of politics in areas marked by hotly contested elections. And the networks and personnel of paramilitarism would readily be summoned to punish the dissident leaders, white and black, if the threat became too great. In one Mississippi county alone, thirteen Republicans and Independents—nine of them black—were targeted by Democratic vigilantes during an election campaign in 1883. Six were threatened, two were beaten, two were shot at, and one had his house torched. Two others, including a black Republican who "had taken a good deal of interest in politics," were murdered.[50]

The risks that militant and effective black leaders still faced in the complex world of post-Reconstruction electoral politics—and those that seemed to confirm the apprehensions of Charles Thomas—were nowhere more brutally apparent than in Choctaw County, part of the violence-ridden western black belt of Alabama. For there, a former slave by the name of Jack Turner was hardly the sort of political boss with whom plantation-district Democrats had looked to come to terms. He was a force to be reckoned with. "Large and powerfully built," a spellbinding orator (despite his lack of formal education) who possessed a "personal magnetism," Turner emerged as an influential local Republican leader in the early 1870s, and continued his organizational activities after Redemption, gnawing away at Democratic control in this closely divided county (53 percent black). Although he preferred a straight Republican ticket, he soon saw the wisdom of cooperating with white Independents and eventually played a leading role in bringing Republicans and Greenbackers together. Leaving nothing to chance, he would march his supporters to the polls and see to it that their ballots were correctly tallied. All the while, he was working as a farm laborer and tenant, raising a family, attending a Methodist church near the small town of Mount Sterling, and accumulating property. In 1881, with the aid of a sympathetic white northerner, he managed to purchase eighty acres of land.

But it was not only Turner's political determination and economic advances that drew the ire of Choctaw County Democrats. It was also his personal toughness, roughness, and independence. Turner was not a man to be trifled with in politics or any walk of life. For him, political discipline involved equal measures of coercion and persuasion. He was said, fearfully by his Democratic enemies, to have had the county's black "mob at his beck and call, ready to do his bidding and carry out his evil designs." And there is little doubt that Turner's volatility and appetites were in part responsible for numerous appearances before the local courts on charges ranging from gambling to intoxication to assault and battery to adultery. On more than one occasion, he was fined or jailed. Yet there is also little doubt that Turner's politics were responsible for his being closely watched and regularly harassed. When his efforts finally helped the Republican-Greenback coalition carry the county in 1882—one of only two black belt counties in Alabama that rejected the Democrats—his enemies had enough.

Within days, Turner and several other black leaders were arrested for conspiring to massacre all of the whites in Choctaw County. But a formal trial was not to be held. Instead, a "mob" of about one thousand, many coming in from the surrounding countryside, gathered at the county seat and began to debate Turner's fate. The few white protectors Turner previously had were now gone—his former master having died several years before and the sympathetic northerner having moved on—and his white Greenback allies seemed nowhere to be found (if they were not among the mob itself). Then, in a grisly parody of democracy, the mob voted to impose the death sentence and had a committee of twenty-four spirit Turner from his cell and parade him to the courthouse square. There, after Turner "cooly" proclaimed his innocence, they hanged him.[51]

In much of the lower South, therefore, black electoral politics in the rural districts came to assume a defensive posture. Militants who had not been cut down or driven off during Reconstruction were often dispatched—like Jack Turner—either in the first wave of white insurgencies or as white Democrats finished the work of Redemption in the localities (the Delta parishes of Louisiana being a prominent example). Only weeks after Turner's lynching, rumors of black insurrectionary activities spread through twenty-three mostly adjacent Alabama counties, fueling a Democratic offensive that by the mid-1880s had snuffed out the Greenback-Republican challenge and claimed control of the black belt. Although African Americans continued to vote in significant numbers there and elsewhere, thus paying tribute to martyrs like Turner, they likely followed leaders who sought accommodations that offered some measure of continuing political influence on the local and state levels together with breathing space for the development of black community life: biracialist "fusions" with Democrats or insurgents, and by the late 1880s chiefly with the Democrats. "We ask but an equal chance before the law, no more, *no less,*" the black Republican editor of the *Huntsville Gazette* wrote in the fall of 1882, reflecting on Jack Turner's murder and on the many travails and obstacles that African Americans had survived and surmounted. "We do not seek your society, we only ask you as Christians, as servants of the Master to help us safely anchor our little boat in some quiet haven." This was the world in which Booker T. Washington began his tenure at the Tuskegee Normal and Industrial Institute, in the Alabama plantation county of Macon.[52]

But Texas, and especially the east-central section, presented a somewhat different picture. During Reconstruction, black majorities (sometimes heavy majorities) in many of these cotton-growing counties, together with active Union League organizing and the presence of small collections of carpetbaggers and white Unionists, a good many of them German immigrants, had enabled the Republicans to wrest control of local governments and send their representatives to the state legislature. It was much like the process that unfolded in the plantation districts of other states in the lower South. Yet unlike those other states, local Republican regimes in east-central Texas not only withstood Redemption; in the years that followed, they became more firmly entrenched, on occasion more militant, and more prone to African-American influence. Indeed, a far greater number of African Americans held state and county offices in Texas after the collapse of Reconstruction than during it: more than double the number of seats in the legislature, and perhaps five times as many places in the counties.[53]

The resilience of local Republican rule in east-central Texas seemed a product of the distinctive dynamics of Reconstruction and Redemption. Although personal and vigilante violence were epidemic in the early postemancipation period, coinciding most notably with Union League and Republican mobilizations, and although a paramilitary showdown nearly exploded in the state capital during the dual government crisis of 1874, Democrats in Texas were not as dependent as their counterparts elsewhere in the lower South on paramilitary operations to achieve state power. On the one hand, whites outnumbered people of color by more than two to one statewide, putting a Democratic electoral majority well within reach. On the other hand, the militia and state police organized by Republican governor Edmund J. Davis, with large contingents of blacks enrolled, appeared to discourage full-scale paramilitary assaults against the party's local leaders and office-holders. The damage that had been inflicted by sporadic Klan-style raids could therefore be repaired, and the popular and institutional foundations of local power preserved. The decade and a half after Redemption would be a time of increasingly intense and consequential black political activity in what was derisively called the Senegambian district.[54]

None of the "Senegambian" counties were more "thoroughly dominated" by black Republicans than Fort Bend. With effective organization and an overwhelming numerical advantage (80 percent of the population), African Americans made their mark from the very first election held under the Reconstruction constitution, enabling the Republican party to carry the county by more than eight hundred votes and putting former slave Walter M. Burton in the offices of sheriff and tax collector. Burton served until 1873, when he was elevated to the state senate, but he was replaced by another former slave, Henry Ferguson, who occupied the offices until 1876, when he began an extended stint as tax assessor. During the 1870s and well into the 1880s, blacks could be seen, almost continuously, as county treasurers, district clerks, court commissioners, justices of the peace, and constables, not to mention as the county's representatives in the state legislature. Three or four were always to be found in countywide offices and many more in the precincts. No other Texas county elected more blacks to political office than did Fort Bend. The black electorate was so fully mobilized that the Democrats did not even bother fielding a ticket between 1871 and 1888; the best that they could hope to do was horse trade for some local offices and exploit bonding requirements to influence an emerging group of black politicians.[55]

African Americans never served as sheriffs in any of the other black—or near-black—majority counties of east-central Texas, and they generally yielded judgeships, seats on the commissioner's court, and offices more directly involved in county finance to their white Republican allies. But they could usually claim at least one seat (and sometimes more) on the four-member commissioner's court together with positions as justices of the peace and constable; on occasion, they won terms as court clerks and treasurers. After all, owing to their numbers, they had a considerable voice in party executive committees and nominating conventions. With the Republicans in power, moreover, they had better opportunities to exercise their political rights, get their grievances aired, and avoid harassment. In Washington County, black churches and schoolhouses were designated as polling places, juries became racially mixed, and black defendants had the prospect of fair trials. One black drayman in the county seat of Brenham, charged with a minor offense by a white farmer, thus demanded a jury and was "triumphantly acquitted." Groaning in the summer of 1878 that "our farmers will experience some difficulty getting the crop gathered," the county's Democratic newspaper had to explain that "the negroes as a general thing have all turned politicians and are out canvassing for their favorite candidates." It made a difference. As late as 1882, when Washington County Republicans "made a clean sweep of everything," they "elected a negro as district clerk, 2 negroes as county commissioners, [and] 2 negro constables." "They seem to have been thoroughly organized," the paper surmised.[56]

As the 1870s wore on, black Republicans in various east-central counties seemed ready to flex their political muscles. Pressing for a more proportionate share in the wielding of local power, they struggled with their white—and especially German—counterparts. Some went so far as to proclaim that "they ought to put none but their race in office." Others thundered that they "would vote for no man who wouldn't vote for a negro for office." So contentious could matters become that Democrats seized the chance to blame blacks for drawing the "color line" in politics. Reports came, too, of disaffection among the Germans, who were said to be questioning "what Republicanism means in county elections" and to have begun entertaining the idea of "a joint movement on the part of the white men."[57]

These circumstances helped give shape to the experience with Greenback insurgency, which made its strongest bid for state power and black support in 1878. Facing poor prospects in the elections that year, the Texas Republican party, with some dissension, embraced fusion with the Greenbackers, and the signs suggested that a great many African Americans were prepared to follow along. Although an early Greenback convention included only a handful of blacks, organizational momentum grew over the spring and summer months. By August, blacks had formed seventy of the nearly five hundred Greenback clubs found throughout the state, and significant activity was in evidence in at least ten of the east-central counties. Yet in most of these, blacks made up just under half of the total population, and few of the clubs appeared to be mixed racially. The Falls County Greenbackers were, according to one observer, "composed principally of negroes." When the McLennan County Greenback convention assembled, 73 of the 111 delegates were black. Elsewhere in the district, African Americans showed divided allegiances and often took their cues from trusted local leaders. In Brazos County, Methodist minister Elias Mayes played a crucial role in rallying most of the black electorate to the Greenbackers, while in Fort Bend County Walter Burton did much the same for the Republicans. In the end, the Greenbackers likely won at least half of the black vote statewide, and more than that in the ten or twelve counties where blacks made up at least one-third of the population. But in well-mobilized counties such as Washington, Harrison, and

Robertson, black ballots were split between the Republicans and the Greenbackers, and conflict between the two sides erupted. Two years later, the state Greenback convention was overwhelmingly white, and most African Americans who had aligned with them returned to the Republican party.[58]

In some respects, the very brief flirtation that black Texans had with Greenback insurgency testified to the loyalties and institutional attachments that a decade of Republican mobilization had created. But, together with the internecine struggles already brewing in the local Republican parties, it also indicated the limits to a biracialism that could alone sustain the viability of black electoral activism in Texas. Without committed white allies, that is, the days of black power and influence in east-central Texas were numbered, however impressive and stable the achievements seemed. And the harbingers of such a defeat were to be seen during the rise and fall of Greenbackism itself. There would, first, be the appearance of "Citizen's," "People's," and "White Man's" tickets in the late 1870s and early 1880s (some resembling previous taxpayers' unions in other states of the lower South), which commenced organizing coalitions of Democrats and white Republicans (with some black adherents) against the "corruption" and other misdeeds they attributed to Republican-dominated county governments. Eventually, a new generation of white Democrats would go still further, resolutely drawing the "color line" and moving to drive off black—and later white insurgent—officeholders through violent confrontations and paramilitary means.[59]

Political biracialism did have its moments in east-central Texas, and we must be sure not to ignore or dismiss them. Much in the manner of the Hamburg Union League lodge in Surry County, North Carolina, they suggested that electoral politics could create openings and possibilities for something approaching egalitarian forms of cooperation even where social relations were anything but egalitarian. In Washington County, this cooperation developed early and quite intensely within the Republican party owing to the remarkable energy and efforts of Stephen A. Hackworth. A native white southerner of modest means, Hackworth organized the local Union League in 1867 while helping African Americans purchase land on credit in neighboring Fort Bend County. Together these activities gave him "great influence" with blacks and established him as the leader of the Republican party in the county. He would come to serve as justice of the peace, as presiding judge on the commissioner's court, and as a postmaster, but, most importantly, he seemed to be the glue that held the party's critical interracial coalition together. When the Republicans united, a Democratic election official acknowledged, they won: that is, "depending on how the German vote cast."

Although it was said that Hackworth and other white Republicans generally met among themselves before consulting "the leading colored men" about nominations and other party affairs, the picture is by no means one of white paternalism. A party committee composed of ten whites and ten blacks forwarded recommendations for the ticket to the county convention; blacks were nominated for seats on the commissioner's court, for positions as treasurer, clerk, justice of the peace and constable, and for most of the places in the state legislature; and white Republicans traditionally "voted solidly for negro nominees" and became sureties on the bonds of black officeholders despite the disapproval of other whites in the county. Hackworth was attentive to the labor problems faced by African Americans, and while he did urge them to "carry out" the contracts they had made, he also instructed them "not to sell your vote with the contract." Even as the white Republicans—notably the Germans—began to peel away in the early 1880s, either "scratching" the Republican ticket or supporting the conservative county People's ticket, and even in the face of growing intimidation and threats, Hackworth stayed the course with the African-American rank and file. Washington County blacks had their own leaders who surely had more influence with them than Hackworth, one observer testified in 1887, assessing the relationship, but they had "faith and confidence in him, and he has been there for twenty years."[60]

The relationship between Garrett Scott and a number of black leaders in Grimes County, Jim Kennard chief among them, originated during the Greenback insurgency rather than Radical Reconstruction. And it exemplified the biracialism that, in the view of white supremacist Democrats, insurgency always threatened. Scott, a member of an antebellum family that had rendered service to the Confederacy and had accumulated moderately large landholdings, seemed an obvious Democrat. But hard times in the 1870s turned him into a Greenbacker, and when he ran for sheriff in 1882, he discovered that Grimes County blacks had built a stable local Republican organization. The initial alliance was therefore a product of political expediency; it developed into something more as Scott joined hands with Kennard, himself just elected as the county's district clerk, and forged an interracial coalition. Little if anything is known about the personal dynamic that linked Scott and Kennard, but Scott and his white followers recognized that their claims to local power depended on black votes and, through Kennard, Scott seems to have learned a good deal about the needs of black constituents. Appointing black deputy sheriffs and attending to the county's black schools and schoolteachers, Scott earned the trust of between 80 and 90 percent of the black voters while holding onto the support of the roughly 30 percent of white voters who inclined to insurgency. For most of the next eighteen years, the coalition—in Greenback, Independent, and Populist phases—would rule Grimes County. A paramilitary offensive, not a discourse of white solidarity, would be required to bring it down.[61]

In the rural areas of the lower South in the late 1870s and 1880s, it clearly required a formidable leader like Garrett Scott or Stephen Hackworth to fashion a political biracialism that blacks could regard as a meaningful alternative to fusionist arrangements with Democrats. For the white folk with whom African Americans might then ally, politically disaffected and economically hard-pressed as many may have been, were accustomed to seeing black folk in subordinate positions and to defining their identities—at least in part—in relation to those conditions of power. Some had owned slaves or belonged to families who had owned slaves. Some had fought for the Confederacy or watched their fathers and brothers go off to fight. Many owned land and employed black labor. And most had been Democrats. The achievements of black communities in constructing their own churches, schools, and associations also meant that there were perilously few settings in which whites and blacks might encounter each other that were not structured by hierarchies of race and class.

The electoral arena did offer a substantial new meeting ground, but it too was surrounded by cultural assumptions that cast black demands for genuine inclusion as illegitimate. One of the reasons that African Americans valued the suffrage so highly—the notion that the franchise "makes them a man," a person of independence capable of standing on an equal footing with whites—was one of the very reasons that so many whites regarded black claims to it with unease or rejection.[62]

In effect, the biracialism of opposition or insurgency required the nur-
turing, even on a small-scale, of new sensibilities and practices, of a
new political culture, that institutions outside the electoral arena did
not reinforce and sustain. Not surprisingly perhaps, such a biracialism
had more significant manifestations during this period in the urban and
industrial areas of the New South—on the docks, in lumber and sawmill camps, and in coal mines, generally under the auspices of fledgling
unions or insurgent parties like the Greenbackers—where whites and
blacks met each other in the workplaces and company stores, in some
cases from the first. Even then, the biracialism was circumscribed,
highly contingent, and often fleeting. In the countryside of plantations
and farms, it was well beyond the imagination and fortitude of all but
a handful of Stephen Hackworths and Garrett Scotts.[63]

It was not beyond the imagination—and surely not beyond the
fortitude—of Virginia's William Mahone. No other southern state
produced an insurgent leader or movement with the compass and
resources of Mahone and the Readjusters. Nor one with the determination to construct the "race" question as a "political" rather than a "social" question: to fashion a language of "rights" that could link Readjusters with divergent goals and regard the aspirations of blacks
among them as legitimate. Unlike their counterparts elsewhere in the
South, the Readjusters not only assumed power at the state and local
levels; they also began to assemble the materials of a new political
culture that could make that power stable and secure. Yet the very
mobilizations and political conduct that enabled the Readjusters to
achieve electoral success simultaneously unleashed issues and pressures
that neither Mahone nor most of the white Readjusters were prepared
to absorb. Before long, they threatened to doom the entire project.[64]

The most salient and potentially corrosive of the issues and pressures came from the ranks of black supporters. Well aware of their
contributions to Readjuster fortunes, many expected suitable and
meaningful rewards. These included greater attention to the problems
facing black communities (such as education), greater influence in precinct and county organizations, and most important, a greater share
of the available political offices, both through party nominations and

patronage appointments. Some local black activists were fired to a new militancy, raising demands and behaving with a confidence and sense of purpose that some white party leaders interpreted as "arrogant" and "boisterous." But in the main, the rewards expected by black Readjusters reflected widely held notions of a just biracialism: recognition of their full and equal political standing in the party and the state, and acknowledgment of their right to exert some control over affairs in the areas where most of them lived. "Now Gen. I am going to ask you to do something for Amelia," a black organizer in that southside county wrote Mahone in the spring of 1883, explaining "that poor Amelia . . . is the only county that has not a colored man holding any Gov't office."[65]

As much as any white Readjusters, Mahone and Governor Cameron seemed to grasp this ("We cannot expect to receive the means of victory from those people and monopolize the fruits," Cameron confided to another party leader), and they moved to make appropriate gestures. Mahone went so far as to concede it "politic to nominate a colored man" for the southside's Fourth Congressional District seat. "They are claiming it," he observed, and "it would help us with that vote not only there . . . but all over the State." The mass of Mahone's and Cameron's white followers were, however, of a different mind.[66]

The dilemmas of Readjuster biracialism became apparent at least as early as 1881, especially in large southside counties like Pittsylvania, where blacks composed just over half of the population and white support was therefore critical. "[I]f the negroes will be true we can get 600 white votes and carry the county by nearly 400 majority," D. M. Pannill, secretary of the Readjuster county executive committee, reported to Mahone a month before that year's election, "but we are between 2 fires." On the one hand, "if we put a negro on the ticket the whites will stampede"; on the other, "if we do not we fear the negroes will not be unanimous." For a time it appeared that "we had the negroes" in the northern part of the county "alright, it being agreed that they should elect the third man, but he should be a white man in order to secure the white vote." Then some of the county's black leaders "came over" and "thwarted" this "well laid scheme," convincing the local blacks that "a negro should be put on the ticket." Given the prevailing racial balances, "their demands had to be complied with." But two of the white Readjuster candidates consequently "declined to run," and the party was left with "no ticket" and with "many leading readjusters going over to the enemy." "If we can put up a good ticket of white men *by the consent of the negroes,* victory is certain," Pannill concluded, adding pointedly, "to get that consent is the obstacle in our way." The "consent" was not obtained. A black candidate was eventually included on the ticket and, according to another party operative, he "brought many more of his color to its support." Predictably, he also "drove off many white votes," and the Readjusters lost the county.[67]

The problem only intensified as the Readjusters sought to consolidate their power by dispensing the spoils to loyalist constituents. In white majority counties of the west, the mere appointment of an African American to a post as deputy collector of internal revenue (the "first" such "instance," as a local paper noted) was enough to jeopardize the party's prospects. Although the action might "do in the lower counties," one correspondent thought, it "wont do here in the mountains where the whites are so opposed to the blacks." But there seemed to be no place in Virginia where black officeholding and official station—where black representation in positions of public authority—did not stir unease, or worse, in coalitionist ranks. "[N]o negro in my judgment ought to be in charge of the county[,] district[,] or precinct chairs," a white Goochland County (61 percent black) Readjuster told Mahone in the fall of 1883; "it drives away many white men and the negro has not the capacity to lead." Indeed, he found "it difficult to get white men to go to the meetings" because "the negroes are at the head and dictate for them." More sympathetic to African-American claims, a Readjuster aspirant for sheriff in a tidewater county similarly learned that "our efforts to do something for the negroes drove many white men from us." Not only did the whites object "to the appointment of negroes on the school board [over] in Richmond"; they also bridled at "my promise to make a colored man . . . one of my deputies," snorting that "the Readjuster party has too much nigger in it for them."[68]

The tobacco-processing town of Danville, in Pittsylvania County, was made to exemplify the racial inversions and aggressiveness that many white Readjusters tended to associate with black public power. With a rapidly growing population in which blacks substantially outnumbered whites, Danville had become a Readjuster stronghold in a

Democratic-leaning county, and, owing to party-sponsored legislation creating three town wards, blacks had gained a significant role in local governance by the spring of 1882. Four African Americans sat on the twelve-member town council (with four white Readjusters), while others served as justices of the peace, policemen, and clerk of the market. For the first time, the needs of black urban dwellers received attention and funding, and schooling for both black and white children was expanded and improved. Black vendors occupied a prominent place in the town marketplace, and Danville generally pulsed with black activity. When some local Democrats complained about the police court being "practically open from morning till night," about "officials of the court, justices and policemen cooperat[ing]" in the work of arresting white men "for the most frivolous acts," and about "swarms of jeering and hooting and mocking negroes" who followed the proceedings and the decisions of the "negro justice," they were also documenting the new dynamic of community participation in the official institutions of town government.[69]

But the Democrats believed they had an audience among white Readjusters, and as the legislative elections of 1883 approached they moved to cultivate it. In a circular entitled "Coalition Rule in Danville," and addressed, conspicuously, "to the Citizens of the Southwest and Valley of Virginia," where Readjusterism appeared comfortably ensconced, they therefore wrote of the "injustice and humiliation to which our white people have been subjected" by the "misrule of the radical or negro party now in absolute power." The manifestations, they charged, were to be seen in many areas of public life: in the taxes whites paid to support social services for improvident blacks, in the "perpetual mockery and disgrace" of the local courts, in the town's infestation by "vagrants" and other "idle and filthy negroes" from the surrounding counties, in the "stench," "drunkenness," and petty thievery run rampant among the once "clean" and "enticing" market stalls, and in the daily flaunting and subverting of racial etiquette. Black women were particularly reviled, set loose by events "to irritate and throw contempt on the white race." Embodying, as it were, the essence of humiliating inversions, they were said "to *force ladies* from the pavement," reminding them that they will "*learn to step aside the next time*," to strike "white children," and, in their domestic employment, to "allude to white ladies and gentlemen as *men* and *women*, and to negroes as *ladies* and *gentlemen*." Yet in the end, the authors of the circular identified black political power and officeholding as the sources of their miseries. When blacks took their places as town councillors and justices of the peace, "then began the deeds which have so humiliated us" and made Danville "a by-word for shame and reproach from one end of this land to the other."[70]

As intended, "Coalition Rule" circulated widely in the days before the election, especially in the counties of the west where it caused "great alarm." "The Funder speakers read it the last week of the campaign from the stump," one Readjuster loyalist in Montgomery County (75 percent white) reported, "and made passionate appeals to the white people to rescue their brothers of the east from the terrible consequences of negro rule, mixed marriages, and mixed schools." But it was Danville that crackled with high tension and anticipations of "serious disturbances." Readjuster leaders there counseled "prudence and precaution," and urged blacks not to "carry weapons of any sort at public meetings or on election day," though their efforts "to prove the falsity of the Danville circular" were deemed, by local Democrats, as "incendiary." One African American was warned by a "prominent white Democrat" that "colored people" who came to the polls to vote the Readjuster ticket "would be shot down like dogs and driven out of the country as the Indians were driven out." Thus, an altercation between a young white man and two black men on the streets of the town the Saturday preceding the election quickly escalated into violence. By that evening, four black men lay dead and bands of armed white Democrats patrolled the area. Virginia had seen nothing quite like this since the advent of black suffrage.[71]

Regarded by black Readjusters as a massacre and by white Democrats as an act of self-defense, the "riot" at Danville had direct effects on the ensuing election—at least in Pittsylvania and neighboring southside counties—emboldening the Democrats and striking terror through the ranks of African-American voters. Carrying double-barreled shotguns and traveling at times in groups of forty to fifty, Democratic vigilantes roamed the precincts and polling places harassing, abusing, and threatening "to shoot" Readjusters. Many blacks, fearing for their lives, chose to stay home. "It was agreed in our club meetings that we would go to vote in companys of ten," a black Readjuster later testified, but reports in circulation about "the shooting and cutting" done "a few nights before" meant that "a large number of my company did not nor would not go to the election." In other black-majority counties, however, preparations only intensified as Readjusters sought to overcome "fear of bloodshed" and turn out a full vote. David Wallace, president of Readjuster Coalition Colored Club No. 1 of Hall Shop precinct in Hanover County, had members gather at the clubhouse the night before the election. With many of their wives also in attendance, they shared information and decided "not to start to the polls till it was broad day lest they might be attacked in the dark." Sometime after dawn, they then marched to the polling place and cast their "77 votes," after which Wallace stayed on "all day" to witness the arrival of other clubs while making sure that black men who did not belong to any clubs could vote the Readjuster ticket.[72]

He was not the only black Readjuster who spent a long election day in service of the cause. Twenty-four-year-old Frank Smedley, who had been appointed by his Halifax County club "to see tickets placed in the hands of the voters and see that they got the genuine Readjuster ticket," reached the polls before sunrise. Over the next many hours, he "stood by the window where the ballots were received," handed "each colored voter a ticket," and saw "each ticket handed to the judge of election" and "deposited in the box," writing "down the name of each man who voted the Readjuster ticket." When the polls closed that night, Medley had a "list of 177 persons." In tidewater Gloucester County, the Readjuster organization needed to make some "modifications" in Mahone's election-day plans, adding "teams to bring colored voters from the rivers on which they have been oystering." Mobilizations over the previous months enabled many black Readjusters outside of the vicinity of Danville to stare down intimidation and perhaps to reject bribes. Offered "the biggest roll of money he ever saw" to switch Readjuster ballots for Democratic ones, Elisha Copeland, "a colored leader of much influence" in the Holy Neck district of Nansemond County, demurred. "I am a poor man but I cannot sell my principles for money," he replied. Despite the atmosphere of violence and coercion, blacks helped provide the coalition with 13,000 more votes in 1883 than it had received in 1881.[73]

The problem was that Democratic vote totals grew even more substantially, by roughly 44,000, and the trend was most pronounced in the white-majority west. In part, this reflected the Democrats' embrace of Readjuster organizational methods and of popular Readjuster issues like debt adjustment and support for public schools. And in part, it reflected—somewhat ironically—the swelling of voter rolls made possible by the abolition of the poll tax. But there can be little doubt that the reverberations of Danville spread widely and influenced the dynamic of electoral behavior. Not only had the Danville circular, detailing the results of "coalition rule," been distributed across the state through the Democratic party apparatus and "Bourbon papers"; stories of the riot as a black rampage, during which "the negroes were murdering the whites," flowed quickly through the same channels. Although we cannot know how individual white men imagined the choice between the Democrats and the Readjusters, we do know that newly participating white voters (those who, in the words of an observer, "had not voted for years") heavily favored the Democrats and that many local Readjuster leaders complained of white defections owing to the "race issue." One of them in Brunswick County (64 percent black) found that the burden of organizational work had fallen almost entirely on the shoulders of black Readjusters because their white counterparts were "not doing anything" and "a large portion of them say they can't vote with us this time." "The Funders predicted that there would be a general uprising of the negroes and that the whites would have to band together for protection," a Spotsylvania County (57 percent white) Readjuster wrote in explaining why "many who had been working for our success" had "turned against us." They "said they could not vote to elevate the negro over the white man."[74]

The Democratic margin of victory statewide in 1883 was a mere 18,000 votes out of more than a quarter of a million cast, but it translated into veto-proof control of the legislature and enabled the Democrats to attack some of the sources of Readjuster electoral strength and political power. Although they did not reimpose the poll tax as a prerequisite for voting, the Democrats quickly amended the charters of Petersburg and Danville, reapportioned congressional districts, and enacted a law that gave them the upper hand in appointing local election boards and registrars. As a party, the Readjusters had clearly suffered a major, and potentially enduring, defeat; as a "movement"— a biracial movement—the Readjusters had plainly reached the end of their tether.[75]

Yet the epitaph was still to be pronounced. Mahone would sit in the U.S. Senate until his term expired, and in Virginia he effectively presided over what was now a reconstituted and reinvigorated Republican party capable of amassing between 40 and 50 percent of the state vote and thus of mounting a serious challenge to the Democrats. While the Democratic party's conquest of the White House in 1884 and the Virginia governorship in 1885 temporarily deprived Mahone of important patronage power and solidified Democratic control in the state, the Democrats would not be able to rest easily or be inclined to draw the "color line." And this was, in good part, because African Americans remained mobilized, especially in the tidewater and southside. "The colored man is a suffragan [*sic*] in Virginia—constitutionally and legally," one official wrote in 1884, "and on the Southside, more particularly, he is a power."[76]

That power found expression in the increasingly independent disposition of the black electorate. The "time has come," a black convention meeting in Lynchburg announced, to "halt unqualified support for the Republican party" and to "declare ourselves politically independent in matters pertaining to us as citizens and voters." A white Republican leader in Brunswick County captured some of the texture of this stance when telling Mahone about a "young man named Harry Green," who might do as a party candidate "if we must have a colored man." "I think our people are all right, but they wont come to the front and show their hand," he admitted in the summer of 1885. More than a few African Americans, complaining that white Readjusters and Republicans had "openly insulted [their] manhood and self-respect," chose to cast their ballots for Democrats. Mahone and his minions, one of them charged, were "renegade Democrats" who had once been "the most violent opponents" of the Republicans. Faced therefore with "two Democratic parties," he selected what he thought to be the "least of the evils." Others held out for a more tangible bid. But a much greater number who wished to break "free" from what was described as Mahone's "political bossism" pressed their interests and agendas within the Republican party and organized, most vociferously, for a black congressional nominee.[77]

Agitation focused on the Second (tidewater) and, especially, the Fourth (southside) Congressional Districts, where African Americans composed the majority of voters and had long demonstrated their partisan allegiance. And it ran directly up against Mahone and his usually well-oiled machine. Despite earlier talk about the need to concede one of those nominations to a black man, Mahone had in fact imagined a racial ceiling: reserving all offices above state legislator for whites so as to avoid alienating white voters across the state or representing the coalition to the world with a black face. Such were the boundaries of his biracialism. But many local black leaders had different ideas, and their militancy, which unsettled politics in the black belt from the time the Readjusters came to power, proved ever more difficult to hold in check. An impressive grassroots campaign, driven in part by a number of black "courthouse rings" (or a "syndicate," as some saw it), took shape in the Fourth District in 1884. Generating the "wildest enthusiasm" in several of the counties, showing considerable strength among likely delegates to the district nominating convention, and winning the endorsements of two black newspapers, only "the basest treachery and bribery" appeared capable of derailing it. "Treachery and bribery"— or what Mahone would have regarded as loyalty and common sense— were, however, sufficiently widespread for the machine to control the convention proceedings and have a white congressional nominee selected. Militants were left with the Independent candidacy of Petersburg's little-known Joseph P. Evans, who went down to an overwhelming defeat. Undeterred, they struggled on to unite the ranks behind an African-American candidate, and in 1888 rallied to John Mercer Langston.[78]

A more formidable challenger to Mahone's machine could hardly have been found. The first African American ever elected to political office in the United States (to the post of town clerk in Brownhelm, Ohio, in 1855), Langston had become a nationally recognized leader and spokesman for black rights. A longtime participant in the black convention movement, a recruiter for the Union army, the leader of the National Equal Rights League, and an educational inspector for the Freedmen's Bureau, he gained greatest prominence and visibility in his work for the Republican party, organizing Union Leagues and campaigning tirelessly across the South. In 1877, President Hayes rewarded him with an appointment as minister to Haiti. Only Frederick Douglass attained more influence and renown among African Americans of the Civil War and Reconstruction era. But Langston was also well acquainted with Virginia. Born a slave in Louisa County in 1829 before being manumitted and taken to Ohio, he returned to the state in carrying out his duties for the Freedman's Bureau and Republican party. At Mahone's invitation, he stumped for the Readjusters in the early 1880s and then in 1885 assumed the presidency of the Virginia Normal and Collegiate Institute in Petersburg, itself a product of Readjuster legislation.[79]

Yet even more consequential were Langston's financial resources (he was worth between $50,000 and $100,000) and his organizational acumen. From experience, he understood the bases and networks of grassroots politics in the southern countryside, and he moved very early to have them mobilized on his behalf. Tapping local black leaders like Mecklenburg County's Ross Hamilton, together with black ministers and their congregations, Langston supervised the formation of political clubs throughout the congressional district that drew in women as well as men, indeed that sought to encompass entire communities. "It was well that this course had been adopted," he later wrote, "since it was true that the women could and did exert large influence in controlling and directing the men in their political conduct." The "Harrison, Morton, and Langston Female Invincibles" thereby took their place alongside the male "Invincibles." At the same time, Langston launched a newspaper to support his candidacy, bought a campaign headquarters to serve as a site for rallies, hired field workers, and circulated other printed materials across the area. His hope, initially, was to win Mahone's backing.[80]

Mahone would offer no such thing, insisting that "it was not time for a Negro Congressman from Virginia yet and even if the time had come Langston was not the man." When the Republican district convention assembled late in the summer, Langston had little chance. Mahone's forces were in command and the official nomination was tendered to R. W. Arnold, a white judge from Sussex County. But Langston was not through. Like Joseph P. Evans in 1884, he remained in the race as an "independent" Republican. Unlike Evans, he was able to press on with a full-scale campaign. Subsequently charging that Langston and "his emissaries had insidiously and industriously played upon the passions and prejudices of the colored people," Arnold nonetheless acknowledged, by his very contempt, the breadth and depth of the undertaking: "He aroused even the women, got up an immense religious fervor in his favor and aroused the prejudice of the large mass of unthinking colored people to such an extent as I never witnessed before and hope never to witness again. It was at white heat in Sussex County the week prior to the election, so much so that . . . they would not even listen to the Lord Jesus Christ, much less vote for him, if he were a white man and appeared against Langston." Local canvassers were directed to make copies of registration books and provided with a veritable map of effective activism. "I want the people everywhere," Langston told them in a confidential letter, "in every house, at every store, in every field, on every road, in every shop, at every lodge, at every schoolhouse, at every church, at every Sunday School, at every marriage gathering, in every factory, at every meeting." There was, one black Mahone loyalist would describe of the results, a "system of organized ostracism."[81]

Election day revealed an operation that Mahone himself would have had to admire. Believing that for each of the one hundred district voting precincts "wise and sufficient scrutiny and surveillance were indispensable," Langston employed about five hundred black men of "education, intelligence, and general qualities of character" to distribute the tickets, observe the balloting process, and record the name of every voter who lent Langston his support. He also seems to have encouraged family participation at the polling places, noting that "in nearly every case where the voter himself by reason of his ignorance or want of understanding as to his duty in the premises, needed help, he was promptly aided by his more intelligent wife or daughter." It was reminiscent, though on a far grander scale, of what rural Union Leagues had set out to accomplish, and it all proved necessary, given the pressure and intimidation that came from every direction. Langston marginalized his machine-backed rival, winning 80 percent of the Republican votes cast, but an official challenge and congressional investigation were required before the Democrat's initial 640 vote lead was overturned and Langston could take his seat. With that, he became the first "Negro representative in Congress from the Old Dominion."[82]

And the last for another century. Langston's campaign demonstrated the persisting vitality of black grassroots electoral activity, and of the social relations and institutions that sustained it. Yet it also showed how difficult it would be for African Americans to claim the signifiers of what most saw as a just biracialism, especially in a white-majority state like Virginia. Such a recognition was already in evidence in the aftermath of the Danville riot and the electoral defeat of 1883, nowhere more strikingly than in the pages of the *Petersburg Lancet.* A black-edited newspaper established in the interests of the Readjusters, the *Lancet* had rallied African Americans to Mahone and the coalition standard, proclaiming that "our alliance with the Liberal party is just and right." Then, in the late summer of 1885, the paper took a sudden turn, announcing that it would no longer take part in "partisan politics" or "champion" any political party. Tired of "worrying over which white man shall represent us" and of "continually being the instrument through which the feelings and prejudice" of whites and blacks were "agitated, chiefly in the interests of white republicans," the *Lancet* looked for another course. And in a version of what would become most closely associated with Booker T. Washington in Tuskegee, it determined "that we can do the masses of the people more good by encouraging our institutions of learning, industry, thrift, economy, and integrity."[83]

A black retreat from the electoral arena in Virginia was clearly under way. But the retreat was slow and uneven, as much the product of Democratic legal and extralegal machinations as of dissatisfactions with white Republican leaders. In cities like Lynchburg and Richmond, the late 1880s still pulsed with black—and working-class biracial—political activism, principally under the auspices of the Knights of Labor. And although Langston's campaign of 1888 suggested a permanent break between southside blacks and Mahone, many African Americans—in the southside and elsewhere in the state—led by their ministers and other local leaders, found it possible to mend fences and support Mahone's failed bid for the governorship the very next year. But there could be no doubting that the bases of black electoral power were very seriously weakened and that the prospects for their repair were dim. In 1891, for the first time since Virginia's readmission to the Union, the state legislature had no African American representatives. Even the tenacious Ross Hamilton had been driven from his seat. It seemed an ominous sign as the 1880s gave way to the 1890s, not only for Virginia but also for the rest of the former Confederate South. Combining elements of the Radical Reconstruction preceding it and of the Populism to follow, the great Readjuster insurgency had surely shown what was possible in postemancipation southern politics. And just as surely what was not.[84]

9

THE VALLEY AND THE SHADOWS

We seldom study the condition of the Negro to-day honestly and carefully. It is so much easier to assume that we know it all. . . . And yet how little we really know of the millions,—of their daily lives and longings, of their homely joys and sorrows and the meaning of their crimes!

W. E. B. Du Bois

For those who labored on the land in areas of the world increasingly ensnared by international commodity markets and Euro-American imperialism, the last quarter of the nineteenth century brought immense turmoil and dislocation. The economic boom of midcentury had accelerated both the advance of commercial agriculture and the assault on customary relations and patterns of rural life that inevitably went along with it. But then boom became bust. During the 1870s there occurred what is generally known as the "first great depression," which was followed by another severe downturn in the 1890s. Together, these developments helped push growing numbers of rural folk out of the countryside and into an ever-expanding circuit of migration and wage labor, while pressing mercilessly on the resources and prospects of those who remained in place. The effects were to be felt with special intensity in the agricultural peripheries of the rapidly industrializing world economy: in Italy, Spain, and Ireland; in China, India, and southern Africa; in the plantation complexes of the Caribbean and South America—and in the American South.[1]

In many respects, the United States proved a microcosm of the social dynamics at play on the international stage. The decisive defeat of the slaveholders' rebellion during the Civil War not only gave the manufacturing and financial interests of the North almost unchallenged control over the policy-making apparatus of the national government, but it also established a quasi-colonial relationship between the industrializing "core" of the Northeast and Middle Atlantic and the agricultural and extractive "hinterlands" of the South and trans-Mississippi West. Thus, as elsewhere in the world, agriculture in the United States would be made to shoulder the chief burdens of industrial development, in this case through tariff and banking policies that favored cities and manufacturers. As elsewhere, rural cultivators would be squeezed by declining prices for their crops and rising interest rates for necessary credit, and thereby threatened with dispossession and further economic dependence. As elsewhere, social differentiation in the countryside would become more pronounced and social tensions there would mount. And, as elsewhere, the tensions would eventually detonate in rebellions that challenged the trajectory of economic change and shaped the social and political reorganization that followed their defeats.[2]

Within the American, and especially within the southern, context, the unfolding of this process has been considered principally from the perspectives of the white farmers who launched the largest of the rebellions (most notably Populism) and the white elites who moved to crush them. African Americans have assumed relatively marginal roles in the telling, represented either as reacting to events well beyond their influence or, more likely, as the victims of them.[3] This is not unreasonable. Black social and political power had been weakened substantially in the decade after Reconstruction, and the examples of subsequent victimization are many. The period between 1877 and 1901 has been called the "nadir" of black life, and it is arguable that African Americans suffered more widespread, multifaceted, and state-sponsored repression in the late nineteenth and early twentieth centuries than at any time since the late seventeenth and early eighteenth centuries.[4]

Yet the repression was inextricably tied to the crisis besetting the countryside and to the intensifying struggles between town and country, industry and agriculture. Even more, it cannot be understood apart from the assertions of rural blacks along an extended political front that began to erupt in the late 1880s and carried on, in one form or another, through the First World War. The organizational product of the late-century crises and struggles—what is called the Jim Crow South—may well have appeared fully formed and firmly planted by 1910, but in ways that can easily be obscured, black men and women were again reconfiguring the political landscape of the South and the nation.

❖

During the late 1880s, just when the insurgencies of the post-Reconstruction period seemed to have expired and white Democrats appeared ensconced in the seats of power, the countryside of the Deep South pulsed with renewed and threatening activity. Most conspicuous were the white landowners and tenant farmers, chiefly in the recently commercialized nonplantation districts, who sought relief from the tyrannies of staple-crop agriculture and flocked in growing numbers to local meetings of the Agricultural Wheel or the Farmers' Alliance. The appeal was powerful. Claiming to stand for the interests of small producers and drawing on the political and intellectual legacies of greenbackism, both the Wheel and the Alliance pressed for monetary inflation and cooperative alternatives to the relations and institutions of the competitive marketplace. Indeed, the organizations first took hold in former Greenback strongholds before they spread explosively across much of the rural South. By the time the Alliance had absorbed the Wheel in 1889, well over half a million white agriculturalists could be counted as members. Their numbers would ultimately exceed one million.[5]

The Alliance specifically excluded African Americans (and required the Wheel to accept the policy as a condition of merger), but there can be little doubt that black communities mobilized on their own. In what appeared to be a parallel development, a Colored Farmers' Alliance, founded in Houston County, Texas, in 1886, soon had a foothold in every southern state and, like the white Alliance, sponsored local cooperatives as well as larger exchanges in Norfolk, Charleston, Mobile, New Orleans, and Houston. In 1889 and 1890, the Alliances convened simultaneously, and both organizations supported a proposal for a federally funded, nationwide system of agricultural cooperatives

known as the subtreasury plan, the centerpiece of white Alliance radicalism.[6] Yet we would be mistaken to see the Colored Alliance as a
mere offshoot or shadow of the white Alliance, for it had a dynamic
of its own and stood as one of several, sometimes interconnected, initiatives that built on established institutional foundations.

There were, in fact, at least three separate Colored Alliances that
took shape in Texas around the same time, in Caldwell and Lee as
well as in Houston counties, before one emerged as dominant, and
these are only the best-known examples of organizational activity that
was widespread, especially in Texas, Arkansas, and North Carolina.
During the early 1880s, blacks in the Arkansas Delta built the Sons
of the Agricultural Star to such a size that the state Agricultural Wheel,
in 1886, dropped its "whites only" eligibility clause to accept the membership (though in racially separate local units). By 1888, two hundred
black Wheels (as they were called) could be identified in Arkansas,
and when the Wheel and Farmers' Alliance merged, resurrecting the
policy of racial exclusion, they went on to form the Colored State
Agricultural Wheel. Although black Wheelers in Alabama and Tennessee did not create statewide bodies after the merger, they did maintain their local chapters, and in Tennessee, apparently because of
strong attachment to their local projects and autonomy, they spurned
overtures from the expanding Colored Farmers' Alliance.[7]

Almost simultaneously, the Knights of Labor, recruiting unskilled
and skilled workers "irrespective of party, race, and sex," moved from
beachheads in Richmond, Raleigh, Birmingham, Little Rock, and Galveston into the small-town and rural South. Before the decade was
out, nearly two thousand local assemblies had been established across
the former Confederate states, about two-thirds of which were to be
found in rural counties. The country districts of Arkansas and Texas
again showed intense organizational activity as did those in lower Louisiana and the Carolinas, and black tenants and laborers (in racially
separate assemblies) appeared to figure prominently among the new
members. Jefferson County, Arkansas, could boast six assemblies composed mainly of "renters, croppers, tenants, [and] plantation employees"; Lonoke County had five, Woodruff County had nine, and Pulaski County had eighteen. Hale County, Alabama, had one black
renters' local and Taliaferro County, Georgia, had one of "farm hands"
and "laborers." The Louisiana sugar parishes had at least twenty (and

probably closer to forty) assemblies made up of "plantation hands,"
"farm hands," and "laborers," while upcountry Aiken County, South
Carolina, had at least one comprised of "renters," "farm hands," and
"laborers." Of more than sixty Knights' assemblies located in the rural
areas of North Carolina, nearly fifty were in counties in which African
Americans represented 40 percent or more of the population; five of
the assemblies were in eastern Pitt County alone, and in one of them
Samuel Perry, an agitator for emigration a decade before, was among
the leaders.[8]

Although relatively little is known about the local experiences of
either the Colored Farmers' Alliance or the rural assemblies of the
Knights of Labor, the dearth of information itself may be suggestive.
Clearly, the prospect of white intervention or retaliation encouraged
a guardedness as to public exposure; but, equally important, these organizations appear to have tapped and fed on an institutional infrastructure of benevolent, church, and political associations commonly known
to African Americans as "secret societies," which had been developing
in the countryside for years. The Sons of the Agricultural Star in Arkansas surely evokes the connection. What we can learn, moreover,
is also indicative of the range and breadth of these experiences and of
how they reflected the specific (and in this period, changing) circumstances of community life. The Colored Alliance and the Knights, together with comparable organizations such as the Cooperative Workers of America, established themselves in a great variety of rural
settings: in the plantation-dominated black belt, in small farming areas
of the piedmont, and in close proximity either to towns and cities or to
new industrial sites growing up in the mineral-rich hills of the southern
Appalachians and in the thick pine forests of the south Atlantic and
Gulf states. In some places, like North Carolina, areas of Colored Alliance and Knights' strength coincided and membership may well have
overlapped. In other places, like Louisiana, one organization or the
other tended to predominate, with the Knights most active in the sugar
parishes and the Colored Alliance in the north-central cotton parishes.
In still others, like the upper piedmont of South Carolina and eastern
Georgia, a patchwork of mobilization seems to have emerged. The
overall social composition of the organizations was, accordingly, somewhat diverse. Black landowners and renters appear to have been disproportionately represented, at least in the Colored Alliance, in the

upper South, while croppers and wage laborers appear to have predominated in the lower South. A great many of the rural Knights' assemblies throughout were designated as "mixed" occupationally.[9]

And "mixed" in other ways too. The ranks of the Colored Alliance and the Knights often included women as well as men and, most everywhere, the organizations became vehicles to advance locally determined goals and encompass locally inflected patterns of life. There can be little doubt that the Colored Alliances' stated objective to find "homes for the families of the colored people" and its promotion of education and improved farming techniques resonated powerfully with the aspirations and sensibilities of blacks throughout the southern countryside. But suballiances and Knights' assemblies became involved in an assortment of issues and struggles of pressing interest to their members. If questions of wages, rents, and the conditions of work usually assumed central importance (one "independent" Alliance in the Alabama black belt resolved "not to hire to white folks and pay less rent"), matters of social welfare, politics, and civil rights were not far behind. In Oktibbeha County, Mississippi, a Colored Alliance established "a Benefit Association for the aid of the needy." In central Georgia, an Alliance meeting "earnestly and sincerely" asked the jury commissioners throughout the state to "draw colored men" for jury service. In upcountry South Carolina, black Alliance members debated the proper stance toward Benjamin Tillman's campaign for governor. The "purpose" of the organization, as blacks in Bellevue, Louisiana, understood it, was to try "to elevate our race, to make us better citizens, better husbands, better fathers and sons, to educate ourselves that we may be able to vote more intelligently on questions that are of vital importance to our people," and to "give us protection for our labor and our crops."[10]

The local Knights' assemblies offer a particularly revealing view not only of the organizational impulse of the late 1880s, but also of the new and shifting sets of social relations into which many rural blacks were entering. In Arkansas, one could identify assemblies of "lumbermen, sawmill & farm hands," of "sawmill, railroad & farm hands, carpenters and teamsters," of "farm & day laborers, & public works hands," and, with women and men, of "farm renters, farm hands, & mechanics," and of "farmers & plantation hands." In Houma, Louisiana; Upshaw, Georgia; Mildred, North Carolina; and Pelham,

North Carolina, individual assembles included "farm hands & washerwomen, cooks & laborers." A Fayetteville, North Carolina, assembly encompassed "turpentine & farm hands," while one in Jefferson County, Georgia, had "farmers, farm hands & factory hands." Assembly 10946 in Halifax County, North Carolina, could boast "renters & farm hands, lumber getters, ditchers & shinglemakers." This is not, in short, a picture of stasis, insularity, or social retreat; it is one of movement, interaction, and assertion, of the linking up of old and new sites of life and work. And one, given the stresses afflicting much of the rural South, vulnerable to violence and repression.[11]

Pulaski County, Arkansas, was a focal point of Knights' recruiting, and cotton-growing Young township, about nine miles south of Little Rock, had three black assemblies with a total of roughly one hundred members. Emboldened, perhaps, by the organizational momentum, thirty of forty workers on the Tate plantation who belonged to the Knights asked for a wage increase in June 1886 and, when rebuffed, went out on strike. Support from some Knights in Little Rock seems to have further encouraged their militance, and word circulated that they had warned the county sheriff not to interfere. He did not heed the warning. Accompanied by several deputies, he hastened to the plantation, accosted the leaders, and wounded one of them with a double-barreled shotgun. When 250 blacks from neighboring plantations, many of them armed, then gathered in the surrounding fields, the sheriff had to summon a posse from Little Rock, which, with a "war correspondent" from the *Arkansas Gazette* in tow, arrived after a three-hour ride. An exchange of gunfire fully dispersed what was left of the black crowd and effectively broke the strike. But it did not crush the spirit of the strikers and their supporters. Running for reelection, the sheriff had another narrow brush: his Republican opponent, who had been endorsed by the Knights, very nearly carried Young township.[12]

About a year later, rumors spread among whites in Spartanburg, Laurens, Pickens, and Greenville counties, South Carolina, about a possible uprising of black farm workers. The blacks, some claimed, had been meeting in secret and planning to "obtain their rights" by murdering the whites, torching white-owned property, or striking for higher wages. It was not entirely far-fetched. For several months, blacks had been organizing lodges of the Cooperative Workers of

America (CWA), quickly known as "Hoover clubs" after Hiram F. Hover (usually reported as "Hoover"), the CWA's president. Hover was white and a former member of the Knights of Labor, but the grassroots operations were carried out by longstanding local black leaders. Most were themselves farm laborers and one was the grandson of a man recognized for having stood up to the Ku Klux Klan. Assembling clandestinely, often in black churches and guarded by armed pickets—much in the manner of earlier Union Leagues—the lodges discussed, among other things, establishing a cooperative store. In some areas, they attracted the support of at least two in three African Americans, many of whom worked on relatively small farms. Then the rumors surfaced and circulated. White vigilance committees began to scour the countryside, rounding up known leaders for interrogation and disbanding the CWA lodges they found, while the state government authorized the formation and arming of new militia units. Only the extent of local organization and the threat of further black emigration west seems to have prevented a reign of intimidation from becoming a bloodbath.[13]

Sugar workers in lower Louisiana were not so fortunate. For more than two decades they had been struggling with plantation owners, in an ever-shifting political environment, over the reconstruction of crop production. And the struggle was only intensifying. Like cotton, the sugar sector felt the effects of the 1870s depression and the generally unfavorable markets for agricultural staples. But it also experienced the distinctive effects of foreign competition and the rise of a domestic sugar trust that was based in New York and increasingly reliant on cheap imports. Seeking to exert more control over labor and modernize operations, the owners formed the Louisiana Sugar Planters' Association (LSPA) in 1877 and pressed to unify pay scales, withhold wages during the crop season, substitute scrip for cash payments, and find a more docile work force.[14]

They met substantial resistance, and by 1886 it was being organized by the Knights of Labor. With an early foothold in New Orleans, the Knights had fanned out into the sugar-growing districts by way of Morgan City (St. Mary Parish), where black and white railroad, clothing, and domestic workers joined local assemblies and enabled Knights-backed candidates to sweep the municipal elections in 1887. Farm laborers and plantation hands were simultaneously being recruited in at least seven other parishes, Terrebonne and Lafourche chief among them, and the staunchly Republican *New Orleans Weekly Pelican* soon announced that the Knights "can carry a third of the parishes . . . in the state." The Knights clearly provided an important vehicle of mobilization in opposition to the planters' offensive. Yet there was even more to the appeal, for the Knights' antimonopoly ideas meshed very well with the sugar workers' aspirations for greater control over the conditions of their labor. "Parcel out gentlemen your large estates among your laborers," a sympathetic black editor advised at the time; "lease a portion to each on reasonable terms and periods long enough to teach them to look upon the place as their home. . . . The large plantations have seen their day." The planters thought otherwise and cut wages. Late in that summer of 1887, the Knights consequently tried to negotiate a boost in harvest wages and the end of payments in scrip: tried, in short, to reclaim some power on the sugar estates. When the planters refused them, the Knights struck.[15]

It was a bold step. The strikes of 1874 and 1880 had taken place early in the crop year; this one was called for November 1, at the beginning of the grinding season, when sugar cane was most vulnerable to loss. Many of the planters, through the auspices of the LSPA, had readied themselves for the showdown, requesting the assistance of state militia companies and searching for strikebreakers in the harvested cotton fields of neighboring Mississippi. The behavior of sugar planter Taylor Beattie was a bad omen. A judge and former Republican candidate for governor, Beattie had once defended African-American voting rights. Now, thundering against "a secret oath-bound association of ignorant and degraded barbarians" and proclaiming that "the question of the supremacy of whites over the blacks" had become paramount, he headed up planter activities in the volatile parishes of Terrebonne and Lafourche, and especially in the environs of Thibodaux.[16]

On November 1, the laborers made an impressive showing. As many as ten thousand of them (90 percent of whom were black, and apparently all members of the Knights of Labor) stopped work. At least some of the planters felt compelled to give in to their demands. Most did not. Indeed, by that afternoon two companies of state militia, dispatched by the Democratic governor "without investigation of any kind" and equipped with a Gatling gun, had arrived on the scene and commenced evicting strikers from the plantations and guarding against "any insurrection of the negroes." It was not long before they were also protecting several hundred strikebreakers. Not surprisingly, indications of the strike's weakening were soon in evidence, as numbers of strikers either began returning to their jobs voluntarily or yielded to ultimatums from their employers. But many still "insisted upon their demands," and the small parish towns steadily filled with evicted strikers, none more so than Thibodaux—in an area of notable militance—where the Knights and black community sympathizers sought to provide food and shelter for the black refugees.[17]

Sporadic violence on the plantations and in a few of the towns added to the tension as the momentum plainly swung in the planters' favor. When one Knights' local of nearly four hundred members leased a plantation to work as a cooperative, they both expressed their vision of "free labor" and tacitly acknowledged the unlikelihood of a strike victory. But the planters were determined to orchestrate the final act. Led by Taylor Beattie, and complaining of the "idle negroes" who filled the streets of Thibodaux, they organized a "peace and order" committee, had the sheriff appoint deputies to patrol the town, declared martial law, and attracted vigilantes from as far off as Shreveport. With pickets stationed along the roads, preventing blacks from either entering or leaving, the eruption of gunfire in the early morning hours of November 23 unleashed a murderous assault that left more than fifty black men, including three of the strike's leaders, dead. For months thereafter, "regulators" terrorized African Americans, particularly their influential and militant leaders, and drove the Knights of Labor to the margins; one year later, only two Knights' local assemblies functioned in Lafourche and Terrebonne parishes, and these in the less technologically advanced sections. White authorities, in the view of a black newspaper, thereby "put into practical effect in southern Louisiana the methods hitherto employed in northern Louisiana to overawe the Negro." Mary Pugh, member of a prominent planter family, was even more direct: "I think this will settle the question of who is to rule the nigger or the white man? for the next 50 years."[18]

In the Mississippi Delta, it appeared that the question had been settled by White League violence and then, after Reconstruction, by the system of fusion. But the arrival of the Colored Farmers' Alliance—what one Democrat saw as an example of the "revival of political activity in the South on the part of the colored men"—disturbed the ostensible stability, nowhere more explosively than in Leflore County. Settled after the Civil War, Leflore County came to have an overwhelming black majority (85 percent black) that worked as tenants, sharecroppers, and laborers on white-owned plantations. Thousands of African Americans had migrated in during the 1880s, and in the summer of 1889, amid the demographic volatility, they could have encountered the black activist Oliver Cromwell. Probably the veteran of Reconstruction-era struggles, including the bloody Clinton riot, Cromwell was fiercely independent and politically resolute, traveling from plantation to plantation delivering militant speeches to rally support for the Colored Alliance. These activities alone would have attracted the attention of white landowners; but when he persuaded newly recruited alliance members to boycott local merchants and trade instead with a white Farmers' Alliance cooperative store in neighboring Holmes County, he became a menace.[19]

The landowners' initial efforts at harassment and intimidation only revealed the solidarity and militancy that had been mobilized. When they attempted to subvert Cromwell's authority by circulating stories about criminal activity in which he had allegedly engaged, the Alliance chapters heard him out and then voted to retain him as their leader. When Cromwell received an anonymous letter threatening his life, the membership vowed "to stand by him." Indeed, the Colored Alliance members expressed their anger and determination by addressing a note of protest to local whites and signing it as "Three Thousand Armed Men." Seventy-five of them marched "in regular military style" into the village of Shell Mound to deliver it. The whites were not amused. Charging that the blacks had collected a large stockpile of weapons and were massing against them, they wired Mississippi's governor for troops while putting out a call for additional reinforcements. In early September, three companies of Mississippi National Guardsmen and the governor himself appeared, together with armed vigilantes from surrounding areas of the Delta. The guardsmen quickly rounded up at least forty blacks, turned them over to the sheriff, and left. For his part, the sheriff assembled a large posse and combed the countryside for the Colored Alliance leaders. Cromwell managed to escape, but five others were captured. They, and most of the other prisoners, were then "shot down like dogs" in what has come to be known as the "Leflore massacre."[20]

The "white citizens and planters" who gathered in the aftermath at the Leflore County village of Red Cross had no doubt about who was to blame for what they called the "recent race trouble," and they took the opportunity to issue a further warning. Insisting that the Colored Farmers' Alliance had been "diverted from its original and supposed purpose" and had instead "caused strife and bloodshed between the races . . . demoralized labor . . . and produced a feeling of uneasiness and insecurity as to the welfare of our wives and little ones," they instructed the white Farmers' Alliance cooperative store to "desist from selling goods or lending money" to the Colored Alliance and ordered the editor of the *Colored Alliance Advocate,* published in the nearby town of Vaiden, to stop sending the paper to subscribers at six of the county's post offices. Disregarding "this notice," they added ominously, would "be treated as it should deserve by a united and outraged community."[21]

A vital Colored Farmers' Alliance movement was thereby destroyed in Leflore County, and Oliver Cromwell appears to have evaporated along with it. But the Colored Alliance continued to grow in much of the Deep South, and it did so in uneasy relationship to white landowners in general and to the white Farmers' Alliance in particular. By 1890, reports claimed 90,000 Colored Alliance members in the founding state of Texas, 20,000 in Arkansas, roughly 50,000 in twenty-seven parishes in Louisiana, another 50,000 in as many as 1,600 local chapters in Alabama, perhaps as many as 30,000 in South Carolina, and about 55,000 in North Carolina. Throughout the South, the Colored Alliance was said to have attracted as many as one million members; it likely attracted substantially fewer. At all events, it was eyed with interest and often suspicion by white planters and farmers and by Democratic political leaders who saw the harbinger of renewed and unsettling activism. "Here is the old Loyal League back upon us again," the *Mobile Register* could fret, "with its yearning for the lands of the white man, with its ambition that the Federal flag shall float over every schoolhouse and over every ballot box. . . . Here is the old secret society going in and out with pass word." Even the white Farmers' Alliance, which cooperated with the Colored Alliance on some projects and at times developed cordial relations on the local level, quickly identified major differences and potential antagonisms: over the question of federal supervision of elections and aid to education, and, especially, over the wisdom of advancing the interests of black rural workers.[22]

Among the issues that local Colored Alliances commonly took up were the wages paid to cotton pickers. With good reason. On the one hand, the cotton harvest offered the prospect of cash income not only to hard-pressed (and often indebted) tenant and cropper families (all of whom would be in the fields), but also to the growing numbers of black wage laborers who either worked seasonally in sawmills, mines, and turpentine camps or had moved to small towns in the plantation belt. On the other hand, wages for picking (by the hundred pounds) had been in recent decline, owing in large measure to the weakening of the international cotton market. The harvest was, therefore, a flash-point of struggle and conflict, and by the summer of 1891 the general superintendent of the Colored Alliance—Richard M. Humphrey, a white Baptist preacher, teacher, farmer, and former Confederate soldier who had close involvements with black churches—moved to build on scattered disturbances and organize a strike across the entire cotton South.[23]

Traveling from state to state and addressing Colored Alliance meetings, Humphrey decried the "starvation wages" that pickers received and quietly encouraged them to act. It was not an easy sell, and some black state leaders, especially in Texas and Georgia, regarding a strike as "perfectly dangerous" and likely ruinous, vehemently opposed him. But Humphrey persisted. Because the Alliance itself seemed so deeply divided, he formed a cotton pickers' league and in early September called upon his followers to "cease" work between September 12 and November 1 "unless their just demands" for "$1 per hundred pounds with board" were accepted. Hoping that "all leagues and unions" might "unite more closely and stand firm together" for the "furtherance of these objects," Humphrey urged the "use of all peaceful and lawful means to secure the sympathy and . . . cooperation of all pickers in every section," and warned strikers to "avoid all public gatherings in public places and insolent displays." "Show yourselves," he counseled, "to be men who seek peace and desire justice."[24]

By September 6, Humphrey informed Colored Alliance members that "600,000 pickers" had "bound themselves together in sacred covenant" to strike, and rumors circulated among planters of "an immense organization of cotton pickers throughout all the states . . . effected through the colored alliance" and "pledged" to its wage demands. It was a great exaggeration on all accounts. Localized strike activity was reported in Texas, Louisiana, Mississippi, and South Carolina, and a bitter conflict erupted in Lee County, Arkansas, just across the Mississippi River from Memphis. Elsewhere, relative quiet prevailed. Yet we must not too quickly discount the wider repercussions or the social and political dynamic at play. The cotton pickers' strike capped a half decade of mobilizations that had reached across the countryside of the Deep South (and had urban and industrial counterparts), and it demonstrated that an African-American political presence would continue to be felt even in the face of the repression it perpetually courted. Organizing traditions found new forms of expression as a generation of men and women who grew up after slavery sought to carve out lives for themselves in a world of change and hardship. And white allies were as difficult to discover and cultivate as they ever had been. Whatever gestures of cooperation it might proffer across the rural color line, the white Farmers' Alliance responded to the cotton pickers' strike, and related black labor agitation, with disapproval and contempt, if not repressive fury. Not a word of protest was uttered when white planters and law enforcement officials in Lee County slaughtered fifteen striking cotton pickers, including their leader Ben Patterson, who was most likely a member of the Colored Alliance.[25]

❖

It was not necessary to strike for higher wages or belong to organizations such as the Knights of Labor and the Colored Farmers' Alliance, for an African American—and principally an African-American man—to run the risk of slaughter in the rural South of the late 1880s and 1890s. It was only necessary to establish relative independence, to stand up to a landlord, to show the signs of literacy, to speak one's mind, or to ignore the local racial etiquette: in short, to behave in any way that could be regarded as nonsubmissive by a white person. For the massacres at Thibodaux, Leflore, and Lee were only the most glaring examples of the organized violence and repression that became facts of life for rural black folk during this period, and remained so for most of the next half century.

No form of violence and repression seemed more characteristic of the time than lynching: the mob execution of an individual or individuals who stood accused of committing an offense against—of, in effect, violating—a self-constituted community. Lynching expressed the tensions not only between white and black or between different groups of whites and blacks, but also between competing ideas of justice and power at a time of great stress and instability. It simultaneously depended on control over the apparatus of the state (or, at least, on the cooperation of the state) while rejecting state institutions as the appropriate channels for enacting popular justice; rejecting, that is, the notion that all individuals should be subject to the authority of the laws and judicial system as opposed to the direct domination of the community. Such tensions were particularly in evidence as white property owners in the aftermath of emancipation and Reconstruction worked to construct new social hierarchies, eyed warily the centralizing trends of the age, and felt the constant pressure from African Americans for inclusion and rights (which they considered illegitimate). Nowhere did those tensions erupt more convulsively than in the countryside.

Scholars have devoted a good deal of energy to studying the causes and trajectories of lynching without reaching very much agreement as to whether economic, social, or political developments (or a combination of these) best account for its surge, character, and eventual decline. Indeed, the search for a clear and singular explanation appears futile. What we do know is that the incidence of lynching began to increase dramatically in the mid-1880s and reached a high point by the mid-1890s; that lynchings were most likely to occur in rural, cotton-growing counties of the Deep South with large and demographically volatile black populations; that victims tended to be young, black men relatively new to the areas in which they lived; and that more of them were accused of murder, assault, arson, and theft than rape or other sexual transgressions. We know that lynch mobs could have been small or very large (sometimes involving many hundreds of people) and that their deeds could have been highly choreographed and ritualized, but that at all events they were public and undisguised, conducted with little fear of punishment, representing themselves as the lethal hand of the local white community's moral judgment. And we know that the tensions and conflicts of the rural economy often figured in their provocation. Strains between landlords and laborers or between debtors and creditors, disputes over hunting privileges and the ownership of livestock, and the influx of plantation, sawmill, or levee workers all made for a combustible mix. In Georgia, one-quarter of the African Americans lynched for murder or assault between 1880 and 1930 had been charged with killing their employer or members of the employer's family. One of the most infamous and gruesome examples, involving a literate plantation hand named Sam Holt who had been in Coweta County for about a year, began with words over Holt's request for an advance in pay.[26]

There is, in short, a sense in which the epidemic of lynching that commenced in the mid-1880s may be seen not so much as the product of this or that "factor," but as part of a phase of struggle in the countryside initiated by assertions and interventions of several types, not least those of African Americans. Feeding on a deep culture of social and political violence, lynch mobs sought to reestablish the boundaries that they believed were being traversed, to crush the attacks and violations they could associate with the weakening of their own leverage. This is, perhaps, why charges of rape and miscegenation reverberated in the discourse of lynching—involving as they did the most intimate and fundamental boundaries and violations—despite the record showing that other forms of assault were more commonly at issue.

It may also be why the surge in lynching coincided not simply with the antilabor violence of the late 1880s and early 1890s, but also with the generally nonlethal, though brutally coercive, phenomenon known as "whitecapping." In the traditions of vigilantism and rough justice, whitecappers were bands of armed white men who engaged in what they viewed as community "regulation" and retaliation, moving against those who violated norms, transgressed boundaries, or threatened livelihoods. Their targets could include prostitutes and racially mixed households, merchants and cotton ginners, and federal revenue agents attempting to shut down moonshiners. But in the early 1890s, as the cotton economy soured further still, some of them launched attacks against blacks who rented farms, owned land, or otherwise worked for merchants and large planters. Seeking, as one group in Mississippi put it, to "gain control of the negro labor, which is by right ours," they tended to be young men of modest means who resided on the edge of the plantation districts or in rapidly developing areas of the piney woods where blacks had a better chance to establish an independent foothold or find alternative employment in newly opened lumber camps and sawmills. If whitecappers did not customarily commit murder, they could wreak havoc: flogging black farmers and laborers, destroying their crops and livestock, torching their barns, churches, and schoolhouses.[27]

Repression of such ferocity and unpredictability left little room for resistance or reprisals, and encouraged silence and submission. The public protests voiced during the 1890s came principally from educated African Americans who, like Ida B. Wells, had already fled the South or, like John L. Mitchell, editor of the *Richmond Planet,* was at a safe distance from the worst of it. They came too, though in more muted tones, from blacks in southern towns—newspaper editors, ministers, and educators prominent among them—who decried lynching and other forms of mob violence and appealed to conservative whites to live up to their professed paternalism and look out for the collective interests of the region. "We believe," the Tuskegee Negro Conference declared in 1893, "that the many acts of lawlessness and the increased frequency of lynchings are not only injurious to the cause of good morals but that they greatly retard the prosperity of the South." Around the same time, "40 of the leading colored men in Texas" who held stock in the *Austin Herald* met in Houston and resolved to "memorialize the Texas legislature on the mob question." By the end of the decade, blacks in Macon, Georgia, had established an "Anti Mob and Lynch Law Association" and invited Booker T. Washington to come and speak on "Mobbing and Lynching and the General Condition of the Country." In 1900, North Carolina's George H. White, the last black southerner to sit in Congress until the 1960s, reported a bill for the "protection of all citizens of the United States against mob violence."[28]

But the black countryside did not suffer the lethal assaults quietly either, and their response often reflected the contours of the social and political landscape. Where blacks had constructed a substantial basis of community life and continued to wield measures of local power— the coasts of South Carolina and Georgia leap out as examples— lynchings were rare and the threat of them could arouse an armed and militant defense. Thus, when a well-known black man in McIntosh County, Georgia, was jailed in the town of Darien on a rape charge in 1899 and put at risk for lynching by the white sheriff, blacks mobilized quickly to protect him. Employing familiar practices and networks, they posted sentinels around the jailhouse and rang the bell of a nearby black Baptist church when emergencies arose. Concerned supporters flocked there from around the county as well as from Sapelo Island to lend their bodies to the effort. Only the intervention of state militia units put an end to what was known as the "Darien insurrection," though not with any loss of black lives. The accused was eventually tried and acquitted.[29]

Blacks in Barnwell County, South Carolina, who had endured more than their share of racial violence, could not prevent the brutal slaughter of eight men imprisoned for the murders of their landlord and a local planter's son in December 1889. But neither were they left in "utter demoralization," as a local white observer seemed to think. At the funeral of two of the victims, more than five hundred blacks lined the streets of the county seat in a show of solidarity and defiance, some expressing rage and praying "that God should burn Barnwell to the ground." Several days later, prominent African Americans from around the state gathered at the Bethel Methodist Episcopal Church in Columbia and added their voices to the protest, blaming the lynchings on "influential leaders among the whites of the State" who have "taught that any treatment of the negro that would tend to impress him with the white man's superior power" was "justifiable." Small wonder that when blacks again assembled at the Barnwell county seat, they passed resolutions recommending emigration.[30]

In both the McIntosh and Barnwell county actions, black women played central roles. Not only were they present in large numbers—they appeared to have outnumbered black men in McIntosh—but they were also conspicuous in their militance and public outrage. They could be described as the "foot soldiers" of resistance, standing doggedly as sentinels around the Darien jailhouse or lashing out verbally at whites in the streets of Barnwell. The record also suggests that they were to be seen in similar stances of defiance elsewhere, again revealing the dynamics and social divisions of black community politics. For as the dangers of public expression and confrontation intensified during the late nineteenth century, black women had somewhat more room to test the boundaries of insubordination than did black men. They were not regarded as dire threats to the hierarchies of power in general or to the security of white women in particular. Thus, they could begin to fashion a grassroots counterpart to the antilynching campaigns of educated, middle-class blacks that focused on molding "public senti-ment"—a counterpart that would ultimately strengthen an increasingly unified effort.[31]

Even so, the space for public protest that black women might claim was perilously delimited and it did not take much for them to invite white retribution. Ida B. Wells, a former slave and the daughter of politically active black Mississippians, learned this in a shocking man-ner when she lashed out at white behavior and hypocrisy in a news-paper editorial in 1892: Her press in Memphis was destroyed and she was driven from Tennessee. Black women and men who resided on farms and plantations scattered across the rural districts—as most in the cotton belt did—were especially at risk if they intended to stand up for themselves or defend one of their number against a lynching. Circumstances demanded that they exercise great caution in their pub-lic demeanor and, better still, that they seek the protection or good offices of a well-placed white patron. But this was not mere "accommo-dation" or "resignation." By enacting the deference and ostensible sub-mission that whites relished, they might limit their vulnerability in the universe of social encounters where a misunderstanding or minor altercation could quickly escalate, and find some way to pursue their own aspirations.[32]

The path was exceedingly precarious, and Ned Cobb, who worked as a tenant farmer in the Alabama black belt, struggled self-consciously to walk it. Determined to "pull myself along . . . to the best of my abilities and knowledge" despite "what people said, regardless to how much I knowed that they was a enemy to me," he at the same "never gived nobody no trouble, tended to my business," and earned "a good name." It made a difference. One Saturday, Cobb traveled into town to buy some shoes for his children. A white female store clerk waited on him, and her willing attention began to irritate one of the other clerks, a white man named Henry Chase. Chase confronted Cobb, told him he was "too hard to suit," tried to hit him with a shoe, and then threatened him with a shovel. Cobb made it clear that he would resist ("when I know I'm right and I aint harmin nobody and nothin else, I'll give you trouble if you try to move me"), and Chase went to fetch a member of the police force, charging that Cobb had a gun hidden in his overalls. Cobb seemed headed for grave difficulty. Although the policeman found no gun, he took the accusation seriously and decided to haul Cobb before the mayor. But when Cobb got up the stairs he saw that the mayor was Dr. Collins who "knowed me well, been knowin me a long time." A few questions later, Collins threw "the little case out." "When a man's mistreated thataway and he got friends and they proves it, he don't need to be scared," Cobb later explained to one of his kinfolk. "Of course," he added with keen recognition and no small understatement, "it's a dangerous situation."[33]

❖

The intensification of struggle and violence in the rural South—and especially the Deep South—during the late 1880s and early 1890s created the context for the emergence of the greatest white insurgency of the postemancipation period: the People's, or Populist, party. A product of both white Alliance mobilizations and increasing disenchantment with the Alliance's ability to advance its aims through the Democratic party, the Populist party burst forth in 1892 with a Greenback-influenced program and a determination to challenge for local, state, and national power. Along with the subtreasury plan of cooperative marketing, the Populists called for the free coinage of silver, the abolition of national (private) banks, the end of alien landownership, and government ownership of the railroads and telegraphs. It was a program that identified exploitation in the exchange, rather than in the production, of goods, and that saw the government as a vehicle for readjusting the increasingly pronounced imbalances of political and economic life. It was also a program that fed on the dislocations and insurgencies of the previous two decades.[34]

The leaders of the party and movement were, for the most part, substantial white landowners, deeply enmeshed in commercial agriculture, who saw themselves economically weakened by low crop prices and high shipping rates and felt powerless to gain redress through the two established political parties. But the Populist mass base was composed of more modest white farm owners and tenants who had experienced tumultuous change. Most resided in hill country or nonplantation districts that had been fully opened to the relations and institutions of the staple-crop economy following the war and emancipation. Railroads increasingly linked them with larger commercial centers while small market towns spread across the countryside in ever-

growing numbers. A tradition of mixed farming and diversified economic activities had steadily given way to an emphasis on cotton culture and especially to a system of production and exchange mediated
by town merchants, crop liens, and exorbitant interest rates.[35]

The great majority of these Populist farmers and tenants had been
Democrats, in good measure because of the party's embrace of state
rights and local control and its ambivalence about the expansion of
market relations. A few had flirted briefly with the Republican party
during Reconstruction; more had been attracted to the insurgencies of
the late 1870s and early 1880s, to Greenbackers and Independents.
They saw themselves squeezed between the predatory demands of
merchants and other commercial interests on the one side and the assertions of freedmen and women on the other. Some of them had already
struck back by joining paramilitary outfits or whitecap raids; some may
even have participated in a lynching. In Populism they seem to have
imagined—as they had in the Farmers' Alliance that preceded it—
the possibility of empowering communities of "producers" (as against
merchants, landlords, and poor black folk) by means of cooperative
endeavors and government resources.[36]

It was not the sort of movement that African Americans could have
found very appealing. By the early 1890s, blacks had a fairly clear idea
as to what they might expect from the people who filled the Populist
ranks. They were people who had ridden with the Klan, the Red Shirts,
and the White Leaguers; people who, as Greenbackers or Independents, had extended them, at best, a limited and often demeaning hand;
who, as Alliancemen, had supported legislation to enforce black submission and had greeted the organization of black cotton pickers with
hostility. They were people commonly known to blacks as "regulators." The Georgia black Republican William Pledger bitterly described the Populists as "the men who have lynched the colored people
in the past; the men who have shot and robbed the colored people;
the men who precipitated the 'Camilla Riot' years ago and who mar-
shalled the red shirter and the night riders."[37]

The Populists, like the Independents and Alliancemen before them,
did regard theirs as a white man's movement. But, again like previous
insurgents, they recognized the need to find sympathetic votes wherever they could, and some turned for help to the black electorate. Much
indeed has been made of the Populist approach to southern blacks,

coming as it did at a time of hardening race relations and widening attempts to mark racial lines of exclusion in social and political life. And there can be little doubt that Populists appropriated a language of protest in which blacks and whites could be imagined as participants in the same civil and political arenas, represented as suffering similar problems and sharing grievances, and seen as having common stakes in change. Populist leaders Tom Watson in Georgia and H. S. P. "Stump" Ashby in Texas were particularly outspoken and direct on these matters, often at considerable risk, and they had counterparts on the local level who also advanced the ideas. After organizing a Populist party in April 1892, "the white people" of Oconee County, Georgia, asked the "cooperation of the colored people in this, our effort to free our country from its present depressed condition and put in office men who will legislate for the masses and not the classes." While disclaiming any "visionary" offer of "forty acres and a mule," they told blacks that "your race today, like ours, is groaning under the oppression of taxation and the low estimate placed on labor," and that "to better our condition means to better yours."[38]

Such language and arguments could certainly command a hearing among African Americans in the 1890s. Many had belonged to the Colored Farmers' Alliance and were quite familiar with the antimonopoly critique of late-nineteenth-century American capitalism put forth by the white Alliance, the Knights of Labor, and the Greenbackers. The national organization of the Colored Alliance had, in fact, moved beyond subtreasury radicalism in "recommending to our people the principles of the single tax party." "We take this occasion," R. M. Humphrey announced at the annual convention in Ocala, Florida, in December 1890, "to distinctly affirm that land is not property; can never be made property; holds no allegiance but to the man who lives on it. The improvements are his. The land belongs to the sovereign people." The Colored Alliance seemed to be even more receptive than the white Alliance to the idea of political insurgency, and, despite the white Alliance's role in the cotton pickers' strike, officially endorsed the third-party effort.[39]

Most rural blacks, whether or not they had become members of the Colored Alliance, appeared more equivocal. However resonant the Populists' language of protest or admirable their intention to unseat the Democrats, rural blacks had to consider the benefits that still might

accrue from their long-standing loyalty to the Republican party and
the vulnerabilities to which they would be exposed should they choose
insurgency. The great majority of them resided in plantation districts
where whites both tended to remain Democrats and were prepared to
preserve their position at all cost. Equally important, the Populists'
concept of biracialism did not go beyond that of the Greenbackers or
Independents, and was a pale shadow of William Mahone's and the
Readjusters' in Virginia. They may have insisted that "our interest is
one," that "to better our condition means to better yours," and that
there were "broad lines of mutual interest," but they rarely addressed
issues of immediate concern to blacks: economic independence, self-
governance, education, lynching, and the general climate of repression.
The radical Texas Populists went as far as any in their platform of
1894, favoring only an "effective system of free schools for six months"
under the control of "each race," a "reformation" of convict leasing,
"amendments" to the vagrant law, "sufficient accommodation" for the
insane "regardless of color," and a "free vote and fair count." Nor
did Populists make much of an effort to include blacks among their
leaders, decision-makers, or organizers. Few black delegates were to
be found at the party's state conventions, and those in attendance
played almost no substantive role in the proceedings. Fewer still were
to be found on the party's executive and campaign committees either
at the state, district, or county levels. And Populists rarely selected a
black man as their candidate for electoral office. What African Americans did learn was that the Populists—even the foremost advocates
of biracialism—took every opportunity to decry "social equality" and
unmistakably refused them direct access to political power.[40]

The local experience of Populism confirmed rather than dispelled
black misgivings. In parts of the Georgia black belt, and especially in
Tom Watson's Tenth Congressional District, Populists simultaneously
courted black voters and intimidated (even terrorized) those who
seemed unlikely to support them. When blacks went to the polls in
Jefferson County in 1892, they found Populists wearing red hats and
carrying sticks, very much evocative of Reconstruction vigilantism. In
Woodruff County, Arkansas, a white Populist reportedly refused to
debate a black Democrat, while in Pulaski County white Populists
opposed the inclusion of any blacks on their county ticket even though

eight had attended their county convention as delegates. Grant Parish, Louisiana, Populists initially won the endorsement of black Republicans, many of whom had been organized into a local branch of a Colored Alliance affiliate. But when blacks approached the parish Populist primary with independence rather than deference, the Populists responded by throwing out the results. Although they quickly reversed course and sought to make amends, the damage was done: when the election took place five months later, most parish blacks abandoned the Populists and cast ballots for one of two tickets put out by the Republicans.[41]

African Americans in Taliaferro County, Georgia, who outnumbered whites by two to one, proved more steadfast. They had organized a chapter of the Colored Alliance in the late 1880s and apparently responded favorably to Populist promises of economic reform and free elections, for after some deliberation their votes enabled the Populists to sweep to local power in 1892 and to maintain it for six years. They did speak well of the first Populist sheriff and some attended county nominating conventions, served on party committees, and represented the county at a Populist state convention. But blacks failed to persuade the Populists to elect or appoint them to political office or to permit them to participate directly in the governance of the county. By the summer of 1898, blacks had had enough. Meeting at the county courthouse, they "resolved themselves back into the Republican party" and effectively opened the door for the return of Democratic rule.[42]

Taliaferro County blacks may have regarded themselves, at least for a time, as Populists. Yet across the South, African Americans who voted Populist did so chiefly without shedding their identities as Republicans. Either they "endorsed" Populist candidates for state and local offices (and sometimes for Congress), or they entered into formal fusion arrangements, trading support for party nominees with a view to wielding a share of power. It made a good deal of sense. Republican party prospects for winning at the state or local levels had deteriorated dramatically, all the more so as white and black wings of the party battled one another; alliances with the insurgents of the 1890s (as in the 1880s) thereby offered new breaths of political life. "Populists, Republicans, and perhaps some Negroes . . . are leagued together," a Democrat in Madison County, Tennessee, scoffed; "*any thing, any way* to beat the Democrats." The only success the Populists had in exercising significant state power came as a result of a well orchestrated and shrewdly implemented plan of fusion in North Carolina.[43]

The Republican party of North Carolina had withstood the Democratic assaults of the 1870s and 1880s and remained better organized than most any of its counterparts in the South. It claimed areas of substantial strength both in the plantation-dominated east (especially in the Second Congressional District) and in the mountain west, which, when combined with some white and black votes in the central piedmont, exceeded 40 percent of the electorate. As early as 1892, there were harbingers of large-scale cooperation with the Populists—cooperation based not so much on economic issues as on the opportunities for real political influence in the state and counties. In heavily black Edgecombe County, Populists nominated an African American for a seat in the legislature. In Vance County, they chose a black man for register of deeds and voted for black county commissioners, and in neighboring Warren County they held out the lure of meaningful local power. "Large numbers of the negroes will vote the third party ticket in the county, including county state national and congressional," a white Warren County Democrat grumbled in the fall of 1892, explaining that the "third partyites tell the Republicans here that if they will cooperate with them that they will capture the legislature and repeal the present system of Co. Government and after the repeal that they will divide the co. offices with the negroes." This, he sighed, "takes like fire with the negroes."[44]

The Democrat's predictions could not have been more prescient, though it was another two years before Populist-Republican fusion took shape and, something in the manner of Virginia's Readjusters, captured control of the legislature. Together, Populists and Republicans won 74 of 110 seats in the house and 42 of 50 seats in the senate in the state elections of 1894. With two blacks among their number, they proceeded—again in the manner of Virginia's Readjusters—to strengthen their political base. They repealed "the present system of Co. Government," restoring the popular selection of county officials that Democrats had awarded to the legislature after Redemption, and replaced an 1889 Democratic election law that had disadvantaged black voters with one that offered new protections. By 1896, the effects had become stunningly apparent. Just when the Populists were succumbing to the Democrats most everywhere else in the South, the fusion project in North Carolina achieved its greatest successes. With record numbers now going to the polls, including nearly nine of ten eligible African-American voters, the fusionists increased their hold on the legislature (and the number of black legislators to eleven), elevated Republican Daniel L. Russell to the governorship, and elected a black man, George H. White, to Congress.[45]

But for African Americans, the results were most visible and pronounced on the local level, where Populist-Republican fusion made considerable gains and, in the eastern counties, black officeholding made a dramatic resurgence. Although no blacks came to serve as sheriffs or superior court clerks and few would serve as county commissioners or registers of deeds, many did win election or appointment to a variety of lesser, though hardly unimportant, posts, especially as magistrates. In Craven County, voters produced perhaps the most startling outcome, choosing blacks for the county commission and the New Bern board of aldermen, and as deputies, constables, register of deeds, high school committeemen, and magistrates (twenty-seven of them for magistrate, to be precise). Throughout the black-majority east there were to be found, along with a handful of black county commissioners, numbers of black postmasters and other federal patronage appointees (thanks to Congressman White), a host of local law enforcement officials, and as many as several hundred school committeemen and magistrates. White supremacist Democrat Furnifold M. Simmons put it differently in his subsequent "Appeal to the Voters of North Carolina": "NEGRO CONGRESSMEN, NEGRO SOLICITORS, NEGRO REVENUE OFFICERS, NEGRO COLLECTORS OF CUSTOMS, NEGROES in charge of white institutions, NEGROES in charge of white schools, NEGROES holdings inquests over white dead. NEGROES controlling the finances of great cities, . . . NEGRO CONSTABLES arresting white women and men, NEGRO MAGISTRATES trying white women and men, white convicts chained to NEGRO CONVICTS, and forced to social equality with them." The bloody backlash would come in the election campaign of 1898 and then in the streets of Wilmington, where armed black Republicans had once chased off the Ku Klux Klan.[46]

Although most North Carolina blacks voted for Republican Daniel Russell in 1896, roughly 20 percent of them supported his Democratic opponent. In states where Republicans did not field an effective ticket, it is likely that the proportion of blacks voting for the Democrats was much larger. In good part, this owed to coercions and submissions: to the manipulations and intimidations that Democrats in the black belt could bring to bear on the electoral process and to the willingness of some African Americans, in the absence of better choices, to placate their white bosses. "It is now pretty generally conceded," one Populist newspaper griped in 1892, "that the Democratic party was saved from defeat in the recent elections in the southern states by its ability to control the negro vote or by its unscrupulous manner of counting that vote once it was cast." Yet we must also recognize that something more may have been at work. The rise of Populist insurgency demanded new mobilizations from the Democrats, who had certainly learned useful lessons about appealing for black votes. Although it was extremely rare for Democrats to advance African Americans for political office, the reformers among them who sympathized with Populist grievances might employ black speakers, reward black supporters, and, most important, address issues of concern to black constituents. In Georgia, Democratic governor William J. Northen, who had belonged to the Alliance and took office in 1890, pushed to increase appropriations for black schools and publicly denounced lynch mobs, threatening to use the state militia to disperse them. Which is to say that black voters could sensibly reject the mostly limited offerings of white Republicans and Populists and side instead with those Democrats prepared to stand against the currents of radical white supremacy. In the end, many African Americans who voted in the 1890s, especially those who resided in the hill-country districts of the Deep South, probably supported Populist candidates at some point. But their support, like the Populist interest in biracialism, tended to be lukewarm and to decline over time.[47]

For it to have been otherwise, the Populists would have had to build on earlier experiments in biracial insurgency and organize rural black communities as those communities saw fit: by winning local black leaders to the Populist cause and encouraging them to cultivate the grass-roots. They needed, that is, to get the help of African Americans like John B. Rayner. Born a slave of mixed parentage in North Carolina in 1850, Rayner gained an education after emancipation and became involved in Republican politics in Reconstruction Edgecombe County, serving as a constable and magistrate. But with his political and economic prospects dimmed by Redemption, he joined the Colored Missionary Baptist Church, was ordained a minister, and then, amid the "exodus fever" that swept the eastern sections of the state in the late 1870s, led a migration of black laborers out to Robertson County, in the Texas black belt. There he taught school, preached, and quietly familiarized himself with county and state politics.[48]

Rayner's lifelong aversion to the Democrats and his experience in Robertson County, which had well-organized Republican and, briefly, Greenback parties, appears to have inclined him to the fledgling Populists. In 1892, he did some local campaigning for them. But few Texas blacks followed his example, dividing their votes instead between rival Democratic claimants to the governorship. One of these had been endorsed by black Republican Norris W. Cuney (the Republicans did not nominate a ticket); the other was the sitting reform governor James S. Hogg, who had curried black support and had a record of opposition to lynching. Beginning in 1894, however, Rayner moved into high gear. Believing that "you must reach the negro through a negro," he traveled tirelessly across east Texas speaking to crowds large and small, stimulating the formation of black Populist clubs, and completing fusion agreements between Populists and Republicans. His reputation as the "Silver-Tongued Orator of the Colored Race" grew apace. "[W]e have a negro speaker who will hold the colored vote to the Republican that he cannot turn to the Populist side," one third-party member said of Rayner, and "he is the ablest speaker for the service I have ever heard. . . . He carries such conviction by his appeals and arguments that few colored men can resist." Steadily, Rayner helped build Populist majorities in at least ten counties, and won black votes to the cause in others.[49]

Rayner likely campaigned in neighboring Grimes County; we know that another black Populist organizer, Melvin Wade, surely did. But there they would have spoken to the converted. Mobilizations among the freedpeople during Reconstruction followed by a decade of Greenback and Independent insurgency during the 1880s composed the foundations of Populism in the 1890s, and enabled Grimes County Populists to achieve on a small scale what the party could not achieve on a larger scale either in Texas or in any other state of the South: a developing coalition of whites and blacks who struggled together to attain and discharge local power. It was a coalition that depended on shared hos-

tility to Democratic rule, on mutual political educations, on the opportunity to occupy the same social and political spaces, and on the fashioning of new political identities. It relied on the courage and political
acumen of white leaders like Garrett Scott, J. W. H. Davis, and J. H.
Teague, and of black leaders like Jim Kennard, Morris Carrington,
and Jack Haynes. And it needed the support of almost the entire black
community. It was a coalition that won power before the advent of
Populism and, owing to its conduct in office, held on to power after
Populism most everywhere else had been left a mere shell. Frustrated
Democrats, led by a defeated candidate for county judge, eventually
decided that paramilitary rather than electoral means would be necessary to reclaim the power that biracial insurgency had denied them.
Thus, following the examples of their counterparts in many other
counties of east Texas, they formed the White Man's Union and commenced a campaign of intimidation. In 1900, in the streets of the small
county seat of Anderson, they brought their campaign to bloody fru-
ition, gunning down much of the Populist leadership, beginning with
the blacks.[50]

❖

The political massacre in Grimes County not only ended Populist rule;
it also ended the tradition of biracial insurgency that had shaped the
county's politics for over two decades, and initiated more than a half-
century reign of power for the White Man's Union. The union's nominees for local office would never suffer electoral defeat, and, at least
in the eyes of the county's whites, became known, not for paramilitarism, but for civic responsibility and governmental reform.[51] Such a
political reinvention was made possible by a newly delimited universe
of official political activity meant to obliterate the world that Radical
Reconstruction had created. For by 1910, in Grimes County, Texas,
and indeed everywhere else in the former Confederacy—whether or
not Populists had tried to fashion a biracial coalition or had mounted
any sort of credible challenge—African Americans had effectively
been driven from political society: from the right to hold office, to
receive the benefits of party patronage, to serve on juries, and, most
consequentially, to cast ballots in local, state, and national elections.
White supremacy was no longer just a rallying cry, a goal, a discourse,

or a description of relations. It had become the very edifice of southern politics.

The removal of African Americans, by constitutional means, from the southern body politic may be seen as the capstone of a lengthy offensive by which white employers and property owners attempted to construct a postemancipation regime of domination and subordination. Beginning with the "black codes" and related legislation enacted under the auspices of Johnsonian Reconstruction, the offensive resumed, albeit unevenly and haphazardly, after the toppling of Republican governments. The most rapid and enduring advances came in the area of labor relations, as post-Reconstruction legislatures and state courts moved to sort out the complexities of the staple-crop economy. Through the adjustment of lien laws and homestead exemption statutes, the adjudication of contract disputes, and the passage of game and stock laws, landowners and in some cases merchants strengthened their leverage over the productive process and the rural surplus, while tenants and especially sharecroppers slipped deeper into dependency. By the mid-1880s across the rural South, landlords had gained first lien on the growing crop for rent and advances, creditors were demanding that debtors waive protection against property seizures, hunting and foraging rights had been dramatically curtailed, and sharecroppers had been relegated to the status of wage laborers, with no claims to the crops that they had cultivated.[52]

Large planters and aspiring rural industrialists also succeeded in using their political clout to commandeer a substantial pool of cheap, coerced black laborers through the leasing of prison convicts and the use of the criminal surety system. Heavily represented in the "modernizing" sectors of the Southern economy, the lessees exploited convicts to build railroads, mine coal and iron, cut lumber, extract turpentine, drain swamps, construct levees, and produce fertilizers, simultaneously enriching themselves and promoting regional "development." At the same time, efforts to restrict black mobility, to bind laborers (not sentenced to penitentiaries) to the estates or to the direct authority of propertyholders, largely proved a failure. Although each of the states enacted anti-enticement statutes, and although the burdens and uses of debt could create circumstances of peonage, their influence was limited. Competition between white employers, struggles on the part of black workers, and the legacy of the Thirteenth Amendment (which ren-

dered "slavery" and "involuntary servitude" unconstitutional) combined to establish precious maneuvering room. The spate of new enticement, emigrant-agent, contract-enforcement, and vagrancy laws
passed by southern legislatures at the turn of the twentieth century
suggests how difficult it was to tie laborers down. Thus, it may be
said that during the age of Jim Crow, a highly repressive regime of
capitalist social relations increasingly engulfed the countryside.[53]

But there occurred, as well, a protracted and, in the end, successful
attack on the standing of African Americans in the official arenas of
southern politics. The attack had two phases. The first commenced
with Redemption in a widespread though uncoordinated manner. Its
principal aim was to weaken black power, place obstacles in the way
of black electoral participation, and wrest control of the balloting process. As best as the circumstances of state politics and federal tolerance
would allow, this could entail the initiation of poll taxes, the gerrymandering of legislative and judicial districts, the encumbrance of registration requirements, the introduction of complicated voting procedures,
and, most important, the centralization of state government authority
over the selection of local election judges, which enabled white Democrats to organize polling venues and count ballots as they thought necessary. Henceforth, poor and illiterate voters would face significant
hurdles, black and dissident candidates for office would have more
trouble winning elections, and Democrats would enjoy a legally sanctioned position from which to intimidate opponents and commit fraud.
Still, in the late 1880s momentum grew for an even more radical and
permanent solution, for "some scheme," as one proponent put it, that
"would effectually remove from the sphere of politics in the state the
ignorant and unpatriotic negro."[54]

The quest for such a "scheme" was driven by a confluence of developments: national, regional, and local. Ever since the 1870s, the middle
and upper classes throughout the United States had been losing faith
in universal manhood suffrage and the democratic political culture that
it nourished. In part, this reflected a growing disillusionment with Reconstruction and an all-too-willing acceptance of the stories about corrupt and incompetent governments that black votes and officeholding
had made possible in the South. But in a larger sense it expressed
fears that the rapid industrialization of the country and the swelling
immigrant working class accompanying it threatened the fate of the

republic. The discourse was of "corruption," "vice," "bossism," and "demogogery," of "honest" government subverted, and the blame fell on enfranchised aliens and proletarians. As social conflict intensified in the 1880s and insurgent labor candidates bid for power in cities and towns across the nation, there were rising calls for "reform," for "purifying" the ballot box, "cleansing" the electorate, and securing "educated men" in their proper place as the governing class. White Southerners who regarded black suffrage as the consummate illegitimacy and the cause of the region's constant turmoil found sympathetic ears and cultural reinforcement in the North and West.[55]

There can, however, be little doubt that the mobilizations and assertions of African Americans across a broad front of political activity in the late 1880s and early 1890s had provoked renewed concerns. The organization of black workers in the cotton and sugar fields, the reinvigoration of black Republicanism in states like Mississippi, Arkansas, and Tennessee, and the early Populist gestures toward biracialism together suggested that white Democrats had not stabilized the political order through statutory and fraudulent means, and that the infrastructures of black politics remained very much intact. In many places, the same grassroots networks and leaders facilitated the work of the Colored Alliance or Knights of Labor *and* the Republican party. As a consequence, constituencies of support—especially among sections of the white elite—began to cohere around the need for more sweeping constitutional revisions. Their rallying cry was "Negro domination": the threat, not so much of direct black power over whites, as of continuing black influence on electoral politics and governance and the openings for insurgent agitation that it made possible. "The question with regard to the colored 'citizens' of South Carolina," the conservative *Charleston News and Courier* pronounced, "is not how to keep them from being elected to office, but how to keep them from voting for other men, white or colored, who are candidates for office and can command their vote."[56]

These provocations were clearly at work in Mississippi, where pressure for black suffrage restriction and other constitutional reforms had been blocked since Redemption by conservatives in the black-majority river counties who, owing to fusion arrangements and advantages in legislative apportionment, believed that the "negro problem" was largely under control. Then, a rapid succession of events in 1888–1889 appears to have shaken their confidence. The national Republican party won control of the presidency and both houses of Congress for the first time since Reconstruction and seemed poised to reimpose federal supervision of southern elections. A "conference of colored men," termed the "largest gathering of its kind ever assembled" in Mississippi, met in Jackson and denounced the violent suppression of the black vote. The black-dominated state Republican party then briefly fielded a full ticket for the first time in years and condemned the hypocrisy of Democrats who howled "Negro domination" but depended on black numbers to exercise disproportionate power in Mississippi and the nation. In Leflore County, Colored Alliance activism evinced a militancy and solidarity that drove white planters to brutal paramilitarism. Within months, a bill providing for a state constitutional convention was racing through the legislature and received the endorsement of the governor; within a year, the convention was in session, the first to gather in the former Confederate states in more than a decade.[57]

There was wide agreement among the delegates, all but four of whom were Democrats and all but one of whom was white, as to the convention's chief object. It was "to devise measures" that would provide "a home government under the control of the white people" and take the blacks "out of politics." But at least two formidable obstacles lay in their path. The measures devised had to be "consistent with the Constitution of the United States," which in the Fifteenth Amendment prohibited denying the "right to vote" on the "grounds of race, color, or previous condition of servitude." And they had to be acceptable to rival party factions: to conservative big planters from the Delta who wished to protect their prerogatives, and to representatives of small planters and farmers from white-majority counties who wished to increase their power and feared that imposing qualifications on the suffrage might injure them. The task was eased by the limited bases of white or biracial insurgency in the state and by franchise precedents already in place. Mississippi had toughened registration requirements in 1876, and the Tennessee legislature had just enacted poll-tax, secret-ballot, and registration laws. In fact, lines of communication with Tennessee had already been opened when the Mississippi convention assembled.[58]

Even so, the delegates hardly seemed sure about how they might "secure a white majority." For a time, they explored proposals to enlarge the white electorate rather than diminish the black one, and they spent more than two weeks debating a plan for modified female suffrage, reflecting currents in the national woman's suffrage movement and anticipating the political logic and discourse of the developing southern variant. But in the end, they legislated "against [the black man's] habits and weaknesses." They used registrars and registration, once the vehicles of black enfranchisement, as the vehicles of black exclusion, and crafted a package of provisions that exploited African-American poverty, illiteracy, and geographical mobility. Thus to qualify, a prospective voter would have to live in the state for two years and the election district for one, to register at least four months before an election, to pay a poll tax of two dollars by February 1 in each of two years preceding an election (a particularly onerous cumulative impost), and "to read" or "to understand" or to "give a reasonable interpretation" of "any section of the [state] constitution" (what was known as an "understanding clause"). The registrar was consequently armed with immense discretionary authority, both to dismiss potentially qualified black voters and, at least in theory, to admit potentially unqualified white voters. So immense was the registrar's discretionary authority that some white Mississippians who favored black disfranchisement nonetheless feared the potential for "fraud," "subterfuge," and "dissatisfaction."[59]

Not even the most enthusiastic of the signatories could claim that Mississippi's new constitution and its franchise provisions represented a groundswell of white popular support. Few white voters bothered to participate in the selection of delegates, and the final document was not submitted for ratification. But the "plan" devised and the dramatic results so rapidly attained (the number of registered black voters plummeted from nearly 190,000 in 1890 to a mere 8,615 in 1892) made it an irresistible model for Democrats in other southern states. Not surprisingly, South Carolina, which closely resembled Mississippi in having a black majority and a weak tradition of white insurgency, held the next convention (1895). In neither state did Populism make much of a showing. Elsewhere, the tenor of political conflict or the scale of political opposition was greater, and the necessary backing for either constitutional conventions (in Louisiana, Alabama, and Virginia) or constitutional amendments (North Carolina, Texas, and Georgia) could not be obtained until very late in the decade or very early in the next century. Nonetheless, the "Mississippi plan," with some variation, was widely embraced.[60]

Although white support for constitutional suffrage restrictions was subdued nearly everywhere in the former Confederacy (only North Carolina, Alabama, and Georgia had referenda, and the turnout was uniformly low), there was a striking absence of significant protest or resistance. The impulse for disfranchisement clearly came from Democratic party leaders, or from leaders of Democratic party factions, who lived in counties or districts with substantial black populations. The local economies that they represented depended on black labor, and they knew firsthand about the disruptions African-American mobilizations might cause. A meeting of Democrats in Virginia's southside Nottoway County in 1900 warned "that while the race question as a political factor is at present under the control of practical conditions," those "conditions are revolutionary in themselves," and "unless adjusted by the organic law, the situation . . . may threaten at any time the supremacy of the Democratic party throughout the whole commonwealth." There, and in the other states, Democrats might fight over the wisdom and effects of particular measures but not over the goal of obliterating the black electorate. Yet what of the insurgents who depended on the votes of humble whites and blacks and whose political prospects would surely suffer too? The record testifies to the limits of their radicalism and the unraveling of their biracialism. For while they rarely joined the charge to disfranchisement, neither did they mount much of a defense against it. The Populist *Dallas Southern Mercury* did denounce the poll tax in the midst of the campaign of 1896, noting that in Mississippi and South Carolina the "poor man, white and black, has been legislated clear out of the right to vote," but many in the rank and file eventually defected. Georgia Populist Tom Watson would become a powerful advocate of black disfranchisement and North Carolina Populist Marion Butler, who worried about the consequences of a proposed constitutional amendment, instead suggested a ban on black officeholding before leading his party into official silence. Ex-Readjuster governor William E. Cameron, who once proposed carrying "Africa" into his "war" against the Funders, played a prominent role in Virginia's constitutional convention of 1901–1902, condemning "negro suffrage as a cancer upon the body politic."[61]

In many states, Democratic intimidation and paramilitarism—the White Man's Union in Texas or the Red Shirt movement of 1898–1900 in North Carolina were conspicuous examples—became part and parcel of the disfranchisement campaign and clearly encouraged white complicity or defeatism. One searches in vain for any strong public voices against the white supremacist storm. The only exceptions were to be found among the intended victims. Acutely aware of the gathering momentum and ferocity of the offensive against them, African Americans struggled to find some way to stem it: to find an ally, a strategy, a means of influencing the discussion and debate. Anger and indignation were widespread, and activity may be detected on a number of fronts. But the murderous atmosphere in much of the countryside, which already had claimed the lives of young militants through lynchings and political repression, produced caution and gave the initiative over to those black leaders most ready to reach an accommodation with whites.[62]

With little hope of derailing the drive for disfranchisement, these black leaders often looked to mitigate the results by aligning with white conservatives, accepting educational or property qualifications, and asking that the qualifications be enacted and enforced in a color-blind fashion. In Mississippi, Isaiah T. Montgomery, the lone black delegate at the constitutional convention, expressed support for efforts to "purify the ballot" and "restrict the franchise to a stable, thoughtful and prudent element of our citizens," even with the "fearful sacrifice" of most black voters, but at the same time challenged white delegates to join him in a quest for racial peace "upon the enduring basis of Truth, Justice, and Equality." On the franchise committee, he opposed the most threatening suffrage proposals and, in full convention, voted against the adoption of the "understanding clause." That he ultimately signed the convention's work owed less to cowardice than to his developing interests and responsibilities, and to the intolerable circumstances in which he found himself. A former slave whose father first managed, then purchased, the 4,000-acre plantation of Joseph Davis, Montgomery had just founded the all-black community of Mound Bayou in the Delta county of Bolivar with the intention of promoting racial self-help, uplift, and autonomy. And he seemed well on his way to doing that with a growing and increasingly prosperous colony. Yet he was also well aware of the escalating repression in the state and could only have felt isolated and vulnerable at the convention: the one other Republican who had actively sought a seat had been assassinated.[63]

African Americans in South Carolina mounted a more substantial and vocal campaign—through the auspices of black ministers and the Republican party—to influence their constitutional convention's proceedings. They succeeded in electing six of the 160 delegates, all from the low country and all well-versed in state and local politics, none more so than William Whipper and Robert Smalls, who had been at it since the earliest days of Reconstruction. In the face of Governor Benjamin Tillman's fulminations about fraud, corruption, and "Negro domination," they defended their claims as rightful citizens, their contributions to the nation's freedom and independence, and their record of governance. Blacks, delegate Thomas E. Miller lectured, "displayed greater conservative force, appreciation for good laws, knowledge for the worth of financial legislation, regard for the rights of his fellow citizens in relation to property and aptitude for honest financial state legislation than has ever been shown by any other people." "We were eight years in power," he said pridefully. "We had built school houses, established charitable institutions, built and maintained the penitentiary system . . . rebuilt the bridges and reestablished the ferries. In short we had reconstructed the state and placed it on the road to prosperity." Robert Smalls boldly submitted to the suffrage committee the provisions from the radical constitution of 1868, and together, the black delegates attacked the convention's franchise scheme as an "act of feudal barbarism," an example of "class legislation," and a "nullification of the fifteenth amendment," taunting the Tillmanites for their hypocrisies. Yet they too ended up proposing literacy and property requirements, offering, as delegate James Wigg pronounced, "the supremacy of law, of intelligence and property" as an alternative to "white supremacy and white degradation."[64]

No other constitutional convention in the former Confederate states had blacks among its delegates, but attempts were made, less conspicuously, to temper the course of radical white racism. In Alabama, Booker T. Washington tried several strategies, including the initiation of a court suit, to influence events. In the spring of 1901, he called a meeting of "representative colored men" and signed their petition to the sitting state convention, which, in supplicating cadences, asked that "the Negro . . . have some humble share in choosing those who shall rule over him." "We beg of your honorable body to keep in mind," the petitioners pleaded, "that as a race, we did not force ourselves upon you," that "we have gotten habits of industry, the English language, and the Christian religion, and at the same time we have tried, in a humble way, to render valuable service to the white man." Admitting that "immediately after the war we made mistakes," they insisted that "we have learned our lesson" and are "not seeking to rule the white man." One of their number soon believed that it might be possible, with clever political manuevers, to register "at least 60000 Negro voters." "I am of the conviction," he told Washington, "that one thing for the Negroes to do is to meet the enemy with the olive branch and beat them at their own game."[65]

This was very much the fear of some disfranchisers: that African Americans would respond to the constitutional challenges by organizing in their "lodges and other secret societies" and "even at the churches and Sunday schools" to pay their poll taxes and ready themselves to " 'answer' every question put to them" by the registrar. Fretting about the need for tighter and more efficient measures, a delegate to the Virginia constitutional convention confided that "Our *negroes more* intelligent, *more money,* & more exposed to *northern inspiration,*" and thus the "chances of being attacked were greater than in Miss. or S.C." Perhaps not. "The only effect of an educational qualification for suffrage," the *Aberdeen Examiner* warned Mississippi's convention delegates in September 1890, "would be to drive thousands of negro men to school." And in the Delta, at least, "night schools for negro men" were reported as being established later that fall, while a black journalist urged his readers to "do away with the midnight dances and cheap excursions . . . and let every negro who can stammer over the alphabet consider himself appointed by the Lord to teach one another of his race so much as he knows." Isaiah T. Montgomery himself lent support to the educational effort in Bolivar County and may have enabled fusion arrangements there and in neighboring Sharkey County to persist for a time. Statewide, the number of registered black voters grew from a scant 8,615 in 1892 to 18,170 in 1899.[66]

Where newly revised constitutions or constitutional amendments were submitted to the voters for ratification, efforts were made to defeat them. In Edgecombe County, North Carolina, a Democratic newspaper complained in July 1900 that blacks were "not only applying

promptly to register, but they usually go to the registrar well schooled"
by "the white fusionists and the local negro bosses." The *Weekly Press,*
published in Mobile, Alabama, urged blacks to "fight the new constitution at the polls, and, if defeated there, carry the matter to the U.S.
Supreme Court." In Georgia, blacks organized a suffrage league in
1908 with the same hope of stimulating a grassroots campaign of registration and opposition. These undertakings and agitations were reflec-
tive of widespread discontent both with the disfranchisement movement and with the willingness of some blacks leaders to accommodate
it. Montgomery came in for angry criticism from blacks in Mississippi
(John R. Lynch most prominently, who instead demanded federal supervision of state elections and the reduction of the state's congressional delegation as mandated by the Fourteenth Amendment) and out,
and more than a few black newspapers, even in the Deep South, expressed "bitterness, indignation, despair, and bewilderment," and
called for "emphatic and continual" protest. One outspoken black Alabama editor, dismayed with the approach of Booker T. Washington,
argued that denying blacks the vote meant taxation without representation and suggested that black property owners refuse to pay their
taxes.[67]

But in truth, there was little that either mobilization or accommodation could achieve, because the few allies that African Americans might
have had either retreated or disappeared. During the 1890s, the U.S.
Congress repealed all of the federal election laws. The Supreme Court
(controlled by northern Republicans) upheld the southern approach to
disfranchisement. New secret ballot laws and prior poll tax statutes
already discouraged black voting. White Populists increasingly fled
from any association with biracialism. And Democratic terrorists
struck where necessary in the rural districts. By the early twentieth
century throughout the former Confederate South, the black electorate
had been reduced to a tiny fraction, the Republican party rendered
virtually insignificant, and the Democrats, by means of black disfranchisement and the white primary, left to fight among themselves over
how to rule their states and localities. The "one-party" Democratic
South had been constructed, and the process of imposing official racial
separation in public life was duly accelerated.[68]

Wherever one stood, it was apparent that a moment of immense
historical importance had arrived, that one historical era had come to

a close and another had been ushered in. "To disfranchise the Negro," a black newspaper correspondent in South Carolina judged at the time of that state's constitutional convention, "is the last act in the bloody drama of intimidation to conquer the southern Negro." In the Alabama black belt, Ned Cobb, who "was a boy [when] I watched em disfranchise the Negro from votin" but still "old enough to look at folks and hear the talk," made the same point with more poignancy. He could remember a time when "they'd always go up . . . to the Chapel Ridge beat, white and colored, to vote," when "the white man would let him vote, wanted him to vote," would "travel around, workin for who they wanted and get the nigger's decision about who they was going to vote for." Cobb understood that votes would be bought, that the white man would be "runnin all about the settlement buyin the niggers' votes," giving "him meat, flour, sugar, coffee, anything the nigger wanted," but he seemed to recognize that even in this relationship power could be operating on both sides. Yet although Cobb "never did hear my daddy" say anything "bout losin the vote," he believed "with all my heart he knowed what it meant." As Cobb "growed to more knowledge," he came to think "that was as bad a thing as ever happened—to disfranchise the nigger." It was like "tellin him he didn't have a right to his thoughts. He just weren't counted to be no more than a dog." The white guardians of Virginia history put it another way. For them, the new constitution of 1902—with its extended residency requirement, cumulative poll tax, and complex "escape" clauses for whites—marked the true end of Reconstruction.[69]

❖

Unable to quell the storm of white supremacy, to halt the violence and repression that seemed to be raining down on them, rural black folk nonetheless refused to sink into the valleys of resignation and fatalism. Their response and protest would not, of course, partake of public militancy and defiance, would not involve a movement to reclaim rights so swiftly stolen from them. There was no longer room for that, even for the bravest and most courageous among them, lest they be suicidal. But the response and protest would draw on deep currents of aspiration and activism, fortified by the belief that their safety and future prospects lay in separating themselves as much as possible from southern whites. It was not that they accepted the destruction of the civil and political rights they had struggled so long and hard to win and retain, nor did they accept or seek accommodation with the official public segregation then being imposed. They regarded all of these developments as despicable indignities and humiliations. It was rather that they saw their survival and growth as families, as communities, and as a people best served by turning inward, by pursuing self-reliance. To this extent, Booker T. Washington articulated a particular version—one designed to gain the financial help and protection of white conservatives, North and South—of sensibilities and goals shared by most African Americans in the countryside, never more so than in the 1890s.

But their responses were not necessarily Washingtonian. Popular interest in African emigrationism (a movement that Washington vehemently opposed) revived dramatically in the mid- to late 1880s. And although that interest could be detected in all of the former Confederate states, some patterns stand out. Blacks in the cities of Hampton, Raleigh, Charlotte, Charleston, Jacksonville, Atlanta, Nashville, Chattanooga, New Orleans, Little Rock, and Galveston sent many inquiries to the offices of the American Colonization Society, reflecting their deepening disenchantment with the segregationism then sweeping over the urban South. But, more generally, the pulse of activity could be felt with special intensity in Arkansas, Mississippi, and Florida. There, emigrationist sentiment had taken hold in the 1870s. There, thousands of black migrants had been flooding in from states (such as the Carolinas) in which emigrationist organizing and discourse had been widespread, some coming in connection with emigrationist projects or as members of "exodus" colonies. There, too, the political and social repression of the period struck with particular force, often against black mobilizations. "[I]n Regards to the negro the times is Getting *very* critical in this *Democratic country*," one black resident of Mississippi County, Arkansas explained in 1892, "our *subsistance are in* they (the *Carcausions*) *Possession* and *money all comes through they hands*. We are very financially *oppressed* and our *Taskes are being Doubled. And we know not what awaits us in the Future*." Across the river in Tunica County, Mississippi, Robert L. Flagg, who claimed that "my only reason for wanting to go [to Liberia] is that our vote is not counted here and our political rights are not regard nor is our legal rights regarded," told of one recent incident as illustration. "A white man came 2 miles the other day and struck a negro who was working for him," Flagg reported, but "the negro stood upon the defence and got the best of the fight that followed. The white man goes to town and gets out a warrant charging the negro with Robery a mob immediately organized to arrest the negro but in reality—to kill him."[70]

As before, the publications and lecturers associated with the American Colonization Society played important roles in stimulating and circulating the idea of African emigration. So too did long-time advocates like the AME Bishop Henry McNeal Turner, who imagined a great black nation emerging in Liberia that would simultaneously uplift the native Africans and fend off new incursions by European imperialists. But, as before, those most likely to respond were poor black farm laborers and tenants concerned less with engaging in civilizationism and resistance against a new form of white supremacy abroad than with simply finding a means of escape from the South. "The Negro in the South . . . is moneyless homeless and he is Friendless," one of them, from Johnson County, Georgia, wrote. "We are . . . lynch and kill. . . . We see No Betterse in the future for the Negro here." "The great question with the Collard in the South," a local organizer in Hamilton County, Tennessee, similarly proclaimed, "is that they are not Able to go Any where." "[H]ow much longer," he asked, "are we to be left hear to suffer and dy and wish to God that there was a Law Passed in the United States to day that would Compell Every collard man to leave the Southern States? . . . we never can live in Peace in the Southern States with the Whytes for they will always wonnt the collard man to look up to them."[71]

It is difficult, if not impossible, to determine how wide the embrace of African emigrationism turned out to be in the 1880s and 1890s. One enthusiastic correspondent in Conway County, Arkansas—sounding very much like Henry Adams—thought it no exaggeration to say, in the summer of 1892, "that there are no less than two million negroes in the South who would leave America, for Africa this Fall, were they able." A more "careful estimate" conducted by the American Colonization Society a year earlier put the number at "one million or more." At the least, there were many more interested parties than the society was prepared to transport, creating a crisis from which the organization would never recover. But one also senses that this time around emigra-

tionist sentiment, while moving through communities of substantial
size, tended to take serious hold among smaller groups of rural families, in good measure because of the immense financial and logistical
hurdles involved. Between 1886 and 1892, the village of Sturgis in
Oktibbeha County, Mississippi, sent 34 people to Liberia; Morrillton,
Arkansas, sent 46; Gainesville, Florida, sent 36; Marengo County, Alabama, sent 16; Fort Mill, South Carolina, sent 15; Conway County,
Arkansas, sent 10; Helena, Arkansas, sent 8; Amorey and Lulu, Mississippi, each sent 4; Columbus, Georgia, sent 7; and Gunnison, Mississippi, sent 2. Lancaster County, South Carolina, stood out in sending
96. In all, about 450 African Americans from the former Confederate
states, together with more than sixty who had recently relocated in
Oklahoma, embarked for Liberia in these years; there would be additional emigrants, perhaps a hundred or two, before interest began to
wane in the mid- to late 1890s.[72]

Yet the separatist impulse manifested itself in other ways. Since the
time of emancipation, some black families and communities had set
out to reconstitute themselves as "colonies" or "towns" in an effort
to establish their independence and integrity in the teeth of white demands for subordination and submission. The challenges usually
proved overwhelming, although fortuitous circumstances—support
from the Union army and Freedmen's Bureau, the generosity of a
former master, the assistance of a sympathetic state agency—could
and did provide a crucial foundation. By the end of Reconstruction,
such settlements were to be found (some on a relatively secure basis),
at such diverse sites as Princeville in eastern North Carolina, Promised
Land in the South Carolina piedmont, and the Cameron plantation in
the Alabama black belt. Then in the mid- to late 1870s, as part of a
developing emigrationism, several black colonies in Kansas were created that were composed of migrants chiefly from the upper South.
But most black towns were launched between 1885 and 1905, both
because black entrepreneurs had by then acquired the necessary capital
and connections and because the conditions of rural life had, for many
African Americans, become increasingly intolerable.[73]

While Oklahoma was at the forefront of this town-building movement (claiming in excess of twenty), most of the towns grew up in
the Deep South. Save for Mound Bayou in the Mississippi Delta,
founded by Isaiah Montgomery and Ben Green in 1887 and supported

by Booker T. Washington, they largely remained in the shadows, little noticed by whites at the time or by historians since, often with names befitting their purposes. There was Freetown, South Carolina; New Rising Star and Klondike, Alabama; Peace, Arkansas; and New Africa, Mississippi. As was true of other emigrationist movements, early residents generally belonged to large family groups, united by strong kinship ties and recruited from the same geographical area. Montgomery and Green were cousins, and the first settlers of Mound Bayou were friends and relatives, most of whom had been slaves of Joseph and Jefferson Davis and then denizens of Davis Bend. Two years earlier, twenty-eight families from Lexington County, South Carolina, under the leadership of William Bookman, established a town (which they would call Bookman) in Grant County, Arkansas.[74]

The black-town movement in Oklahoma was part of a much larger migration of roughly 100,000 African Americans who traveled there from the states to the east and south between 1890 and 1910. More than a few came from the neighboring, and turbulent, state of Arkansas, and some of them may well have considered Liberia as a potential site for relocation. "[T]he peoples are Greatly stirred up in this country about Oklanhoma," the "acting scribe" of a community in Poplar Grove, Arkansas, wrote in June 1892, "but we are bound for [Liberia]." Yet although government sponsored land rushes gave Oklahoma special appeal, the scale of the movement must alert us to a far wider field of demographic activity and social separation: to the early rumblings of what has come to be called "the Great Migration."[75]

Blacks had been moving within and between states of the former Confederate South since the Civil War, and a stream of growing significance started flowing out of the countryside and into cities and towns in the years after Reconstruction. But something new seemed to be happening from the mid-1880s, and especially from the early 1890s, as to volume, direction, composition, and political meaning. To begin with, the numbers leapt substantially as the combined net outmigration of the individual states increased nearly threefold between the 1880s and the 1890s, and then spiked an additional 50 percent between the 1890s and the first decade of the twentieth century. To be sure, many of these migrants moved from one southern state to another, for the most part on a westerly vector; but, especially in the states of the upper South, a northward shift was now in evidence, as thousands of African Americans moved into New York, New Jersey, Massachusetts, Pennsylvania, West Virginia, Ohio, Indiana, and Illinois around the turn of the century.[76]

Black and white observers alike took keen note of the phenomenon, particularly the age profile of those on the move. For there appeared to be a pronounced generational aspect to the migrations. "There is a tendency around Calhoun, [Alabama,]" went a common refrain, "in the young men and women to leave the farms." Without "money enough to think of going North," they headed, first, to nearby towns and cities, hoping for better schools, better economic prospects, and better social circumstances. While the newer commercial and manufacturing centers of the South—Atlanta, Nashville, Charlotte, Lynchburg, and Birmingham—may have held special allure, surges of black population growth also occurred in much smaller places, in close proximity to friends and kin who remained in the agricultural hinterlands. But these, in turn, would become stepping stones on roads leading east, north, and west. When W. E. B. Du Bois conducted a detailed social study in 1897 of Farmville in Virginia's southside, he found that one black family in eight had arrived in the town within the previous five years, that one in three had arrived within the previous ten, and that half had moved there since 1880. "Such a town in the midst of a large farming district," he wrote, "has a great attraction for young countrymen, on account of its larger life and the prospect of better wages in its manufacturing and trading establishments." At the same time, Du Bois discovered that Farmville already acted "as a sort of clearing house" for the "boys and girls" inevitably "attracted by the large city life of Richmond, Norfolk, Baltimore, and New York."[77]

It would be another two decades before the first wave of the Great Migration swept across the South, carrying thousands to the cities of the Northeast and Middle West. Yet the flow in evidence in the 1890s and 1900s should suggest that this movement followed paths carved out imaginatively and directly over many years. Its political character could be clearly and painfully apparent, as in Grimes County, Texas, where the violent seizure of power by the White Man's Union in 1900 sparked an "exodus" of hundreds (perhaps one-third) of the black inhabitants. More commonly, the politics were to be found in smaller-scale rejections of the hardships, humiliations, and coercions that black migrants believed whites were determined to inflict on them and in the established institutions and social networks that were their vehicles of change. Theirs was a response "to the totality of their experience in the South." In their own way, that is, the first generation of African Americans born and bred in freedom began to construct and enact a dream of community reconstitution much as their parents had struggled to do at the dawn of emancipation.[78]

❖

But African Americans did not have to leave the rural South or formally organize a black town in order to pursue important measures of a community dream. There remained very powerful attachments, even among freedom's first generation, to people, to place, and more generally to the land. And despite the terror and repression of the century's last decades, there had been significant gains and social achievements over time. Often ignored or overlooked—obscured by more vivid and tumultuous setbacks—these gains created dense webs of black community life in many parts of the rural South, giving tangible meaning to the notion of uplift through social separation and testifying to the value of their many and varied mobilizations.

Perhaps the most remarkable gain, especially in view of the economic and political obstacles put in the way, was the acquisition of land. By the turn of the twentieth century, more than one in five African-American "farm operators" in the South owned some or all of the soil they tilled, and the proportion was considerably higher in certain parts of the region. Prospects for black landownership were more favorable in the upper and border South (Virginia, Florida, North Carolina, Arkansas, Tennessee, and Texas) than in the Deep South—especially in Virginia, where nearly 60 percent of black farm operators had become owners. Within states, prospects were best in those counties and districts where blacks were in the minority and land values (and therefore prices) were lowest. But even in the Deep South, and in the plantation districts of those states, accumulations of real and personal property grew steadily, if slowly. In Georgia, which had the smallest proportion of owners among black farm operators (14 percent) of any former Confederate state, the land acreage owned by blacks nearly tripled while its value nearly quadrupled between 1875 and 1900. Significant increases were registered during this period in the heart of the plantation belt, as well as in the wiregrass and pine barrens of the southeast and in the hill country of the northwest. In Burke County (80 percent black), black-owned acreage quadrupled; in Greene County (69 percent black), it nearly tripled; and in Macon County (70 percent black), it more than doubled. Throughout the rural South, by 1900, a substantial portion of the African-American population (77 percent in the upper and border South, 35 percent in the Deep South, 53 percent overall) lived in counties in which at least 20 percent of the black farm operators owned land.[79]

The process of land acquisition followed no single course, and it could vary as to crop culture, demography, economic cycles, local culture, and politics. In some cases, white patronage and ancestry proved critical; in others, the economic woes or seasonal labor requirements of white owners; and in still others, the low population density and general availability of vacant land. But everywhere land ownership demanded the toleration and involvement of white people; and almost always, it demanded a protracted and precarious effort on the part of black households and, often, extended black families. In Alabama, Ned Cobb "watched and scuffled four years first one way then another— makin baskets, cuttin stove wood for people—until I could buy me a mule so I could rent me a little land and go to work and run my own affairs." Then, with the help of his wife, children, and nephew, he could "come up from the bottom" and pay "cash rent," making a "heavier crop," a "better crop," a "profit from my farmin," to be supplemented by hauling logs, cultivating provisions, blacksmithing, and, on occasion, subrenting a portion of the tract he had leased. But the Cobb family still had to endure this for fifteen years—and in the face of many trials and setbacks—before they managed to buy the eighty-acre Pollard place. Even then, the land "was so rough" that Ned had to rent "some smooth land in the piney woods" to keep afloat. In Natchitoches Parish, Louisiana, Daniel and Rose Trotter, with the aid of two nephews, one niece, and some other kin (they had no surviving children of their own), also labored for fifteen years as renters on at least five different plantations until they could purchase, in 1900, thirty-five acres on the "lower end of the Tatum Place." The "cash-books" that Daniel so meticulously kept reveal what it took for them to accumulate the $700 used as a down payment: picking cotton, selling eggs, raising chickens, sewing dresses, and blacksmithing, year in and year out.[80]

The experiences of the Cobbs and the Trotters suggest that literacy (in the Cobbs' case, Ned's wife Hannah; in the Trotters' case, at the least Daniel) was vital to the task of acquiring land, both in marshaling the necessary resources and in defending against the fraudulent practices of employers and creditors. Trotter appears to have recorded every bale of cotton the family produced, every odd job he and other members of his household performed, every cent they earned for years. But the experiences also suggest that landownership took place in a context of relationships involving family, neighbors, and community institutions, and cannot be understood apart from them. Longtime residents of the Cane River section of Natchitoches Parish, the Trotters belonged to St. Mary's Baptist Church, as well as to the church's benevolent association (organized "to benefit Our Selves and permote the Genal welfair to Our Selves and Our posterity"). Together with depending on the labor of kinfolk, they engaged in many social and economic exchanges with other members of the church: with the Loves, the Golstons, the Stewarts, the Adamses, the Paytons, the Maslands, the Dicksons, and the Monroes, some of whom lived very close by, principally as tenant farmers.[81]

Like the Cobbs and the Trotters, the holdings of most black landowners tended to be small. The great majority included far fewer than 100 acres, and usually fewer than 50 or even 25 acres. But rather than being scattered vulnerably across the countryside, the holdings generally occurred in clusters of two or more, and were commonly delimited by kinship as much as proximity. The clustered farms, that is, would be owned by members of extended families, and in turn became the hubs around which larger enclaves (often kin-based as well) of tenants, croppers, and laborers took shape, usually in close connection to a church. "As a rule," W. E. B. Du Bois observed of Newton County, Georgia, in 1899, "the Negroes live in neighborhoods by themselves," and in the country surrounding the town of Covington, "there are many small communities composed entirely of Negroes, which form clans of blood relatives."[82]

Black neighborhoods and enclaves such as these offered welcome distance, and some semblance of safety, from regular contacts with whites—so long as they did not seem threatening—and on occasion they moved quite deliberately to constitute themselves as virtually self-sustaining communities. Thus, in the early twentieth century, several families of Archers in the hills just outside of the Mississippi Delta established what they called a "family rent group" and leased a hilltop of more than four hundred acres known to them as the "Place." Led by their "patriarch," John Perry Archer, who also happened to be a Baptist minister, they not only produced cotton and corn but also planted potato, vegetable, and orchard crops, tended livestock, and built smokehouses and a blacksmith shop. As best as possible, they avoided borrowing and faithfully paid all of their bills on time so as to keep white creditors—and much of the "outside world"—at bay. When, therefore, one of the Perrys traveled to Mound Bayou to hear Booker T. Washington speak, he found much with which to agree, but adamantly rejected Washington's "philosophy of casting down one's bucket wherever one was." "This smacked of the white man's idea that black people should be satisfied with what they had," he charged, "rather than make any attempt to better themselves."[83]

The cohesiveness and self-consciousness of the families on the "Place" may have been a rarity in the rural South of the late nineteenth and early twentieth centuries. But the petty accumulations of land and personal property that African Americans had struggled mightily to attain, as well as the tendency of landlords in many of the plantation districts to move their residences to nearby towns, clearly created a basis for variations. Even in "forlorn and forsaken" Dougherty County, in Georgia's southwestern cotton belt, where the rack-renting remnants of an older plantation regime seemed to be squeezing everything but the life out of ten thousand black denizens, W. E. B. Du Bois found that most had lifted themselves out of the "submerged tenth" of sharecroppers and that somewhat more than an "upper tenth" had become cash renters and freeholders. Black-owned acreage in the county had increased from 752 in 1875 to over 10,000 in 1900, while the value of all black property more than tripled. Three-quarters of the black landowners had purchased their holdings during the 1890s. A few, perhaps, anchored the "hundred cabin homes" surrounding Shepherd's church, "a great whitewashed barn of a thing," where, "of a Sunday," five hundred worshippers "from far and near" would gather "to talk and eat and sing." There, too, was a schoolhouse, "a very airy, empty shed," which could still be regarded as an "improvement" over the usual practice of holding school in the church. And back of it was a "lodge-house two stories high and not quite finished" where "societies to care for the sick and bury the dead" would meet: societies, Du Bois noted, that "grow and flourish."[84]

Grow and flourish they did. Following the earlier lead of urban areas, the rural South experienced, during the last two decades of the nineteenth century a remarkable "thickening" of African-American civic and associational life. Despite the financial burdens that became even more cumbersome after Reconstruction, blacks managed to scrape together resources and build churches, open schools, and establish benevolent societies across the countryside. The results could be seen in fairly isolated black settlements, at crossroads villages, and in small county seats. Of the nearly sixty black churches that would eventually be found in Panola County, Mississippi (43 Baptist, 15 Methodist, and 1 Primitive Baptist), only six were located in the towns of Sardis, Como, or Batesville, but virtually all could boast a Sunday school and a women's missionary society. The Tuskegee Negro Conference of 1893 received reports from "little country settlements" in Alabama of the hundreds of dollars raised for schools and of efforts to extend the school year "from the three months allowed by the county to four and five months." In organizing a school in Utica, Mississippi, the educator William H. Holtzclaw met every Monday night with a group of black farmers, nearly all of whom were tenants. Visiting black neighborhoods in Covington, Georgia, W. E. B. Du Bois discovered, in addition to four churches, "a beneficial society twenty years old which owns some property; a lodge of Masons, and one of Odd Fellows."[85]

This may help account for an enormous explosion in the publication of African-American newspapers and religious journals between 1890 and 1910, one that far surpassed in both number and scope anything that had happened before. Most of the papers were issued from larger cities, but a growing number across the South were published in smaller towns for the benefit of a largely rural readership. Commonly claiming two to three hundred subscribers at one dollar per year, the papers circulated more widely still, as they were passed from hand-to-hand and household-to-household, and read aloud in groups. There were, to name just a few, the *Staunton Valley Index* and the *Pulaski*

Enterprise in Virginia; the *Shreveport Record* and the *Lake Charles Searchlight* in Louisiana; the *Hot Springs Crystal* and the *Forest City Herald* in Arkansas; the *Opelika People's Choice* and the *Selma New Idea* in Alabama; and the *Eatonton Blade* and the *Valdosta Afro-American Mouthpiece* in Georgia.[86]

But the picture is fullest and most revealing for the poor and over-whelmingly rural state of Mississippi. For there, in the twenty-year period following the constitutional convention of 1890, African Americans published nearly 150 newspapers and journals in forty-four counties, chiefly (110) outside the cities of Jackson, Vicksburg, Natchez, and Biloxi. Attala County had two, Bolivar County twelve, Chickasaw County four, Coahoma County four, Holmes County five, Leflore County four, Marshall County five, Pike County four, Washington County fourteen, and Wilkinson County two. In the hard years after disfranchisement, at least fourteen of the papers publicly claimed loyalty to the Republican party.[87]

Politics thus continued to be pursued in all of its former venues, though there were necessarily significant reorientations. Especially in southern towns and cities with developing black middle classes ("better" classes, as they would have identified themselves), it may well have been that the exclusion of black men from the official arenas of politics in the 1890s and early 1900s brought about a shift in the gender dynamics of social and political life. New voice and authority appears to have been lent to black women who, for years, had been actively involved in community mobilizations through churches, schools, charitable organizations, and auxiliaries, not to mention Union Leagues, Republican parties, and benevolent societies. There can be little doubt that, in the highly charged atmosphere of segregation and lynching, black women were perhaps best suited to act as what has been termed "ambassadors" to white society and what was left of an "interracial public sphere." Disfranchisement may well have ended that role for the local black bosses and other male intermediaries who had helped negotiate the complex world of post-Reconstruction electoral politics.[88]

But such a shift in gender dynamics is not nearly so evident in the rural areas. Indeed, what we can see in the wake of disfranchisement is less a shift of gender participation and authority than one in the fields of activity: away from political parties and elections and even more decidedly toward churches, schools, and lodges as means of community definition, sustenance, and reproduction. This is not surprising. It should only remind us of how interconnected the male-dominated official arenas of politics were with the more diverse and inclusive arenas of African-American public life. There was, in other words, not so much a stepping back of the men and a stepping forward of the women as a necessary redeployment to terrain in which both had recognized roles and authority, although the roles and authority still tilted power and leadership toward the men.

In Edgecombe County, North Carolina, blacks had been building local institutions since Reconstruction. They built churches, public and private schools, all-black teacher organizations, church-and-community-supported normal schools, and fraternal orders replete with women's auxiliaries and youth groups. By the time of disfranchisement, these institutions composed a formidable and intermeshed infrastructure of social and political engagement. Republican party activists and officeholders belonged to, and generally led, lodges of the Masons, Good Templars, Odd Fellows, Elks, and Knights of Pythias, and in a couple of cases edited local newspapers. Church congregations, whose members were predominately female, along with women's auxiliaries and benevolent associations, spoke regularly to the issues of the day, aiding mobilizations and recommending courses of action.[89]

In Edgecombe County, and in most other parts of the rural South after disfranchisement, blacks turned a face of moderation and ostensible deference to the outside world of whites, quite mindful of the power that whites had, and were ready to, unleash. They often took their cues from Booker T. Washington in emphasizing that education, industry, solidarity, and economic self-sufficiency would not only nourish their communities but also offer the best chance for ultimately regaining their political and civil rights. "The wiser heads among our people can hardly fail to see," the *Helena* (Ark.) *Reporter* announced in 1900, "that our political preferment must not precede but follow our advancement in other walks of life." Increasingly marginalized by the state and local governments, their "ambassadors" had little to negotiate. Their chief responsibilities were to arrange labor contracts and tenancy agreements with white employers, to obtain goods and credit from white merchants, and perhaps to purchase land from a white property owner. And so, the "ambassadors" were more likely to be men than women. If anything, they sought to keep these contacts to a minimum, avoiding as much as possible the trip to town where, as Ned Cobb learned, the indignities and vulnerabilities of Jim Crow were most likely to be felt.[90]

Yet beyond the shadows, African Americans in the rural south struggled among themselves to reckon and respond. At times, the struggles could become intense and divisive, based as they often were not only in conflicting sensibilities but also in rival kinship groups and community institutions that set clan against clan and lodge against church.[91] But in the process, they also sustained and enhanced, with immense fortitude and creativity, a political culture deeply rooted in the period of their enslavement and early freedom; and in so doing, they constructed, simultaneously, launching pads for the Great Migration North and foundations for new forms of activism within the South.

EPILOGUE

"UP, YOU MIGHTY RACE"

The migration of a million and a half African Americans from the South to the North between 1915 and 1930 initiated a new era in black—and American—political life. Once overwhelmingly southern, the African-American population would become national; once overwhelmingly rural and agricultural, it would become urban and industrial; once overwhelmingly subject to formal and informal repression, coercion, and exclusion, it would find precious new space for civic and political activism. The results would be seen not simply in the extension and reconstitution of black communities, but also in the changing social and political face of the country as a whole. Many of the landmark political developments of twentieth-century America—electoral realignments, the New Deal, industrial unionism, the Great Society, and, of course, the battle for civil rights—would be difficult to imagine outside of this massive demographic shift that then continued, and accelerated, over the next three decades.

Yet the Great Migration not only allowed for the construction of newly vibrant political arenas; it also served as a large and powerful political transmission belt that moved and redeployed the experiences, expectations, institutions, and networks crucial to the early shape and character of the arenas themselves. African Americans may have carried no more valuable and consequential baggage as they headed from countryside to town, from town to city, and from South to North and West than their political sensibilities and know-how: the ways they had come to understand the world, define their goals, and mobilize their energies. Together, these intellectual and cultural possessions mediated their encounters with new settings, people, and projects—some involving other recent arrivals of African descent. And together, they made for a remarkable moment of consciousness and convergence in the 1920s, now national in scope, that looked back on nearly a century of political education and struggle while at the same time marking political courses for the future.

The Great Migration is commonly understood as the product of a very specific set of circumstances that coalesced in the mid-1910s, chiefly as a result of the First World War. The war created, simultaneously, a massive industrial labor shortage in the Northeast and Midwest owing to conscription and the interruption of European immigration, and a massive demand for industrial production owing to militarization. For the first time in the nation's history, meaningful employment outside of the South beckoned for large numbers of African Americans and, encouraged by labor recruiters, railroad companies, and a climate of repression at home, thousands responded with their feet. But we must remember that a northward shift in black migration was already in evidence in the 1890s, and that it was closely connected to a substantial trend, beginning in the 1880s, that took growing numbers—sometimes temporarily, sometimes permanently—from the rural districts to the towns and cities of the South, and from plantations and farms to lumber camps, sawmills, turpentine camps, and coal mines stretching from the Atlantic and Gulf Coasts up through the Appalachians.[1]

These demographic phenomena were certainly consequences of economic transformations and dislocations felt in much of the rural world of the Americas, Europe, Africa, and south Asia, and cannot be understood apart from them. Yet there also appeared to be a pronounced self-consciousness that compels us to see them as social and political, as well as economic and demographic, movements: as searches for new circumstances of life and labor, new sites of family and community building, new opportunities to escape economic dependence, often initiated by the first generation of African Americans to grow up in freedom. It can hardly be accidental that these movements began to erupt at a time when emigrationist activity was acquiring a mass base, when small-scale exoduses were being carried out, and when black towns began to multiply. Indeed, if we consider the Great Migration as a process, we can detect striking resemblances to the grassroots emigrationism of an earlier period.

Like the emigrationism of the 1870s and 1880s, the Great Migration reflected collective sensibilities, social networks, organizational activism, and circuits of communication and deliberation. From the outset, African Americans widely imagined their moves as family and community strategies, and, even when departing as individuals, they laid out links in a developing chain of kin, neighbors, and friends that would guide and support those who followed. By the mid-1910s, they had built substantial bases across the urban South, and had established beachheads in the urban North. Back and forth along the chains flowed people, resources, and information about living conditions, job prospects, and the civil and political atmosphere. Letters, reverse migrations, and visitations alike told rural folk what they might expect and who might help them in Atlanta and Birmingham, Norfolk and Nashville, Harlem and Pittsburgh, Cleveland and Chicago. But the reverberations would also be heard through more extended circuits, new and old. Black railroad workers—sleeping car porters, cooks, dining car waiters, freight handlers, and track hands—employed by the Illinois Central, the Louisville and Nashville, the Southern, and the Seaboard Air Line railroads brought stories, handbills, and newspapers such as the *Chicago Defender* and the *Pittsburgh Courier,* which gained a growing readership in the South. The newspapers, together with rumors about the North, the South, and the war, then traveled farther into the rural areas, doubtless following circuits that had previously carried the *African Repository* and, earlier still, anticipations of land and emancipation.[2]

Again as was true of grassroots emigrationism, the circuits of communication that helped facilitate the Great Migration had important institutional connectors that enabled wider dissemination. Churches, benevolent societies, lodges, and local associations became centers of discussion and debate, places where newspapers and letters could be read aloud, rumors assessed and validated. In some cases—the precedent of emigrationism once more comes to mind—migration clubs were formed to pool resources and lend the undertaking greater effectiveness. Club organizers were generally African Americans with some education, resources, and influence, although this time women were among them, perhaps because they were more likely than men to go straight from the rural or small-town South to the North. At the same time, their efforts provoked divisions and tensions, often of the kind of which Henry Adams had once complained, between established ministers, businessmen, professionals, and self-designated race spokesmen on the one side, who, like Booker T. Washington, urged blacks to remain in the South, and humbler folk and the leaders closest to them on the other, who, with new urgency and expectation, looked to the North.[3]

The chains of migration allowed for family and community reconstitution, as urban blocks and neighborhoods, often taking shape around transplanted storefront churches, became magnets for African Americans who had lived in the same rural districts or small towns of the South. Difficult transitions were thereby eased and enclaves of familiarity established in an otherwise unfamiliar environment. But by making dense concentrations of blacks in sections of northern cities, the migrations also created new meeting grounds, new political and cultural encounters between black people who had lived in different parts of the South, different parts of the country, and different parts of the world. During the very period of the Great Migration, thousands of people of African descent, chiefly from the Caribbean, arrived in the United States. Responding to economic distress, natural disasters, and changes in colonial policies, they traveled from Barbados, Cuba, Puerto Rico, St. Kitts, Nevis, Antigua, Montserrat, and Jamaica principally to the Northeast, and, in greatest numbers, to New York. What then developed seemed reminiscent of the political contact zones previously found in the contraband camps and Union army units of the Civil War and, even before, in the port cities and hinterlands of the late-eighteenth and early-nineteenth-century Atlantic.[4]

The most politically significant of the contacts and encounters made possible by the streams of migration involved an African Jamaican named Marcus Garvey and his organization, the Universal Negro Improvement Association (UNIA). An artisan and political agitator from rural St. Ann's Bay who spent time in Kingston and London, Garvey came to New York in 1916 along with the early waves of migrants from the South. Almost immediately, he set off on a year-long, thirty-eight-state speaking tour of the nation, but then returned to Harlem where he established a UNIA branch and, a little over a year later, began to publish a newspaper, the *Negro World*. By the early 1920s, the membership of UNIA numbered in the many thousands, and Garvey's following in the United States alone may have exceeded one million. Ultimately encompassing forty-two countries and colonies, mainly in the Caribbean, Latin America, and Africa, Garvey's has been judged the largest and most powerful pan-African movement the world has seen.[5]

Although relatively little is known about the social base of Garvey's movement in the United States, it seems to have been attractive to the first generation of southern migrants to the urban North. In part, its appeal owed to the moment of encounter, a moment when racial discrimination became fully inscribed in the bureaucracy of the federal government, when ferocious racist violence exploded North and South, and when a deep sense of alienation was to be found among black Americans even as they struck out in search of new possibilities. But the attraction may have had more to do with a profound resonance between the experiences and sensibilities of many southern blacks and the ideas and culture of Garvey and the UNIA. Organizationally, Garvey honored the black struggle against slavery, the practices of black institutional life, and the religious fervor that could infuse black community events. Annual UNIA conventions were held on August 1, the anniversary of British slave emancipation, and the meetings of local chapters employed rituals highly evocative of Union Leagues and, especially, fraternal and benevolent societies, with their oaths and pledges, their use of UNIA's *Constitution and Book of Laws*, and, on occasion, their resplendent quasi-military displays. Garvey similarly incorporated religious, indeed messianic, language and style into his speeches and convocations, preaching personal as well as collective redemption, so that his Sunday evening meetings were likened to conversion experiences and he came to be regarded as a black Moses. Ideologically, Garvey tapped long-developing traditions of thought and aspiration as he tried to construct a newly expansive race consciousness.[6]

Garvey is best known as an advocate of African repatriation, and this alone would have made his voice familiar to those from the rural South. Yet he managed to tie repatriation not only to a grim, and for many blacks realistic, assessment of their prospects in the United States, but also to a notion of revitalization that did not necessarily require repatriation itself. Influenced by Booker T. Washington's ethic of self-help and material improvement, as well as by nineteenth-century "civilizationism," Garvey nonetheless rejected the possibility of a meaningful accommodation with whites. Only when blacks could claim an independent and formidable African nation of their own would they be able to prosper and achieve rights and respect either there or anywhere else; only by redeeming Africa from white domination could a black race fully make and redeem itself. "We may make progress in America, the West Indies and other foreign countries," Garvey wrote, "but there will never be any real lasting progress until the Negro makes of Africa a strong and powerful Republic to lend protection to the success we make in foreign lands." He therefore called for agitation and collective struggle toward that end, electrifying audiences with a sense of their potential might, with the likelihood of allies in China, India, Egypt, and Ireland, and with the notion that they could again harness the forces of history.[7]

Garvey's ideas were sweeping and internationalist, remarkably bold in the vision of racial solidarity and identity that they offered. But they also seemed very close to a great many African Americans, especially to those from the South. In various forms, the ideas had been advanced by Paul Cuffe, David Walker, Henry Highland Garnet, Martin Delany, and Alexander Crummell, by major intellectuals and organizers who had begun to mark out the terrain of repatriation, civilizationism, and pan-Africanism. But they had also been nourished, very much at the grassroots, by the black ministers who met with William T. Sherman in Savannah, Georgia, in 1865, by Tunis Campbell and Henry McNeal Turner, by Henry Adams, Samuel Perry, and the local emigrationists, by Ned Cobb in Alabama and the Archers in Mississippi, by those who believed that separatism, self-governance, family and community uplift, racial solidarity, and perhaps relocation were necessary to the success of their struggles. Indeed, Garvey and his movement may well have allowed their many ideas to come together in a particular way, to make particular sense at a particular time, to be interpreted and energized anew, with a scope and power previously impossible. "It was when the Garveyites spoke fervently of building their own country, of someday living within the boundaries of a culture of their own making," recalled Richard Wright, himself a Mississippian who migrated to Chicago, "that I sensed the passionate hunger of their lives, that I caught a glimpse of the potential strength of the American Negro."[8]

The reach and significance of this moment of political consciousness are, however, most apparent when we consider the geography of Garveyism. For although Garvey's movement is generally understood to have taken hold largely in the black urban North, its most extensive bases were in fact to be found in the rural and small-town South. By the mid-1920s, about half of all UNIA divisions were located in the southern states (more than in the Northeast and Midwest combined), chiefly in a great arc from Virginia down the southeastern seaboard, through the Deep South, and up again into the lower Mississippi Valley. Louisiana ranked first with seventy-five divisions, followed by North Carolina (61), Mississippi (56), Virginia (43), Arkansas (42), Georgia (35), Florida (30), South Carolina (25), and Alabama (14). As might be expected, Atlanta and Savannah, New Orleans and Baton Rouge, Raleigh and Charlotte, Norfolk and Richmond all had organizational activity. But by far the greatest pulse was felt in the countryside: in Blytheville, Cotton Plant, Earl, Hughes, and Postelle, Arkansas; in Adel, Camilla, Fitzgerald, Limerick, and Ty Ty, Georgia; in Armistead, Brusly, Clouterville, Hymel, Mareno, Natchitoches, and Trinity, Louisiana; in Aberdeen, Clarksdale, East Mound Bayou, Greenville, Shelby, and Vance, Mississippi; in Acme, Gaylord, Kinston, Parmele, Spencer, and Windsor, North Carolina; in Arringdale, Capron, Kenbridge, Roxbury, and Tabbs, Virginia. Of the roughly four hundred UNIA divisions that can be identified in the region, well over three hundred (more than 80 percent) were in locations such as these.[9]

The process by which UNIA spread across the rural South remains to be studied, but the circulation of the *Negro World*, itself made possible by the Great Migration, appears to have played a crucial role. The newspaper began to reach rural areas by late 1920 and spread about thereafter. Those who gravitated to Garvey's message and then led the work of local organizing seem to have been older, predominately male, farmers and tenants who were literate, had financial ties, and were mostly longtime denizens. Like many African Americans who headed North, they had been hardened to the pervasiveness of white racism and had no illusions about the prospects of integration. The perspective of the fledgling National Association for the Advancement of Colored People (NAACP) therefore had little appeal (and the NAACP had little interest in moving outside of the urban South, where it recruited among a sympathetic black middle class), whereas Garvey's views comported with their own experiences. Yet unlike many African Americans who headed North, they had more substantial roots and obligations, would have found it more difficult to leave, and had determined to pursue their objectives and defend their dignity where they already lived.[10]

The UNIA chapters that they built often had modest-sized memberships, although acquaintance with Garvey became far more widespread owing to the *Negro World*, word-of-mouth, and communication networks linked to migrants in the urban North. Local UNIA meetings generally took place in churches (depending on the views of the minister), lodges, or farmhouses, and although the leaders tended to be men, women also assumed important roles as officers and correspondents. Relative secrecy in the conduct of business was undoubtedly desirable—although probably not essential because UNIA did not engage in a confrontational politics that would threaten or unsettle neighboring whites. Indeed, UNIA in the rural and small-town South may be regarded as a political underground of activity and education, rarely attracting public notice—Garveyites in the South did not generally stage the parades, processions, and mass assemblies that were common to the movement in the North—which is why it has largely escaped later scholarly detection. At all events, Garvey seems to have attracted a following in these areas that remained remarkably loyal despite the scandals and internecine struggles that quickly surrounded him.[11]

But popular attraction to Garvey and UNIA may well have had an even deeper history. Garveyism was not simply a movement of the rural and small-town black South. It was a movement that appeared to take special hold in sections of the rural and small-town black South where emigrationism had developed a base of support more than four decades earlier. UNIA divisions, spread as they were throughout the region, therefore tended to cluster in southeast Virginia and eastern North Carolina, in southwest Georgia, and in the delta and surrounding areas of Mississippi and Arkansas. And they were most numerous of all across black Louisiana, where Henry Adams had lived, labored, and organized for much of his life.[12]

Garveyism became the most important intellectual and political thoroughfare to popular forms of what we call black nationalism in twentieth-century America. The routes have yet to be fully elaborated—Elijah Muhammed who grew up the son of a preacher and sharecropper in Washington County, Georgia, and lived in Macon during the early 1920s, and Malcolm X, whose Garveyite father was born and raised in Taylor County, Georgia, are only among the best-known examples—but they surely would help us understand how nationalist ideas have developed so powerfully in African-American political thought and culture, especially among workers and the poor. These ideas emphasize, in varying degrees, the centrality of race and racism as markers of experience in American society, the importance of black self-determination as a goal and vehicle of change, and the perils of seeking alliances outside of the African-American community. They often assign Africa a special place in historical memory and destiny, and generally embrace some version of pan-Africanism. They are not so much state-oriented as group-oriented, not so much about nationhood as about peoplehood, not so much about structures as about solidarities. And they have left their imprint, often decisively, on every significant black social and political movement for the past eighty years.[13]

Yet even more broadly, Garveyism exemplified the vitality and adaptability of popular "organizing traditions" whose genealogies extend deep into the history of slavery and early emancipation. For a long time, these traditions were cultivated underground, out of the view of white slaveowners and the public world of politics and civic life, to be transmitted generationally as family and community resources, as growing funds of knowledge. With emancipation, they began to come to public light, expand and develop formal institutional bases, cross into new arenas of activity, and carve out new circuits of mobilization and communication. They established sufficiently strong foundations to withstand the terrors and onslaughts of Reconstruction and the emerging era of Jim Crow, leaving a far denser network than anything that had been known before. But the underground not only remained important; by the early twentieth century it appeared to assume an increasingly encompassing character as black communities turned ever inward, avoiding as much as possible the gaze and potential fury of whites, though it was ready to generate new rounds of activism as changing circumstances might allow.[14]

The Arkansas Delta offers a compelling example of how, even in the face of demographic volatility, these traditions may have been replenished and, at different points, enabled political mobilization. In 1919, amid postwar labor struggles that engulfed both sides of the Atlantic, black sharecroppers and tenants in Phillips County joined the Progressive Farmers and Household Union of America in an effort to secure better settlements from their landlords. Many of the black workers already belonged to fraternal societies, and the union appeared, in its rituals and conduct, very much like one of them. But this was not the first time that Phillips and the surrounding counties had given rise to African-American activism. During Reconstruction, black Republicans elected local officeholders and representatives to the state legislature. Soon thereafter, two of the legislators, one from Phillips County and one from neighboring Monroe County, helped spark an emigration movement that began with a convention at the Third Baptist Church of Helena (the seat of Phillips County) and eventuated in the formation of the Liberian Exodus Arkansas Colony. In the late 1880s, the Knights of Labor established two local assemblies (and at least ten others nearby), and in 1891, the Colored Farmers' Alliance organized a cotton pickers' strike in Lee County, just north of Phillips.[15]

The Progressive Farmers and Household Union, seeking legal redress and contemplating a strike in 1919, provoked a murderous response from Phillips County planters that has come to be called the Elaine Massacre. The survivors may then have joined one of the numerous UNIA chapters that sprouted up in the area during the 1920s, five or more in Phillips County alone. Some did become actively involved with the Southern Tenant Farmers' Union (STFU) in the mid-1930s, and they brought important things with them. "Because of his long experience in other organizations such as churches, burial, fraternal organizations and the like," a white STFU founder wrote in explaining the political acumen he saw among the black members, "the

Negro generally knows how to run meetings as they should be run." Their traditions would later be carried by some of the younger black STFU faithful, women and men alike, into the local movement for civil rights.[16]

Political traditions and genealogies such as these may be identified almost endlessly over time and space in the South. They became embedded in long-established communities, branched out across the countryside, and, especially with the rural enclosures of the Depression decade, which left many thousands of tenants and sharecroppers evicted from plantations, swept into towns and cities. Kept vital by family stories, shared memories, and ongoing struggles, they offered knowledge, fortitude, and creativity as new possibilities arose. Ella Baker, who grew up in Norfolk, Virginia, and rural North Carolina in the early twentieth century and eventually helped found both the Southern Christian Leadership Conference (SCLC) and the Student Nonviolent Coordinating Committee (SNCC), very much embodied them. She learned that her maternal grandparents had been slaves, and that soon after emancipation her grandfather had purchased 250 acres of his old plantation, which he then parceled out in small tracts to other family members, constructing an enclave of kinship in which Baker spent much of her youth. She learned, as well, that he pastored the community church, mortgaged his own land to provide for local people in need, felt pride in his blackness, and would submit to no indignity. "[In] my grandpa's community there was a sense of independence," she remembered. "When they were beginning to permit the Negroes to vote after Emancipation, he and his sons got into quite a battle with somebody who called him 'nigger.' You see, they would fight back . . . [and] it provided you with a sense of your own worth and you weren't brow-beaten."[17]

Young SNCC organizers were deeply influenced by Ella Baker's wisdom, but when they went into the field they discovered that political traditions and genealogies seemed to be everywhere, that the "older people" had the networks, experience, and credibility without which SNCC organizing would have been impossible. "One of the things that happened in the movement," SNCC's Bob Moses later observed, "was that there was a joining of a younger generation of people with an older generation that nurtured and sustained them." Moses was referring to what he learned during a very difficult voter registration campaign in southwest Mississippi in 1961.[18] There, not far from the Woodville area where a century earlier freedpeople had defied their employer's orders and marched twenty-five miles to a political meeting, rural and small-town black folk again commenced to struggle for their rights. Relying on the relations and institutions that they had built and that enabled them over many decades to endure repression and make themselves as a people, they challenged the nation—as their slave and freed forebears had done—to confront the meaning of its own democracy. Their challenge remains with us. And they are still to be thanked.

APPENDIX

NOTES

ACKNOWLEDGMENTS

INDEX

APPENDIX:
BLACK LEADERS DATA SET

My discussions of African-American politics are based in part on information derived from a large data set on local and state black leaders
that I compiled in the course of research. The data set is certainly not
exhaustive; indeed, it became increasingly clear that accounting for no
more than black state and local officeholders during the period considered was an enormous and difficult undertaking, requiring the most
intensive archival detective work at the county and precinct levels. I
have done a good deal of it, and along with what I could learn from
a range of published sources (local and family histories, legislative
records, newspapers, almanacs, autobiographies, memoirs, oral histories, and secondary literature), I feel confident of the generalizations
and assessments I have made. Precision, on the other hand, is very
elusive, and for that reason I have refrained from presenting the data
in the form of numerical or statistical tables (although there are detailed
discussions and representations in both the text and the notes). But I
would be happy to make available both the data set and the results to
anyone whose interests and scholarship would consequently be aided
and advanced.

My Black Leaders Data Set includes 3,878 individuals distributed
among the southern states as follows:

Alabama	345	North Carolina	700
Arkansas	91	South Carolina	394
Florida	85	Tennessee	120
Georgia	127	Texas	224
Louisiana	430	Virginia	987
Mississippi	375		

For each of them, I attempted to record information about the county (ies) in which they lived, the dates of their birth and death, their color, antebellum status (slave, freeborn, or manumitted), Civil War careers, antebellum and postbellum occupations, literacy, education, property ownership, religion, party affiliations, attendance at political conventions, organizational activities, and terms of office. In some cases, I was able to find out a great deal; in many others, I could find but very little. At all events, I supplemented my own findings with those of historians who have done some of this empirical research for the South as a whole or for discrete states and counties. Especially valuable was Eric Foner's *Freedom's Lawmakers: A Directory of Black Officeholders during Reconstruction,* published in 1993, a remarkably rich and wide-ranging scholarly contribution.

Leadership is, of course, not only about the markers of status, personal attribute, and accomplishment, but also about the worlds and relations in which people are embedded. These are even more resistant to quantitative analysis, though immensely important to our understanding of political life.

NOTES

ABBREVIATIONS

[A-3274]   Freedmen and Southern Society Project Document Number, College Park, Md.

ACS   Papers of the American Colonization Society, Incoming Correspondence

ADAH   Alabama Department of Archives and History, Montgomery, Ala.

AFIC   American Freedmen's Inquiry Commission, Record Group 94

AgH   *Agricultural History*

AHQ   *Arkansas Historical Quarterly*

AHR   *American Historical Review*

AMA   American Missionary Association Papers

AR   *African Repository*

ARC   Amistad Research Center, New Orleans, La.

BLDS   Black Leaders Data Set

BRFAL   Bureau of Refugees, Freedmen, and Abandoned Lands, Record Group 105

BTHC   Barker Texas History Center, Austin, Tex.

CWH   *Civil War History*

DU   Duke University Archives, Perkins Library, Durham, N.C.

ECU   East Carolina University Archives, Greenville, N.C.

EU   Emory University Archives, Woodruff Library, Atlanta, Ga.

FU   Fisk University Archives, Nashville, Tenn.

GDAH   Georgia Department of Archives and History, Atlanta, Ga.

GHQ   *Georgia Historical Quarterly*

HU   Howard University Archives, Washington, D.C.

JAH   *Journal of American History*

JEH	*Journal of Economic History*
JMH	*Journal of Mississippi History*
JNH	*Journal of Negro History*
JSH	*Journal of Southern History*
JSoH	*Journal of Social History*
JSwGH	*Journal of Southwest Georgia History*
LaH	*Louisiana History*
LC	Library of Congress, Washington, D.C.
LH	*Labor History*
LSU	Louisiana State University Archives, Baton Rouge, La.
MDAH	Mississippi Department of Archives and History, Jackson, Miss.
NA	National Archives, Washington, D.C.
NCDAH	North Carolina Department of Archives and History, Raleigh
NCHR	*North Carolina Historical Review*
PMHS	*Publications of the Mississippi Historical Society*
RHR	*Radical History Review*
S&A	*Slavery and Abolition*
SCC	Southern Claims Commission, Record Group 217
SCDAH	South Carolina Department of Archives and History, Columbia
SCHM	*South Carolina Historical Magazine*
SCL	South Caroliniana Library, Columbia
SHC	Southern Historical Collection, Chapel Hill, North Carolina
SmLNY	Schomberg Library, New York Public Library, New York City
SWHQ	*Southwestern Historical Quarterly*
TSLA	Tennessee State Library and Archives, Nashville, Tenn.
TxSLA	Texas State Library and Archives, Austin, Tex.
UGa	University of Georgia Archives, Athens, Ga.
VHS	Virginia Historical Society, Richmond, Va.
VMHB	*Virginia Magazine of History and Biography*
VSLA	Virginia State Library and Archives, Richmond
WMP	William Mahone Papers
WMQ	*William and Mary Quarterly*

PROLOGUE

1. P. P. Berguin, "Report," 31 Jan. 1868, BRFAL, Miss. Asst. Comr., roll 32, NA.

2. Feminist and women's historians have done pioneering work in advancing our understanding of these problems. The relevant literature is very large, but for some of the most important work that has influenced my own thinking, see Joan Wallach Scott, *Gender and the Politics of History* (New York, 1988); Christine

Stansell, *City of Women: Sex and Class in New York, 1789–1860* (New York, 1982); Stephanie McCurry, *Masters of Small Worlds: Yeoman Households, Gender Relations, and the Political Culture of the Antebellum South Carolina Low Country* (New York, 1995); Nancy A. Hewitt, *Women's Activism and Social Change: Rochester, New York, 1822–1872* (Ithaca, N.Y., 1984); Amy Dru Stanley, *From Bondage to Contract: Wage Labor, Marriage, and the Market in the Age of Slave Emancipation* (New York, 1998); Laura Edwards, *Gendered Strife and Confusion: The Political Culture of Reconstruction* (Urbana, Ill., 1997); Elsa Barkley Brown, "Negotiating and Transforming the Public Sphere: African-American Political Life in the Transition from Slavery to Freedom," in Black Public Sphere Collective, ed., *The Black Public Sphere: A Public Culture Book* (Chicago, 1995); Tera Hunter, *To 'Joy My Freedom: Southern Black Women's Lives and Labors after the Civil War* (Cambridge, Mass., 1997); Evelyn Brooks Higginbotham, *Righteous Discontent: The Women's Movement in the Black Baptist Church, 1880–1920* (Cambridge, Mass., 1993); Glenda E. Gilmore, *Gender and Jim Crow: Women and the Politics of White Supremacy in North Carolina, 1896–1920* (Chapel Hill, N.C., 1996); Jacquelyn Dowd Hall, *Revolt against Chivalry: Jessie Daniel Ames and the Women's Campaign against Lynching* (New York, 1979).

3. My thinking on these issues, even when I have disagreements, has been most influenced by James C. Scott, *Domination and the Arts of Resistance: Hidden Transcripts* (New Haven, Conn., 1990); Ranajit Guha, *Elementary Aspects of Peasant Insurgency in Colonial India* (New York, 1983); Emilia Viotti da Costa, *Crowns of Glory, Tears of Blood: The Demerara Slave Rebellion of 1823* (New York, 1994); William Beinart and Colin Bundy, *Hidden Struggles in Rural South Africa* (Berkeley, Calif., 1987); Eugene D. Genovese, *Roll, Jordan, Roll: The World the Slaves Made* (New York, 1974); Robin D. G. Kelley, *Race Rebels: Culture, Politics, and the Black Working Class* (New York, 1994); Florencia Mallon, *Peasant and Nation: The Making of Postcolonial Mexico and Peru* (Berkeley, Calif., 1995); E. P. Thompson, *The Making of the English Working Class* (New York, 1963); and E. P. Thompson, *Customs in Common* (London, 1991).

4. This is characteristic of the major works covering the Civil War and post-emancipation periods, including the most brilliant and influential ones. For important examples, see Eric Foner, *Reconstruction: America's Unfinished Revolution, 1863–1877* (New York, 1988); David W. Blight, *Race and Reunion: The Civil War in American Memory* (Cambridge, Mass., 2001); Leon F. Litwack, *Been in the Storm so Long: The Aftermath of Slavery* (New York, 1979); Joel Williamson, *After Slavery: The Negro in South Carolina during Reconstruction* (Chapel Hill, N.C., 1965); Neil R. McMillen, *Dark Journey: Black Mississippians in the Age of Jim Crow* (Urbana, Ill., 1989). Even Michael Dawson's recent work, which emphasizes the significance of black nationalism in African-American history and culture and offers a powerful critique of liberalism, nonetheless tends to see black nationalism, historically, as "reactive." See *Black Visions: The Roots of Contemporary African-American Political*

Ideologies (Chicago, 2001), esp. 86. But for a different view see V. P. Franklin, *Black Self-Determination: A Cultural History of the Faith of the Founders* (Westport, Conn., 1984).

5. For important exceptions, see Herbert G. Gutman, *The Black Family in Slavery and Freedom* (New York, 1976); David Montgomery, *Citizen Worker: The Experience of Workers in the United States with Democracy and the Free Market during the Nineteenth Century* (New York, 1993); and Ira Berlin, *Many Thousands Gone: The First Two Centuries of Slavery in North America* (Cambridge, Mass., 1998).

I. OF CHAINS AND THREADS

The title for Part 1 is taken from Eugene D. Genovese, *From Rebellion to Revolution: Afro-American Slave Revolts in the Making of the Modern World* (Baton Rouge, 1979), 6. The full quotation: " 'Let it never be forgotten,' Edwin C. Holland, editor of the *Charleston Times* warned in the early 1820s, 'that our NEGROES are truly the *Jacobins* of the country; that they are the *Anarchists* and the *Domestic* enemy: the *common enemy of civilized society,* and the *barbarians* who *would if they could, become the destroyers of our race.*' " The epigraph for Chapter 1 is from William F. Allen et al., *Slave Songs of the United States* (1867; New York, 1951), 22–23.

1. Merton Dillon, *Slavery Attacked: Southern Slaves and Their Allies, 1619–1865* (Baton Rouge, 1990), 240–242; Charles L. Perdue, Jr. et al., eds., *Weevils in the Wheat: Interviews with Virginia Ex-Slaves* (Bloomington, Ind., 1976), 216; Armstead L. Robinson, "Day of Jubilo: Civil War and the Demise of Slavery in the Mississippi Valley, 1861–1865," Ph.D. diss., University of Rochester, 1977, 14–91; John K. Betterworth, *Confederate Mississippi: The People and Policies of a Cotton State in Wartime* (Baton Rouge, 1943), 162; John Q. Anderson, ed., *Brokenburn: The Journal of Kate Stone, 1861–1868* (Baton Rouge, 1955), 28, 33.

2. Ira Berlin et al., eds., *Freedom: A Documentary History of Emancipation, 1861–1867,* ser. 1, vol. 1: *The Destruction of Slavery* (Cambridge, Eng., 1985), 11–13, 71, and generally 1–156, 187–243; Edward McPherson, *The Political History of the United States of America during the Great Rebellion* (New York, 1864), 123–129; Testimony of Col. Thomas Wentworth Higginson, AFIC, ser. 12, Letters Rec'd, filed with O-328 1863, NA [K-81].

3. John Houston Bills Diary, 1863–1864, SHC.

4. Joseph C. G. Kennedy, *Preliminary Report on the Eighth Census, 1860* (Washington, D.C., 1862), 245–289; *Eighth Census of the United States: Agriculture* (Washington, D.C., 1864), 223–248; Michael P. Johnson, "Work, Culture, and the Slave Community: Slave Occupations in the Cotton Belt in 1860," *LH* 27 (Summer 1986): 325–355.

5. For an important and highly pertinent comparison, see Peter Kolchin, *Unfree Labor: American Slavery and Russian Serfdom* (Cambridge, Mass., 1987). Also see Eugene D. Genovese, *Roll, Jordan, Roll: The World the Slaves Made* (New York, 1974), 3–7, 25–70, 450–458; and Orlando Patterson, *Slavery and Social Death: A Comparative Study* (Cambridge, Mass., 1982).

6. See Michael Mullin, *Africa in America: Slave Acculturation and Resistance in the American South and the British Caribbean, 1736–1831* (Urbana, Ill., 1992), 159–173; Allan Kulikoff, *Tobacco and Slaves: The Development of Southern Cultures in the Chesapeake, 1680–1800* (Chapel Hill, N.C., 1986), 317–334; Peter Wood, *Black Majority: Negroes in Colonial South Carolina from 1670 through the Stono Rebellion* (New York, 1974); 131–166; Peter Kolchin, *American Slavery, 1619–1877* (New York, 1993), 28–62.

7. See especially Herbert G. Gutman, *The Black Family in Slavery and Freedom, 1750–1925* (New York, 1976); Kulikoff, *Tobacco and Slaves,* 319–379; Ann Patton Malone, *Sweet Chariot: Slave Family and Household Structure in Nineteenth-Century Louisiana* (Chapel Hill, N.C., 1992); Charles Wetherell, "Slave Kinship: A Case Study of the South Carolina Good Hope Plantation, 1835–1856," *Journal of Family History* 6 (Fall 1981): 294–307.

8. Frederick Douglass, *My Bondage and My Freedom,* ed. William L. Andrews (1855; Urbana, Ill., 1987), 48–49; Elizabeth Hyde Botume, *First Days amongst the Contrabands* (Boston, 1893), 48–49. Also see Gutman, *Black Family,* 216–220.

9. Malone, *Sweet Chariot,* 1–68; Michael Tadman, *Speculators and Slaves: Masters, Traders, and Slaves in the Old South* (Madison, Wisc., 1989), 41–42, 45, 136–137, 169–171; Brenda Stevenson, *Life in Black and White: Family and Community in the Slave South* (New York, 1996), 206–257; Allan Kulikoff, "Uprooted Peoples: Black Migrants in the Age of the American Revolution," in Ira Berlin and Ronald Hoffman, eds., *Slavery and Freedom in the Age of the American Revolution* (Charlottesville, Va., 1983), 167; Walter Johnson, *Soul by Soul: Life inside the Antebellum Slave Market* (Cambridge, Mass., 1999), 1–18; Steven F. Miller, "Plantation Labor Organization and Slave Life on the Cotton Frontier: The Alabama-Mississippi Black Belt, 1815–1840," in Ira Berlin and Philip D. Morgan, eds., *Cultivation and Culture: Labor and the Shaping of Slave Life in the Americas* (Charlottesville, Va., 1993), 156–160.

10. To write this way of the slaves' "political objectives" is not to suggest that the desire to live in a world free from slavery was not always one of those objectives. Nor is it to suggest that fleeing from slavery was not an important political objective of individuals or small groups of slaves. Indeed, flight from slavery was a powerful objective early on, and it continued to be in those areas bordering on free states or on international boundaries. I mean simply to highlight the direction of the slaves' ongoing collective struggle to shape the relations of power both between them and their masters and among themselves. The meaning and consequences of this struggle

would, of course, change as other political conditions and circumstances changed, as I hope to show here and in Chapter 2.

11. The point is cogently made in Ira Berlin and Philip D. Morgan, "Labor and the Shaping of Slave Life in the Americas," in Berlin and Morgan, *Cultivation and Culture*, 1; Ira Berlin, *Many Thousands Gone: The First Two Centuries of Slavery in North America* (Cambridge, Mass., 1998).

12. The best treatment of this dynamic in southern slave society remains Genovese, *Roll, Jordan, Roll*, but see also the important work of Emilia Viotti da Costa, *Crowns of Glory, Tears of Blood: The Demerara Slave Rebellion of 1823* (New York, 1994), 39–86.

13. Lewis Cecil Gray, *History of Agriculture in the Southern United States to 1860*, 2 vols. (Washington, D.C., 1933), 545–556; V. Alton Moody, *Slavery on Louisiana Sugar Plantations* (1924; New York, 1976), 45–46.

14. Charles Joyner, *Down by the Riverside: A South Carolina Slave Community* (Urbana, Ill., 1984), 43–45; Philip D. Morgan, "Work and Culture: The Task System and the World of Lowcountry Blacks, 1700–1880, *WMQ*, 3d ser., 39 (Oct. 1982): 563–599; Berlin and Morgan, "Labor and Shaping of Slave Life," 14–15. The organization of agricultural labor by tasks could also be found on cotton and tobacco plantations, especially during harvest, as well as on diversified farms.

15. See, for example, *DeBow's Review* 1 (October 1851): 369–372; vol. 4 (October 1854): 421–426; 1 (June 1855): 713–719; 2 (September 1855): 358–363; 1 (December 1856): 617–620; 2 (April 1857): 376–381; 1 (May 1859): 579–581; 24 (September 1860): 357–368. Also see Miller, "Plantation Labor Organization," 163–165.

16. Perdue et al., *Weevils in the Wheat*, 26; Johnson, "Work, Culture, and Slave Community," 341–345, 348–349; Miller, "Plantation Labor Organization," 165–167; William L. Van Deburg, *The Slave Drivers: Black Agricultural Labor Supervisors in the Antebellum South* (Westport, Conn., 1979), 16–19; Kulikoff, *Tobacco and Slaves*, 366.

17. Frederick Law Olmsted, *The Cotton Kingdom*, ed. Arthur M. Schlesinger, Sr. (New York, 1984), 191–193. On the role of kinship in task labor, see Philip D. Morgan, "The Ownership of Property by Slaves in the Mid-Nineteenth-Century Low Country," *JSH* 49 (August 1983): 402–405; Leslie A. Schwalm, *A Hard Fight for We: Women's Transition from Slavery to Freedom in South Carolina* (Urbana, Ill., 1997), 19–46.

18. Douglass, *My Bondage and My Freedom*, 187–194; Lynda J. Morgan, *Emancipation in Virginia's Tobacco Belt, 1850–1870* (Athens, Ga., 1992), 57–76; Barbara J. Fields, *Slavery and Freedom on the Middle Ground: Maryland during the Nineteenth Century* (New Haven, Conn., 1985), 40–89; Charles Dew, *Bond of Iron: Master and Slave at Buffalo Forge* (New York, 1994), 108–121; Michael P. Johnson and James L. Roark, *Black Masters: A Free Family of Color in the Old South* (New York, 1984), 175–178.

19. Testimony of Stephen Brooke, SCC, 1877–1883, entry 732, claim 16293, box

197, NA; John C. Inscoe, *Mountain Masters, Slavery, and the Sectional Crisis in Western North Carolina* (Knoxville, Tenn., 1989), 74–78.

20. Charles Ball, *Fifty Years in Chains; or, The Life of an American Slave* (New York, 1859), 147–148; *DeBow's Review* 4 (October 1854): 424; Testimony of James Speed, AFIC, ser. 12, Letters Rec'd, filed with O-328 1863 [K-91].

21. Solomon Northup, *Twelve Years a Slave*, ed. Sue Eakin and Joseph Logsdon (Baton Rouge, 1968), 148; George P. Rawick, ed., *The American Slave: A Composite Autobiography*, ser. 1, vol. 7 (Westport, Conn., 1972), 22–23, 77; Stephanie McCurry, *Masters of Small Worlds: Yeoman Households, Gender Relations, and the Political Culture of the Antebellum South Carolina Low Country* (New York, 1995), 25, 62; Joseph P. Reidy, *From Slavery to Agrarian Capitalism in the Cotton Plantation South: Central Georgia, 1800–1880* (Chapel Hill, N.C., 1992), 61.

22. Although we are deeply indebted to the pioneering work that they have done, some historians who have identified and examined what they term "internal economies" or "independent production by slaves" raise problematic conceptual issues. First and foremost, they suggest that the slaves' production of goods either for their own consumption or for petty sale is somehow to be considered a sphere of economic activity at least partially distinct from the social relations of slavery and the slave/plantation economy. See, for example, Morgan, "Work and Culture," 385–399; and Roderick A. McDonald, "Independent Economic Production by Slaves on Antebellum Louisiana Sugar Plantations," in Berlin and Morgan, *Cultivation and Culture*, 275–299. I believe this is mistaken and, oddly enough, understates the ways in which slaves gave shape to the social and economic system as a whole.

23. J. M. Gibson, *Memoirs of J. M. Gibson: Terrors of the Civil War and Reconstruction Days* (n.p., 1966), 13; Olmsted, *Cotton Kingdom*, 184–185; Nelson M. Ferebee Memoir, 1850s, Nelson M. Ferebee Papers, ECU; Dylan C. Penningroth, "Claiming Kin and Property: African-American Life before and after Emancipation," Ph.D. diss., Johns Hopkins University, 1999; Roderick A. McDonald, *The Economy and Material Culture of Slaves: Goods and Chattel on the Sugar Plantations of Jamaica and Louisiana* (Baton Rouge, 1993), 51–52; Reidy, *Slavery to Agrarian Capitalism*, 71; Joyner, *Down by the Riverside*, 128–133; Julie Saville, *The Work of Reconstruction: From Slave to Wage Laborer in South Carolina, 1860–1870* (Cambridge, Eng., 1994), 5–11; John T. Schlotterbeck, "The Internal Economy of Slavery in Rural Piedmont Virginia," in Ira Berlin and Philip D. Morgan, eds., *The Slaves' Economy: Independent Production by Slaves in the Americas* (London, 1991), 170–173.

24. John D. Campbell, "The Gender Division of Labor, Slave Reproduction, and the Slave Family on Southern Cotton Plantations, 1800–1865," Ph.D. diss., University of Minnesota, 1988, 167, 238–267; Rawick, *American Slave*, ser. 1, vol. 4, pt. 1, 71, 85, and vol. 7, 58; Testimony of Elijah Hooker, SCC, 1877–1883, entry 732, claim 12453, box 198.

25. Berlin and Morgan, "Labor and Shaping of Slave Life," 35–38; Genovese,

Roll, Jordan, Roll, 535–540; Reidy, *Slavery to Agrarian Capitalism,* 60, 69–71; Northup, *Twelve Years a Slave,* 153; Rawick, *American Slave,* ser. 1, vol. 11, 115–116, and vol. 13, pt. 3, 240–241; Ferebee Memoir, 1850s.

26. Ball, *Fifty Years in Chains,* 131–133.

27. On the West Indian examples, see Sidney Mintz, *Caribbean Transformations* (New York, 1974), 131–250; McDonald, *Economy and Material Culture,* 16–49; Woodville K. Marshall, "Provision Ground and Plantation Labor in Four Windward Islands: Competition for Resources during Slavery," in Berlin and Morgan, *Cultivation and Culture,* 203–220; Dale W. Tomich, *Slavery in the Circuit of Sugar: Martinique and the World Economy, 1830–1848* (Baltimore, 1990), 259–280; Carolyn E. Fick, *The Making of Haiti: The Saint Domingue Revolution from Below* (Knoxville, Tenn., 1990), 31–33.

28. *DeBow's Review* 10 (June 1851): 624; Larry E. Hudson, Jr., " 'All That Cash': Work and Status in the Slave Quarters," in Larry E. Hudson, Jr., ed., *Working toward Freedom: Slave Society and Domestic Economy in the American South* (Rochester, N.Y., 1994), 77–94. On the efforts of slaveholders to restrict the slaves from engaging in trading relations off of the plantation and farm, see McCurry, *Masters of Small Worlds,* 112, 292–294; J. William Harris, *Plain Folk and Gentry in a Slave Society: White Liberty and Black Slavery in Augusta's Hinterlands* (Middletown, Conn., 1985), 52–61.

29. Olmsted, *Cotton Kingdom,* 81; Schlotterbeck, "Internal Economy of Slavery in Rural Piedmont Virginia," 176; Gibson, *Memoirs,* 13; Testimony of Samuel B. Smith, AFIC, ser. 12, Letters Rec'd, filed with O-328 1863 [K-90].

30. Ball, *Fifty Years in Chains,* 128–130; Rawick, *American Slave,* ser. 1, vol. 7, pt. 2, 343, and 11, 50; Olmsted, *Cotton Kingdom,* 258; *DeBow's Review* 4 (October 1854): 424, and 2 (September 1855): 362; McCurry, *Masters of Small Worlds,* 15, 19, 293–294; Charles C. Bolton, *Poor Whites of the Antebellum South: Tenants and Laborers in Central North Carolina and Northeast Mississippi* (Durham, N.C., 1994), 46–47, 107–108.

31. Olmsted, *Cotton Kingdom,* 197–198; McDonald, *Economy and Material Culture,* 57. Also see Rawick, *American Slave,* ser. 1, vol. 4, pt. 1, 2; Testimony of Alexander Kenner, AFIC, ser. 12, Letters Rec'd, filed with O-328 1863 [K-201].

32. Ball, *Fifty Years in Chains,* 204–205; Schwalm, *Hard Fight for We,* 57–63. Also see Mullin, *Africa in America,* 134–136.

33. Thorpe quoted in McDonald, *Economy and Material Culture,* 76; Ferebee Memoir, 1850s, 8; Charles Joyner, *Shared Traditions: Southern Folk History and Folk Culture* (Urbana, Ill., 1999), 68–69; Stephen Nissenbaum, *The Battle for Christmas* (New York, 1996), 258–291. This dynamic, with its symbolic inversions and appropriations, received more ritualized and agonistic display in the festive rite variously called "Jonkonnu," "John Canoe," "John Kuner," or "John Canno." With West African and Caribbean roots, "Jonkonnu" was celebrated in eastern North Carolina

and southern Virginia, though we do not know when it first surfaced in North America or why it appears to have remained confined to this relatively small geographical area. For the most thorough, complex, and provocative treatments, see Elizabeth A. Fenn, "'A Perfect Equality Seemed to Reign': Slave Society and Jonkonnu," *NCHR* 65 (April 1988): 127–153; Robert Dirks, *Black Saturnalia: Conflict and Its Ritual Expression on British West Indian Slave Plantations* (Gainesville, Fla., 1987); Michael Craton, "Decoding Pitchy-Patchy: The Roots, Branches, and Essence of Junkanoo," *S&A* 16 (April 1995): 14–44. But also see Lawrence W. Levine, *Black Culture and Black Consciousness: Afro-American Folk Thought from Slavery to Freedom* (New York, 1977), 13; and Sterling Stuckey, *Slave Culture: Nationalist Theory and the Foundations of Black America* (New York, 1987), 67–73.

34. Ball, *Fifty Years in Chains*, 202–203; Campbell, "Gender Division of Labor," 238–291; Hudson, "All That Cash," 77–94.

35. Ball, *Fifty Years in Chains*, 132–133; John Campbell, "As 'A Kind of Freeman'? Slaves' Market-Related Activities in the South Carolina Upcountry, 1800–1860," in Berlin and Morgan, *Cultivation and Culture*, 268–271; Schlotterbeck, "Internal Economy of Slavery in Rural Piedmont Virginia," 177–178; Leslie S. Rowland, "'My Pappy Gave Me a Start': Inheritance, Gift, and Exchange among Slaves in Lowcountry Georgia and South Carolina," unpublished paper in author's possession, 1991, 6.

36. See Rowland, "My Pappy," 16; Morgan, "Ownership of Property By Slaves," 416–417. For a particularly insightful analysis, see Penningroth, "Claiming Kin and Property," 36–130.

37. For an unusually thoughtful discussion of rural communities as historical and analytical phenomena, see Victor V. Magagna, *Communities of Grain: Rural Rebellion in Comparative Perspective* (Ithaca, N.Y., 1991), 12–21.

38. Gerald W. Mullin, *Flight and Rebellion: Slave Resistance in Eighteenth-Century Virginia* (New York, 1972), 3–33; Roger D. Abrahams, *Singing the Master: The Emergence of African-American Culture in the Plantation South* (New York, 1992), 46–47; Douglass, *My Bondage and My Freedom*, 44–45, 76.

39. Kennedy, *Preliminary Report of Eighth Census*, 245–289; *Eighth Census: Agriculture*, 223–247; Steven Hahn, *The Roots of Southern Populism: Yeoman Farmers and the Transformation of the Georgia Upcountry, 1850–1890* (New York, 1983), 31; Stevenson, *Life in Black and White*, 208–212, 231–234; Gutman, *Black Family*, 135–138.

40. *DeBow's Review* 2 (September 1855): 362; Rawick, *American Slave*, ser. 2, vol. 18, 55, and supp. ser. 1, vol. 11, 16; Ball, *Fifty Years in Chains*, 21; Kolchin, *Unfree Labor*, 211; Stevenson, *Life in Black and White*, 231–234.

41. Perdue et al., *Weevils in the Wheat*, 53; Luther Porter Jackson, *Free Negro Labor and Property Holding in Virginia, 1830–1860* (1942; New York, 1969), 70–136; Morgan, *Emancipation in Virginia's Tobacco Belt*, 34; Fields, *Slavery and Free-*

dom, 23–39; Schlotterbeck, "Internal Economy of Slavery in Rural Piedmont Virginia," 172.

42. Ball, *Fifty Years in Chains,* 206–207. For a thoughtful treatment of this problem, see Anthony Kaye, "The Personality of Power: The Ideology of Slaves in the Natchez District and in the Mississippi Delta, 1830–1865," Ph.D. diss., Columbia University, 1999.

43. Botume, *First Days amongst the Contrabands,* 121; Rev. Charles Colcock Jones, *The Religious Instruction of the Negroes in the United States* (1842; New York, 1969), 135–136; Margaret Washington Creel, *"A Peculiar People": Slave Religion and Community Culture among the Gullahs* (New York, 1988), 240.

44. Saville, *Work of Reconstruction,* 87–97; Janet Sharp Hermann, *The Pursuit of a Dream* (New York, 1981), 12–18; Jones, *Religious Instruction,* 130–131.

45. Mechal Sobel, *Trabelin' On: The Slave Journey to an Afro-Baptist Faith* (Westport, Conn., 1979), 223; John E. Bryant to Sister, 15 Sept. 1862, John E. Bryant Papers, box 1, folder 3, DU.

46. Rawick, *American Slave,* supp. ser. 1, vol. 11, 130; Northup, *Twelve Years a Slave,* 116–117; Testimony of Mandy Rollins, WPA Ex-Slave Narratives, LSU; Campbell, "Gender Division of Labor," 140–141. Also see Jacqueline Jones, *Labor of Love, Labor of Sorrow: Black Women, Work, and the Family from Slavery to the Present* (New York, 1985), 11–43.

47. Deborah Gray White, *Ar'n't I a Woman: Female Slaves in the Plantation South* (New York, 1985), 114–115; Schwalm, *Hard Fight for We,* 47–72; Elizabeth Fox-Genovese, "Strategies and Forms of Resistance: Focus on Slave Women in the United States," in Gary Y. Okihiro, ed., *In Resistance: Studies in African, Caribbean, and Afro-American History* (Amherst, Mass., 1986), 156–157.

48. White, *Ar'n't I a Woman,* 76, 153–159; Rawick, *American Slave,* ser. 2, vol. 18, 55, and supp. ser. 1, vol. 11, 16; Ball, *Fifty Years in Chains,* 21; John Brown, *Slave Life in Georgia: A Narrative of the Life of John Brown,* ed. L. A. Chamerovzow (1855; New York, 1971), 1–2; Kolchin, *Unfree Labor,* 210.

49. John W. Blassingame, "Status and Social Structure in the Slave Community: Evidence from New Sources," in Harry P. Owens, ed., *Perspectives and Irony in American Slavery* (Jackson, Miss., 1976), 137–151; Abrahams, *Singing the Master,* 107–130; Van Deburg, *Slave Drivers,* 24; Thomas L. Webber, *Deep Like the Rivers: Education in the Slave Quarter Community, 1831–1865* (New York, 1978), 207–243.

50. Peter Wood, " 'The Dream Deferred': Black Freedom Struggles on the Eve of White Independence," in Okihiro, *In Resistance,* 176; Botume, *First Days amongst the Contrabands,* 6; Rawick, *American Slave,* ser. 1, vol. 7, pt. 2, 12; Testimony of Elizabeth Rose Hite, WPA Ex-Slave Narratives, 13, LSU.

51. Rawick, *American Slave,* ser. 1, vol. 7, pt. 2, 6, and supp. ser. 1, vol. 6, 60; Perdue et al., *Weevils in the Wheat,* 166–167; Kaye, "Personality of Power," 93–94; Barbara Bush, *Slave Women in Caribbean Society, 1650–1838* (Bloomington, Ind.,

1990), 49; Morgan, *Emancipation in Virginia's Tobacco Belt*, 73–75; Louis R. Harlan, *Booker T. Washington: The Making of a Black Leader, 1856–1901* (New York, 1972), 17–18.

52. Janet Duitsman Cornelius, *When I Can Read My Title Clear: Literacy, Slavery, and Religion in the Antebellum South* (Columbia, S.C., 1991), esp. 3, 8–9, 12, 24, 33–34, 37, 54–57, 61, 67, 77–78, and 90–93. Also see Webber, *Deep Like the Rivers*, 131–138; Genovese, *Roll, Jordan, Roll*, 561–566; and Kolchin, *American Slavery*, 116–117, 127–129.

53. David Macrae, *Americans at Home* (1871; New York, 1952), 328–329; George Teamoh, "Autobiography," 43–46, Carter Woodson Papers, LC; Rawick, *American Slave*, ser. 1, vol. 7, pt. 2, 127, supp. ser. 1, vol. 6, pt. 1, 10, and supp. ser. 1, vol. 6, pt. 2, 497; Douglass, *My Bondage and My Freedom*, 42, 92–98, 161–164; Cornelius, *When I Can Read My Title Clear*, 8–9, 90–91. Cornelius, who makes the point about male predominance among literate slaves, adds that women in slave communities who could read were considered to be leaders and teachers.

54. Albert Raboteau, *Slave Religion: The "Invisible Institution" in the Antebellum South* (New York, 1978), 4–35; Sobel, *Trabelin' On*, 5–48; Levine, *Black Culture and Black Consciousness*, 59–60; Creel, *"Peculiar People,"* 6–62.

55. Sylvia R. Frey, *Water from the Rock: Black Resistance in a Revolutionary Age* (Princeton, N.J., 1991), 284–297; Mechal Sobel, *The World They Made Together: Black and White Values in Eighteenth-Century Virginia* (Princeton, N.J., 1987), 174–180; Luther Porter Jackson, "Religious Developments of the Negro in Virginia from 1760 to 1860," *JNH* 16 (1931): 236–246; Rhys Isaac, "Evangelical Revolt: The Nature of the Baptists' Challenge to the Traditional Order in Virginia, 1765–1775," *WMQ*, 3d ser., 31 (July 1974): 345–368.

56. Sobel, *Trabelin' On*, 188–191; Frey, *Water from the Rock*, 285–294; Creel, *"Peculiar People,"* 114–234; Rachel Klein, *Unification of a Slave State: The Rise of the Planter Class in the South Carolina Backcountry, 1760–1808* (Chapel Hill, N.C., 1990), 269–302; C. Eric Lincoln and Lawrence H. Mamiya, *The Black Church in the African American Experience* (Durham, N.C., 1990), 21–30, 47–68; William E. Montgomery, *Under Their Own Vine and Fig Tree: The African-American Church in the South, 1865–1900* (Baton Rouge, 1993), 27–33.

57. Genovese, *Roll, Jordan, Roll*, 183–193; Sobel, *Trabelin' On*, 182–183, 221–222; John C. Willis, "From the Dictates of Pride to the Paths of Righteousness: Slave Honor and Christianity in Antebellum Virginia," in Edward L. Ayers and John C. Willis, eds., *The Edge of the South: Life in Nineteenth-Century Virginia* (Charlottesville, Va., 1991), 37–55; Jones, *Religious Instruction*, 125; Macrae, *Americans at Home*, 370.

58. Peter W. Williams, *Popular Religion in America: Symbolic Change and the Modernization Process in Historical Perspective* (Urbana, Ill., 1989), 40–42; Macrae, *Americans at Home*, 353; Sobel, *Trabelin' On*, 79–135.

59. Creel, *"Peculiar People,"* 249–50; Jones, *Religious Instruction,* 125–126. On the antinomian tradition, see E. P. Thompson, *Witness against the Beast: William Blake and the Moral Law* (New York, 1993), 3–21.

60. Macrae, *Americans at Home,* 344, 370; Levine, *Black Culture and Black Consciousness,* 30–54; Williams, *Popular Religion in America,* 42; John Jentz, "A Note on Genovese's Account of the Slaves' Religion," *CWH* 28 (1977): 161–169. See also Sobel, *Trabelin' On,* 108–109.

61. Anna A. Carter to Rev. S. S. Jocelyn, 13 June 1864, AMA, South Carolina, roll 1, ARC; John Conant to Messrs. Whipple and Jocelyn, 7 Aug. 1862, AMA, South Carolina, roll 1, ARC; Testimony of Hite, WPA Ex-Slave Narratives, 9–11.

62. Willis, "From Dictates of Pride," 37–39; Jones, *Religious Instruction,* 113; Creel, *"Peculiar People,"* 279.

63. Creel, *"Peculiar People,"* 249–250, 286; Ferebee Memoir, 7; Macrae, *Americans at Home,* 365; Schwalm, *Hard Fight for We,* 69–71.

64. Olmsted, *Cotton Kingdom,* 201–202; John Conant to Messrs. Whipple and Jocelyn, 7 Aug. 1862; Genovese, *Roll, Jordan, Roll,* 258; Peter Randolph, *From Slave Cabin to the Pulpit: The Autobiography of Reverend Peter Randolph* (Boston, 1893), 9–11; Cornelius, *When I Can Read My Title Clear,* 88; Testimony of Hite, WPA Ex-Slave Narratives, 11.

65. James L. Smith, *The Autobiography of James L. Smith* (Norwich, Conn., 1881), 26–27; Jones, *Religious Instruction,* 117; Laura M. Towne, *Letters and Diary of Laura M. Towne: Written from the Sea Islands of South Carolina, 1862–1884,* ed. Rupert S. Holland (1912; New York, 1969), 20–23. Also see Stuckey, *Slave Culture,* 3–97; and Genovese, *Roll, Jordan, Roll,* 232–279.

66. Jones, *Religious Instruction,* 135–136; American Missionary Association, "Annual Report, 1862," roll 1, ARC; Creel, *"Peculiar People,"* 181.

67. Robin Blackburn, *The Overthrow of Colonial Slavery, 1776–1848* (London, 1988); da Costa, *Crowns of Glory, Tears of Blood,* 39–124; Dillon, *Slavery Attacked,* 85–86; Steven Hahn, "Class and State in Postemancipation Societies: Southern Planters in Comparative Perspective," *AHR* 95 (February 1990): 78–83.

68. Julius S. Scott, "The Common Wind: Currents of Afro-American Communication in the Age of the Haitian Revolution," Ph.D. diss., Duke University, 1986; Frey, *Water from the Rock,* 181–193; Alfred N. Hunt, *Haiti's Influence on Antebellum America: Slumbering Volcano in the Caribbean* (Baton Rouge, 1988), 37–83; Peter Linebaugh and Marcus Rediker, *The Many-Headed Hydra: Sailors, Slaves, Commoners, and the Hidden History of the Revolutionary Atlantic* (Boston, 2000); W. Jeffrey Bolster, *Black Jacks: African American Seamen in the Age of Sail* (Cambridge, Mass., 1997); Klein, *Unification of a Slave State,* 203–237. On the notion of a "contact zone," see Mary Louise Pratt, *Imperial Eyes: Travel Writing and Transculturation* (London, 1992), 6–7; and Paul Gilroy, *The Black Atlantic: Modernity and Double Consciousness* (Cambridge, Mass., 1993), 1–40.

69. Mullin, *Africa in America*, 226–227; Testimony of Ben Woolfolk, October 1800, Executive Papers, Gov. James Monroe, box 114, VSLA; Douglas R. Egerton, *Gabriel's Rebellion: The Virginia Slave Conspiracies of 1800 and 1802* (Chapel Hill, N.C., 1993), 3–51; James Sidbury, *Ploughshares into Swords: Race, Rebellion, and Identity in Gabriel's Virginia, 1730–1810* (New York, 1997), 55–117; Vincent Harding, *There Is a River: The Black Struggle for Freedom in America* (New York, 1981), 55–56; Michael P. Johnson, "Denmark Vesey and His Co-Conspirators," *WMQ*, 3d ser., 58 (October 2001): 960–971; Creel, *"Peculiar People,"* 148–166; David Walker, *Appeal . . . to the Coloured Citizens of the World*, ed. Charles M. Wiltse (1829; New York, 1965); Peter Hinks, *To Awaken My Afflicted Brethren: David Walker and the Problem of Antebellum Slave Resistance* (University Park, Pa., 1997).

70. Douglass, *My Bondage and My Freedom*, 103–104, 106–107; Ball, *Fifty Years in Chains*, 19–20; Dillon, *Slavery Attacked*, 76, 139–141; John W. Blassingame, ed., *Slave Testimony: Two Centuries of Letters, Speeches, Interviews, and Autobiographies* (Baton Rouge, 1977), 135.

71. Olmsted, *Cotton Kingdom*, 321; Scott, "Common Wind," 272–274; James T. McGowan, "Creation of a Slave Society: Louisiana Plantations in the Eighteenth Century," Ph.D. diss., University of Rochester, 1976, 347–392; Thomas Fiehrer, "St. Domingue/Haiti: Louisiana's Caribbean Connection," *LaH* 30 (February 1989): 431–437; James H. Dormon, "The Persistent Specter: Slave Rebellion in Territorial Louisiana," *LaH* 18 (Fall 1977): 389–404. "The old negroes," local historian Lubin F. Laurent wrote, "still relate the story of the slave insurrection of 1811 as they heard it from their grandfathers." See Laurent, "A History of St. John the Baptist Parish," unpublished ms., LSU, n.d., 71–73.

72. Creel, *"Peculiar People,"* 267; Northup, *Twelve Years a Slave*, 188–190; Rawick, *American Slave*, supp. ser. 1, vol. 7, 11, and vol. 7, 581.

73. Genovese, *Roll, Jordan, Roll*, 49–70; Kenneth Wiggins Porter, *The Negro on the American Frontier* (New York, 1971), 182–261; William W. Freehling, *The Road to Disunion: The Secessionists at Bay, 1776–1854* (New York, 1990), 289–452; William J. Cooper, *The South and the Politics of Slavery, 1828–1856* (Baton Rouge, 1978), 62–69, 225–268; Joe B. Wilkins, "Window on Freedom: The South's Response to the Emancipation of Slaves in the British West Indies, 1833–1861," Ph.D. diss., University of South Carolina, 1977; Hunt, *Haiti's Influence*, 107–146; Ronald T. Takaki, *A Pro-Slavery Crusade: The Agitation to Reopen the African Slave Trade* (New York, 1971); and McCurry, *Masters of Small Worlds*, 239–304.

74. See, for example, H. C. Bruce, *The New Man: Twenty-Nine Years a Slave, Twenty-Nine Years a Free Man* (1895; New York, 1969), 28–31; Rawick, *American Slave*, ser. 1, vol. 2, pt. 1, 14, vol. 3, pt. 4, 224, 254, vol. 6, 106, 279, vol. 14, 264, 267, and vol. 15, 345; Clement Eaton, *The Freedom-of-Thought Struggle in the Old South* (New York, 1964); as well as Mia Bay, *The White Image in the Black Mind: African-American Ideas about White People, 1830–1925* (New York, 2000), 150–183.

75. J. D. B. DeBow, *Statistical View of the United States* (Washington, D.C., 1854), 64; James Oliver Horton, *Free People of Color: Inside the African American Community* (Washington, D.C., 1993), 25–39, 53–74; Jane H. Pease and William H. Pease, *They Who Would Be Free: Blacks' Search for Freedom, 1830–1861* (New York, 1974); Patrick Rael, *Black Identity and Black Protest in the Antebellum North* (Chapel Hill, N.C., 2002), 19–81; James Oakes, "The Political Significance of Slave Resistance," *History Workshop Journal* 22 (1986): 314–317. Horton estimates that in midwestern cities like Cincinnati and Detroit half of the blacks were southern-born in 1850, though the proportion seems to be lower in Northeast with somewhere between one-fifth and one-fourth.

76. Gordon W. Allport and Leo Postman, *The Psychology of Rumor* (New York, 1947), ix; James C. Scott, *Domination and the Arts of Resistance: Hidden Transcripts* (New Haven, Conn., 1990), 144–145. Also see Ranajit Guha, *Elementary Aspects of Peasant Insurgency in Colonial India* (Delhi, 1983), 220–264; Anand A. Young, "A Conversation of Rumors: The Language of Popular *Mentalités* in Late-Nineteenth-Century Colonial India," *JSoH* 20 (Spring 1987): 485–500; Georges Lefebvre, *The Great Fear of 1789: Rural Panic in Revolutionary France*, trans. Joan White (1932; New York, 1973); Clay Ramsay, *The Ideology of the Great Fear: Soissonais in 1789* (Baltimore, 1992).

77. Wendell Addington, "Slave Insurrections in Texas," *JNH* 35 (October 1950): 413; Dillon, *Slavery Attacked*, 156. Also see John Scott Strickland, "The Great Revival and Insurrectionary Fears in North Carolina: An Examination of Antebellum Southern Society and Slave Revolt Panics," and Laurence Shore, "Making Mississippi Safe for Slavery: The Insurrectionary Panic of 1835," both in Orville Vernon Burton and Robert C. McMath Jr., eds., *Class, Conflict, and Consensus: Antebellum Southern Community Studies* (Westport, Conn., 1982), 57–127; Harvey Wish, "American Slave Insurrections before 1861," *JNH* 22 (July 1937): 299–320; and Herbert Aptheker's still impressive *American Negro Slave Revolts* (New York, 1943), which commenced the serious discussion of the subject.

78. Dillon, *Slavery Attacked*, 135, 187–188; Eugene D. Genovese, *From Rebellion to Revolution: Afro-American Slave Revolts in the Making of the Modern World* (Baton Rouge, 1979), 128–129.

79. Aptheker, *American Negro Slave Revolts*, 345–350; Addington, "Slave Insurrections in Texas," 414–417; Genovese, *Rebellion to Revolution*, 128–129; William Webb, *The History of William Webb, Composed by Himself* (Detroit, 1873), 14, 23, 26.

80. Michael Craton, *Testing the Chains: Resistance to Slavery in the British West Indies* (Ithaca, N.Y., 1982), 243–244, 260–262, 278–280, 295–296; Fick, *Making of Haiti*, 86; da Costa, *Crowns of Glory, Tears of Blood*, 78–79, 174–178; Mary Turner, *Slaves and Missionaries: The Disintegration of Jamaican Slave Society, 1787–1834* (Urbana, Ill., 1982), 150–151; Johnson, "Vesey and Co-Conspirators," 962–964. On

the role of such rumors in peasant unrest, see Yves-Marie Berce, *History of Peasant Revolts*, trans. Amanda Whitmore (1986; Ithaca, N.Y., 1990), 244–319; Jerome Blum, *The End of the Old Order in Rural Europe* (Princeton, N.J., 1978), 333–335; and Kolchin, *Unfree Labor*, 284. On "naive monarchism," see Daniel Field, *Rebels in the Name of the Tsar* (1975; Boston, 1989), 1–29; Scott, *Domination and the Arts of Resistance*, 96–103.

81. For important conceptual and comparative points see Field, *Rebels in the Name of the Tsar*, 12–13; Scott, *Domination and the Arts of Resistance*, 148.

2. "THE CHOKED VOICE OF A RACE AT LAST UNLOOSED"

1. See, for example, E. J. Hobsbawm, *The Age of Capital, 1848–1875* (New York, 1975), 9–26; Dorothy Thompson, *The Chartists: Popular Politics in the Industrial Revolution* (New York, 1984); Jerome Blum, *The End of the Old Order in Rural Europe* (Princeton, N.J., 1978), 357–417; Robin Blackburn, *The Overthrow of Colonial Slavery, 1776–1848* (London, 1988), 331–379, 473–550; Eric Foner, *Nothing but Freedom: Emancipation and Its Legacy* (Baton Rouge, 1983), 8–38; David Eltis, "Abolitionist Perceptions of Society after Slavery," in James Walvin, ed., *Slavery and British Society, 1776–1846* (London, 1982), 195–213; Steven Hahn, "Emancipation and the Development of Capitalist Agriculture: The South in Comparative Perspective," in Kees Gispen, ed., *What Made the South Different?* (Jackson, Miss., 1990), 71–88.

2. See, for example, Lori Ginzburg, *Women and the Work of Benevolence: Morality, Politics, and Class in the Nineteenth Century* (New Haven, Conn., 1990), 11–132; Ellen Carol DuBois, *Feminism and Suffrage: The Emergence of an Independent Women's Movement in America, 1848–1869* (Ithaca, N.Y., 1978), 21–52; Jane H. Pease and William H. Pease, *They Who Would Be Free: Blacks' Search for Freedom, 1830–1861* (New York, 1974), 120–123, 173–185, 236; James Oliver Horton and Lois E. Horton, *In Hope of Liberty: Culture, Community, and Protest among Northern Free Blacks, 1700–1860* (New York, 1997), 155–176; David Montgomery, *Citizen Worker: The Experience of Workers in the United States with Democracy and the Free Market during the Nineteenth Century* (New York, 1993), 18–21; and generally, Alexander Keyssar, *The Right to Vote: The Contested History of Democracy in the United States* (New York, 2000), 26–87.

3. Eugene D. Genovese, "Slavery: The World's Burden," in Harry P. Owens, ed., *Perspectives and Irony in American Slavery* (Jackson, Miss., 1976), 38–39; Ira Berlin, *Slaves without Masters: Free Negroes in the Antebellum South* (New York, 1974), 343–380; Donald E. Fehrenbacher, *The Dred Scott Case: Its Significance in American Law and Politics* (New York, 1978); Michael A. Morrison, *Slavery and the American West: The Eclipse of Manifest Destiny and the Coming of the Civil War* (Chapel Hill, N.C., 1997), 188–218.

4. Keyssar, *Right to Vote*, 53–87; Tyler Anbinder, *Nativism and Slavery: The*

Northern Know Nothings and the Politics of the 1850s (New York, 1992); Joe B. Wilkins, "Window on Freedom: The South's Response to the Emancipation of the Slaves in the British West Indies, 1833–61," Ph.D. diss., University of South Carolina, 1977; Alfred N. Hunt, *Haiti's Influence on Antebellum America: Slumbering Volcano in the Caribbean* (Baton Rouge, 1988), 123–146.

5. See, variously, Michael P. Johnson, *Toward a Patriarchal Republic: The Secession of Georgia* (Baton Rouge, 1977); William L. Barney, *The Secessionist Impulse: Alabama and Mississippi in 1860* (Princeton, N.J., 1974); and Stephanie McCurry, *Masters of Small Worlds: Yeoman Households, Gender Relations, and the Political Culture of the Antebellum South Carolina Low Country* (New York, 1995), 239–304.

6. Merton Dillon, *Slavery Attacked: Southern Slaves and Their Allies* (Baton Rouge, 1990), 240–242; Clarence L. Mohr, *On the Threshold of Freedom: Masters and Slaves in Civil War Georgia* (Athens, Ga., 1986), 36–37; Randolph B. Campbell, *An Empire for Slavery: The Peculiar Institution in Texas, 1821–1865* (Baton Rouge, 1989), 224–228; Booker T. Washington, *Up from Slavery: An Autobiography* (New York, 1900), 7–8.

7. John Q. Anderson, ed., *Brokenburn: The Journal of Kate Stone, 1861–1868* (Baton Rouge, 1955), 37; Testimony of Elizabeth Rose Hite, WPA Ex-Slave Narratives, LSU.

8. Testimony of George Braxton, SCC, 1877–1878, entry 732, claim 4329, box 190B, NA; Susie King Taylor, *A Black Woman's Civil War Memoirs*, ed. Patricia W. Romero and Willie Lee Rose (1902; New York, 1988), 29–32; C. Vann Woodward, ed., *Mary Chesnut's Civil War* (New Haven, Conn., 1981), 36, 234; Armstead L. Robinson, "Day of Jubilo: Civil War and the Demise of Slavery in the Mississippi Valley, 1861–1865," Ph.D. diss., University of Rochester, 1977, 36; Robert Russa Moton, *What the Negro Thinks* (New York, 1929), 10–11.

9. Lynda J. Morgan, *Emancipation in Virginia's Tobacco Belt, 1850–1870* (Athens, Ga., 1992), 87–89, 98–101; Mohr, *On the Threshold*, 120–122, 161–162; Leon F. Litwack, *Been in the Storm So Long: The Aftermath of Slavery* (New York, 1979), 36–39; and especially, Ira Berlin et al., *Freedom: A Documentary History of Emancipation, 1861–1867*, ser. 1, vol. 1: *The Destruction of Slavery* (Cambridge, Eng., 1985), 663–818.

10. Dillon, *Slavery Attacked*, 240; Bell I. Wiley, *Southern Negroes, 1861–1865* (New Haven, Conn., 1938), 82; Vincent Harding, *There Is a River: The Black Struggle for Freedom in America* (New York, 1981), 230; Winthrop D. Jordan, *Tumult and Silence at Second Creek: An Inquiry into a Civil War Slave Conspiracy* (Baton Rouge, 1993); Robinson, "Day of Jubilo," 39.

11. For an extremely insightful discussion of the relationship between "day-to-day forms of resistance" and rebellion among slaves, see Emilia Viotti da Costa, *Crowns of Glory, Tears of Blood: The Demerara Slave Rebellion of 1823* (New York, 1994), 75–85. On flight from the plantations as a crucial aspect of slave rebellion,

see Carolyn E. Fick, *The Making of Haiti: The San Domingue Revolution from Below* (Knoxville, Tenn., 1990), 91–117.

12. Louis Gerteis, *From Contraband to Freedman: Federal Policy toward Southern Blacks, 1861–1865* (Westport, Conn., 1973), 11–14; Berlin et al., *Freedom*, ser. 1, vol. 1, 59–61, 72; Robert F. Engs, *Freedom's First Generation: Black Hampton, Virginia, 1861–1890* (Philadelphia, 1979), 25–28.

13. Berlin et al., *Freedom*, ser. 1, vol. 1, 61; Edward McPherson, *The Political History of the United States of America during the Great Rebellion* (New York, 1864), 195–196; John W. Blassingame, ed., *Slave Testimony: Two Centuries of Letters, Speeches, Interviews, and Autobiographies* (Baton Rouge, 1977), 607–608.

14. McPherson, *Political History*, 195; Benjamin F. Butler to Lt. Gen. Scott, 27 May 1861, in Berlin et al., *Freedom*, ser. 1, vol. 1, 71; Blassingame, *Slave Testimony*, 608–609.

15. Simon Cameron to Maj. Gen. B. F. Butler, 8 Aug. 1861, in Berlin et al., *Freedom*, ser. 1, vol. 1, 74; Morgan, *Emancipation in Virginia's Tobacco Belt*, 79–82.

16. Berlin et al, *Freedom*, ser. 1, vol. 1, 17–19, 251, 398–400; Stephen V. Ash, *Middle Tennessee Society Transformed, 1860–1870: War and Peace in the Upper South* (Baton Rouge, 1988), 107; Robinson, "Day of Jubilo," 250–253. On antebellum runaways, see John Hope Franklin and Loren Schweninger, *Runaway Slaves: Rebels on the Plantation* (New York, 1999), 209–213.

17. McPherson, *Political History*, 196–197, 237–238; Berlin et al., *Freedom*, ser. 1, vol. 1, 22–27, 103–107; 187–199, 249–256; James M. McPherson, *What They Fought For, 1861–1865* (Baton Rouge, 1994), 59–60; Robinson, "Day of Jubilo," 318–320; Joel Williamson, *After Slavery: The Negro in South Carolina during Reconstruction, 1861–1877* (Chapel Hill, N.C., 1965), 4–5; John Eaton, *Grant, Lincoln, and the Freedmen: Reminiscences of the Civil War* (1907; New York, 1969), 1–2.

18. L. S. Livermore to George B. Fields, 19 Feb. 1863, Geo. B. Field to Hon. E. M. Stanton, 20 Mar. 1863, John Eaton Jr. to Col. Jno. A. Rawlins, 29 Apr. 1863, all in Ira Berlin et al., *Freedom*, ser. 1, vol. 3: *The Wartime Genesis of Free Labor: The Lower South* (Cambridge, Eng., 1990), 680–683, 686; Henry Crydenwise to Parents and All, 5 June 1863, Henry Crydenwise Letters, folder 6, EU.

19. Eaton to Rawlins, 29 Apr. 1863, in Berlin et al., *Freedom*, ser. 1, vol. 3, 692.

20. "Annual Report, 1862," AMA, roll 1, ARC, 41; Wiley, *Southern Negroes*, 260–261; Joe M. Richardson, *Christian Reconstruction: The American Missionary Association and Southern Blacks, 1861–1890* (Athens, Ga., 1986), 3–14; Willie Lee Rose, *Rehearsal for Reconstruction: The Port Royal Experiment* (Indianapolis, 1964).

21. G. H. Hyde to Mr. Whiting, 28 Feb. 1862, AMA, Virginia, roll 1; Berlin et al., *Freedom*, ser. 1, vol. 3, 14–17, 687–697; Blassingame, *Slave Testimony*, 367–444; John Cimprich, *Slavery's End in Tennessee, 1861–1865* (University, Ala., 1985), 71.

22. "Annual Report, 1862," AMA, roll 1, 43; John Eaton to Revd. S. S. Jocelyn, 18 May 1863, in Berlin et al., *Freedom*, ser. 1, vol. 3, 704–706; Supt. C. B. Wilder to Dr. Brethren, 1 Oct. 1862, AMA, Virginia, roll 1.

23. Eaton to Rawlins, 29 Apr. 1863, James Bryan to Edwin M. Stanton, 27 July 1863, Rear Admiral David D. Porter to Gen. Lorenzo Thomas, 21 Oct. 1863, Testimony of Charles A. Dana to AFIC, 4 Jan. 1864, all in Berlin et al., *Freedom*, ser. 1, vol. 3, 687–697, 716–717, 746; Testimony of Capt. E. W. Hooper, 1863, AFIC, ser. 12, Letters Received, filed with O-328 1863, [K-82], NA.

24. Porter to Thomas, 21 Oct. 1863, in Berlin et al., *Freedom*, ser. 1, vol. 3, 746. For the best treatments, see Gerteis, *Contraband to Freedman*, 65–98; Rose, *Rehearsal for Reconstruction*, 217–319; Lawrence N. Powell, *New Masters: Northern Planters during the Civil War and Reconstruction* (New Haven, Conn., 1980), 8–34, 73–96; Julie Saville, *The Work of Reconstruction: From Slave to Wage Laborer in South Carolina, 1860–1870* (Cambridge, Eng., 1994), 32–71; Eric Foner, *Reconstruction: America's Unfinished Revolution, 1863–1877* (New York, 1988), 50–60; and especially Berlin et al., *Freedom*, ser. 1, vol. 3.

25. Julian E. Bryant to Captain, 10 Oct. 1863, in Berlin et al., *Freedom*, ser. 1, vol. 3, 729, 96; Laura M. Towne, *Letters and Diary of Laura M. Towne: Written from the Sea Islands of South Carolina, 1862–1884*, ed. Rupert S. Holland (1912; New York, 1969), 9.

26. Capt. John W. Ela to Brig. Gen. James Bowen, 11 June 1863, in Berlin et al., *Freedom*, ser. 1, vol. 3, 455–456; Thomas W. Knox, *Camp-Fire and Cotton-Field: A Southern Adventure in Time of War* (New York, 1865), 372–373, 411.

27. U.S. Senate, *Report of the Secretary of War*, Exec. Doc. no. 53, 38th Cong., 1st sess. (Washington, D.C., 1864), 8.

28. Knox, *Camp-Fire*, 320; *New Orleans Tribune*, 13 Aug. 1864; Report by Sgt. Moses Proctor, 13–14 June 1864, Chaplain J. I. Herrick to Brig. Gen. Buford, 30 Nov. 1864, Col. Samuel Thomas to Brig. Gen. L. Thomas, 15 June 1864, all in Berlin et al., *Freedom*, ser. 1, vol. 3, 830–832, 838–839, 862; Paul K. Eiss, "A Share in the Land: Freedpeople and the Government of Labour in Southern Louisiana, 1862–1865," *S&A* 19 (April 1998): 46–89.

29. Eaton, *Grant, Lincoln, and the Freedmen*, 163; S. Thomas to L. Thomas, 15 June 1864, Herrick to Buford, 30 Nov. 1864, both in Berlin et al., *Freedom*, ser. 1, vol. 3, 838, 862; C. Peter Ripley, *Slaves and Freedmen in Civil War Louisiana* (Baton Rouge, 1976), 138.

30. Janet Sharp Hermann, *The Pursuit of a Dream* (New York, 1981), 3–60; Eaton, *Grant, Lincoln, and the Freedmen*, 85–86; Vernon Lane Wharton, *The Negro in Mississippi, 1865–1890* (Chapel Hill, N.C., 1947), 38–41; Foner, *Reconstruction*, 58–59; Knox, *Camp-Fire*, 353; Steven J. Ross, "Freed Soil, Freed Labor, Freed Men: John Eaton and the Davis Bend Experiment," *JSH* 44 (May 1978): 213–232.

31. Edward Magdol, *A Right to the Land: Essays on the Freedmen's Community* (Westport, Conn., 1977), 102–103, 176–180; Saville, *Work of Reconstruction*, 32–71; Berlin et al., *Freedom*, ser. 1, vol. 3, 105–109; Foner, *Reconstruction*, 76.

32. "Annual Report, 1863," 39–43, AMA; Magdol, *Right to the Land*, 90–108; Berlin et al., *Freedom*, ser. 1, vol. 2: *The Wartime Genesis of Free Labor: The Upper South* (Cambridge, Eng., 1993), 42–43, 85–110, 243–262; Ash, *Middle Tennessee*, 135; David S. Cecelski, "Abraham Galloway: Wilmington's Lost Prophet and the Rise of Black Radicalism in the American South," in David S. Cecelski and Timothy B. Tyson, eds., *Democracy Betrayed: The Wilmington Race Riot of 1898 and Its Legacy* (Chapel Hill, N.C., 1998), 49–53.

33. The best estimates on the number of slaves who had reached Union lines by this point are to be found in Berlin et al., *Freedom*, ser. 1, vol. 3, 77–80. The editors of *Freedom* count those who served "as soldiers, military laborers, residents of contraband camps, urban workers, or agricultural laborers on government supervised plantations and farms." By the spring of 1865, at least 475,000 former slaves and free blacks fell into these categories, though there are figures from mid-1864, along with some adjustments made to compensate for the time differentiation, that suggest that the totals were probably around 400,000 at that point. Well over 200,000 had reached Union lines in the Mississippi Valley and lower Louisiana, well over 50,000 had in Virginia, nearly 40,000 had in the Carolinas, and well over 50,000 had in Kentucky and Tennessee. Together, their numbers represented at least 15 percent of the combined slave population in those states, based on the 1860 federal census.

34. On agitation for the reform of slavery in the Confederacy, see Drew Gilpin Faust, *The Creation of Confederate Nationalism* (Baton Rouge, 1988), 58–81; Robert F. Durden, *The Gray and the Black: The Confederate Debate on Emancipation* (Baton Rouge, 1972), 29–73; and Mohr, *On the Threshold*, 235–271.

35. Robert A. Tyson Diary, 2 Feb. 1864, LSU; Robinson, "Day of Jubilo," 235, 243–247.

36. Robinson, "Day of Jubilo," 235; Admiral David Dixon Porter, *Incidents and Anecdotes of the Civil War* (New York, 1886), 89–91.

37. John Houston Bills Diary, 1863, SHC.

38. Wiley, *Southern Negroes*, 74–75; Ripley, *Slaves and Freedmen*, 22–23; J. Carlyle Sitterson, *Sugar Country: The Cane Sugar Industry in the South, 1753–1950* (Lexington, Ky., 1953), 209–210.

39. George H. Hepworth, *The Whip, Hoe, and Sword; The Gulf Department in '63* (Boston, 1864), 29–30; Testimony of John King, 16 Nov. 1871, in Berlin et al., *Freedom*, ser. 1, vol. 3, 479–480.

40. Ash, *Middle Tennessee*, 139; W. Bosson to Maj. Genl. Thomas, 27 Jan. 1864, and Testimony of Alfred Scruggs, 31 July 1872, both in Berlin et al., *Freedom*, ser. 1, vol. 2, 437, 445, 636; Labor Contract: William R. Steen and Freedpeople, 26 Jan. 1864, in Berlin et al., *Freedom*, ser. 1, vol. 3, 785.

41. Washington, *Up from Slavery*, 8–9; George P. Rawick, ed., *The American Slave: A Composite Autobiography* (Westport, Conn., 1972), ser. 1, vol. 4, pt. 1, 52, and supp. ser. 1, vol. 4, 12; Campbell, *Empire for Slavery*, 246–247; Morgan, *Emancipation in Virginia's Tobacco Belt*, 108.

42. Carol Bleser, ed., *Secret and Sacred: The Diaries of James Henry Hammond, a Southern Slaveholder* (New York, 1988), 289–290; Adam B. Davidson to William Alexander Graham, 30 Jan. 1864, in Max R. Williams, ed., *The Papers of William Alexander Graham*, 8 vols. (Raleigh, N.C., 1957–1992), vol. 6, 21.

43. See, for example, Robinson, "Day of Jubilo," 522–571; Litwack, *Been in the Storm So Long*, 104–166; George C. Rable, *The Confederate Republic: A Revolution against Politics* (Chapel Hill, N.C., 1994), 154–194; Drew Gilpin Faust, *Mothers of Invention: Women of the Slaveholding South in the American Civil War* (Chapel Hill, N.C., 1996), 53–79.

44. James L. Smith, *Autobiography of James L. Smith* (Norwich, Conn., 1881), 116–117; Hepworth, *Whip, Hoe, and Sword*, 142–144, 259–260; Wayne K. Durrill, *War of Another Kind: A Southern Community in the Great Rebellion* (New York, 1990).

45. Rawick, ed., *The American Slave*, ser. 1, vol. 12, 12–13.

46. James M. McPherson, *The Battle Cry of Freedom: The Civil War Era* (New York, 1988), 312–313; James M. McPherson, *The Struggle for Equality: Abolitionists and the Negro in the Civil War and Reconstruction* (Princeton, N.J., 1964), 192.

47. Benjamin Quarles, *The Negro in the Civil War* (Boston, 1953), 22–35; William Cheek and Aimee Lee Cheek, *John Mercer Langston and the Fight for Black Freedom, 1829–1865* (Urbana, Ill., 1989), 383–387.

48. *Christian Recorder*, 18 January 1862; Brig. Gen. J. W. Phelps to Capt. R. S. Davis, 16 June 1862, in Joseph T. Wilson, *The Black Phalanx: A History of Negro Soldiers of the United States in the Wars of 1775–1812, 1861–1865* (Hartford, Conn., 1890), 187–188; Berlin et al., *Freedom*, ser. 2, vol. 1: *The Black Military Experience* (Cambridge, Eng., 1982), 37–73.

49. The best and most comprehensive treatment of the black military experience during the Civil War is Berlin et al., *Freedom*, ser. 2. For other important contributions see Quarles, *Negro in the Civil War*; Wilson, *Black Phalanx*; George W. Williams, *A History of the Negro Troops in the War of the Rebellion, 1861–1865* (New York, 1888); James M. McPherson, *The Negro's Civil War: How American Negroes Felt and Acted during the War for the Union* (New York, 1965); Dudley Taylor Cornish, *The Sable Arm: Negro Troops in the Union Army, 1861–1865* (1956; New York, 1966); W. E. B. Du Bois, *Black Reconstruction in America, 1860–1880* (1935; New York, 1971), 55–127; Litwack, *Been in the Storm So Long*, 64–103; and McPherson, *Political History*, 228–229. We can only estimate the proportion of black soldiers in the Union army by the last year of the war, and the estimate itself is somewhat

contingent. In January 1865, 959,460 soldiers were enrolled in the Union army, of whom 123,156 were black (12.8 percent), but of the total only 620,924 soldiers were "present," pushing the black portion to 19.8 percent. See Thomas L. Livermore, *Numbers and Losses in the Civil War in America: 1861–1865* (Bloomington, Ind., 1957), 47; E. B. Long, *The Civil War Day by Day: An Almanac, 1861–1865,* with Barbara Long (New York, 1971), 706; Berlin et al., *Freedom,* ser. 2, 733.

50. See, for example, Berlin et al., *Freedom,* ser. 2, 113–278.

51. Quarles, *Negro in the Civil War,* 109–110; Mohr, *On the Threshold,* 84–85; Berlin et al., *Freedom,* ser. 2, 118–120.

52. Wilson, *Black Phalanx,* 130–131; Joseph T. Glatthaar, *Forged in Battle: The Civil War Alliance of Black Soldiers and White Officers* (New York, 1990), 72–75; Edwin S. Redkey, ed., *A Grand Army of Black Men: Letters from African-American Soldiers in the Union Army, 1861–1865* (Cambridge, Eng., 1992), 84–85; "Abstract of a visit of Major Yarrington to plantations of Dr. Knapp, Ducross et al.," 3 Sept. 1863, in Berlin et al., *Freedom,* ser. 1, vol. 3, 461.

53. Berlin et al., *Freedom,* ser. 2, 13, 55–56, 116–122.

54. Cornish, *Sable Arm,* 75–78, 130–131; Glatthaar, *Forged in Battle,* 270–274; Bobby L. Lovett, "The Negro in Tennessee, 1861–1866," Ph.D. diss., University of Arkansas, 1978, viii–ix, 110–113.

55. See, for example, Samuel J. Kirkwood to Gen. Henry W. Halleck, 5 Aug. 1862, in Berlin et al., *Freedom,* ser. 2, 85.

56. Rawick, *American Slave,* ser. 1, vol. 7, 566; *Christian Recorder,* 25 July 1864, quoted in Redkey, *Grand Army of Black Men,* 66; Berlin et al., *Freedom,* ser. 2, 1–2; Cornish, *Sable Arm,* 161–162.

57. In mid-June 1864, Congress equalized the pay of black and white soldiers retroactive to 1 Jan. 1864, and permitted the attorney general to compensate blacks who were free when the war began from the time of their enlistment. See Berlin et al., *Freedom,* ser. 2, 362–405; McPherson, *Negro's Civil War,* 193–204; Litwack, *Been in the Storm So Long,* 79–87; Glatthaar, *Forged in Battle,* 169–176. On General Orders No. 100, see Cornish, *Sable Arm,* 160–180. "It was understood amongst us," one Confederate soldier wrote in 1864 from North Carolina, "that we take no negro prisoners." See John W. Graham to William A. Graham, 13 Mar. 1864, in Williams, *Papers of William Alexander Graham,* vol. 6, 42–43.

58. Edwin S. Williams to Rev. S. S. Jocelyn, 26 Apr. 1863, AMA, South Carolina, roll 1; Berlin et al., *Freedom,* ser. 2, 21; McPherson, *Struggle for Equality,* 217.

59. Testimony of Thomas Wentworth Higginson, 1863, AFIC, Letters Rec'd, [K-81].

60. Wilson, *Black Phalanx,* 504. Service in "people's armies" of several types has historically been seen as an immensely politicizing experience for previously unfranchised groups. See, for example, Alan Forest, *Soldiers of the French Revolution*

(Durham, N.C., 1990), 89–124; Eric Foner, *Tom Paine and Revolutionary America* (New York, 1976), 62–69; Christopher Hill, *The World Turned Upside Down: Radical Ideas during the English Revolution* (New York, 1972).

61. Wilson, *Black Phalanx*, 504–505; Fannie J. Scott to Rev. C. H. Fowler, 1 Feb. 1864, AMA, Mississippi, roll 1; Cimprich, *Slavery's End in Tennessee*, 89; "Sergeant" to *Liberator*, 26 July 1864, quoted in Redkey, *Grand Army of Black Men*, 69; Ripley, *Slaves and Freedmen*, 122; David Macrae, *The Americans at Home* (1871; New York, 1952), 330; Berlin et al., *Freedom*, ser. 2, 611–612.

62. Berlin et al., *Freedom*, ser. 2, 613; Col. T. H. Barrett to the Officers and Men of the 62d U.S. Colored Infantry, 4 Jan. 1866, in Berlin et al., *Freedom*, ser. 2, 782–783; *Christian Recorder*, 31 Dec. 1864.

63. Your Big Uncle Sam White to Annie, 22 May 1863, Civil War Soldiers' Letters, LSU; Berlin et al., *Freedom*, ser. 2, 517–566.

64. *Nashville Times*, quoted in *New Orleans Tribune*, 30 July 1864.

65. Wilson, *Black Phalanx*, 291–303.

66. George Thomas to *Weekly Anglo-African*, 18 July 1865, quoted in Redkey, *Grand Army of Black Men*, 188–189.

67. Thomas Wentworth Higginson, *Army Life in a Black Regiment*, intro. by John Hope Franklin (1869; Boston, 1962), 22–23.

68. Smith, *Autobiography*, viii–ix. See also Charles L. Perdue et al., eds., *Weevils in the Wheat: Interviews with Virginia Ex-Slaves* (Bloomington, Ind., 1976), 103–104.

69. Joel H. Silbey, *A Respectable Minority: The Democratic Party in the Civil War Era, 1860–1868* (New York, 1977), 115–139; Harding, *There Is a River*, 246.

70. For the best brief discussion of the emergence of these early Reconstruction regimes, see Foner, *Reconstruction*, 37–43. But also see Barbara Fields, *Slavery and Freedom on the Middle Ground: Maryland during the Nineteenth Century* (New Haven, Conn., 1985), 131–166; Jean H. Baker, *The Politics of Continuity: Maryland Political Parties from 1858 to 1870* (Baltimore, 1973); and Richard O. Curry, ed., *Radicalism, Racism, and Party Realignment: The Border States during Reconstruction* (Baltimore, 1969).

71. Announced on 8 Dec. 1863, Lincoln's Proclamation of Amnesty and Reconstruction offered pardons for Confederates who took an oath of loyalty to the United States and provided for the establishment of new governments in the former Confederate states when the number of those pardoned equaled at least 10 percent of the total votes cast in the election of 1860. See Foner, *Reconstruction*, 35–36.

72. Carl H. Moneyhon, *The Impact of the Civil War and Reconstruction on Arkansas: Persistence in the Midst of Ruin* (Baton Rouge, 1994), 156–167; John William Graves, *Town and Country: Race Relations in an Urban-Rural Context, Arkansas, 1865–1905* (Fayetteville, Ark., 1990), 7–9; Thomas B. Alexander, *Political Recon-*

struction in Tennessee (Nashville, 1950), 15–77; Ash, *Middle Tennessee*, 152–161; Foner, *Reconstruction*, 43–45; Berlin et al., *Freedom*, ser. 2, 12.

73. Joe Gray Taylor, *Louisiana Reconstructed, 1863–1877* (Baton Rouge, 1974), 21–41; Ted Tunnell, *Crucible of Reconstruction: War, Radicalism, and Race in Louisiana, 1862–1877* (Baton Rouge, 1984), 35–37; Foner, *Reconstruction*, 46–50; *Christian Recorder*, 26 Mar. 1864.

74. Taylor, *Louisiana Reconstructed*, 42–52; Tunnell, *Crucible of Reconstruction*, 51–65; Foner, *Reconstruction*, 48–50.

75. Tunnell, *Crucible of Reconstruction*, 37; McPherson, *Struggle for Equality*, 238–246; Testimony of Charles A. Dana, 4 Jan. 1864, in Berlin et al., *Freedom*, ser. 1, vol. 3, 770–771.

76. *New Orleans Tribune*, 28 July 1864; Du Bois, *Black Reconstruction*, 153; Cheek and Cheek, *Langston*, 425–429.

77. *New Orleans Tribune*, 25 Oct. 1864, 27 Oct. 1864; *Christian Recorder*, 1 Oct. 1864; Cheek and Cheek, *Langston*, 429–436. On the political climate and divisions of the 1850s, see Pease and Pease, *They Who Would Be Free*, 206–277; William S. McFeely, *Frederick Douglass* (New York, 1991), 163–216; and Wilson Jeremiah Moses, *The Golden Age of Black Nationalism, 1850–1925* (New York, 1988), 32–55.

78. Cimprich, *Slavery's End in Tennessee*, 104–110; Ash, *Middle Tennessee*, 138.

79. Petition of the Colored Citizens of Nashville, 9 Jan. 1865, in Berlin et al., *Freedom*, ser. 2, 811–816; Alrutheus Ambush Taylor, *The Negro in Tennessee, 1865–1880* (Washington, D.C., 1941), 1–2.

80. *New Orleans Tribune*, 29 Dec. 1864, 4 Jan. 1865; "Proceedings of the State Convention of the Colored People of Louisiana," in Philip S. Foner and George E. Walker, eds., *Proceedings of the Black State Conventions 1840–1865*, 2 vols. (Philadelphia, 1979–1980), vol. 2, 243–245; Tunnell, *Crucible of Reconstruction*, 76–77; Jean-Charles Houzeau, *My Passage at the* New Orleans Tribune: *A Memoir of the Civil War Era*, ed. David Rankin (Baton Rouge, 1984), 96–97.

81. "State Convention of the Colored People of Louisiana," 245–249; *New Orleans Tribune*, 12 Jan. 1865; Roger A. Fischer, *The Segregation Struggle in Louisiana, 1862–1877* (Urbana, Ill., 1974), 30–32.

82. "State Convention of the Colored People of Louisiana," 249–250; *New Orleans Tribune*, 14 Jan. 1865, 15 Jan. 1865, Tunnell, *Crucible of Reconstruction*, 81–86.

83. *New Orleans Tribune*, 29 Dec. 1864, 15 Jan. 1865, 15 Nov. 1864.

84. "Annual Report, 1862," 54, AMA, roll 1; Washington, *Up from Slavery*, 19–20; Testimony of William J. Minor, 25 Apr. 1865, Smith-Brady Commission, record group 94, ser. 736, [AA–3], NA.

85. Rev. Horace F. James, *Annual Report of the Superintendent of Negro Affairs in North Carolina, 1864* (Boston, 1865), 45; William T. Sherman to Ellen, 25 Dec. 1864, William Tecumseh Sherman Letters, UGa.

86. Elizabeth Hyde Botume, *First Days amongst the Contrabands* (Boston, 1893), 102, 108–109, 174; Testimony of Capt. E. W. Hooper, [1863], AFIC, Letters Rec'd, [K-82].

87. Mrs. F. L. Williams to Rev. Jocelyn, 28 Apr. 1863, AMA, South Carolina, roll 1; W. T. Richardson to Rev. George Whipple, 25 Aug. 1864, AMA, South Carolina, roll 1; Towne, *Letters and Diary of Laura Towne*, 162.

88. *Christian Recorder*, 16 Jan. 1864; *New York National Anti-Slavery Standard*, 16 Jan. 1864; Williamson, *After Slavery*, 31.

89. *New York National Anti-Slavery Standard*, 4 Feb. 1865; Botume, *First Days amongst the Contrabands*, 75–76.

3. OF RUMORS AND REVELATIONS

1. Frederick Douglass, "What to the Slave Is the Fourth of July? An Address Delivered in Rochester, New York, on 5 July 1852," in John W. Blassingame, ed., *The Frederick Douglass Papers*, ser. 1, vol. 2 (New Haven, Conn., 1982), 371.

2. Brig. Gen. Edwin A. Wild to Bvt. Maj. Gen. Rufus Saxton, 14 July 1865, BRFAL, SC Asst. Comr., ser. 2929, Reports of Conditions and Operations, NA [A-7006]; Nimrod Porter Diary, 4 July 1865, SHC; *Christian Recorder*, 22 July 1865, 29 July 1865, 2 Sept. 1865; "Statement of Brig. Gen. Thomas Kirby Smith," 14 Sept. 1865, *Senate Executive Documents*, doc. no. 2, 39th Cong., 1st sess. (Washington, D.C., 1865), 58; David L. Swain to William A. Graham, 4 July 1865, in Max R. Williams, ed., *The Papers of William Alexander Graham*, 8 vols. (Raleigh, N.C., 1957–1992), vol. 6, 324.

3. Wild to Saxton, 14 July 1865, BRFAL, South Carolina Asst. Comr. [A-7006]; *Christian Recorder*, 6 July 1865, 15 July 1865, 22 July 1865.

4. *New Orleans Tribune*, 4 July 1865; Fields Cook et al. to Andrew Johnson, 10 June 1865, in Paul H. Bergeron, ed., *The Papers of Andrew Johnson*, 10 vols. (Knoxville, Tenn., 1989), vol. 8, 210–212; Eric Foner, *Reconstruction: America's Unfinished Revolution, 1863–1877* (New York, 1988), 110–111; Euline Williams Brock, "Black Political Leadership during Reconstruction," Ph.D. diss., North Texas State University, 1974, 42–48; Roberta Sue Alexander, *North Carolina Faces the Freedmen: Race Relations during Presidential Reconstruction, 1865–1867* (Durham, N.C., 1985), 16–18; W. McKee Evans, *Ballots and Fence Rails: Reconstruction on the Lower Cape Fear* (Chapel Hill, N.C., 1966), 18–51; Armstead L. Robinson, "Plans Dat Comed from God: Institution Building and the Emergence of Black Leadership in Reconstruction Memphis," in Orville Vernon Burton and Robert C. McMath, eds., *Toward a New South? Studies in Post–Civil War Southern Communities* (Westport, Conn., 1982), 71–102; Herbert Aptheker, "Organizational Activities of Southern Negroes, 1865," in his *To Be Free: Studies in American Negro History* (New York, 1948), 136–162.

5. Newspaper Clippings from December 1865, John Mercer Langston Papers,

box 6, scrapbook 1, FU; John Mercer Langston, *From the Virginia Plantation to the National Capitol; or, The First and Only Negro Representative in Congress from the Old Dominion* (Hartford, Conn., 1894), 245.

6. Howard Rabinowitz, *Race Relations in the Urban South, 1865–1890* (New York, 1978), 18–20; Leon Litwack, *Been in the Storm So Long: The Aftermath of Slavery* (New York, 1979), 310–316; Alrutheus A. Taylor, *The Negro in the Reconstruction of Virginia* (Washington, D.C., 1926), 34; Alrutheus A. Taylor, *The Negro in Tennessee, 1865–1880* (Washington, D.C., 1941), 27; Vernon L. Wharton, *The Negro in Mississippi, 1865–1890* (Chapel Hill, N.C., 1947), 106; John W. Graves, *Town and Country: Race Relations in an Urban-Rural Context, Arkansas, 1865–1905* (Fayetteville, Ark., 1990), 103; Orville Vernon Burton, "The Rise and Fall of Afro-American Town Life: Town and Country in Reconstruction Edgefield, South Carolina," in Burton and McMath, *Toward a New South?*, 158–160; Peter J. Rachleff, *Black Labor in the South: Richmond, Virginia, 1865–1890* (Philadelphia, 1984), 14.

7. Ira Berlin, *Slaves without Masters: The Free Negro in the Antebellum South* (New York, 1974), 284–315; Rachleff, *Black Labor*, 13–39; Joseph P. Reidy, *From Slavery to Agrarian Capitalism in the Cotton Plantation South: Central Georgia, 1800–1880* (Chapel Hill, N.C., 1992), 76–78; Foner, *Reconstruction*, 78–110.

8. *Nashville Daily Press and Times*, 8 Aug. 1865. On the "jacobin" tradition, see Dorothy Thompson, "Seceding from the Seceders: The Decline of the Jacobin Tradition in Ireland, 1790–1850," in her *Outsiders: Class, Gender, and Nation* (London, 1993), 140–142.

9. *Christian Recorder*, 9 Sept. 1865; Sidney Andrews, *The South since the War: As Shown by Fourteen Weeks of Travel and Observation in Georgia and the Carolinas*, intro. David Donald (1866; Boston, 1971), 119–120; *Proceedings of the Colored People's Convention of the State of South Carolina, Held in Zion Church, Charleston, South Carolina, November 1865* (Charleston, S.C., 1865), 6–7, 28, 30–31; "Proceedings of the Convention of the Colored People of Virginia, Held in the City of Alexandria, August 2–5, 1865," in Philip S. Foner and George E. Walker, eds., *Proceedings of the Black State Conventions, 1840–1865* (Philadelphia, 1980), vol. 2, 262–263, 264–265, 271–274; Thomas Holt, *Black over White: Negro Political Leadership in South Carolina during Reconstruction* (Urbana, Ill., 1977), 14–20.

10. *Convention of the Freedmen of North Carolina: Official Proceedings* (Raleigh, N.C., 1865), 5; *Proceedings of Colored People's Convention of South Carolina*, 6–7, 23–25; "Proceedings of Convention of Colored People of Virginia," 259–260, 270; Alexander, *North Carolina Faces the Freedmen*, 17–31; Holt, *Black over White*, 14–20. The best general treatments of the conventions are to be found in Foner, *Reconstruction*, 112–119; and especially in Litwack, *Been in the Storm So Long*, 503–524.

11. "Proceedings of Convention of Colored People of Virginia," 270; *Proceedings of Colored People's Convention of South Carolina*, 24–25; *Journal of Freedom*, 28 Oct. 1865; Litwack, *Been in the Storm So Long*, 520.

12. *Proceedings of Colored People's Convention of South Carolina*, 6–7; *Athens (Ga.) Southern Watchman*, 31 Jan. 1866; *Nashville Daily Press and Times*, 8 Aug. 1865; Peter Kolchin, *First Freedom: The Responses of Alabama Blacks to Emancipation and Reconstruction* (Westport, Conn., 1973), 152–153; Hannah Rosen, "The Gender of Reconstruction: Rape, Race, and Citizenship in the Postemancipation South," Ph.D. diss., University of Chicago, 1999, 184–189.

13. *Convention of Freedmen of North Carolina*, 4; Andrews, *South since the War*, 121, 131. Also see John R. Dennett, *The South as It Is, 1865–1866* (1866; New York, 1965), 148–153. According to the *Official Proceedings*, there were 106 delegates representing 34 counties. But owing to the admission of delegates without regular credentials, Sidney Andrews claimed that there were 117 delegates representing 42 counties, while John R. Dennett estimated "about 120 delegates." In any case, it was the largest of all the early freedmen's conventions.

14. Alexander, *North Carolina Faces the Freedmen*, 21–25; Andrews, *South since the War*, 123; *Convention of Freedmen of North Carolina*, 6, 12–14, 16–17, 22; Dennett, *South as It Is*, 148–153; Horace W. Raper, *William W. Holden: North Carolina's Political Enigma* (Chapel Hill, N.C., 1985), 71–72.

15. *New Orleans Tribune*, 8 Sept. 1865, 20 Sept. 1865, 15 Oct. 1865, 6 Nov. 1865; Henry Clay Warmoth, *War, Politics and Reconstruction: Stormy Days in Louisiana* (New York, 1930), 42–45; Joe Gray Taylor, *Louisiana Reconstructed, 1863–1877* (Baton Rouge, 1974), 60–61, 74–76.

16. Lt. William E. Dougherty to Lt. L. Crooker, 18 Oct. 1865, BRFAL, La. Asst. Comr., Ser. 1303, Letters Rec'd, L-259 1865 [A-8577]; Capt. Jo. Rhodes to Capt. B. B. Campbell, 21 Oct. 1865, Dept. of Louisiana, RG 393, pt. 1, ser. 1757, Letters Rec'd, L-516 1865, NA [C-653]; Lt. William E. Doughtery to Lt. L. Crooker, 7 Nov. 1865, Dept. of Louisiana, RG 393, pt. 1, ser. 1845, Letters Rec'd, D-6 1865 [C-805]; *New Orleans Tribune*, 9 Nov. 1865, 10 Nov. 1865; Warmoth, *War, Politics and Reconstruction*, 45.

17. Andrews, *South since the War*, 130–131, 159–161.

18. See, for example, Eric L. McKitrick, *Andrew Johnson and Reconstruction* (Chicago, 1960), 166–170; Foner, *Reconstruction*, 193–204.

19. Capt. Thos. Kanady to Lt. Z. K. Wood, 23 Dec. 1865, Dept. of the Gulf, RG 393, pt. 1, ser. 1757, Letters Rec'd, L-896 1865 [C-655]; Carl Schurz to President Andrew Johnson, 13 Aug. 1865, in Brooks D. Simpson et al., eds., *Advice after Appomattox: Letters to Andrew Johnson, 1865–66* (Knoxville, Tenn., 1987), 95; John J. Robertson et al. to Maj. Gen. James B. Steedman, 27 Apr. 1865, BRFAL, Ga. Asst. Comr., ser. 653, Affidavits and Petitions [A-5166]; Robert Cartmell Diaries, 30 Oct. 1865, TSLA; *Senate Executive Documents*, no. 2, 39th Cong., 1st sess. (Washington, D.C., 1866), 31.

20. Samuel A. Agnew Diary, 3 Nov. 1865, SHC; William S. Thomson to W. A. Thomson, 7 Dec. 1865, William S. Thomson Papers, box 1, folder 8, EU; C. C.

Emerson to Gov. William W. Holden, 3 June 1865, Governors' Papers, box 185, NCDAH.

21. See, for example, Lt. D. H. Reese to Lt. D. G. Fenno, 31 Oct. 1865, BRFAL, La. Asst. Comr., ser. 1303, Letters Rec'd [A-8589]; Chaplain Thos. Smith to Lt. S. D. Barnes, 2 Oct. 1865, BRFAL, Acting Asst. Comr. for the Northern Dist. of Miss., ser. 2188, Reg. Letters Rec'd [A-9317]; H. M. Spofford to Maj. Gen. R. W. Johnson, 10 July 1865, BRFAL, Tenn. Asst. Comr., ser. 3379, Reg. Letters Rec'd [A-6194]; Andrew J. Hamilton to President Andrew Johnson, 21 Oct. 1865, in Bergeron, *Papers of Andrew Johnson*, vol. 9, 263–264; H. H. Montgomery to Gov. Sharkey, 16 Aug. 1865, Governors' Records, RG 27, box 62, MDAH; *Report of the Joint Committee on Reconstruction*, 39th Cong., 1st sess. (Washington, D.C., 1866), pt. 3, 31, 160.

22. *Report of Joint Committee*, pt. 3, 31. Also see C. C. Emerson to Gov. William W. Holden, 3 June 1865, and A. M. Waddell to Gov. William W. Holden, 18 June 1865, both in Governors' Papers, box 185; Richard Jones et al. to Gov. Lewis Parsons, 26 Sept. 1865, Gov. Lewis Parsons Papers, ADAH; *New Orleans Tribune*, 21 Oct. 1865; F. Marion Shields to Pres. Andrew Johnson, 25 Oct. 1865, BRFAL, Miss. Asst. Comr., ser. 2052, Letters Rec'd [A-9065]; *Senate Executive Documents*, no. 27, 39th Cong., 1st sess. (Washington, D.C., 1866), 83–84; Dan T. Carter, "The Anatomy of Fear: The Christmas Insurrection Scare of 1865," *JSH* 42 (August 1976): 345–364.

23. George P. Rawick, ed., *The American Slave: A Composite Autobiography* (Westport, Conn., 1972), ser. 1, vol. 7, 103. On the importance of credibility in the circulation of rumors, see Clay Ramsay, *The Ideology of the Great Fear: The Soissonnais in 1789* (Baltimore, 1992), xxvii, 123–127.

24. Swain to Graham, 4 July 1865, in Williams, *Papers of William A. Graham*, vol. 6, 324. On federal land and confiscation policy during this period, see Edward McPherson, *The Political History of the United States of America during the Great Rebellion* (Washington, D.C., 1865), pp. 195–208; James M. McPherson, *The Struggle for Equality: Abolitionists and the Negro in the Civil War and Reconstruction* (Princeton, N.J., 1964), 246–259; Edward Magdol, *A Right to the Land: Essays on the Freedmen's Community* (Westport, Conn., 1977), 139–173; Claude F. Oubre, *Forty Acres and a Mule: The Freedmen's Bureau and Black Landownership* (Baton Rouge, 1978), 1–71; William S. McFeely, *Yankee Stepfather: O. O. Howard and the Freedmen* (New Haven, Conn., 1968), 211–244; Foner, *Reconstruction*, 158–159, 183–184.

25. James C. Scott, *Domination and the Arts of Resistance: Hidden Transcripts* (New Haven, Conn., 1990), 144–148; Gordon W. Allport and Leo Postman, *The Psychology of Rumor* (New York, 1947), 33–47.

26. T. William Lewis to Maj. Gen. Devens, 26 Dec. 1865, Dept. of the South, RG 393, pt. 1, ser. 4112, Letters Rec'd, box 1; W. J. Minor et al. to Maj. Gen. Banks, 14 Jan. 1863, in Ira Berlin et al., eds., *Freedom: A Documentary History of Emancipation, 1861–1867*, ser. 1, vol. 3: *The Wartime Genesis of Free Labor: The*

Lower South (Cambridge, Eng., 1990), 408–409; Saxton quoted in *Report of Joint Committee*, pt. 2, 221; Elizabeth Hyde Botume, *First Days amongst the Contrabands* (Boston, 1893), 170; Magdol, *Right to the Land*, 169–170; John K. Betterworth, *Confederate Mississippi: The People and Policies of a Cotton State in Wartime* (Baton Rouge, 1943), 163–164.

27. *Report of Joint Committee*, pt. 2, 177. For a pioneering study of communications networks among slaves and free blacks in the Atlantic world of the late eighteenth century, see Julius S. Scott III, "The Common Wind: Currents of Afro-American Communication in the Age of the Haitian Revolution," Ph.D. diss., Duke University, 1986. For broader comparisons, see Georges Lefebvre, *The Great Fear of 1789: Rural Panic in Revolutionary France* (1932; New York, 1973), 67–74, 148–155; Ranajit Guha, *Elementary Aspects of Peasant Insurgency in Colonial India* (Delhi, 1983), 220–277.

28. Charles L. Perdue Jr. et al., ed., *Weevils in the Wheat: Interviews with Virginia Ex-Slaves* (Bloomington, Ind., 1976), 167–168; George H. Hepworth, *The Whip, Hoe, and Sword; or, The Gulf Department in '63* (Boston, 1864), 25–26.

29. *Savannah Republican*, 5 Feb. 1865, enclosed in Mansfield French to Samuel Breck, 28 Feb. 1865, RG 94, ser. 12, Letters Rec'd, F-174 1865, NA [K-504]; Spofford to Johnson, 10 July 1865, BRFAL, Tenn. Asst. Comr.; S. G. Wright to Rev. H. E. Fairchild, 10 Dec. 1865, AMA, Mississippi, roll 1, ARC; Capt. C. B. Wilder to Col. Orlando Brown, 17 Nov. 1865, BRFAL, Va. Asst. Comr., ser. 3799, Unreg. Letters and Telegrams Rec'd [A-7521]; E. B. Hayward to Gen. Wade Hampton, 15 Nov. 1865, enclosed in Hayward to Gen. D. E. Sickles, 13 Dec. 1865, Dept. of S.C., RG 393, pt. 1, Letters Rec'd, H-147 1865 [C-1383].

30. Lt. Col. F. H. Whittier to Lt. C. B. Fillebrown, 4 Nov. 1865, Dept. of the South and South Carolina, RG 393, pt. 1, ser. 4112, Letters Rec'd, box 1; Capt. J. J. Upham to Lt. J. W. Clous, 4 Sept. 1865, Subdist. of Coosawhatchie, RG 393, ser. 2383, Letters Sent [C-1595].

31. E. G. Baker to Messrs. Irby and Ellis and Mosely, 22 Oct. 1865 in Ira Berlin et al., eds., *Freedom: A Documentary History of Emancipation, 1861–1867*, ser. 2: *The Black Military Experience* (Cambridge, Eng., 1982), 747–748; Henry William Ravenel, Private Journal, 21 June 1865, 24 June 1865, 25 June 1865, vol. 8, SCL; Gen. U.S. Grant to President Johnson, 18 Dec. 1865, *Congressional Globe*, 39th Cong., 1st sess. (Washington, D.C., 1865), 78; Schurz to Johnson, 29 Aug. 1865, in Simpson et al., *Advice after Appomattox*, 113–114. More generally on blacks in the army of occupation, see Berlin et al., *Freedom*, ser. 2, 733–736; Joseph T. Glatthaar, *Forged in Battle: The Civil War Alliance of Black Soldiers and White Officers* (New York, 1990), 207–230; Edwin S. Redkey, ed., *A Grand Army of Black Men: Letters from African-American Soldiers in the Union Army, 1861–1865* (Cambridge, Eng., 1992), 281–296. Black troops were disproportionately represented in the army of occupation because of the relatively late date at which most were inducted into the service.

32. Rev. Horace F. James, *Annual Report of the Superintendent of Negro Affairs in North Carolina, 1864* (Boston, 1865); Capt. Henry Sweeney to Col. Levering, June 1865, Dept. of Arkansas and 7th Army Corps, RG 393, pt. 1, ser. 269, Letters Rec'd, S-119 1865 [C-232]; Porter Diary, 26 Aug. 1865, SHC; John J. Robertson et al. to Maj. Gen. James B. Steedman, 27 Sept. 1865, BRFAL, Ga. Asst. Comr., ser. 653, Affidavits and Petitions [A-5166]; Kanady to Wood, 23 Dec. 1865, Dept. of the Gulf [C-655].

33. Willard to Hooker, 19 Nov. 1865, Dept. of the South and South Carolina, RG 393, pt. 1, ser. 4112, Letters Rec'd, box 1; F. M. Garrett to Col. Whittlesey, 25 Sept. 1865, BRFAL, NC Asst. Comr., ser. 2453, Unreg. Letters Rec'd [A-645]; Capt. W. L. Cadle to Maj. Gen. D. Reynolds, 10 Dec. 1865, BRFAL, Recs. of Subasst. Comr. for Southern Dist. of Miss., ser. 2268, Reg. Letters Rec'd, C-14 1865 [A-9446].

34. We the colorde peple to the govener of Mississippi, 3 Dec. 1865, BRFAL, Miss. Asst. Comr., ser. 2052, Reg. Letters Rec'd [A-9035]; *Proceedings of Colored People's Convention of South Carolina*, 17; Dennett, *South as It Is*, 175–177; R. H. Cain to Maj. Gen. Devens, 29 Dec. 1865, Dept. of South and South Carolina, RG 393, pt. 1, ser. 4112, Letters Rec'd, box 1; *Report of Joint Committee*, pt. 2, 62.

35. For some related conceptual points, see Colin Seymour-Ure, "Rumour and Politics," *Politics* 17 (1982): 1; Anand A. Yang, "A Conversation of Rumors: The Language of Popular *Mentalités* in Late Nineteenth-Century Colonial India," *JSoH*, 20 (Spring 1987): 485.

36. Foner, *Reconstruction*, 105; Bvt. Maj. Gen. Jon. E. Smith to Maj. Gen. O. O. Howard, 22 June 1865, Military Division of the Tennessee, RG 393, pt. 1, ser. 926, Letters Rec'd, W-20 1865 [C-57].

37. See, for example, Michael Craton, "Proto-Peasant Revolts? The Late Slave Rebellions in the British West Indies, 1816–1832," *Past and Present* 85 (November 1979): 99–125; Thomas C. Holt, *The Problem of Freedom: Race, Labor, and Politics in Jamaica and Britain, 1832–1938* (Baltimore, 1992), 143–176; Eric Foner, *Nothing but Freedom: Emancipation and Its Legacy* (Baton Rouge, 1983); Jerome Blum, *The End of the Old Order in Rural Europe* (Princeton, N.J., 1978), 332–376; Sidney W. Mintz, *Caribbean Transformation* (1974; New York, 1989), 146–250.

38. "And you shall . . . proclaim liberty throughout the land to all its inhabitants; it shall be a jubilee for you, when each of you shall return to his property and each of you shall return to his family." Leviticus 25:10–12. On the jubilee, see Lawence W. Levine, *Black Culture and Black Consciousness: Afro-American Folk Thought from Slavery to Freedom* (New York, 1977), 137–138; Peter Linebaugh, "Jubilating; or, How the Atlantic Working Class Used the Bible Jubilee against Capitalism, with Some Success," *RHR* 50 (1991): 143–180; Armstead L. Robinson, "Day of Jubilo: Civil War and the Demise of Slavery in the Mississippi Valley, 1861–1865," Ph.D. diss., University of Rochester, 1977. On the conflation of secular and spiritual figures see James, *Annual Report of Negro Affairs*, 45; Botume, *First Days amongst the Contra-*

bands, 102; Laura M. Towne, *Letters and Diary of Laura M. Towne: Written from the Sea Islands of South Carolina, 1862–1884,* ed. Rupert S. Holland (1912; New York, 1969), 162.

39. Capt. C. C. Richardson to Capt. W. W. Deane, 28 Nov. 1865, BRFAL, Ga. Asst. Comr., ser. 632, Unreg. Letters Rec'd [A-5256]; Lt. S. D. Barnes to Lt. E. Bamberger, 30 Dec. 1865, BRFAL, Acting Asst. Comr. of Northern Dist. of Mississippi, ser. 2188, Reg. Letters Rec'd, B-23 1865 [A-9292]; Thomas Wentworth Higginson, *Army Life in a Black Regiment,* notes and intro. John Hope Franklin (1869; Boston, 1962), 205. In the Book of Revelation, also known as Apocalypse, there is a scroll with seven seals opened to reveal the prophecies of the Second Coming of Christ. But the idea of "four" seals may indicate simply a mixing of prophetic allegorical imagery. Thus, around the throne where the scroll is held are four living creatures, harking back as well to the prophetic dream in Daniel 7:1–27. I am greatly indebted to Harold S. Forsythe of Fairfield University for a number of important suggestions.

40. F. Marion Shields to Andrew Johnson, 25 Oct. 1865, BRFAL, Mississippi Asst. Comr., ser. 2052, Letters Rec'd [A-9065]; Lt. D. H. Reese to Lt. D. G. Fenno, 31 Oct. 1865, BRFAL, La. Asst. Comr., ser. 1303, Letters Rec'd, R-233 1865 [A-8589]; Circular by G. D. Reynolds, 22 Nov. 1865, BRFAL, Asst. Comr. for Southern Dist. of Miss., ser. 2265, Letters Sent [A-9475]. Also see Scott, *Domination and the Arts of Resistance,* 96–103; and especially Daniel Field, *Rebels in the Name of the Tsar* (1975; Boston, 1989), 1–29.

41. On the Christmas rites under slavery, see Stephen Nissenbaum, *The Battle for Christmas* (New York, 1996), 258–301; Eugene D. Genovese, *Roll, Jordan, Roll: The World the Slaves Made* (New York, 1974), 573–584; Charles Joyner, *Down by the Riverside: A South Carolina Slave Community* (Urbana, Ill., 1984), 134–187; Roger D. Abrahams, *Singing the Master: The Emergence of African-American Culture in the Plantation South* (New York, 1992), 30–32; Frederick Law Olmsted, *The Cotton Kingdom: A Traveller's Observations on Cotton and Slavery in the American Slave States,* ed. Arthur M. Schlesinger Sr., intro. Lawrence N. Powell (1860; New York, 1984), 76–77, 433–434.

42. Carter, "Anatomy of Fear," 358; Herbert Aptheker, *American Negro Slave Revolts* (1943; New York, 1974), 345–348; Michael Craton, *Testing the Chains: Resistance to Slavery in the British West Indies* (Ithaca, N.Y., 1982), 291–321; Robert Dirks, *Black Saturnalia: Conflict and Its Ritual Expression on British West Indian Slave Plantations* (Gainesville, Fla., 1987), 167–168.

43. Affidavit of J. Burcard and G. Chabaud, 21 Dec. 1862, Louisiana Prov. Marshall Field Organizations, RG 393, pt. 4, ser. 1390, Letters Rec'd, C-90 1862 [C-962]; Thos. D. Hailes to Col. Richard D. Irwin, 20 Dec. 1862, Dept. of the Gulf, RG 393, pt. 1, Field Records-Banks' Expedition, ser. 1956, Letters Rec'd, H-65 1862 [C-824].

44. See, for example, Natalie Zemon Davis, *Society and Culture in Early Modern France* (Stanford, Calif., 1975), 97–123; Peter Burke, *Popular Culture in Early Modern Europe* (New York, 1978), 116–204; Edward Muir, *Ritual in Early Modern Europe* (New York, 1997), 85–116.

45. On Jonkonnu see Chapter 1, as well as Ellizabeth A. Fenn, "'A Perfect Equality Seemed to Reign': Slave Society and Jonkonnu," *NCHR* 65 (April 1988): 127–153.

46. On the ex-slaves' attachments to their old homes, see Dennett, *South as It Is*, 229; *Report of Joint Committee*, pt. 1, 108, pt. 2, 185, and pt. 3, 122; Lygon N. Low to Wm. E. Whiting, 20 Sept. 1865, AMA, South Carolina, roll 2.

47. *Report of Joint Committee*, pt. 2, 248; James M. McPherson, *The Negro's Civil War: How American Negroes Felt and Acted during the War for the Union* (New York, 1965), 298; Julie Saville, *The Work of Reconstruction: From Slave to Wage Laborer in South Carolina, 1860–1870* (Cambridge, Eng., 1994), 72–101.

48. See Robert Cartmell Diaries, 1 Jan. 1866, vol. 3, TSLA; Saville, *Work of Reconstruction*, 102–110. On slavery in nonplantation areas also see Ash, *Middle Tennessee Society Transformed*, 53–54; Steven Hahn, *The Roots of Southern Populism: Yeoman Farmers and the Transformation of the Georgia Upcountry, 1850–1890* (New York, 1983), 29–32, 56–57; and John Inscoe, *Mountain Masters, Slavery, and the Sectional Crisis in Western North Carolina* (Knoxville, Tenn., 1989).

49. John Dobbins to Elisha Lowrey, 29 Jan. 1866, John S. Dobbins Papers, EU; W. W. Lawson to Capt. Ed. N. Ketchum, 1 Jan. 1866, BRFAL, Office of the Subasst. Comr. for Waynesboro, Ga., ser. 1055, Letters Rec'd [A-5064]; W. Longworth to Capt. Wm. Sinclair, 28 Mar. 1866, BRFAL, Texas Asst. Comr., ser. 3620, Letters Rec'd, L-5 1866 [A-3264]; Moses Scott to Lilly Ann Scott, 17 Dec. 1865, BRFAL, Office of Subasst. Comr. for Charlottesville, Va., ser. 3922, Letters Rec'd [A-3922]; David Schenck Diary, 14 June 1865, SHC.

50. Chaplain Thos. Smith to Lt. S. D. Barnes, 2 Oct. 1865, BRFAL, Acting Asst. Comr. of the Northern Dist. of Miss., ser. 2188, Reg. Letters Rec'd [A-9317]; *Report of Joint Committee*, pt. 3, 174; James, *Annual Report of Negro Affairs*, 45; *New York Tribune*, 22 July 1865.

51. Thomas W. Conway, *The Freedmen of Louisiana: Final Report of the Bureau of Free Labor, Department of the Gulf* (New Orleans, 1865), 16–17; Anthony Blunt et al. to Comr. of Freedmen, 7 Aug. 1865, BRFAL, North Carolina Asst. Comr., ser. 2452, Letters Rec'd, B-15 1865 [A-509]; J. T. Trowbridge, *The South: A Tour of Its Battle-fields and Ruined Cities* (Hartford, Conn., 1866), 362. On other associations formed by freedpeople to lease or purchase land, see Brig. Gen. Davis Tillson to Major Hastings, 15 Nov. 1865, BRFAL, Ga. Asst. Comr., ser. 625, Letters Sent, vol. 11 [A-5196]; Magdol, *Right to the Land*, 174–199.

52. *New Orleans Tribune*, 16 July 1865, 15 Nov. 1864, 24 Sept. 1864, 6 May 1864, 19 Apr. 1865, 1 Mar. 1865.

53. Ibid., 14 Oct. 1865.

54. It is not entirely clear when or how this committee was constituted, but it may have been in connection with the state freedmen's convention that met in Charleston in late November, for Bram, Moultrie, and Simpson were listed as delegates from the Colleton district. See *Proceedings of Colored People's Convention of South Carolina*, 6–7. It should also be noted that by late August, according to a Freedmen's Bureau agent, "the people of [Edisto] Island" had established "a simple form of Gov[ernment] among themselves" with "selectmen and constables . . . elected by the people," as well as a "court comprising three of the most intelligent colored men." See John A. Alden to Bvt. Maj. Gen. Rufus Saxton, 30 Aug. 1865, BRFAL, SC Asst. Comr., ser. 2929, Reports of Conditions and Operations [A-7009].

55. Henry Bram et al. to Maj. Gen. O. O. Howard [Oct. 1865], and Henry Bram et al. to the President of these United States, 28 Oct. 1865, BRFAL, Washington Hdqrs., ser. 15, Letters Rec'd, B-53 1865 and P-27 1865. On October 19, following Johnson's orders, Howard went to Edisto Island to inform the black settlers that their old masters had received presidential pardons and would have their property restored. The petitions appear to have gone through several drafts and benefited from the advice and editorial assistance of a local Freedmen's Bureau agent. Howard quickly responded to the committee, arguing that "you are right in wanting homesteads and will surely be defended in the possession of every one which you shall purchase or have already purchased." But in the end, he could only maintain that although "the Government does not wish to befriend its enemies and injure its friends," it "considers a forgiven man in the light of a citizen restored to rights of property excepting as to slaves," and urge that "the people had better enter into contracts, leasing or for wages or purchase when possible for next year." Johnson simply forwarded the committee's petition to Howard without comment. Excerpts from an earlier draft of the petitions can be found in Mary Ames, *From a New England Woman's Diary in Dixie in* 1865 (1906; New York, 1969), 99–103. For a close and insightful treatment of the episode, see Saville, *Work of Reconstruction*, 90–98.

56. William Tecumseh Sherman, *Memoirs of General William T. Sherman*, ed. Charles Royster, 2 vols. (1875; New York, 1990), vol. 1, 725–730.

57. For an account of the meeting in Savannah, see New York *National Anti-Slavery Standard*, 18 Feb. 1865. For Special Field Orders No. 15, issued 16 Jan. 1865, see *Official Records of the War of the Rebellion*, vol. 47, pt. 2 (Washington, D.C., 1895), 60–62.

58. See, for example, Circular no. 15, 12 Sept. 1865, BRFAL, Washington Hdqrs., ser. 27, Printed Circulars and Circular Letters Issued by the Bureau [A-10711]; Eric Foner, *Politics and Ideology in the Age of the Civil War* (New York, 1980), 138; McFeely, *Yankee Stepfather*, 220–244; Oubre, *Forty Acres and a Mule*, 32–45; C. Vann Woodward, *The Future of the Past* (New York, 1990), 190–191.

59. See, for example, Laurence Shore, "Making Mississippi Safe for Slavery: The Insurrectionary Panic of 1835," and John Scott Strickland, "The Great Revival and Insurrectionary Fears in North Carolina: An Examination of Antebellum Southern Society and Slave Revolt Panics," both in Orville Vernon Burton and Robert C. McMath, Jr., eds., *Class, Conflict, and Consensus: Antebellum Southern Community Studies* (Westport, Conn., 1982), 57–127; Charles B. Dew, "Black Ironworkers and the Slave Insurrection Panic of 1856," *JSH* 41 (Summer 1975): 321–338; Shula Marks, *Reluctant Rebellion: The 1906–08 Disturbances in Natal* (Oxford, Eng., 1970), 144–168.

60. Col. H. Schofield to Lt. Z. N. Wood, 30 Dec. 1865, Dept. of Louisiana, RG 393, pt. 1, ser. 1757, Letters Rec'd [C-656].

61. See, for instance, Peter Kolchin, *Unfree Labor: American Slavery and Russian Serfdom* (Cambridge, Mass., 1987); Genovese, *Roll, Jordan, Roll*, 3–7, 70–97; William W. Freehling, *The Road to Disunion: Secessionists at Bay, 1776–1854* (New York, 1990), 59–76; Drew Gilpin Faust, "Culture, Conflict, and Community: The Meaning of Power on an Antebellum Plantation," *JSoH*, 14 (Fall 1980): 83–97.

62. Steven Hahn, "Class and State in Postemancipation Societies: Southern Planters in Comparative Perspective," *AHR* 95 (February 1990): 75–98; Foner, *Nothing but Freedom*, 8–38; Woodward, *Future of the Past*, 145–166; Amy Dru Stanley, *From Bondage to Contract: Wage Labor, Marriage, and the Market in the Age of Emancipation* (Cambridge, Eng., 1998).

63. Trowbridge, *The South*, 369. See also Christopher Memminger to Andrew Johnson, 4 Sept. 1865, in Bergeron, *Papers of Andrew Johnson*, vol. 9, 25; John Martin to Andrew Johnson, 28 May 1865, in Bergeron, *Papers of Andrew Johnson*, vol. 8, 26; Agnew Diary, 15 Dec. 1865; *Report of Joint Committee*, pt. 3, 5; C. W. Buckley to Thomas W. Conway, June 1865, BRFAL, Ala. Asst. Comr., roll 18.

64. Alfred R. Wynne to Andrew Johnson, 8 Sept. 1865, in Bergeron, *Papers of Andrew Johnson*, vol. 9, 50; Schenck Diary, 14 June 1865; Dennett, *South as It Is*, 74–75.

65. Capt. Andrew Geddes to Col. C. Cadle, Jr., 6 Oct. 1865, BRFAL, Ala. Asst. Comr., roll 18.

66. *New Orleans Tribune*, 21 Oct. 1865. Also see H. H. Montgomery to Gov. William Sharkey, 16 Aug. 1865, Governors' Records, RG 27, box 62; Carl Schurz to Andrew Johnson, 29 Aug. 1865, in Simpson et al., *Advice after Appomattox*, 113–114; Richard Jones et al. to Gov. Lewis Parsons, 26 Sept. 1865, Gov. Lewis Parsons Papers, ADAH; Thomas W. Holloway to Gov. James L. Orr, 18 Dec. 1865, Governor Orr Papers, Letters Rec'd, box 1, SCDAH.

67. Gov. William L. Sharkey to Andrew Johnson, 20 Aug. 1865, 28 Aug. 1865, in Bergeron, *Papers of Andrew Johnson*, vol. 8, 627–628, 666–667; Gov. William L. Sharkey to Gen. O. O. Howard, 10 Oct. 1865, BRFAL, Miss. Asst. Comr., ser. 2052, Letters Rec'd [A-9062]; Gov. Lewis E. Parsons to Andrew Johnson, 2 Oct.

1865, in Bergeron, *Papers of Andrew Johnson*, vol. 9, 171; Resolution of the Constitutional Convention, 20 Sept. 1865, Governor Parsons Papers; *New Orleans Tribune*, 27 Aug. 1865.

68. Col. Samuel Thomas to Maj. Gen. O. O. Howard, 2 Nov. 1865, BRFAL, Washington Hdqrs., ser. 15, Letters Rec'd [A-9219]. Also see Col. Eliphalet Whittlesey to Dr. Garrott, 19 Aug. 1865, BRFAL, NC Asst. Comr., ser. 2446, Letters Sent, vol. 7, pp. 46–47 [A-531]; *Report of Joint Committee*, pt. 2, 128.

69. Circular no. 2, 3 Oct. 1865, BRFAL, Ga. Asst. Comr., ser. 636, General Orders, Special Orders and Circulars Issued, vol. 26, 325–326 [A-480]; Circular no. 5, 19 Oct. 1865, South Carolina Asst. Comr., Reconstruction Scrapbook, SCL; General Orders no. 13, 31 Oct. 1865, BRFAL, Miss. Asst. Comr., ser. 2055, General Orders and Circulars [A-9536]; Circular Letter, 11 Nov. 1865, BRFAL, Fla. Asst. Comr., Ser. 586, Letters Rec'd [A-1115]; Circular no. 1, 12 Oct. 1865, BRFAL, Tex. Asst. Comr., ser. 3622, General and Special Orders and Circulars Issued and Rostered; *Athens (Ga.) Southern Banner*, 15 Nov. 1865; Dennett, *South as It Is*, 250; *Sen. Exec. Docs.*, no. 27, 39th Cong., 1st sess., 36, 82.

70. Schurz to Johnson, 29 Aug. 1865, 2 Sept. 1865, in Simpson et al., *Advice after Appomattox*, 105, 109, 112, 119; Johnson to Sharkey, 21 Aug. 1865, and Sharkey to Johnson, 30 Aug. 1865, both in Bergeron, *Papers of Andrew Johnson*, vol. 8, 635, 685; Johnson to Parsons, 1 Sept. 1865, in Bergeron, *Papers of Andrew Johnson*, vol. 9, 12; McPherson, *Struggle for Equality*, 332–333; Michael Perman, *Reunion without Compromise: The South and Reconstruction*, 1865–1868 (Cambridge, Eng., 1973), 134–136.

71. Lt. Spencer Smith to Col. C. Cadle, 25 Nov. 1865, BRFAL, Ala. Asst. Comr., ser. 17, Repts. of Operations from the Subdistricts [A-1608]. On Johnson's policies, see Perman, *Reunion without Compromise*, 57–143; Dan T. Carter, *When the War Was Over: The Failure of Self-Reconstruction in the South, 1865–1867* (Baton Rouge, 1985); and Foner, *Reconstruction*, 176–227.

72. Capt. J. H. Mathews to Lt. Stuart Eldridge, 12 Jan. 1866, BRFAL, Miss. Asst. Comr., Ser. 2052, Reg. Letters Rec'd, M-6 1866 [A-9124]; Capt. Warren Peck to Lt. Col. R. S. Donaldson, 16 Dec. 1865, BRFAL, Acting Asst. Comr. of the Northern Dist. of Miss., ser. 2188, Reg. Letters Rec'd, P-24 1865 [A-9312]; Capt. A. C. Bardwell to Col. H. F. Sickles, 14 Dec. 1865, BRFAL, Subasst. Comr. in Savannah, ser. 1013, Unreg. Letters Rec'd [A-5022]; Agnew Diary, 15 Dec. 1865; *Hinds County (Miss.) Gazette*, 25 Nov. 1865; Thomas J. Parrish to Gov. F. W. Peirpont, 15 Dec. 1865, Exec. Corresp., Peirpont, box 1, VSLA.

73. Dennett, *South as It Is*, 240–241; W. R. Swain et al. to Gov. William Marvin, 23 Dec. 1865, BRFAL, Fla. Asst. Comr., ser. 586, Letters Rec'd, S-9 1865 [A-1282]; L. M. Hobbs to Col. T. W. Osborn, 26 Dec. 1865, BRFAL, Fla. Asst. Comr., ser. 586, Letters Rec'd, H-33 1865 [A-1116]. Also see Bvt. Brig. Genl. Samuel A. Duncan to Maj. C. C. Cilly, 26 July 1865, Dist. of Wilmington, RG 393, pt. 2, ser. 1821,

Letters Sent [C-3173]; Towne, *Letters and Diary of Laura M. Towne*, 164–165; Trowbridge, *The South*, 374; *Report of Joint Committee*, pt. 3, 30, 72.

74. Agnew Diary, 31 July 1865, 25 Dec. 1865; Williams, *Papers of William Alexander Graham*, vol. 6, 363; Earl C. Branaugh et al. to Gov. Isaac Murphy, 31 Oct. 1865, BRFAL, Ark. Asst. Comr., ser. 230, Letters Rec'd [A-2409]; Andrews, *South since the War*, 179.

75. Lt. O. B. Fisher to Capt. J. H. Weber, 30 Nov. 1865, BRFAL, Asst. Comr. for the Western Dist. of Miss., ser. 2347, Reg. Letters Rec'd [A-9251]; Cartmell Diaries, vol. 3, 30 Oct. 1865; Lt. S. D. Barnes to Lt. E. Bamberger, 28 Nov. 1865, BRFAL, Acting Asst. Comr. of the Northern Dist. of Miss., ser. 2188, Reg. Letters Rec'd [A-9291].

76. Dennett, *South as It Is*, 187–189.

77. *Sen. Exec. Docs.*, no. 27, 64–65; Capt. J. H. Mathews to Lt. Stuart Eldridge, 12 Jan. 1866, BRFAL, Miss. Asst. Comr., ser. 2052, Reg. Letters Rec'd, M-6 1866 [A-9124]; Dennett, *South as It Is*, 275.

78. Brig. Gen. Wager Swayne to Maj. Gen. O. O. Howard, 22 Dec. 1865, BRFAL, Ala. Asst. Comr., Weekly Reports, roll 2; Foner, *Reconstruction*, 185–208; Perman, *Reunion without Compromise*, 78–81.

79. *South Carolina Leader*, 16 Dec. 1865; *Franklin (La.) Planters' Banner*, quoted in *New Orleans Tribune*, 19 Dec. 1865; Oubre, *Forty Acres and a Mule*, 37; Berlin et al., *Freedom*, ser. 2, 733–736; James E. Sefton, *The Army and Reconstruction, 1865–1877* (Baton Rouge, 1967), 50–53, 261.

80. Capt. Buel C. Carter to Lt. Col. H. B. Scott, 7 Nov. 1865, BRFAL, Va. Asst. Comr., ser. 3799, Unreg. Letters and Telegrams Rec'd [A-7489].

81. J. C. Caruthers to Robert L. Caruthers, 2 Jan. 1866, Robert L. Caruthers Papers, folder 48, SHC; Lt. William E. Dougherty to Capt. A. F. Hayden, 31 Jan. 1866, BRFAL, La. Asst. Comr., Reports of Conditions, roll 28; Clinton A. Cilly to Lt. Beecher, 23 Dec. 1865, BRFAL, NC Asst. Comr., ser. 2453, Unreg. Letters Rec'd [A-640]; Brig. Gen. Wager Swayne to Maj. Gen. O. O. Howard, 2 Jan. 1866, BRFAL, Ala. Asst. Comr., Weekly Reports, roll 2; Col. E. A. Koylay to Maj. W. H. Smith, 29 Jan. 1866, BRFAL, Subasst. Comr. in Orangeburg, S. C., Letters Sent, vol. 250, 3–4 [A-7274].

82. *Report of Joint Committee*, xv; McPherson, *Struggle for Equality*, 329–340; Foner, *Reconstruction*, 193–197; J. Michael Quill, *Prelude to the Radicals: The North and Reconstruction during 1865* (Washington, D.C., 1980), 43–102; Georges Clemenceau, *American Reconstruction, 1865–1870*, ed. and intro. Fernand Baldensperger, and trans. Margaret MacVeagh (1928; New York, 1969), 35–36.

83. *Cincinnati Daily Gazette*, 2 Dec. 1865; Quill, *Prelude to the Radicals*, 122–135.

84. Charles Sumner to John Bright, 5 Nov. 1865, in Beverly W. Palmer, ed., *The Selected Letters of Charles Sumner*, 2 vols. (Boston, 1990), vol. 2, 341–342; "Message to Congress," 4 Dec. 1865, in Bergeron, *Papers of Andrew Johnson*, vol. 9, 472;

William H. Barnes, *History of the Thirty-ninth Congress of the United States* (1868; New York, 1969). Also see W. R. Brock, *An American Crisis: Congress and Recon-struction, 1865–1867* (New York, 1963), 44–48; Perman, *Reunion without Compromise,* 104–109; and McKitrick, *Johnson and Reconstruction,* 253–260.

85. *New York Times,* 1 Dec. 1865; Foner, *Reconstruction,* 176–216; Theodore B. Wilson, *The Black Codes of the South* (University, Ala., 1965); Francis Newton Thorpe, ed., *The Federal and State Constitutions, Colonial Charters, and Other Organic Laws of the . . . United States of America,* 7 vols. (Washington, D.C., 1909), 116–132, 685–704, 809–822; *Report of Joint Committee,* xiii.

86. *Report of Joint Committee,* iii; *Congressional Globe,* 39th Cong., 1st sess., 61.

4. RECONSTRUCTING THE BODY POLITIC

The epigraph is from Lt. Jno. W. Jordan to Maj. J. R. Stone, 30 Apr. 1867, BRFAL, Va. AC, Monthly Repts., roll 47.

1. On the politics of the Military Reconstruction Acts, see W. R. Brock, *An American Crisis: Congress and Reconstruction, 1865–1867* (New York, 1963), 153–211; Michael Les Benedict, *A Compromise of Principle: Congressional Republicans and Reconstruction, 1863–1869* (New York, 1974), 210–243; Michael Perman, *Reunion without Compromise: The South and Reconstruction, 1865–1868* (Cambridge, Eng., 1973), 229–303; Henry Wilson, *History of the Reconstruction Measures of the Thirty-ninth and Fortieth Congresses, 1865–1868* (1868; Westport, Conn., 1970), 314–459; and Eric Foner, *Reconstruction: America's Unfinished Revolution, 1863–1877* (New York, 1988), 228–280.

2. Charles Sumner, *His Complete Works* (Boston, 1874), vol. 13, 282–283, vol. 14, 304–305, 314–315.

3. David Medlock to James P. Newcomb, 29 May 1872, James P. Newcomb Papers, box 2F106, folder 3, BTHC; Federal Manuscript Census, Limestone County, Texas, Schedule of Population, 1870, NA; Walter F. Cotton, *History of Negroes of Limestone County, from 1860 to 1939* (Mexia, Tex., 1939), 2–10; Doris Hollis Pember-ton, *Juneteenth at Comanche Crossing* (Austin, Tex., 1983), 2–3, 47–52, 56–57; Mer-line Pitre, *Through Many Dangers, Toils and Snares: Black Leadership in Texas, 1868–1900* (Austin, Tex., 1985), 24, 28, 205.

4. Medlock represented Texas's Nineteenth Legislative District in 1870–1871. The district included Limestone, Falls, and McLennan counties, where together blacks composed about 35 percent of the population. In Limestone County blacks made up just under 20 percent. See Pitre, *Through Many Dangers,* 205; *Statistics of the Population of the United States at the Tenth Census* (Washington, D.C., 1883), 409–410.

5. This point is made with particular clarity in Laura F. Edwards, *Gendered Strife and Confusion: The Politics of Reconstruction* (Urbana, Ill., 1997), 24–65; and Edwards, "'The Marriage Covenant Is at the Foundation of All Our Rights': The Politics of Slave Marriages in North Carolina after Emancipation," *Law and History Review* 14 (Spring 1996): 81–124. But also see Leon F. Litwack, *Been in the Storm So Long: The Aftermath of Slavery* (New York, 1979), 229–251; Herbert G. Gutman, *The Black Family in Slavery and Freedom, 1750–1925* (New York, 1976), 363–431; Julie Saville, *The Work of Reconstruction: From Slave to Wage Laborer in South Carolina, 1860–1870* (Cambridge, Eng., 1994), 105–106; Peter W. Bardaglio, *Reconstructing the Household: Families, Sex, and the Law in the Nineteenth-Century South* (Chapel Hill, N.C., 1995), 132–134; Susan E. O'Donovan, "Transforming Work: Slavery, Free Labor, and the Household in Southwest Georgia, 1850–1880," Ph.D. diss., University of California, San Diego, 1997, chap. 3; Ira Berlin et al., eds., "Afro-American Families in the Transition from Slavery to Freedom," *RHR* 42 (Fall 1988): 92–97.

6. Edward Magdol, *A Right to the Land: Essays on the Freedmen's Community* (Westport, Conn., 1977), 181–186; Brig. Gen. Davis Tillson to Major Hastings, 15 Nov. 1865, BRFAL, Ga. Asst. Comr., ser. 625, Letters Sent, vol. 11, NA [A-5196]; Paul A. Cimbala, "A Black Colony in Dougherty County: The Freedmen's Bureau and the Failure of Reconstruction in Southwest Georgia," *JSwGH* 4 (Fall 1986): 72–89; James Davison to Gen. Tillson, 6 Dec. 1866, BRFAL, Ga. Asst. Comr., ser. 632, Unreg. Letters Rec'd [A-217].

7. Labor Contract: W. R. Capehart and Freedpeople, 29 Dec. 1866, BRFAL, NC Asst. Comr., Letters Rec'd, roll 10; Labor Contract: Edgar G. Dawson and Freedmen and Women, 1870, Edgar Dawson Labor Contracts, BTHC. Also see O'Donovan, "Transforming Work," chaps. 3–5. On early interest in emigration to Liberia, see Col. E. Whittlesey to Rev. Gurley, 19 July 1865, BRFAL, NC Asst. Comr., ser. 2446, Letters Sent, vol. 7, 11 [A-725]; Joseph Williams to Gen. Tillson, 15 Nov. 1865, BRFAL, Ga. Asst. Comr., ser. 632, Unreg. Letters Rec'd [A-5281]; R. T. Smith to Bvt. Brig. Gen. O. L. Shepherd, 2 May 1868, BRFAL, Ala. Asst. Comr., roll 18; *Christian Recorder*, 1 Sept. 1866. Also see Chapter 7.

8. Labor Contract: George W. Swepson and R. Y. McAden, 31 Dec. 1866, enclosed in Capt. Chas. Wolff to Col. A. G. Bready, BRFAL, NC Asst. Comr., Letters Rec'd, roll 13; Linda Morgan, *Emancipation in Virginia's Tobacco Belt, 1850–1870* (Athens, Ga., 1992), 192; Johnson County Tax Digest, 1874, GDAH; J. C. Caruthers to Robert L. Caruthers, 2 Jan. 1866, Robert L. Caruthers Papers, folder 48, SHC.

9. Lt. Albert Metzner to Lt. J. T. Kirkman, 31 Jan. 1867, BRFAL, Tex. Asst. Comr., Reg. Reports on Operations, roll 20; H. C. Smart to Lt. L. Baker, 18 July 1866, Dept. of the South, RG 393, pt. I, ser. 4112, Letters and Reports Rec'd, box 1, NA; Frances Butler Leigh, *Ten Years on a Georgia Plantation since the War* (Lon-

don, 1883), 87–88, 139. Also see Orville Vernon Burton, *In My Father's House Are Many Mansions: Family and Community in Edgefield, South Carolina* (Chapel Hill, N.C., 1985), 230–232.

10. Some of the earliest research on squads was done by Ralph Shlomowitz, "The Squad System on Postbellum Cotton Plantations," in Orville Vernon Burton and Robert C. McMath Jr., eds., *Toward a New South? Studies in Post–Civil War Southern Communities* (Westport, Conn., 1982), 265–280; Shlomowitz, "The Transition from Slave to Freedman Labor Arrangements in Southern Agriculture, 1865–1870," Ph.D. diss., University of Chicago, 1978. But also see Peter Kolchin, *First Freedom: The Response of Alabama's Blacks to Emancipation and Reconstruction* (Westport, Conn., 1972), 45–47; Charles E. Orser Jr., *The Material Basis of the Postbellum Tenant Plantation: Historical Archaeology in the South Carolina Piedmont* (Athens, Ga., 1988), 54–55. For the most penetrating and challenging treatment, see Gerald D. Jaynes, *Branches without Roots: Genesis of the Black Working Class in the American South, 1862–1882* (New York, 1986), 158–190. More generally, see Saville, *Work of Reconstruction*, 109–110.

11. William A. Graham Jr. to William A. Graham, 15 Sept. 1866, 11 Dec. 1867, in Max R. Williams, ed., *The Papers of William Alexander Graham*, 8 vols. (Raleigh, N.C., 1957–1992), vol. 7, 211, 410; Charles Stearns, *The Black Man of the South and the Rebels* (1872; New York, 1969), 516–517; Robert Somers, *The Southern States since the War, 1870–1871*, intro. Malcolm C. McMillan (1871; University, Ala., 1965), 120.

12. P. F. Duggan to Lt. J. T. Kirkman, 1 Aug. 1867, BRFAL, Tex. Asst. Comr., Reg. Repts. of Operations and Conditions, M821, roll 21; Capt. Samuel W. Carpenter to Bvt. Maj. W. R. Morse, 28 Feb. 1867, BRFAL, Va. Asst. Comr., Monthly Reports, roll 46; Lt. A. S. Bennett to Maj. George Shockley, 31 Mar. 1868, BRFAL, Ala. Asst. Comr., roll 18. Also see Thavolia Glymph, " 'I'se Mrs. Tatom Now': Freedom and Black Women's Reconstruction," unpublished paper presented to the Annual Meeting of the Southern Historical Association, 1992, in author's possession.

13. Jacqueline Jones, *Labor of Love, Labor of Sorrow: Black Women, Work, and the Family from Slavery to the Present* (New York, 1985), 44–78; Roger Ransom and Richard Sutch, *One Kind of Freedom: The Economic Consequences of Emancipation* (Cambridge, Eng., 1977), 44–45; Leslie A. Schwalm, *A Hard Fight for We: Women's Transition from Slavery to Freedom in South Carolina* (Urbana, Ill., 1997), 194–207; Noralee Frankel, *Freedom's Women: Black Women and Families in Civil War Era Mississippi* (Bloomington, Ind., 1999), 56–78.

14. Schwalm, *Hard Fight for We*, 226–233; John Scott Strickland, "Traditional Culture and Moral Economy: Social and Economic Change in the South Carolina Low Country, 1865–1910," in Steven Hahn and Jonathan Prude, eds., *The Countryside in the Age of Capitalist Transformation: Essays in the Social History of Rural America* (Chapel Hill, N.C., 1985), 153–162; Saville, *Work of Reconstruction*, 130–

135; W. W. Lawson to Capt. Ed. N. Ketchum, 1 Jan. 1866, BRFAL, Waynesboro Ga. Agt, ser. 1055, Letters Rec'd [A-5064]; ? to Bvt. Brig. Gen. Orlando Brown, 28 Feb. 1867, BRFAL, Va. Asst. Comr., Monthly Reports, roll 46.

15. W. E. Connelly to Col. O. D. Kinsman, 1 Aug. 1867, BRFAL, Ala. Asst. Comr., roll 18; Bvt. Lt. Col. Jno. W. Jordan to Maj. J. R. Stone, 28 Feb. 1867, BRFAL, Va. Asst. Comr., Monthly Repts., roll 46; Joel Mathews to Brig. Gen. Davis Tillson, 6 Dec. 1865, BRFAL, Ga. Asst. Comr., ser. 632, Unreg. Letters Rec'd [A-5247]. Also see Susan A. Mann, "Slavery, Sharecropping, and Sexual Inequality," in Darlene Clark Hine et al., eds., *"We Specialize in the Wholly Impossible": A Reader in Black Women's History* (New York, 1995), 281–396; Edwards, *"Gendered Strife,"* 24–106, 145–183.

16. Russell Duncan, *Freedom's Shore: Tunis Campbell and the Georgia Freedmen* (Athens, Ga., 1986); Mary Ames, *From a New England Woman's Diary in Dixie in 1865* (1906; New York, 1969), 99–103; Henry W. Anderson et al. to ?, enclosed in Stephen Moore to Bvt. Lt. Col. J. F. Chur, 2 Feb. 1868, BRFAL, NC Asst. Comr., Letters Rec'd, roll 13; Bvt. Maj. Gen. Davis Tillson to Gen. O. O. Howard, 1 Nov. 1866, BRFAL, Washington Hdqrs, ser. 32, Annual Repts. [A-5001–8]; Manuel Gottlieb, "The Land Question in Georgia during Reconstruction," *Science and Society* 3 (Summer 1939): 364–375.

17. See, for example, Chs. E. Chovin to Maj. Gen. Canby, 3 Dec. 1867, Second Military Dist., RG 393, pt. I, ser. 4111, Letters Rec'd, C-122, box 6, NA; *Christian Recorder*, 25 May 1867; H. H. Means et al. to Col. O. D. Greene, 2 Dec. 1867, Fourth Military Dist., RG 393, pt. I, ser. 385, Letters Rec'd, A-173, box 1; Gov. Jonathan Worth to Col. Bernford, ? Dec. 1866, BRFAL, NC Asst. Comr., Letters Rec'd, roll 13.

18. Bvt. Maj. Gen. R. K. Scott to Maj. Gen. O. O. Howard, 23 Jan. 1867, Dept. of the South, RG 393, pt. I, ser. 4112, Letters and Repts. Rec'd, box 1, NA; James L. Orr to Gen. E. R. S. Canby, 31 Oct. 1867, Second Military Dist., ser. 4111, Letters Rec'd, S-25, box 12; Bvt. Maj. Gen. Canby to Gov. James Orr, 25 Nov. 1867, Governor Orr Papers, Letters Rec'd, box 11, folder 6, SCDAH.

19. Worth to Bernford, ? Dec. 1866. Also see Alex D. Bailie to Maj. J. R. Stone, 31 May 1867, BRFAL, Va. Asst. Comr., Monthly Repts., NA, roll 47; Lt. David P. Scott to Gen. Orlando Brown, NA, roll 48; Jonathan M. Bryant, *How Curious a Land: Conflict and Change in Greene County, Georgia, 1850–1885* (Chapel Hill, N.C., 1996), 118–119; Capt. John Power to Maj. O. D. Greene, 20 Dec. 1867, Fourth Military Dist., ser. 385, Letters Rec'd, H-201, box 1; "Speech of Gen. C. C. Andrews," 20 July 1865, *Early Steps in Reconstruction: Speeches by Gen. C. C. Andrews of Minnesota, in Texas and Arkansas* (Austin, Tex.: BTHC, n.d.).

20. Worth to Bernford, ? Dec. 1866.

21. For the best treatment of these quasi-military associations during the early postemancipation period, see Saville, *Work of Reconstruction*, 147–151. On slaves'

familiarity with the militia and their appropriation of military titles during community festivities like corn shuckings, see Roger D. Abrahams, *Singing the Master: The Emergence of African-American Culture in the Plantation South* (New York, 1992), 10–11, 107–130. See also Gad Heuman, *"The Killing Time": The Morant Bay Rebellion in Jamaica* (Knoxville, Tenn., 1994), 88–91 for evidence of these activities in Jamaica.

22. See, for example, Saville, *Work of Reconstruction*, 99–100; Schwalm, *Hard Fight for We*, 190–194; Lawrence N. Powell, *New Masters: Northern Planters during the Civil War and Reconstruction* (New Haven, Conn., 1980), 108–109. See also, Thomas C. Holt, *The Problem of Freedom: Race, Labor, and Politics in Jamaica and Britain, 1832–1938* (Baltimore, 1992) 64–65; Walter Rodney, *A History of the Guyanese Working People, 1881–1905* (Baltimore, 1981), 206–207; Barbara Bush, *Slave Women in Caribbean Society, 1650–1838* (Bloomington, Ind., 1990), 79–82.

23. Lt. Ira D. McClary to Capt. Wm. H. Sterling, 10 Mar. 1867, BRFAL, La. Asst. Comr., Repts., roll 27; Petition of S. Wilson and Family et al., 11 Apr. 1867, BRFAL, Savannah Ga. Subasst. Comr., ser. 1012, Letters Rec'd [A-248].

24. Daybook 2, Jan.–Mar. 1866; Daybook 1, 1850s; Record Book 5, 1854–1855; and Box 1, 22 July 1854, all in George B. Marshall Family Papers, LSU.

25. Capt. D. J. Connolly to Bvt. Maj. G. Mallory, 31 Aug. 1867, BRFAL, Va. Asst. Comr., Monthly Repts., roll 47; Lt. R. G. Rutherford to Bvt. Capt. W. A. Coulter, 30 June 1868, BRFAL, Va. Asst. Comr., Monthly Reports, roll 49; David Schenck Diary, 26 May 1867, 17 June 1867, SHC; Jno. R. Cook to Lt. Louis V. Caziarc, 27 Sept. 1867, Second Military Dist., ser. 4111, Letters Rec'd, R-20, box 9; Gov. Jonathan Worth to Gen. D. E. Sickles, 29 Apr. 1867, Second Military Dist., ser. 4111, Letters Rec'd, N-119, box 3; Bvt. Maj. Geo. W. Smith to Lt. J. T. Kirkman, 31 May 1867, BRFAL, Tex. Asst. Comr., ser. 3624, Repts. [A-3094].

26. Allan Nevins, *The War for the Union: The Organized War, 1863–1864* (New York, 1971), 161–167; Michael W. Fitzgerald, *The Union League Movement in the Deep South: Politics and Agricultural Change during Reconstruction* (Baton Rouge, 1989), 2–22; Susie Lee Owens, "The Union League of America: Political Activities in Tennessee, the Carolinas, and Virginia, 1865–1870," Ph.D. diss., New York University, 1943, 7–25; "Constitution of the National Council of U.L.A.," in Walter L. Fleming, ed., *Documents Relating to Reconstruction: Union League Documents* (Morgantown, W.Va., 1904), 6–10; Joseph Reidy, *From Slavery to Agrarian Capitalism in the Cotton Plantation South: Central Georgia, 1800–1880* (Chapel Hill, N.C., 1992), 178–179; Thomas Alexander, *Political Reconstruction in Tennessee* (Nashville, Tenn., 1950), 143–144; Richard Lowe, *Republicans and Reconstruction in Virginia, 1856–1870* (Charlottesville, Va., 1991), 40; Joe Richardson, *The Negro in the Reconstruction of Florida, 1865–1877* (Tallahassee, Fla., 1965), 142–144; *Christian Recorder*, 27 Jan. 1866.

27. Richard Abbott, ed., "Black Ministers and the Organization of the Republican

Party in the South in 1867: Letters from the Field," *Hayes Historical Journal* 6 (1986): 24–27; James D. Lynch to Dear Sir, 9 July 1867, in *Hayes Historical Journal* 6 (1986): 30; Fitzgerald, *Union League Movement*, 38–46; Horace W. Raper, *William W. Holden: North Carolina's Political Enigma* (Chapel Hill, N.C., 1985), 95; Thos. Haughey to John C. Keffer, 12 July 1867, Wager Swayne Papers, ADAH.

28. Lynch to Dear Sir, 9 July 1867, in Abbott, "Black Ministers," 30; Fitzgerald, *Union League Movement*, 58.

29. John Givens to Mr. Tullock, 15 July 1867, in Abbott, "Black Ministers," 29; C. D. Morris to James P. Newcomb, 30 Oct. 1870, Newcomb Papers, box 2F105, folder 2a.

30. John Costin to Dear Sir, 25 July 1867, in Abbott, "Black Ministers," 31.

31. "Constitution of Alabama State Council," and "The Ritual of the Union League," both in Fleming, *Documents Relating to Reconstruction*, 14–27; Thos. G. Baker to James P. Newcomb, 20 June 1870, Newcomb Papers, box 2F105, folder 2; Edmund L. Drago, *Black Politicians and Reconstruction in Georgia: A Splendid Failure* (Baton Rouge, 1982), 77–78.

32. U.S. Senate, *Testimony Taken by the Joint Select Committee to Inquire into the Affairs of the Late Insurrectionary States*, 42d Cong., 2d sess., 13 vols. (Washington, D.C., 1872), vol. 2, 140–141, 145; Capt. H. C. Cook to Lt. John E. Hosmer, 4 Dec. 1867, enclosed in Geo. P. Screven et al. to Col. Maloney, 11 Nov. 1867, Third Military Dist., RG 393, pt. I, ser. 5738, Letters Rec'd, S-136, 1867, NA; *Tarrboro (N.C.) Southerner*, 16 May 1867.

33. *Affairs of Late Insurrectionary States*, vol. 1, 443–445; G. H. Stacy to James P. Newcomb, 24 May 1871, Newcomb Papers, box 2F105, folder 3; G. F. Steifer to Gov. James Orr, 8 Nov. 1867, Orr Papers, Letters Rec'd, box 10, folder 43; Nimrod Porter Diary, 20 Apr. 1867, SHC; Fitzgerald, *Union League Movement*, 58–59; Jacqueline Jones, *Soldiers of Light and Love: Northern Teachers and Georgia Blacks, 1865–1873* (Chapel Hill, N.C., 1980), 77; Vernon L. Wharton, *The Negro in Mississippi, 1865–1890* (Chapel Hill, N.C., 1947), 165–166.

34. George C. Rives to James P. Newcomb, 14 Sept. 1869, Newcomb Papers, box 2F105, folder 1; W. M. Waddell to Newcomb, 2 July 1870, Newcomb Papers, box 2F105, folder 2; G. H. Stacy to Newcomb, 24 May 1871, Newcomb Papers, box 2F105, folder 3; Minutes of the Hamburg Lodge of the Union League, 1867, Surry County, N.C., Brower Papers, SHC; Richard Bailey, *Neither Carpetbaggers nor Scalawags: Black Officeholders during the Reconstruction of Alabama, 1867–1878* (Montgomery, Ala., 1991), 43–44; Fitzgerald, *Union League Movement*, 58.

35. Rev. Henry M. Turner to Dear Sir, 8 July 1867, in Abbott, "Black Ministers," 33.

36. Frank Yancey et al. to Gov. William Holden, n.d., Governors' Papers, GP 226, NCDAH; Federal Manuscript Census, Caswell County, N.C., Schedule of Population, 1870, NCDAH; W. M. Waddell to James P. Newcomb, 28 Sept. 1870,

Newcomb Papers, box 2F105, folder 2a; Election of Officers for Union League of Groesbuck, Limestone County, 7 June 1871, Newcomb Papers, box 2F108; Cotton, *Negroes of Limestone County,* 9–12; Pemberton, *Juneteenth,* 62–83.

37. Capt. Wm. P. Austin to Capt. G. Mallory, 31 July 1867, and Lt. Jno. W. Jordan to Maj. J. R. Stone, 30 Apr. 1867, both in BRFAL, Va. Asst. Comr., Monthly Repts., roll 47; South Carolinian, "Political Conditions of South Carolina," *Atlantic Monthly* (February 1877): 192–193; Stearns, *Black Man of the South,* 343; "Ritual of the Union League," in Fleming, *Documents Relating to Reconstruction,* 17–23; Fitzgerald, *Union League Movement,* 61.

38. "Loyal League Catechism," in Fleming, *Documents Relating to Reconstruction,* 28–33; Turner to Dear Sir, 8 July 1867, in Abbott, "Black Ministers," 33; O'Donovan, "Transforming Work," chap. 6; South Carolinian, "Political Conditions of South Carolina," 192–193.

39. Cook to Hosmer, 4 Dec. 1867, Third Military Dist., Letters Rec'd; Morris to Newcomb, 30 Oct. 1870, Newcomb Papers, box 2F105, folder 2a; Rev. Henry M. Turner to Dear Sir, 9 July 1867, in Abbott, "Black Ministers," 33; Robert Hinton, "Cotton Culture on the Tar River: The Politics of Agricultural Labor in the Coastal Plain of North Carolina, 1862–1902," Ph.D. diss., Yale University, 1993, 102; Reidy, *Slavery to Agrarian Capitalism,* 178–179.

40. J. R. Grady to ?, 27 Aug. 1867, BRFAL, NC Asst. Comr., Letters Rec'd, roll 10; F. Z. Browne, "Reconstruction in Oktibbeha County," *PMHS* 13 (Jackson, Miss., 1913), 277–278, 282–286; W. E. Connelly to Maj. Gen. Swayne, 15 Apr. 1867, Swayne Papers; Wm. Strander to James P. Newcomb, 24 Jan. 1871, Newcomb Papers, box 2F105, folder 3; Roberta F. Cason, "The Loyal League in Georgia," *GHQ* 20 (June 1936): 140; William George Matton Memoirs, 1867, DU; Cook to Caziarc, 27 Sept. 1867, Second Military Dist., ser. 4111, Letters Rec'd; *Richmond Enquirer,* 5 Dec. 1867.

41. Rev. Samuel Lewis to Gov. W. W. Holden, 4 Jan. 1869, Governors' Papers, box 215; W. E. Wiggins to Lt. Geo. Wagner, 11 June 1867, BRFAL, LaGrange Ga. Agt., ser. 924, Letters Rec'd [A-5615]; Susan E. O'Donovan, "Philip Joiner: Southwest Georgia Black Republican," *JSwGH* 4 (Fall 1986): 58–59; Fitzgerald, *Union League Movement,* 136–176; Foner, *Reconstruction,* 285. Fitzgerald makes the strongest case for the Union League's role in the shift from gang labor to tenancy and cropping.

42. See, for example, Stacey to Newcomb, 24 May 1871, Waddell to Newcomb, 28 Sept. 1870, Chas. W. Winn to Newcomb, 19 June 1870, H. C. Hunt to Newcomb, 2 May 1871, and David C. Claiborne to Newcomb, 10 Aug. 1870, all in Newcomb Papers, box 2F105; John W. Kyle, "Reconstruction in Panola County," *PMHS* 13 (Jackson, Miss., 1913), 49–50; Albert T. Morgan, *Yazoo; or, On the Picket Line of Freedom in the South* (Washington, D.C., 1884), 201; Fitzgerald, *Union League Movement,* 108–109; William Harris, *Day of the Carpetbagger: Republican*

Reconstruction in Mississippi (Baton Rouge, 1979), 102; Lawrence N. Powell, "The Politics of Livelihood: Carpetbaggers in the Deep South," in J. Morgan Kousser and James M. McPherson, eds., *Region, Race, and Reconstruction: Essays in Honor of C. Vann Woodward* (New York, 1982), 315–348.

43. Claiborne to Newcomb, 10 Aug. 1870, Newcomb Papers, box 2F105; Alexander, *Political Reconstruction in Tennessee*, 144; Foner, *Reconstruction*, 284–85.

44. *Eighth Census of the United States, 1860: Agriculture* (Washington, D.C., 1864), 236; *Ninth Census of the United States, 1870: Population* (Washington, D.C., 1872), 52–54, 359; Marc W. Kruman, *Parties and Politics in North Carolina, 1836–1865* (Baton Rouge, 1983), 277.

45. Minutes of Hamburg Lodge, 13 Apr. 1867, 4 May 1867, 18 May 1867, ? June 1867, Brower Papers; Federal Manuscript Census, Surry County, N.C., Schedule of Population, 1870, NA. I was able to identify 94 of 168 white members in the federal manuscript census. Fifty-one were property-owning farmers, 26 were either landless farmers or laborers, and 11 were tradesmen of various sorts. In all, 34 owned no land, 29 owned less than $500 worth of land, 10 owned between $500 and $1,000 worth of land, 18 owned between $1,000 and $5,000 worth of land, and only 3 owned land of greater value.

46. Federal Manuscript Census, Surry Co., 1870. I identified 62 of 106 black lodge members in the federal manuscript census. Almost 80 percent were either landless "farmers" or laborers, and 89 percent owned no real property. I concluded that most black members had been slaves because in 1860 only 10 percent of the county's black population was free and a large number of black lodge members shared surnames with whites in the county, though significantly few if any of those whites were in the lodge.

47. Jacob W. Brower to Officers of the Grand Council of North Carolina, 15 June 1867, BRFAL, NC Asst. Comr., Letters Rec'd, roll 10; Minutes of Hamburg Lodge, 15 June 1867, 6 July 1867, 14 Sept. 1867, 12 Oct. 1867.

48. See, for example, Minutes of Hamburg Lodge, 18 May 1867, 25 May 1867, 6 July 1867, 20 July 1867, 10 Aug. 1867, 5 Oct. 1867, 12 Oct. 1867; Wilson, *History of the Reconstruction Measures*, 385–388.

49. Frances Fox Piven and Richard A. Cloward, *Why Americans Don't Vote* (New York, 1989), 18–21; Chilton Williamson, *American Suffrage: From Property to Democracy, 1760–1860* (Princeton, N.J., 1960); Alexander Keyssar, *The Right to Vote: The Contested History of Democracy in the United States* (New York, 2001), 26–52.

50. See Edward McPherson, *The Political History of the United States of America during the Period of Reconstruction* (Washington, D.C., 1875), 191–194; Wilson, *History of the Reconstruction Measures*, 385. The provisions for voter registration were not included in the first Reconstruction Act passed on 2 Mar. 1867 but were instead written into the Supplemental Reconstruction Act, passed three weeks later, which was designed "to provide the machinery for carrying into effect" the original law.

51. *Richmond (Va.) New Nation,* 18 Apr. 1867; U.S. House, *Condition of Affairs in Mississippi,* Misc. Doc. no. 53, 40th Cong., 3d sess. (Washington, D.C., 1869), 116; Capt. Allen Rutherford to Col. J. F. Chur, 18 May 1867, BRFAL, NC Asst. Comr., roll 32; Bvt. Maj. Gen. Wm. P. Carlin to Gen. O. O. Howard, 18 Mar. 1867, BRFAL, Tenn. Asst. Comr., Repts., roll 16; Bvt. Maj. R. K. Scott to Gen. O. O. Howard, 25 Sept. 1867, Second Military Dist., ser. 4139, Repts. Rec'd; Robert A. Hill to Gen. Ord, 4 July 1867, E. O. C. Ord Papers, box 3, Bancroft Library, University of California, Berkeley; J. W. Barney to John Little, BRFAL, Ga. Asst. Comr., Letters Rec'd, M818.

52. Harris, *Day of the Carpetbagger,* 67–76; Bvt. Maj. Wm. L. Bryan to Lt. Col. H. W. Smith, 1 Sept. 1867, and Lt. George Haller to Col. H. W. Smith, 4 Sept. 1867, both in BRFAL, Miss. Asst. Comr., Repts., roll 30; Lt. John G. S. White to Lt. D. H. Williams, 2 July 1867, Swayne Papers; *New Bern (N.C.) Republican,* 2 May 1867; Capt. H. M. Lazelle to Capt. J. W. Clous, 18 May 1867, Second Military Dist., ser. 4111, Letters Rec'd, C-59, box 1; Lewis N. Wynne and Milly St. Julien, "The Camilla Race Riot and the Failure of Reconstruction in Georgia," *JSwGH* 5 (Fall 1987): 26.

53. William A. Graham to William A. Graham Jr., 29 Aug. 1867, in Williams, *Papers of William A. Graham,* 360; John Houston Bills Diary, 16–17 July 1867, SHC; Susan Sillers Darden Diary, 22 July 1867, MDAH; Alexandre E. de Clouet Diary, 3 May 1867, LSU; Capt. Edw. Collins to Lt. J. T. Kirkman, 30 June 1867, BRFAL, Tex. Asst. Comr., Reg. Repts. of Opers., roll 21.

54. Lt. E. W. Busby to Bvt. Brig. Gen. O. Brown, 26 July 1867, and Capt. N. M. Brooks to Brown, 25 Apr. 1867, both in BRFAL, Va. Asst. Comr., Monthly Repts., roll 47; C. Smith to Gov. James L. Orr, 25 Apr. 1867, Orr Papers, Letters Rec'd, box 7, folder 31; Lt. Wm. F. Martin to Capt. Eugene Pickett, 22 Aug. 1867, BRFAL, Subfield Off. Newnan Ga., ser. 967, Letters Sent, vol. 328, 48–49; Reidy, *Slavery to Agrarian Capitalism,* 191; *Christian Recorder,* 8 June 1867.

55. Capt. Wm. L. Tidball to Bvt. Lt. Col. H. W. Smith, 31 Aug. 1867, BRFAL, Miss. Asst. Comr., Repts., roll 30.

56. Francis B. Simkins and Robert B. Woody, *South Carolina during Reconstruction* (New York, 1932), 88; *Tarrboro (N.C.) Southerner,* 2 May 1867; Charles R. Holcombe to Lt. J. M. Hoag, 5 Sept. 1867, BRFAL, Savannah Ga. Subasst. Comr., ser. 1013, Unreg. Letters Rec'd [A-193].

57. Lt. D. M. White to Lt. J. F. Conyngham, 31 Aug. 1867, BRFAL, Miss. Asst. Comr., Repts., roll 30; *Memphis (Tenn.) Avalanche,* quoted in *Cartersville (Ga.) Express,* 7 June 1867; Simkins and Woody, *South Carolina during Reconstruction,* 88; Lt. Jno. W. Jordan to Maj. J. R. Stone, 30 May 1867, BRFAL, Va. Asst. Comr., Monthly Repts., roll 47; Hill to Ord, 4 July 1867, Ord Papers, box 3; Lt. J. W. Keller to Capt. W. H. Sterling, 10 Apr. 1867, BRFAL, La. Asst. Comr., Repts., roll 27.

58. "Reports on Prominent Whites and Freedmen," Mar.–May 1867, BRFAL, Va. Asst. Comr., Misc. Recs., NA; Registers and Repts. of Registrars Recommended for the Election of Delegates to the Constit'l Conv. of 1868, BRFAL, NC Asst. Comr., roll 32. My findings, which suggest a mean age of 41 for Virginia and 38 for North Carolina, and over 95 percent born in their respective states, comport with those of Richard Lowe, who worked with the Virginia material. See Lowe, "The Freedmen's Bureau and Local Black Leadership," *JAH* 80 (December 1993): 989–998.

59. Registers and Repts. of Registrars, BRFAL, NC Asst. Comr., roll 32; Minutes of Hamburg Lodge, 25 May 1867; Loren Schweninger, *James T. Rapier and Reconstruction* (Chicago, 1978), 1–46; *Huntsville Advocate,* ? June 1867; Thos. M. Peters to Gen. W. Swayne, 29 May 1867, Thos. Haughey to Wm. H. Smith, 3 May 1867, Bvt. Maj. C. W. Pierce to Wm. H. Smith, 24 May 1867, all in Swayne Papers.

60. Josiah Gorgas Journal, 9 July 1867, SHC. According to the meticulous research done by Lawrence N. Powell, blacks formed a majority of the registered electorate in Alabama, Florida, Louisiana, Mississippi, and South Carolina, and over 45 percent of it everywhere else except North Carolina (41 percent) and Arkansas (35 percent). Powell's compilation and interpolation of registration rates shows 83 percent for Mississippi, 91 percent for Arkansas and Georgia, 93 percent for South Carolina and Virginia, 95 percent for Louisiana and North Carolina, 96 percent for Alabama, and 97 percent for Texas. I am grateful to Professor Powell for sharing with me this material from his work-in-progress on Reconstruction.

61. Wade Hampton to My Dear Connor, 24 Mar. 1867, Hampton Family Papers, box 5, SCL; Foner, *Reconstruction,* 291–293; Perman, *Reunion without Compromise,* 269–293.

62. Lt. W. S. Chase to Capt. S. P. Lee, 31 Mar. 1867, BRFAL, Va. Asst. Comr., Monthly Repts., roll 46; F. L. Childs to Samuel A'Court Ashe, 5 June 1867, Samuel A'Court Ashe Papers, 51.1, NCDAH; *Richmond Enquirer,* 16 Apr. 1867; *New Bern (N.C.) Republican,* 9 May 1867; Harris, *Day of the Carpetbagger,* 80–83.

63. Alrutheus Ambush Taylor, *The Negro in Tennessee, 1865–1880* (Washington, D.C., 1941), 48–49; *Richmond Enquirer,* 16 Apr. 1867; *Raleigh Republican,* 30 Nov. 1867, in Charles N. Hunter Papers, box 13, Scrapbooks, DU; Foner, *Reconstruction,* 292; Stearns, *Black Man of the South,* 186–187; Bvt. Lt. Col. W. H. Eldridge to Lt. J. F. Conyngham, 31 Oct. 1867, BRFAL, Miss. Asst. Comr., Repts., roll 30; J. L. Randall to Lt. J. T. Kirkman, 31 May 1867, BRFAL, Tex. Asst. Comr., ser. 3624, Regis. Narr. Repts. [A-3093A].

64. Taylor, *Negro in Tennessee,* 48–49.

65. *New Bern Republican,* 2 May 1867, 9 May 1867, 14 May 1867, 9 July 1867; David Schenck Diary, 24 May 1867, SHC.

66. *Christian Recorder,* 4 May 1867; Morgan, *Emancipation in Virginia's Tobacco Belt,* 160–161; Porter Diary, 30 July 1867.

67. *Richmond New Nation*, 18 Apr. 1867, 2 May 1867; *New Bern Republican*, 7 Nov. 1867; Eric Foner, *Freedom's Lawmakers: A Directory of Black Officeholders during Reconstruction* (New York, 1993), 81.

68. See, for example, Schweninger, *Rapier and Reconstruction*, 49–50; Bailey, *Neither Carpetbaggers nor Scalawags*, 38; Carl H. Moneyhon, *Republicanism in Reconstruction Texas* (Austin, Tex., 1980), 65–67; Joel Williamson, *After Slavery: The Negro in South Carolina during Reconstruction, 1861–1877* (Chapel Hill, N.C., 1965), 357; Drago, *Black Politicians and Reconstruction*, 30–31; Richardson, *The Negro in the Reconstruction of Florida*, 148; Harris, *Day of the Carpetbagger*, 103–106; Wharton, *Negro in Mississippi*, 145; Richard Lowe, *Republicans and Reconstruction in Virginia, 1856–1870* (Charlottesville, Va., 1991), 77–79, 90–91; Carl H. Moneyhon, *The Impact of the Civil War and Reconstruction on Arkansas: Persistence in the Midst of Ruins* (Baton Rouge, 1994), 243–244. In Mississippi, blacks made up roughly one-third of the delegates.

69. Lt. George Haller to Col. H. W. Smith, 31 Aug. 1867, BRFAL, Miss. Asst. Comr., Repts., reel 30; W. E. Connelly to Col. O. D. Kinsman, 1 Oct. 1867, BRFAL, Ala. Asst. Comr., roll 18. Also see Bvt. Col. Ira Ayer to Lt. P. R. Hambrick, 28 Dec. 1867, BRFAL, Va. Asst. Comr., Monthly Repts., roll 48; Thad Preuss to Bvt. Col. H. W. Smith, 31 Aug. 1867, BRFAL, Miss. Asst. Comr., Repts., roll 30.

70. Connelly to Kinsman, 1 Oct. 1867, BRFAL, Ala. Asst, Comr., roll 18; Lt. W. F. DeKnight to Bvt. Brig. Gen. O. Brown, 31 July 1867, BRFAL, Va. Asst. Comr., Monthly Repts., roll 47; Lt. James Hough to Lt. L. O. Parker, 20 Aug. 1867, BRFAL, La. Asst. Comr., Repts., roll 27; Lt. D. M. Whites to Capt. J. W. Sunderland, 31 Oct. 1867, BRFAL, Miss. Asst. Comr., Repts., roll 30; Joseph Crews to Gen. E. R. S. Canby, 11 Nov. 1867, Second Military Dist., ser. 4111, Letters Rec'd, C-89, box 6; Wm. H. Austin to Wm. H. Smith, 5 Sept. 1867, and Wm. Hurter to Wm. H. Smith, 12 Sept. 1867, both in Swayne Papers; Morgan, *Yazoo*, 134–135, 138; Stearns, *Black Man of the South*, 186–187; Fitzgerald, *Union League Movement*, 59–60.

71. Charles Vincent, *Black Legislators in Louisiana during Reconstruction* (Baton Rouge, 1976), 46–47; Lowe, *Republicans and Reconstruction in Virginia*, 122–127; C. Mildred Thompson, *Reconstruction in Georgia: Economic, Social, and Political, 1865–1872* (1915; Gloucester, Mass., 1964), 188–189; Bailey, *Neither Carpetbaggers nor Scalawags*, 57–58; Harris, *Day of the Carpetbagger*, 108–109; Joe Gray Taylor, *Louisiana Reconstructed, 1863–1877* (Baton Rouge, 1974), 147; Charles W. Ramsdell, *Reconstruction in Texas* (1910; Gloucester, Mass., 1964), 198–199; Bvt. Maj. C. A. de la Mesa to Bvt. Lt. Col. Jno. Ritter, 1 Nov. 1867, BRFAL, Ga. Subdist. of Rome, ser. 991, vol. 341, Letters Sent, 358; Thos. F. Monroe to Lt. L. O. Parker, 30 Sept. 1867, BRFAL, La. Asst. Comr., Repts., roll 27; Jack R. Wilson to Wm. H. Smith, 5 Oct. 1867, Swayne Papers.

72. Bvt. Capt. B. G. Cook to Lt. Paul Hambrick, 31 Oct. 1867, BRFAL, Va. Asst. Comr., Monthly Repts., roll 48.

73. David Macrae, *The Americans at Home* (1871; New York, 1952), 138–139; Foner, *Reconstruction*, 193; Perman, *Reunion without Compromise*, 71–103; Dan T. Carter, *When the War Was Over: The Failure of Self-Reconstruction in the South, 1865–1867* (Baton Rouge, 1985), 63–85.

74. Jean-Charles Houzeau, *My Passage at the* New Orleans Tribune: *A Memoir of the Civil War Era*, ed. and intro. David Rankin, trans. Gerard F. Denault (Baton Rouge, 1984), 142; William A. Graham to Messrs. Pell and Gates, 10 Oct. 1867, in Williams, *Papers of William A. Graham*, vol. 7, 384–385.

75. My characterization of the black delegations is drawn from Richard L. Hume, "The 'Black and Tan' Constitutional Conventions of 1867–1869 in Ten Former Confederate States: A Study of Their Membership," Ph.D. diss., University of Washington, 1969, 52–85, 110–127, 177–203, 250–268, 306–324, 428–467, 514–528, 569–590, 631–654; Richard L. Hume, "Negro Delegates to the State Constitutional Conventions of 1867–1869," in Howard N. Rabinowitz, ed., *Southern Black Leaders of the Reconstruction Era* (Urbana, Ill., 1982), 129–153; Euline Williams Brock, "Black Political Leadership during Reconstruction," Ph.D. diss., North Texas State, 1974, 161–167; Foner, *Reconstruction*, 316–319; Foner, *Freedom's Lawmakers;* Thomas Holt, *Black over White: Negro Political Leadership in South Carolina during Reconstruction* (Urbana, Ill., 1977), app. A; Drago, *Black Politicians and Reconstruction*, app.; and from my BLDS (see Appendix).

76. Budd, "The Negro in Politics in Texas, 1867–1898," master's thesis, University of Texas, 1925, 16–19; Lt. W. F. DeKnight to Bvt. Brig. Gen. O. Brown, 31 July 1867, BRFAL, Va. Asst. Comr., Monthly Repts., roll 47; Morgan, *Yazoo*, 134–135, 138; Richard Nelson Current, *Those Terrible Carpetbaggers: A Reinterpretation* (New York, 1988), 78–83; Foner, *Reconstruction*, 317–318.

77. C. W. Wesson to Wm. H. Smith, 4 Oct. 1867, Swayne Papers; Minutes of Hamburg Lodge, 5 Oct. 1867; Hume, "The 'Black and Tan' Constitutional Conventions," 518, 522.

78. See, for example, Richard H. Abbott, *The Republican Party and the South, 1855–1877* (Chapel Hill, N.C., 1986), 110–174; Foner, *Reconstruction*, 316–333.

79. *Debates and Proceedings of the Constitutional Convention of the State of Virginia, 1867–68* (Richmond, 1868), 519; Brock, "Black Political Leadership," 184–201; Paul D. Escott, *Many Excellent People: Power and Privilege in North Carolina, 1850–1900* (Chapel Hill, N.C., 1985), 142–144; Richard L. Morton, *The Negro in Virginia Politics, 1865–1902* (Charlottesville, Va., 1919), 54–59; *Proceedings of the Constitutional Convention of South Carolina, Held at Charleston, South Carolina, Beginning January 14th and Ending March 17th, 1868* (Charleston, S.C., 1868), 99, 835; Holt, *Black over White*, 131–132.

80. Hume, "Negro Delegates," 144; Ted Tunnell, *Crucible of Reconstruction: War, Radicalism, and Race in Louisiana, 1862–1877* (Baton Rouge, 1984), 117–119; Vincent, *Black Legislators in Louisiana*, 48–66; Williamson, *After Slavery*, 213–221, 279, 293; Harris, *Day of the Carpetbagger*, 149–152; Schweninger, *Rapier and Reconstruction*, 58–62; Lowe, *Republicans and Reconstruction in Virginia*, 133–135; W. E. B. Du Bois, *Black Reconstruction in America, 1860–1880* (1935; New York, 1971), 395–400; Pitre, *Through Many Dangers*, 19–20.

81. Union League leaders included George Ruby of Texas (president of the state league), Henry Jacobs of Mississippi, Francis L. Cardozo of South Carolina (eventual president of the state league), and James H. Harris of North Carolina. Newspaper editors included Ruby, Ceasar Antoine of Louisiana, and Richard H. Cain and Robert Elliott of South Carolina. Republican party leaders and activists included Jonathan C. Gibbs of Florida, Henry McNeal Turner of Georgia, James Rapier of Alabama, Abraham H. Galloway of North Carolina, Lewis Lindsey of Virginia, and James H. Ingraham of Louisiana. According to my BLDS, at least 10 percent of the delegates at the conventions in Virginia, Texas, North Carolina, Mississippi, and Alabama, and a somewhat smaller percentage in Florida, Georgia, and South Carolina, were active in the Union League. And between 10 and 50 percent of the delegates at the conventions in South Carolina, Louisiana, North Carolina, Arkansas, Mississippi, and Texas were local political organizers either for the league or the Republican party. See also Foner, *Freedom's Lawmakers*, 35–36, 39, 69–70, 81, 84, 96–97, 114, 116, 134, 177, 187, 215.

82. Macrae, *Americans at Home*, 138–139; Peter J. Rachleff, *Black Labor in the South: Richmond, Virginia, 1865–1890* (Philadelphia, 1984), 45–49; Elsa Barkley Brown, "Negotiating and Transforming the Public Sphere: African American Political Life in the Transition from Slavery to Freedom," in Black Public Sphere Collective, ed., *The Black Public Sphere: A Public Culture Book* (Chicago, 1995), 122–123; *Richmond Enquirer*, 3 Dec. 1867.

83. *Debates and Proceedings of Virginia Constitutional Convention*, 673, 713–714; *Proceedings of South Carolina Constitutional Convention*, 40, 43, 213, 376–381, 401–406; Schweninger, *Rapier and Reconstruction*, 58–62; Hume, "The 'Black and Tan' Constitutional Conventions," 100–101; Vincent, *Black Legislators in Louisiana*, 63–64; Lowe, *Republicans and Reconstruction in Virginia*, 133–135; John W. Graves, *Town and Country: Race Relations in an Urban-Rural Context, Arkansas, 1865–1905* (Little Rock, Ark., 1990), 75; Foner, *Reconstruction*, 328–329; Eric Foner, *Politics and Ideology in the Age of the Civil War* (New York, 1980), 146–147.

84. *Debates and Proceedings of Virginia Constitutional Convention*, 523–526; *Proceedings of South Carolina Constitutional Convention*, 836, 838; Brock, "Black Political Leadership," 184–185; Barkley Brown, "Negotiating and Transforming," 125. The issue of women's suffrage also seems to have come up at the constitutional convention in North Carolina.

85. Elsa Barkley Brown has made the most compelling case for the notion of a "collective" possession of the franchise. See "Negotiating and Transforming," esp. 128. On the disfranchisement of former Confederates, see Foner, *Reconstruction,* 323–324; Brock, "Black Political Leadership," 182–185; Bailey, *Neither Carpetbaggers nor Scalawags,* 72–80; Lowe, *Republicans and Reconstruction in Virginia,* 137–138; and Tunnell, *Crucible of Reconstruction,* 130–131.

86. The Georgia constitutional convention at once rejected political disabilities for southern whites and refused to guarantee officeholding rights for blacks. This set the stage for the legislative expulsion of black members and for Georgia being again remanded to military rule. See Hume, "The 'Black and Tan' Constitutional Conventions," 222–225; and Thompson, *Reconstruction in Georgia,* 196–197.

87. P. P. Bergevin, "Report," 31 Jan. 1868, BRFAL, Miss. Asst. Comr., Repts., roll 32; James D. McCormack to O. E. C. Ord, 3 Jan. 1868, Fourth Military Dist., ser. 385, Letters Rec'd, M-2, box 6; Lt. David P. Scott to Gen. O. Brown, 31 Jan. 1868, BRFAL, Va. Asst, Comr., Monthly Repts., reel 48; F. A. Clover to Lt. J. M. Lee, 7 Oct. 1867, BRFAL, La. Asst. Comr., Repts., roll 27; Gov. Benj. G. Humphreys to Gen. Ord, 26 Nov. 1867, Ord Papers, box 4; *Richmond Enquirer,* 6 Dec. 1867; Bvt. Maj. Gen. R. K. Scott to Gen. O. O. Howard, 26 Mar. 1868, Second Military Dist., ser. 4139, Repts. Rec'd.

88. J. Rives Wade to Capt. J. W. Clous, 17 June 1867, Second Military Dist, ser. 4111, Letters Rec'd, W-93, box 5; Escott, *Many Excellent People,* 142–144; Morton, *Negro in Virginia Politics,* 54–59.

5. "A SOCIETY TURNED BOTTOMSIDE UP"

1. Newspaper Clippings, 1870, Hiram Revels Papers, SmLNY; Hiram Revels Autobiography, Carter G. Woodson Collection, LC; Eric Foner, *Freedom's Lawmakers: A Directory of Black Officeholders during Reconstruction* (New York, 1993), 180–181; William C. Harris, *Day of the Carpetbagger: Republican Reconstruction in Mississippi* (Baton Rouge, 1979), 268–269; David Herbert Donald, *Charles Sumner and the Rights of Man* (New York, 1970), 426–427; George Washington Williams, *A History of the Negro Race in America, 1619–1880* (1883; New York, 1968), 423.

2. John R. Lynch, *The Facts of Reconstruction* (1913; New York, 1968), 46–47; Harris, *Day of the Carpetbagger,* 264–265.

3. Alrutheus Ambush Taylor, *The Negro in Tennessee, 1865–1880* (Washington, D.C., 1941), 247–248; Charles P. Vincent, *Black Legislators in Louisiana during Reconstruction* (Baton Rouge, 1976), 228–229, 236–237. Tennessee's Sampson W. Keeble, representing Davidson County, was elected to the General Assembly in 1872, after the state had been redeemed by the Democrats. He was the only African American to serve before 1880.

4. James S. Pike, *The Prostrate State: South Carolina under Negro Government,*

ed. and intro. Robert F. Durden (1874; New York, 1968), 11–16; Thomas Holt, *Black over White: Negro Political Leadership in South Carolina during Reconstruction* (Urbana, Ill., 1977), 96–97.

5. U.S. Senate, *Testimony Taken by the Joint Select Committee to Inquire into the Affairs of the Late Insurrectionary States,* 42d Cong., 2nd sess., 13 vols. (Washington, D.C., 1872), vol. 7, 1037–1038; Edmund L. Drago, *Black Politicians and Reconstruction in Georgia: A Splendid Failure* (Baton Rouge, 1982), 78–79.

6. I rely here and elsewhere on Foner, *Freedom's Lawmakers,* esp. xi–xxxii, and on my BLDS. Foner and I reached comparable though not identical conclusions. For more on the scope and organization of my data set, see the Appendix. A precise number of local black officeholders is almost impossible to obtain because the secondary literature is incomplete and in some cases unreliable, and because the pertinent records housed in state and local archives generally do not make racial distinctions. Only the most intense local research in any one place, conducted by a scholar with in-depth knowledge of local politics and genealogy, could come up with reliable and nearly precise figures.

7. See, for example, "Information," Issaquena County, Mississippi, WPA Histories, RG 60, box 304, MDAH.

8. See, for example, Francis N. Thorpe, *The Federal and State Constitutions, Colonial Charters, and Other Organic Laws of the States, Territories, and Colonies Now or Heretofore Forming the United States of America,* 7 vols. (Washington, D.C., 1909), 143, 300, 320, 714, 834, 2079, 2813, 2815; Eric Foner, *Reconstruction: America's Unfinished Revolution, 1863–1877* (New York, 1988), 355; Alrutheus Ambush Taylor, *The Negro in the Reconstruction of Virginia* (Washington, D.C., 1926), 16–17; Mingo Scott, *The Negro in Tennessee Politics and Governmental Affairs, 1865–1965* (Nashville, 1964), 45; Randolph Campbell, "Grass Roots Reconstruction," *JSH* 58 (February 1992): 102.

9. Scott, *Negro in Tennessee Politics,* 44.

10. Marion L. Durden, *A History of St. George Parish, Colony of Georgia, Jefferson County, State of Georgia* (Swainsboro, Ga., 1983), 86–90; A. D. Tinsley to James P. Newcomb, 25 May 1871, James P. Newcomb Papers, box 2F105, folder 3, BTHC; Harold S. Forsythe, "Fraternity in the Service of Liberty and Equality: The Social and Political Functions of African-American Fraternal and Mutual Aid Societies in Virginia, 1865–1890," paper presented to Annual Meeting of the Southern Historical Association, Atlanta, November 1997; *Affairs of Late Insurrectionary States,* vol. 7, 607–618. Also see David Montgomery, *Citizen Worker: The Experience of Workers in the United States with Democracy and the Free Market during the Nineteenth Century* (Cambridge, Eng., 1993), 123–125.

11. Elizabeth Hyde Botume, *First Days amongst the Contrabands* (Boston, 1893), 272–273; BLDS.

12. *Affairs of Late Insurrectionary States,* vol. 7, 607–618; George P. Rawick, ed.,

The American Slave: A Composite Autobiography, supp. ser. 1, 12 vols. (Westport, Conn., 1977), vol. 6, pt. 1, 17–18; Foner, *Freedom's Lawmakers,* 2–3, 6.

13. *Affairs of Late Insurrectionary States,* vol. 2, 1168, vol. 7, 695–702, vol. 9, 1004–1006; and vol. 11, pt. 1, 576–577; Foner, *Freedom's Lawmakers,* 47–48.

14. See, for example, F. P. Hilliard to Maj. John Tyler, 23 June 1868, Fourth Military Dist., RG 393, pt. 1, ser. 385, Letters Rec'd, Y-47, box 9, NA; R. J. Alcorn to Maj. John Tyler, 24 June 1868, Fourth Military Dist., RG 393, pt. 1, ser. 385, Letters Rec'd, A-199, box 6; U.S. House, *House Executive Documents,* no. 303, 40th Cong., 2d sess. (Washington, D.C., 1868), 4–5; Affidavit of Richard Reese, 7 Nov. 1868, Exec. Dept., Incoming Corresp., Gov. Bullock, box 57, GDAH; Charles Stearns, *The Black Man of the South, and the Rebels* (1872; New York, 1969), 252.

15. *House Executive Documents,* no. 303, 66. Also see *Athens (Ga.) Southern Watchman,* 29 Apr. 1868; C. B. Blacker to Gov. Rufus Bullock, 30 Oct. 1868, BRFAL, Ga. Sub. Field Office, ser. 824, Letters Sent, vol. 215, 65, NA; ? to Benjamin F. Butler, 14 Jan. 1870, Gov. E. J. Davis Papers, RG 301, box 60, folder 12, TxSLA.

16. ? to Adelbert Ames, 12 Nov. 1871, Adelbert Ames Papers, Sophie Smith Collection, Smith College, Northampton, Mass.; *House Executive Documents,* no. 303, 67; U.S. House, *House Reports,* no. 262, 43d Cong., 2d sess. (Washington, D.C., 1875), 214.

17. ? to Butler, 14 Jan. 1870, Gov. Davis Papers; F. Z. Browne, "Reconstruction in Oktibbeha County," *PMHS* 13 (Jackson, Miss., 1913), 278–279; U.S. House, *Condition of Affairs in Mississippi,* Misc. Doc. no. 53, 40th Cong., 3d sess. (Washington, D.C., 1869), 5, 13–14; Nimrod Porter Diary, 1 Aug. 1867, SHC; Jonathan M. Bryant, *How Curious a Land: Conflict and Change in Greene County, Georgia, 1850–1885* (Chapel Hill, N.C., 1996), 126–128.

18. Alexandre E. de Clouet Diary, 20 Sept. 1868, 15 Oct. 1868, Alexandre E. de Clouet Papers, LSU; Henry Marston Diary, 2 Nov. 1872, Henry Marston Papers, LSU; E. E. Platt to Bvt. Maj. S. C. Greene, 20 Aug. 1868, BRFAL, Miss. Asst. Comr., Repts., roll 33; Testimony of Dr. John A. Moore in *State v. William M. Andrews et al.,* Sept. 1870, Ku Klux Klan Papers, DU; David Schenck Diary, 4 Aug. 1871, SHC.

19. *Affairs of Late Insurrectionary States,* vol. 7, pt. 2, 725, and vol. 2, II, 368–369; *Christian Recorder,* 31 July 1869; Taylor, *Negro in Reconstruction of Virginia,* 270; Julie Saville, *The Work of Reconstruction: From Slave to Wage Laborer in South Carolina, 1860–1870* (New York, 1994), 170.

20. Saville, *Work of Reconstruction,* 167–170; Ella G. (Clanton) Thomas Journal, 1 Nov. 1868, DU; U.S. Senate, *Report of the Select Committee to Enquire into the Mississippi Election of 1875,* Rept. no. 527, 44th Cong., 1st sess. (Washington, D.C., 1876), 210, 902–903. Also see Ranajit Guha, *Elementary Aspects of Peasant Insurgency in Colonial India* (1983; Durham, 1999), 190–191, 195.

21. *Affairs of Late Insurrectionary States,* vol. 9, 1015, and vol. 7, 735–738; Saville,

Work of Reconstruction, 169–170; Tera Hunter, *To 'Joy My Freedom: Southern Black Women's Lives and Labors after the Civil War* (Cambridge, Mass., 1997), 32. On the idea of the franchise as a "collective possession" and on the relation between what she calls "internal" and "external" arenas of politics among African Americans in postemancipation Richmond, see Elsa Barkley Brown, "Negotiating and Transforming the Public Sphere: African American Political Life in the Transition from Slavery to Freedom," in Black Public Sphere Collective, ed., *The Black Public Sphere* (Chicago, 1995), 124–128.

22. Albert T. Morgan, *Yazoo; or, On the Picket Line of Freedom in the South* (Washington, D.C., 1884), 230, 232.

23. *Affairs of Late Insurrectionary States*, vol. 9, 684–686; *House Reports*, no. 262, 58–59; [B. O. Townshend], "Political Condition of South Carolina," *Atlantic Monthly* (February 1877): 193.

24. *Christian Recorder*, 15 June 1867; *Condition of Affairs in Mississippi*, 23; Henry William Ravenel Private Journal, 1 Oct. 1868, vol. 9, SCL; *Affairs of Late Insurrectionary States*, vol. 9, 1072–1077; Joseph P. Reidy, *From Slavery to Agrarian Capitalism in the Cotton Plantation South: Central Georgia, 1800–1880* (Chapel Hill, N.C., 1992), 196–197; *Mississippi Election of 1875*, 16; *Warrenton (N.C.) Indicator*, 1 May 1868. Also see Taylor, *Negro in Reconstruction of Virginia*, 269–270.

25. E. B. Dwyer to Gov. E. J. Davis, 4 Jan. 1870, Gov. E. J. Davis Papers, RG 301, box 60, folder 7, TxSLA; R. K. Scott to Maj. Gen. O. O. Howard, 20 July 1868, Second Military Dist., RG 393 pt. 1, ser. 4139, Repts. Rec'd for BRFAL, NA; Morgan, *Yazoo*, 285–287; *Affairs of Late Insurrectionary States*, vol. 9, 1113–1114; *House Reports*, no. 262, 202–206; Rawick, *American Slave*, supp. ser. 1, vol. 11, 101–104; *Mississippi Election of 1875*, 210.

26. John R. Cochran to Gen. R. K. Scott, 28 Apr. 1868, Second Military Dist., ser. 4111, Letters Rec'd, C-10, box 23; W. Lankford to Gov. William Holden, 14 Sept. 1870, Governors' Papers, Holden, GP 225, NCDAH; *Affairs of Late Insurrectionary States*, vol. 9, 684–686; *Condition of Affairs in Mississippi*, 146.

27. Philip S. Foner and George E. Walker, eds., *Proceedings of the Black State Conventions, 1840–1865*, 2 vols. (Philadelphia, 1979), vol. 2, 284–287; Edward Magdol, *A Right to the Land: Essays on the Freedmen's Community* (Westport, Conn., 1977), 73–77; *Nashville Daily Press and Times*, 8 Aug. 1865, 12 Aug. 1865; Peter Kolchin, *First Freedom: The Responses of Alabama Blacks to Emancipation and Reconstruction* (Westport, Conn., 1972), 152–153; Katharine L. Dvorak, *An African-American Exodus: The Segregation of the Southern Churches* (New York, 1991), 69–119.

28. Stearns, *Black Man of the South*, 345; *Report of the Joint Committee on Reconstruction*, 39th Cong., 1st sess. (Washington, D.C., 1866), pt. 2, 183, 247; Peter Randolph, *From Slave Cabin to the Pulpit: The Autobiography of Reverend Peter Randolph*

(Boston, 1893), 107; Joe M. Richardson, *Christian Reconstruction: The American Missionary Association and Southern Blacks, 1861–1890* (Athens, Ga., 1986), 143–147.

29. Reidy, *From Slavery to Agrarian Capitalism*, 166–168; "Churches," Issaquena County, WPA Histories, RG 60, box 304, MDAH; Leon F. Litwack, *Been in the Storm So Long: The Aftermath of Slavery* (New York, 1979), 455–476. Also see John L. Bell, Jr., "Baptists and the Negro in North Carolina during Reconstruction," *NCHR* 42 (Autumn 1965): 391–409; Philip S. Foner and Ronald L. Lewis, eds., *The Black Worker during the Era of the National Labor Union* (Philadelphia, 1978), 125.

30. Litwack, *Been in the Storm So Long*, 468; William George Matton Memoirs, 1867, 23–24, DU; Harold S. Forsythe, " 'But My Friends Are Poor': Ross Hamilton and Freedpeople's Politics in Mecklenburg County, Virginia, 1869–1901," *VMHB* 105 (Autumn 1997): 427; J. W. Wiley to Maj. Gen. Pope, 10 Sept. 1867, Third Military Dist., RG 393, Pt. 1, Ser. 5738, Letters Rec'd, Box 2.

31. Randall C. Luce, "Racial Relations and Political Change: A Social History of a Southern County, 1886–1981," Ph.D. diss., University of California, Santa Barbara, 1983), 34–35; Augustine Roots to Rev. S. S. Jocelyn, 8 Feb. 1863, AMA, South Carolina, roll 1, ARC.

32. William E. Montgomery, *Under Their Own Vine and Fig Tree: The African-American Church in the South, 1865–1900* (Baton Rouge, 1993), 254–255; Magdol, *Right to the Land*, 73–75; Randolph, *Slave Cabin to Pulpit*, 88–89; James M. Washington, *Frustrated Fellowship: The Black Baptist Quest for Social Power* (Mercer, Ga., 1985), 109; Cheryl Townshend Gilkes, "The Politics of 'Silence': Dual-Sex Political Systems and Women's Traditions of Conflict in African-American Religion," in Paul E. Johnson, ed., *African-American Christianity: Essays in History* (Berkeley, Calif., 1994), 91–93.

33. Forsythe, " 'But My Friends Are Poor,' " 423; *House Reports*, no. 262, 46; Lt. Henry Ayres to Bvt. Lt. Col. James Johnson, 31 May 1867, BRFAL, Va. Asst. Comr., Monthly Repts., roll 47; *Christian Recorder*, 3 Oct. 1868; Reginald F. Hildebrand, *The Times Were Strange and Stirring: Methodist Preachers and the Crisis of Emancipation* (Durham, N.C., 1995), 67–71.

34. Testimony of William J. Minor, 25 Apr. 1865, Smith-Brady Commission, RG 94, ser. 736, NA; *Affairs of Late Insurrectionary States*, vol. 1, 174.

35. Rev. Horace James, *Annual Report of the Superintendent of Negro Affairs in North Carolina, 1864* (Boston, 1865), 47; Reidy, *From Slavery to Agrarian Capitalism*, 169–170; *Affairs of Late Insurrectionary States*, vol. 1, 15–16; *Mississippi Election of 1875*, 902–903.

36. Eric Foner, *Nothing but Freedom: Emancipation and Its Legacy* (Baton Rouge, 1983), 8–73; Steven Hahn, "Hunting, Fishing, and Foraging: Common Rights and Class Relations in the Postbellum South," *RHR* 26 (1982): 37–64; Edward L. Ayers,

Vengeance and Justice: Crime and Punishment in the Nineteenth-Century American South (New York, 1984), 141–184; Dan T. Carter, *When the War Was Over: The Failure of Self-Reconstruction in the South, 1865–1867* (Baton Rouge, 1985), 176–193; *New Orleans Tribune*, 6 Aug. 1865. Even in Texas, nearly half of the local officeholders had owned slaves, more than one-third had held political office before the Civil War, and most owned substantial tracts of land. See Campbell, "Grass Roots Reconstruction," 106–110.

37. Litwack, *Been in the Storm So Long*, 364–368; Maj. Gen. O. O. Howard to Bvt. Maj. Gen. J. C. Robinson, 21 Nov. 1866, BRFAL, NC Asst. Comr., Letters Rec'd, roll 13; Jas. C. Devine to Wm. H. Sinclair, 12 Jan. 1867, BRFAL, Tex. Asst. Comr., Reg. Repts of Opers., roll 20; Lt. Amos S. Collins to Capt. W. H. Sterling, 10 Feb. 1867, BRFAL, La. Asst. Comr., Repts., roll 27.

38. Committee of Freedmen to Bvt. Maj. Gen. John Pope, 7 July 1867, BRFAL, Ga. Asst. Comr., roll 18; Harry H. Burton to Col. O. D. Kinsman, 1 July 1867, BRFAL, Ala. Asst. Comr., roll 18; H. de F. Young to Capt. M. Frank Gallagher, 16 Oct. 1868, Exec. Dept., Incoming Corresp., Gov. Bullock, box 57, GDAH.

39. See, for example, Kenneth Stampp, *The Era of Reconstruction, 1865–1877* (New York, 1965); Foner, *Reconstruction*, 346–364; Joel Williamson, *After Slavery: Negroes in South Carolina during Reconstruction, 1861–1877* (Chapel Hill, N.C., 1965), 326–417.

40. Michael Perman, *Reunion without Compromise: The South and Reconstruction, 1865–1868* (Cambridge, Eng., 1973); Foner, *Reconstruction*, 291–307; Paul D. Escott, *Many Excellent People: Power and Privilege in North Carolina, 1850–1900* (Chapel Hill, N.C., 1985), 136–150; Campbell, "Grass Roots Reconstruction," 106–112.

41. Russell Duncan, *Freedom's Shore: Tunis Campbell and the Georgia Freedmen* (Athens, Ga., 1986), 1–11; Albert E. Smith, "Down Freedom's Road: The Contours of Race, Class, and Property Crime in Black-Belt Georgia, 1866–1910," Ph.D. diss., University of Georgia, 1982, 120. In 1860, there were 4,063 slaves and 1,429 free whites in McIntosh County. See *Preliminary Report on the Eighth Census of the United States, 1860* (Washington, D.C., 1861), 251.

42. Duncan, *Freedom's Shore*, 12–41; William S. McFeely, *Sapelo's People: A Long Walk into Freedom* (New York, 1994), 94–98; Paul A. Cimbala, *Under the Guardianship of the Nation: The Freedmen's Bureau and the Reconstruction of Georgia, 1865–1870* (Athens, Ga., 1997), 177–188.

43. Tunis G. Campbell, "Declaration of BelleVille Farmers Association," 4 Mar. 1867, BRFAL, Savannah Subasst. Comr., ser. 1021, Misc. Recs [A-5788]; Charles R. Holcombe to Col. C. C. Sibley, 21 July 1867, BRFAL, Ga. Asst. Comr., roll 18; Frances Butler Leigh, *Ten Years on a Georgia Plantation since the War* (London, 1883), 133–134; Duncan, *Freedom's Shore*, 21–38. The initial registration tallies for McIntosh County had 675 blacks and 128 whites.

44. Lectured Crawford et al. to Honorable Committee of the Senate, 20 May 1872,

and Lt. James H. Bradley to Bvt. Col. J. H. Taylor, 13 June 1872, both in Tunis G. Campbell File, folder 1, GDAH; Leigh, *Ten Years on a Georgia Plantation*, 135–137; Duncan, *Freedom's Shore*, 64–67; Smith, "Down Freedom's Road," 120.

45. *Affairs of Late Insurrectionary States*, vol. 7, 858; Leigh, *Ten Years on a Georgia Plantation*, 133–134; Testimony of William R. Gignilliat, 18 May 1872, Campbell File, folder 1; Duncan, *Freedom's Shore*, 77; Smith, "Down Freedom's Road," 118–120.

46. According to my BLDS, Mississippi could claim at least 157 black local office-holders during Reconstruction and at least thirteen counties as bases of black political power. Also see Buford Satcher, *Blacks in Mississippi Politics, 1865–1900* (Washington, D.C., 1978), 38–39.

47. Claude F. Oubre, *Forty Acres and a Mule: The Freedmen's Bureau and Black Landownership* (Baton Rouge, 1978), 37; William C. Harris, *Day of the Carpetbagger: Republican Reconstruction in Mississippi* (Baton Rouge, 1979), 55–57, 256–258; W. E. B. Du Bois, *Black Reconstruction in America, 1860–1880* (1935; New York, 1962), 431–433; Ira Berlin et al., *Slaves No More: Three Essays on Emancipation and the Civil War* (Cambridge, Eng., 1992), 101–186.

48. John W. Kyle, "Reconstruction in Panola County," *PMHS* 13 (Jackson, Miss., 1913), 16, 19, 24–25, 36–38, 44–45, 49–50, 60–65; Secretary of State, Register of Commissions, RG 60, Panola County, 437, MDAH; Harris, *Day of the Carpetbagger*, 123–124.

49. *Mississippi Election of 1875*, 184–185, 875–876; John E. Rodabough, "A History of the Negroes of Aberdeen and Monroe County, Mississippi, 1790–1916," master's thesis, Mississippi State University, 1964, 26–27; Sec. of State, Register of Commissions, RG 60, Warren County, 556–557; *Christian Recorder*, 6 May 1871; *New York Sun*, quoted in *Brenham (Tex.) Banner*, 19 Mar. 1875; WPA, Bolivar County, RG 60, box 239, MDAH; Eric Foner, "Black Reconstruction Leaders at the Grassroots," in Leon Litwack and August Meier, eds., *Black Leaders of the Nineteenth Century* (Urbana, Ill., 1988), 230.

50. Kyle, "Reconstruction in Panola County," 86–87, 90–91; Irby C. Nichols, "Reconstruction in Desoto County," *PMHS* 11 (Jackson, Miss., 1910), 309–315; E. F. Puckett, "Reconstruction in Monroe County," *PMHS* 11 (Jackson, Miss., 1910), 111–113; Rodabough, "History of Negroes," 26–27; M. G. Abney, "Reconstruction in Pontotoc County," *PMHS* 11 (Jackson, Miss., 1910), 255–259; John R. Lynch, *Reminiscences of an Active Life: The Autobiography of John Roy Lynch*, ed. John Hope Franklin (Chicago, 1970), 59–61.

51. *Warrenton Indicator*, 7 Feb. 1868, 21 Feb. 1868, 17 Apr. 1868, 24 July 1868; Board of Commissioner Minutes, Warren County, North Carolina, 7 Aug. 1868, 29 Sept. 1868, 5 Jan. 1869, 6 Aug. 1869, 7 Dec. 1869, 8 June 1870, Aug. 1870, 12 Sept. 1870, 7 Nov. 1870, 1 May 1871, 19 June 1871, 5 Aug. 1871, 2 Oct. 1871, 3 Aug. 1872, 9 Aug. 1873, and for superior and inferior court jurors, pp. 184, 212, 221, 251–252,

291, 300–301, 336–337, 344–345, 357, 387–388, 393–394, 398–99, 406, 458, 484, 498, NCDAH; Thorpe, *Federal and State Constitutions*, 2809–2813; Marc W. Kruman, *Parties and Politics in North Carolina, 1836–1865* (Baton Rouge, 1983), 276–278.

52. In 1870, more than seven of ten Warren County inhabitants were black. Although we do not know the extent of Union League activity in the county, we do know that the league was very active in this area of the state. See Horace W. Raper, *William W. Holden: North Carolina's Political Enigma* (Chapel Hill, N.C., 1985), 95; Thorpe, *Federal and State Constitutions*, 2815–2816; William H. Dougherty, "Monthly Report," 25 July 1868, BRFAL, N.C. Asst. Comr., Repts., roll 22; Board of Commissioner Minutes, Warren County, 8 Feb. 1871; Federal Manuscript Census, North Carolina, Warren County, 1870, Schedule of Population, NA; Eric Anderson, *Race and Politics in North Carolina, 1872–1901: The Black Second* (Baton Rouge, 1981), 3–33.

53. Orville Vernon Burton, *In My Father's House Are Many Mansions: Family and Community in Edgefield, South Carolina* (Chapel Hill, N.C., 1985), 251–254; Vernon Burton, "Race and Reconstruction: Edgefield, South Carolina," *JSoH* 12 (Fall 1978): 31–56; Foner, *Freedom's Lawmakers*, 183–184; Donald G. Nieman, "Black Political Power and Criminal Justice: Washington County, Texas, 1868–1884," *JSH* 55 (August 1989): 395–415.

54. D. C. Rugg to Bvt. Lt. Col. Edwin Belcher, 31 Aug. 1868, BRFAL, Ala. Asst. Comr., roll 18; Ted Tunnell, ed., *Carpetbagger from Vermont: The Autobiography of Marshall Harvey Twitchell* (Baton Rouge, 1989), 127–130; Laura F. Edwards, *Gendered Strife and Confusion: The Political Culture of Reconstruction* (Urbana, Ill., 1997), 63–65.

55. Capt. Ripley to Bvt. Brig. Gen. O. Brown, 31 July 1867, BRFAL, Va. Asst. Comr., Monthly Repts., roll 47; C. S. Mooring to Gen. Miles, 4 Dec. 1867, BRFAL, N.C. Asst. Comr., Letters Rec'd, roll 11; Freedmen's Burial Association, 20 July 1868, Governors' Papers, box 214, NCDAH; Smith, "Down Freedom's Road," 61–62; M. G. Abney, "Reconstruction in Pontotoc County," *PMHS* 11 (Jackson, Miss., 1910), 254; Rev. Charles R. Edwards to John E. Bryant, 27 Dec. 1869, John E. Bryant Papers, box 2, DU.

56. Marcus S. Hopkins to Gen. Brown, 31 Dec. 1868, BRFAL, Va. Asst. Comr., Monthly Repts., roll 49.

57. Henry William Ravenel Private Journal, 14 May 1870, vol. 10, SCL; *Beaufort Republican*, 21 May 1870.

58. Montgomery, *Citizen Worker*, 118; Taylor, *Negro in Tennessee*, 52, 59; J. W. Bailey to Gov. DeWitt Senter, 15 May 1869, Gov. Senter Papers, box 1, folder 2, TSLA; Kush, *The Political Battle Axe for the Use of the Colored Men of the State of South Carolina in the Year 1872 with the Constitution of the Progressive Association* (Columbia, S.C., 1872), 3–12. Readmitted to the Union in 1866, the State of Tennes-

see was not subject to Radical Reconstruction, but freedmen there did not gain the franchise by state law until late February 1867, only days before congressional passage of the Military Reconstruction Acts.

59. *Charleston Free Press*, 4 Apr. 1868; W. R. Wentworth to Bvt. Brig. Gen. O. Brown, 30 Apr. 1868, BRFAL, Va. Asst. Comr., Monthly Repts., roll 48; *Cartersville (Ga.) Express*, 21 Feb. 1868; L. Pace to Gov. Holden, 22 Aug. 1868, Governors' Papers, Holden, box 212; J. R. Burns to James P. Newcomb, 18 Sept. 1872, James P. Newcomb Papers, box 2F106, folder 4, BTHC; *Affairs of Late Insurrectionary States*, vol. 2, 82.

60. See, for example, J. Allen Ross to Adelbert Ames, 9 June 1872, Sophie Smith Collection; *Affairs of Late Insurrectionary States*, vol. 2, 55, vol. 7, 863; W. D. Morgan to Gov. W. W. Holden, 1 Sept. 1868, Gov. Papers, Holden, box 213; Osborn A. Giles to Gov. W. W. Holden, 22 Feb. 1870, Gov. Papers, Holden, box 222; Williamson, *After Slavery*, 174; Bryant, *How Curious a Land*, 121–122; Lawrence N. Powell, "The Politics of Livelihood: Carpetbaggers in the Deep South," in J. Morgan Kousser and James M. McPherson, eds., *Region, Race, and Reconstruction: Essays in Honor of C. Vann Woodward* (New York, 1982), 315–348; Joel Sipress, "The Triumph of Reaction: Political Struggle in a New South Community, 1865–1898," Ph.D. diss., University of North Carolina, 1993, 37–59; Michael W. Fitzgerald, "Radical Republicanism and the White Yeomanry during Alabama Reconstruction," *JSH* 54 (November 1988), 595–596.

61. A. J. Glover to Gov. W. W. Holden, 24 Oct. 1868, Gov. Papers, Holden, box 213; R. Beverly Frayser to Gov. W. W. Holden, 28 Dec. 1868, Gov. Papers, Holden, box 214; L. S. Ellington to Father, 23 Nov. 1868, L. S. Ellington Papers, DU; Calton Sessomes to Daniel L. Russell, 27 June 1874, Daniel L. Russell Papers, box 1, folder 2, SHC; Roll of Members, Republican Central Club, Ward 12, Minute Book, 1876, J. P. Breda Papers, LSU; *Affairs of Late Insurrectionary States*, vol. 7, 704.

62. Bryant, *How Curious a Land*, 121; Elizabeth Studley Nathans, *Losing the Peace: Georgia Republicans and Reconstruction, 1865–1871* (Baton Rouge, 1968), 121–126; Jordan H. Parker to Gov. W. W. Holden, 13 Aug. 1869, Gov. Papers, Holden, box 220; *Semi-Weekly Brenham (Tex.) Banner*, 4 Aug. 1871; Harrel Budd, "The Negro in Texas Politics, 1867–1898," master's thesis, University of Texas, 1925, 49.

63. Lynch, *Reminiscences of an Active Life*, 142; Richard Bailey, *Neither Carpetbaggers nor Scalawags: Black Officeholders during the Reconstruction of Alabama, 1867–1878* (Montgomery, Ala., 1991), 171–172; Foner, *Freedom's Lawmakers*, 132.

64. Morgan, *Yazoo*, 366; D. E. J. Parkerville to Gov. W. W. Holden, 24 Jan. 1869, Gov. Papers, Holden, box 215; *Selma (Ala.) Southern Argus*, 16 June 1869; S. A. Hackworth to James P. Newcomb, 24 June 1871, Newcomb Papers, box 2F105, folder 3; U.S. Senate, *Mississippi Election of 1875*, 50; Carl H. Moneyhon, *Republicanism in Reconstruction Texas* (Austin, Tex., 1980), 179.

65. [Townshend], "Political Condition of South Carolina," 193–194; Charles Nordhoff, *The Cotton States in the Spring and Summer of 1875* (New York, 1876), 66.

66. Harris, *Day of the Carpetbagger*, 624–631; Joe Gray Taylor, *Louisiana Reconstructed, 1863–1877* (Baton Rouge, 1974), 227–240; Holt, *Black over White*, 141–142.

67. See, for example, Lawrence N. Powell, "The Centralization of Local Government in Warmoth's Louisiana: Machine Politics, Black Power, and Republican Factionalism," 1990, unpublished paper in author's possession, 10–11; Morgan, *Yazoo*, 376–381.

68. Charles Stearns to Gov. Rufus Bullock, 18 Sept. 1868, Exec. Dept., Incoming Corresp., Bullock, Box 56, GDAH; Stearns, *Black Man of the South*, 208–228; B. C. Thomas to Gov. William H. Smith, 1 Sept. 1868, Samuel Macartney to Gov. Smith, 11 Sept. 1868, Samuel L. Gardner to Gov. Smith, 24 Sept. 1868, S. J. Rogers to Gov. Smith, 19 Aug. 1868, all in Gov. William H. Smith Papers, ADAH.

69. Capt. Thos. H. Norton to Bvt. Maj. John Tyler, 9 June 1868, Fourth Military Dist., ser. 385, Letters Rec'd, N-49, box 7; *Affairs of Late Insurrectionary States*, vol. 7, 859–860; J. C. Norris to Gov. Rufus Bullock, 9 Oct. 1868, and Maj. Gen. George Meade to Gov. Bullock, 18 Nov. 1868, both in Exec. Dept., Incoming Corresp., Bullock, box 57.

70. See, for example, John J. Ormond et al., *The Code of Alabama* (Montgomery, Ala., 1852), 188, 190–194; Josiah Gould, *A Digest of the Statutes of Arkansas* (Little Rock, Ark., 1858), 271, 296, 298, 918, 1021; R. H. Clark et al., *The Code of the State of Georgia* (Atlanta, Ga., 1861), 69–70, 161–164, 680–687; *Revised Code of the Statute Laws of the State of Mississippi* (Jackson, Miss., 1857), 121–136; *Code of Tennessee* (Nashville, Tenn., 1858), 140–144; *The Code of Virginia* (Richmond, Va., 1860), 279. The older states of the upper South and southeastern seaboard generally required higher bonds, as did urban incorporations and plantation counties. To my knowledge, almost nothing substantial has been written about officer bonds and their relation to the structure of local power for any part of the United States.

71. Osborn A. Giles to Gov. Holden, 9 Sept. 1868, box 213; Jonathan W. Alberton to Gov. Holden, 10 Nov. 1868, box 214; Noah Hicks to Gov. Holden, 7 Jan. 1869, box 215; Allen G. Ward to Gov. Holden, 3 July 1869, box 219; James H. Reynolds to Gov. Holden, 21 Aug. 1869, box 220, all in Gov. Papers, Holden; J. M. Coleman to Gov. Rufus Bullock, 4 Nov. 1868, Exec. Dept. Incoming Corresp., Bullock, box 57; D. Hall Rice to Gov. Bullock, 16 Aug. 1868, Bullock, box 56.

72. *Mississippi Election of 1875*, 158–161.

73. Nichols, "Reconstruction in DeSoto County," 307; Shade Croome to James P. Newcomb, 24 June 1870, Newcomb Papers, box 2F105, folder 2; Clarence R. Wharton, *History of Fort Bend County* (San Antonio, Tex., 1939), 182; A. T. Morgan to Adelbert Ames, 9 Dec. 1873, Sophie Smith Collection.

74. Powell, "Centralization of Local Government," 11. Also see Budd, "The Negro in Politics in Texas," 50–51.

75. Foner, *Reconstruction*, 372–373; Lester Salamon, "Protest, Politics, and Modernization: Mississippi as a Developing Society," Ph.D. diss., Harvard University, 1972, 180–185; R. T. Smith to Col. O. D. Kinsman, 29 June 1867, BRFAL, Ala. Asst. Comr., roll 18; J. Mills Thornton III, "Fiscal Policy and the Failure of Reconstruction in the Lower South," in Kousser and McPherson, *Region, Race, and Reconstruction*, 349–394; Hahn, "Hunting, Fishing, and Foraging," 37–64.

76. Holt, *Black over White*, 95–151; Williamson, *After Slavery*, 113–114, 150–156; Carol K. Rothrock Bleser, *The Promised Land: The History of the South Carolina Land Commission, 1869–1890* (Columbia, S.C., 1969), 25–46; F. L. Cardozo, *Address before the Grand Council of the Union Leagues at Their Annual Meeting Held July 27, 1870* (Columbia, S.C., 1870), 11.

77. Satcher, *Blacks in Mississippi Politics*, 53–56; Salamon, "Protest, Politics, and Modernization," 180–185, 197–200; A. T. Morgan to Adelbert Ames, 24 Mar. 1872, Sophie Smith Collection; Harris, *Day of the Carpetbagger*, 609–610; Foner, *Freedom's Lawmakers*, 29.

78. Foner, *Reconstruction*, 364–379; Richard H. Abbott, *The Republican Party and the South: 1855–1877* (Chapel Hill, N.C., 1986), 204–244; Holt, *Black over White*, 143–144, 152–154; Vincent, *Black Legislators in Louisiana*, 71, 98–101. See also Drago, *Black Politicians and Reconstruction*, 86–87; John William Graves, *Town and Country: Race Relations in an Urban-Rural Context, Arkansas, 1865–1905* (Fayetteville, Ark., 1990), 28–35.

79. According to my BLDS, roughly one-quarter (27 percent) of all the black state legislators in the former Confederate states claimed agricultural occupations (farmer, tenant, cropper, laborer), and only in Alabama, South Carolina, and Virginia did more than one-third.

80. Drago, *Black Politicians and Reconstruction*, 86; Scott, *Negro in Tennessee Politics*, 29; Elizabeth Balanoff, "Negro Legislators in the North Carolina General Assembly, July 1868–February 1872," *NCHR* 49 (January 1972): 22–55; Alwyn Barr, "Black Legislators of Reconstruction Texas," *CWH* 32 (December 1986): 340–351; Budd, "Negro in Texas Politics," 44–51; Joe Louis Caldwell, "A Social, Economic, and Political Study of Blacks in the Louisiana Delta, 1865–1880," Ph.D. diss., Tulane University, 1989, 312–313. Except for South Carolina, in no southern state did the proportion of blacks in the state legislatures, even at the height of black power, come near to matching the proportion of blacks in the respective state populations.

81. Euline W. Brock, "Black Political Leadership during Reconstruction," Ph.D. diss., North Texas State, 1974, 84–87; Dorothy V. Smith, "Black Reconstruction in Mississippi, 1862–1870," Ph.D. diss., University of Kansas, 1985, 240–241; *Christian Recorder*, 25 May 1867. The black labor conventions of 1869 responded, in part, to the racial insensitivities of the fledgling National Labor Union and to a consequent

call for the formation of a Colored National Labor Union. See Foner and Lewis, *Black Worker during the Era of the National Labor Union*, 2–3.

82. Foner and Lewis, *Black Worker during the Era of the National Labor Union*, 4–14; *Alabama State Journal*, 6 Nov. 1869; C. Mildred Thompson, *Reconstruction in Georgia: Economic, Social, Political, 1865–1872* (1915; Gloucester, Mass. 1964), 297; Reidy, *From Slavery to Agrarian Capitalism*, 208–209. The reports of delegates in attendance ranged from 232 to 236, and of counties represented from 56 to 80.

83. Foner and Lewis, *Black Worker during the Era of the National Labor Union*, 22–27; Holt, *Black over White*, 158–159; Peggy Lamson, *The Glorious Failure: Black Congressman Robert Brown Elliott and the Reconstruction in South Carolina* (New York, 1973), 77–78.

84. Foner and Lewis, *Black Worker during the Era of the National Labor Union*, 20–21, 29–30, 120–127; Loren Schweninger, *James T. Rapier and Reconstruction* (Chicago, 1978), 88–89; Taylor, *Negro in Tennessee*, 109–113.

85. Foner and Lewis, *Black Worker during the Era of the National Labor Union*, 121–122, 127–128, 132.

6. OF PARAMILITARY POLITICS

The epigraph is from C. L. R. James, *The Black Jacobins: Toussaint L'Ouverture and the San Domingo Revolution* (1938; New York, 1989), 88–89.

1. See, for example, U.S. Senate, *Testimony Taken by the Joint Select Committee to Inquire into the Affairs of the Late Insurrectionary States*, 42nd Cong., 2d sess., 13 vols. (Washington, D.C., 1872), vol. 2, 317–321, 385, vol. 6, 308–309, 320–321; William A. Graham to Messrs. Pell and Gales, 10 Oct. 1867, in Max R. Williams, ed., *The Papers of William Alexander Graham*, 8 vols. (Raleigh, N.C., 1957–1992), vol. 7, 384–385; John W. Kyle, "Reconstruction in Panola County," *PMHS* 13 (Jackson, Miss., 1913), 51–52; C. Mildred Thompson, *Reconstruction in Georgia: Economic, Social, Political, 1865–1872* (1915; Gloucester, Mass., 1964), 386–393.

2. Lt. Col. Dexter E. Clapp to Lt. Fred H. Beecher, 7 Aug. 1865, BRFAL, N.C. Asst. Comr., Repts., roll 22, NA; *New Orleans Tribune*, 22 Sept. 1865; *Hinds County (Miss.) Gazette*, 25 Nov. 1865; Rev. J. H. Caldwell to Bvt. Maj. Gen. Davis Tillson, 3 Sept. 1866, BRFAL, Ga. Asst. Comr., Repts., roll 13; Lt. Allan Rutherford to Col. J. F. Chur, 12 Feb. 1867, BRFAL, N.C. Asst. Comr., Letters Rec'd, roll 12; Fred M. Witty, "Reconstruction in Carroll and Montgomery Counties," *PMHS* 10 (Jackson, Miss., 1909), 129–130; *Franklin (La.) Planters' Banner*, quoted in *New Orleans Tribune*, 19 Dec. 1865.

3. James E. Sefton, *The United States Army and Reconstruction, 1865–1877* (Baton Rouge, 1967), 112; Allen W. Trelease, *White Terror: The Ku Klux Klan Conspiracy and Southern Reconstruction* (New York, 1971), 10–14; Paul D. Escott, *Many Excel-*

lent People: Power and Privilege in North Carolina, 1850–1900 (Chapel Hill, N.C., 1985), 154–155; Ted Tunnell, *Crucible of Reconstruction: War, Radicalism, and Race in Louisiana, 1862–1877* (Baton Rouge, 1984), 153–157; Vernon Lane Wharton, *The Negro in Mississippi, 1865–1890* (Chapel Hill, N.C., 1947), 219; George C. Wright, *Racial Violence in Kentucky, 1865–1940: Lynchings, Mob Rule, and 'Legal Lynchings'* (Baton Rouge, 1990), 25–26.

4. For differences in historical experience and scholarly interpretation, see Trelease, *White Terror;* Edward L. Ayers, *Vengeance and Justice: Crime and Punishment in the Nineteenth-Century American South* (New York, 1984), 151–165; Charles L. Flynn, Jr., *White Land, Black Labor: Caste and Class in Late Nineteenth-Century Georgia* (Baton Rouge, 1983), 29–56; Richard Zuczek, *State of Rebellion: Reconstruction in South Carolina* (Columbia, S.C., 1996), 55–63; Scott Reynolds Nelson, *Iron Confederacies: Southern Railways, Klan Violence, and Reconstruction* (Chapel Hill, N.C., 1999), 95–138; Martha Hodes, *White Women, Black Men: Illicit Sex in the Nineteenth-Century South* (New Haven, Conn., 1997), 147–175; Samuel C. Hyde, Jr., *Pistols and Politics: The Dilemma of Democracy in Louisiana's Florida Parishes, 1810–1899* (Baton Rouge, 1996), 164–172; Otto H. Olsen, "The Ku Klux Klan: A Study in Reconstruction Politics and Propaganda," *NCHR* 39 (Summer 1962): 340–362; J. C. A. Stagg, "The Problem of Klan Violence: The South Carolina Upcountry, 1868–1871," *Journal of American Studies* 8 (1974): 303–316.

5. *Affairs of Late Insurrectionary States,* vol. 2, 385; David Schenck Diary, 30 Sept. 1871, SHC; Greg Cantrell, "Racial Violence and Reconstruction Politics in Texas, 1867–1868," *SWHQ* 93 (January 1990): 334–353.

6. Trelease, *White Terror,* 3–5; Lt. J. S. McEwan to U.S. Attorney General, 18 Oct. 1871, Dept. of Justice, RG 60, Source-Chronological file, North Carolina, 1345, roll 1, NA; Witty, "Reconstruction in Carroll and Montgomery Counties," 129–130; Nelson, *Iron Confederacies,* 109–110; Powell Clayton, *The Aftermath of the Civil War, in Arkansas* (New York, 1915), 109–110; Otto H. Olsen, "North Carolina: An Incongruous Presence," in Otto H. Olsen, ed., *Reconstruction and Redemption in the South* (Baton Rouge, 1980), 178–179.

7. We still know relatively little about either the militia or the patrol system. John Hope Franklin's *The Militant South, 1800–1861* (Cambridge, Mass., 1956), esp. 73–74, 173, however, remains invaluable, and Sally E. Hadden, *Slave Patrols: Law and Violence in Virginia and the Carolinas* (Cambridge, Mass., 2001), is an important recent contribution. But also see Joel Williamson, *The Crucible of Race: Black-White Relations in the American South since Emancipation* (New York, 1984), 18–20; Bertram Wyatt-Brown, *Southern Honor: Ethics and Behavior in the Old South* (New York, 1982), 402–434; Robert C. Kenzer, *Kinship and Neighborhood in a Southern Community: Orange County, North Carolina, 1849–1881* (Knoxville, Tenn., 1987), 71–73; Howell M. Henry, *Police Control of the Slave in South Carolina* (Emory, Va., 1914); J. Michael Crane, "Controlling the Night: Perceptions of the Slave Patrol

System in Mississippi," *JMH* 61 (Summer 1999): 119–136; E. Russ Williams, Jr., ed., "Slave Patrol Ordinances of St. Tammany Parish, Louisana, 1835–1838," *LaH* 13 (Fall 1972): 399–412.

8. Franklin, *Militant South.* The best treatment of the role of the militia in antebellum politics is Stephanie McCurry, *Masters of Small Worlds: Yeoman Households, Gender Relations, and the Political Culture of the Antebellum South Carolina Low Country* (New York, 1995), 265–271. Also see Williamson, *Crucible of Race,* 18–19; Lacy Ford, *Origins of Southern Radicalism: The South Carolina Upcountry, 1800–1860* (New York, 1988), 303–304; Rachel N. Klein, *Unification of a Slave State: The Rise of the Planter Class in the South Carolina Backcountry, 1760–1808* (Chapel Hill, N.C., 1990), 162–163.

9. See, for example, Hadden, *Slave Patrols,* 203–220; Lou Falkner Williams, *The Great South Carolina Ku Klux Klan Trials, 1871–1872* (Athens, Ga., 1996), 28–29; Gladys-Marie Fry, *Night Riders in Black Folk History* (Athens, Ga., 1975), 147–157. Fry shows that some former slaves went so far as to insist that the Ku Klux itself existed before the war, and while she admits that such claims cannot be corroborated, she suggests that the matter deserves further investigation.

10. C. G. McClelland to James Johnson, 29 Feb. 1868, BRFAL, Va. Asst. Comr., Monthly Repts., roll 48; Jonathan Bryant, *How Curious a Land: Conflict and Change in Greene County, Georgia, 1850–1885* (Chapel Hill, N.C., 1996), 120–121; Deposition of Edward Brown and Cambridge Williams, 14 Nov. 1868, Gov. William H. Smith Papers, ADAH; Rev. T. H. Ball, *A Glance into the Great Southeast; or, Clark County, Alabama, 1540–1877* (Grove Hill, Ala., 1882), 263–264, 290; Federal Manuscript Census, Schedule of Population, Clark County, Ala., 1870, NA; Testimony of John W. Long in *State v. W. C. Tarpley et al.,* 29 Aug. 1870, Ku Klux Klan Papers, DU; *Affairs of Late Insurrectionary States,* vol. 2, 122–147, 214; Testimony of Elijah Smith, 1871, Dept. of Justice, RG 60, Source-Chronological file, Mississippi, roll 1; U.S. House, *Condition of Affairs in Mississippi,* Misc. Doc. no. 53, 40th Cong., 3d sess. (Washington, D.C., 1869), vol. 1, 241–242.

11. Trelease, *White Terror,* 51–54; William Stanley Hoole, ed., *Reconstruction in West Alabama: The Memoirs of John L. Hunnicutt* (Tuscaloosa, Ala., 1959), 56, 71–73; M. G. Abney, "Reconstruction in Pontotoc County," *PMHS* 11 (Jackson, Miss., 1910), 246–248.

12. James Dauphine, "The Knights of the White Camelia and the Election of 1868: Louisiana's White Terrorists; a Benighted Legacy," *LaH* 30 (Spring 1989): 180–181; A. P. Parsons to James P. Newcomb, 12 Sept. 1871, James P. Newcomb Papers, box 2F105, folder 4; Charles W. Winn to George T. Ruby, 1 June 1870, Newcomb Papers, box 2F105, folder 2, BTHC, emphasis mine.

13. Escott, *Many Excellent People,* 152–58; Albion W. Tourgee, *A Fool's Errand: By One of the Fools* (New York, 1879), 130. For a thought-provoking account of

the role of fascist squads, see Anthony Cardoza, *Agrarian Elites and Italian Fascism: The Province of Bologna, 1901–1926* (Cambridge, Eng., 1982), esp. 290–339.

14. See, for example, Eric Foner, *Reconstruction: America's Unfinished Revolution, 1863–1877* (New York, 1988), 425–444; Michael Fitzgerald, *The Union League Movement in the Deep South: Politics and Agricultural Change during Reconstruction* (Baton Rouge, 1989), 200–233; George C. Rable, *But There Was No Peace: The Role of Violence in the Politics of Reconstruction* (Athens, Ga., 1984), 85–86; Trelease, *White Terror*, xxx–xxxi, xlvii, 28–29; Stagg, "Problem of Klan Violence," 303–316; Zuczek, *State of Rebellion*, 53–57.

15. Samuel P. Harvey to Gen. A. C. Gillem, 19 May 1868, Fourth Military Dist., RG 393, pt. 1, ser. 385, Letters Rec'd, H-154, box 4, NA; Bvt. Maj. Gen. William P. Carlin to Gen. O. O. Howard, 13 Jan. 1868, BRFAL, Tenn. Asst. Comr., Repts., roll 16; Witty, "Reconstruction in Carroll and Montgomery Counties," 123; D. A. Self to William H. Smith, 23 May 1867, Wager Swayne Papers, ADAH; H. M. Majers to James P. Newcomb, 15 Sept. 1870, Newcomb Papers, box 2F105, folder 2a; Miles Welch to Gov. W. W. Holden, 12 Sept. 1868, Governors' Papers, box 213, NCDAH.

16. When the Tennessee state senate investigated the Klan in 1868, Lewis Powell of Hickman County testified that a "masked band" that had been "roaming around the country, taking arms from the colored men" came to his house and claimed his wife "was at the head of the Loyal League, and at once shot two balls through her, killing her instantly." See *Tennessee State Journal*, extra session, 35th General Assembly, 1868 (Nashville, 1868), 137.

17. W. A. McNulty to Bvt. Brig. Gen. O. Brown, 30 Apr. 1868, BRFAL, Va. Asst. Comr., Monthly Repts., roll 48; Barry Crouch, "Self-Determination and Local Black Leaders in Texas," *Phylon* 39 (December 1978): 349–351; Melinda Meek Hennessey, "To Live and Die in Dixie: Reconstruction Race Riots in the South," Ph.D. diss., Kent State University, 1978, 78–80; Eric Foner, *Freedom's Lawmakers: A Directory of Black Officeholders during Reconstruction* (New York, 1993), 27, 56.

18. *Affairs of Late Insurrectionary States*, vol. 7, 655–665.

19. The best treatment of Outlaw is to be found in Nelson, *Iron Confederacies*, 100–113. But also see Horace W. Raper, *William W. Holden: North Carolina's Political Enigma* (Chapel Hill, N.C., 1985), 174–175; Otto H. Olsen, *Carpetbagger's Crusade: The Life of Albion Winegar Tourgee* (Baltimore, 1965), 161; Foner, *Freedom's Lawmakers*, 165.

20. K. K. Klan to Ben Turner, [n.d.], Governors' Papers, Holden, GP 226; *Affairs of Late Insurrectionary States*, vol. 7, 668–671, vol. 9, 686–694, 814, 951, 983, 994, vol. 11, 471–472, 482, vol. 12, 809, 814; *Tennessee State Journal*, extra session, 1868, 154; *Condition of Affairs in Mississippi*, 233–234, 244–245; Daniel Price to Gov.

William H. Smith, 7 Oct. 1868, Smith Papers. On Klan rituals of punishment and terror see Nelson, *Iron Confederacies*, 111–112; Flynn, *White Land, Black Labor*, 45–46.

21. Rable, *But There Was No Peace*, 96–97; John E. Rodabough, "A History of Negroes of Aberdeen and Monroe County, Mississippi, 1790–1916," master's thesis, Mississippi State University, 1964, 24; *Tennessee State Journal*, extra session, 1868, 132.

22. Herbert G. Gutman, "Schools for Freedom: The Post-Emancipation Origins of Afro-American Education," in *Power and Culture: Essays on the American Working Class*, ed. Ira Berlin (New York, 1987), 261; J. W. Alvord to Maj. Gen. O. O. Howard, 1 Jan. 1866, *Senate Executive Documents*, no. 27, 39th Cong., 1st sess. (Washington, D.C., 1866), 115; J. T. Trowbridge, *The South: A Tour of Its Battlefields and Ruined Cities* (Hartford, Conn, 1866), 289; American Missionary Association, "Annual Report 1866," AMA Manuscripts, ARC; James D. Anderson, *The Education of Blacks in the South, 1860–1935* (Chapel Hill, N.C., 1988), 6–15; Joe M. Richardson, *Christian Reconstruction: The American Missionary Association and Southern Blacks, 1861–1890* (Athens, Ga., 1986).

23. Lt. L. D. McAlpine to Col. ?, 25 Nov. 1867, BRFAL, NC Asst. Comr., Letters Rec'd, roll 11; John W. Barney to J. J. Knox, 4 Feb. 1868, BRFAL, Ga. Asst. Comr., Letters Rec'd, M-818; Lt. Jas. Hutchinson to Lt. J. T. Kirkman, 1 Apr. 1867, BRFAL, Tex. Asst. Comr., Reg. Repts. of Operations, roll 20; R. T. Smith to Col. O. D. Kinsman, 1 Nov. 1867, BRFAL, Ala. Asst. Comr., roll 18; *Christian Recorder*, 18 July 1868; Leon F. Litwack, *Been in the Storm So Long: The Aftermath of Slavery* (New York, 1979), 475–476; Bvt. Maj. Gen. R. K. Scott to Maj. Gen. O. O. Howard, 20 May 1868, Second Military Dist., RG 393, pt. 1, ser. 4139, Repts. Rec'd; Schenck Diary, 4 July 1873; Gutman, "Schools for Freedom," 293. Also see Alrutheus Ambush Taylor, *The Negro in the Reconstruction of Virginia* (Washington, D.C., 1926), 142.

24. Elizabeth Hyde Botume, *First Days amongst the Contrabands* (Boston, 1893), 259; Smith to Kinsman, 1 Nov. 1867, BRFAL, Ala. Asst. Comr., roll 18; Alvord to Howard, 1 Jan. 1866, *Senate Executive Documents*, no. 27, 107; David Macrae, *The Americans at Home* (1871; New York, 1952), 334.

25. Green Hester et al. to Rev. F. A. Fiske, 17 Aug. 1867, BRFAL, N.C. Asst. Comr., Letters Rec'd, roll 11; Jacqueline Jones, *Labor of Love, Labor of Sorrow: Black Women, Work, and the Family from Slavery to the Present* (New York, 1985), 76; G. L. Eberhart to Col. C. C. Sibley, 30 July 1867, BRFAL, Ga. Asst. Comr., roll 17.

26. Foner, *Reconstruction*, 147–148; Robert C. Morris, *Reading, 'Riting, and Reconstruction: The Education of Freedmen in the South, 1861–1870* (Chicago, 1976), 174–212; Jacqueline Jones, *Soldiers of Light and Love: Northern Teachers and Georgia*

Blacks, 1865–1873 (Chapel Hill, N.C., 1980), 77–78; *New Bern (N.C.) Republican*, 30 July 1867.

27. Hunnicutt, *Reconstruction in West Alabama*, 51–55; James Martin et al. to Gov. William H. Smith, 25 May 1869, Smith Papers; Jones, *Soldiers of Light and Love*, 82.

28. J. W. Alvord, *Third Semi-Annual Report on Schools for Freedmen, January 1, 1867* (Washington, D.C., 1867), 6–35; Kyle, "Reconstruction in Panola County," 89–91. Also see Albert T. Morgan, *Yazoo; or, On the Picket Line of Freedom in the South* (Washington, D.C., 1884), 420–422; William C. Harris, *Day of the Carpetbagger: Republican Reconstruction in Mississippi* (Baton Rouge, 1979), 311–334; Joel Williamson, *After Slavery: The Negro in South Carolina during Reconstruction, 1861–1877* (Chapel Hill, N.C., 1965), 223–229.

29. E. H. Adams to James P. Newcomb, 26 Aug. 1871, Newcomb Papers, box 2F105, folder 4; Jennie Shaw to My Beloved Sister, 30 Mar. 1871, Rollins Papers, MDAH.

30. J. F. Wilson to Bvt. Brig. Gen. O. Brown, 30 Apr. 1868, BRFAL, Va. Asst. Comr., Monthly Repts., roll 48; Williams, *Great South Carolina Ku Klux Klan Trials*, 19; *Affairs of Late Insurrectionary States*, vol. 7, 611; U.S. House, *House Miscellaneous Documents*, no. 111, 40th Cong., 2d sess. (Washington, D.C., 1868); *Tennessee State Journal*, extra session, 1868, 131; G. Wiley Wells to A. J. Falls, 2 Jan. 1873, Dept. of Justice, RG 60, Source-Chronological file, Mississippi, roll 1.

31. Witty, "Reconstruction in Carroll and Montgomery Counties," 123; Trelease, *White Terror*, 30–31; H. H. Howard to Maj. Gen. Irwin McDowell, ? June 1868, Fourth Military Dist., ser. 385, Letters Rec'd, H-218, box 6; *Tennessee State Journal*, extra session, 1868, 155; T. B. Johnston and William H. Gardner to Gov. Scott, 26 Oct. 1869, Gov. Robert K. Scott Papers, Letters Rec'd, box 9, Folder 29, SCDAH; Charles Stearns, *The Black Man of the South, and the Rebels* (1872; New York, 1969), 247–248; Trelease, *White Terror*, 208.

32. Hunnicutt, *Reconstruction in West Alabama*, 79–80; Zuczek, *State of Rebellion*, 58–59; Raper, *Holden*, 157; A. T. Morgan to Sen. Adelbert Ames, ? Mar. 1871, Sophie Smith Collection, Smith College, Northampton, Mass.; Silas L. Curtis et al. to Gov. W. W. Holden, 11 Oct. 1868, Governors' Papers, box 213; Laura Edwards, *Gendered Strife and Confusion: The Political Culture of Reconstruction* (Urbana, Ill., 1997), 220. Also see Paul A. Cimbala, *Under the Guardianship of the Nation: The Freedmen's Bureau and the Reconstruction of Georgia, 1865–1870* (Athens, Ga., 1997), 209–210.

33. *Affairs of Late Insurrectionary States*, vol. 7, 846; Trelease, *White Terror*, 64.

34. W. McKee Evans, *Ballots and Fence Rails: Reconstruction on the Lower Cape Fear* (Chapel Hill, N.C., 1966), 63–102.

35. Not surprisingly, the Klan, much like earlier vigilantes and white militia units,

quickly moved to disarm the freedpeople, confiscating at gunpoint pistols, muskets, and shotguns. See Nimrod Porter Diary, 23 Apr. 1868; Dept. of the South, RG 393, pt. 1, ser. 4116, Letters Rec'd, D-95, box 2; *Affairs of Late Insurrectionary States,* vol. 9, 868.

36. Sefton, *United States Army and Reconstruction,* 261–262; Otis A. Singletary, *Negro Militia and Reconstruction* (Austin, Tex., 1957), 6–9. The number of federal troops and posts in fact overstate those available to fend off vigilantes and protect blacks and white Republicans because the most sizable contingent was to be found in Texas, where most of the troops and posts were located on the state's western frontier. In March 1867, Congress ordered the disbandment of all militia forces in the former Confederate states, and although the prohibition was repealed in July 1868 for the Carolinas, Florida, Alabama, Louisiana, and Arkansas, those state assemblies had to enact the appropriate legislation before mobilization could again begin.

37. Thomas B. Alexander, *Political Reconstruction in Tennessee* (Nashville, 1950), 122–160; J. W. Brown to William G. Brownlow, 21 May 1867, and Capt. John T. Robeson to Brownlow, 22 June 1867, both in Gov. Brownlow Papers, box 2, TSLA; Porter Diary, 1 Aug. 1867; Bvt. Maj. Gen. William P. Carlin to Gen. O. O. Howard, 14 Aug. 1868, BRFAL, Tenn. Asst. Comr., Repts., roll 16; Trelease, *White Terror,* 32, 43–44, 176–183; Alrutheus Ambush Taylor, *The Negro in Tennessee, 1865–1880* (Washington, D.C., 1941), 61. A new militia law was required in September 1868 because the legislature, trying to appease Conservatives, repealed the earlier one.

38. Trelease, *White Terror,* 149–74; Richard N. Current, *Those Terrible Carpetbaggers: A Reinterpretation* (New York, 1988), 132–142; Clayton, *Aftermath of the Civil War,* 63–116; Randy Finley, *From Slavery to Uncertain Freedom: The Freedmen's Bureau in Arkansas, 1865–1869* (Fayetteville, Ark., 1996), 159–160.

39. Williams, *Great South Carolina Ku Klux Klan Trials,* 18, 22–26; Williamson, *After Slavery,* 261–262; Trelease, *White Terror,* 148; Charles Ramsdell, *Reconstruction in Texas* (1910; Gloucester, Mass., 1964), 295–297, 310, 316; Joe Gray Taylor, *Louisiana Reconstructed, 1863–1877* (Baton Rouge, 1974), 176–178.

40. Taylor, *Louisiana Reconstructed,* 176–178; Singletary, *Negro Militia,* 35–36; Rable, *But There Was No Peace,* 103–110.

41. Raper, *Holden,* 106–107, 156–223; Trelease, *White Terror,* 208–225; Otto H. Olsen, "North Carolina: An Incongruous Presence," in Otto H. Olsen, ed., *Reconstruction and Redemption in the South* (Baton Rouge, 1980), 179–184; Evans, *Ballots and Fence Rails,* 134–139.

42. Harris, *Day of the Carpetbagger,* 391–394; Trelease, *White Terror,* 246–273; Sarah Woolfolk Wiggins, "Alabama: Democratic Bulldozing and Republican Folly," in Olsen, *Reconstruction and Redemption,* 54; Elizabeth S. Nathans, *Losing the Peace: Georgia Republicans and Reconstruction, 1865–1871* (Baton Rouge, 1968), 196–197.

43. Singletary, *Negro Militia,* 27–29; Clayton, *Aftermath of Civil War,* 106–108;

Trelease, *White Terror*, 119–120, 156–158, 383–384; Current, *Those Terrible Carpet-baggers*, 140–141.

44. *House Report*, no. 261, 11–12; Ted Tunnell, ed., *Carpetbagger from Vermont: The Autobiography of Marshall Harvey Twitchell* (Baton Rouge, 1989), 121; Dauphine, "Knights of the White Camelia," 174–177; Foner, *Reconstruction*, 454–459; Trelease, *White Terror*, 127–136, 185, 383–418.

45. See, for example, *Affairs of Late Insurrectionary States*, vol. 2, 24, vol. 4, 798–799, vol. 7, 515–519; Klan Warning to D. P. Baldwin, Aug.–Sept. 1868, Exec. Dept. Incoming Corresp., Gov. Rufus Bullock, box 56, GDAH; Richard H. Cain to Gov. R. K. Scott, 24 Oct. 1868, folder 12, and Joseph Crews to Gov. R. K. Scott, 2 Nov. 1868, folder 21, both in Gov. Scott Papers, Letters Rec'd, box 3, SCDAH; Mrs. J. Ward Molte to Robert, 22 Oct. 1870, Lalla Pelot Papers, folder 5, DU.

46. *Affairs of Late Insurrectionary States*, vol. 2, 139; Edmund L. Drago, *Black Politicians and Reconstruction in Georgia: A Splendid Failure* (Baton Rouge, 1982), 146–156; Joseph P. Reidy, *From Slavery to Agrarian Capitalism in the Cotton Plantation South: Central Georgia, 1800–1880* (Chapel Hill, N.C., 1992), 203–206; Fitzgerald, *Union League Movement in the Deep South*, 200–233; R. M. Saunders to James P. Newcomb, 12 Jan. 1871, Newcomb Papers, box 2F105, folder 3.

47. Six of seven riots took place in Louisiana: in Bossier, St. Landry, Orleans, Caddo, Jefferson, and St. Bernard parishes. The seventh took place in Mitchell County, Georgia. See *House Reports*, no. 261, 11–12; Rable, *But There Was No Peace*, 73–75.

48. The best secondary account of the Camilla riot is Lee W. Formwalt, "The Camilla Massacre of 1868: Racial Violence as Political Propaganda," *GHQ* 21 (Fall 1987): 399–426. But also see Hennessey, "To Live and Die in Dixie," 123–131; Drago, *Black Politicians*, 51–53; Lewis N. Wynne and Milly St. Julien, "The Camilla Race Riot and the Failure of Reconstruction in Georgia," *JSwGH* 5 (Fall 1987): 15–37; and Carolyn E. DeLatte, "The St. Landry Riot: A Forgotten Incident of Reconstruction Violence," *LaH* 17 (Winter 1976): 41–49.

49. Capt. William Mills to Bvt. Brig. Gen. R. C. Drum, 29 Sept. 1868, Affidavit of Lewis Smith, 24 Sept. 1868, Affidavit of Goliah Kendrick, 23 Sept. 1868, Affidavit of Washington Jones, 23 Sept. 1868, and Affidavit of Plenty Arnold, 25 Sept. 1868, all in Exec. Dept., Incoming Correspondence, Governor Bullock, box 56, GDAH; Formwalt, "Camilla Massacre," 403–408; Susan E. O'Donovan, "Philip Joiner: Southwest Georgia Black Republican," *JSwGH* 4 (Fall 1986): 57–62.

50. Affidavit of Davis Sneed, 25 Sept. 1868, Affidavit of Squire Acre, 25 Sept. 1868; Affidavit of Kendrick and Mills to Drum, all in Exec. Dept., Incoming Correspondence, Bullock, box 56; Hennessey, "To Live and Die in Dixie," 123–124. Also see Julie Saville, "Rites and Power: Reflections on Slavery, Freedom, and Political Ritual," *S&A* 20 (April 1999): 81–102.

51. Deposition of M. S. Poore, 25 Sept. 1868, Exec. Dept., Incoming Correspondence, Bullock, box 56; Formwalt, "Camilla Massacre," 408–410; Hennessey, "To Live and Die in Dixie," 124–125.

52. Deposition of Poore, Mills to Drum, Affidavit of Acre, all in Exec. Dept., Incoming Correspondence, Bullock, box 56; P. Joiner to John E. Bryant, 30 Sept. 1868, John E. Bryant Papers, box 2, folder 3, DU; Formwalt, "Camilla Massacre," 410–414; O'Donovan, "Philip Joiner," 60–62.

53. Affidavit of Richard Hobbs, 27 Sept. 1868, and Mills to Drum, both in Exec. Dept., Incoming Correspondence, Bullock, box 56; Formwalt, "Camilla Massacre," 414–426; Hennessey, "To Live and Die in Dixie," 126–130.

54. Although it expressed contempt for the behavior of the Republicans, *The Nation* nonetheless saw Colfax as illustrative "of the state of things which has converted Louisiana into a South American republic." See *The Nation* 408 (24 Apr. 1873): 277.

55. *House Report*, no. 261, pt. 3, 411–412, 419. The best and most detailed study of Grant Parish and the Colfax riot is Joel M. Sipress, "The Triumph of Reaction: Political Struggle in a New South Community, 1865–1898," Ph.D. diss., University of North Carolina, 1993. But on this and related developments in Louisiana see Taylor, *Louisiana Reconstructed*, 267–273; Tunnell, *Crucible of Reconstruction*, 153–172; Hennessey, "To Live and Die in Dixie," 211–228; and Lawrence Powell, "The Centralization of Local Government in Warmoth's Louisiana: Machine Politics, Black Power, and Republican Factionalism," unpublished manuscript in author's possession.

56. Sipress, "Triumph of Reaction," 74–77.

57. *House Report*, no. 261, pt. 3, 893–894; Sipress, "Triumph of Reaction," 83–91; Taylor, *Louisiana Reconstructed*, 268.

58. On the election of 1872, its aftermath, and the struggles between rival governments in New Orleans, see Taylor, *Louisiana Reconstructed*, 241–257; Tunnell, *Crucible of Reconstruction*, 169–172.

59. Manie White Johnson, "The Colfax Riot of 1873," *LHQ* 13 (July 1930): 407; *House Reports*, no. 261, pt. 3, 12–13; Sipress, "Triumph of Reaction," 92–99.

60. *House Reports*, no. 261, pt. 3, 413, 895; Sipress, "Triumph of Reaction," 94–99.

61. *House Reports*, no. 261, pt. 3, 12–13, 416–417; Hennessey, "To Live and Die in Dixie," 223–227; Sipress, "Triumph of Reaction," 100–105; Johnson, "Colfax Riot," 411–419.

62. Taylor, *Louisiana Reconstructed*, 269–271; Tunnell, *Crucible of Reconstruction*, 192–194; Sipress, "Triumph of Reaction," 105–118; Hennessey, "To Live and Die in Dixie," 232–238.

63. *House Reports*, no. 261, pt. 3, 873–874; Gen. Hugh J. Campbell, *The White League Conspiracy against Free Government*, 11 Jan. 1875, Tulane Library Collection; C. P. Lincoln to J. E. Carpenter, 4 Sept. 1874, Dept. of Justice, RG 60, Source-

Chronological file, Mississippi, roll 1; Taylor, *Louisiana Reconstructed*, 281–283; Wharton, *Negro in Mississippi*, 181–183; Lester Salamon, "Protest, Politics, and Modernization: Mississippi as a Developing Society," Ph.D. diss., Harvard University, 1972, 227–229.

64. *House Reports*, no. 261, pt. 3, 873–874; Wharton, *Negro in Mississippi*, 181–183. According to my BLDS, the total number of black state and county officeholders grew from at least 331 in 1869 to at least 664 in 1874, after which it began a steep decline. In 1874, about 85 percent of the officeholders were to be found in Mississippi, South Carolina, Alabama, and Louisiana.

65. Lawrence N. Powell, "Reinventing Tradition: Liberty Place, Historical Memory, and Silk-Stocking Vigilantism in New Orleans Politics," *S&A* 20 (April 1999): 127–131; Tunnell, *Crucible of Reconstruction*, 193–205; Taylor, *Louisiana Reconstructed*, 287–296; Tunnell, *Carpetbagger from Vermont*, 137–153; Harris, *Day of the Carpetbagger*, 634–636; *Opelousas Courier*, 15 Aug. 1874, quoted in *House Reports*, no. 261, pt. 3, 877; *New Orleans Weekly Louisianian*, 22 Aug. 1874, 5 Sept. 1874. Grant's decision not to intervene militarily in the Vicksburg municipal elections of August 1874 was also consequential and plainly noticed by White Leaguers.

66. Executive Order of Adelbert Ames, 4 Dec. 1874, Gov. Recs., RG 27, box 96, MDAH; Harris, *Day of the Carpetbagger*, 643–649; Hennessey, "To Live and Die in Dixie," 271–273; Foner, *Freedom's Lawmakers*, 54; John R. Lynch, *Reminiscences of an Active Life: The Autobiography of John Roy Lynch*, ed. John Hope Franklin (Chicago, 1970), 164.

67. J. M. B. to Albert Batchelor, 4 Jan. 1875, Albert A. Batchelor Papers, box 5, LSU; A. J. Packer to Gov. Ames, 7 Dec. 1874, and O. S. Lee to Gov. Ames, 7 Dec. 1874, both in Gov. Recs., RG 27, box 96; Hennessey, "To Live and Die in Dixie," 272–278; Rable, *But There Was No Peace*, 145–149; Current, *Those Terrible Carpetbaggers*, 314–317. Estimates of the black death toll in this Vicksburg riot range as high as 300.

68. Proclamation of Governor Ames, 8 Dec. 1874, and Pres. U.S. Grant to Ames, 19 Dec. 1874, both in Gov. Recs., RG 27, box 96; *Alexandria (Va.) People's Advocate*, 9 Sept. 1876; *Mississippi Election of 1875*, 9; Harris, *Day of the Carpetbagger*, 645–649, 686; Wharton, *Negro in Mississippi*, 185–188.

69. Kyle, "Reconstruction in Panola County," 73–74; E. F. Puckett, "Reconstruction in Monroe County," *PMHS* 11 (Jackson, Miss., 1910), 143–156; Interview with Mrs. J. T. Chamberlain, WPA, RG 60, box 312, MDAH; *Mississippi Election of 1875*, 520; J. B. Allgood to Gov. Ames, 12 Sept. 1875, Gov. Recs., RG 27, box 99.

70. *Mississippi Election of 1875*, 429–430, 790–793, 859–861; William H. Harney to Gov. Adelbert Ames, 6 Sept. 1875, box 99, Affidavit of John P. Matthews, 13 Sept. 1875, box 99, and Monk Joseph to Gov. Ames, 6 Jan. 1876, box 101, all in Gov. Recs., RG 27; F. Z. Browne, "Reconstruction in Oktibbeha County," *PMHS* 13 (Jackson, Miss., 1913), 286; Foner, *Freedom's Lawmakers*, 87.

71. *Mississippi Election of 1875,* 106–114; A. Parker to Blanche K. Bruce, 6 Jan. 1876, Gov. Recs., RG 27, box 101. The achievement was all the more impressive given the political conditions in the county as late as June 1868. One correspondent who had gone to live there at the time "found the Loyal Colored People . . . in utter darkness as regards their duty as citizens" and the "Rebels determined that reconstruction shall never succeed." See Joseph B. Lott to Maj. Gen. McDowell, ? June 1868, Fourth Military Dist., ser. 385, Letters Rec'd, L-102, box 2.

72. *Mississippi Election of 1875,* 107, 112; Parker to Bruce, 6 Jan. 1876, Gov. Recs., RG 27, box 101; A. Parker to Gov. A. Ames, 19 Sept. 1875, Dept. of Justice, RG 60, Source-Chronological file, Mississippi, roll 1, NA.

73. *Mississippi Election of 1875,* 102, 104; William Deshields et al. to Gov. Ames, 23 Oct. 1875, Gov. Recs., RG 27, box 99; Federal Manuscript Census, Schedule of Population, Mississippi, Amite County, 1870, NA.

74. *Mississippi Election of 1875,* 13, 106–114; Current, *Those Terrible Carpetbaggers,* 321–324; Harris, *Day of the Carpetbagger,* 660–673; Singletary, *Negro Militia,* 83–99.

75. *Mississippi Election of 1875,* 9, 44, 138–145, 883–887; James W. Lee to Gov. Ames, 2 Nov. 1875, Gov. Recs., RG 27, box 100; Morgan, *Yazoo,* 487; Puckett, "Reconstruction in Monroe County," 143–156; William D. Frazee to Judge R. A. Hill, 8 July 1876, Dept. of Justice, RG 60, Source-Chronological file, Mississippi, roll 2; Harris, *Day of the Carpetbagger,* 684–687.

76. Current, *Those Terrible Carpetbaggers,* 324–327; Harris, *Day of the Carpetbagger,* 691–698.

77. The best treatment of the Republicans in South Carolina is Thomas Holt, *Black over White: Negro Political Leadership in South Carolina during Reconstruction* (Urbana, Ill., 1977). But also see Joel Williamson, *After Slavery: The Negro in South Carolina during Reconstruction, 1861–1877* (Chapel Hill, N.C., 1965), 363–417; as well as Francis B. Simkins and Robert H. Woody, *South Carolina during Reconstruction* (Chapel Hill, N.C., 1932). On the low country, see Julie Saville, *The Work of Reconstruction: From Slave to Wage Laborer in South Carolina, 1860–1870* (Cambridge, Eng., 1994); and Edward A. Miller, Jr., *Gullah Statesman: Robert Smalls from Slavery to Congress, 1839–1915* (Columbia, S.C., 1995), 35–107. On the regulators, see Rachel N. Klein, *Unification of a Slave State: The Rise of the Planter Class in the South Carolina Backcountry, 1760–1808* (Chapel Hill, N.C., 1990).

78. Zuczek, *State of Rebellion,* 136–139; Stephen Kantrowitz, *Ben Tillman and the Reconstruction of White Supremacy* (Chapel Hill, N.C., 2000), 60–61; Simkins and Woody, *South Carolina during Reconstruction,* 499–501; Rable, *But There Was No Peace,* 174.

79. W. M. Porcher et al. to Gov. R. K. Scott, 6 Sept. 1868, box 2, folder 12, and Lawrence Cain et al. to Gov. Scott, 2 Nov. 1868, box 3, folder 20, both in Scott Papers, Letters Rec'd; *Affairs of Late Insurrectionary States,* vol. 3, 146; Mrs. J. Ward

Motte to Robert, 2 Aug. 1870, Pelot Papers, folder 5; Nelson, *Iron Confederacies,* 126–128; Zuczek, *State of Rebellion,* 74.

80. *Affairs of Late Insurrectionary States,* vol. 3, 146–147; Orville Vernon Burton, *In My Father's House Are Many Mansions: Family and Community in Edgefield, South Carolina* (Chapel Hill, N.C., 1985), 256–257; Foner, *Freedom's Lawmakers,* 35, 89, 96, 194–195. On the potentially tense relationship between the militia companies and state government authorities, see Saville, *Work of Reconstruction,* 197–198.

81. Francis Butler Simkins, *Pitchfork Ben Tillman: South Carolinian* (Baton Rouge, 1944), 58–61; Kantrowitz, *Ben Tillman,* 61–62; Orville Vernon Burton, "The Rise and Fall of Afro-American Town Life: Town and Country in Reconstruction Edgefield, South Carolina," in Orville Vernon Burton and Robert C. McMath Jr., eds., *Toward a New South? Studies in Post–Civil War Southern Communities* (Westport, Conn., 1982), 167; Vernon Burton, "Race and Reconstruction: Edgefield County, South Carolina," *JSoH* 12 (Fall 1978): 41; Foner, *Freedom's Lawmakers,* 210.

82. U.S. Senate, *South Carolina in 1876: Testimony as to the Denial of the Elective Franchise in South Carolina at the Elections of 1875 and 1876,* Senate Misc. Doc. no. 48, 44th Cong., 2d sess., 3 vols. (Washington, D.C., 1877), vol. 1, 34–35, 45, 47–49; Kantrowitz, *Ben Tillman,* 64–66; Foner, *Freedom's Lawmakers,* 1, 183–184; Williamson, *After Slavery,* 266–267. Adams's militia company had been organized six or seven years earlier in the Ninth Regiment under Rivers's command. Although Adams claimed that he reorganized it as Company A of the Eighteenth Regiment, it may not have been officially sanctioned, instead operating at least semi-independently.

83. *South Carolina in 1876,* vol. 1, 28–29. For accounts of the battle at Hamburg, see Kantrowitz, *Ben Tillman,* 67–69; Williamson, *After Slavery,* 268–269; Rable, *But There Was No Peace,* 165–167; and Foner, *Reconstruction,* 570–571.

84. *South Carolina in 1876,* vol. 1, 13, 20; D. T. Corbin to Gov. Chamberlain, 9 Oct. 1876, box 15, folder 7, S. J. Patterson et al. to Gov. Chamberlain, 22 Aug. 1876, box 14, folder 8, and E. J. Black to Gov. Chamberlain, 2 Oct. 1876, box 15, folder 2, all in Gov. Chamberlain Papers, SCDAH; Kantrowitz, *Ben Tillman,* 74; Simkins, *Pitchfork Ben Tillman,* 66; Zuczek, *State of Rebellion,* 175–176; Simkins and Woody, *South Carolina during Reconstruction,* 482–491.

85. Melinda Meeks Hennessey, "Racial Violence during Reconstruction: The 1876 Riots in Charleston and Cainhoy," *SCHM* 86 (April 1985): 100–112; Zuczek, *State of Rebellion,* 177–178; Julius P. Strobel to Gov. Chamberlain, 11 Sept. 1876, Chamberlain Papers, box 14, folder 28; L. R. Ragsdale to Gov. Hampton, 13 Jan. 1877, Gov. Hampton Papers, box 2, folder 33, SCDAH.

86. Wade Hampton, *Free Men! Free Ballots!! Free Schools!!! The Pledges of General Wade Hampton . . . to the Colored People of South Carolina* (n.p., 1876); Richland Democratic Club Minutes and Scrapbook, 7 Sept. 1876, 21 Sept. 1876, and 28 Sept. 1876, SCL; F. E. Thomas to J. H. Aycock, 25 Sept. 1876, Aycock Family Papers, box 1, folder 13, SCL; Barnwell County Democratic Executive Committee, 1 Aug.

1876, SCL; Hampton M. Jarrell, *Wade Hampton and the Negro: The Road Not Taken* (Columbia, S.C., 1949), 46–62; Burton, "Race and Reconstruction," 43.

87. Nell Irvin Painter, "Martin R. Delany: Elitism and Black Nationalism," in Leon F. Litwack and August Meier, eds., *Black Leaders of the Nineteenth Century* (Urbana, Ill., 1988), 149–171; Edmund L. Drago, *Hurrah for Hampton: Black Red Shirts in South Carolina during Reconstruction* (Fayetteville, Ark., 1998), 13–24.

88. Richland Democratic Club Minutes and Scrapbook, 5 Oct. 1876; Barnwell County Democratic Executive Committee, 1 Aug. *1876; South Carolina in 1876*, vol. 1, 7.

89. Richland Democratic Club Minutes and Scrapbook, 28 Sept. 1876; Hennessey, "Racial Violence during Reconstruction," 104–109; Drago, *Hurrah for Hampton*, 13–45; Williamson, *After Slavery*, 408–412.

90. Hennessey, "Racial Violence during Reconstruction," 110; Kantrowitz, *Ben Tillman*, 75–76.

91. Taylor, *Louisiana Reconstructed*, 495–498; Simkins and Woody, *South Carolina during Reconstruction*, 525–541; Zuczek, *State of Rebellion*, 195–197; Rable, *But There Was No Peace*, 183–185.

92. *The Nation* 617 (26 Apr. 1877).

93. Foner, *Reconstruction*, 582–87; Eric Foner, *Nothing but Freedom: Emancipation and Its Legacy* (Baton Rouge, 1983), 106–107; Joe Louis Caldwell, "A Social, Economic, and Political Study of Blacks in the Louisiana Delta, 1865–1880," Ph.D. diss., Tulane University, 1989, 345; John C. Rodrigue, *Reconstruction in the Cane Fields: From Slavery to Free Labor in Louisiana's Sugar Parishes, 1862–1880* (Baton Rouge, 2001), 159–191.

94. I have tried to develop some of these points in Steven Hahn, "Class and State in Postemancipation Societies: Southern Planters in Comparative Perspective," *AHR* 95 (February 1990): 75–98; and Steven Hahn, "Emancipation and the Development of Capitalist Agriculture: The South in Comparative Perspective," in Kees Gispen, ed., *What Made the South Different?* (Jackson, Miss., 1990), 71–88.

7. THE EDUCATION OF HENRY ADAMS

The epigraph is from U.S. Senate, *Report and Testimony of the Select Committee of the United States Senate to Investigate the Causes of the Removal of the Negroes from the Southern States to the Northern States*, Senate Rept. no. 693, 46th Cong., 2d sess. (Washington, D.C., 1880), pt. 2, 186.

1. Convention Circular enclosed in Henry Adams to William Coppinger, 16 Nov. 1878, ACS, roll 18, LC; U.S. Senate, *Louisiana in 1878*, no. 855, 45th Cong., 3d sess. (Washington, D.C., 1879).

2. The one work that takes this seriously as a political phenomenon is Nell Irvin

Painter, *Exodusters: Black Migration to Kansas after Reconstruction* (New York, 1976). But also see William Cohen, *At Freedom's Edge: Black Mobility and the Southern White Quest for Racial Control, 1861–1915* (Baton Rouge, 1991), 138–197; and August Meier, *Negro Thought in America, 1880–1915: Racial Ideologies in the Age of Booker T. Washington* (Ann Arbor, Mich., 1963), 59–68.

3. We do not know the precise circumstances that took Adams (initially Henry Houston) and his family from Georgia to Louisiana, but it appears that, once in Louisiana, one of their masters died in 1858. Henry Adams and his father then became the property of the teenaged Nancy Emily Adams and were both hired out to a man named Ferguson, who owned a plantation near Logansport. Adams's mother, however, belonged to the teenaged girl's brother and lived on one of his properties. At the time of emancipation, Henry Adams seems to have had "three horses and a fine buggy, and a good deal of money, both gold and silver." This, and most of what else we have discovered about Adams, is derived from his extraordinary testimony before a select committee of the U.S. Senate investigating the "removal" of southern blacks to the northern states in 1880. See *Report and Testimony* no. 693, pt. 2, 101, 175, 189–192, and generally 101–214. The most authoritative secondary treatment of Adams is Painter, *Exodusters*, 71–255.

4. *Report and Testimony*, no. 693, pt. 2, 101, 153–154, 175–177.

5. Ibid., 101–104, 114, 148, 158–159, 186; Henry Adams et al. to President Rutherford B. Hayes, enclosed in Henry Adams to William Coppinger, 5 Jan. 1878, ACS, roll 117; Painter, *Exodusters*, 77–81; Cohen, *At Freedom's Edge*, 161. Adams and the council had sent a petition to Hayes, with "over 3,000 of our solid names in it," earlier in the summer, but "never have seen a publication of it." See Henry Adams et al. to John H. B. Latrobe, 31 Aug. 1877, ACS, roll 116A.

6. See, for example, Wilson Jeremiah Moses, *The Golden Age of Black Nationalism, 1850–1925* (Hamden, Conn., 1978), 15–55; Jane H. Pease and William H. Pease, *They Who Would Be Free: Blacks' Search for Freedom, 1830–1861* (New York, 1974), 120–121, 251–277; Floyd J. Miller, *The Search for a Black Nationality: Black Emigration and Colonization, 1787–1863* (Urbana, Ill., 1975); James T. Campbell, *Songs of Zion: The African Methodist Episcopal Church in the United States and South Africa* (Chapel Hill, N.C., 1998), 66–75; Nell Irvin Painter, "Martin R. Delany: Elitism and Black Nationalism," in Leon Litwack and August Meier, eds., *Black Leaders of the Nineteenth Century* (Urbana, Ill., 1988), 149–163; William Cheek and Aimee Lee Cheek, *John Mercer Langston and the Fight for Black Freedom, 1829–1865* (Urbana, Ill., 1989), 113–114, 170–175, 186–193, 231–233; Sterling Stuckey, *Slave Culture: Nationalist Theory and the Foundations of Black America* (New York, 1987), 138–192; Howard Temperley, "African-American Aspirations and the Settlement of Liberia," *S&A* 21 (August 2000): 67–92.

7. *AR* 41 (September 1865): 284; *AR* 41 (December 1865): 362–365; *AR* 42 (July 1866): 222; *AR* 42 (October 1866): 315; *AR* 43 (January 1867): 11–23; *AR* 43 (Febru-

ary 1867): 39; *AR* 43 (April 1867): 109–117; *AR* 43 (July 1867): 204–211; *AR* 43 (December 1867): 366–372; *AR* 44 (March 1868): 70–71; *AR* 44 (June 1868): 173–183. Applications for emigration were also received from parties in Alabama, Mississippi, and Florida, as well as from Pennsylvania, Massachusetts, New York, Maryland, and the District of Columbia, although they were far fewer. Of the 10,595 who emigrated between 1820 and 1861, 7,263 (69 percent) were from the states of Virginia, North Carolina, South Carolina, Georgia, and Tennessee.

8. G. W. Samson to Rev. William McLain, 3 Aug. 1866, ACS, roll 99; E. M. Pendleton to Rev. Dr. McLain, 20 June 1866, ACS, roll 98; Henry M. Turner to Mr. Coppinger, 18 July 1866, ACS, roll 99; Joseph P. Reidy, *From Slavery to Agrarian Captialism in the Cotton Plantation South: Central Georgia, 1800–1880* (Chapel Hill, N.C., 1992), 182–184.

9. James Davison to Gen. Tillson, 6 Dec. 1866, BRFAL, Ga. Asst. Comr., ser. 632, Unreg. Letters Rec'd, [A-217]; W. W. Granger to George W. Denison, 19 Mar. 1867, BRFAL, Ark. Asst. Comr., ser. 231 [A-5539]; Edward Magdol, *A Right to the Land: Essays on the Freedmen's Community* (Westport, Conn., 1977), 174–199.

10. John Averill to William Coppinger, 1 June 1866, ACS, roll 98; H. A. Crane to William McLain, 9 Jan. 1866, ACS, roll 98; Thomas Holt, *The Problem of Freedom: Race, Labor, and Politics in Jamaica and Britain, 1832–1938* (Baltimore, 1992), 143–176; Walter Rodney, *A History of the Guyanese Working People, 1881–1905* (Baltimore, 1981), 60–89; Sidney Mintz, *Caribbean Transformations* (New York, 1974), 146–224. According to the reports of the American Colonization Society, 346 Barbadians were settled in Liberia in 1865. See *AR* 42 (July 1866): 222.

11. *AR* 44 (March 1868): 68. Between 1868 and 1873, annual emigration to Liberia averaged 187, or 67 percent less than during the previous four years.

12. *AR* 49 (March 1873): 66–67; Allen Trelease, *White Terror: The Ku Klux Klan Conspiracy and Southern Reconstruction* (New York, 1971), 372; Philip S. Foner and Ronald L. Lewis, eds., *The Black Worker during the Era of the National Labor Union* (Philadelphia, 1978), 20–21, 29–30, 120–128, 132; Loren Schweninger, *James T. Rapier and Reconstruction* (Chicago, 1978), 88–89; Alrutheus Ambush Taylor, *The Negro in Tennessee, 1865–1880* (Washington, D.C., 1941), 109–113. Also see Chapter 5.

13. *Report and Testimony*, no. 693, pt. 2, 108–109, 114, 135–138, 142, 148, 151, 178, 182, 187, 538–539; Minutes of General Colonization Council Meeting, 27 Apr. 1878, ACS, roll 117; Henry Adams to William Coppinger, 16 Nov. 1878, ACS, roll 118.

14. *Report and Testimony*, no. 693, pt. 1, 280–281, 287, 294; *Alexandria (Va.) People's Advocate*, 20 Dec. 1879; Frenise A. Logan, *The Negro in North Carolina, 1876–1894* (Chapel Hill, N.C., 1964), 123–124.

15. Unus Hubbard to William Coppinger, 2 June 1878, ACS, roll 117; *AR* 3 (November 1827), 283–284; *AR* 25 (January 1849), 4–6; *AR* 27 (March 1851), 67–68;

AR 42 (October 1866), 312; *AR* 46 (March 1870), 68–69; *Savannah Republican,* 27 June 1865; *Report and Testimony,* no. 693, pt. 2, 342; R. T. Smith to Bvt. Brig. Gen. O. L. Shepherd, 2 May 1868, BRFAL, Ala. Asst. Comr., roll 18, NA; Ted Tunnell, ed., *Carpetbagger from Vermont: The Autobiography of Marshall Harvey Twitchell* (Baton Rouge, 1989), 117.

16. The 1880 federal census presents data on the number of African Americans over the age of ten (and in various age categories) who were unable to write, thus exaggerating the extent of illiteracy since some of those who were unable to write were able to read. The highest rates of illiteracy were to be found in Georgia (81.6 percent) and Alabama (80.6 percent) and the lowest in Florida (70.7 percent) and Tennessee (71.7 percent). Illiteracy rates were substantially lower in the fifteen- to twenty-year-old category, ranging from a high of 76.4 percent in Georgia to a low of 61.2 percent in Virginia, while they were higher in the age twenty-one and over category, ranging from a high of 84.3 percent in Georgia to a low of 73.8 percent in Florida. See Department of the Interior, *Compendium of the Tenth Census* (Washington, D.C., 1883), pt. 2, 1650–1653.

17. See, for example, Vilma Raskin Potter, *A Reference Guide to Afro-American Publications and Editors, 1827–1946* (Ames, Iowa, 1993); Julius E. Thompson, *The Black Press in Mississippi, 1865–1985* (Gainesville, Fla., 1993), 1–22; and the essays in Henry Lewis Suggs, ed., *The Black Press in the South, 1865–1979* (Westport, Conn., 1983), especially those by Julius E. Thompson on Mississippi, Allen Woodrow Jones on Alabama, Jerrell Shofner on Florida, and Alton Hornsby Jr. on Georgia.

18. *Report and Testimony,* no. 693, pt. 3, 226, 353–354, 381–382, 513, and pt. 2, 342; ? McStokes et al. to William Coppinger, 25 Mar. 1878, ACS, roll 117; Joab Brown to William Coppinger, 10 July 1879, ACS, roll 119.

19. Henry Foster to William Coppinger, 14 Oct. 1878, ACS, roll 118; Richard Stokes to William Coppinger, 5 Dec. 1877, ACS, roll 116B; H. M. Gates to William Coppinger, 2 Dec. 1877, ACS, roll 116B; Bud Steven to William Coppinger, June 1877, ACS, roll 116A; Richard T. Hyman to William Coppinger, 17 Mar. 1880, ACS, roll 120. "I have heard a great talk a bout Liberia and it society and I wish to learn the facts a bout it," a local leader in Waller County, Texas, also wrote. "Sir Please send document stating all the facts a bout Liberia." See A. G. Randell to William Coppinger, 28 May 1882, ACS, roll 123.

20. J. C. Hazely to William Coppinger, 17 July 1879, ACS, roll 119; Henry B. DaCoster to William Coppinger, 11 Sept. 1880, ACS, roll 120; Reuben R. Wynne to William Coppinger, 11 Feb. 1878, ACS, roll 117; Bud Steven to William Coppinger, June 1877, ACS, roll 116A; Eli Morrow to William Coppinger, 4 Aug. 1877, ACS, roll 116A; S. S. Boorum to Mr. Editor, 9 Oct. 1877, ACS, roll 116B; *Report and Testimony,* no. 693, pt. 2, 148, 151.

21. Morrow to Coppinger, 4 Aug. 1877, ACS, roll 116A; Charles Martin to Gentle-

men, 8 Nov. 1877, ACS, roll 116B; P. P. Ervin to William Coppinger, 27 Apr. 1877, ACS, roll 116A; L. G. Goodwin to William Coppinger, 10 Jan. 1880, ACS, roll 120; "Notice to the Colored People of Warren County," enclosed in Hazely to Coppinger, 17 July 1879, ACS, roll 119; *Brenham (Tex.) Weekly Banner*, 13 June 1879.

22. Allen M. Jones to William Coppinger, 16 Aug. 1878, ACS, roll 117; *Report and Testimony*, no. 693, pt. 2, 517–518; Adell Patton, Jr., "The 'Back to Africa' Movement in Arkansas," *AHQ* 51 (Summer 1992): 167; M. C. Simpson et al. to American Colonization Society, 5 Oct. 1879, ACS, roll 119; J. H. Rivers to William Coppinger, 8 Aug. 1877, ACS, roll 116A; C. L. Paine to William Coppinger, 27 June 1877, ACS, roll 116A.

23. *Report and Testimony*, no. 693, pt. 3, 51, pt. 1, 301; John W. H. Lee to William Coppinger, 3 Apr. 1878, ACS, roll 117.

24. W. E. B. Du Bois, ed., *The Negro Church: Report of a Social Study Made under the Direction of Atlanta University* (Atlanta, 1903), 57; *Report and Testimony*, no. 693, pt. 2, 351; F. R. Guernsey, "The Negro Exodus," *International Review* 7 (October 1879): 378–379.

25. *Report and Testimony*, no. 693, pt. 2, 517–518, 539, 542; Organization Metin of Emigrants, 27 Sept. 1879, ACS, roll 119; Steven to Coppinger, 4 June 1877, ACS, roll 116A; William E. Montgomery, *Under Their Own Vine and Fig Tree: The African-American Church in the South, 1865–1900* (Baton Rouge, 1993), 197–223; Stephen Ward Angell, *Bishop Henry McNeal Turner and African-American Religion in the South* (Knoxville, Tenn., 1992), 136–141; Campbell, *Songs of Zion*, 79–87.

26. See, for example, *New Orleans Weekly Louisianian*, 26 Apr. 1879, 17 May 1879; *Huntsville (Ala.) Gazette*, 14 Feb. 1880; *Report and Testimony*, pts. 1–3; William Ivy Hair, *Bourbonism and Agrarian Protest: Louisiana Politics, 1877–1900* (Baton Rouge, 1969), 83–92; Logan, *Negro in North Carolina*, 119–120; James C. Cobb, *The Most Southern Place on Earth: The Mississippi Delta and the Roots of Regional Identity* (New York, 1992), 69.

27. See, for example, Vernon Lane Wharton, *The Negro in Mississippi, 1865–1890* (Chapel Hill, N.C., 1947), 11–16; Logan, *Negro in North Carolina*, 119–125; Hair, *Bourbonism and Agrarian Protest*, 83–106; John William Graves, *Town and Country: Race Relations in an Urban-Rural Context, Arkansas, 1865–1905* (Fayetteville, Ark., 1990), 59–60. Some of the most important recent treatments of the South and of African Americans in this period either ignore or slight emigrationist activity. See Edward Ayers, *The Promise of the New South: Life after Reconstruction* (New York, 1992); Leon Litwack, *Trouble in Mind: Black Southerners in the Age of Jim Crow* (New York, 1998), 135, 484–486; Jacqueline Jones, *Labor of Love, Labor of Sorrow: Black Women, Work, and the Family from Slavery to the Present* (New York, 1985), 81–82. The major exception to this tendency is Painter, *Exodusters*. Although she focuses on the Kansas exodus and is modest as to the "wider applicability" of her findings, she both suggests important links between the Kansas and Liberia

movements and casts them in a broader political context. But also see Cohen, *At Freedom's Edge,* 138–197; and Meier, *Negro Thought in America,* 59–68.

28. I kept close track of the counties and localities from which expressions of interest in emigration, or outright emigrationist activity, came between 1876 and 1882, and these included the states of Kentucky, Maryland, Tennessee, Virginia, and Missouri; the cities of Baltimore, Nashville, Knoxville, St. Louis, Richmond, Norfolk, Savannah, New Orleans, and Galveston; and white majority counties such as Escambia County, Alabama, Cherokee County, Georgia, Santa Rosa County, Florida, Lamar County, Texas, and Marshall County, Kentucky.

29. This seems plain from the incoming correspondence of the American Colonization Society, as well as from testimony taken by the Senate committee investigating the exodus. But see also George Tindall, *South Carolina Negroes, 1877–1900* (Columbia, S.C., 1952), 153–185; George A. Devlin, *South Carolina and Black Migration, 1865–1940: In Search of the Promised Land* (New York, 1989), 88–94; Lawrence D. Rice, *The Negro in Texas, 1874–1900* (Baton Rouge, 1971), 198–208; Joe Louis Caldwell, "A Social, Economic, and Political Study of Blacks in the Louisiana Delta, 1865–1880," Ph.D. diss., Tulane University, 1989, 372–388. More than 80 percent of the affected counties produced at least 1,000 bales of cotton per year, and more than 70 percent produced at least 5,000 bales. See Department of the Interior, *Tenth Census of the United States: Report on the Production of Cotton* (Washington, D.C., 1884), vols. 5–6.

30. *Report and Testimony,* no. 693, pt. 1, iii–viii, 116, 310–313, and pt. 2, 60, 365, 439; *New Orleans Weekly Louisianian,* 15 Mar. 1879, 13 Dec. 1879; E. D. Sawyer to William Coppinger, 18 Jan. 1878, ACS, roll 117; Cain Gibbs to Rev. William McLain, 7 Mar. 1878, ACS, roll 117; William H. Holt to William Coppinger, 2 Dec. 1878, ACS, roll 118; *Alexandria People's Advocate,* 14 Feb. 1880.

31. See Chapters 6 and 8; Eric Foner, *Reconstruction: America's Unfinished Revolution, 1863–1877* (New York, 1988), 425–444, 548–553, 569–575, 587–601; Michael Perman, *The Road to Redemption: Southern Politics, 1869–1879* (Chapel Hill, N.C., 1984), 237–263; Steven Hahn, "Class and State in Postemancipation Societies: Southern Planters in Comparative Perspective," *AHR* 95 (February 1990): 85–86.

32. *Report and Testimony,* no. 693, pt. 2, 214–219, 237, pt. 3, 433–434; *New Orleans Weekly Louisianian,* 15 Nov. 1879.

33. *Cincinnati Commercial,* quoted in *New Orleans Weekly Louisianian,* 1 Jan. 1881; *Report and Testimony,* no. 693, pt. 3, 1–2; *Brenham Weekly Banner,* 20 June 1879; Polk and Gillespie to William Coppinger, 27 Jan. 1878, ACS, roll 117.

34. D. W. Frias to William Coppinger, 8 May 1880, ACS, roll 120; Jeremiah Jenkins to Lardner Gibbon, 1 Aug. 1879, ACS, roll 119; A. G. Randolph to American Colonization Society, 15 Feb. 1880, ACS, roll 120; Jackson Caesar to W. N. Coppinger, 2 Jan. 1878, ACS, roll 117; Simon Davis to William Coppinger, 21 Apr. 1880, ACS, roll 120; William Mohr to William Coppinger, 6 Mar. 1880, ACS, roll 120.

35. *Report and Testimony*, no. 693, pt. 2, 343. These aspirations closely resemble what scholars of late-nineteenth and early-twentieth-century Russia and South Africa have called the "peasant dream." See Teodor Shanin, "The Peasant Dream: Russia, 1905–07," in Raphael Samuel and Gareth Stedman Jones, eds., *Culture, Ideology, and Politics: Essays for Eric Hobsbawm* (London, 1982), 227–243; and William Beinart and Colin Bundy, *Hidden Struggles in Rural South Africa: Politics and Popular Movements in the Transkei and Eastern Cape, 1890–1930* (Berkeley, Calif., 1987), 35–36.

36. *New Orleans Weekly Louisianian*, 1 Feb. 1879; *Report and Testimony*, no. 693, pt. 3, 4–12, 122, 134, 509, and pt. 2, 343; Painter, *Exodusters*, 175–176; Cohen, *At Freedom's Edge*, 177–180.

37. Painter, *Exodusters*, 195; Guernsey, "Negro Exodus," 375.

38. *Report and Testimony*, no. 693, pt. 3, 4–12, 509; Robert Evans to William Coppinger, 8 July 1879, ACS, roll 119.

39. Painter, *Exodusters*, 179; William Benson to William Coppinger, 23 Apr. 1877, ACS, roll 116A.

40. A. B. Coleman to William Coppinger, 13 Apr. 1880, ACS, roll 120; A. G. Randolph to American Colonization Society, 15 Feb. 1880, ACS, roll 120.

41. *Report and Testimony*, no. 693, pt. 2, 186, 104; Henry Adams to William Coppinger, 28 Mar. 1879, ACS, roll 118; Adams to Coppinger, 9 July 1879, ACS, roll 119; Adams to Coppinger, 17 July 1879, roll 119; Adams to Coppinger, 12 July 1880, ACS, roll 120.

42. Those who sought to emigrate individually or as single families tended to be young, to be literate, to have skills or a professional identity, and to have resources in the way of money or property. Teachers were especially prominent, as were city and village dwellers. They may also have been targets of political persecution, like John Milton Brown. Brown taught school and served as the sheriff of Coahoma County, Mississippi, in the early 1870s, but when he was renominated in 1875, between 1,000 and 1,500 armed whites drove him out of the state. After a brief stay in Helena, Arkansas, Brown settled in Topeka, Kansas. See James C. Noisette to Colonization Society, 11 Aug. 1877, R. J. Braden to William Coppinger, 7 Apr. 1877, and H. H. Montgomery to William Coppinger, 18 Apr. 1877, all in ACS, roll 116A; *Report and Testimony*, no. 693, pt. 2, 351–355.

43. *New Orleans Weekly Louisianian*, 31 May 1879; Nelson Davies to William Coppinger, 23 Aug. 1877, ACS, roll 116A; H. C. Rogers to William Coppinger, 9 Mar. 1879, ACS, roll 118; Allen M. Jones to William Coppinger, 29 Aug. 1877, ACS, roll 116A. See also *AR* 51 (October 1875): 120, which reported, "The applicants [for emigration to Liberia] are mostly in families and neighborhoods."

44. Cary Bellamy to William Coppinger, n.d. [Feb. 1879], ACS, roll 118; Miles Morgan to William Coppinger, 26 Aug. 1879, ACS, roll 119; Samuel Brown to William Coppinger, 11 Sept. 1877, ACS, roll 116A.

45. See, for example, Jones to Coppinger, 29 Aug. 1877, ACS, roll 116A; and William P. Casis to William Coppinger, 14 Jan. 1878, ACS, roll 117.

46. C. W. Jones to William Coppinger, 19 Nov. 1877, ACS, roll 116B; *Report and Testimony*, no. 693, pt. 2, 512–513; W. R. Long and J. D. Thompson to William Coppinger, 28 May 1877, ACS, roll 116A; Simon Davis to William Coppinger, 21 Apr. 1880, ACS, roll 120. In Bolivar County, Mississippi, the superintendent of education noticed that while "only a few persons . . . left" for Kansas, "the movement was confined to one plantation, and there was a little movement over at Col. Stoke's plantation." See *Report and Testimony*, no. 693, pt. 3, 509.

47. Jones to Coppinger, 19 Nov. 1877, ACS, roll 116B; Morgan to Coppinger, 26 Aug. 1879, ACS, roll 119; Bellamy to Coppinger, n.d., ACS, roll 118; Skinner to Coppinger, 30 July 1877, ACS, roll 116A; Brown to Coppinger, 11 Sept. 1877, ACS, roll 116A; Norfleet Browne to William Coppinger, 25 Aug. 1879, ACS, roll 119; Robinson to Coppinger, 29 Oct. 1878, ACS, roll 118. The denominational distinctions could also be more refined. A party of fourteen families looking to leave Craven County, North Carolina, included Regular, Primitive, New Light, and Missionary Baptists. See William Hayes to William Coppinger, 16 July 1878, ACS, roll 117. On the interdenominational aspects of religious experience, see Montgomery, *Under Their Own Vine and Fig Tree*, 275–277, 293–295. See also Elizabeth R. Bethel, *Promiseland: A Century of Life in a Negro Community* (Philadelphia, 1981), 77–80.

48. William Hayes to William Coppinger, 16 July 1878, ACS, roll 117; M. C. Simpson et al. to American Colonization Society, 5 Oct. 1879, roll 119; and Jones to Coppinger, 29 Aug. 1877, ACS, roll 116A.

49. *Report and Testimony*, no. 693, pt. 2, 182.

50. G. W. Hayden to William Coppinger, 5 Jan. 1880, ACS, roll 120; *Report and Testimony*, no. 693, pt. 3, 67. Also see Jones, *Labor of Love, Labor of Sorrow*, 44–109; Sharon Ann Holt, *Making Freedom Pay: North Carolina Freedpeople Working for Themselves, 1865–1900* (Athens, Ga., 2000), 1–24.

51. *Report and Testimony*, no. 693, pt. 2, 232–233.

52. Frederick Douglass, "Southern Questions: The Negro Exodus from the Gulf States," *Journal of Social Science* 11 (May 1880): 7–19. Also see William S. McFeely, *Frederick Douglass* (New York, 1991), 299–304; David W. Blight, *Frederick Douglass' Civil War: Keeping Faith in Jubilee* (Baton Rouge, 1989), 122–147.

53. *Christian Recorder*, 31 Jan. 1878, 11 Apr. 1878, 18 Apr. 1878, 22 Aug. 1878; *New Orleans Weekly Louisianian*, 24 May 1879, 7 June 1879; Turner to Coppinger, 18 July 1866, ACS, roll 99; Angell, *Bishop Turner*, 136–141; Montgomery, *Under Their Own Vine and Fig Tree*, 199–209; Meier, *Negro Thought in America*, 65–67; Robert G. Athearn, *In Search of Canaan: Black Migration to Kansas, 1879–1880* (Lawrence, Kan., 1978), 182–184; Campbell, *Songs of Zion*, 79–87.

54. *New Orleans Weekly Louisianian*, 17 May 1879.

55. Ibid., 26 Apr. 1879, 10 May 1879; William A. Pledger to Editor, 22 Sept. 1877,

William A. Pledger Letterbooks, John E. Bryant Papers, box 9, DU; Caldwell, "Blacks in Louisiana Delta," 378–388; Hair, *Bourbonism and Agrarian Protest*, 89–92; Schweninger, *Rapier and Reconstruction*, 160–165; Meier, *Negro Thought in America*, 60–61.

56. *Report and Testimony*, no. 693, pt. 1, 52–53, 103–107; *Alexandria People's Advocate*, 10 Jan. 1880; Logan, *Negro in North Carolina*, 119–120; John H. Haley, *Charles N. Hunter and Race Relations in North Carolina* (Chapel Hill, N.C., 1987), 47–56; Eric Anderson, *Race and Politics in North Carolina, 1872–1901: The Black Second* (Baton Rouge, 1981).

57. *Report and Testimony*, no. 693, pt. 1, 280–281, and pt. 2, 105, 109–110. On "representative colored men" see Painter, *Exodusters*, esp. 14–16.

58. *Report and Testimony*, no. 693, pt. 3, 520–521; Eric Foner, *Freedom's Lawmakers: A Directory of Black Officeholders during Reconstruction* (New York, 1993), 207; Wharton, *Negro in Mississippi*, 113.

59. Painter, *Exodusters*, 187–189.

60. *Report and Testimony*, no. 693, pt. 2, 528; Foner, *Freedom's Lawmakers*, 156–157. After the bulldozing and outrages that marked the parish elections of 1878, Murrell changed his mind about the exodus.

61. *AR* 3 (November 1827): 284; *AR* 25 (February 1849): 34; *AR* 41 (September 1865): 273; *AR* 42 (October 1866): 312; *AR* 43 (January 1867): 37–38; Philip D. Morgan, *Slave Counterpoint: Black Culture in the Eighteenth Century Chesapeake and Lowcountry* (Chapel Hill, N.C., 1998), 441–658; Charles Joyner, *Down by the Riverside: A South Carolina Slave Community* (Urbana, Ill., 1984); Margaret Washington Creel, *"A Peculiar People": Slave Religion and Community-Culture among the Gullahs* (New York, 1988).

62. Ira Berlin, *Many Thousands Gone: The First Two Centuries of Slavery in North America* (Cambridge, Mass., 1998), 142–176; Morgan, *Slave Counterpoint*, 179–187, 358–376; Peter A. Coclanis, *Shadow of a Dream: Economic Life and Death in the South Carolina Low Country, 1670–1920* (New York, 1989); John Scott Strickland, "Traditional Culture and Moral Economy: Social and Economic Change in the South Carolina Low Country, 1865–1910," in Steven Hahn and Jonathan Prude, eds., *The Countryside in the Age of Capitalist Transformation: Essays in the Social History of Rural America* (Chapel Hill, N.C., 1985), 142–147.

63. Julie Saville, *The Work of Reconstruction: From Slave to Wage Laborer in South Carolina, 1860–1870* (Cambridge, Eng., 1994); Ira Berlin et al., *Freedom: A Documentary History of Emancipation, 1861–1867*, ser. 1, vol. 3: *The Wartime Genesis of Free Labor: The Lower South* (Cambridge, Eng., 1990), 87–344; Leslie A. Schwalm, *A Hard Fight for We: Women's Transition from Slavery to Freedom in South Carolina* (Urbana, Ill., 1997), 75–268; Eric Foner, *Nothing but Freedom: Emancipation and Its Legacy* (Baton Rouge, 1983), 76–90; Strickland, "Traditional Culture and Moral

Economy," 150–155. On the postemancipation Caribbean, see Holt, *Problem of Freedom*, 143–176; Sidney W. Mintz, *Caribbean Transformations* (New York, 1989), 146–213; Dale Tomich, "Contested Terrains: Houses, Provision Grounds, and the Reconstitution of Labour in Post-Emancipation Martinique," in Mary Turner, ed., *From Chattel Slaves to Wage Slaves: The Dynamics of Labour Bargaining in the Americas* (Kingston, West Indies, 1995), 241–257.

64. John Burbridge to Gov. Chamberlain, 13 Sept. 1876, Gov. Daniel Chamberlain Papers, box 14, folder 30, SCDAH; Thomas Holt, *Black over White: Negro Political Leadership in South Carolina during Reconstruction* (Urbana, Ill., 1977), 168–169. Easily the best treatment of the rice strikes is Foner, *Nothing but Freedom*, 74–110. But also see Edward A. Miller, Jr., *Gullah Statesman: Robert Smalls from Slavery to Congress, 1839–1915* (Columbia, S.C., 1995), 104–105; Strickland, "Traditional Culture and Moral Economy," 155–156.

65. William Elliott to Gov. Chamberlain, 12 Sept. 1876, folder 29, James Low to Chamberlain, 14 Sept. 1876, folder 31, and William Stone to Chamberlain, 14 Sept. 1876, folder 31, all in Chamberlain Papers, box 14; Foner, *Nothing but Freedom*, 95–96.

66. Stone to Chamberlain, 12 Sept. 1876, Chamberlain Papers, box 14, folder 30; Robert Smalls to Gov. D. H. Chamberlain, 24 Aug. 1876, box 14, folder 9; Elliott to Chamberlain, 12 Sept. 1876, box 14, folder 9; Miller, *Gullah Statesman*, 105–106; Foner, *Nothing but Freedom*, 97–99.

67. *Alexandria People's Advocate*, 21 Aug. 1880; Strickland, "Traditional Culture and Moral Economy," 159–168; Foner, *Nothing but Freedom*, 104–110.

68. Aleck Boazenau (?) to Henry Clay Warmoth, 10 May 1879, Henry Clay Warmoth Papers, roll 4, SHC; *AR* 6 (February 1831): 383; *AR* 23 (March 1847): 35; *AR* 25 (February 1849): 34; *AR* 27 (March 1851): 67–68.

69. Berlin, *Many Thousands Gone*, 77–92, 195–215, 325–357; Gwendolyn Midlo Hall, *Africans in Colonial Louisiana: The Development of Afro-Creole Culture in the Eighteenth Century* (Baton Rouge, 1992); Ann Patton Malone, *Sweet Chariot: Slave Family and Household Structure in Nineteenth-Century Louisiana* (Chapel Hill, N.C., 1992); Roderick A. McDonald, *The Economy and Material Culture of Slaves: Goods and Chattels on the Sugar Plantations of Jamaica and Louisiana* (Baton Rouge, 1993).

70. Berlin et al., *Freedom: Wartime Genesis of Free Labor in Lower South*, 347–618; C. Peter Ripley, *Slaves and Freedmen in Civil War Louisiana* (Baton Rouge, 1976), 25–90; Paul K. Eiss, "A Share in the Land: Freedpeople and the Government of Labour in Southern Louisiana, 1862–65," *S&A* 19 (April 1998): 46–86.

71. On the postemancipation sugar economy, see John C. Rodrigue, *Reconstruction in the Cane Fields: From Slavery to Free Labor in Louisiana's Sugar Parishes, 1862–1880* (Baton Rouge, 2001); J. Carlyle Sitterson, *Sugar Country: The Cane Sugar Industry in the South, 1753–1950* (Lexington, Ky., 1953), 231–342; Louis Ferleger,

"Farm Mechanization in the Sugar Sector after the Civil War," *LH* 23 (Winter 1982): 21–34; Joseph P. Reidy, "Mules and Men: Field Labor on Louisiana Sugar Plantations, 1887–1915," *AgH* 72 (Spring 1998): 183–196.

72. *New Orleans Daily Picayune* reports in Philip S. Foner and Ronald L. Lewis, eds., *The Black Worker during the Era of the National Labor Union* (Philadelphia, 1978), 152–160; Rodrigue, *Reconstruction in the Cane Fields*, 159–182; Rebecca J. Scott, "Defining the Boundaries of Freedom in the World of Cane: Cuba, Brazil, and Louisiana after Emancipation," *AHR* 99 (February 1994): 76–77; Sitterson, *Sugar Country*, 245–246; Thomas Becnel, *Labor, Church, and the Sugar Establishment: Louisiana, 1887–1976* (Baton Rouge, 1980), 4–5; BLDS, Louisiana. Seven of Terrebonne Parish's "most prominent citizens" apparently called on Kellogg for assistance, claiming that the strikers "had broken into open riot and were murdering white people, burning houses, plantation mills and committing the wildest outrages." Kellogg replied, saying that he would send in "a strong force of militia." But according to the *Picayune*, he first sent only two officers to investigate and "see whether troops were necessary." Eventually, Kellogg dispatched a detachment of forty infantry with one piece of artillery along with a squad of cavalry.

73. Foner and Lewis, *Black Worker*, 158–159; Eiss, "Share in the Land," 77–78; Scott, "Defining the Boundaries of Freedom," 77.

74. Rodrigue, *Reconstruction in the Cane Fields*, 139–158; Reidy, "Mules and Men," 184; Sitterson, *Sugar Country*, 323; Charles Nordhoff, *The Cotton States in the Spring and Summer of 1875* (New York, 1876), 70. According to Rodrigue, the gross earnings of freed sugar workers ranged between $325 and $350 a year, nearly comparable to the average annual earnings of nonagricultural workers nationwide (about $380 per year) and far more than the less than $200 per year earned by sharecroppers and tenants.

75. Rodrigue, *Reconstruction in the Cane Fields*, 78–103, 159–182; Hair, *Bourbonism and Agrarian Protest*, 171–172. Despite the attractions of Republican tariff policy and the importance of prewar Whiggery among them, most of the sugar planters aligned with the Democratic party. See Sitterson, *Sugar Country*, 332–334.

76. *Louisiana in 1878*, no. 855, xxi; Rodrigue, *Reconstruction in the Cane Fields*, 159–182.

77. *New Orleans Daily Picayune*, 20 Mar. 1880, 29 Mar. 1880, 31 Mar. 1880; Foner, *Freedom's Lawmakers*, 61; Rodrigue, *Reconstruction in the Cane Fields* 159–182; Becnel, *Labor, Church, and Sugar Establishment*, 6–7.

78. *New Orleans Daily Picayune*, 29 Mar. 1880, 1 Apr. 1880; Hair, *Bourbonism and Agrarian Protest*, 173–175.

79. *New Orleans Daily Picayune*, 2 Apr. 1880; *New Orleans Weekly Louisianian*, 3 Apr. 1880, 24 Apr. 1880, 28 Apr. 1880, 5 Nov. 1881, 19 Nov. 1881; Rodrigue, *Reconstruction in the Cane Fields*, 158–182; Jonathan Garlock, ed., *Guide to the Local Assemblies of the Knights of Labor* (Westport, Conn., 1982), 161–167.

80. *New Orleans Daily Picayune,* 20 Mar. 1880; *Chicago Inter-Ocean,* quoted in *New Orleans Weekly Louisianian,* 5 Mar. 1881; Cohen, *At Freedom's Edge,* 169, 187–194, 196, 301–311; Painter, *Exodusters,* 147; *AR* 54 (April 1878): 53; *AR* 54 (July 1878): 86; *AR* 54 (January 1879): 28; *AR* 55 (July 1879): 88; *AR* 56 (January 1880): 30; *AR* 56 (August 1880): 82–83, 129; P. J. Staudenraus, *The African Colonization Movement, 1816–1865* (New York, 1961), 251. Cohen's close analysis of the census returns leads him to conclude that "the total black influx to Kansas *throughout the 1870s* can hardly have numbered more than 25,000," and "the number that came in 1879 and 1880 would be about 22,000. Of these 22,000, no more than 8,474 came from the Deep South, roughly 4,500 of whom arrived from Mississippi and Louisiana."

81. Jones to Coppinger, 5 July 1877, ACS, roll 116A; H. N. Bouey to William Coppinger, 10 July 1877, ACS, roll 116A.

82. B. K. McKeever to William Coppinger, 18 Jan. 1879, 10 Feb. 1879, ACS, roll 118; *New Orleans Southwestern Christian Advocate,* quoted in *Report and Testimony,* no. 693, pt. 2, 254; Adams to Coppinger, 28 Feb. 1878, ACS, roll 117.

83. Athearn, *In Search of Canaan,* 91–95, 144–147; Painter, *Exodusters,* 196–200.

84. Hardy Hogan Helper to William Coppinger, 30 Sept. 1880, ACS, roll 120. Historian William Cohen, who generally emphasizes white solidarity in the work of subordinating southern blacks, nonetheless suggests that white plain folk often foiled efforts to restrict black mobility. See his *At Freedom's Edge,* 236–237, 298. Also see James C. Davis to William Coppinger, 20 May 1878, ACS, roll 117. The subject deserves further investigation.

85. *Brenham (Tex.) Weekly Banner,* 25 July 1879; *New Orleans Times,* 22 Apr. 1879, quoted in *Report and Testimony,* no. 693, pt. 2, 253; *New Orleans Times,* 20 Apr. 1879 and *St. Louis Post-Dispatch,* 17 Apr. 1879, both quoted in Athearn, *In Search of Canaan,* 95; *New Orleans Weekly Louisianian,* 10 May 1879.

86. See, for example, George Lewis to William Coppinger, 30 May 1877, ACS, roll 116A; C. W. Joshua to Coppinger, 15 Aug. 1877, ACS, roll 116A; Isaac Skinner to Coppinger, 10 Oct. 1877, ACS, roll 116B; A. A. Constantine to Coppinger, 14 Feb. 1878, ACS, roll 117; Charles Boyle to Coppinger, 28 June 1878, ACS, roll 117; Jones to Coppinger, 16 Aug. 1878, ACS, roll 117. The American Colonization Society had customarily afforded "to intelligent, enterprising, and worthy colored people . . . without charge, a comfortable passage with food on the voyage, and shelter and support for six months after arrival." Once in Liberia, each unmarried adult emigrant would receive ten acres of land and each family twenty-five acres. But it was not long before the society noted the "disastrous" effect of the "financial depression," and by 1879 required adult males to furnish at least half the cost of his emigration (estimated at about $100) and at least $10 per capita for other family members. The cost of transportation to the point of embarkation had to be shouldered entirely by the emigrants. See, *AR* 41 (September 1865): 284; *AR* 49 (February 1873): 40; *AR* 51 (April 1875): 56; *AR* 55 (April 1879): 49; *AR* 56 (January 1880): 22.

87. American Colonization Society vessels to Liberia usually departed in very late December or very early January, in late May or June, and in late October or November. See, *AR* 49 (December 1873): 371–372; *AR* 50 (November 1874): 350; *AR* 52 (April 1876): 55; *AR* 53 (January 1877): 27; *AR* 54 (April 1878): 53; *AR* 54 (July 1878): 86; *AR* 55 (January 1879): 28; *AR* 55 (July 1879): 88; *AR* 56 (January 1880): 30; *AR* 56 (August 1880): 83. On problems in harvesting and disposing of the crops, see Ceasar to Coppinger, 18 July 1878, ACS, roll 117; Ceaser Harvey to Coppinger, 24 Mar. 1879, ACS, roll 118.

88. L. G. Goodwin to William Coppinger, 10 Jan. 1880, ACS, roll 120. A family of five would have needed between $50 and $100 in addition to the cost of travel from their residence to the port of departure. See also W. R. Long and J. D. Thompson to Coppinger, 28 May 1877, ACS, roll 116A; E. D. Sawyer to Coppinger, 18 Jan. 1878, ACS, roll 117; and Limerick Long to Coppinger, 14 Mar. 1879, ACS, roll 118.

89. *Chicago Inter-Ocean*, quoted in *New Orleans Weekly Louisianian*, 5 Mar. 1881; *Report and Testimony*, no. 693, pt. 2, 359. The colonies that the Kansas Freedmen's Relief Association tried to set up are to be distinguished from the black colonies, the best known being Nicodemus, formed earlier in the decade. See Athearn, *In Search of Canaan*, 78–79, 173–177. Also see Thomas C. Cox, *Blacks in Topeka, Kansas, 1865–1915: A Social History* (Baton Rouge, 1982), 46–81; Painter, *Exodusters*, 148–153.

90. *AR* 55 (April 1879): 49; Guernsey, "Negro Exodus," 381. Thus, although it appears that only about 1,400 Louisiana blacks migrated to Kansas, the historian William Ivy Hair claims that more than "ten thousand left the state" in 1879 and "probably five times as many tried, futilely, to depart." See Hair, *Bourbonism and Agrarian Protest*, 83.

91. *New Orleans Daily Picayune*, 20 Mar. 1880; *New Orleans Weekly Louisianian*, 24 Apr. 1880, 21 Jan. 1882; Painter, *Exodusters*, 209–210; Caldwell, "Blacks in Louisiana Delta," 389–390.

92. *New Orleans Weekly Louisianian*, 15 Feb. 1879, 29 Mar. 1879, 5 July 1879, 19 July 1879; *Report and Testimony*, no. 693, pt. 2, 221.

93. *Chicago Inter-Ocean*, quoted in *New Orleans Weekly Louisianian*, 14 Jan. 1882; *Charleston News and Courier*, 12 Jan. 1882, 14 Jan. 1882; Orville Vernon Burton, *In My Father's House Are Many Mansions: Family and Community in Edgefield County, South Carolina* (Chapel Hill, N.C., 1985), 237–238; Tindall, *South Carolina Negroes*, 170–173; *Huntsville (Ala.) Gazette*, 17 Nov. 1883, 23 Jan. 1886, 30 Jan. 1886, 20 Feb. 1886. Some of those who stayed behind in Edgefield County expressed their anger at the stock law by engaging in "ku kluxism" against "white farmers, good Democrats, men of wealth and standing in the communities in which they reside." See *Savannah (Ga.) Echo*, quoted in *Huntsville Gazette*, 8 Apr. 1882.

94. See, for example, Jacqueline Jones, *The Dispossessed: America's Underclass from the Civil War to the Present* (New York, 1992), 38–39, 142–143, 158; Jones,

Labor of Love, Labor of Sorrow, 92–99; Cohen, *At Freedom's Edge*, 248–273; Ayers, *Promise of the New South*, 108–109, 120; and Daniel Letwin, *The Challenge of Interracial Unionism: Alabama Coal Miners, 1878–1921* (Chapel Hill, N.C., 1998), 23–26.

95. *Report and Testimony*, no. 693, pt. 3, 220; *New Orleans Weekly Pelican*, 26 Nov. 1887, 2 Mar. 1889; *New York Sun*, quoted in *New Orleans Weekly Pelican*, 15 Jan. 1887.

96. Adams et al. to John H. B. Latrobe, 31 Aug. 1877, ACS, roll 116A; Adams et al. to President Hayes, enclosed in Adams to Coppinger, 5 Jan. 1878, ACS, roll 117; Adams to Coppinger, 9 July 1879, ACS, roll 119; Adams to Coppinger, 27 May 1879, ACS, roll 118; *Report and Testimony*, no. 693, pt. 2, 108–109.

8. OF BALLOTS AND BIRACIALISM

1. According to records of the American Colonization Society, 3,560 of the 10,595 African Americans who emigrated to Liberia before the outbreak of the Civil War were from the State of Virginia, accounting for 33.6 percent of the total. North Carolina ranked second to Virginia in total emigrants during the period with 1,371, followed by Georgia (1,147) and Tennessee (721). In 1865, almost all of the African Americans who emigrated to Liberia under the auspices of the American Colonization Society were from Virginia. See, *AR* 41 XLI (September 1865): 284; *AR* 41 (December 1865), 362–365; *AR* 42 (July 1866): 222; *AR* 42 (September 1866): 283; *AR* 42 (October 1866): 315; *AR* 43 (January 1867): 11–23; *AR* 43 (February 1867): 39; *AR* 43 (April 1867): 109–117; *AR* 43 (July 1867): 204–211; *AR* 43 (December 1867): 366–372; *AR* 44 (March 1868): 70–71; *AR* 44 (June 1868): 173–183; *AR* 45 (December 1869): 373; *AR* 46 (December 1870), 373; *AR* 52 (April 1876): 35; *AR* 54 (January 1878): 34.

2. Sir George Campbell, *In White and Black: The Outcome of a Visit to the United States* (New York, 1879), 277; Resolutions of Bellefonte Grange, no. 15, 22 Aug. 1874, Harvie Family Papers, box 3, VHS. For more on black landownership and acquisition in Virginia, see Lynda J. Morgan, *Emancipation in Virginia's Tobacco Belt, 1850–1870* (Athens, Ga., 1992), 206–207; Jeffrey R. Kerr-Ritchie, *Freedpeople in the Tobacco South: Virginia, 1860–1900* (Chapel Hill, N.C., 1999), 210–223; Crandall A. Shiflett, *Patronage and Poverty in the Tobacco South: Louisa County, Virginia, 1860–1900* (Knoxville, Tenn., 1992), 39–66; Samuel T. Bitting, *Rural Landownership among Negroes in Virginia* (Charlottesville, Va., 1915). In 1900, 26,432 blacks owned all or part of the land they farmed, making up 59.1 percent of the state's black farm operators. Mississippi ranked second to Virginia in the absolute number of black landowning farmers with 20,827, followed closely by Texas with 20,023. Florida ranked second in the proportion of black owner-operators with 48.1 percent, followed by North Carolina (31.8 percent) and Texas (30.6 percent). In all of the former Confederate states, there were 165,749 blacks who owned all or part of the land they

farmed, making up 23.4 percent of all black farm operators. See *Twelfth Census of the United States: Agriculture* (Washington, D.C., 1901), pt. 1, 4–14. Also see Loren Schweninger, *Black Property Owners in the South, 1790–1915* (Urbana, Ill., 1990), 143–184.

3. See, for example, Edward L. Ayers, *The Promise of the New South: Life after Reconstruction* (New York, 1992), 34–54; Michael R. Hyman, *The Anti-Redeemers: Hill-Country Political Dissenters in the Lower South from Redemption to Populism* (Baton Rouge, 1990); Steven Hahn, *The Roots of Southern Populism: Yeoman Farmers and the Transformation of the Georgia Upcountry, 1850–1890* (New York, 1983), 204–238; Brooks M. Barnes, "Triumph of the New South: Independent Movements in Post-Reconstruction Politics," Ph.D. diss., University of Virginia, 1991; James Tice Moore, *Two Paths to the New South: The Virginia Debt Controversy, 1870–1883* (Lexington, Ky., 1974); Richard Franklin Bensel, *The Political Economy of American Industrialization, 1877–1900* (Cambridge, Eng., 2000), 101–288.

4. Michael Perman, *The Road to Redemption: Southern Politics, 1869–1879* (Chapel Hill, N.C., 1984), 178–220; Lawrence D. Rice, *The Negro in Texas, 1874–1900* (Baton Rouge, 1971), 16–25; John William Graves, *Town and Country in Arkansas: Race Relations in an Urban-Rural Context, 1865–1905* (Fayetteville, Ark., 1990), 47–49; Clara L. Campbell, "The Political Life of Louisiana Negroes, 1865–1890," Ph.D. diss., Tulane University, 1971, 198–207.

5. Perman, *Road to Redemption*, 198; Paul D. Escott, *Many Excellent People: Power and Privilege in North Carolina, 1850–1900* (Chapel Hill, N.C., 1985), 163–170; George B. Tindall, *South Carolina Negroes, 1877–1900* (Columbia, S.C., 1952), 68–69; Vernon L. Wharton, *The Negro in Mississippi, 1865–1890* (Chapel Hill, N.C., 1947), 199–200; William Harris, *The Day of the Carpetbagger: Republican Reconstruction in Mississippi* (Baton Rouge, 1979), 694–701; Alrutheus Ambush Taylor, *The Negro in Tennessee, 1865–1880* (Washington, D.C., 1941), 74–75; Charles E. Wynes, *Race Relations in Virginia, 1870–1902* (Charlottesville, Va., 1961), 12–14.

6. See, for example, J. Morgan Kousser, *The Shaping of Southern Politics: Suffrage Restriction and the Establishment of the One-Party South, 1880–1910* (New Haven, Conn., 1974), 15. I part company here with those who see the advent of Jim Crow in the 1890s and first decade of the twentieth century, principally in connection with state-mandated segregation and full-scale black disfranchisement. These did, of course, represent the "triumph" of Jim Crow, but such a view privileges the reordering of urban society (where segregation could most clearly choreograph daily life), and tends to see Jim Crow more as an imposition than as a product of struggle: struggle not only among different social and racial groups but also among individual, community, and state authority.

7. There is still no modern scholarly monograph on Reconstruction in Virginia, but much of the political history can be found in Jack P. Maddex Jr., *The Virginia Conservatives, 1867–1879: A Study in Reconstruction Politics* (Chapel Hill, N.C.,

1970); Jack P. Maddex Jr., "Virginia: The Persistence of Centrist Hegemony," in Otto H. Olsen, ed., *Reconstruction and Redemption in the South* (Baton Rouge, 1980), 113–150; Richard Lowe, *Republicans and Reconstruction in Virginia, 1856–1870* (Charlottesville, Va., 1991); Richard Lowe, "Another Look at Reconstruction in Virginia," *CWH* 32 (March 1986): 56–76; and the valuable Alrutheus Ambush Taylor, *The Negro in the Reconstruction of Virginia* (Lancaster, Pa., 1926).

8. Fields Cook et al. to President Andrew Johnson, 10 June 1865, in Paul Bergeron, ed., *The Papers of Andrew Johnson* (Knoxville, Tenn., 1989), vol. 8, 210–212; *New Orleans Tribune*, 4 July 1865; A. W. R. to Jefferson W. Stubbs, 25 July 1865, Jefferson W. Stubbs Papers, folder 2, LSU; Colored Mass Meeting, 1 Dec. 1865, RG 92, ser. 225, Central Recs, NA [Y-8]; Proceedings of a Mass Meeting of Freedpeople, 12 Dec. 1865, BRFAL, Washington Hdqrs., ser. 15, Letters Rec'd, L-76 1865 [A-7471]; *Richmond New Nation*, 22 Mar. 1866. Also see Peter J. Rachleff, *Black Labor in the South: Richmond, Virginia, 1865–1890* (Philadelphia, 1984), 13–54; John T. O'Brien, "Reconstruction in Richmond: White Restoration and Black Protest, April–June 1865," *VMHB* 89 (July 1981): 259–281; Elsa Barkley Brown, "Negotiating and Transforming the Public Sphere: African-American Political Life in the Transition from Slavery to Freedom," in Black Public Sphere Collective, *The Black Public Sphere: A Public Culture Book* (Chicago, 1995), 111–120.

9. Maddex, *Virginia Conservatives*, 46–85; Lowe, *Republicans and Reconstruction in Virginia*, 121–182; Taylor, *Negro in Reconstruction of Virginia*, 208–261.

10. On black legislative representation, see BLDS and Luther Porter Jackson's valuable *Negro Office-Holders in Virginia, 1865–1895* (Norfolk, Va., 1945), 1–44. In 1876, the Conservatives successfully amended the state constitution to make the poll tax a qualification for voting, to disfranchise voters convicted of petty larceny, and to reduce the number of local offices as well as the number of seats in the House of Delegates. See Wynes, *Race Relations in Virginia*, 12–14; Maddex, *Virginia Conservatives*, 97–98. Also see John Hammond Moore, "The Norfolk Riot: 16 April 1866," *VMHB* 90 (April 1982): 155–164.

11. On the legislators, see Jackson, *Negro Office-Holders*, 1–44. On free blacks in antebellum Virginia, see Luther Porter Jackson, *Free Negro Labor and Property Holding in Virginia, 1830–1860* (1942; New York, 1969), 70–136; Ira Berlin, *Slaves without Masters: The Free Negro in the Antebellum South* (New York, 1974), esp., 15–78, 217–249.

12. Jackson, *Negro Office-Holders*, 1–44. On Hamilton, see Harold Forsythe, " 'But My Friends Are Poor': Ross Hamilton and Freedpeople's Politics in Mecklenburg County, Virginia, 1869–1901," *VMHB* 105 (Autumn 1997): 409–438, easily the best treatment of local black politics in rural Virginia.

13. Barnes, "Triumph of the New South," 99–104; Jackson, *Negro Office-Holders*, 7.

14. Marilyn M. White, " 'We Lived on an Island': An Afro-American Family and

Community in Rural Virginia, 1865–1940," Ph.D. diss., University of Texas, 1983, 59–101; Jackson, *Negro Office-Holders*, 13.

15. Jackson, *Negro Office-Holders*, 39.

16. Ibid., 13, 33–34,

17. ? to William Mahone, April 1883, WMP, box 189, DU; Colored Societies, April 1883, WMP, box 189; W. E. B. Du Bois, "The Negroes of Farmville, Virginia: A Social Study," *Bulletin of the Department of Labor* 14 (January 1898): 35–36. On developments in urban Virginia, see Rachleff, *Black Labor in the South*, 13–33; Lawrence L. Hartzell, "The Exploration of Freedom in Black Petersburg, Virginia, 1865–1902," in Edward L. Ayers and John C. Willis, eds., *The Edge of the South: Life in Nineteenth-Century Virginia* (Charlottesville, Va., 1991), 134–140; Earl Lewis, *In Their Own Interests: Race, Class, and Power in Twentieth-Century Norfolk, Virginia* (Berkeley, Calif., 1991), 8–28.

18. T. E. Chambliss to Judge Peirpont, 12 Oct. 1875, Chambliss to Peirpont, 27 Oct. 1875, both in Justice Dept., RG 60, Source-Chronological File, Virginia, roll 2, NA; *Alexandria (Va.) People's Advocate*, 17 June 1876, 15 July 1876, 22 July 1876, 29 July 1876, and 12 Aug. 1876; BLDS; Jackson, *Negro Office-Holders*, 61–67; Joseph P. Harahan, "Politics, Political Parties, and Voter Participation in Tidewater Virginia during Reconstruction, 1865–1900," Ph.D. diss., Michigan State University, 1973, 169–185, 284–288. I have been able to identify about 135 local officeholders in the rural counties, about 102 of whom (76 percent) were either justices of the peace, constables, or overseers of the poor. This probably includes blacks who served in local office after 1880, since the dates of their terms are very hard to recover.

19. On Virginia's debt, see Moore, *Two Paths to the New South;* Maddex, *Virginia Conservatives*, 218–275; Charles C. Pearson, *The Readjuster Movement in Virginia* (New Haven, Conn., 1917), 1–67; and Barnes, "Triumph of the New South," 5–8, 43–44.

20. On the state debt issue in the South of this period, see C. Vann Woodward, *Origins of the New South, 1877–1913* (Baton Rouge, 1951), 86–98; Perman, *Road to Redemption*, 228–232; and Roger L. Hart, *Redeemers, Bourbons, and Populists: Tennessee, 1870–1896* (Baton Rouge, 1975), 1–55.

21. The best treatment of the Readjusters is Jane Dailey, *Before Jim Crow: The Politics of Race in Postemancipation Virginia* (Chapel Hill, N.C., 2000). But also see Moore, *Two Paths to the New South;* Pearson, *Readjuster Movement;* Barnes, "Triumph of the New South," 2–266; Hampton D. Carey, "New Voices in the Old Dominion: Black Politics in the Southside Region and the City of Richmond, 1867–1902," Ph.D. diss., Columbia University, 2000; and Woodward, *Origins of the New South*, 92–98.

22. On these struggles over the political economy of postbellum America, see David Montgomery, *Beyond Equality: Labor and the Radical Republicans, 1862–1872* (New York, 1967); Robert L. Sharkey, *Money, Class, and Party: An Economic Study*

of the Civil War and Reconstruction (Baltimore, 1959); Richard F. Bensel, *Yankee Leviathan: The Origins of Central State Authority in America, 1859–1877* (Cambridge, Eng., 1990); and Irwin Unger, *The Greenback Era: A Social and Political History of American Finance, 1865–1879* (Princeton, N.J., 1964).

23. Ayers, *Promise of the New South*, 43–48; Steven Hahn, "Class and State in Postemancipation Societies: Southern Planters in Comparative Perspective," *AHR* 90 (February 1990): 75–98; Hahn, *Roots of Southern Populism*, 137–203; Jonathan Wiener, *Social Origins of the New South: Alabama, 1860–1885* (Baton Rouge, 1978).

24. Hahn, *Roots of Southern Populism*, 204–238; Woodward, *Origins of the New South*, 75–106; Hyman, *Anti-Redeemers;* Alwyn Barr, *Reconstruction to Reform: Texas Politics, 1876– 1906* (Austin, Tex., 1971), 38–76; William Warren Rogers, *The One-Gallused Rebellion: Agrarianism in Alabama, 1865–1896* (Baton Rouge, 1970), 31–55; Stephen Cresswell, *Multiparty Politics in Mississippi, 1877–1902* (Jackson, Miss., 1995), 22–99; Carl H. Moneyhon, *Arkansas and the New South, 1874–1929* (Fayetteville, Ind., 1997), 78–79.

25. *Richmond Whig*, 27 Feb. 1879; Wynes, *Race Relations in Virginia*, 19; Pearson, *Readjuster Movement*, 98–99, 127–128; Dailey, *Before Jim Crow*, 43–44; Carey, "New Voices in Old Dominion," 73–74.

26. J. M. Gills to Lewis E. Harvie, 6 Dec. 1879, Harvie Family Papers, box 3; Moore, *Two Paths to the New South*, 63–67; Wynes, *Race Relations in Virginia*, 20–21.

27. William Mahone to William M. Burwell, 12 Nov. 1880, WMP, box 23; Barnes, "Triumph of the New South," 57–64; Dailey, *Before Jim Crow*, 40–42. There has been no biography of Mahone since Nelson M. Blake, *William Mahone of Virginia: Soldier and Political Insurgent* (Richmond, Va., 1935).

28. S. Flournoy to William Mahone, 6 Nov. 1879, W. W. Newman to Mahone, 10 Nov. 1879 G. R. C. Phillips, 13 Nov. 1879 D. J. Godwin, 12 Nov. 1879 R. P. Hughes to Mahone, 13 Nov. 1879 and C. L. Davis to Mahone, 14 Nov. 1879, all in WMP, box 16; Daniel W. Lewis to Mahone, 6 Dec. 1879, WMP, box 17; W. R. Roberts to Mahone, 9 Dec. 1879, WMP, box 17; Dailey, *Before Jim Crow*, 46–47.

29. *Huntsville (Ala.) Gazette*, 20 Dec. 1879; *Alexandria People's Advocate*, 15 Nov. 1879; R. F. Mays to William Mahone, 18 Oct. 1880, WMP, box 23; Pearson, *Readjuster Movement*, 132–141; Barnes, "Triumph of the New South," 89–95.

30. William Mahone to H. H. Riddleberger, 25 Nov. 1880, H. H. Riddleberger Papers, box 1, folder 7, College of William and Mary Archives, Williamsburg, Va.; Mahone to Riddleberger, 12 Jan. 1881, Riddleberger Papers, box 1, folder 8; William Mahone to Lewis E. Harvie, 31 Aug. 1881, Harvie Papers; "The Lightning Vat," 30 Dec. 1880, Riddleberger Papers, box 1, folder 8; *Huntsville Gazette*, 26 Mar. 1881; Barnes, "Triumph of the New South," 123–124.

31. William Mahone to Dear Sir, 12 Sept. 1881, WMP, box 187; Mahone to Dear

Sir, 24 Mar. 1883, WMP, box 189; George E. Winder to Mahone, 30 Sept. 1881, WMP, box 35; Edward Taylor to Mahone, 1 Oct. 1881, WMP, box 35; Barnes, "Triumph of the New South," 123; Pearson, *Readjuster Movement*, 138–141. Much of the correspondence identifying influential black local leaders can be found in WMP, box 187.

32. See, for example, Dr. William H. Henning to William Mahone, 14 July 1881, WMP, box 187; County Canvassers, Lunenberg County, 1881, WMP, box 187; County Canvassers, Buckingham County, 1881, WMP, box 187; Local Readjuster Organization and Expenses, Louisa County, n.d., WMP, box 188; Readjuster Organization, King and Queen County, n.d., WMP, box 189; Readjuster Organization, Southampton County, n.d., WMP, box 189. Also see Dailey, *Before Jim Crow*, 62.

33. William Mahone to H. H. Riddleberger, 28 June 1881, Riddleberger Papers, box 1, folder 9; A. A. Bell to Mahone, Oct. 1881, WMP, box 187; Bell to Mahone, 1881, WMP, box 188; G. W. Hoge to Mahone, 1881, WMP, box 188; Meredith Watson to Mahone, Sept. 1881, WMP, box 187; Peter Reckerd et al. to Mahone, 18 Oct. 1881, WMP, box 187. I compiled the figures of the number of likely black Readjusters who had failed to pay their poll tax from reports to Mahone that can be found in his papers, boxes 187 and 188. In Powhatan and Brunswick counties, the delinquents made up only 5 and 14 percent, respectively, of the likely black Readjusters. But in Amelia it was 25 percent, in Westmoreland 26 percent, Halifax 31 percent, King and Queen 44 percent, Northampton 47 percent, Accomac 60 percent, and Hanover 63 percent.

34. J. C. Dearn to William Mahone, 13 Nov. 1881, WMP, box 37; J. M. Gills to Mahone, 5 Oct. 1881, S. W. McChesney to W. C. Elam, 3 Oct. 1881, and Albert McDaniel to Mahone, 20 Oct. 1881, all in WMP, box 35.

35. E. W. Early to William Mahone, 4 Oct. 1881, WMP, box 35; Rev. J. L. Barksdale, 5 Oct. 1881, WMP, box 35. By 1883, the Readjuster organization was paying county lieutenants between $10 and $25 and squad captains between $2 and $5 for the campaign. See Readjuster Organization for King and Queen County, Southampton County, and Louisa County, all in WMP, box 189. On the changes occasioned by Arthur's ascendancy, see Barnes, "Triumph of the New South," 145–146; Moore, *Two Paths to the New South*, 82; Dailey, *Before Jim Crow*, 61–64; and more generally, Vincent P. DeSantis, *Republicans Face the Southern Question: The New Departure Years, 1877–1897* (Baltimore, 1959); and Stanley P. Hirshon, *Farewell to the Bloody Shirt: Northern Republicans and the Southern Negro, 1877–1893* (Bloomington, Ind., 1962).

36. On the estimates of likely black Readjuster voters, see the correspondence in WMP, boxes 35, 187, and 188. On the county vote in Virginia in the 1881 state election, as well as the figures on the voting age population by race, see *Warrock-Richardson Almanack* (Richmond, Va., 1882), 30–33. Also see James Tice Moore, "Black Militancy in Readjuster Virginia, 1879–1883," *JSH* 41 (May 1975): 178–179.

Although Virginia had forty-one counties in 1880 with black population majorities (thirty of which supported the Readjusters), only thirty-two had majorities of black voting-age males, twenty-seven of which sided with the Readjusters. Three counties with black population majorities but with majorities of white voting age males also supported the Readjusters.

37. *New Orleans Weekly Louisianian*, 19 Mar. 1881; *Alexandria People's Advocate*, 21 May 1881, 11 June 1881; Pearson, *Readjuster Movement*, 142–159; Moore, *Two Paths to the New South*, 87–92; Moore, "Black Militancy in Readjuster Virginia," 178–179; Barnes, "Triumph of the New South," 150–152.

38. William H. Hening to William Mahone, 8 June 1883, Vernon J'Anson to Mahone, 14 June 1883, William F. Jones to Mahone, June 1883, and J. M. Gills to Mahone, June 1883, all in WMP, box 191; *Petersburg (Va.) Lancet*, 9 June 1883; *Huntsville Gazette*, 21 Aug. 1880; Dailey, *Before Jim Crow*, 69–70; Moore, "Black Militancy in Readjuster Virginia," 181–182; Lawrence L. Hartzell, "The Exploration of Freedom in Black Petersburg, Virginia, 1865–1902," in Edward L. Ayers and John C. Willis, eds., *The Edge of the South: Life in Nineteenth-Century Virginia* (Charlottesville, Va., 1991), 140–143; Michael J. Schewel, "Local Politics in Lynchburg, Virginia, in the 1880s," *VMHB* 89 (April 1981): 172–175.

39. Dailey, *Before Jim Crow*, 57–59, 72–75, 96–99; Samuel Matthews to William Mahone, 12 Nov. 1881, WMP, box 37; *Petersburg Lancet*, 15 July 1882, 19 Aug. 1882; Moore, "Black Militancy in Readjuster Virginia," 180–183; Pearson, *Readjuster Movement*, 154–164.

40. *Petersburg Lancet*, 9 Sept. 1882; *Alexandria People's Advocate*, 14 Jan. 1882; Moore, "Black Militancy in Readjuster Virginia," 182–183.

41. Tindall, *South Carolina Negroes*, 62–64; *Huntsville Gazette*, 7 July 1883; *New Orleans Weekly Pelican*, 12 July 1889; Wharton, *Negro in Mississippi*, 202–203; Graves, *Town and Country*, 54; Gilles Vandal, "Politics and Violence in Bourbon Louisiana: The Loreauville Riot of 1884 as a Case Study," *LaH* 30 (Winter 1989): 31; Eric Anderson, *Race and Politics in North Carolina: The Black Second* (Baton Rouge, 1981), 86–93; Alan B. Bromberg, " 'Pure Democracy and White Supremacy': The Redeemer Period in North Carolina, 1876–1894," Ph.D. diss., University of Virginia, 1977, 232–232; Frenise A. Logan, *The Negro in North Carolina, 1876–1894* (Chapel Hill, N.C., 1964), 29–31. Also see Albert E. Smith, "Down Freedom's Road: The Contours of Race, Class, and Property Crime in Black-Belt Georgia," Ph.D. diss., University of Georgia, 1982, 128–132.

42. *New Orleans Weekly Pelican*, 12 July 1889; Wharton, *Negro in Mississippi*, 202; Tindall, *South Carolina Negroes*, 54–55, 58, 309–310; Buford Satcher, *Blacks in Mississippi Politics, 1865–1900* (Washington, D.C., 1978); Logan, *Negro in North Carolina*, 26–28; Helen G. Edmonds, *The Negro and Fusion Politics in North Carolina, 1894–1901* (Chapel Hill, N.C., 1951), 97–112; Merline Pitre, *Through Many Dangers, Toils, and Snares: Black Leadership in Texas, 1868–1900* (Austin, Tex.,

1985), 206–208; Charles Vincent, "Black Louisianians during the Civil War and Reconstruction," in Vincent, ed., *The African American Experience in Louisiana*, part B (Lafayette, La., 2000), 128; Taylor, *Negro in Tennessee*, 247–248; Joseph H. Cartwright, *The Triumph of Jim Crow: Tennessee Race Relations in the 1880s* (Knoxville, Tenn., 1976), 101–118; *Huntsville Gazette*, 22 May 1880, 12 Feb. 1881, 14 May 1881, 2 July 1881, 8 Apr. 1882, 12 May 1883, 7 Feb. 1885, 24 Apr. 1886, 25 Sept. 1886, 25 June 1887; Board of Commissioners, Warren County, Minutes, 1870–1878, NCDAH.

43. See, for example, John Hope Franklin, "John Roy Lynch: Republican Stalwart from Mississippi," in Howard Rabinowitz, ed., *Southern Black Leaders of the Reconstruction Period* (Urbana, Ill., 1982), 39–58; Edward A. Miller, Jr., *Gullah Statesman: Robert Smalls from Slavery to Congress, 1839–1915* (Columbia, S.C., 1995), 163–170; Anderson, *Race and Politics*, 86–87; Joe L. Caldwell, "A Social, Economic, and Political Study of Blacks in the Louisiana Delta, 1865–1880," Ph.D. diss., Tulane University, 1989, 370–393.

44. On these tensions and conflicts among rural African Americans, see Thomas F. Armstrong, "The Building of a Black Church: Community in Post Civil War Liberty County, Georgia," *GHQ* 66 (Fall 1982): 346–367; Susan A. Mann, "Slavery, Sharecropping, and Sexual Inequality," in Darlene Clark Hine et al., eds., *We Specialize in the Wholly Impossible: A Reader in Black Women's History* (New York, 1995), 281–302.

45. *Montgomery Advance*, 11 Sept. 1880; U.S. Senate, *Mississippi in 1883: Report of the Special Commission to Inquire into the Mississippi Election of 1883*, Report no. 512, 48th Cong., 1st sess. (Washington, D.C., 1884), 309–311; Garrett D. Sadler to Gov. William Bate, 17 Nov. 1884, Gov. William B. Bate Papers, box 5, folder 3, TSLA; A. D. Lister to Oran M. Roberts, 25 July 1878, Oran M. Roberts Papers, 2F476, BTHC; Charles Nordhoff, *The Cotton States in the Spring and Summer of 1875* (New York, 1876), 92; Caldwell, "Blacks in the Louisiana Delta," 370–371.

46. On the logic of black support for the Democrats, see August Meier, *Negro Thought in America, 1880–1915* (Ann Arbor, Mich., 1963), 26–32; Cartwright, *Triumph of Jim Crow*, 34–44; Peter Eisenstadt, "Southern Black Conservatism: 1865–1945, an Introduction," in Peter Eisenstadt, ed., *Black Conservatism: Essays in Intellectual and Political History* (New York, 1999), 52–62. On Democrats vying with Republicans and insurgents for black votes, see, *Mississippi in 1883*, xxxvii; *Nashville American*, quoted in *Huntsville Gazette*, 4 Apr. 1885; Randolph B. Campbell, *A Southern Community in Crisis: Harrison County, Texas, 1850–1880* (Austin, Tex., 1983), 361; and Logan, *Negro in North Carolina*, 20. On the social bases of insurgency, see Hyman, *Anti-Redeemers*, 10–74; Hahn, *Roots of Southern Populism*, 216–238.

47. *Huntsville Gazette*, 19 June 1880, 18 Dec. 1880; Judson C. Ward, "The Republican Party in Bourbon Georgia, 1872–1890" *JSH* 9 (May 1943): 201; Olin B. Adams, "The Negro and the Agrarian Movement in Georgia, 1874–1908," Ph.D. diss., Florida State University, 1973, 42; Stephen Kantrowitz, "Ben Tillman and Hendrix

McLane, Agrarian Rebels: White Manhood, 'The Farmers,' and the Limits of Southern Populism," *JSH* 66 (August 2000): 505–507.

48. *Huntsville Gazette,* 22 May 1880, 17 July 1880, 24 July 1880, 28 Aug. 1880, 12 Feb. 1881, 14 May 1881, 2 July 1882, 11 Nov. 1882; *Gwinnett (Ga.) Herald,* 13 Nov. 1878; Hyman, *Anti-Redeemers,* 181–188.

49. *Mississippi in 1883,* 261–262; Cresswell, *Multiparty Politics in Mississippi,* 24–41; Vandal, "Politics and Violence in Bourbon Louisiana," 28–32; Joel M. Sipress, "The Triumph of Reaction: Political Struggle in a New South Community, 1865–1898," Ph.D. diss., University of North Carolina, 1993, 195–227.

50. Sipress, "Triumph of Reaction," 224–225; G. C. Candler to Attorney General, Nov. 1882, Department of Justice, RG 60, Source-Chronological File, Mississippi, roll 2, NA; *Mississippi in 1883,* xviii–xxv. On bulldozing and related political practices, see William Ivy Hair, *Bourbonism and Agrarian Protest: Louisiana Politics, 1877–1900* (Baton Rouge, 1969), 5, 62, 73, 84, 88, 92, 105, 192; Woodward, *Origins of the New South,* 103–106; and Kousser, *Shaping of Southern Politics,* 16–17. Although the derivation of the term "bulldozing" is unclear, Hair claims it was first applied to the methods of political vigilantism during the Louisiana campaign of 1876. It may well be a construction implying a "dose" of the bullwhip.

51. On Turner see William Warren Rogers and Robert David Ward, *August Reckoning: Jack Turner and Racism in Post–Civil War Alabama* (Baton Rouge, 1973); Gerald L. Roush, "Aftermath of Reconstruction: Race, Violence, and Politics in Alabama, 1874–1884," Ph.D. diss., Auburn University, 1973," 311–312, 385. The other black leaders arrested with Turner were spared the lynching, and they demanded to be brought to trial. But it was five years before the charges were dismissed and they were released. According to reports, the mob also appears to have included some blacks, though their motives or role was not clear. Turner undoubtedly had enemies among blacks as well as whites, and some of them may well have taken the opportunity to even a score.

52. U.S. Senate, *Louisiana in 1878,* no. 855, 45th Cong., 3d sess. (Washington, D.C., 1879); Caldwell, "Blacks in the Louisiana Delta," 331–371; Rogers and Ward, *August Reckoning,* 157–167; Roush, "Aftermath of Reconstruction," 319–358; *Huntsville Gazette,* 23 Sept. 1882; Louis R. Harlan, *Booker T. Washington: The Making of a Black Leader, 1856–1901* (New York, 1972), 109–133. According to Morgan Kousser's estimates, the turnout rates of eligible black voters in the 1880s ranged from a low of about 30 percent in South Carolina to a high of more than 85 percent in North Carolina and Florida. See Kousser, *Shaping of Southern Politics,* 28.

53. On the Reconstruction experience in east-central Texas, see Randolph B. Campbell, *Grass-Roots Reconstruction in Texas, 1865–1880* (Baton Rouge, 1997), 1–62, 98–141, 163–192; Pitre, *Through Many Dangers,* 7–52; Carl H. Moneyhon, *Republicanism in Reconstruction Texas* (Austin, Tex., 1980); James M. Smallwood, *Time of Hope, Time of Despair: Black Texans during Reconstruction* (Port Washington,

N.Y., 1981); Alwyn Barr, "Black Legislators of Reconstruction," *CWH* 32 (December 1986): 340–351. Blacks occupied 14 seats (2 senate, 12 house) in Texas's Twelfth Legislature, the only one that had a Republican majority; if we include the Thirteenth Legislature that had a Democratic majority but met before the Democrats had claimed the governorship, blacks occupied ten additional seats, for a generous Reconstruction total of 24. But from the Fourteenth Legislature to the Twenty-fifth Legislature (1874–1897), blacks occupied 49 seats (6 senate, 43 house). My BLDS shows that blacks served 59 local office terms before 1874, and 293 local office terms between 1874 and 1897.

54. Gregg Cantrell, "Racial Violence and Reconstruction Politics in Texas, 1867–1868," *SWHQ* 93 (January 1990): 334–352; Barry A. Crouch, "Self-Determination and Local Black Leaders in Texas," *Phylon* 38 (December 1978): 345–355; Otis A. Singletary, *Negro Militia and Reconstruction* (Austin, Tex., 1957), 18, 38–39; Harrel Budd, "Negro in Politics in Texas 1867–1898," master's thesis, University of Texas, 1925, 98; Rice, *Negro in Texas*, 35.

55. Clarence R. Wharton, *History of Fort Bend County* (San Antonio, Tex., 1939), 174–186; "Elected Officials of Fort Bend County from 1869–1888," BTHC; *Burke's Texas Almanac* (Houston, 1878–1883); Budd, "Negro in Politics in Texas," 96–98; Rice, *Negro in Texas*, 88–91; Pauline Yelderman, *The Jay Bird Democratic Association of Fort Bend County* (Waco, Tex., 1979), 45–55. By the late 1870s, the Republicans had acquired sufficient resources to make each other's bonds.

56. *Brenham Banner*, 21 Jan. 1876, 4 Feb. 1876, 25 Feb. 1876, 26 July 1878, 9 Aug. 1878, 11 July 1879, 9 Nov. 1882; Donald G. Nieman, "Black Political Power and Criminal Justice: Washington County, Texas, 1868–1884," *JSH* 55 (August 1989): 392–420; Rice, *Negro in Texas*, 93–94.

57. *Brenham Weekly Banner*, 31 May 1878, 12 July 1878, 9 Aug. 1878, 27 Sept. 1878; *Navasota Tablet*, 29 Mar. 1878, 7 June 1878.

58. *Navasota Tablet*, 21 June 1878; *Brenham Weekly Banner*, 23 Aug. 1878; Alwyn Barr, *Reconstruction to Reform: Texas Politics, 1876–1906* (Austin, Tex., 1971), 38–62; Rice, *Negro in Texas*, 55–61; Budd, "Negro in Politics in Texas," 70–77; Pitre, *Through Many Dangers*, 58, 116–119.

59. *Brenham Weekly Banner*, 12 July 1878; U.S. Senate, *Testimony of the Alleged Outrages in Texas*, Sen. Misc. Doc. 62, vol. 3, 50th Cong., 2d sess. (Washington, D.C., 1889); Barr, *Reconstruction to Reform*, 194–199; Randolph B. Campbell, *A Southern Community in Crisis: Harrison County, Texas, 1850–1880* (Austin, Tex., 1983), 338–362; Yelderman, *Jay Bird Democratic Association*, 38–109.

60. *Alleged Outrages in Texas*, 136–137, 164–165, 216, 234–242; *Brenham Banner*, 25 Feb. 1876, 24 Mar. 1876, 28 Apr. 1876, 9 Nov. 1882; Nieman, "Black Political Power," 396–397.

61. On Scott, Kennard, and the Grimes County experience, see Lawrence Goodwyn's extraordinary article, "Populist Dreams and Negro Rights: East Texas as a Case Study," *AHR* 76 (December 1971): 1435–1456.

62. U.S. Senate, *Louisiana in 1878*, no. 855, 45th Cong., 3d sess. (Washington, D.C., 1879), xxviii; U.S. Senate, *Report and Testimony of the Select Committee of the United States Senate to Investigate the Causes of the Removal of the Negroes from the Southern States to the Northern States*, Senate Rept. no. 693, 46th Cong., 2d sess., 3 pts. (Washington, D.C., 1880), pt. 2, 441.

63. For important work on the biracialism in the urban and industrial New South, see Eric Arnesen, *Waterfront Workers of New Orleans: Race, Class, and Politics* (New York, 1991); Eric Arnesen, "Biracial Waterfront Unionism in the Age of Segregation," in Calvin Winslow, ed., *Waterfront Workers: New Perspectives on Race and Class* (Urbana, Ill., 1998), 19–61; Daniel Letwin, *The Challenge of Interracial Unionism: Alabama Coal Miners, 1878–1921* (Chapel Hill, N.C., 1998); Jacqueline Jones, *The Dispossessed: America's Underclass from the Civil War to the Present* (New York, 1992), 129–130; Stephen H. Norwood, "Bogalusa Burning: The War against Biracial Unionism in the Deep South, 1919," *JSH* 63 (August 1997): 591–628; Ronald Lewis, *Black Coal Miners in America: Race, Class, and Community Conflict, 1780–1980* (Lexington, Ky., 1987); Rachleff, *Black Labor in the South*, 86–156.

64. On the Readjusters' language of rights, see Dailey's insightful discussion in *Before Jim Crow*, 77–102, and in "The Limits of Liberalism in the New South: The Politics of Race, Sex, and Patronage in Virginia, 1879–1883," in Jane Dailey, Glenda Gilmore, and Bryant Simon, eds., *Jumpin' Jim Crow: Southern Politics from Civil War to Civil Rights* (Princeton, N.J., 2000), 88–114.

65. Jefferson Bragg to William Mahone, April 1883, WMP, box 71; Goodman Brown to Mahone, 14 May 1883, WMP, box 72; C. E. Wilson et al. to Mahone, June 1882, WMP, box 191; *Alexandria People's Advocate*, 21 May 1881; Moore, "Black Militancy in Readjuster Virginia," 181–182.

66. William E. Cameron to H. H. Riddleberger, 22 Mar. 1881, Riddleberger Papers, box 1, folder 8; Moore, "Black Militancy in Readjuster Virginia," 181–183.

67. D. M. Pannill to William Mahone, 3 Oct. 1881, WMP, box 35; Horatio Davis to Mahone, 12 Nov. 1881, WMP, box 37.

68. C. H. Ingles to William Mahone, 15 Nov. 1881, WMP, box 37; A. M. Lybrook to Mahone, 18 Nov. 1881, WMP, box 37; *Martinsville (Va.) Herald*, 18 Nov. 1881, WMP, box 37; Robert B. Winston to Mahone, 15 Oct. 1883, WMP, box 79; Thomas H. Cross to Mahone, 26 May 1883, WMP, box 72.

69. Statements of Col. J. B. Raulston and John D. Blackwell, Nov. 1883, WMP, box 175; "Coalition Rule in Danville," October 1883, WMP, box 80; Dailey, *Before Jim Crow*, 111–114; Moore, "Black Militancy in Readjuster Virginia," 181–182.

70. "Coalition Rule in Danville." The circular may also be seen in U.S. Senate, *Testimony in Regard to Alleged Outrages in Danville, Virginia*, Rept. no. 579, 48th Cong., 1st sess. (Washington, D.C., 1884), vii–ix.

71. Statement of C. S. Hurmans, 1883, WMP, box 175. See the statements from the following counties in the same box that testify to the distribution of "Coalition Rule": Rappahonnock (62 percent white), Tazewell (85 percent white), Pulaski

(72 percent white), Bland (95 percent white), Craig (94 percent white), Grayson (92 percent white), Madison (57 percent white), Floyd (90 percent white), Henry (54 percent white), Spottsylvania (57 percent white), Montgomery (75 percent white), Warren (80 percent white), and Fairfax (67 percent white)—most of which supported the Readjusters in the election of 1881. On the Danville riot, see Statement of Mr. Wheeler, Nov. 1883, WMP, box 175; Statement of Edward Lewis, Nov. 1883, WMP, box 175, "Report of the Committee of Forty," Nov. 1883, WMP, box 175; W. E. Sims to Mahone, Nov. 1883, WMP, box 192; *Testimony in Regard to Outrages in Danville*, ix–lxxv. The fullest and best treatment of the riot is Jane Dailey, "Deference and Violence in the Postbellum Urban South: Manners and Massacres in Danville, Virginia," *JSH* 58 (August 1997): 553–590. But also see Carey, "New Voices in Old Dominion," 126–149.

72. *Testimony in Regard to Outrages in Danville*, xl–xli; *Alexandria People's Advocate*, 10 Nov. 1883; Statement of Isaac Cabaniss, 26 Nov. 1883, Affidavit of David Wallace, 13 Nov. 1883, and Statement of Frank Chappell, 19 Nov. 1883, all in WMP, box 192.

73. Statement of Frank Medley, 16 Nov. 1883, WMP, box 192; J. F. Ross to William Mahone, 22 Oct. 1883, WMP, box 80; George Colvin to Mr. Raulston, 30 Oct. 1883, WMP, box 80; Statement of C. H. Causey, 10 Dec. 1883, WMP, box 192; Moore, *Two Paths to the New South*, 117. On mobilizations, see Richard A. Wise to Mahone, 5 Oct. 1883, W. C. Franklin to Mahone, 12 Oct. 1883; A. W. Brady to Mahone, 12 Oct. 1883, J. G. Cannon to Mahone, 3 Oct. 1883, and V. J'Anson to Mahone, 9 Oct. 1883, all in WMP, box 79; William H. Vaughn to Mahone, 13 Oct. 1883, WMP, box 80.

74. *Alexandria People's Advocate*, 10 Nov. 1883; Statement of V. J. Anson, 1883, WMP, box 175; C. L. Pritchard to William Mahone, 19 Nov. 1883, WMP, box 192; R. H. Whitaker to Mahone, 12 Oct. 1883, WMP, box 79; Statement of S. J. Quinn, 1883, WMP, box 175; Barnes, "Triumph of the New South," 194–200.

75. Wynes, *Race Relations in Virginia*, 38–50; Andrew Buni, *The Negro in Virginia Politics, 1902–1965* (Charlottesville, Va., 1967), 7–8; Pearson, *Readjuster Movement*, 164–168.

76. G. K. Gilmer to Lewis E. Harvie, 10 Mar. 1884, Harvie Papers, box 3; Dailey, *Before Jim Crow*, 156–158; Buni, *Negro in Virginia Politics*, 7–9.

77. R. A. Raney to William Mahone, 3 Aug. 1885, WMP, box 190; Alfred Washington to Mahone, 26 Oct. 1885, WMP, box 189; George Strother to Mahone, 29 Oct. 1885, WMP, box 189; *Petersburg Lancet*, 10 Oct. 1885, 24 Oct. 1885; *New York Freeman*, quoted in *Petersburg Lancet*, 14 Nov. 1885.

78. *Alexandria People's Advocate*, 22 Mar. 1884; *Petersburg Lancet*, 24 May 1884, 7 June 1884, 2 Aug. 1884, 9 Aug. 1884, 16 Aug. 1884, 13 Sept. 1884, 20 Sept. 1884, 27 Sept. 1884, 1 Nov. 1884, 8 Nov. 1884; F. S. Collins to William Mahone, 24 June 1889, WMP, box 136; Harold S. Forsythe, "African American Churches, Fusion

Politics in Virginia, and the Republican Gubernatorial Campaign in 1889," in John Saillant, ed., *Afro-Virginian History and Culture* (New York, 1999), 214–215. For a treatment of the Evans campaign, see Carey, "New Voices in Old Dominion," 154–172. The black voting population outnumbered the white in 1880 in the Second Congressional District by 19,071 to 18,845, and in the Fourth Congressional District by 19,855 to 13,770. See *Warrock-Richardson Almanack* (Richmond, Va., 1889), 32–33.

79. On Langston's career, see John Mercer Langston, *From the Virginia Plantation to the National Capitol; or, The First and Only Negro Representative in Congress from the Old Dominion* (1894; New York, 1968); William Cheek and Aimee Lee Cheek, *John Mercer Langston and the Fight for Black Freedom, 1829–1865* (Urbana, Ill., 1989); William Cheek and Aimee Lee Cheek, "John Mercer Langston: Principles and Politics," in Leon Litwack and August Meier, eds., *Black Leaders of the Nineteenth Century* (Urbana, Ill., 1988), 103–126.

80. Langston, *From the Virginia Plantation*, 438–458; U.S. House of Representatives, *John M. Langston vs. E. C. Venable,* House Rept. no. 2462, 51st Cong., 1st sess. (Washington, D.C., 1890); William Cheek, "A Negro Runs for Congress: John Mercer Langston and the Virginia Campaign of 1888," *JNH* 52 (January 1967): 17–19; Cheek and Cheek, "John Mercer Langston," 122–123; Carey, "New Voices in Old Dominion," 213–241; Forsythe, "African American Churches," 216–217. There was, as Harold Forsythe points out, some opposition to Langston among black ministers who accused him of waging "war against every white man in this congressional district."

81. Langston, *From the Virginia Plantation,* 471; Cheek, "A Negro Runs for Congress," 22–25; Forsythe, "African American Churches," 216–217.

82. Langston, *From the Virginia Plantation,* 477–478; *Langston vs. Venable;* Cheek, "A Negro Runs for Congress," 26–31.

83. *Petersburg Lancet,* 25 Aug. 1883, 12 Sept. 1885. Emigrationist sentiment was also being cultivated. See *Petersburg Lancet,* 22 Dec. 1883.

84. Schewel, "Local Politics in Lynchburg," 174–178; Rachleff, *Black Labor in the South,* 109–191; Forsythe, "African American Churches," 218–223; Wynes, *Race Relations in Virginia,* 44–46; Dailey, *Before Jim Crow,* 155–162.

9. THE VALLEY AND THE SHADOWS

The epigraph is from W. E. B. Du Bois, *The Souls of Black Folk* (1903; New York, 1986), 457.

1. See, for example, Eric Hobsbawm, *The Age of Empire, 1875–1914* (New York, 1987), 34–83; Victor V. Magagna, *Communities of Grain: Rural Rebellion in Comparative Perspective* (Ithaca, N.Y., 1991), 162–189; Walter Rodney, *A History of the Guya-*

nese Working People, 1881–1905 (Baltimore, 1981); César J. Ayala, *American Sugar Kingdom: The Plantation Economy of the Spanish Caribbean, 1898–1934* (Chapel Hill, N.C., 1999); Thomas C. Holt, *The Problem of Freedom: Race, Labor, and Politics in Jamaica and Britain, 1832–1938* (Baltimore, 1992), 313–379; Winston James, *Holding Aloft the Banner of Ethiopia: Caribbean Radicalism in Early Twentieth-Century America* (London, 1998), 9–49; David Montgomery, *The Fall of the House of Labor: The Workplace, the State, and American Labor Activism, 1865–1925* (New York, 1987), 70–74; Steven Hahn, "Emancipation and the Development of Capitalist Agriculture: The South in Comparative Perspective," in Kees Gispen, ed., *What Made the South Different?* (Jackson, Miss., 1990), 71–88.

2. Richard Franklin Bensel, *Sectionalism and American Political Development, 1880–1980* (Madison, Wisc., 1984); Richard Franklin Bensel, *The Political Economy of American Industrialization, 1877–1900* (New York, 2000); C. Vann Woodward, *Origins of the New South, 1877–1913* (Baton Rouge, 1951), 291–320; Steven Hahn, "Class and State in Postemancipation Societies: Southern Planters in Comparative Perspective," *AHR* 95 (February 1990): 75–98.

3. Woodward, *Origins of the New South;* Lawrence Goodwyn, *Democratic Promise: The Populist Moment in America* (New York, 1976); Robert C. McMath, Jr., *American Populism: A Social History, 1877–1898* (New York, 1993).

4. Rayford W. Logan, *The Negro in American Life and Thought: The Nadir, 1877–1901* (New York, 1954). See also Leon F. Litwack, *Trouble in Mind: Black Southerners in the Age of Jim Crow* (New York, 1998).

5. On the Wheel and the Alliance, see Edward L. Ayers, *The Promise of the New South: Life after Reconstruction* (New York, 1992), 214–248; Woodward, *Origins of the New South,* 188–204; Robert C. McMath, Jr., *Populist Vanguard: A History of the Southern Farmers' Alliance* (Chapel Hill, N.C., 1975); Goodwyn, *Democratic Promise,* 25–272; Steven Hahn, *The Roots of Southern Populism: Yeoman Farmers and the Transformation of the Georgia Upcountry, 1850–1890* (New York, 1983), 269–276.

6. *National Economist,* 14 Dec. 1889, 7 June 1890, 1 Nov. 1890; McMath, *Populist Vanguard,* 44–46; Michael Schwartz, *Radical Protest and Social Structure: The Southern Farmers' Alliance and Cotton Tenancy, 1880–1890* (New York, 1976), 100–102; William F. Holmes, "The Demise of the Colored Farmers' Alliance," *JSH* 41 (May 1975): 187–190.

7. McMath, *Populist Vanguard,* 44–45; Ayers, *Promise of the New South,* 234–236; Holmes, "Demise," 188; Fon Louise Gordon, "From Slavery to Uncertain Freedom: Blacks in the Delta," in Jeannie Whayne and Willard B. Gatewood, eds., *The Arkansas Delta: Land of Paradox* (Fayetteville, Ark., 1993), 107–108.

8. Kenneth Kann, "The Knights of Labor and the Southern Black Worker," *LH* 18 (Winter 1977): 49–70; Melton A. McLaurin, *The Knights of Labor in the South* (Westport, Conn., 1978), 131–148; Jonathan Garlock, ed., *A Guide to the Local As-*

semblies of the Knights of Labor (Westport, Conn., 1982), 3–21, 48–59, 161–167, 235–238, 353–368, 479–481, 484–513, 517–527; Robert C. McMath, Jr., "Southern White Farmers and the Organization of Black Farm Workers: A North Carolina Document," *LH* 18 (Winter 1977): 115–119. Taliaferro County, Georgia, also experienced the organization of the Colored Farmers' Alliance.

9. Martin Dann, "Black Populism: A Study of the Colored Farmers' Alliance through 1891," *Journal of Ethnic Studies* 2 (Fall 1974): 59–61; Harold G. Sugg, "The Colored Farmers' Alliance, 1888–1892: With Special Reference to North Carolina," master's thesis, Old Dominion University, 1971, 90–92; Bruce E. Baker, "The 'Hoover Scare' in South Carolina, 1887: An Attempt to Organize Black Farm Labor," *LH* 40 (August 1999): 261–282; Jeffrey R. Kerr-Ritchie, *Freedpeople in the Tobacco South: Virginia, 1870–1900* (Chapel Hill, N.C., 1999), 204–206; William Ivy Hair, *Bourbonism and Agrarian Protest: Louisiana Politics, 1877–1900* (Baton Rouge, 1969), 194–195; Garlock, *Guide to the Local Assemblies*.

10. *National Economist*, 2 Aug. 1890, 27 Dec. 1890; *Huntsville (Ala.) Gazette*, 24 Jan. 1891; *Dallas (Tex.) Southern Mercury*, 21 Feb. 1889; Stephen Kantrowitz, *Ben Tillman and the Reconstruction of White Supremacy* (Chapel Hill, N.C., 2000), 142–144; *St. Landry (La.) Clarion*, 27 June 1891.

11. On the Knights' assemblies, see Garlock, *Guide to the Local Assemblies*, 11–21, 53–56, 166, 353–368. For a pioneering study of the organization of black domestic workers, see Tera Hunter, *To 'Joy My Freedom: Southern Black Women's Lives and Labors after the Civil War* (Cambridge, Mass., 1997). See also Mark V. Wetherington, *The New South Comes to Wiregrass Georgia, 1860–1910* (Knoxville, Tenn., 1994), 162–163, 240–241.

12. William Warren Rogers, "Negro Knights of Labor in Arkansas: A Case Study of the 'Miscellaneous' Strike," *LH* 10 (Summer 1969): 498–505.

13. The best and most careful treatment of this episode is Baker, "The 'Hoover Scare' in South Carolina," 261–282. But also see *New Orleans Weekly Pelican*, 2 July 1887; Thomas W. Kremm and Diane Neal, "Clandestine Black Labor Societies and White Fear: Hiram F. Hoover and the 'Cooperative Workers of America' in the South," *LH* 19 (Spring 1978): 226–237; and Kantrowitz, *Ben Tillman*, 141–142. Hover himself was shot and wounded while recruiting for the CWA in Warrenton, Georgia.

14. See Jeffrey Gould, "Sugar War: The Strike of 1887, Louisiana," *Southern Exposure* 12 (November–December 1984): 45–48; John A. Heitmann, *The Modernization of the Louisiana Sugar Industry, 1830–1910* (Baton Rouge, 1987), 68–97; Rebecca J. Scott, " 'Stubborn and Disposed to Stand their Ground': Black Militia, Sugar Workers, and the Dynamics of Collective Action in the Louisiana Sugar Bowl, 1863–1887," *S&A* 20 (April 1999): 115–119.

15. *New Orleans Weekly Pelican*, 6 Dec. 1886, 7 May 1887, 5 Nov. 1887; *New Orleans Daily Picayune*, 29 Oct. 1887, 31 Oct. 1887; Gould, "Sugar War," 49–50;

Garlock, *Guide to the Local Assemblies,* 161–167; Hair, *Bourbonism and Agrarian Protest,* 176–180; John C. Rodrigue, *Reconstruction in the Cane Fields: From Slavery to Free Labor in Louisiana's Sugar Parishes, 1862–1880* (Baton Rouge, 2001), 182–191.

16. *New Orleans Daily Picayune,* 28 Oct. 1887, 31 Oct. 1887, 3 Dec. 1887; Hair, *Bourbonism and Agrarian Protest,* 182–183; Rodrigue, *Reconstruction in the Cane Fields,* 182–191; Thomas Becnel, *Labor, Church, and the Sugar Establishment: Louisiana, 1887–1976* (Baton Rouge, 1980), 7–9.

17. *New Orleans Weekly Pelican,* 5 Nov. 1887, 26 Nov. 1887; *New Orleans Daily Picayune,* 2 Nov. 1887, 4 Nov. 1887, 5 Nov. 1887, 6 Nov. 1887, 11 Nov. 1887; Hair, *Bourbonism and Agrarian Protest,* 181–182.

18. *New Orleans Daily Picayune,* 7 Nov. 1887, 21 Nov. 1887, 24 Nov. 1887; *New Orleans Weekly Pelican,* 12 Nov. 1887, 19 Nov. 1887, 26 Nov. 1887; Mrs. Mary W. Pugh to Son, 25 Nov. 1887, Mrs. Mary W. Pugh Papers, LSU; Gould, "Sugar War," 50–55; Hair, *Bourbonism and Agrarian Protest,* 183–185; Rebecca J. Scott, "Defining the Boundaries of Freedom in the World of Cane: Cuba, Brazil, and Louisiana after Emancipation," *AHR* 99 (February 1994): 78–80.

19. See, for example, Clark L. Miller, " 'Let Us Die to Make Men Free': Political Terrorism in Post-Reconstruction Mississippi, 1877–1896," Ph.D. diss., University of Minnesota, 1983, 529–531; William Holmes, "The Leflore County Massacre and the Demise of the Colored Farmers' Alliance," *Phylon* 34 (September 1973): 269–270; John C. Willis, *Forgotten Time: The Yazoo-Mississippi Delta after the Civil War* (Charlottesville, Va., 2000), 129–130.

20. *Greenwood (Miss.) Yazoo Valley Flag,* 21 Sept. 1889; Miller, "Let Us Die to Make Men Free," 531–537; Holmes, "Leflore Massacre," 272–274; Willis, *Forgotten Time,* 130–136.

21. *Greenwood (Miss.) Yazoo Valley Flag,* 14 Sept. 1889.

22. *National Economist,* 7 June 1890, 10 Jan. 1891, 7 Mar. 1891; *Mobile (Ala.) Register,* quoted in William Warren Rogers, "The Negro Alliance in Alabama," *JNH* 45 (January 1960): 43; Gerald Gaither, *Blacks and the Populist Revolt: Ballots and Bigotry in the New South* (University, Ala., 1977), 12–13; Dann, "Black Populism," 61–62; Hair, *Bourbonism and Agrarian Protest,* 194–195; Frenise A. Logan, *The Negro in North Carolina, 1876–1894* (Chapel Hill, N.C., 1964), 84; George B. Tindall, *South Carolina Negroes, 1877–1900* (Columbia, S.C., 1952), 117–118; Lawrence D. Rice, *The Negro in Texas, 1874–1900* (Baton Rouge, 1971), 182; John W. Graves, *Town and Country: Race Relations in an Urban-Rural Context, Arkansas, 1865–1905* (Fayetteville, Ark., 1990), 205; McMath, *Populist Vanguard,* 45.

23. Tindall, *South Carolina Negroes,* 118–119; Kantrowitz, *Ben Tillman,* 141–142. On the growing importance of rural black wage laborers, see Department of the Interior, *Twelfth Census of the United States: Occupations* (Washington, D.C., 1904), 220–406. Almost all of the other Colored Alliance leaders were black.

24. *Houston Daily Post*, 8 Sept. 1891, 11 Sept. 1891, 12 Sept. 1891; Dann, "Black Populism," 65–66; Holmes, "Demise of Colored Farmers' Alliance," 196–197; Ayers, *Promise of the New South*, 257–259.

25. *Houston Daily Post*, 6 Sept. 1891, 8 Sept. 1891, 12 Sept. 1891, 13 Sept. 1891, 29 Sept. 1891, 30 Sept. 1891; *Galveston (Tex.) Daily News*, 9 Sept. 1891; *National Economist*, 26 Sept. 1891; Dann, "Black Populism," 65–66; Holmes, "Demise of Colored Farmers' Alliance," 198; William F. Holmes, "The Arkansas Cotton Pickers' Strike of 1891 and the Demise of the Colored Farmers' Alliance," *AHQ* 32 (Summer 1973): 107–119.

26. The most thorough, thoughtful, and imaginative treatment of the subject is W. Fitzhugh Brundage, *Lynching in the New South: Georgia and Virginia, 1880–1930* (Urbana, Ill., 1993). But see also Stewart E. Tolnay and E. M. Beck, *A Festival of Violence: An Analysis of Southern Lynchings, 1880–1930* (Urbana, Ill., 1995); Ayers, *Promise of the New South*, 156–158; Edward L. Ayers, *Vengeance and Justice: Crime and Punishment in the Nineteenth-Century South* (New York, 1984), 238–255; Litwack, *Trouble in Mind*, 280–312; Willis, *Forgotten Time*, 156–157; Joel Williamson, *The Crucible of Race: Black-White Relations in the American South since Emancipation* (New York, 1984), 183–189; Terence Finnegan, "Lynching and Political Power in Mississippi and South Carolina," in W. Fitzhugh Brundage, ed., *Under the Sentence of Death: Lynching in the South* (Chapel Hill, N.C., 1997), 191–214. Study of the subject begins with the seminal investigative work of Ida B. Wells, *Southern Horrors: Lynch Law in All Its Phases* (New York, 1892).

27. We still very much need more study of whitecapping. The most important work to date has been done by William F. Holmes—see Holmes, "Whitecapping in Mississippi: Agrarian Violence in the Populist Era," *Mid-America* 55 (April 1973): 134–148; Holmes, "Whitecapping in Georgia: Carroll and Houston Counties, 1893," *GHQ* 64 (Winter 1980): 387–404; and Holmes, "Whitecapping: Agrarian Violence in Mississippi," *JSH* 25 (May 1969): 165–185. But also see Litwack, *Trouble in Mind*, 157–158; Neil R. McMillen, *Dark Journey: Black Mississippians in the Age of Jim Crow* (Urbana, Ill., 1989), 120–121; Bryan D. Palmer, "Discordant Music: Charivaris and Whitecapping in Nineteenth-Century North America," *Labour/Le Travailleur* 3 (1978).

28. Brundage, *Lynching in the New South*, 161–207; Account of the Tuskegee Negro Conference, 21 Feb. 1893, in Louis Harlan, ed., *The Papers of Booker T. Washington*, 14 vols. (Urbana, Ill., 1974), vol. 3, 298; Benjamin J. Bridgers to Booker T. Washington, 19 Mar. 1898, in Harlan, *Booker T. Washington Papers*, vol. 4, 393; *Austin Herald*, 25 Mar. 1893, 1 Apr. 1893; *Birmingham (Ala.) Wide-Awake*, 24 Jan. 1900.

29. See W. Fitzhugh Brundage, "The Darien 'Insurrection' of 1899: Black Protest during the Nadir of Race Relations," *GHQ* 74 (Summer 1990): 234–253; J. William

Harris, *Deep Souths: Delta, Piedmont, and Sea Island Society in the Age of Segregation* (Baltimore, 2001), 78–80.

30. Finnegan, "Lynching and Political Power," 196–198; Tindall, *South Carolina Negroes*, 248–249.

31. W. Fitzhugh Brundage, "The Roar on the Other Side of Silence: Black Resistance and White Violence in the American South, 1880–1940," in Brundage, *Under the Sentence of Death*, 278–282; Finnegan, "Lynching and Political Power," 197–198.

32. On Wells, see Jacqueline Jones Royster, ed., *Southern Horrors and Other Writings: The Anti-Lynching Campaign of Ida B. Wells, 1892–1900* (Boston, 1997), 14–19, 50–54.

33. Theodore Rosengarten, *All God's Dangers: The Life of Nate Shaw* (New York, 1975), 162–170, 193.

34. The story of the emergence of the Populist party in the South has been told many times and there is no reason to repeat it here. For the best and most influential discussions, see Woodward, *Origins of the New South*, 175–204, 235–263; Goodwyn, *Democratic Promise*, 154–272; Ayers, *Promise of the New South*, 214–282; and McMath, *American Populism*, 83–179.

35. See Hahn, *Roots of Southern Populism*, 137–289; Hahn, "Emancipation and the Development of Capitalist Agriculture," 71–88; C. Vann Woodward, *Tom Watson: Agrarian Rebel* (New York, 1938), 73–215; Barton C. Shaw, *The Wool-Hat Boys: Georgia's Populist Party* (Baton Rouge, 1984), 98–101; McMath, *American Populism*, 19–49.

36. The best treatment of Populist ideas and sensibilities is Bruce Palmer, *"Man over Money": The Southern Populist Critique of American Capitalism* (Chapel Hill, N.C., 1980). But also see Goodwyn, *Democratic Promise*, 307–386; Theodore R. Mitchell, *Political Education in the Southern Farmers' Alliance, 1887–1900* (Madison, Wisc., 1987), 69–92; and Woodward, *Origins of the New South*, 235–263.

37. Shaw, *Wool-Hat Boys*, 83; *St. Landry (La.) Clarion*, 8 Aug. 1891; William F. Holmes, "The Southern Farmers' Alliance: The Georgia Experience," *GHQ* 72 (Winter 1988): 649–652.

38. Palmer, *"Man over Money,"* 51. C. Vann Woodward was the first to write seriously and largely sympathetically about the Populist efforts to forge a biracial political coalition in the South. Almost all historians since have acknowledged this as an important aspect of the Populist experience. But recent historians have been more attentive, in varying degrees, to the limitations of these efforts. See Woodward, *Tom Watson*, 216–243; Woodward, *Origins of the New South*, 254–259; Goodwyn, *Democratic Promise*, 276–306; Palmer, *"Man over Money,"* 50–66; Ayers, *Promise of the New South*, 269–277; Shaw, *Wool-Hat Boys*, 78–90; and McMath, *American Populism*, 172–175.

39. *National Economist*, 27 Dec. 1890; Gaither, *Blacks and the Populist Revolt*, 22–23.

40. *Dallas Southern Mercury*, 30 Aug. 1894; Gaither, *Blacks and the Populist Revolt*, 73–74, 84–86, 97–98; Palmer, *"Man over Money,"* 50–53; Shaw, *Wool-Hat Boys*, 79–80; Roger L. Hart, *Redeemers, Bourbons, and Populists: Tennessee, 1870–1896* (Baton Rouge, 1975), 190–191.

41. Shaw, *Wool-Hat Boys*, 86–87; Graves, *Town and Country in Arkansas*, 213–214; Joel M. Sipress, "The Triumph of Reaction: Political Struggle in a New South Community, 1865–1898," Ph.D. diss., University of North Carolina, 1993, 244–285.

42. See William F. Holmes, "Populism in Black Belt Georgia: Racial Dynamics in Taliaferro County Politics, 1890–1900," *GHQ* 83 (Summer 1999): 242–262.

43. Robert Cartmell Diary, 28 July 1894, TSLA; Ayers, *Promise of the New South*, 290–293.

44. R. B. Shaw to Furnifold M. Simmons, 1 Nov. 1892, Marmaduke J. Hawkins Papers, 106.2, NCDAH; Eric Anderson, *Race and Politics in North Carolina, 1872–1901: The Black Second* (Baton Rouge, 1981), 198–199; Alan B. Bromberg, " 'Pure Democracy and White Supremacy': The Redeemer Period in North Carolina, 1876–1894," Ph.D. diss., University of Virginia, 1977, 503–504; Paul D. Escott, *Many Excellent People: Power and Privilege in North Carolina, 1850–1900* (Chapel Hill, N.C., 1985), 181.

45. Anderson, *Race and Politics in North Carolina*, 227–228; Helen G. Edmonds, *The Negro and Fusion Politics in North Carolina, 1894–1901* (Chapel Hill, N.C., 1951), 37–45, 67–81; Jeffrey J. Crow, " 'Fusion, Confusion, and Negroism': Schisms among Negro Republicans in the North Carolina Election of 1896," *NCHR* 53 (October 1976): 383.

46. Anderson, *Race and Politics in North Carolina*, 227–251; Glenda Elizabeth Gilmore, *Gender and Jim Crow: Women and the Politics of White Supremacy in North Carolina, 1896–1920* (Chapel Hill, N.C., 1996), 77–78, 91–118; Escott, *Many Excellent People*, 255.

47. *Lampassas (Tex.) People's Journal*, 21 Oct. 1892; Ayers, *Promise of the New South*, 274–280; Shaw, *Wool-Hat Boys*, 82–83; John Dittmer, *Black Georgia in the Progressive Era, 1900–1920* (Urbana, Ill., 1977), 90; Hahn, *Roots of Southern Populism*, 283–286; McMath, *American Populism*, 197–198; Palmer, *"Man over Money,"* 50–66.

48. On Rayner, see Gregg Cantrell, *Kenneth and John B. Rayner and the Limits of Southern Dissent* (Urbana, Ill., 1993). Rayner's father and master, a political dissident in his own right, helped John get an education and aided him politically in North Carolina.

49. W. P. Laughler to Vachel Weldon, 1 Oct. 1894, J. B. Rayner to Vachel Weldon, 8 Oct. 1894, and J. A. Orederdonk to Vachel Weldon, 16 Oct. 1894, all in

Vachel Weldon Papers, 3C144, BTHC; *Dallas Southern Mercury*, 20 Sept. 1894, 4 Oct. 1894, 11 Oct. 1894, 30 Jan. 1896, 16 Apr. 1896, 19 Nov. 1896; Cantrell, *Kenneth and John B. Rayner*, 200–243; Gregg Cantrell and D. Scott Barton, "Texas Populists and the Failure of Biracial Politics," *JSH* 55 (November 1989): 662–672; Alwyn Barr, *Reconstruction to Reform: Texas Politics, 1876–1906* (Austin, Tex., 1971), 136–139; Douglass G. Perry, "Black Populism: The Negro in the People's Party in Texas," master's thesis, Prairie View University, 1945, 41–43.

50. *Dallas Southern Mercury*, 24 Sept. 1896; Lawrence C. Goodwyn, "Populist Dreams and Negro Rights: East Texas as a Case Study," *AHR* 76 (December 1971): 1435–1456; C. H. Chernosky to Dr. Charles W. Ramsdell, 4 Aug. 1922, Jaybird Association Papers, box 2H428, BTHC.

51. Goodwyn, "Populist Dreams," 1446; Barr, *Reconstruction to Reform*, 200–201; Roscoe Martin, *The People's Party in Texas: A Study in Third-Party Politics* (Austin, Tex., 1933), 236–237.

52. See, for example, Harold D. Woodman, *New South—New Law: The Legal Foundations of Credit and Labor Relations in the Postbellum Agricultural South* (Baton Rouge, 1995); Jonathan M. Wiener, *Social Origins of the New South: Alabama, 1860–1885* (Baton Rouge, 1978), 35–133; Kerr-Ritchie, *Freedpeople in the Tobacco South*, 157–158, 164–178; Steven Hahn, "Hunting, Fishing, and Foraging: Common Rights and Class Relations in the Postbellum South," *RHR* 26 (1982): 37–67; Hahn, "Emancipation and the Development of Capitalist Agriculture," 84–85.

53. See Alex Lichtenstein, *Twice the Work of Free Labor: The Political Economy of Convict Labor in the New South* (London, 1996); Ayers, *Vengeance and Justice*, 185–222; William Cohen, *At Freedom's Edge: Black Mobility and the Southern White Quest for Racial Control, 1861–1915* (Baton Rouge, 1991), 201–298.

54. *Proceedings of the Reunion of the Survivors of the Constitutional Convention of 1890* (Jackson, Miss., 1910), 12. The best and most thorough treatment of the attack on black voting rights is Michael Perman, *Struggle for Mastery: Disfranchisement in the South, 1888–1908* (Chapel Hill, N.C., 2001). But also see Woodward, *Origins of the New South*, 321–349; Ayers, *Promise of the New South*, 51–54, 146–149, 289–309; J. Morgan Kousser, *The Shaping of Southern Politics: Suffrage Restriction and the Establishment of the One-Party South, 1880–1910* (New Haven, Conn., 1974). Although the initiatives varied considerably from one state to another, all except Georgia (which had enacted a retroactive poll tax) and Tennessee gave the power to appoint local election judges to the governor, the state legislature, or to a state election board.

55. For national developments, see Alexander Keyssar, *The Right to Vote: The Contested History of Democracy in the United States* (New York, 2000), 117–171; Michael McGerr, *The Decline of Popular Politics: The North, 1865–1930* (New York, 1986); Leon Fink, *Workingmen's Democracy: The Knights of Labor and American*

Politics (Urbana, Ill., 1983); Sven Beckert, *The Monied Metropolis: New York City and the Consolidation of the American Bourgeoisie, 1850–1896* (New York, 2001).

56. *Charleston (S.C.) News and Courier,* 11 Sept. 1895; *Richmond Dispatch,* 3 Sept. 1901; Perman, *Struggle for Mastery,* 24, 60–61. Black Republican militancy in Tennessee during this period was chiefly an urban phenomenon. See Joseph H. Cartwright, *The Triumph of Jim Crow: Tennessee Race Relations in the 1880s* (Knoxville, Tenn., 1976), 63–99. On the involvements of grassroots networks and leaders, see Sipress, "Triumph of Reaction," 245–246.

57. *New Orleans Weekly Pelican,* 22 June, 1889, 28 Sept. 1889; McMillen, *Dark Journey,* 40–41; Vernon L. Wharton, *The Negro in Mississippi, 1865–1890* (Chapel Hill, N.C., 1948), 208–212; Miller, "Let Us Die to Make Men Free," 556–567; Willis, *Forgotten Time,* 136–137; Kousser, *Shaping of Southern Politics,* 139–142.

58. *Jackson (Miss.) Clarion-Ledger,* 17 July 1890, 14 Aug. 1890; 229 *Federal Supplement* 985 (1964); *Mississippi Laws,* 1876, chap. 67, sec. 5, 66; Perman, *Struggle for Mastery,* 53–56, 70–74.

59. *Proceedings of the Reunion,* 34–35; Francis N. Thorpe, *Federal and State Constitutions, Colonial Charters and Other Organic Laws of the . . . United States,* 7 vols. (Washington, D.C., 1909), 2120–2121; *Jackson Clarion-Ledger,* 11 Sept. 1890, 9 Oct. 1890. On the convention debate over modified female suffrage and the developing relation between the woman suffrage campaign in the South and the quest for white supremacy, see *Jackson Clarion-Ledger,* 21 Aug. 1890, 23 Aug. 1890, 25 Aug. 1890, 26 Aug. 1890, 28 Aug. 1890, 1 Sept. 1890, 2 Sept. 1890, 4 Sept. 1890, 5 Sept. 1890. Delegate J. W. Fewell had proposed to enfranchise women who owned, or had husbands who owned, real estate valued at $300 over encumbrances, though the ballot would be cast by an authorized male elector. Also see Marjorie Spruill Wheeler, *New Women of the New South: The Leaders of the Woman Suffrage Movement in the Southern States* (New York, 1993); Gilmore, *Gender and Jim Crow,* 203–224.

60. Perman, *Struggle for Mastery,* esp. 73–74, 88–90; U.S. Commission on Civil Rights, *Voting in Mississippi* (Washington, D.C., 1965), 8; Justin J. Behrend, "Losing the Vote: Disfranchisement in Natchez, Mississippi," master's thesis, California State University, Northridge, 2000, 35–98; Woodward, *Origins of the New South,* 321–349; Sheldon Hackney, *Populism to Progressivism in Alabama* (Princeton, N.J., 1969), 147–208.

61. Ralph C. McDaniel, *The Virginia Constitutional Convention of 1901–1902* (Baltimore, 1928), 33; *Dallas Southern Mercury,* 3 Sept. 1896; Cantrell and Barton, "Texas Populists and Failure of Biracial Politics," 690–691; Woodward, *Tom Watson,* 370–395; Perman, *Struggle for Mastery,* 170–171; *Richmond Dispatch,* 1 Nov. 1901. Michael Perman has argued convincingly that disfranchisement was the work of the Democratic party and that the social and political dynamics in achieving the result varied from one state to another. Still, the black-belt thesis, advanced more than

two decades ago by J. Morgan Kousser, retains a good deal of force. In Mississippi, the leader of the "agrarian" faction in pushing for a constitutional convention hailed from Chickasaw County, where blacks outnumbered whites by nearly two to one. In South Carolina, the driving force was Governor Benjamin Tillman and other Democrats from the "upcountry," where blacks generally outnumbered whites and racial conflict had been long-standing and intense. In North Carolina, the leaders of the disfranchisement campaign came principally from the black-majority Second Congressional District. And in Alabama, Virginia, and Texas, black-belt Democrats played crucial parts. See Kousser, *Shaping of Southern Politics*.

62. Barr, *Reconstruction to Reform*, 193–208; H. Leon Prather, Sr., "The Red Shirt Movement in North Carolina, 1898–1900," *JNH* 62 (April 1977): 174–184; Gilmore, *Gender and Jim Crow*, 123–124; Michael Honey, "Class, Race, and Power in the New South: Racial Violence and the Delusions of White Supremacy," in David S. Cecelski and Timothy B. Tyson, eds., *Democracy Betrayed: The Wilmington Race Riot of 1898 and Its Legacy* (Chapel Hill, N.C., 1998), 163–184.

63. McMillen, *Dark Journey*, 48–53, 186–187; Willis, *Forgotten Time*, 71–73, 137–139; Miller, "Let Us Die to Make Men Free," 606–609; Wharton, *Negro in Mississippi*, 211–212. There is some dispute as to whether the assassinated Republican, F. M. B. Cook of Jasper County, was black or white. Along with McMillen, see Stephen Cresswell, *Multiparty Politics in Mississippi, 1877–1902* (Jackson, Miss., 1995), 100–101.

64. *Journal of the Constitutional Convention of the State of South Carolina* (Columbia, S.C., 1895), 111, 293, 411–413, 420; Mary J. Miller, ed., *The Suffrage: Speeches by Negroes in the Constitutional Convention* (n.p., n.d), 7–9, 10–15, 19, 21; Tindall, *South Carolina Negroes*, 76–86; Kantrowitz, *Ben Tillman*, 209–211, 221, 226.

65. Charles O. Boothe et al. to Alabama Constitutional Convention, 28 May 1901, Addison Wimbs to Booker T. Washington, 6 July 1901, both in Harlan and Smock, *Booker T. Washington Papers*, vol. 6, 130–133, 166–168; Louis R. Harlan, *Booker T. Washington: The Making of a Black Leader, 1856–1901* (New York, 1972), 292–303.

66. Laura K. Rebbe, "The Negro and Politics in Edgecombe County, North Carolina before and after Disfranchisement, 1870–1920," honors thesis, Duke University, 1985, 64; Ayers, *Promise of the New South*, 307–308; Perman, *Struggle for Mastery*, 210–211; John E. Rodabough, "A History of the Negroes of Aberdeen and Monroe Counties, Mississippi, 1790–1916," master's thesis, Mississippi State University, 1964; McMillen, *Dark Journey*, 53–54; Willis, *Forgotten Time*, 140–143; U.S. Commission on Civil Rights, *Voting in Mississippi*, 8; Litwack, *Trouble in Mind*, 369–370.

67. Rebbe, "Negro and Politics in Edgecombe County," 64; John Dittmer, *Black Georgia in the Progressive Era, 1900–1920* (Urbana, Ill., 1977) 101–103; *Richmond Planet*, 18 Oct. 1890; McMillen, *Dark Journey*, 52–53; *Huntsville (Ala.) Star*, 26 Jan.

1900; Allen Woodrow Jones, "Alabama," in Henry Lewis Suggs, ed., *The Black Press in the South, 1865–1979* (Westport, Conn., 1983), 37–38.

68. Perman, *Struggle for Mastery*, 37–47, 121–123, 299–328; Kousser, *Shaping of Southern Politics*, 224–265; C. Vann Woodward, *The Strange Career of Jim Crow*, 3d ed. (New York, 1974), 67–109.

69. *Austin (Tex.) Herald*, 18 Oct. 1895; Rosengarten, *All God's Dangers*, 34–35.

70. James A. Miller to American Colonization Society, 20 Dec. 1892, ACS, roll 141, NA; Robert L. Flagg to William Coppinger, 1 Aug. 1890, ACS, roll 134. From 1889 through 1891, for example, over one thousand letters came into the office of the American Colonization Society from correspondents in the former Confederate states. Of these, 226 (23 percent) came from Arkansas, 194 (19 percent) from Florida, and 151 (15 percent) from Mississippi. Then the most came from Georgia (84), Virginia (71), and North Carolina (65). The counties in Arkansas and Mississippi that showed the most activity also tended to be areas in which Knights of Labor, Colored Farmers' Alliance, or Republican party organizing had been notable and in which lynching and political violence had erupted; and the counties showing the most activity in Florida had experienced Knights of Labor organizing and were almost identical with those experiencing a high incidence of lynching. These factors do not fully explain why Arkansas, Mississippi, and Florida stood out, but they offer an important context. See ACS, rolls 133–135; Garlock, *Guide to Local Assemblies*, 48–51.

71. C. H. Hicks to J. Ormond Wilson, 29 Aug. 1899, ACS, roll 149; James Dubose to William Coppinger, 15 Sept. 1889, ACS, roll 133. See, too, the important study by Edwin S. Redkey, *Black Exodus: Black Nationalist and Back-to-Africa Movements, 1890–1910* (New Haven, Conn., 1969).

72. J. H. Harris to J. Ormond Wilson, 14 July 1892, ACS, roll 141; *AR* 67 (April 1891): 36; *AR* 63 (January 1887): 28–29; *AR* 63 (April 1887): 63; *AR* 64 (January 1888): 39–40; *AR* 64 (July 1888): 105; *AR* 65 (July 1889): 94–95; *AR* 66 (January 1890): 32; *AR* 66 (July 1890): 94–95; *AR* 67 (January 1891): 31; *AR* 67 (April 1891): 63; *AR* 67 (July 1891): 94–95; *AR* 68 (January 1892), 30–31. The American Colonization Society reported that its "actual applications" for emigration to Liberia began to jump substantially in the mid-1880s. Also see Redkey, *Black Exodus*, 73–149.

73. Joe A. Mobley, "In the Shadow of White Society: Princeville, a Black Town in North Carolina, 1865–1915," *NCHR* 63 (July 1986): 340–378; Elizabeth Rauh Bethel, *Promiseland: A Century of Life in a Negro Community* (Philadelphia, 1981); Sydney Nathans, "Fortress without Walls: A Black Community after Slavery," in Robert L. Hall and Carol B. Stack, eds., *Holding on to the Land and the Lord: Kinship, Ritual, Land Tenure, and Social Policy in the Rural South* (Athens, Ga., 1982), 55–65; Robert G. Athearn, *In Search of Canaan: Black Migration to Kansas, 1879–1880* (Lawrence, Kan., 1978), 69–88.

74. See, for example, Norman L. Crockett, *The Black Towns* (Lawrence, Kan., 1979), esp. xii–xiii, 48–49, and 64; Carter G. Woodson, *The Rural Negro* (Washington, D.C., 1930), 110–130; Murray R. Wickett, *Contested Territory: Whites, Native Americans, and African Americans in Oklahoma, 1865–1907* (Baton Rouge, 2000), 30–34; Gatewood, "Arkansas Negroes in the 1890s," 300; John Leftwich to Booker T. Washington, 17 Jan. 1887, in Harlan, *Booker T. Washington Papers*, vol. 2, 323; Willis, *Forgotten Time*, 71–73; McMillen, *Dark Journey*, 186–88; Rauh Bethel, *Promiseland*, 5.

75. J. W. Turner to American Colonization Society, 20 June 1892, ACS, roll 141; *Indianapolis (Ind.) Freeman*, 16 Apr. 1892, quoted in Gatewood, "Arkansas Negroes in the 1890s," 309; Cohen, *At Freedom's Edge*, 252–256; Wickett, *Contested Territory*, 54–59.

76. During the 1880s, the combined net outmigration of the eleven former Confederate states was about 68,000. During the 1890s, it jumped to about 181,000, or by 166 percent. And during the 1900s, it increased to about 256,000 or by another 41 percent. See Cohen, *At Freedom's Edge*, 295; *Helena (Ark.) Reporter*, 1 Feb. 1900. Also see Ayers, *Promise of the New South*, 24.

77. Testimony of Thomas B. Patterson, 25 May 1894, Testimony of George E. Stephens, 25 May 1894, both in Harlan, *Booker T. Washington Papers*, vol. 3, 431–432; *Huntsville (Ala.) Gazette*, 10 Feb. 1883; Howard Rabinowitz, *Race Relations in the Urban South, 1865–1890* (Urbana, Ill., 1980), 18–30; Louis M. Kyriakoudes, "Southern Black Rural-Urban Migration in the Era of the Great Migration: Nashville and Middle Tennessee, 1890–1930," *AgH* 72 (Spring 1998): 341–351; W. E. B. Du Bois, "The Negroes of Farmville, Virginia: A Social Study," *Bulletin of the Department of Labor* 14 (Washington, D.C., January 1898), 5, 9. Du Bois made the same point about Covington, in Newton County, Georgia, when he completed a study there in 1899. See "The Negro in the Black Belt: Some Social Sketches," *Bulletin of the Department of Labor* 22 (Washington, D.C., May 1899), 406.

78. Goodwyn, "Populist Dreams," 1446–1447; U.S. Bureau of the Census, *Negro Population, 1790–1915* (Washington, D.C., 1918), 790; Litwack, *Trouble in Mind*, 490–492.

79. *Twelfth Census of the United States: Agriculture* (Washington, D.C., 1901), pt. 1, 4–14; W. E. B. Du Bois, "The Negro Landholder of Georgia," *Bulletin of the Department of Labor* 35 (Washington, D.C., July 1901), 665, 694, 723, 742. It should be pointed out that black "farm operators" includes those who farmed units as either owners, part owners, managers, cash tenants, or share tenants. It does not include those (whether or not they were household heads) who worked as agricultural wage laborers or as sharecroppers on undifferentiated plantations. Thus, the proportion of farm operators who were owners exaggerates their significance in the total universe of black agricultural workers. For a pioneering study of property accumulation among African Americans in the nineteenth-century South, which puts this process

in broad perspective, see Loren Schweninger, *Black Property Owners in the South, 1790–1915* (Urbana, Ill., 1990).

80. Rosengarten, *All God's Dangers*, 113–282; Cashbooks, Daniel Trotter Papers, LSU; McMillen, *Dark Journey*, 115–119; Willis, *Forgotten Time*, 47–68. A particularly careful and evocative treatment of this process can be found in Sharon Ann Holt, *Making Freedom Pay: North Carolina Freedpeople Working for Themselves, 1865–1900* (Athens, Ga., 2000). See also Mark R. Schultz, "The Dream Realized? African-American Landownership in Central Georgia between Reconstruction and the Second World War," *AgH* 72 (Spring 1998): 301–310.

81. Rosengarten, *All God's Dangers*, 91, 266–268; Membership Roll, St. Mary's Baptist Church Benevolent Association, January 1892, Cashbook no. 12, Record Book no. 69, Trotter Papers; Federal Manuscript Census, Population, Louisiana, Natchitoches Parish, Ward One West of Cane River, 1900, NA.

82. Du Bois, "Negro Landholder of Georgia," 670–677; Schweninger, *Black Property Owners*, 161–176; Holt, *Making Freedom Pay*, 58–59; Du Bois, "Negro in the Black Belt," 410–411. On the clustering of black-owned farms, see Charles S. Aiken, *The Cotton Plantation South since the Civil War* (Baltimore, 1998), 158–159.

83. See Chalmers Archer Jr., *Growing Up in Rural Mississippi: Memories of a Family, Heritage of a Place* (New York, 1992), 3, 5, 12, 17, 27, 62, 67.

84. Du Bois, *Souls of Black Folk*, 443–445, 448–449, 458–474; Du Bois, "Negro Landholder of Georgia," 712.

85. Black Churches, Panola County, WPA Histories, RG 60, box 372, MDAH; Account of the Tuskegee Negro Conference, 21 Feb. 1893, in Harlan, *Booker T. Washington Papers*, vol. 3, 296; William H. Holtzclaw, *The Black Man's Burden* (New York, 1915), 100; Du Bois, "Negro in the Black Belt," 410–411.

86. See, for example, Suggs, *Black Press in the South;* Gatewood, "Arkansas Negroes in the 1890s," 293.

87. Julius E. Thompson, *The Black Press in Mississippi, 1865–1985: A Directory* (West Cornwall, Conn., 1988).

88. Gilmore, *Gender and Jim Crow*, 147–224; Evelyn Brooks Higginbotham, *Righteous Discontent: The Women's Movement in the Black Baptist Church, 1880–1920* (Cambridge, Mass., 1993).

89. See, for example, Rebbe, "Negro and Politics in Edgecombe County," 26–68.

90. *Helena (Ark.) Reporter*, 1 Feb. 1900.

91. See, for example, Harold S. Forsythe, "Kingfish's Elders: Freedpeople Constructing a World of Institutionalized Power and Meaning in Virginia and the South, 1865–1900," unpublished paper in author's possession, 1999; Harold S. Forsythe, "African-American Churches, Fusion Politics in Virginia, and the Republican Gubernatorial Campaign in 1889," in John Saillant, ed., *Afro-Virginian History and Culture* (New York, 1999), 211–226; and Thomas F. Armstrong, "The Building of a Black

Church: Community in Post–Civil War Liberty County, Georgia," *GHQ* 66 (Fall 1982): 346–367.

EPILOGUE

1. There is a very large literature on the Great Migration and related population movements within the South, but for some of the best recent contributions, see James R. Grossman, *Land of Hope: Chicago, Black Southerners, and the Great Migration* (Chicago, 1989); Peter Gottlieb, *Making Their Own Way: Southern Blacks' Migration to Pittsburgh, 1916–1930* (Urbana, Ill., 1987); Neil Fligstein, *Going North: Migration of Blacks and Whites from the South, 1900–1950* (New York, 1981); Earl Lewis, *In Their Own Interests: Race, Class, and Power in Twentieth-Century Norfolk, Virginia* (Berkeley, Calif., 1991); Joe William Trotter Jr., *Coal, Class, and Color: Blacks in Southern West Virginia, 1915–1932* (Urbana, Ill., 1990); Jacqueline Jones, *Labor of Love, Labor of Sorrow: Black Women, Work, and the Family from Slavery to the Present* (New York, 1985), 110–195; Edward L. Ayers, *The Promise of the New South: Life after Reconstruction* (New York, 1992), 55–131; William Cohen, *At Freedom's Edge: Black Mobility and the Southern White Quest for Racial Control, 1861–1915* (Baton Rouge, 1991), 248–298; Leon Litwack, *Trouble in Mind: Black Southerners in the Age of Jim Crow* (New York, 1998), 480–496; Milton C. Sernett, *Bound for the Promised Land: African American Religion and the Great Migration* (Durham, N.C., 1997).

2. Grossman, *Land of Hope*, 13–119; Kimberley L. Phillips, *AlabamaNorth: African-American Migrants, Community, and Working-Class Activism in Cleveland, 1915–1945* (Urbana, Ill., 1999), 17–40; Gottlieb, *Making Their Own Way*, 12–62; Earl Lewis, "Expectations, Economic Opportunities, and Life in the Industrial Age: Black Migration to Norfolk, Virginia, 1910–1945," and Joe William Trotter Jr., "Race, Class, and Industrial Change: Black Migration to Southern West Virginia, 1915–1932," both in Joe William Trotter Jr., ed., *The Great Migration in Historical Perspective: New Dimensions of Race, Class, and Gender* (Bloomington, Ind., 1991), 22–26, 46–57; Eric Arnesen, *Brotherhoods of Color: Black Railroad Workers and the Struggle for Equality* (Cambridge, Mass., 2001), 5–41.

3. Grossman, *Land of Hope*, 56–58, 89–97; Darlene Clark Hine, "Black Migration to the Urban Midwest: The Gender Dimension, 1915–1945," in Trotter, *Great Migration*, 128–131; Gottlieb, *Making Their Own Way*, 46–47; Sernett, *Bound for Promised Land*, 142.

4. See especially Winston James, *Holding Aloft the Banner of Ethiopia: Caribbean Radicalism in Early Twentieth-Century America* (London, 1998), 9–49. But also see Grossman, *Land of Hope*, 123–160; Sernett, *Bound for Promised Land*, 188–189; Gottlieb, *Making Their Own Way*, 63–88; Thomas J. Sugrue, *Origins of the Urban Crisis: Race and Inequality in Postwar Detroit* (Princeton, N.J., 1996), 23–25.

5. There is a great deal written on Garvey and the UNIA, but very good introductions may be found in Robert A. Hill, ed., *The Marcus Garvey and Universal Negro Improvement Association Papers*, 9 vols. (Berkeley, Calif., 1983–1891), vol. 1, xxxv–cxvii; E. David Cronon, *Black Moses: The Story of Marcus Garvey and the Universal Negro Improvement Association* (Madison, Wisc., 1955); Tony Martin, *Race First: The Ideological and Organizational Struggles of Marcus Garvey and the Universal Negro Improvement Association* (Westport, Conn., 1976); Judith Stein, *The World of Marcus Garvey: Race and Class in Modern Society* (Baton Rouge, 1986); James, *Holding Aloft*, 122–194; Lawrence W. Levine, "Marcus Garvey and the Politics of Revitalization," in John Hope Franklin and August Meier, eds., *Black Leaders of the Twentieth Century* (Urbana, Ill., 1982), 105–138; George M. Fredrickson, *Black Liberation: A Comparative History of Black Ideologies in the United States and South Africa* (New York, 1995), 137–178; and Eric J. Sundquist, *To Wake the Nations: Race in the Making of American Literature* (Cambridge, Mass., 1993), 540–625.

6. See, for example, Report of James O. Peyronnin, 8 Oct. 1919, in Hill, *Garvey Papers*, vol. 2, 61; Hill, "General Introduction," in Hill, *Garvey Papers*, xxxvii, lxi–lxiii; Levine, "Marcus Garvey," 122–125.

7. Levine, "Marcus Garvey," 119–120, 129–130; Hill, *Garvey Papers*, vol. 1, lxix–lxxviii, lxxxvii, 461; Fredrickson, *Black Liberation*, 160–161; Wilson Jeremiah Wilson, *The Golden Age of Black Nationalism, 1850–1925* (New York, 1978), 262–267.

8. Richard Wright, *Black Boy* (1945; New York, 1993), 337.

9. See, Hill, *Garvey Papers*, vol. 7, 986–1002. But also see James, *Holding Aloft*, 365; Barbara Bair, "Garveyism and Contested Political Terrain in 1920s Virginia," in John Saillant, ed., *Afro-Virginian History and Culture* (New York, 1999), 227–249; Neil McMillen, *Dark Journey: Black Mississippian in the Age of Jim Crow* (Urbana, Ill., 1989), 312; and especially Mary L. Gambrell, "U.N.I.A. Divisions in the Southern United States: Strongholds of Garveyism," master's thesis, University of Georgia, 1989. Tony Martin pointed to the importance of the South nearly two decades ago, but his finding did not seem to register in the historical literature. See his *Race First*, 15–17. The "division" was the organizational base of UNIA. To be granted a charter, a division needed at least seven members but could have many more. See "Constitution and Book of Laws," in Hill, *Garvey Papers*, vol. 1, 256–257. If we just include the states of Alabama, Arkansas, Florida, Georgia, Kentucky, Louisiana, Mississippi, North Carolina, South Carolina, Tennessee, Texas, and Virginia, the South would claim 401 of 936 divisions nationwide (43 percent). If we add Oklahoma (31) and West Virginia (50), the number increases to 482 (52 percent). New England (27), the Mid-Atlantic (138), and the Midwest (241) together had 406 (43 percent).

10. *Negro World*, 24 May 1924, 30 Aug. 1924, 13 Sept. 1924, 4 July 1925. The best and most suggestive treatment of the experience of Garveyism in the South is

to be found in Mary Gambrell Rolinson, "The Universal Negro Improvement Association in Georgia: Southern Strongholds of Garveyism," in John Inscoe, ed., *Georgia in Black and White* (Athens, Ga., 1994), 202–224; and Gambrell, "U.N.I.A. Divisions." But also see Lewis, *In Their Own Interests*, 74–76; and Bair, "Garveyism," 227–49. In the urban South, UNIA seems to have recruited support mainly among skilled and unskilled black workers.

11. *Negro World*, 30 Aug. 1924. Gambrell, "U.N.I.A. Divisions," 17–48. UNIA's Constitution called for a "Lady President" and a "Male President" in each division. See "Constitution and Book of Laws," in Hill, *Garvey Papers*, vol. 1, 268–270. Women appear to have served widely at least as organizational secretaries, and correspondence with the *Negro World* suggests further activism and leadership.

12. Gambrell, "U.N.I.A. Divisions," 69–74; Hill, *Garvey Papers*, vol. 7, 986–1002.

13. Michael C. Dawson has recently made a very compelling case for the importance of nationalism in contemporary black thought and politics. See his *Black Visions: The Roots of Contemporary African-American Political Ideologies* (Chicago, 2001), esp. 14–22. But also see Wilson, *Golden Age*, 15–31; Eddie S. Glaude Jr., *Exodus! Religion, Race, and Nation in Early Nineteenth-Century Black America* (Chicago, 2000), 8–9, 16; Robin D. G. Kelley, *Freedom Dreams: The Black Radical Imagination* (Boston, 2002), 13–35; Rolinson, "Universal Negro Improvement Association in Georgia," 220; Malcolm X, *The Autobiography of Malcolm X*, as told to Alex Haley (1964; New York, 1987), 1–2.

14. I borrow this concept of "organizing traditions" from Charles Payne's pioneering book on the Civil Rights Movement, *I've Got the Light of Freedom: The Organizing Tradition and the Mississippi Freedom Struggle* (Berkeley, Calif., 1995).

15. See M. Langley Biegert, "Legacy of Resistance: Uncovering the History of Collective Action by Black Agricultural Workers in Central East Arkansas from the 1860s to the 1930s," *JSoH* 32 (Fall 1998): 73–99; *AR* 54 (January 1878), 29–30; H. H. Robinson to William Coppinger, 3 May 1879, ACS, roll 118, LC; Charles H. Hicks to Coppinger, 3 July 1879, ACS, roll 119; Nan Elizabeth Woodruff, *American Congo: The Black Freedom Struggle in the Arkansas and Mississippi Delta, 1900–1950* (Cambridge, Mass., 2003), chap. 3. Also see Jeannie M. Whayne, *A New Plantation South: Land, Labor, and Federal Favor in Twentieth-Century Arkansas* (Charlottesville, Va., 1996), 47–77.

16. Woodruff, *American Congo*, chap 3; Hill, *Garvey Papers*, vol. 7, 986–987; Biegert, "Legacy of Resistance," 88–89; Mark D. Naison, "Black Agrarian Radicalism in the Great Depression: The Threads of a Lost Tradition," *Journal of Ethnic Studies* 1 (Fall 1973): 60–61. Also see Greta de Jong, " 'With the Aid of God and the F.S.A.': The Louisiana Farmers' Union and the African American Freedom Struggle in the New Deal Era," *JSoH* 34 (Fall 2000): 123–125.

17. Payne, *Got the Light of Freedom*, 79–80; Joanne Grant, *Ella Baker: Freedom*

Bound (New York, 1998), 7–20. Baker's grandfather apparently purchased the land with four other relatives in 1872, and deeded some of it to Roanoke Chapel, where he was minister. For a different, though interconnecting, political trajectory, see Timothy B. Tyson, *Radio Free Dixie: Robert F. Williams and the Roots of Black Power* (Chapel Hill, N.C., 1999).

18. Payne, *Got the Light of Freedom*, 102, 128, 145, 178; John Dittmer, *Local People: The Struggle for Civil Rights in Mississippi* (Urbana, Ill., 1994), 90–115.

ACKNOWLEDGMENTS

I have been at work on this book for longer than I like to recall, but I feel quite certain that it never would have been completed if not for the incredible support I have received from so many people and institutions. To offer my deep thanks to them here hardly seems adequate for the time, energies, and resources that they have extended to me, but for the moment it will have to do.

All scholars are dependent on the knowledge and assistance of librarians and archivists, and I have been particularly fortunate in my travels. Thanks go to those at the many repositories I have visited from New York to Texas, but I am especially grateful to the late Sara Dunlap Jackson of the National Archives in Washington, D.C., whose command of the collections was awe-inspiring and who made it possible for me to have access to the many relevant records of the War Department.

The research and writing of this book could hardly have been undertaken, let alone completed, without generous financial support. I should like to thank, first, the Academic Senate of the University of California, San Diego (particularly Dean Stanley Chodorow), and most recently the Dean's Office at Northwestern University (particularly Dean Eric Sundquist), for helping me find the time to travel to libraries and archives and then to write portions of the manuscript. I must thank, as well, the American Council of Learned Societies, the John Simon Guggenheim Memorial Foundation, and the Center for

Advanced Study in the Behavioral Sciences at Stanford, for honoring me with fellowships that allowed me to conduct the research and begin the writing. The Center at Stanford was a remarkably wonderful place to work, and I should like to offer special thanks to Bob Scott and Neil Smelser for adding so much to what was already both a beautiful and stimulating environment.

The book uses material from two of my previously published essays: "The Politics of Black Rural Laborers in the Postemancipation South," in Enrico Dal Lago and Rick Halpern, eds., *The American South and the Italian Mezzogiorno: Essays in Comparative History* (New York: Palgrave, 2002), by permission of Palgrave Macmillan; and "'Extravagant Expectations' of Freedom: Rumor, Political Struggle, and the Christmas Insurrection Scare of 1865 in the American South," *Past and Present*, no. 157 (November 1997), pp. 122–158, by permission of The Past and Present Society.

Over the years, I have had the help of several excellent research assistants who have enabled me to compile bibliography, find information on black leaders, make that information machine-readable, identify and process illustrations, and track down a host of leads in original sources. Some of them are now history professors in their own right, but all deserve recognition for their creative efforts: Justin Behrend, Robert Chase, Greg Downs, Carole Emberton, Megan Glick, Max Grivno, Rene Hayden, Natalie Ring, Gerald Shenk, Jeannie Whayne, and especially Michael Gorman.

Even before I began this book, I had the great fortune to work as an associate editor at the Freedmen and Southern Society Project at the University of Maryland, where I benefited enormously from the talents, expertise, imaginative thinking, and friendship of Ira Berlin, Leslie Rowland, Steven Miller, Joseph Reidy, Barbara Fields, Thavolia Glymph, and, a bit later, Susan O'Donovan and John Rodrigue. Lunchtime invariably turned into a free-wheeling seminar, and the intellectual nourishment has helped sustain me since.

Portions of what would become this book were presented to the Agrarian Studies Seminar at Yale University; the Seminar in the Comparative History of Labor, Technology, and Society in Atlanta; the Commonwealth Fund Conference on the Comparative Study of the American South and the Italian Mezzogiorno at University College, London; and the Departments of History at the University of California, San Diego, Emory University, the Johns Hopkins University, Harvard University, the University of Chicago, Northwestern University, the University of Oregon, and the University of Pennsylvania. The opportunity to try out my ideas in these settings was immensely valuable, and I should like to thank those in attendance for their searching questions and critical engagement. Thanks, too, to my friends at the Odyssey Project on Chicago's North Side, especially Carol Bolton El, John Dick, Rod Mathis, and Pat Taylor, who moved, challenged, and energized me as the book was being completed.

A number of other friends and colleagues very kindly took time from their own busy schedules to read all or part of a large manuscript and offer sharp criticisms, incisive comments, and extremely helpful suggestions. The book is far better for their contributions: William Andrews, Edward Ayers, Justin Behrend, Jane Dailey, Greg Downs, Gary Fine, Harold Forsythe, Robert Gooding-Williams, Rene Hayden, Michael Johnson, Stephen Kantrowitz, Nancy MacLean, Susan O'Donovan, Dylan Penningroth, James Scott, Thomas Summerhill, Eric Van Young, and the anonymous readers for the press. But very special and heartfelt thanks go to Ira Berlin, Adam Green, Rachel Klein, Lawrence Powell, and Jonathan Prude, who not only gave me the benefit of their wisdom, insight, imagination, and friendship for what was in most cases many years on end, who not only read countless drafts and answered what must have seemed like endless questions, but who, in various ways, also gave me the confidence to struggle on with a project that at times looked impossible to finish.

When I met Joyce Seltzer of Harvard University Press I had written only about one-third of this book, but her enthusiasm for what I was trying to do has been a great boost throughout and her "book sense" has never ceased to astonish me. This is still a much longer book than she would have preferred, but not nearly so long and untidy as it would have been without her guidance. Great appreciation goes, as well, to Julie Carlson, my copy editor at the press, who invariably helped me to say what I wanted to far better than I had initially managed to do.

My son, Declan, and my daughter, Saoirse, were born during the years when I had begun to write this book, and it is a sobering measure of how long the writing process has taken to know that they will both be able to read at least some of the book when it appears in print. I'm not quite sure how much more quickly the chapters would have come were it not for the sleep deprivation and all else that goes into parenting, but I wouldn't give up a second of the time that I spent with them for an earlier publication date. They have filled me with joy and taught me more about the important things in life than I could ever have imagined.

Stephanie McCurry has been in my life for about as long as this book has, and she may be even more relieved than I finally to see it off. But she has meant more to me and to the book than I can possibly convey: with her brilliance, wisdom, humor, and encouragement at all the right moments. We have shared a very special, and encompassing, kind of relationship, and she has enabled me to encounter the world (past and present) with new eyes, new questions, new thoughts, and a bigger heart. With much love, this book is for her.

INDEX

Abbeville County, S.C., 181, 309

Adams, Dock, 306

Adams, Henry, 317, 387, 452, 470; early life, 318, 553; army and secret committee, 318–319; forms Colonization Council, 319–320; petitions federal government, 320; organizing for emigration, 323, 327, 330–331, 333, 335–336, 341, 343, 362

Adams County, Miss., 95, 242, 244

Africa: West Africa, influence of, 17, 44, 50, 346; emigration to, 263–264, 317–346, 355–363, 452–454, 470–471, 473; southern Africa, 412; dislocations in, 466

African-American celebrations and processions, 107, 113–117

African-American conventions, 106–107; freedmen's conventions, 120–127; labor conventions, 262–264

African-American drilling companies, 173–175, 177–182. *See also* Freed politics; Union League

African-American migrations: Reconstruction, 119–120; within South, 362, 455; South to North, 363, 455–457

African-American newspapers, 108–110, 325–326, 461–462, 467–469, 471–472

African-American officeholding: congressional, 216, 437; state, 217–219, 237, 254, 369–373, 381, 386, 394–395, 436–437, 474, 530, 539; local, 218–220, 237, 244–246, 254, 369, 371–373, 381, 394–395, 437, 530, 535; geography of, 219; and power, 220–221; and electioneering, 221–222; jurors, 245–246; obstacles to, 255–258; officer bonds, 256–259; decline of, 367

African-American political leaders: under slavery, 37–40, 49–51; gender and, 38–40, 185, 339–341; Reconstruction and, 165–166, 173–174, 176, 178–179, 182–183, 185, 188–189, 195–197, 222–226, 249–258; post-Reconstruction and, 317–320, 323–324, 327–329, 342–345, 347–349, 351, 354, 369–372, 387, 391–393, 396–397, 398–400, 405, 408–411, 419, 422–423, 438–440, 472–476; data set, 479–480

African-American suffrage: issue during Civil War, 105–111; advent of, 163–198; exercise of, 204–206, 220–230, 237–249, 253–257, 265–266, 379–384; attacks on, 366–367, 440–451

African-American troops: history in military, 90; recruitment of, 91–94; struggles against racism, 95; literacy of, 97–98; political education of, 98–102; in army of occupation, 132–133, 501; in Reconstruction politics, 133; mustered out, 155